CATHERINE THE GREAT

ALSO BY ROBERT K. MASSIE

Nicholas and Alexandra
Peter the Great
Dreadnought
The Romanovs
Castles of Steel
Journey (co-author)

CATHERINE THE GREAT

Portrait of a Woman

ROBERT K. MASSIE

HEAD
of ZEUS

First published in 2011 in the United States of America by Random House, Inc.
First published in the United Kingdom in 2012 by Head of Zeus Ltd.

This edition published in the United Kingdom in 2013
by Head of Zeus Ltd.

1 3 5 7 9 10 8 6 4 2

A CIP catalogue record for this book is available from the British Library.

Trade Paperback ISBN: 9781908800015
eBook ISBN: 9781908800947

Printed in the United Kingdom
by CPI Anthony Rowe.

Head of Zeus Ltd
Clerkenwell House
45–47, Clerkenwell Green
London EC1R 0HT

www.headofzeus.com

Book design by Carole Lowenstein

For Deborah

And for Bob Loomis.
Twenty-four years, four books.
Thank you.

*Perhaps the best description of her is
that she is a woman as well as an empress.*

—The Earl of Buckinghamshire,
British ambassador to Russia, 1762–65

CONTENTS

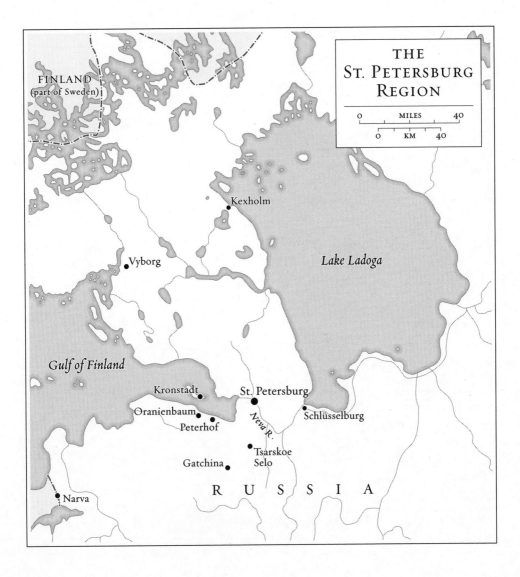

THE
 St. Petersburg
Region

0   MILES   40

0   KM   40

FINLAND
(part of Sweden)

Kexholm

Lake Ladoga

Vyborg

Gulf of Finland

Kronstadt

St. Petersburg

Oranienbaum

Schlüsselburg

Peterhof

Neva R.

Tsarskoe
Selo

Gatchina

R   U   S   S   I   A

Narva

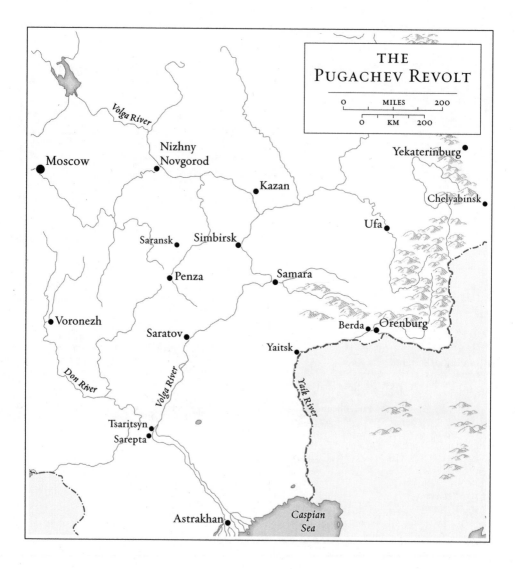

THE
PUGACHEV REVOLT

0   MILES   200

0   KM   200

Moscow

Nizhny
Novgorod

Volga River

Kazan

Yekaterinburg

Chelyabinsk

Ufa

Saransk   Simbirsk

Penza

Samara

Berda   Orenburg

Voronezh

Saratov

Yaitsk

Don River

Volga River

Yaik River

Tsaritsyn
Sarepta

Astrakhan

Caspian
Sea

POLAND

AUSTRIA

Kiev

RUSSIA

Dnieper River

Dniester River

Bug River

Ekaterinoslav

Pruth River

JASSY

BENDER

MOLDAVIA

Nikolaev

Ochakov

Odessa

Kherson

Taganrog

Don R.

AKKERMAN

Kinburn

THE LIMAN

Azov

ISMAIL

SEA OF
AZOV

WALLACHIA

CRIMEA

Kerch

Danube River

Silistria

Bakhchiserai

Kuchuk
Kainardzhi

Sebastopol

BLACK SEA

OTTOMAN
EMPIRE

Constantinople

POTEMKIN'S SOUTHERN
CONQUESTS AND EMPIRE

X Battles   Potemkin's conquests

0   MILES   200

0   KM   200

European Russia
and the
Three Partitions of Poland

0   MILES   200

0   KM   200

WHITE SEA

SWEDEN

FINLAND
(part of Sweden)

Vyborg   Lake
Ladoga

Gulf of Finland

Revel
ESTONIA

St. Petersburg

BALTIC SEA

Novgorod

LIVONIA

Pskov

RUSSIA

COURLAND

Riga

Mitau

To Russia in
First Partition
1772

Tver

Volga River

Yaroslavl

EAST
PRUSSIA

Vilna

Vladimir

Moscow

(TO
PRUSSIA)

Minsk

Smolensk

Mogilev

Tula

Warsaw

P O L A N D
(BEFORE FIRST PARTITION IN 1772)

Orel

Bug River

To Russia in
Second Partition
1793

Voronezh

Kursk

(TO
AUSTRIA)

To Russia in
Third Partition
1795

Kiev

Dnieper River

AUSTRIA

Dniester River

Bug River

Ekaterinoslav

Pruth River

Ochakov

Kherson

OTTOMAN
EMPIRE

Kinburn

SEA OF
AZOV

Danube River

CRIMEA

BLACK
SEA

Sebastopol

Don River

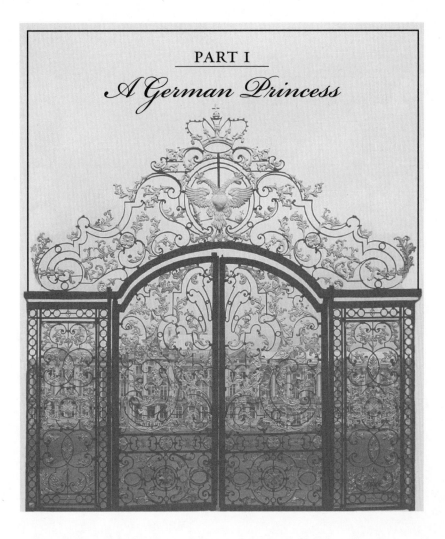

PART I

A German Princess

Sophia's Childhood

P RINCE CHRISTIAN AUGUSTUS of Anhalt-Zerbst was hardly distinguishable in the swarm of obscure, penurious noblemen who cluttered the landscape and society of politically fragmented eighteenth-century Germany. Possessed neither of exceptional virtues nor alarming vices, Prince Christian exhibited the solid virtues of his Junker lineage: a stern sense of order, discipline, integrity, thrift, and piety, along with an unshakable lack of interest in gossip, intrigue, literature, and the wider world in general. Born in 1690, he had made a career as a professional soldier in the army of King Frederick William of Prussia. His military service in campaigns against Sweden, France, and Austria was meticulously conscientious, but his exploits on the battlefield were unremarkable, and nothing occurred either to accelerate or retard his career. When peace came, the king, who was once heard to refer to his loyal officer as "that idiot, Zerbst," gave him command of an infantry regiment garrisoning the port of Stettin, recently acquired from Sweden, on the Baltic coast of Pomerania. There, in 1727, Prince Christian, still a bachelor at thirty-seven, bowed to the pleas of his family and set himself to produce an heir. Wearing his best blue uniform and his shining ceremonial sword, he married fifteen-year-old Princess Johanna Elizabeth of Holstein-Gottorp, whom he scarcely knew. His family, which had arranged the match with hers, was giddy with delight; not only did the line of Anhalt-Zerbst seem assured, but Johanna's family stood a rung above them on the ladder of rank.

It was a poor match. There were the problems of difference in age; pairing an adolescent girl with a man in middle age usually stems from a confusion of motives and expectations. When Johanna, of a good family with little money, reached adolescence and her parents, without consulting her, arranged a match to a respectable man almost three times her age, Johanna could only consent. Even more unpromising, the characters and temperaments of the two were almost entirely opposite. Christian Augustus was simple, honest, ponderous, reclusive, and thrifty; Johanna Elizabeth was complicated, vivacious, pleasure-loving, and extravagant.

She was considered beautiful, and with arched eyebrows, fair, curly hair, charm, and an exuberant eagerness to please, she attracted people easily. In company, she felt a need to captivate, but as she grew older, she tried too hard. In time, other flaws appeared. Too much gay talk revealed her as shallow; when she was thwarted, her charm soured to irritability and her quick temper suddenly exploded. Underlying this behavior, and Johanna had known this from the beginning, was the fact that her marriage had been a terrible—and was now an inescapable—mistake.

Confirmation first came when she saw the house in Stettin to which her new husband brought her. Johanna had spent her youth in unusually elegant surroundings. Because she was one of twelve children in a family that formed a minor branch of the ducal Holsteins, her father, the Lutheran bishop of Lübeck, had passed her along for upbringing to her godmother, the childless Duchess of Brunswick. Here, in the most sumptuously magnificent court in north Germany, she had become accustomed to a life of beautiful clothes, sophisticated company, balls, operas, concerts, fireworks, hunting parties, and constant, tittering gossip.

Her new husband, Christian Augustus, a career officer existing on his meager army pay, could provide none of this. The best he could manage was a modest gray stone house on a cobbled street constantly swept by wind and rain. The walled fortress town of Stettin, overlooking a bleak northern sea and dominated by a rigid military atmosphere, was not a place where gaiety, graciousness, or any of the social refinements could flourish. Garrison wives led dull lives; the lives of the wives of the town were duller still. And here, a lively young woman, fresh from the luxury and distractions of the court of Brunswick, was asked to exist on a tiny income with a puritanical husband who was devoted to soldiering, addicted to rigid economy, equipped to give orders but not to converse, and eager to see his wife succeed in the enterprise for which he had married her: the bearing of an heir. In this endeavor, Johanna did her best—she was a dutiful if unhappy wife. But always, underneath, she yearned to be free: free of her boring husband, free of their relative penury, free of the narrow, provincial world of Stettin. Always, she was certain that she deserved something better. And then, eighteen months after her marriage, she had a baby.

Johanna, at sixteen, was unprepared for the realities of motherhood. She had dealt with her pregnancy by wrapping herself in dreams: that her children would grow into extensions of herself and that their lives eventually would supply the broad avenue on which she would travel to achieve her own ambitions. In these dreams, she took it for granted that the baby she was carrying—her firstborn—would be a son, an heir for his father, but more important a handsome and exceptional boy whose brilliant career she would guide and ultimately share.

At 2:30 a.m. on April 21, 1729, in the chill, gray atmosphere of a Baltic dawn, Johanna's child was born. Alas, the little person was a daughter. Johanna and a more accepting Christian Augustus managed to give the baby a name, Sophia Augusta Fredericka, but from the beginning, Johanna could not find or express any maternal feeling. She did not nurse or caress her little daughter; she spent no time watching over her cradle or holding her; instead, abruptly, she handed the child over to servants and wet nurses.

One explanation may be that the process of childbirth nearly cost Johanna her life; for nineteen weeks after Sophia was born, the adolescent mother remained confined to her bed. A second is that Johanna was still very young and her own bright ambitions in life were far from fulfilled. But the stark, underlying reason was that her child was a girl, not a boy. Ironically, although she could not know it then, the birth of this daughter was the crowning achievement of Johanna's life. Had the baby been the son she so passionately desired, and had he lived to adulthood, he would have succeeded his father as Prince of Anhalt-Zerbst. Then the history of Russia would have been different and the small niche in history that Johanna Elizabeth earned for herself never would have existed.

Eighteen months after the birth of her first child, Johanna gave birth to the son upon whom she had set her heart. Her fondness for this second infant, Wilhelm Christian, became all the more intense when she realized that something about the child was seriously wrong. The boy, who appeared to suffer from rickets, became her obsession; she petted him, spoiled him, and scarcely let him out of her sight, lavishing on him all the affection she had denied her daughter. Sophia, already keenly aware that her own birth had been a disappointment to her mother, now observed the love with which Johanna surrounded her little brother. Gentle kisses, whispered endearments, tender caresses all were bestowed on the boy—while Sophia watched. It is, of course, common for the mother of a handicapped or chronically ill child to spend more time with that child, just as it is normal for other children in the family to resent this disproportionate attention. But Johanna's rejection of Sophia began before Wilhelm's birth, and then continued in aggravated form. The result of this maternal favoritism was a permanent wound. Most children, rejected or neglected in favor of a sibling, react more or less as Sophia did: to avoid more hurt, she sealed off her emotions; nothing was being given her and nothing was expected. Little Wilhelm, who simply accepted his mother's affection as normal, was quite innocent of any wrongdoing; even so, Sophia hated him. Forty years later, writing her *Memoirs,* her resentments still simmered:

> It was told me that I was not very joyfully welcomed. . . . My father thought I was an angel; my mother did not pay much attention to me. A year and a half later, she [Johanna] gave birth to a son whom she idolized. I was merely tolerated and often I was scolded with a violence and anger I did not deserve. I felt this without being perfectly clear why in my mind.

Thereafter, Wilhelm Christian goes unmentioned in her *Memoirs* until his death in 1742 at the age of twelve. Then, her brief account is unemotionally clinical:

> He lived to be only twelve and died of spotted [scarlet] fever. It was not until after his death that they learned the cause of an illness which had compelled him to walk always with crutches and for which remedies had been constantly given him in vain and the most famous physicians in Germany consulted. They advised that he be sent to baths at Baden and Karlsbad, but he came home each time as lame as before he went away and his leg became smaller in proportion as he grew taller. After his death, his body was dissected and it was found that his hip was dislocated and must have been so from infancy. . . . At his death, my mother was inconsolable and the presence of the entire family was necessary to help her bear her grief.

This bitterness only hints at Sophia's enormous resentment against her mother. The harm done to this small daughter by Johanna's open display of preference marked Sophia's character profoundly. Her rejection as a child helps to explain her constant search as a woman for what she had missed. Even as Empress Catherine, at the height of her autocratic power, she wished not only to be admired for her extraordinary mind and obeyed as an empress, but also to find the elemental creature warmth that her brother—but not she—had been given by her mother.

Even minor eighteenth-century princely families maintained the trappings of rank. Children of the nobility were provided with nurses, governesses, tutors, instructors in music, dancing, riding, and religion to drill them in the protocol, manners, and beliefs of European courts. Etiquette was foremost; the little students practiced bowing and curtseying hundreds of times until perfection was automatic. Language lessons were paramount. Young princes and princesses had to be able to speak and write in French, the language of the European intelligentsia; in aristocratic German families, the German language was regarded as vulgar.

The influence of her governess, Elizabeth (Babet) Cardel, was critical at this time in Sophia's life. Babet, a Huguenot Frenchwoman who found Protestant Germany safer and more congenial than Catholic France, was entrusted with overseeing Sophia's education. Babet quickly understood that her pupil's frequent belligerence arose out of loneliness and a craving for encouragement and warmth. Babet provided these things. She also began to give Sophia what became her permanent love of the French language, with all its possibilities for logic, subtlety, wit, and liveliness in writing and conversation. Lessons began with *Les Fables de La Fontaine;* then they moved on to Corneille, Racine, and Molière. Too much of her education, Sophia decided later, had been sheer memorization: "Very early it was noticed that I had a good memory; therefore I was incessantly tormented with learning everything by heart. I still possess a German Bible in which all the verses I had to memorize are underlined with red ink."

Babet's approach to teaching was gentle compared to that of Pastor Wagner, a pedantic army chaplain chosen by Sophia's fervently Lutheran father to instruct his daughter in religion, geography, and history. Wagner's rigid methodology—memorize and repeat—made little headway against a pupil whom Babet had already described as an *esprit gauche* and who asked embarrassing questions: Why were great men of antiquity such as Marcus Aurelius eternally damned because they had not known of Christ's salvation and therefore could not have been redeemed? Wagner replied that this was God's will. What was the nature of the universe before the Creation? Wagner replied that it had been in a state of chaos. Sophia asked for a description of this original chaos; Wagner had none. The word "circumcision" used by Wagner naturally triggered the question: What does that mean? Wagner, appalled at the position in which he found himself, refused to answer. By elaborating on the horrors of the Last Judgment and the difficulty of being saved, Wagner so frightened his pupil that "every night at dusk I would go and cry by the window." The next day, however, she retaliated: How can the infinite goodness of God be reconciled with the terrors of the Last Judgment? Wagner, shouting that there were no rational answers to such questions, and that what he told her must be accepted on faith, threatened his pupil with his cane. Babet intervened. Later Sophia wrote, "I am convinced in my inmost soul that Herr Wagner was a blockhead." She added, "All my life I have had this inclination to yield only to gentleness and reason—and to resist all pressure."

Nothing, however, neither gentleness nor pressure, could assist her music teacher, Herr Roellig, in his task. "He always brought with him a creature who roared bass," she later wrote to her friend Friedrich Melchior Grimm. "He had him sing in my room. I listened to him and said to myself, 'he roars like a bull,' but Herr Roellig was beside himself with delight whenever this bass throat was in action." She never overcame her inability to appreciate harmony. "I long to hear and enjoy music," Sophia-Catherine wrote in her *Memoirs,* "but I try in vain. It is noise to my ears and that is all."

Babet Cardel's approach to teaching children lived on in the empress Catherine, and, years later, she poured out her gratitude: "She had a noble soul, a cultured mind, a heart of gold; she was patient, gentle, cheerful, just, consistent—in short the kind of governess one would wish every child to have." To Voltaire, she wrote that she was "the pupil of Mademoiselle Cardel." And in 1776, when she was forty-seven, she wrote to Grimm:

> One cannot always know what children are thinking. Children are hard to understand, especially when careful training has accustomed them to obedience and experience has made them cautious in conversation with their teachers. Will you not draw from that the fine maxim that one should not scold children too much but should make them trustful, so that they will not conceal their stupidities from us?

The more independence Sophia displayed, the more she worried her mother. The girl was arrogant and rebellious, Johanna decided; these qualities must be stamped out before her daughter could be offered in marriage. As marriage was a minor princess's only destiny, Johanna was determined "to drive the devil of pride out of her." She repeatedly told her daughter that she was ugly as well as impertinent. Sophia was forbidden to speak unless spoken to or to express opinions to adults; she was made to kneel and kiss the hem of the skirt of all visiting women of rank. Sophia obeyed. Bereft of affection and approval, she nevertheless maintained a respectful attitude toward her mother, remained silent, submitted to Johanna's commands, and smothered her own opinions. Later, concealment of pride in humility came to be recognized as a deliberate and useful tactic which Sophia—renamed Catherine—used when confronting crisis and danger. Threatened, she drew around herself a cloak of meekness, deference, and temporary submission. Here, too, an example was set by Babet Cardel: a woman of gentle birth who accepted her inferior position as a governess but still managed to preserve a self-respect, dignity, and pride that raised her, in Sophia's eyes, higher than her own mother.

Outwardly, in these years, Sophia was a cheerful child. In part this sprang from the ebullient curiosity of her mind and in part from her sheer physical energy. She needed a great deal of exercise. Walks in the park with Babet Cardel were not enough, and her parents allowed her to play games with children of the town. Sophia easily took command of these little bands of boys and girls, not simply because she was a princess but because she was a natural leader and her imagination created the games that everyone liked to play.

Eventually, Christian Augustus was promoted from commander of the garrison to governor of the town of Stettin, an advance that entitled him to move his family into a wing of the granite castle on the town's main square. For Johanna, the move to the castle did not help. She was still unhappy, still unable to reconcile herself to the situation in which life had deposited her. She had married beneath her, and instead of the brilliant life she had dreamed of she was now no more than a provincial lady in a garrison town. Two more children had followed her first two—another son and another daughter—but they brought no added happiness.

In her longing to escape, her thoughts turned to the high connections she still possessed. By birth, Johanna belonged to one of the great families of Germany, the ducal house of Holstein-Gottorp, and she remained convinced that with her family rank, her cleverness, her charm and vivacity, she still might create a better place for herself in the world. She began spending time cultivating her relatives by writing frequent letters and by paying regular visits. She went often to Brunswick, the glittering court of her girlhood, where Rembrandts and Van Dycks hung on the walls. Then, every February at carnival time, she visited Berlin to pay her respects to the king of Prussia. She had a passion for intrigue, and, from the perspective of Stettin, even the gossipy intrigues of petty German courts, where she thought she would shine, attracted her. But somehow, wherever she went, Johanna was always aware that she was no more than a poor relation, a girl of good family who had made an unpromising marriage.

When Sophia was eight, Johanna began taking her along on these travels. Arranging a marriage was a duty Johanna meant to fulfill, and it could do no harm, even at an early stage, to let society know that an available little princess was growing up in Stettin. And, indeed, marriage was a major conversational topic as mother and daughter made these rounds. By the time Sophia was ten, talk of this or that potential husband was commonplace among her aunts and uncles. Sophia never objected to traveling with her mother; indeed, she enjoyed it. As she grew older, she was not only well aware of the purpose of their visits, she wholeheartedly approved. Not only did marriage offer the best avenue of escape from her mother and family, but Sophia had been introduced to another dreadful alternative. This was the condition of her spinster aunts, surplus daughters of the north German petty nobility, who had been put away in the farthest wings of family castles or permanently stabled in remote Protestant convents. Sophia remembered visiting one of these unfortunates, an older sister of her mother's, who owned sixteen pug dogs, all of whom slept, ate, and performed their natural functions in the same room as their mistress. "A large number of parrots besides lived in the same room," Sophia wrote. "One can imagine the fragrance which reigned there."

Despite her own wish to marry, Sophia's chances of an excellent match appeared only marginal. Each year produced a new crop of eligible adolescent European princesses, most of whom offered far more of substance to reigning royal and noble families than a union with the insignificant house of tiny Zerbst. Nor was Sophia a child with remarkable physical attractions. At ten, she had a plain face with a thin, pointed chin, which Babet Cardel had advised her to keep carefully tucked in. Sophia understood the problem of her appearance. Later, she wrote:

> I do not know whether as a child I was really ugly, but I remember well that I was often told that I was and that I must therefore strive to show inward virtues and intelligence. Up to the age of fourteen or fifteen, I was firmly convinced of my ugliness and was therefore more concerned with acquiring inward accomplishments and was less mindful of my outward appearance. I have seen a portrait of myself painted when I was ten years old and that is certainly very ugly. If it really resembled me, they told me nothing false.

And so it was that, despite mediocre prospects and a plain appearance, Sophia trailed around north Germany after her mother. During these journeys, she added new subjects to her education. Listening to adults gossiping, she learned the genealogy of most of the royal families of Europe. One visit was of particular interest. In 1739, Johanna's brother, Adolphus Frederick, the Prince-Bishop of Lübeck, was appointed guardian of the newly orphaned young Duke of Holstein, eleven-year-old Charles Peter Ulrich. This was an extraordinarily well-connected boy, presumably destined for an exalted future. He was the only living grandson of Peter the Great of Russia, and he also stood first in line to become heir to the throne of Sweden. A year older than Sophia, he was also her second cousin on her mother's side. Once he became her brother's ward, Johanna lost no time in gathering up Sophia and paying the prince-bishop a visit. In her *Memoirs,* Sophia-Catherine described Peter Ulrich as "agreeable and well-bred, although his liking for drink was already noticeable." This description of the eleven-year-old orphan was far from complete. In reality, Peter Ulrich was small, delicate, and sickly, with protuberant eyes, no jaw, and thin, blond hair falling to his shoulders. Emotionally as well as physically, he was underdeveloped. He was shy and lonely, he lived surrounded by tutors and drillmasters, he had no contact with anyone his own age, he read nothing, and he was greedy at meals. But Johanna, like every other mother of an eligible daughter, watched every movement he made, and her heart soared when she saw her own ten-year-old Sophia talking to him. Afterward, Sophia saw her mother and her aunts whispering. Even at her age, she knew that they were discussing the possibility of a match between herself and this strange boy. She did not mind; already she had begun letting her own imagination wander:

> I knew that one day he would become king of Sweden, and although I was still a child, the title of queen fell sweetly on my ears. From that time on, the people around me teased me about him and gradually I grew accustomed to thinking that I was destined to be his wife.

Meanwhile, Sophia's appearance was improving. At thirteen, she was slender, her hair was a silky, dark chestnut, she had a high forehead, brilliant dark blue eyes, and a curved rosebud mouth. Her pointed chin had become less prominent. Her other qualities had begun to attract attention; she was intelligent and had a ready wit. Not everyone thought her insignificant. A Swedish diplomat, Count Henning Gyllenborg, who met Sophia at her grandmother's house in Hamburg, was impressed by her intelligence and told Johanna in Sophia's presence, "Madame, you do not know the child. I assure you she has more mind and character than you give her credit for. I beg you therefore to pay more attention to your daughter for she deserves it in every respect." Johanna was unimpressed, but Sophia never forgot these words.

She was discovering the way to make people like her, and, once she had learned the skill, she practiced it brilliantly. It was not a matter of behaving seductively. Sophia—and, later, Catherine—was never a coquette; it was not sexual interest she wished to arouse but warm, sympathetic understanding of the kind Count Gyllenborg had given her. To produce these reactions in other people, she used means so conventional and modest that they appear almost sublime. She realized that people preferred to talk rather than to listen and to talk about themselves rather than anything else. In this respect, her mother, pathetically anxious to be considered important, had provided a telling example of how not to behave.

Other feelings were stirring within her. Sophia was awakening to sensuality. At thirteen and fourteen, she often went to her room at night, still restless with nervous energy. Attempting to find some release, she sat up in bed, placed a hard pillow between her legs, and, astride an imaginary horse, "galloped until I was quite worn out." When maids outside her room came in to investigate the noise, they found her lying quietly, pretending to be asleep. "I was never caught in the act," she said. There was a reason for her steely control in public. Sophia had a single, overriding desire: to escape her mother. She understood that her only avenue of escape would be marriage. To achieve that, she must marry—and marry not just any husband, but one who would raise her in rank as far as possible above Johanna.

She succumbed, however, to one episode of adolescent infatuation. At fourteen, she flirted briefly with a handsome young uncle, her mother's younger brother, George Lewis. Ten years older than Sophia and attracted by the fresh innocence of his blossoming niece, this pomaded lieutenant of cuirassiers began to pay court. Sophia describes the progress of this little romance, which ended with her uncle George suddenly asking her to marry him. She was dumbfounded. "I knew nothing about love and never associated it with him." Flattered, she hesitated; this man was her mother's brother. "My parents will not wish it," she said. George Lewis pointed out that their family relationship was not an obstacle; unions of this kind often occurred in the aristocratic families of Europe. Sophia was confused and allowed Uncle George to continue his suit. "He was very good looking at the time, had beautiful eyes, and knew my disposition. I was accustomed to him. I began to feel attracted by him and did not avoid him." In the end, she tentatively accepted her uncle's proposal, provided "my father and mother give their consent. At that point, my uncle abandoned himself entirely to his passion which was extreme. He seized every opportunity of embracing me and was skilled at creating them, but apart from a few kisses, it was all very innocent."

Was Sophia really prepared to set aside her ambition to become a queen in order to become her own mother's sister-in-law? For a moment, she teetered. Perhaps she might have given in, permitted George Lewis to have his way, and married him. But before anything final had happened, a letter arrived from St. Petersburg.

※2※

Summoned to Russia

THE LETTER FROM RUSSIA was a surprise, but its message was one Johanna had been dreaming of and hoping for. Even as the ambitious mother was trooping her daughter through the petty courts of north Germany, she had been reaching out to make use of a more exalted connection. There was a family history involving Johanna's relatives in the house of Holstein with the Romanov dynasty of Imperial Russia. In December 1741, when Sophia was twelve, Elizabeth, the younger daughter of Peter the Great, had seized the Russian throne in a midnight coup d'état. The new empress had several strong ties to the house of Holstein. The first was through Elizabeth's beloved older sister, Anne, Peter the Great's eldest daughter, who had married Johanna's cousin Charles Frederick, Duke of Holstein. This marriage had produced the sad little Peter Ulrich; three months after her child was born, Anne was dead.

Elizabeth had an even closer personal bond with the house of Holstein. At seventeen, she had been betrothed to Johanna's older brother, Charles Augustus. In 1726, this Holstein prince had traveled to St. Petersburg to be married, but a few weeks before the wedding, the prospective bridegroom had caught smallpox in the Russian capital and died there. Elizabeth was left with a grief she never entirely overcame, and thereafter she regarded the house of Holstein as almost a part of her own family.

Now, when the news arrived that this same Elizabeth had suddenly ascended the Russian throne, Johanna immediately wrote to congratulate the new empress, who, at one time, had been about to become her sister-in-law. Elizabeth's reply was amiable and affectionate. The relationship continued to prosper. Johanna had in her possession a portrait of Elizabeth's dead sister, Anne, which the empress wanted. When Elizabeth wrote to her "dear niece" and asked whether the picture might be returned to Russia, Johanna was overjoyed to do this favor. Soon after, a secretary from the Russian embassy in Berlin arrived in Stettin bringing Johanna a miniature portrait of Elizabeth set in a magnificent frame of diamonds worth eighteen thousand rubles.

Determined to nurture this promising connection, Johanna took her daughter to Berlin, where the Prussian court painter Antoine Pesne painted a portrait of Sophia to be sent as a gift to the empress. The portrait was unremarkable; the subjects of most of Pesne's paintings wound up on his canvases looking almost identical, and his portrait of Sophia emerged as a generic eighteenth-century portrait of a pleasant young woman. Nevertheless, once the likeness had been dispatched to St. Petersburg, the desired response came back: "The empress is charmed by the expressive features of the young princess."

Thereafter, Johanna passed up no opportunity to forge new links in this family chain. At the end of 1742, she gave birth to a second daughter, Sophia's only sister. As soon as the infant's gender was known, Johanna wrote to the empress, saying that the child was to be named Elizabeth and asking Her Majesty to consent to act as the baby's godmother. Elizabeth agreed and soon another portrait of the empress, again set in diamonds, arrived in Stettin.

Meanwhile, another series of events favorable to Johanna was taking place. In January 1742, young Peter Ulrich of Holstein, the orphaned boy whom Sophia had met three years before, suddenly disappeared from Kiel and reappeared in St. Petersburg, where he was adopted by his aunt Elizabeth and proclaimed heir to the Russian throne. This boy, now a future emperor of Russia, was Johanna's cousin (and, by extension, Sophia's). In 1743, there was another wonderful surprise for Johanna. As a condition of Peter Ulrich's becoming heir to the Russian throne, the little Holstein prince renounced his claim to the crown of Sweden. By the terms of a treaty concluded between Russia and Sweden, Empress Elizabeth was permitted to designate her nephew's replacement as heir to the Swedish throne. She chose Johanna's brother, Adolphus Frederick, Prince-Bishop of Lübeck, who had been Peter Ulrich's guardian. Thus it was that when all these proclamations, changes, and replacements were in place, Johanna found herself at the center of a wheel of astonishing good fortune. She had lost to smallpox a brother who would have been the consort of the new Russian empress, but now she possessed a cousin who would one day be the Russian emperor and a living elder brother who would become the king of Sweden.

As his wife was courting St. Petersburg and escorting their daughter through north Germany, Prince Christian Augustus, husband and father, remained at home. Now over fifty, unchanging in his disciplined, frugal way of life, he survived a temporary paralytic stroke, recovered, and lived to see his own rank and status improve. In July 1742, the new king of Prussia, Frederick II, promoted him to the rank of field marshal in the Prussian army. In November of the same year, the prince and his elder brother succeeded to joint sovereignty of the little principality of Anhalt-Zerbst, a town southwest of Berlin with medieval walls and towers, a moat, and gabled houses. Resigning from the army and leaving Stettin, Christian Augustus moved his family to Zerbst and devoted himself to the welfare of his twenty thousand subjects. Johanna was mildly pleased; now she was a reigning princess of a small—very small— sovereign German state. She lived in a small—very small—baroque palace. Despite her correspondence with an empress and her visits to her well-placed relatives, she still worried that life was passing her by.

Then, on January 1, 1744, after a service in the castle chapel, the family had just sat down to New Year's Day dinner when a courier brought a sealed letter for Johanna. She opened it immediately. It was from St. Petersburg and had been written by Otto Brümmer, grand marshal of the court of Peter Ulrich, the young Duke of Holstein, now heir apparent to the Russian throne. Brümmer wrote:

> At the explicit command of Her Imperial Majesty [the Empress Elizabeth], I have to inform you, Madame, that the empress desires Your Highness, accompanied by the princess, your eldest daughter, to come to Russia as soon as possible and repair without loss of time to whatever place the Imperial Court may then be found. Your Highness is too intelligent not to understand the true meaning of the impatience of the empress to see you here soon as well as the princess your daughter of whom report has said much that is lovely. At the same time, our incomparable monarch has expressly charged me to inform Your Highness that His Highness the prince shall under no circumstances take part in the journey. Her Majesty has very important reasons for wishing it so. A word from Your Highness will, I believe, be all that is necessary to fulfill the will of our divine empress.

Brümmer's letter contained other requests. He asked that Johanna travel incognito as far as Riga, on the Russian frontier, and that, if possible, she keep her destination a secret. If, somehow, the destination became known, she was to explain that duty and etiquette required her to thank the Russian empress personally for her generosity to the house of Holstein. To cover Johanna's expenses, Brümmer enclosed a bill of exchange for ten thousand rubles on a Berlin bank. The letter did not specify the ultimate purpose of the summons, but a second letter, arriving by another courier only a few hours later, made the purpose clear. This letter came from Frederick II of Prussia and also was addressed only to Johanna:

I will no longer conceal the fact that in addition to the respect I have always cherished for you and for the princess your
daughter, I have always had the wish to bestow some unusual
good fortune upon the latter; and the thought came to me that
it might be possible to arrange a match for her with her cousin,
the Grand Duke Peter of Russia.

Brümmer's specific exclusion of Prince Christian Augustus from
the empress's invitation, reinforced by Frederick's having written only
to Johanna, was, of course, humiliating for the nominal head of the
family. And the wording of both letters made it clear that everyone involved seemed confident that the wife could manage to override whatever objections her stolid husband might raise, not only to his exclusion
from the invitation but to other aspects of this possible marriage. These
objections, they feared, would center on the requirement that a German princess marrying a future tsar would have to abandon her Protestant faith and convert to Greek Orthodoxy. Christian Augustus's
devout Lutheranism was well known, and all parties understood that he
would oppose his daughter's setting it aside.

For Johanna, this was a glorious day. After fifteen years of a de-
pressing marriage, an empress and a king had put before her the prospect that all her dreams of excitement and adventure were to be
realized. She was to be a person of importance, a performer on the
world stage; all the heretofore wasted treasures of her personality
were to be put to use. She was euphoric. As the days passed, messages
from Russia and Berlin urging haste continued to arrive in Zerbst. In
St. Petersburg, Brümmer, now under constant pressure from an impatient empress, told Elizabeth that Johanna had written that "she
lacked only wings, otherwise she would fly to Russia." And this was
almost true: it took Johanna only ten days to make preparations for
the journey.

While Sophia's mother savored her crowning moment, her father
secluded himself in his study. The old soldier had always known how to
behave on a battlefield, but he did not know how to behave now. He
resented his exclusion from the invitation, yet he wished to support his
daughter. He abhorred the prospect of her being forced to change her
religion, and was uneasy at the idea of her being sent far from home to
a country as politically unstable as Russia. Ultimately, despite all these
worries and reservations, the old, good soldier felt that he had no
choice; he must listen to his wife and obey the orders of King Frederick

II. He locked his study door and began composing cautionary advice to his daughter as to how she should behave at the Russian court:

> Next to the empress, Her Majesty, you must respect the Grand Duke [Peter, her future husband] above all as your Lord, Father, and Sovereign; and withal win by care and tenderness at every opportunity his confidence and love. Your Lord and his will are to be preferred to all the pleasures and treasures of the world and nothing is to be done which he dislikes.

Within three days, Johanna was able to report to Frederick: "The prince, my husband, has signified his approval. The journey, which at this time of year is an exceedingly dangerous one, holds no terrors for me. I have made my decision and am firmly convinced that everything is happening in the best interests of Providence."

Prince Christian was not the only member of the Zerbst family whose role in this momentous undertaking was unmistakably secondary. As Johanna read and wrote, ordered and tried on clothes, Sophia was ignored. The money available went into improving her mother's wardrobe; nothing was left for the daughter. Sophia's clothing—what might have been considered her trousseau—consisted of three old dresses, a dozen chemises, some pairs of stockings, and a few handkerchiefs. Her bridal linen was made up of a few of her mother's used sheets. Altogether, these fabrics filled half of a small trunk of a size that a local girl might carry with her when she traveled to be married in the next village.

Sophia already knew what was happening. She had caught a glimpse of Brümmer's letter and saw that it came from Russia. As her mother was opening it, she had read the words, "accompanied by the princess, your eldest daughter." Moreover, her mother's subsequent breathless behavior and her parents' hasty withdrawal to whisper together encouraged her belief that the letter concerned her future. She knew the importance of marriage; she remembered the excitement her mother had shown four years earlier when she met the little duke Peter Ulrich; she knew that her portrait had been sent to Russia. Eventually, unable to contain her curiosity, she confronted her mother. Johanna admitted what the letters said and confirmed what they implied. "She told me," Catherine wrote later, "that there was also a considerable risk involved, given the instability of that country. I answered that God would provide for stability, if such was his will; and that I had sufficient courage to face the risk, and that my heart told me that all would be well." The matter that tormented her father—the question of a change in her religion—did not trouble Sophia. Her approach to religion was, as Pastor Wagner already knew, pragmatic.

During this week, which was to be their last together, Sophia did not tell Babet Cardel about her imminent departure. Her parents had forbidden her to mention it; they put it about that they and their daughter were leaving Zerbst simply to pay their annual visit to Berlin. Babet, keenly attuned to her pupil's character, realized that no one was being straightforward. But the pupil, in her tearful farewell to her beloved teacher, still would not reveal the truth. And teacher and pupil were never to see each other again.

On January 10, 1744, mother, father, and daughter entered a carriage for the ride to Berlin, where they were to see King Frederick. Sophia now was as eager as her mother. This was the escape she had dreamed of, the beginning of her climb toward a higher destiny. When she left Zerbst for the Prussian capital, there were no painful scenes. She kissed her nine-year-old brother, Frederick (Wilhelm, the brother she hated, was already dead), and her new little sister, Elizabeth. Her uncle, George Lewis, whom she had kissed and promised to marry, was already forgotten. As the carriage rolled through the city gates and onto the high road, Sophia never turned to look back. And in the more than five decades of her life that lay before her, she never returned.

❧3❧

Frederick II and the Journey to Russia

THREE AND A HALF YEARS before Sophia and her parents visited Berlin, when twenty-eight-year-old Frederick II ascended the throne of Prussia, Europe confronted an intriguing bundle of contradictions. The new monarch possessed an enlightened mind, restless energy, political astuteness, and remarkable—if thus far unrevealed—military genius. When this introspective lover of philosophy, literature, and the arts, who was also a ruthless practitioner of Machiavellian statecraft, came to the throne, his small kingdom was already pulsing with militant energy, ready to expand and make its mark on the history of Europe. Frederick had only to give the order to march.

This was not what Europe or Prussia had expected. In his childhood, Frederick had been a dreamy, delicate boy, often beaten by his father, King Frederick William I, for being unmanly. As an adolescent, he wore his hair in long curls hanging down to his waist, and costumed himself in embroidered velvet. He read French writers, wrote French poetry, and performed chamber music on the violin, the harpsichord, and the flute. (The flute was a lifelong passion; he wrote more than a hundred flute sonatas and concerti.) At twenty-five, he accepted his royal destiny and took command of an infantry regiment. On May 31, 1740, he became Frederick II, king of Prussia. His appearance was un-impressive—he was five feet seven inches tall and had a thin face, high forehead, and large, slightly protruding blue eyes—but this mattered to no one, least of all, by then, to Frederick. He had no time for finery or nonsense; there was no formal coronation. Six months later, Frederick suddenly plunged his kingdom into war.

The Prussia Frederick inherited was a small state, poor in popula-tion and natural resources, scattered in disconnected fragments from the Rhine to the Baltic. In the center lay the electorate of Brandenburg, whose capital was Berlin. To the east lay East Prussia, separated from Brandenburg by a corridor of land belonging to the kingdom of Poland. To the west were a number of separate enclaves on the Rhine, in West-phalia, in East Frisia, and on the North Sea. But if lack of territorial cohesion was a national weakness, Frederick also possessed an impor-tant instrument of strength. The Prussian army, man for man, was the best in Europe: eighty-three thousand well-trained, professional sol-diers, an efficient officer corps, and armories stocked with modern weapons. Frederick's intention was to use Prussia's formidable military strength to address his country's geographical weaknesses.

Opportunity quickly thrust itself upon him. On October 20, 1740, five months after Frederick ascended the Prussian throne, the Holy Roman Emperor, Charles VI of Austria, suddenly died. Charles, the last Hapsburg in the male line, was survived by two daughters, and the elder, twenty-three-year-old Maria Theresa, assumed the Austrian throne. Frederick, seeing his chance, immediately summoned his gen-erals. By October 28, he had decided to seize the province of Silesia, one of the richest Hapsburg possessions. His arguments were prag-matic: his own army was ready while Austria seemed leaderless, weak, and impoverished. Other considerations Frederick put aside; the fact that he had solemnly sworn to recognize Maria Theresa's title to all the Hapsburg dominions did not restrain him. Later, in his *Histoire de Mon Temps,* he candidly admitted that "ambition, the opportunity for gain, the desire to establish my reputation—these were decisive and thus war became certain." He chose Silesia because it was next door and because its agricultural and industrial riches and largely Protestant population would constitute a substantial reinforcement to his small kingdom.

On December 16, in an icy, drenching rain, Frederick led thirty-two thousand soldiers across the Silesian frontier. He met practically no resistance; the campaign was more an occupation than an invasion. By the end of January, Frederick was back in Berlin. But in making his prewar calculations, the young king lacked one important piece of information: he had not known the character of the woman he had made his enemy. Maria Theresa, archduchess of Austria and queen of Hungary, possessed a deceptive, doll-like beauty, with blue eyes and golden hair. Under stress, she managed to appear unusually calm, which led some observers to conclude that she was stupid. They were mistaken. She possessed intelligence, courage, and tenacity. When Frederick attacked and seized Silesia, everyone in Vienna was paralyzed—except Maria Theresa. Although in an advanced state of pregnancy, she reacted with the energy of the enraged. She raised money, mobilized troops, and inspired her subjects, meanwhile giving birth to the future emperor Joseph II. Frederick was surprised by this inexperienced young woman's stubborn refusal to surrender the province he had stolen from her. He was even more surprised when in April an Austrian army crossed the Bohemian mountains and reentered Silesia. The Prussians defeated the Austrians again, and, in the temporary peace that followed, Frederick kept Silesia, with its fourteen thousand miles of productive farmland, its rich vein of coal mines, its prosperous towns, and a population of 1,500,000, most of them German Protestants. Added to the number of subjects Frederick had inherited from his father, Prussia now grew to a population of four million. But these spoils came at a cost. Maria Theresa regarded her Hapsburg inheritance as a sacred trust. What Frederick's aggressive war created was her lifelong hatred of him and a Prussian-Austrian antagonism that lasted a century.

Despite his victory in Silesia, Frederick was in a dangerous position. Prussia remained a small country, her territories continued to be fragmented, and her growing strength was making her powerful neighbors uneasy. Two great empires, each larger and potentially stronger than Prussia, were potential enemies. One was Austria under an embittered Maria Theresa. The other was Russia, the immense, sprawling empire that lay on his northern and eastern flank, ruled by the newly crowned Empress Elizabeth. In this situation, nothing was of greater importance to Frederick than the friendship, or at least the neutrality, of Russia. He remembered that on his deathbed his father had passed along a cautionary maxim: that there would always be more to lose than to gain by going to war with Russia. And at this point, Frederick could not be sure what Empress Elizabeth would do.

Immediately after taking the throne, the empress had placed at the head of her political affairs a man who hated Prussia, her new vice-chancellor, Count Alexis Bestuzhev-Ryumin. Bestuzhev's lifelong ambition was to create an alliance linking Russia to the sea powers, England and Holland, and to the central European land powers, Austria and Saxony-Poland. Aware of Bestuzhev's views, Frederick believed that only the vice-chancellor stood in the way of a diplomatic arrangement between himself and the empress. It seemed imperative, therefore, that this obstacle be removed.

Some of these diplomatic tangles, Frederick calculated, might be smoothed if he involved himself in the Russian empress's search for a bride for her fifteen-year-old nephew and heir. Over a year before, the Prussian ambassador in St. Petersburg had reported that Bestuzhev was pressing Elizabeth to choose a daughter of Augustus III, elector of Saxony and king of Poland. Such a marriage, if it took place, could become a critical element in the vice-chancellor's policy of building his alliance against Prussia. Frederick was determined to prevent this Saxon marriage. To do this, he needed a German princess of some reasonably distinguished ducal house. Empress Elizabeth's choice of Sophia, the convenient little pawn from Anhalt-Zerbst, suited Frederick admirably.

By New Year's Day, 1744, the timing of these negotiations had become critical. The emphasis on speed and secrecy in Brümmer's first letter to Johanna, reiterated by Frederick's letter, arose from the fact that Bestuzhev was continuing to press the empress on behalf of the Polish-Saxon Marianne. Now that Elizabeth's choice of Sophia had been made, both she and Frederick wanted the two Holstein princesses to reach St. Petersburg as soon as possible. For Frederick, it was essential that the empress not have time to change her mind.

Frederick II was anxious to see the little princess from Zerbst in order to judge for himself how she might be received in St. Petersburg. On arriving in Berlin, however, Johanna, either because she feared that Sophia might fail to measure up to the king's expectations or because she simply could not imagine that Frederick's interest would be more in her daughter than in herself, rushed immediately to present herself at court—alone. When Frederick asked about Sophia, Johanna said that her daughter was ill. The next day she offered the same excuse; pressed, she said that her daughter could not be presented at court because she had brought no court dress. Losing patience, Frederick ordered that a gown belonging to one of his sisters be provided and that Sophia come immediately.

When at last Sophia appeared before him, Frederick saw a girl neither plain nor beautiful, wearing a gown that did not fit, adorned with no jewelry, her hair unpowdered. Sophia's shyness turned to surprise when she learned that she—but neither her mother nor her father—was to sit at the king's table. Surprise turned into astonishment when she found herself actually sitting next to the monarch himself. Frederick made an effort to put the nervous girl at ease. He spoke to her, she wrote later, about "opera, plays, poetry, dancing and I don't know what, but anyway a thousand things that one usually does not talk about to entertain a girl of fourteen." Gradually gaining confidence, Sophia managed to answer intelligently and, she proudly said later, "the entire company stared in amazement to see the king engaged in conversation with a child." Frederick was pleased with her; when he asked her to pass a dish of jam to another guest, he smiled and said to this person, "Accept this gift from the hand of the Loves and Graces." For Sophia, the evening was a triumph. And Frederick was not indulging his young dinner partner; to Empress Elizabeth he wrote, "The little princess of Zerbst combines the gaiety and spontaneity natural to her age with intelligence and wit surprising in one so young." Sophia was then only a political pawn, but one day, he knew, she might play a greater role. She was fourteen and he was thirty-two, and this was the first and only meeting of these two remarkable monarchs. Both would eventually be accorded the title "the Great." And between them, for decades, they would dominate the history of central and eastern Europe.

Despite the public attention Frederick paid to Sophia, the king's private business was with her mother. It was Frederick's plan that in St. Petersburg Johanna should become an unofficial Prussian diplomatic agent. Thus, quite apart from the long-term advantage of marrying Sophia to the heir to the Russian throne, Johanna, being close to the Russian empress, would be able to exercise an influence on Prussia's behalf. He explained to her about Bestuzhev and his policies. He emphasized that as a sworn enemy of Prussia, the vice-chancellor would do everything in his power to prevent Sophia's marriage. If for no other reason than this, the king insisted, it was in Johanna's interest to do everything she could to undermine Bestuzhev's position.

It was not difficult for Frederick to fire Johanna's enthusiasm. The secret mission entrusted to her delighted her. She was no longer traveling to Russia as a secondary personage, her daughter's chaperone, but as the central figure of a great diplomatic enterprise: the toppling of an imperial chancellor. Carried away, Johanna lost her bearings. She forgot her oft-proclaimed gratitude and devotion to Elizabeth; forgot the advice of her earnest, provincial husband that she take no part in politics; and forgot that the real purpose of her journey was to escort her daughter to Russia.

On Friday, January 16, Sophia left Berlin with her mother and father in a little procession of four coaches. In accordance with Brümmer's instructions, the small group going to Russia was limited in number: the two princesses, one officer, a lady-in-waiting, two maids, a valet, and a cook. As arranged, Johanna was traveling under the assumed name Countess Reinbeck. Fifty miles east of Berlin, at Schwest on the Oder River, Prince Christian Augustus said goodbye to his daughter. Both wept on parting; they were not aware that they would never see each other again. Sophia's feelings about her father, although formally expressed, shine through a letter she wrote two weeks later from Königsberg. She makes a promise that she knows will please him: that she will try to fulfill his wish that she remain a Lutheran.

> My Lord: I beg you to assure yourself that your advice and exhortation will remain forever engraved on my heart, as the seeds of the holy faith will in my soul, to which I pray God to lend all the strength it will need to sustain me through the temptations to which I expect to be exposed. . . . I hope to have the consolation of being worthy of it, and likewise of continuing to receive good news of my dear Papa, and I am, as long as I live, and in an inviolable respect, my lord, your Highness's most humble, most obedient, and faithful daughter and servant, Sophia.

Traveling toward an unknown country, propelled by an empress's sentimentality, a mother's ambition, and the intrigues of the king of Prussia, an adolescent girl was launched on a great adventure. And once the sadness of parting with her father had passed, Sophia was filled with excitement. She had no fear of the long journey or the complications of marrying a boy whom she had met only briefly four years before. If her future husband was considered ignorant and willful, if his health was delicate, if he was miserable in Russia, none of this mattered to Sophia. Peter Ulrich was not the reason she was traveling to Russia. The reason was Russia itself and proximity to the throne of Peter the Great.

In summer, the road from Berlin to St. Petersburg was so primitive that most travelers chose to go by sea; in winter, no one used the road except diplomatic and postal couriers on urgent errands. Johanna, spurred by the empress's demand for haste, had no choice. Although it was already mid-January, no snow had fallen, and sledges designed to glide across a packed surface could not be used. Instead, the travelers lumbered along day after day in heavy carriages, lurching and jolting over frozen ruts while freezing wind sweeping down from the Baltic whistled through cracks in the floor and sides. Inside one carriage, mother and daughter huddled together, muffled in heavy coats, with wool masks pulled over their cheeks and noses. Often, Sophia's feet were so numbed by cold that she had to be carried from the carriage when they stopped to rest.

Frederick had instructed that everything possible be done to ease the journey of "Countess Reinbeck" and her daughter, and in the Germanic towns of Danzig and Königsberg, his orders produced considerable comfort. After a day of creaking wheels and whips cracking on the horses' backs, the travelers were met with warm rooms, pitchers of hot chocolate, and suppers of roasted fowl. Farther east along the frozen road, they found only crude postal stations, each with a single giant stove in its central common room. "The bedchambers were unheated and icy," Johanna reported to her husband, "and we had to take refuge in the postmaster's own room which was little different from a pigsty. . . . He, his wife, the watchdog, and a few children, all lay on top of each other like cabbages and turnips. . . . I had a bench brought for myself and lay down in the middle of the room." Where Sophia slept, Johanna did not report.

In fact, Sophia, healthy and curious, saw everything as part of her great adventure. While passing through Courland (now in Latvia), Sophia watched the giant comet of 1744 blaze across the dark night sky. "I had never seen anything so grand," she wrote in her *Memoirs*. "It seemed very close to earth." During one part of the journey, she made herself sick. "In these last days I had a little indigestion because I had drunk all the beer I could find," she wrote her father. "Dear mama has put a stop to that and I am well again."

The cold grew worse but still it did not snow. From dawn to darkness, they rattled over the frozen ruts. Beyond Memel, there were no more postal stops, and relays of horses had to be hired from peasants. On February 6, they reached Mitau, on the frontier between Polish Lithuania and the Russian empire. Here, they were greeted by a Russian colonel, the commander of the frontier garrison. Farther down the road, they were met by Prince Semyon Naryshkin, a court chamberlain and the former Russian ambassador to London, who welcomed them officially in the name of the empress. He handed Johanna a letter from Brümmer, who reminded her not to forget, when she was presented to the empress, to show "extraordinary respect" by kissing the sovereign's hand. On the bank of the frozen Dvina River across from the city of Riga, the city's vice-governor and a civic delegation awaited them, along with a handsome state coach for the travelers' use. Inside, reported Johanna, "I found ready to wrap us two splendid sables covered with gold brocade . . . two collars of the same fur, and a coverlet of another fur, quite as beautiful." Mother and daughter then rode across the ice into the city while the guns of the fortress roared in salute; this was the moment at which the unknown Countess Reinbeck was transformed into Princess Johanna of Anhalt-Zerbst, mother of the wife-to-be of the future emperor of Russia.

In Riga, the travelers moved their calendar back eleven days because Russia used the Julian calendar, which followed eleven days behind the Gregorian calendar employed in western Europe. In Riga, too, the snow finally began to fall. On January 29 (February 9 in Berlin and Zerbst), the two princesses left Riga for St. Petersburg. They traveled now in a magnificent imperial sledge—actually a wooden hut on runners, pulled by ten horses—hung inside with scarlet draperies trimmed with gold and silver braid and so roomy that it was possible for passengers to completely stretch out on quilted feather beds with silk and satin cushions. In this comfortable vehicle, with a squadron of cavalry galloping alongside, they proceeded to St. Petersburg. They reached the

Winter Palace at noon on February 3. Their approach was signaled by the thunder of the guns of the Peter and Paul Fortress facing the ice-bound Neva River. Outside the palace, a guard of honor presented arms; inside, a crowd of people in bright-colored uniforms and silks and velvet smiled and bowed.

Empress Elizabeth was not there; she had gone ahead to Moscow two weeks earlier, but many in the court and diplomatic corps remained behind, and Elizabeth had commanded that the visitors be given an imperial welcome. Johanna wrote to her husband:

> Here everything goes on in such magnificent and respectful style that it seemed to me . . . as if it all were only a dream. . . . I dine alone with the ladies and gentlemen whom Her Imperial Majesty has given me; I am served like a queen. . . . When I go in to dinner, the trumpets inside the house, and the drums of the guard outside sound a salute. . . . It does not seem real that all this can happen to poor me, for whom at only a few places a drum was ever stirred.

It was not all for "poor me," of course, but while her mother draped herself in these honors, Sophia stood by and watched. The truth was that she was more interested in the antics of fourteen elephants, presented to the empress by the Shah of Persia, performing tricks in the Winter Palace courtyard.

To Frederick in Berlin, Johanna wrote in a different tone, presenting herself as his dutiful subject, working on his behalf. While the German princesses were being fitted with Russian wardrobes before proceeding to Moscow, Johanna had conversations with the two men in Russia whom Frederick had assigned to guide her. One was his own ambassador, Baron Mardefeld, the other the French minister, the Marquis de La Chétardie. The ambassadors reiterated that Vice-Chancellor Bestuzhev was fiercely opposed to the choice of Sophia as the bride of the heir. For this reason, they emphasized, he must be removed, and they counted on her assistance. Meanwhile, to put herself on the most amiable possible terms with the empress, they urged that she and her daughter hurry to Moscow in time to celebrate the new grand duke Peter's sixteenth birthday on February 10.

Guided by this advice, the two travelers left for Moscow on the night of February 5 in a cavalcade of thirty sledges. This time, they traveled smoothly and swiftly over four hundred miles of hard-packed snow on the best-maintained road in Russia, the winter highway used by the empress. When they stopped to change horses, village people stared and told each other, "It is the bride of the grand duke."

At four o'clock on the fourth day—it was the afternoon of February 9, 1744—the cavalcade reached a rest house forty-five miles from Moscow. There they found a message from the empress requesting that they delay their entrance into Moscow until after dark. While waiting, they drank fish soup and coffee and dressed for their presentation to the monarch; Sophia put on a rose-colored silk gown trimmed with silver. Meanwhile, to increase the speed of their sledge, sixteen fresh horses replaced the relays of ten that had brought them this far. Back in their sledge, they hurtled forward, reaching the walls of Moscow before eight. The city was dark until they reached the Golovin Palace, whose courtyard was lit by flaring torches. The journey was over. Now, at the foot of a wide staircase in the entrance hall, stood Otto Brümmer, the writer of the empress's summons, to welcome them. They had only a little time to speak, to remove their furs and smooth their gowns. Within a few minutes, fourteen-year-old Sophia would stand before the empress Elizabeth and her nephew, Grand Duke Peter, the two people who, for the next eighteen years, would dominate her life.

✤4✤

Empress Elizabeth

E LIZABETH HAD A FLAIR for the dramatic. On December 18, 1709, her father, Peter the Great, was just setting out through snowy streets of Moscow at the head of a parade celebrating his astonishing victory at Poltava the previous summer over his formidable enemy Charles XII of Sweden. Behind the tsar marched the regiments of the Russian Imperial Guard, followed by other Russian soldiers dragging three hundred captured Swedish battle flags through the snow, a file of defeated Swedish generals, and finally, by a long column of more than seventeen thousand Swedish prisoners, the remnants of the formerly invincible army that had invaded Russia two years before.

Suddenly, an officer rode up to the tsar and delivered a message.

Peter's hand went up. The parade halted. The tsar spoke a few words, then galloped away. Soon after, Peter reined his frothing horse before the great wooden Kolomenskoe Palace outside Moscow and burst through the door. In a room, he found his wife just emerging from childbirth. Beside her in the bed lay an infant baby girl. Her name was to be Elizabeth and, thirty-two years later, she would become empress of Russia.

Elizabeth was the fifth child born to Peter and the peasant who became his wife—the fifth of twelve, six boys and six girls, only two of whom lived beyond the age of seven. The other survivor was Elizabeth's sister Anne, one year older. As far as the world knew, Elizabeth and Anne were both illegitimate; their father said that he had "not found the time" to publicly marry her mother, the buxom Livonian peasant Martha Skavronskya, renamed Catherine. In fact, in November 1707, Peter had married Catherine in private, but the secret was kept for reasons of state. Peter had already been married as a very young man, and his first wife, Eudoxia, to whom he was grievously ill-suited, had been divorced and placed in a convent. In 1707, with the Swedish army on the march, many traditional Russians would have found it shocking for the tsar to choose that moment to marry an illiterate foreign peasant. Five years later, with the victory at Poltava accomplished, Peter felt differently. On February 9, 1712, he married Catherine again, this time with public fanfare. At the second wedding, the two little girls, Anne and Elizabeth, then four and two, wearing jewels in their hair, served as their mother's bridesmaids.

Peter always said that he "loved both his girls like his own soul." On January 28, 1722, when he declared thirteen-year-old Elizabeth to be of age, she was fair-haired, blue-eyed, brimming with energy and health. She delighted everyone with her laughter and high spirits; this in contrast to her more sedate older sister, Anne, whom she worshipped. Both Anne and Elizabeth received the education of European princesses: languages, manners, and dancing. They learned French as well as Russian, and Anne, the better pupil, also learned some Italian and Swedish. Many years later, the empress Elizabeth recalled the keen interest her father had taken in his daughters' education. He came frequently to their rooms to see them and often asked what they had learned in the course of the day. When he was satisfied, he praised them, kissed them, and sometimes gave each a present. Elizabeth also remembered how greatly Peter regretted the neglect of his own formal education. "My father often repeated," she said, "that he would have given one of his fingers if his education had not been neglected. Not a day passed in which he did not feel this deficiency."

When she reached fifteen, Elizabeth was not as tall and stately as her sister Anne, yet there were many who preferred the radiance of the lively blonde to the grace and majesty of the statuesque brunette. The Duke of Liria, the Spanish ambassador, described Elizabeth in superlatives: "She is a beauty the like of which I have never seen. An amazing complexion, glowing eyes, a perfect mouth, a throat and bosom of rare whiteness. She is tall and her temperament is lively. She is always with one foot in the air. One senses in her a great deal of intelligence and affability, but also a certain ambition." The Saxon minister, Lefort, praised her large and brilliant blue eyes and he found irresistible her high spirits and her lighthearted sense of fun.

At fifteen, she was considered ready for marriage. From the time of Peter the Great's visit to Paris in 1717, the great tsar had hoped to marry Elizabeth to Louis XV, who was two months younger than she. Elizabeth had been schooled with this marriage in mind. She was taught the French language and court manners along with French history and literature. Campredon, the French ambassador to St. Petersburg, wholeheartedly endorsed the tsar's plan: "There is nothing but what is agreeable in the person of the Princess Elizabeth," he wrote to Paris. "It may be said that she is a beauty in her figure, her complexion, her eyes and her hands. Her defects, if she has any, are on the side of education and manners, but I am assured that she is so intelligent that it will be easy to rectify what is lacking by the care of some skillful and experienced person who should be placed near her if the affair should be concluded." Yet despite this recommendation and the girl's manifest charms, at Versailles her credentials were tarnished: her mother was a peasant, and the daughter may have been born out of wedlock. France did not want a bastard on or near the throne.

Peter's hope for Elizabeth was thwarted, but one of his two daughters was to marry. In 1721, when Elizabeth was not quite twelve and Anne was thirteen, Duke Charles Frederick of Holstein, the only nephew of Peter the Great's legendary adversary Charles XII of Sweden, had come to St. Petersburg. When King Charles had died, the duke had been displaced in Stockholm as heir to his dead uncle's throne.

In Russia, Peter welcomed the young man with a pension and a place of honor. To further advance his own cause, the duke began to pay court to Elizabeth's sister Anne. Four years later, when Anne was seventeen—and despite Anne's lack of enthusiasm for this suitor—the couple were betrothed in a service in which the emperor himself took rings from each partner and exchanged them with the other. Then, suddenly, on January 25, 1725, Peter the Great, fifty-two years old, died. Anne's wedding was postponed while her mother assumed the throne as Empress Catherine I. On May 21, four months after her father's death, Anna married Charles Frederick. Her fifteen-year-old sister, Elizabeth, was her bridesmaid.

The death of Peter the Great and the marriage of his daughter Anne plunged the already complicated Russian succession into greater confusion. In a decree in February 1722, Peter had denounced as a dangerous practice, unfounded in scripture, the rule of male primogeniture, the ancient, time-honored sequence by which the grand dukes of Muscovy and later the Russian tsars had passed down the throne from father to eldest son. Henceforth, Peter declared, every reigning sovereign would have the power to designate his or her successor. Following his proclamation, Peter placed a crown on Catherine's head and declared her empress.

Her father's early death profoundly affected Elizabeth's future. The prospect of a brilliant match for Elizabeth became remote. Her mother still hoped for a French marriage, but Louis XV had married a Polish princess. At this point in St. Petersburg, Elizabeth's new brother-in-law, Duke Charles Frederick of Holstein, began praising the merits of his twenty-year-old cousin, Prince Charles Augustus of Holstein (who happened to be a brother of Princess Johanna of Anhalt-Zerbst). Catherine I, who was fond of her son-in-law, agreed to invite this second young Holstein nobleman to Russia.

Charles Augustus reached St. Petersburg on October 16, 1726, and made a favorable impression. Elizabeth saw him as the kinsman of her adored older sister's husband, which made it easy for her to fall in love. The engagement announcement had been set for January 6, 1727, when Empress Catherine I was stricken by a series of chills and fevers. The ceremony was postponed until she recovered. The empress did not recover; instead, she grew worse, and in April, after reigning only twenty-seven months, she died. In May, only a month after her mother's death, Elizabeth decided to go ahead with her marriage. Then, on May 27, on the eve of her engagement announcement, her prospective husband, Charles Augustus, was stricken; several hours later, the doctors diagnosed smallpox; four days later, he, too, was dead. Elizabeth, her happiness shattered at seventeen, cherished his memory for the rest of her life—although as her hopes for a conventional marriage slipped away, her sadness did not prevent her from seeking consolation with other men.

When Catherine I died, the throne passed to Peter the Great's eleven-year-old grandson, who became Emperor Peter II. In July 1727, soon after Catherine's death, the Duke of Holstein decided that he had been in Russia long enough. Having spent his childhood in Sweden and six years of his young manhood in Russia, the hereditary duke was belatedly accepted as the ruler of his German duchy. He and his wife, Anne, departed for Kiel, the capital of Holstein, with a generous Russian pension.

Left behind, Elizabeth was plunged into grief. Within six months, her mother, her future husband, and her beloved sister had all abandoned her. Although, by her mother's will, she now was next in line to the throne after Peter II, she posed no political threat to the youthful tsar. Indeed, she turned to him for friendship, and soon she and her nephew, a handsome, physically robust boy, tall for his age, became companions. Peter enjoyed his aunt's beauty and bubbling high spirits and liked having her nearby. In March 1728, when the court moved to Moscow, Elizabeth accompanied him. She shared the young emperor's passion for hunting, and together they galloped through the hills of the Moscow countryside. In summer, they went boating together; in winter, sledging and tobogganing. When Peter was not there, Elizabeth sought other male companions. She confessed that she was "content only when she was in love," and there was talk that she had been generous in giving pleasure to the young emperor himself.

To the world, she might seem madcap, but despite her frivolity, there was another side to Elizabeth. She was a serious religious believer, and her moods of precipitous pleasure-seeking were followed by extended retreats into prayer. When in a mood of piety, she would spend hours on her knees in churches and convents. Then life would reach out for her again in the form of some laughing Guards officer. She was endowed with her father's ardent impetuosity and never hesitated to gratify her desires; before she was twenty, there were reports that she had given herself to six young men. She was unashamed; she told herself that she had been made beautiful for a reason and that fate had robbed her of the only man she had ever really loved.

She remained indifferent to power and responsibility. The friends who urged her to take more interest in her future were turned away. Then, there was a moment when the throne itself seemed there for the taking. On the night of January 11, 1730, fourteen-year-old Peter II, dangerously ill, died of smallpox. Elizabeth, then twenty, was asleep nearby. Her French physician, Armand Lestocq, burst into her bedroom, saying that if she arose, presented herself to the Guards, showed herself to the people, hurried to the Senate, and proclaimed herself empress, she could not fail. Elizabeth sent him away and went back to sleep. By morning, the opportunity had evaporated. The Imperial Council had elected her thirty-six-year-old cousin, Anne of Courland, as empress. Elizabeth's failure to act was based partly on her apprehension that if she moved and failed, there was the chance of disgrace, even imprisonment. The stronger reason was that she was not ready. She did not want power and protocol; she preferred freedom. She never regretted that night's decision. Later, she said, "I was too young then. I am very glad that I did not assert my right to the throne earlier; I was too young and my people would never have borne with me."

The council had pushed Anne of Courland forward that night because it believed that Anne would prove a weaker, more docile monarch than the daughter of Peter the Great. Anne, who had left Russia twenty years before as a seventeen-year-old widow and who had remained unmarried and had no children, was the daughter of Peter's gentle, weak-minded half-brother and co-tsar, Ivan V. Peter had been fond of Ivan, and when his hapless brother died, Peter swore to take care of his wife and her three young daughters. Peter kept his word. In 1710, after his victory at Poltava, he arranged the marriage of his half-niece, seventeen-year-old Anne, to nineteen-year-old Frederick William, Duke of Courland. The marriage, however, was brief. Peter himself arranged a gargantuan wedding feast at which the new bridegroom drank himself into a stupor. On leaving Russia a few days later, he developed colic, went into paroxysms, and died on the road. His young widow begged to be allowed to remain with her mother in St. Petersburg, but Peter insisted that she take up her position in Courland. She obeyed and, supported by Russian money and military power, became the ruler of the duchy. Twenty years later, she still was there, governing with the aid of her German secretary and lover, Count Ernst Johann Biron. When the Imperial Council of Russia offered her the throne, the offer was hedged with many conditions: she was not to marry or appoint her successor, and the council was to retain approval over war and peace, levying taxes, spending money, granting estates, and the appointment of all officers over the rank of colonel. Anne accepted these conditions and was crowned in Moscow in the spring of 1730. Then, with the support of the Guards regiments, she tore up the documents she had signed and reestablished the autocracy.

Despite her crown, Anne was always wary of Elizabeth. Concerned that her twenty-one-year-old cousin might constitute a threat, she took Elizabeth aside when the younger woman came to pay her respects. "My sister," Anne said, "we have very few princesses of the Imperial House remaining and it therefore behooves us to live together in the strictest union and harmony, whereto I mean to contribute with all my power." Elizabeth's cheerful, open reply partially convinced the empress that her own fears were exaggerated.

For eleven years, from the age of twenty to the age of thirty-one, Elizabeth lived under the rule of Empress Anne. At first, she was expected to attend court on formal occasions and sit demurely near the empress. Elizabeth did her best, but nothing could prevent her outshining her cousin. Not only was she the only living child of Peter the Great, she was also the undisputed belle of the imperial court. Eventually, she wearied of the strain of living at court and retreated to a country estate, where she resumed her independent life, and her behavior and morals were free of court surveillance. A magnificent horsewoman, she often rode dressed as a man; her purpose was to display her legs, which were shapely and could best be admired in male breeches. Elizabeth loved the Russian countryside, with its primeval forests and wide meadowlands. She joined in the lives of the peasants and shared their amusements: dancing and singing, mushrooming in summer, tobogganing and skating in winter, sitting before a fire, eating roasted nuts and butter cakes.

Because she was an unmarried young woman, her private life subject to no rules or authority, she became a subject of court gossip—and, inevitably, of the empress's attention. Anne was offended by Elizabeth's frivolity, jealous of her appeal to men, nervous about her popularity, and uncertain of her loyalty. At one point, Anne was so incensed by tales of Elizabeth's behavior that she threatened to shut her up in a convent. For her part, Elizabeth understood that her status was changing when her yearly income was cut, then cut again. Anne's hostility, veiled at first, turned to personal meanness. When Elizabeth was infatuated with a young sergeant named Alexis Shubin, the empress banished the young man to Kamchatka, on the Pacific, five thousand miles away. Elizabeth herself was commanded to return immediately to St. Petersburg.

Elizabeth obeyed, taking a house in the capital, where she made a point of getting to know the soldiers in the Guards regiments. The officers who had served under her father and who had known Elizabeth since childhood were delighted to see the last surviving child of their hero. She visited and spent time in their barracks, became familiar with the speech and habits of soldiers as well as officers, flattered them, reminisced with them, lost money to them at cards, stood godmother to many of their children, and soon had dazzled and conquered them. As much as her beauty and generosity, they admired and trusted the fact that she was Russian. No one knew whether, at this stage, she had an ulterior motive, a plan. Empress Anne was on the throne; the idea of dislodging her must have been remote, if it existed at all. Probably the obvious was true: Elizabeth was spontaneous, generous, and hospitable; she loved people and wanted to be surrounded by people who admired her. In any case, she was constantly about in the streets of the capital. And the more she was seen, the more popular she became.

Ironically, this handsome, much-admired young woman now found herself unable to marry. That she was the daughter and a potential heir of Peter the Great should have given her a glittering marital allure. But with Anne of Courland on the throne, Elizabeth faced insurmountable obstacles to any gilded marriage. No royal house in Europe could allow a son to pay her court lest this be interpreted as an unfriendly act toward Empress Anne. A different handicap affected the possibility of marriage to a son of the Russian nobility. The danger here was that by marrying a countryman of lesser rank, a woman who was a potential sovereign could undermine any potential future claim to the throne.

Elizabeth's reaction was to reject any thought of marriage and choose freedom instead. If she could not have a royal or a noble husband, she would have a soldier of the Guards, a coachman, a handsome lackey. Indeed, a man appeared whom she was to love devotedly and to whom her attachment was to be lifelong. As her father had found happiness with a peasant wife, Elizabeth discovered her own companion of humble origin. One morning she heard a powerful new voice, a deep, rich bass, singing in the choir of the court chapel. The voice, she discovered, belonged to a tall young man with black eyes, black hair, and an appealing smile. He was a son of Ukrainian peasants, born the same year as Elizabeth; his name was Alexis Razumovsky. Elizabeth immediately made him a member of the choir in her private chapel. Soon, he had a room near her apartment.

As a favorite, Razumovsky was ideal for Elizabeth, not only because of his extraordinary good looks but because he was a genuinely decent and simple man, universally liked for his kindliness, good nature, and tact. Untroubled by education, he was wholly lacking in ambition and never interfered in politics. Later, Catherine the Great wrote of Alexis Razumovsky and his younger brother Kyril that she "knew of no other family enjoying the sovereign's favor to a like degree, who were so much loved, by so many people, as the two brothers." Elizabeth loved his handsome face, his gentle manner, his magnificent voice. He became her lover, and possibly, after a secret marriage, her morganatic husband; between themselves, courtiers called him "the Emperor of the Night." Once she was on the throne, Elizabeth made him a count, a prince, and a field marshal. But while his sovereign loaded him with titles, Razumovsky said to her, "Your Majesty may create me a field marshal, but I defy you or anyone to make even a tolerable captain out of me."

In her mid-twenties, Elizabeth still seemed all froth and exuberance in comparison to the austere, forbidding Empress Anne. In a different sphere, the contrast was more striking: Anne was surrounded by Germans; Elizabeth was heart and soul a Russian, a lover of the language, the people, the customs. Although there remained no external sign that she was eager to assert her claim to the throne, beneath her outer calm, some thought they saw something else. "In public, she has an unaffected gaiety, and a certain air of giddiness that seems to possess her whole mind," said the wife of the British ambassador. "But in private I have heard her talk with such a strain of good sense and steady reasoning that I am persuaded the other behavior is a feint."

Another shadow fell across Elizabeth's future when Empress Anne, a childless widow, brought to St. Petersburg her German niece, the daughter of her sister, Catherine of Mecklenburg, and converted her to Orthodoxy under the name Anna Leopoldovna. Next, the empress proposed that Anna Leopoldovna marry the German prince Anthony Ulrich of Brunswick-Wolfenbüttel. Anna Leopoldovna, who was in love with someone else, refused, but Empress Anne insisted, and in the spring of 1738 the engagement was announced. The months before her marriage saw Anna Leopoldovna transformed from a lively, pleasant girl into a plain, silent, unhappy bride-to-be, bitterly resentful of her aunt's decision. Elizabeth, in contrast, continued to appear confident and charming, and her beauty, if not quite as fresh as a decade before, remained sufficiently striking to irritate the empress.

In July 1739, Anna Leopoldovna married Anthony Ulrich, and on August 24, 1740, she gave birth to a son. Overjoyed, Empress Anne insisted that the boy be named Ivan after her own father. Scarcely a month later, the empress suffered a stroke. She recovered temporarily and, in feverish haste, declared her infant grandnephew to be her heir; the baby's mother, Anna Leopoldovna, would be named regent if the boy came to the throne while still a minor. On October 16, Empress Anna suffered a second stroke. This time her doctors pronounced her condition hopeless, and, at the age of forty-seven, she died. The following day, the empress's will was read publicly. The two-month-old baby was proclaimed Emperor Ivan VI. Elizabeth, then thirty, and the baby's parents dutifully swore allegiance to their new sovereign.

Turmoil followed. The infant's mother, Anna Leopoldovna, swallowed her chagrin at not being awarded the crown herself and assumed the office of regent. She appointed her German husband, Anthony Ulrich of Brunswick, commander in chief of the Russian army and then resumed her relationship with her lover, the Saxon ambassador, Count Lynar. Her husband's humiliation was public; soldiers, visible to all, were posted to bar him from his wife's apartments whenever her lover was with her.

Elizabeth, Peter the Great's closest descendant by blood, had now been passed over three times, and still she seemed not to care. She did not challenge the new regent's authority. Nor, on the other hand, did she alter her own way of life. She was often seen in the streets of St. Petersburg; she walked every day on the parade ground of the Preobrazhensky Guards barracks, close to her palace. Diplomats and foreign capitals hummed with speculation. The British ambassador reported to London that Elizabeth was "extremely obliging and affable, and in consequence much personally beloved and extremely popular. She has also the additional advantage of being the daughter of Peter the Great who, though he was more feared than any former prince of this century, was at the same time more beloved also. . . . This love certainly descends to his posterity and gives a general bent to the minds of the common people and of the soldiery, too."

At first, the relationship between Anna Leopoldovna and Elizabeth was correct. Elizabeth was frequently invited to the Winter Palace, but she soon became more reserved and went only for ceremonies she could not avoid. By February 1741, the regent had given orders that Elizabeth be watched; these constraints did not escape the notice of the court and the diplomatic community. During the summer of 1741, the relationship worsened. Anna Leopoldovna now surrounded herself only with foreigners. Count Lynar continually pressed her to order Elizabeth's arrest. The restrictions placed on Elizabeth became more onerous. In July, her income was reduced. In early autumn, she heard rumors that the regent was planning to insist that she put in writing a renunciation of her claim to the throne. A tale circulated that Anna Leopoldovna was about to force her to become a nun and enter a convent. On the morning of November 24, Dr. Lestocq came into Elizabeth's bedroom, awakened her, and handed her a paper. On one side, he had drawn a picture of her as empress, seated on the throne; on the other, he had depicted her dressed as a nun, and behind her he had drawn a rack and a gibbet. "Madam," he said, "you must choose finally now whether to be empress or to be relegated to a convent and see your servants perish under torture." Elizabeth decided to act. At midnight, she set off for the barracks of the Preobrazhensky Guards. There, she said, "You know whose daughter I am. Follow me!"

"We are ready," shouted the soldiers. "We will kill them all."

"No," said Elizabeth, "no Russian blood is to be spilled." Followed by three hundred men, she made her way through a bitterly cold night to the Winter Palace. Walking past the unprotesting palace guards, she led the way to Anna Leopoldovna's bedroom, where she touched the sleeping regent on the shoulder and said, "Little sister, it is time to rise." Realizing that all was lost, Anna Leopoldovna begged for mercy for herself and her son. Elizabeth assured her that no harm would come to any member of the Brunswick family. To the nation she announced that she had ascended her father's throne and that the usurpers had been apprehended and would be charged with having deprived her of her hereditary rights. On November 25, 1741, at three o'clock in the afternoon, Elizabeth reentered the Winter Palace. At thirty-two, the daughter of Peter the Great was the empress of Russia.

Her first act as sovereign was to shower gratitude on those who had supported her during the long years of waiting. Promotions, titles, jewels, and other rewards poured out in a rich stream. Each of the Preobrazhensky Guardsmen who had marched with her to the Winter Palace was promoted. Lestocq was made a privy councillor and physician in chief to the sovereign, besides receiving a portrait of the empress set in diamonds and a handsome annuity. Razumovsky became a count, a court chamberlain, and the Grand Master of the Hunt. Other privy councillors were appointed, other counts created, and more jewel-encrusted portraits, snuff boxes, and rings placed in eager hands.

But Elizabeth's most pressing problem could not be resolved with largesse. A living tsar, Ivan VI, remained in St. Petersburg. He had inherited the throne at the age of two months, he was dethroned at fifteen months, he did not know he was emperor, but he had been anointed, his likeness had been scattered through the country on coins, and prayers had been offered for him in all the churches of Russia. From the beginning, Ivan haunted Elizabeth. She had originally intended to send him abroad with his parents, and, for this reason, she packed the entire Brunswick family off to Riga as a first stage of their journey west. Once they arrived in Riga, however, she had a second thought: perhaps it would be safer to keep her small, dangerous prisoner securely under guard in her own country. The child was removed from his parents and classified as a secret state prisoner, a status he retained for the remaining twenty-two years of his life. He was moved from one prison to another; even then, Elizabeth could not know when an attempt to liberate him and restore him to the throne might be made. Almost immediately, a solution suggested itself: if Ivan was to live and still be rendered permanently harmless, a new heir to the throne must be found, a successor to Elizabeth who would anchor the future of her dynasty and be recognized by the Russian nation and the world. Such an heir, Elizabeth knew by then, would never come from her own body. She had no acknowledged husband; it was late now, and no one suitable would ever be found. Furthermore, in spite of her many years as a carefree voluptuary, she had never known pregnancy. The heir she must have, therefore, must be the child of another woman. And there was such a child: the son of her beloved sister, Anne; the grandson of her revered father, Peter the Great. The heir whom she would bring to Russia, nurture, and proclaim was a fourteen-year-old boy living in Holstein.

❧ 5 ❧

The Making of a Grand Duke

THERE WAS NO ONE Elizabeth loved better than her sister Anne. Just as the younger of the two sisters had inspired rhapsodic descriptions of her beauty and high spirits, the elder also found euphoric admirers. "I don't believe there is a princess in Europe at the present time who could vie with Princess Anne in majestic beauty," wrote Baron Mardefeld, Prussian minister in St. Petersburg. "She is a brunette, but of a vividly white and quite un-artificial complexion. Her features are so perfectly beautiful that an accomplished artist, judging them by the severest classical standards, could desire nothing more. Even when she is silent, one can read the amiability and magnanimity of her character in her large and beautiful eyes. Her behavior is without affectation, she is always the same and serious rather than gay. From her youth up she has striven to cultivate her mind. . . . She speaks French and German perfectly."

Anne's life was shorter than Elizabeth's. She was married at seventeen to Charles Frederick, Duke of Holstein, a young man of exalted prospects and moderate abilities. He was the only son of Hedwig Sophia, the sister of the legendary King Charles XII of Sweden, and Frederick IV, Duke of Holstein, who died fighting in King Charles's army. Educated in Sweden, he had good reason to believe that his childless uncle, Charles XII, intended him to be his heir. When King Charles died and Frederick, Prince of Hesse, was given the Swedish throne, the rejected nineteen-year-old Charles Frederick retreated to St. Petersburg to seek the protection of Peter the Great. The tsar received the duke, who, being a pretender to the Swedish crown, could serve as a useful political weapon.

The visiting duke, whose ambition exceeded his abilities, had not been at the Russian court long before he began intriguing for the hand of one of the emperor's daughters. Peter opposed any such marriage, but his wife, Catherine, liked the duke and persuaded her daughter Anne that he would be a good match. The princess yielded to her mother and an engagement was agreed upon.

Suddenly, in January 1725, Peter the Great fell mortally ill. On his deathbed, he awoke from delirium and cried, "Where's little Annie. I would see her." His daughter was summoned, but before she arrived, her father was delirious again, and he never recovered consciousness. The betrothal and marriage were postponed, but only briefly. On May 21, 1725, Anne married the duke.

During her mother's short reign, Anne and her husband lived in St. Petersburg. When Catherine died in 1727, the duke and his wife left Russia for Holstein. Anne was sorry to leave her sister, Elizabeth, but pleased to find herself pregnant. On February 21, 1728, six months after her arrival in Holstein, she gave birth to a son, who, the following day, was christened in the Lutheran church in Kiel. The baby's name, Charles Peter Ulrich, proclaimed his illustrious lineage: "Charles" came from his father, but also from his great-uncle, Charles XII; "Peter" from his grandfather, Peter the Great; "Ulrich" from Ulrica, the reigning queen of Sweden.

While Anne was recovering, a ball was given in honor of the new prince. It was February, and although the weather was damp and icy, the happy nineteen-year-old mother insisted on standing at an open window to watch the fireworks that followed the ball. When her ladies protested, she laughed and said, "I am Russian, remember, and my health is used to a ruder climate than this." She caught a chill, which aggravated a tubercular condition; three months after the birth of her son, she was dead. In her will, she had asked to be buried next to her father, and a Russian frigate arrived to carry her body up the Baltic to St. Petersburg.

When Anne died, Charles Frederick mourned not only the loss of his young wife but also the shutting off of the golden stream flowing to Kiel from the imperial treasury in St. Petersburg. The duke's expenses were high; he maintained a crowd of servants and gaudily uniformed bodyguards, all justified by the fact that he still considered himself the heir to the crown of Sweden. Preoccupied by these concerns, Charles Frederick took little interest in his infant son. The boy was handed over to nurses and then, until he was seven, to French governesses, who taught him to speak a serviceable French, although he was always more at home in his native German. At seven, Peter began military training, learning to stand erect at guard posts and to strut about with a miniature sword and musket. Soon, he came to love the forms and atmosphere of military drill. Sitting with a tutor, he would leap up from his lessons and run to the window to watch soldiers drilling in the court-yard. He was happiest on the parade ground himself, wearing a soldier's uniform. But Peter had little endurance. Frequently ill, he had to sit in his room and substitute the lining up and maneuvering of toy soldiers for real parade ground drill. Eventually, his father noticed him. One day when Peter was nine and had reached the rank of sergeant, he was standing guard at the door of a room where the duke was dining with his officers. When the meal began, the hungry boy did nothing but stare at the procession of dishes being carried past him to the table. Then, during the second course, his father rose and brought him to the table, where he solemnly promoted his son to the rank of lieutenant and invited him to sit down among the officers. Years later, in Russia, Peter said that this was "the happiest day of my life."

Peter received a haphazard education. He mastered Swedish as well as French and learned to translate that language into German. He loved music, although his interest was not encouraged. He delighted in play-ing the violin but he was never taught to play properly. Instead, he prac-ticed on his own, playing his favorite melodies as best he could, tormenting all within earshot.

As a child, Peter was pulled in many directions. He was the heir, after his father, to the dukedom of Holstein, and on his father's death, he would also inherit his father's claim to the throne of Sweden. Through his mother, he was the only surviving male descendant of Peter the Great, and therefore he also remained a potential heir to the Russian throne. But when, on the death of his cousin Tsar Peter II, the Russian Imperial Council ignored the claim of the little Holstein prince, along with the claim of Peter's daughter Elizabeth, and elected Anne of Courland to the Russian throne, the Holstein court, which had hoped for benefits from little Peter's Russian connection, reacted bitterly. Thereafter, in Kiel, Russia was ridiculed in the boy's presence as a nation of barbarians.

This multiplicity of possible futures placed too many demands on Peter. It was almost as if nature had failed him: the child who was the nearest male blood relation of both of the towering adversaries in the Great Northern War—the grandson of the great Peter, that dynamo of human energy, and the grandnephew of the invincible Charles, the most brilliant soldier of his day—was a puny, sickly boy with protruding eyes, a weak chin, and little energy. The life he was forced to lead, the immense legacy he was forced to carry, were too great a burden. In any subordinate position, he would have performed his duty unflinchingly. Command of a regiment would have delighted him. An empire, even a kingdom, would be too much.

In 1739, when Peter was eleven, his father died and the boy became, in name at least, Duke of Holstein. In addition to the dukedom, his father's claim to the Swedish crown passed to the son. His uncle, Prince Adolphus Frederick of Holstein, the Lutheran bishop of Eutin, was appointed his guardian. Obviously, the bishop should have devoted particular care to the upbringing of a boy who was the possible heir to two thrones, but Adolphus was good-natured and lazy, and he shirked this duty. The task was delegated to a group of officers and tutors working under the authority of the grand marshal of the ducal court, a former cavalry officer named Otto Brümmer. This man, a rough, choleric martinet, abused his little sovereign without mercy; the young duke's French tutor observed that Brümmer was "better suited to train a horse than a prince." Brümmer assaulted his young charge with harsh punishment, mockery, public humiliation, and malnutrition. When, as frequently happened, the young prince performed poorly at his lessons, Brümmer would appear in the dining room and threaten to punish his pupil as soon as the meal was over. The frightened boy, unable to continue eating, would leave the table, vomiting. Thereupon, his master would order that he be given no food the next day. Throughout that day, the hungry child would be compelled to stand by the door at mealtimes with a picture of a donkey hung around his neck, watching his own courtiers eat. Brümmer routinely beat the boy with a stick or a whip and made him kneel for hours on hard, dried peas until his naked knees were red and swollen. The violence which Brümmer constantly inflicted on him produced a pathetic, twisted child. He became fearful, deceitful, antagonistic, boastful, cowardly, duplicitous, and cruel. He made friends only with the lowest of his servants, those whom he was allowed to strike. He tortured pet animals.

Brümmer's senseless regime, his pleasure in tormenting a child who might one day become king of Sweden or emperor of Russia, has never been explained. If by ill-treatment he hoped to steel the boy's character, the result was the opposite. Life was made too hard for Peter. His mind rebelled at every effort to pound knowledge or obedience into his head by beating and humiliating him. In all the chapters of

Peter's unhappy life, the worst monster he had to face was Otto Brümmer. The damage inflicted would be revealed in the future.

Just before his thirteenth birthday, Peter's life changed. On the night of
December 6, 1741, his aunt Elizabeth put an end to the reign of little
Tsar Ivan VI and to the regency of Ivan's mother, Anna Leopoldovna.
One of the new empress's first acts on the throne was to summon her
nephew, Peter, her last remaining male kinsman, whom she intended to
adopt and proclaim her successor. Her command was obeyed, and her
nephew was secretly hurried from Kiel to St. Petersburg; Elizabeth neither consulted nor revealed her intention to anyone until she had the
boy in safekeeping. Diplomats, obliged to explain her action to their
courts, suggested reasons: they cited the threat of Ivan VI; they noted
her devotion to her sister Anne. They also mentioned another, less
noble motive: self-preservation. With Ivan under guard, Peter was
Elizabeth's only competitor for the throne. If he remained in Holstein
and his Russian claim were to be backed by foreign powers, it could be
dangerous for her. But if he became a Russian grand duke, living under
her eye, it was she who would control his future.

As for Peter himself, Elizabeth's coup d'état turned the boy's life
upside down. At fourteen, he left the castle in Kiel and his native Holstein, of which he was still nominally the ruler, and, accompanied by
Brümmer, his tormentor, traveled to St. Petersburg. His departure from
Holstein was sudden and stealthy, almost an abduction; his subjects did
not know he was gone until three days after he was across the frontier.
Peter reached St. Petersburg at the beginning of January 1742. There, in
an emotional reception at the Winter Palace, the empress held out her
arms, shed tears, and promised to cherish her sister's only child as if he
were her own.

Elizabeth had never seen Peter before that moment. When she examined him, she saw what Sophia had seen four years before. He was
still an odd little figure, short for his age, pale, thin, and gawky. His
straggling blond hair was combed straight down to his shoulders. Attempting to show respect, he held his puny body as stiff as a wooden
soldier. When spoken to, Peter responded in a squeaking, prepubescent
mixture of German and French.

Surprised and disappointed by the appearance of the adolescent
standing before her, Elizabeth was even more appalled by his ignorance.

She herself was far from a scholar and even regarded excessive bookishness as injurious to health; she worried that this had caused the premature death of her sister Anne. She assigned Professor Staehlin, of the Imperial Academy of Sciences in St. Petersburg, an amiable Saxon, to accept chief responsibility for Peter's education. Introducing Staehlin to the boy, she said, "I see that Your Highness has still a great many pretty things to learn and Monsieur Staehlin here will teach them to you in such a pleasant manner that it will be a mere pastime for you." Staehlin began examining his new pupil, and it was immediately apparent that the boy was ignorant in almost every branch of knowledge. Staehlin also discovered that while his pupil was astonishingly childish for his age and so fidgety that it was difficult to fix his attention on anything, he nevertheless had a passion for everything relating to soldiers and warfare. On arrival, Elizabeth had made him a lieutenant colonel in the Preobrazhensky Guards, the senior regiment of the Russian Imperial Guard. Peter was unimpressed; he sneered at the loose, bottle-green uniforms of the Russian soldiers, so different from the tight-fitting, blue, Germanic uniforms of Holstein and Prussia.

Staehlin adapted as best he could. He made everything as easy as possible. He exposed his pupil to the history of Russia using books filled with maps and pictures, and by showing his pupil collections of old coins and medals borrowed from the art gallery. He gave Peter an idea of the geography of the country he was one day to rule by showing him a huge folio displaying all the fortresses of the empire, from Riga to the Turkish and Chinese frontiers. To broaden his pupil's horizons, he read news items from diplomatic dispatches and foreign gazettes, using maps or a globe to point out where these events were taking place. He taught geometry and mechanical sciences by making scale models; natural science by strolling with Peter in the palace gardens to point out categories of plants, trees, and flowers; architecture by taking him through the palace to explain how it was designed and built. As the boy was unable to sit quietly and listen while the tutor was talking, most of Peter's lessons were conducted with the teacher and his pupil walking up and down, side by side. The attempt to teach Peter to dance, a project removed from Staehlin's responsibility but one particularly close to the empress's heart, was a spectacular failure. Elizabeth, a consummate dancer, required her nephew to take intensive training in performing quadrilles and minuets. Four times a week, Peter was forced to drop whatever he was doing when the dancing master and a violinist arrived in his room. The result was disaster. Throughout his life, his dancing was comical.

For three years, Staehlin kept at his task. That he had little success was not his fault; the mischief had been done earlier when his student's spirit and interest in learning had been twisted and broken. To Peter, life seemed an oppressive round of instruction in matters about which he cared nothing. In his journal, Staehlin wrote that his pupil was "utterly frivolous" and "altogether unruly." Nevertheless, Staehlin was the only person in Peter's young life who made any attempt to understand the boy and handle him with intelligence and sympathy. And, although Peter learned little, he remained on friendly terms with this tutor for the rest of his life.

During his first year in Russia, Peter's schooling was affected by his delicate health. In October 1743, Staehlin wrote, "He is extremely weak and has lost the taste for everything that pleased him, even music." Once on a Saturday, when music was being played in the young duke's antechamber and a castrato was singing Peter's favorite air, the boy, lying with his eyes closed said in a barely audible whisper, "Will they stop playing soon?" Elizabeth hurried to his side and burst into tears.

Even when Peter was not ill, other problems afflicted him. He had no friends; indeed, he knew no one his age. And Brümmer, whose real character had not been seen or understood by Elizabeth, was always nearby. The boy's nerves, weakened by illness, were constantly threatened by Brümmer's violent behavior. Staehlin reports that one day Brümmer attacked and began to beat the young duke with his fists. When Staehlin intervened, Peter ran to the window and called for help from the guards in the courtyard. Then he fled to his own room and returned with a sword, shouting at Brümmer, "This will be your last piece of insolence. The next time you dare to raise your hand to me I will run you through with this sword." Nevertheless, the empress allowed Brümmer to stay. Peter realized that he had gained no respite from persecution by coming to Russia. If anything, his situation was worse: however unhappy he might have been with Brümmer in Kiel, at least he was home.

Elizabeth was distressed by her nephew's failure to make any discernable progress. She was not a patient woman; she wanted favorable results, and her nagging anxiety about the existence of Ivan VI drove her to push Peter and his tutors harder. Why, she asked herself, was her nephew such a difficult, unpromising boy? Surely, soon he would change. Sometimes, attempting to calm her anxiety and convince herself that all was well, Elizabeth showered exaggerated praise on her nephew's progress. "I cannot express in words the pleasure I feel when I see you employing your time so well," she would say. But as the months went by and there was no improvement, her hopes were sinking.

Elizabeth's principal grievance was her nephew's open dislike of everything Russian. She appointed teachers to instruct him in the Russian language and Orthodox religion and worked tutors and priests overtime to see that he learned. Studying theology two hours a day, he learned to babble bits of Orthodox doctrine, but he despised this new religion and felt nothing but contempt for its bearded priests. Cynically, he told the Austrian and Prussian ambassadors, "One promised priests a great many things that one could not perform." He approached the Russian language with the same attitude. He was given lessons, but he hated the language and made no effort to speak it grammatically. When he could, he surrounded himself with as many Holstein officials as possible and conversed with them only in German.

Peter's difficulty ran deeper than dislike and cynicism. It was not merely a matter of acquiring the Russian language; given sufficient time, he might have mastered it. But behind every task his teachers set him loomed the greater obstacle: the prospect of succeeding to the Russian throne; it was against this future that Peter rebelled. He had not the least interest in governing a vast and—as he saw it—primitive, foreign empire. He was homesick for Germany and Holstein. He longed for the simple, straightforward life of the barracks in Kiel, where life required only uniforms and drums, command and obedience. Chosen to be the future ruler of the greatest empire on earth, he remained at heart a little Holstein soldier. His hero was not his own towering Russian grandfather but the idol of every German soldier, Frederick of Prussia.

Nevertheless, the empress eventually had her way. On November 18, 1742, in the court chapel of the Kremlin, Peter Charles Ulrich was solemnly baptized and received into the Orthodox Church under the Russian name of Peter Fedorovich—a Romanov name intended to wipe away the taint of his Lutheran beginnings. Empress Elizabeth then formally proclaimed him heir to the Russian throne, raised him to the rank of Imperial Highness, and granted him the title of grand duke. Peter, speaking in memorized Russian, promised to reject all doctrines contrary to the teaching of the Orthodox Church, whereupon, at the end of the service, the assembled court took the oath of allegiance to him. Throughout the ceremony and at the public audience afterward, he displayed an unmistakable sullenness; foreign ambassadors, noting his mood, said that "as he spoke with his customary petulance, one may conclude he will not be a fanatical believer." That day, at least, Elizabeth simply refused to see these negative signs. When Peter was confirmed, she wept. Afterward, when the new grand duke returned to his apartment, he found waiting for him a draft for three hundred thousand rubles.

Despite her passionate display of emotion, Elizabeth still did not trust her nephew. To make his Russian commitments irrevocable and cut off all possibility of retreat, she liquidated his claim to the Swedish throne by making it a condition of a Russian-Swedish treaty that her nephew's Swedish rights be transferred to his former guardian, Johanna's brother, Adolphus Frederick of Holstein, Bishop of Lübeck. The bishop became heir to the Swedish throne in Peter's place.

The more obvious it became that Peter was miserable in Russia, the more Elizabeth worried. She had removed from the throne a branch of her family hated for its German connections only to find that the new heir she had chosen was even more German. Every possible Russian influence had been brought to bear on Peter, yet his ideas, tastes, prejudices, and outlook remained stubbornly German. She was bitterly disappointed, but she had to accept him. She could not send him back to Holstein. Peter was her closest living relative; he was newly Orthodox, newly proclaimed the heir, now the future hope of the Romanov dynasty. And when, in October 1743, he became seriously ill—not leaving his bed until mid-November—she realized how very much she needed him.

Indeed, the poor condition of Peter's health pushed Elizabeth into further action. He was always ailing; suppose he were to die? What then? A solution—the best, perhaps the only, solution—was to find him a wife. He was fifteen, and the presence of the right young wife might not only help him mature but might serve an even greater purpose by providing a new infant heir, a child better equipped than his father to guarantee the succession. Elizabeth decided to follow this path: a wife must be found quickly and an heir begotten. Hence the empress's haste to choose a bride for Peter; hence the urgent dispatches that Brümmer wrote at her behest to Johanna in Zerbst: Come to Russia! Bring your daughter! Make haste! Make haste! Make haste!

❧ 6 ❧

Meeting Elizabeth and Peter

WHILE SOPHIA AND HER MOTHER waited, Peter suddenly appeared. "I could wait no longer," he declared in German with an exaggerated smile. His enthusiasm seemed genuine, however, and both Sophia and her mother were pleased. As he stood before them, nervously fidgeting, Sophia looked carefully at the future husband whom she had seen only once before, as a boy of ten. Now, at fifteen, he was still unusually short and thin, and his features—pale face, wide mouth, sharply receding chin—had not changed greatly since she had seen him five years before. The warmth of his greeting might be explained by the fact that she was a cousin near his own age, someone with whom he could speak German and who had shared, and therefore understood, the background from which he had come. He may have believed that this little cousin would become his ally in resisting the demands that Russia was making on him. Walking back and forth, talking incessantly, he stopped only when Dr. Lestocq arrived to say that the empress was ready to receive them. Peter offered his arm to Johanna, a lady-in-waiting gave hers to Sophia, and they passed through a succession of candlelit halls, filled with people bowing and curtsying. At last, they reached the portal of the imperial apartments, and the double doors were flung open. Before them stood Elizabeth, empress of Russia.

Sophia and her mother were dazzled. Elizabeth was tall, with a full, rounded figure. She had large, brilliant blue eyes, a broad forehead, a full mouth, red lips, white teeth, and a clear, rosy complexion. Her hair, naturally blond, now was dyed a luxuriant black. She was dressed in an immense, hoop-skirted gown of silver trimmed with gold lace, and her hair, neck, and ample bosom were covered with diamonds. The effect of this woman, standing before her in a blaze of silver, gold embroidery, and jewels, was overwhelming. And Sophia still managed to notice and would always remember a particular crowning touch: a black feather standing upright from her hair on one side of her head, then curving to cover part of her face.

Johanna, remembering Brümmer's advice, kissed Elizabeth's hand and stammered her thanks for the favors showered on her and her daughter. Elizabeth embraced her and said, "All that I have done for you so far is nothing compared to what I shall do for your family in the future. My own blood is not dearer to me than yours." When Elizabeth turned to Sophia, the fourteen-year-old bowed from the waist and curtsied. Elizabeth, smiling, noticed the girl's freshness, intelligence, and discreet, submissive manner. Sophia meanwhile had made her own judgment, and, thirty years later, she wrote, "It was quite impossible on seeing her for the first time not to be astonished by her beauty and the majesty of her bearing." Here, in this woman covered with jewels and radiating power, she saw the embodiment of what she hoped someday to become.

The next day was Peter's sixteenth birthday. The empress, appearing in a brown dress embroidered with silver, "her head, neck, and bosom covered with jewels," presented both mother and daughter with the Order of St. Catherine. Alexis Razumovsky, costumed as Master of the Hunt, bore the ribbons and insignia of the order on a golden plate. As he approached, Sophia passed another judgment: Razumovsky, the official lover, the "Emperor of the Night," was, in Sophia's words, "one of the most handsome men I have seen in my life." Again, Elizabeth was in an excellent humor. Smiling broadly, she beckoned Sophia and Johanna and hung the ribbon of the order around their necks.

The empress's display of warmth to Johanna and Sophia came from something deeper than her satisfaction that a promising political marriage seemed in the offing. Elizabeth had not had children. Two years before, she had reached out to her sister's child, Peter, brought him to Russia, and made him her heir. But Peter had not responded to the kind of maternal love she had tried to give. Now she had chosen for him a bride who was the niece of the man she had loved. Alone on her throne, the empress of Russia was hoping to create around herself a family.

Johanna perceived the empress's welcome as a part of her own political triumph. She found herself at the center of a glittering court, favored by a monarch whose generosity was legendary. Mother and daughter were given their own household, with chamberlains, ladies- and gentlemen-in-waiting, and a staff of lesser servants. "We are living like queens," Johanna wrote to her husband. "Everything is bedecked, inlaid with gold, wonderful. We drive out in marvelous style."

Johanna's ambition for herself and her daughter was approaching fruition. As to the private, intimate side of this coming marriage, and the obligation to give her daughter useful advice, the thirty-two-year-old mother had given the matter little thought; after all, no one had cared about her feelings when, years earlier, she had married a man almost twice her age. She knew little about the real character of the future bridegroom; the fact that he was to be an emperor was sufficient. If Johanna had asked herself whether these two adolescents were likely to develop any mutual romantic passion, her honest answer would have been a shrug. In arranged royal marriages, these questions were irrelevant. Johanna knew this; Sophia sensed it. The only figure who still believed in love and hoped that passion as well as politics would bind this youthful relationship was Elizabeth.

Sophia later remembered of Peter that "for the first ten days, he seemed glad to see my mother and me. . . . In that short space of time I became aware that he cared little for the nation over which he was destined to rule, that he remained a convinced Lutheran, did not like his entourage, and was very childish. I kept silent and listened which helped gain his confidence."

What did Peter think of Sophia and their approaching betrothal? It is true that on the night of her arrival, he had made a pretty speech. And in the days that followed, he repeatedly expressed his delight at having a relative his own age to whom he could talk freely. But soon her polite interest in him encouraged him to speak freely, too freely. At the first opportunity, he told her that he was really in love with someone else, the daughter of a former lady-in-waiting of Elizabeth's. He still wanted to marry this girl, he said, but, sadly, her mother had recently been disgraced and exiled to Siberia. Now his aunt, the empress, would not permit a marriage to the daughter. He went on to say that he was now resigned to marrying Sophia "because his aunt wished it."

Peter, still regarding Sophia more as a playmate than as a future wife, had not meant to hurt her; he was simply, in his way, being honest. "I blushed to hear these confidences," Sophia wrote in her *Memoirs*, "and thanked him for his trust in me, but in my heart I was astonished at his imprudence and want of judgment." If she was wounded by his mindless insensitivity, she did not show this. She had learned to deal with absence of love in her own family, and now she was prepared to deal with it in this new situation. Besides, her father's parting command had been that she should respect the grand duke as her "master, father and sovereign lord" and seek to win his love "through meekness and docility."

Sophia was only fourteen, but she was wise and practical. For the moment, she adapted herself to Peter's ways and accepted her role as a friend and playmate. But there was no trace of love, not even the fumbling version she had experienced with her uncle George.

❧ 7 ❧

Pneumonia

I T DID NOT TAKE Sophia long to understand two underlying facts about her position in Russia: first, that it was Elizabeth, not Peter, whom she had to please; and, second, that if she wanted to succeed in this new country, she must learn its language and practice its religious faith. Within a week of her arrival in Moscow, her education began. A professor was provided to teach her to read and speak Russian, and a scholarly priest was assigned to instruct her in the doctrines and liturgy of the Russian Orthodox Church. In contrast to Peter, who had bucked and rebelled against everything his teachers tried to teach him, Sophia was eager to learn.

The more urgent task, in the empress's thinking, was conversion to Orthodoxy, and the religious figure chosen to teach was specifically equipped to calm the apprehensions of a young Protestant being asked to abandon her Lutheran faith. Simon Todorsky, bishop of Pskov, was a cultivated, broad-minded man who spoke fluent German, having spent four years studying at the University of Halle in Germany. There he had come to believe that what mattered in religion was not the differences between creeds but the inner, fundamental message of Christianity. He counseled Sophia that the Orthodox faith was not so different from the Lutheran and that she would not be betraying her promise to her father if she converted. Impressed, Sophia wrote to her father that she had come to realize that the discrepancy between Lutheranism and Orthodoxy was only that "the external rites are quite different, but the Church here is bound to them by the uncouthness of the people." Christian Augustus, alarmed at the speed with which his daughter's Protestantism seemed to be slipping away, wrote back:

Search yourself with care whether you are really in your heart inspired by religious inclination or whether, perhaps, without being aware of it, the marks of favor shown you by the empress . . . have influenced you in that direction. We human beings often see only what is before our eyes. But God in His infinite justice searches the heart and our secret motives and manifests accordingly to us His mercy.

Sophia, struggling to reconcile the opposing beliefs of two men she respected and honored, had difficulty finding her way. "The change of religion gives the princess infinite pain," Mardefeld, the Prussian ambassador, wrote to King Frederick. "Her tears flow abundantly."

While studying with Todorsky, Sophia also flung herself into study of the Russian language. The day was too short for her; she begged that her lessons be prolonged. She began rising from bed at night, taking a book and a candle, and walking barefoot on the cold stone floor, repeating and memorizing Russian words. Not surprisingly, this being Moscow in early March, she caught a cold. At first, Johanna, alarmed that her daughter might be criticized as too susceptible to illness, tried to conceal her sickness. Sophia developed a fever, her teeth began to chatter, she was bathed in sweat—eventually, she fainted. Doctors, summoned belatedly, diagnosed acute pneumonia and demanded that the unconscious patient be bled. Johanna vehemently refused, claiming that excessive bleeding had caused the death of her brother Charles, about to be betrothed to the young Elizabeth, and that she would not permit other doctors to kill her daughter. "There I lay with a high fever between my mother and the doctors, arguing," Sophia wrote later. "I could not help groaning, for which I was scolded by my mother who expected me to suffer in silence."

Word that Sophia's life was in danger reached the empress in retreat at the thirteenth-century Troitsa Monastery, forty miles away. She rushed back to Moscow, hurried to the sickroom, and walked in on an argument still raging between Johanna and the physicians. Elizabeth immediately intervened and commanded that whatever the medical men considered necessary must be done. Berating Johanna for daring to oppose *her* doctors, she ordered an immediate bloodletting. When Johanna continued to protest, the empress had the girl's mother evicted from the room. Elizabeth then cradled Sophia's head while a doctor opened a vein in her foot and took two ounces of blood. From that day on, for the four weeks that followed, Elizabeth nursed Sophia herself. Because the fever persisted, Elizabeth prescribed repeated bleeding—and the fourteen-year-old girl was bled sixteen times in twenty-seven days.

With the patient slipping in and out of consciousness, Elizabeth sat by her bed. When the physicians shook their heads, the empress wept. The childless woman was filled with a kind of maternal love for this young girl whom she scarcely knew and whom she thought she was about to lose. When Sophia awoke, it was in Elizabeth's arms. Afterward, Sophia always remembered these moments of intimacy. Through all she was to enjoy and endure over the years at Elizabeth's hands—generosity and kindness, alternating with pettiness and harsh disapproval—Sophia was never to forget the woman who, during these uncertain days, had leaned over her, stroked her hair, and kissed her forehead.

There were some for whom Sophia's illness was a cause for joy, not grief. The vice-chancellor, Alexis Bestuzhev, and those who had favored a Saxon marriage for Peter were jubilant, although Elizabeth quickly dampened their glee by declaring that no matter what happened—even if she had the misfortune to lose Sophia—"the devil would take her before she would ever have any princess of Saxony." In Berlin, Frederick of Prussia began thinking of replacement candidates; he wrote to the landgrave of Hesse-Darmstadt asking about his daughter's availability in case Sophia should die.

Meanwhile, the youthful invalid was—without awareness of the fact—winning hearts. Her ladies-in-waiting knew how she had contracted this illness; they told the chambermaids, who told the lackeys, who passed it through the palace and thence out into the city: the little foreign princess loved Russia so much that now she was lying at death's door because she had risen from bed every night in order to learn the Russian language more quickly! In the space of a few weeks, this story won Sophia the affection of many who had been repelled by the aloof, negative attitude of Grand Duke Peter.

Another incident in the sickroom, widely reported, further burnished Sophia's reputation. At a moment when the worst was feared, Johanna spoke of bringing a Lutheran pastor to comfort her daughter. Sophia, still exhausted by fever and bloodletting, nevertheless managed to whisper, "Why do that? Call Simon Todorsky instead. I would rather talk to him." Elizabeth, hearing this, burst into tears. Soon, Sophia's request was the talk of the court and the city, and people who had regarded the arrival of the Protestant German girl with apprehension now were filled with sympathy.

Whether Sophia knew what she was doing and understood the possible effect of her words cannot be known. It is unlikely that in the few weeks she had been in Russia she had become a genuine convert to the Orthodox faith. And yet the fact remains that, lying close to death, she had the extraordinary luck—or the extraordinary presence of mind—to use the most effective means of winning the sympathy of her future countrymen: "Call Simon Todorsky."

In her *Memoirs,* Catherine, looking back, seems to suggest that the fourteen-year-old girl did, in fact, understand the impact of her request. She admits that there were times during her illness when she did deceive. Sometimes, she would shut her eyes, pretending to be asleep in order to listen to the conversation of the ladies by her bedside. French, which she spoke, was commonly used at the Russian court. Together, she said, "the ladies would speak their minds freely and in that way I learned a great many things."

Perhaps the explanation is even simpler. There is no apparent reason that Sophia's spirits should have been raised or her health improved by the appearance at her bedside of an unknown Lutheran clergyman. And if Lutheranism and Orthodoxy were essentially similar, as Todorsky had explained to her, why not ask Todorsky himself, a man she liked and whose conversation she enjoyed, to come and comfort her?

By the first week in April, Sophia's fever had passed. As she was regaining her strength, she noticed changes in the attitudes of people around her. Not only were the ladies in the sickroom more sympathetic; she also noticed that "my mother's behavior during my illness had lowered her in everyone's esteem." Unfortunately, just at this point, Johanna chose to create more difficulty for herself. Johanna's concern for her daughter's life had been genuine, but while the young girl was quietly winning praise and admirers, her mother, barred from the sickroom, had become querulous. One day when Sophia was recovering, Johanna sent a maid to ask her daughter to give her a piece of blue and silver brocade that had been a parting gift from Sophia's uncle, her father's brother. Sophia surrendered the cloth, but she did so reluctantly, saying that she treasured it, not only because her uncle had given it to her but because it was the only beautiful thing she had brought with her to Russia. Indignant, the ladies in the sickroom repeated the incident to Elizabeth, who immediately sent Sophia a large quantity of beautiful material, including a new length of rich blue silk woven with silver flowers, similar to, but much finer than, the original fabric.

On April 21, her fifteenth birthday, Sophia appeared at court for the first time since her illness. "I cannot imagine that the world found me a very edifying sight," she wrote later. "I had become as thin as a skeleton. I had grown taller, but my face and all its features were drawn; my hair was falling out and I was deathly pale. I appeared to myself as frightfully ugly; I didn't even recognize my own face. The empress sent me a pot of rouge that day and ordered me to use it." To reward Sophia for her courage and to celebrate her recovery, Elizabeth gave her a diamond necklace and pair of earrings worth twenty thousand rubles. Grand Duke Peter sent her a watch encrusted with rubies.

When she emerged into the world that birthday evening, Sophia was perhaps not a picture of youthful beauty, but as she entered the reception rooms of the palace, she became aware that something had changed. In the look on every face, the warm pressure of every touched hand, she saw and felt the sympathy and respect she had won. She was no longer a stranger, an object of curiosity and suspicion; she was one of them, returned to them, welcomed back. In those weeks of suffering, Russians had begun to think of her as a Russian.

The next morning she was back at work with Simon Todorsky. She had agreed to enter the Orthodox Church, and a brisk correspondence ensued between Moscow and Zerbst in order to obtain her father's formal consent to her change of religion. She knew that Christian Augustus would be deeply grieved, but Zerbst was far away and she was now committed to Russia. At the beginning of May, she wrote to her father:

> My Lord, I make so bold as to write to Your Highness to ask your consent to Her Imperial Majesty's intentions with regard to me. I can assure you that your will shall always be my own, and that no one shall make me fail in my duty to you. Since I can find almost no difference between the Orthodox faith and the Lutheran, I am resolved (with all due regard to Your Highness's gracious instructions) to change, and shall send you my confession of faith on the first day. I may flatter myself that Your Highness will be pleased with it and I remain, while I live, with profound respect, my lord, Your Highness's very obedient and very humble daughter and servant. Sophia.

Christian Augustus was slow to agree. Frederick of Prussia, who had a great interest in the marriage, wrote of the situation to the landgrave of Hesse-Darmstadt, "Our good prince is entirely obstinate on this point. I have gone to endless trouble to overcome his religious scruples. His answer to all my arguments is 'My daughter shall not enter the Orthodox church.'" Frederick eventually found an obliging Lutheran minister to persuade Christian Augustus that there was "no essential difference" between the Lutheran and Orthodox faiths, and Christian Augustus gave his consent. Later, Frederick wrote, "I have had more trouble in accomplishing this business than if it had been the most important matter in the world."

❧ 8 ❧

Intercepted Letters

N O SOONER HAD Frederick of Prussia managed the successful massaging of Christian Augustus's religious scruples than Sophia's other parent, Johanna, believing herself to be Frederick's primary secret agent in Russia, participated in the botching of his larger diplomatic enterprise. Frederick had recruited Johanna to help bring about the fall of Bestuzhev by telling her that the Russian vice-chancellor was hostile to Prussia and therefore to Sophia's marriage, which he would do his best to prevent. Once in Russia, Johanna had joined the French and Prussian ambassadors in an anti-Bestuzhev conspiracy. When this plot was uncovered, the consequences were disastrous for the two ambassadors and seriously damaging for Johanna.

Elizabeth's behavior during Sophia's illness had made plain to everyone the empress's affection for the young princess. With the betrothal about to take place, Johanna might have asked herself what danger to the marriage now could come from Bestuzhev. A moment's reflection might have told her that there was little; that Bestuzhev, no matter how opposed, could not possibly at this point have prevailed on the empress to cancel the German marriage. Johanna, therefore, should have been gracious to a defeated enemy; indeed, wisdom would have dictated that she work to win him to her daughter's support. But Johanna was incapable of such a reversal. From the moment she arrived in

St. Petersburg, Bestuzhev's enemies, Mardefeld and La Chétardie, had become her confidants. There had been secret meetings, plans had been hatched, coded letters sent to Paris and Berlin. Johanna was not a woman to turn away from this heady brew. In any case, it was too late to change. She was already ensnared.

Alexis Bestuzhev-Ryumin, then almost fifty-one, was one of the most gifted Russians of his day. His diplomatic talents ranked high; his political ability to survive in the swirling currents of domestic policy and court intrigue placed him higher still. As a boy, he had shown outstanding ability in languages. At fifteen, he had been sent abroad by Peter the Great to be educated and begin a long apprenticeship in diplomacy. In 1720, Peter appointed him, at twenty-seven, as Russian ambassador in Copenhagen. Five years later, after Peter's death, he was shunted off to the minor post of resident in Hamburg, where he remained for fifteen years. When Elizabeth succeeded the two German women, empress and regent, she meant to restore the foreign policies of her father. In order to administer these policies, she plucked Bestuzhev, her father's protégé, from the backwater of Hamburg and placed him at the head of foreign affairs as vice-chancellor.

A thin-lipped man with a large nose, sharp chin, and broad, sloping forehead, Bestuzhev was an epicure, an amateur chemist, and a hypochondriac. By nature, he was moody, secretive, irascible, and ruthless. A master of intrigue, by the time he returned to power, he was so silent and efficient in wielding power that he was more feared than loved. But while merciless in dealing with his enemies, he was devoted to his country and to Elizabeth. Before Sophia became the empress Catherine, he first opposed and then befriended her, and she came to understand the two sides of his character: blunt, headstrong, even despotic, but also an excellent psychologist and judge of men, a fanatical worker of selfless devotion, a passionate Russian nationalist, and a faithful servant of the autocrat.

During her reign, Elizabeth's was the only opinion that counted. She may have disliked her vice-chancellor as a man, but she trusted him as her chief adviser, and rejected all attempts of Frederick's ambassador and agents to undermine her confidence in him. She allowed him to have his way in most things, but there were occasions when she asserted herself. She did not, for example, consult him when she brought her nephew to Russia to become her heir, and she acted against Bestuzhev's advice when she chose Sophia to be Peter's bride. On both these occasions she acted impulsively on her own intuition and initiative. On the other hand, there were long periods when she chose to be no more than a beautiful woman at the center of a glittering, admiring court, a woman who demanded no more than to be constantly entertained. Sometimes, when she was in this mood, Bestuzhev had to wait for weeks, even months, to get her signature on important documents. "If the empress would give to government affairs only one one-hundredth of the time Maria Theresa devotes to them, I should be the happiest man on earth," Bestuzhev once told an Austrian diplomat.

Frederick's instructions to Johanna in Berlin had been to assist his ambassador to get rid of the vice-chancellor. But none of the conspirators had any real knowledge of their enemy. They thought him a man of moderate gifts and many failings: a gambler, a drinker, and a bumbling intriguer. Accordingly, they imagined that it would take only a slight, well-timed effort to push him over the edge. They never imagined that he knew about their secret meetings, that he was astute enough to have guessed their purpose, that he was expertly on guard, and that he, not they, would strike first.

Bestuzhev's precautions were simple: he intercepted their letters, had them decoded, read them, and then had them copied. The work of decoding was done by a German specialist in the Foreign Office, who deciphered, copied, and resealed the letters so well that no trace of interference could be seen. Thus it was that innumerable letters passed between Moscow and Europe without either writer or recipient having the slightest suspicion that Bestuzhev had read and recorded every word.

Bestuzhev had no need to fear what was disclosed about himself in these letters; their most prominent feature was a string of snide comments and irreverent attacks La Chétardie had made about the empress. Elizabeth, the marquis informed his government, was lazy, extravagant, and immoral; she changed her clothes four or five times a day; she put her signature on letters she had not even read; she was "frivolous, indolent, running to fat" and "and no longer had sufficient energy to rule the country." Written with a supercilious rancor intended to titillate Louis XV and his ministers at Versailles, they were letters to infuriate a far less sensitive and irascible monarch than the daughter of Peter the Great.

Beyond personal insults, La Chétardie's letters also thrust into light the political conspiracy to overthrow Bestuzhev and his pro-Austrian policy. In this connection the clandestine involvement of the Princess of Anhalt-Zerbst was revealed. By citing her support of his opinions and referring to her correspondence with Frederick in Berlin, the marquis laid bare Johanna's role as a Prussian agent.

Bestuzhev did not hurry; he gave his enemies plenty of time to incriminate themselves. Not until he had collected about fifty of these poisonous letters, mostly from the pen of La Chétardie, did he carry the evidence to the empress. On June 1, 1744, Elizabeth took Peter, Sophia, and Johanna with her on retreat to the Troitsa Monastery. Here, calculating that in the seclusion of this religious place the empress would have more time to read, Bestuzhev placed before her the evidence he had gathered. What Elizabeth saw, along with the effort to overthrow her vice-chancellor, was that Sophia's mother, while being overwhelmed with generosity and luxury, was scheming against Russia in the interests of a foreign power.

On June 3, Sophia, Peter, and Johanna had just finished their midday dinner when the empress, followed by Lestocq, entered their room and commanded Johanna to follow her. Left alone, Sophia and Peter climbed onto a window ledge and sat, side by side, legs dangling, talking and joking. Sophia was laughing at something Peter had said when suddenly the door burst open and Lestocq appeared. "This horseplay will stop at once!" he shouted. Turning to Sophia, he said, "You can go pack your bags. You will be leaving for home immediately." The two young people were stunned.

"What is this about?" Peter asked.

"You will find out," Lestocq said grimly and stalked away.

Neither Peter nor Sophia could imagine what had happened; for even a highly placed courtier to speak with this insolence to the heir to the throne and his future wife seemed unthinkable. Groping for an explanation, Peter said, "If your mother has done something wrong, that does not mean that you have."

Frightened, Sophia replied, "My duty is to follow my mother and obey her commands." Feeling that she was about to be sent back to

Zerbst, she looked at Peter, wondering how he would feel if this happened. Years later, she wrote, "I saw clearly that he would have parted from me without regret."

The two were still sitting there, bewildered and trembling, when the empress, her blue eyes flashing, her face crimson with rage, emerged from her apartment. Behind her came Johanna, her eyes red with tears. As the empress stood over them beneath the low ceiling, the two children jumped down from their perch and bowed their heads in respect. This gesture seemed to disarm Elizabeth, and impulsively she smiled and kissed them. Sophia understood that she was not being held responsible for whatever her mother had done.

There was no forgiveness, however, for those who had insulted and betrayed the empress. She struck first at La Chétardie. The French ambassador was ordered to leave Moscow within twenty-four hours, going directly to the frontier at Riga without passing through St. Petersburg. Elizabeth's anger against this former friend was so great that she commanded him to return the portrait of herself set in diamonds that she had given him. He returned the portrait and kept the diamonds. Mardefeld, the Prussian ambassador, was allowed to linger, but he, too, was sent home within a year. Johanna was permitted to remain, but only because she was Sophia's mother, and only until her daughter married the grand duke.

With his political enemies overthrown and scattered, Bestuzhev rose higher. He was promoted from vice-chancellor to chancellor; he was awarded a new palace and estates; the downfall of his diplomatic enemies meant the success of his pro-Austrian, anti-Prussian policy. Secure in his new power, he no longer felt it necessary to oppose Peter's marriage to Sophia. He could see that this was a project the empress was determined to carry out; to attempt to block it would be dangerous. Further, even after the marriage, the girl's mother would be harmless.

Princess Johanna's brief career in diplomacy had ended in ruin: the French ambassador had been summarily banished; the Prussian ambassador, a veteran of twenty years at the Russian court, had been stripped of influence; Bestuzhev had been promoted to chancellor. Finally, there was the downfall of Johanna herself. Elizabeth's friendship for the sister of the man she had loved had now been replaced by an intense desire to send Sophia's mother back to Germany as soon as possible.

❧ 9 ❧

Conversion and Betrothal

T HE EMPRESS, wishing to hurry events along, fixed the date of Sophia's betrothal to Peter for June 29. Accordingly, on the day just
before, June 28, 1744, the young German princess was scheduled to
formally and publicly disavow the Lutheran faith and be admitted into
the Orthodox Church. Almost to the last minute, Sophia worried
about the irreversible step she was about to take. Then, on the night
before the ceremony, her hesitations seemed to disappear. "She slept
soundly the whole night," Johanna wrote to her husband, "a sure sign
that her mind is at peace."

The next morning, the empress sent for Sophia to be dressed under
her supervision. Elizabeth had ordered the young woman a gown identical to her own; both were made of heavy, scarlet, silk taffeta, embroidered with silver threads along the seams. The difference was that
Elizabeth's dress was ablaze with diamonds, while Sophia's only jewels
were the pendants and brooch that the empress had given her after her
pneumonia. Sophia was pale from the required three days of fasting
before the service, and she wore only a white ribbon in her unpowdered
hair, but, Johanna wrote, "I must say, I thought she was lovely." Indeed,
many that day were struck by the elegance of the slender figure with her
dark hair, pale skin, blue eyes, and scarlet dress.

Elizabeth reached for her hand and together they led a long procession through many halls to the crowded palace chapel. There, Sophia
kneeled on a square cushion and the long ceremony began. Johanna
described parts of it to her absent husband: "The forehead, eyes, neck,
throat, and palms and backs of hands are anointed with oil. The oil is
wiped off with a piece of cotton immediately after application."

Kneeling on the cushion, Sophia performed her role expertly.
Speaking in a firm, clear voice, she recited the creed of her new faith. "I
had learned it by heart in Russian. Like a parrot," she admitted later.
The empress cried, but, said the young convert, "I remained quite in
control for which I was highly praised." For her, this ceremony was
another challenging piece of schoolwork, the kind of performance at

which she excelled. Johanna was proud of her daughter: "Her bearing... through the entire ceremony was so full of nobility and dignity that I should have admired her [even] had she not been to me what she is."

In this way, Sophia Augusta Fredericka of Anhalt-Zerbst became Ekaterina, or, in English, Catherine. Sophia could have been baptized with her own name, Sophia, which was a common name in Russia. But Elizabeth had rejected this because Sophia had been the name of her own aunt, the half-sister and rival of Peter the Great who had struggled for the throne with the young tsar fifty-five years before. Instead, Elizabeth chose the name of her own mother, Catherine.

As she left the chapel, the new convert was presented with a diamond necklace and brooch by the empress. Despite her gratitude, the new Catherine was so exhausted that, in order to save her strength for the morrow, she asked permission to be excused from the banquet following the ceremony. Later that night, she drove with the empress, the grand duke, and her mother to the Kremlin, where her betrothal was to be celebrated the following day.

The next morning, Catherine opened her eyes and was handed two miniature portraits, one of Elizabeth, the other of Peter, both framed with diamonds, both gifts from the empress. Soon, Peter himself arrived to escort her to the empress, who was wearing the imperial crown and, over her shoulders, an imperial mantle. Leaving the Kremlin palace, Elizabeth walked under a canopy of solid silver whose great weight required eight generals to carry it. Behind the empress came Catherine and Peter, followed by Johanna, the court, the Synod, and the Senate. The procession descended the famous Red Staircase, crossed the square lined by men of the Guards regiments, and entered the Assumption Cathedral, where Russian tsars were crowned. Once inside, Elizabeth took the two young people by the hand and led them to a velvet-carpeted dais erected between the massive pillars in the center of church. The archbishop of Novgorod conducted the service, and the betrothal rings exchanged by the couple were handed to them by the empress herself. Johanna, with her appraising eye, observed that the rings were "real little monsters, both of them"; her daughter noted specifically, "The one he gave me was worth twelve thousand rubles, the one he received from me, fourteen thousand." At the end of the ceremony, a court official read an imperial decree granting Catherine the rank of grand duchess and the title of imperial highness.

Johanna's report on the betrothal service was a litany of complaint:

The ceremony lasted four hours during which it was impossible to sit down for a moment. It is no exaggeration to say
that my back was numb from all the bowing I had been obliged
to do as I embraced all the numerous ladies and that there was
a red mark the size of a German flourin on my right hand from
all the times it had been kissed.

Johanna's mixed feelings about her daughter, now the central figure
in this ceremonial pageantry, should have been mollified when Elizabeth went out of her way to be gracious to a woman she despised. In the
cathedral, the empress had prevented Johanna from kneeling before
her, saying, "Our situation is the same; our vows are the same." But
when the ceremony was over, with the cannon thundering, the church
bells pealing, and the court moving to the adjacent Granovitaya Palace
for the betrothal banquet, Johanna's unhappiness burst out. By rank,
the bride's mother could not sit at the imperial table with the empress,
the grand duke, and the newly proclaimed grand duchess. When this
was explained to her, Johanna protested, declaring that her place could
not be among mere ladies of the court. The master of ceremonies was
uncertain what to do, and Catherine witnessed and suffered her mother's behavior in silence. Elizabeth, again infuriated by the presumption
of this ungrateful, deceitful guest, ordered a separate table set up in a
private alcove where Johanna could watch from a window.

The ball that evening was in the Hall of Facets of the Granovitaya
Palace, a room constructed with a single central pillar, filling one quarter
of the room, supporting the low ceiling. In this place, said Catherine,
"one was almost suffocated by the heat and the crowd," Then, walking
back to the state apartments, other new rules of precedence took effect.
Catherine now was Her Imperial Highness, a Grand Duchess of Russia,
the future wife of Heir to the Throne; Johanna, therefore, was obliged
to walk behind her daughter. Catherine attempted to avoid these situations, and Johanna recognized Catherine's effort. "My daughter conducts herself very intelligently in her new situation," she wrote to her
husband. "She blushes each time she is forced to walk in front of me."

Elizabeth continued to be generous. "There was not a day on which
I did not receive presents from the empress," Catherine said later. "Silver and jewels, cloth and so forth, indeed everything that one can imag-

ine, the least of which was worth from ten to fifteen thousand rubles. She showed me extreme affection." Soon afterward, the empress gave Catherine thirty thousand rubles for personal expenses. She, who had never had any pocket money at all, was awed by this sum. She immediately sent money to her father to help with the education and medical care of her younger brother. "I know that Your Highness has sent my brother to Hamburg and that this has entailed heavy expenses," she wrote to Christian Augustus. "I beg Your Highness to leave my brother there as long as is necessary to restore him to health. I will undertake to pay all his expenses."

Elizabeth also gave the new grand duchess a small court of her own, including young chamberlains and maids-in-waiting. Peter already had his own court, and in the apartments of the grand duke and grand duchess, the young people played blindman's buff and other games, laughing, jumping, dancing, running—even taking the lid off a big harpsichord, placing it on pillows, and using it as a toboggan to slide along the floor. By participating in these frolics, Catherine was trying to please her future husband. Peter was friendly toward this willing playmate; he was also intelligent enough to know that any fondness he showed his fiancée would please the empress. Even Brümmer, observing them together and deciding that she might help him deal with his rebellious charge, asked her to "use my influence to correct and reprimand the Grand Duke." She refused. "I told him it was impossible for in that case, I should become as hateful to him [Peter] as the rest of his entourage already were." She understood that to have any influence on Peter, she must be the opposite of those who tried to "correct" him. He could not come to her looking for friendship only to find he had another watchdog.

Johanna became more distant. Now, when she wanted to see her daughter, she had to have herself announced. Reluctant to do this, she stayed away, declaring that the young court around Catherine was too wild and noisy. Meanwhile, Johanna herself was making new friends. She joined a circle of people of whom the empress and most of the court disapproved. It was not long before her intimacy with the chamberlain, Count Ivan Betskoy, began to cause talk; eventually, the two were so often together that some at court began saying that they were having an affair—and even whispering that the thirty-two-year-old Princess of Anhalt-Zerbst was pregnant.

❧ 10 ❧

A Pilgrimage to Kiev and Transvestite Balls

THE BRIDE HAD ARRIVED in Russia, she was young, her health was restored, and the difficulties involving her conversion to Orthodoxy had been overcome. Now that she and Peter were betrothed, what stood in the way of an immediate marriage? One obstacle, difficult to surmount even for an empress, was the doctors' strong cautionary opinion regarding Peter. At sixteen, the grand duke looked more like fourteen, and the medical men still could not detect in him any convincing signs of puberty. It would be at least a year, they believed, before he could father a child. Even if a pregnancy occurred, there must be another nine months before an infant could be born. To Elizabeth, this length of time—twenty-one months—seemed an eternity. And because the wedding had to be postponed, the empress also had to postpone Johanna's departure.

Reluctantly accepting these disappointments, Elizabeth decided on another means of presenting her new dynasty to the public eye. In August 1744 she set out on a pilgrimage to Kiev, the oldest and holiest of Russian cities, where Christianity was first introduced by Grand Prince Vladimir in A.D. 800. The journey of almost six hundred miles between Moscow and Kiev had been suggested by Elizabeth's Ukrainian lover, Razumovsky, and the trek included Peter, Catherine, and Johanna and their respective retainers, along with two hundred and thirty courtiers and hundreds of servants. Once under way, the cavalcade of carriages and wagons loaded with baggage jolted and swayed day after day over the endless roads, inflicting weariness, boredom, hunger, and thirst on the passengers. The horses were frequently exchanged; at every relay station, eight hundred fresh animals awaited the arrival of the imperial caravan.

While the grandees of the Russian court rode in velvet-cushioned carriages, one figure made most of the journey on foot. Elizabeth took penance and pilgrimages seriously. Walking along the hot, shadeless Russian roads, sweating in the heat and murmuring prayers, Elizabeth stopped to pray at every village church and wayside shrine. Meanwhile, Razumovsky, as practical and modest in his heavenly as in his earthly expectations, preferred to ride behind her in his comfortable carriage.

Catherine and Johanna began the journey riding in a carriage with two ladies-in-waiting; Peter was in a separate carriage with Brümmer and two of his tutors. One afternoon, Peter tired of his "pedagogues," as Catherine called them, and decided to join the two German princesses, whose company he thought would be more lively. He abandoned his carriage, "got into ours and refused to leave," bringing with him one of the spirited young men of his entourage. Very soon, Johanna, irritated by the company of the young people, reshuffled the arrangements. She had one of the carts that was loaded with beds rearranged with boards and pillows so that as many as ten people could sit in it. To Johanna's annoyance, Peter and Catherine insisted on filling the cart with other young people. "We allowed only the most amusing and entertaining of the entourage to join us," she said. "From morning till night, we did nothing but laugh, play and make merry." Brümmer, Peter's tutors, and Johanna's ladies-in waiting were insulted by this reshuffle, which ignored court precedence. "While we were enjoying ourselves, they were, all four of them, in one carriage where they sulked, scolded, condemned, and made sour remarks at our expense. In our carriage we knew this, but we just laughed at them."

For Catherine, Peter, and their friends, this journey became not a religious pilgrimage but an excursion, a lark. There was no need to hurry; Elizabeth walked no more than a few hours a day. At the end of three weeks, the main cavalcade arrived at Alexis Razumovsky's large mansion in Koseletz, where they waited three additional weeks for the empress to appear. When she finally arrived on August 15, the religious complexion of the pilgrimage was temporarily suspended; for two weeks, the "pilgrims" joined in a succession of balls, concerts, and, from morning to night, card games so feverish that sometimes forty or fifty thousand rubles lay on the tables.

While they were staying in Koseletz, an incident occurred that drove a permanent wedge between Johanna and Peter. It began when the grand duke entered a room where Johanna was writing. On a low stool beside her, she had placed her jewel case, in which she kept the small things that were important to her, including her letters. Peter, romping and frisking in an attempt to make Catherine laugh, made as if to rummage through the case and snatch the letters. Johanna fiercely told him not to touch it. The grand duke, still prancing, started across the room, but in pirouetting away from Johanna, his coat caught the open lid of the little case and tipped it and its contents onto the floor. Johanna, thinking he had done it intentionally, flew into a rage. Peter tried at first to apologize, but when she refused to believe that it had been an accident, he, too, became angry. The two began to shout at each other, and Peter, turning to Catherine, appealed to her to verify his innocence.

Catherine was caught in the middle.

"Knowing how easily excited my mother was and that her first impulses were always very violent, I feared she would slap me if I disagreed with her. Wanting neither to lie to her nor to offend the grand duke, I kept silent. Nevertheless, I did tell my mother that I did not think the grand duke had done it intentionally."

Johanna then turned on Catherine:

When my mother was in a temper, she had to find someone to quarrel with. I remained silent and then burst into tears. At first, my silence angered them both. Then, the grand duke, seeing that all my mother's anger was now directed at me because I had taken his part and that I was crying, accused my mother of being an unjust, over-bearing shrew. She hurled back that he was "an ill-bred little boy." It would have been impossible to quarrel more violently without coming to blows.

From that moment on, the grand duke took a great dislike to my mother and he never forgot this quarrel. My mother, in turn, bore him an unforgiving grudge. Their strained relationship became one of ever-worsening bitterness and suspicion, liable to turn sour at any moment. Neither of them could hide their feelings from me. And, as hard as I worked to obey the one and please the other—and somehow to reconcile them—I succeeded only for short periods. Each always had some sarcastic or malicious barb ready to let fly. My own position became more and more painful every day.

Catherine was torn, but her mother's bad temper and her sympathy for the grand duke had an effect: "In truth, at that time, the grand duke opened his heart to me more than to anyone else. He could see that my mother often attacked and scolded me when she was unable to find fault with him. This placed me high in his estimation; he believed he could rely on me."

At the climax of the pilgrimage, the empress and the court spent ten days in Kiev. Catherine first saw the magnificent city in panorama, its golden domes rising from a bluff on the western bank of the Dnieper River. Elizabeth, Peter, and Catherine entered the city on foot, walking with a crowd of priests and monks behind a large cross. Everywhere in this holiest of Russian cities, in a period when the church was immensely rich and the people devoutly pious, the empress was welcomed with extravagant pomp. At the famous Pecharsky Monastery Church of the Assumption, Catherine was awed by the majesty of the religious processions, the beauty of the religious ceremonies, the incomparable splendor of the church themselves. "Never in my whole life," she wrote later, "have I been so impressed as by the extraordinary magnificence of this church. Every icon was covered with solid gold, silver, pearls and encrusted with precious stones."

Impressed though she was by this visual display, Catherine never in her lifetime was devoutly religious. Neither the strict Lutheran beliefs of her father nor the passionate Orthodox faith of Empress Elizabeth ever took possession of her mind. What she saw and admired in the Russian church was the majesty of architecture, art, and music merged into a splendid unity of inspired—but still man-made—beauty.

No sooner had Elizabeth and the court returned from Kiev than another round of operas, balls, and masquerades began in Moscow. Every evening, Catherine appeared in a new dress and was told how well she looked. She was shrewd enough to recognize that flattery was the lubricating oil of court life, and she was also aware that some people still disapproved of her: Bestuzhev and his followers; jealous court ladies who envied a rising star; parasites who kept careful count of the distribution of favors. Catherine worked hard to disarm her critics. "I was afraid of not being liked and did everything in my power to win those with whom I was to spend my life," she wrote later. Above all, she never forgot to whom she owed primary allegiance. "My respect for the empress and my gratitude to her were extreme," she said. "And she used to say that she loved me almost more than the grand duke."

A sure way to please the empress was to dance. For Catherine, this was easy; she, like Elizabeth, was passionately fond of dancing. Every morning at seven, Monsieur Landé, the French ballet master of the court, arrived with his violin and, for two hours, taught her the latest steps from Paris. From four to six in the afternoon, he returned to teach again. And then, in the evenings, Catherine would impress the court with her graceful dancing.

Some of these evening balls were bizarre. Every Tuesday by decree of the empress, men would attend dressed as women and women would dance dressed as men. Catherine, then fifteen, was delighted by this change of costume: "I must say that there was nothing more hideous and at the same time more comical than to see most men dressed this way and nothing more miserable than to see women in men's clothes." Most of the court roundly detested these evenings, but Elizabeth had a reason for this caprice: she looked superb in male clothing. Though she was far from slender, her full-bosomed figure was set off by a pair of slim, splendidly shaped legs. Her vanity demanded that these elegant limbs should not remain hidden, and the only way to display them was in a pair of tight male trousers.

Catherine described the hazards she encountered on one of these evenings:

> The very tall Monsieur Sievers, who was wearing a hoop skirt the empress had lent him, was dancing a Polonaise with me. Countess Hendrikova, who was dancing behind me, stumbled over the hoop skirt of Monsieur Sievers as he turned around with his hand in mine. In falling, she struck me so hard that I fell beneath the hoop skirt of Monsieur Sievers which had sprung upright beside me. Sievers himself became entangled in his own long skirts which were in great disorder and there we were, all three of us, sprawling on the floor with me entirely covered by his skirt. I was dying of laughter trying to get up, but people had to come and help us up because the three of us were so entangled in Monsieur Sievers's clothing that no one could get up without causing the other two to fall down.

That autumn, however, Catherine saw and felt the darker side of Elizabeth's personality. The empress's vanity demanded that she should be not only the most powerful woman in the empire but the most beautiful. She could not tolerate hearing another woman's beauty praised. Catherine's triumphs had not escaped her notice, and her annoyance found an outlet. One evening at the opera, the empress was sitting with Lestocq in the royal box opposite the box in which Catherine, Johanna, and Peter were seated. During the intermission, the empress noticed Catherine talking gaily to Peter. Could this young woman, a picture of glowing health and confidence, now so popular at court, be the same shy girl who had come to Russia less than a year ago? Suddenly, the empress's jealousy flared. Staring at the younger woman, she seized on the first grievance that popped into her head. As if the matter were something that could not wait, Elizabeth dispatched Lestocq to Catherine's box to tell Catherine that the empress was furious with her because she had run up unacceptable debts. Elizabeth had given her thirty thousand rubles; where had it all gone? In delivering this message, Lestocq made certain that Peter and everyone else within earshot could hear. Tears sprang to Catherine's eyes and, even as she wept, more humiliation was added. Peter, instead of consoling her, said that he agreed with his aunt and thought it appropriate that his betrothed had been reprimanded. Johanna then declared that as Catherine no longer consulted her as to how a daughter should behave, she "washed her hands" of the matter.

The fall was sudden and steep. What had happened? What crime had the fifteen-year-old girl whose one thought was to please everyone, particularly the empress, committed? Catherine checked and found that she was in debt for two thousand rubles. The sum was absurd, in view of Elizabeth's own extravagance and generosity, and the reprimand was an obvious excuse to cloak another grievance. It was true that Catherine had spent freely. She had sent money to her father to help pay expenses for her brother. She had spent money on herself. Arriving in Russia with only four dresses and a dozen chemises in her trunk, and taking her place at a court where women changed clothes three times a day, she had used some of her allowance to create a wardrobe. But the greater part had been spent showering presents on her mother, her ladies-in-waiting, and even on Peter himself. She had discovered that the most effective way of pacifying her mother's temper and of stopping the constant bickering between Johanna and Peter was to give them both presents. She had realized that in this court, gifts could win her friends. She had noticed, too, that most of the people around her did not object to receiving gifts. Accordingly, eager to find favor, she saw no reason to scorn this simple, blatant method. In a few months, she had learned not only the language but also the customs of Russia.

This sudden blow from the empress was difficult for her to understand and accept. It revealed to her the two faces of the empress, a woman who, alternately and with no warning, charmed and intimidated. Afterward, when Catherine remembered that evening, she also remembered the lesson it had taught: that in dealing with a massive ego such as Elizabeth's, all other women at court had to beware of succeeding too well. She worked hard to reingratiate herself with her patron. And Elizabeth, when her fit of jealousy subsided, relented and eventually forgot the incident.

❧ 11 ❧

Smallpox

I N NOVEMBER, while the court was still in Moscow, Peter came down with measles and, since Catherine had never had the disease, all contact between the two was forbidden. During his illness, Catherine was told, Peter "was uncontrollable in his whims and passions." Confined to his room and neglected by his tutors, he spent his time ordering his servants, dwarfs, and gentlemen-in-waiting to march and countermarch in parade ground drill around his bed. When, after six weeks of convalescence, Catherine saw him again, "he confided his childish pranks to me and it was not my business to restrain him; I let him do and say what he wished." Peter was pleased by her attitude. He felt no romantic attraction for her, but she was his comrade and the only person to whom he dared speak freely.

Toward the end of December 1744, when Peter recovered from the measles, the empress decided that the court should leave Moscow and return to St. Petersburg. A heavy snowfall lay over the city, and the temperature was bitterly cold. Catherine and Johanna were to travel together with two ladies-in-waiting; Peter was in another sledge with Brümmer and a tutor. As the women were taking their seats, the empress, who was traveling separately, leaned in and tucked Catherine's furs tightly around her; then, worried that these still might be insufficient against the cold, she wrapped her own magnificent ermine cloak over Catherine's shoulders.

Four days later, between the towns of Tver and Novgorod, Catherine and Peter's little procession halted for the night at the village of Khotilovo. That evening, Peter began to shiver; then he fainted and was put to bed. The next day, when Catherine and Johanna went to see him, Brümmer stopped them in the doorway. The grand duke, he said, had developed a high fever during the night, and spots—symptoms of smallpox—had appeared on his face. Johanna turned pale. Terrified of the disease that had killed her brother, she instantly pulled Catherine away from the door, ordered their sledge, and left immediately for St. Petersburg, leaving Peter to be cared for by Brümmer and the two ladies-in-waiting. A courier galloped ahead to inform the empress, who had already reached the capital. As soon as Elizabeth was told, she ordered her sledge and, with the horses under the lash, raced back toward Khotilovo. The two sledges, Catherine's and Elizabeth's, hurtling across the snow in opposite directions, met in the middle of the night on the road. They stopped and Johanna told Elizabeth what she knew. The empress listened, nodded, then gave the signal to proceed. As the horses pounded forward, Elizabeth stared into blackness—not just the blackness of the night outside, but also the blackness of the future of her dynasty if Peter should die.

But it was more than self-interest that drove the empress to behave as she did once she reached Khotilovo. On arriving, she seated herself by the patient's bed and declared that she would care for her nephew herself. She was to remain at Peter's side for six weeks, rarely lying down, hardly changing her clothes. Elizabeth, who had seemed to care for nothing as much as the preservation of her beauty, now took on all the menial duties of a sick nurse. Dismissing the risk of smallpox and consequent disfigurement, she hovered over the bed where her nephew lay. This was the same warm, maternal impulse that had compelled her to sit by Catherine's bedside when the little German princess collapsed with pneumonia. While Peter slept, she sent couriers galloping with messages to the one person who, she believed, fully shared her affection and fears.

In St. Petersburg, Catherine waited anxiously for news. Could the grand duke, just recovered from measles, survive this more ominous disease? Catherine's anxiety was genuine; although she found Peter childish and often irritating, she had accepted her fiancé. There was, of course, more to it than that; she was anxious for her own future. If Peter died, her life would change. Her position at court, all the honors heaped upon her, were bestowed on the wife of the future tsar. Already in St. Petersburg, certain courtiers, foreseeing the death of the grand duke, were turning away from her. Powerless to do anything else, she wrote respectful, affectionate letters to Elizabeth, asking about Peter's health. The letters, in Russian, were drafted by her teacher, then copied by

Catherine in her own hand into Russian. Elizabeth, who may or may not have known this, was touched.

Meanwhile, Johanna continued to create trouble. The empress had assigned Catherine a suite of four rooms in the Winter Palace; these rooms were separated from the four rooms assigned to her mother. Johanna's rooms were of the same size, furnished with the same furniture, and the same fabric of blue and red cloth; the only difference was that Catherine's were to the right of a stairway and Johanna's to the left. Nevertheless, when Johanna discovered the arrangement, she complained. Her daughter's rooms were grander than hers, she said. Furthermore, why was Catherine being separated from her at all? She had not proposed it; she had not approved it. When Catherine told her mother that the separation had been ordered and the rooms specifically assigned by the empress, who did not want her to share her mother's quarters, Johanna's indignation mounted. She regarded this new arrangement as a form of criticism of her conduct at court and of her influence on her daughter. Unable to direct her anger at Elizabeth, Johanna poured it out on Catherine. She picked constant quarrels "and was on such bad terms with everybody that she no longer joined us for meals but had them served in her apartment." Catherine confessed, however, that the separation "was very much to my liking. I was not at all at ease in my mother's rooms and had no good opinion of the group of intimate friends which she gathered around herself."

Catherine's separation from her mother and her careful avoidance of her mother's friends meant that there were areas of Johanna's life of which her daughter had little knowledge. The nature and extent of Johanna's relationship with Count Betskoy was one of these. Catherine was aware that her mother was fond of Betskoy and saw him constantly, and that many people at court, including the empress, believed that the relationship had become too intimate. Of the rumors that Johanna had become pregnant by Betskoy, Catherine says nothing in her *Memoirs*. She does, however, tell this story:

One morning, Johanna's German chambermaid rushed into Catherine's room to say that her mother had fainted. Catherine ran to her mother's room and found Johanna, pale but conscious, lying on a mattress on the floor. Catherine asked what had happened. Johanna said that she had asked to be bled and that the surgeon had been clumsy. "He had not succeeded with two veins on her arms and then had tried to open two on her feet" and failed again. She had fainted. Catherine knew that Johanna was afraid of bloodletting and had violently opposed it as treatment for her own pneumonia; she did not understand why her mother had wanted it done now to herself—or as treatment for what illness. Johanna, becoming hysterical, refused to answer further questions and began to scream. She accused her daughter of caring nothing about her and then "she ordered me to go."

Here, Catherine ends her account, hinting at what had happened. Johanna offered a flimsy excuse that she had contracted a sudden, unspecified illness. It is unlikely that this particular woman would ever ask to be bled. There is the accusation of gross surgical incompetence to explain heavy bleeding. There is the placement of a titled patient on a mattress on the floor rather than on a bed, suggesting that Johanna had suddenly staggered and collapsed. There is Johanna's rage and hysteria when confronting her daughter. And, finally, in the days that followed, there is the absence of any further symptoms of the illness that this surgical bleeding might have been intended to cure or alleviate. A possible explanation of this sequence is that Johanna had suffered a miscarriage.

Not long after this episode, Johanna suffered another blow. From Zerbst came the news that her two-and-a-half-year-old daughter, Elizabeth, Catherine's younger sister, had died suddenly. Johanna had been away from home for over a year. In his letters, her husband had repeatedly asked her to come home. Always, she replied that her primary obligation was to shepherd and oversee the brilliant marriage being offered to her eldest daughter.

Eventually, a message from the empress at Khotilovo reached Catherine:

> Your Highness, my very dear niece, I am infinitely obliged to Your Highness for your agreeable messages. I have delayed replying to them because I could not reassure you with regard to the health of His Highness, the Grand Duke. Now this day, I can assure you that, to our joy, God be Praised, we may hope for his recovery. He has come back to us.

On reading this letter, Catherine's natural cheerfulness returned, and that evening she went to a ball. When she appeared, the whole room crowded around her; the news had spread that the danger was over, the grand duke was recovering. Relieved, Catherine saw the Moscow days repeat themselves: every evening a ball or masquerade; every evening another triumph.

In the midst of this whirlwind, the Swedish diplomat Count Adolf Gyllenborg arrived in St. Petersburg. He came as an official envoy to announce the marriage of the new crown prince of Sweden, Adolphus Frederick of Holstein (Johanna's brother and Catherine's uncle) to Princess Louisa Ulrika, sister of Frederick II of Prussia. It was Catherine's second encounter with Gyllenborg; they had met five years before at her grandmother's house in Hamburg, when she was ten. It was then that she had so impressed him with her precocious intelligence that he had advised her mother to pay her more attention.

As Catherine described their second encounter:

> He was a man of great intelligence, who was no longer young [Gyllenborg then was thirty-two]. . . . He noticed that I accepted without protest all the intrigues and customs of the court and it seemed to him that I was showing less intelligence in Petersburg than he had given me credit for in Hamburg. He told me one day that he was surprised by the prodigious change that had taken place in me. "How is it," he said, "that your character, so vigorous and strong in Hamburg, has allowed itself to deteriorate. You busy yourself now only with superficialities, with luxury and pleasure. You must recover the natural inclination of your mind. Your genius is destined for great achievements and you are wasting yourself on trifles. I would wager that you have not read a book since you have been in Russia."
>
> I told him of the hours I spent in my room, reading. He said that a philosopher of fifteen was too young yet for self-knowledge and that I was surrounded by so many pitfalls that I would stumble unless my soul was of an utterly superior metal; that I should nourish it with the best possible reading. He recommended Plutarch's *Parallel Lives,* a life of Cicero, and *The Causes of the Grandeur and Decline of the Roman Republic* by Montesquieu. I promised to read them and actually did look for them. I found the life of Cicero in German and read a few pages; then I was brought the Montesquieu. When I began to read, it caused me to reflect, but I could not read it straight through because it made me yawn and I tossed it aside. . . .

I was not able to find Plutarch's *Lives;* I read it only two years later.

To prove to Gyllenborg that she was not superficial, Catherine composed an essay about herself, "so that he would see whether I knew myself or not." The next day, she wrote and handed to Gyllenborg an essay titled "Portrait of a Fifteen-Year-Old Philosopher." He was impressed and returned it with a dozen pages of comments, mostly favorable. "I read his remarks again and again, many times; I impressed them on my consciousness and resolved to follow his advice. In addition, there was something else surprising: one day, while conversing with me, he allowed the following sentence to slip out: 'What a pity that you will marry!' I wanted to find out what he meant, but he would not tell me."

Early in February, Peter was finally well enough to travel, and the empress brought him back to St. Petersburg. Catherine went to meet them in a reception hall of the Winter Palace. It was after four in the afternoon and the light was failing; they met, Catherine says, in "semi-darkness." Until that moment, absence and anxiety had softened Catherine's image of the man she was to marry. Peter had never been handsome, but he had possessed a certain nondescript, inoffensive blandness. Sometimes he wore a surly grin, sometimes a slight smile that might be inane or could be merely shy. Overall, his appearance had not been not wholly displeasing. Catherine was eager to see him.

The figure now standing before her in the gloom was quite different; it filled her "almost with terror.... His face was practically unrecognizable." It was ravaged, swollen and pitted with still unhealed pockmarks. It was evident that he would be deeply scarred. His head had been shaved, and the enormous wig he was wearing made him appear even more terrifying. Despite the poor light, Catherine was unable to mask her horror; later, she described her future husband as "hideous." As she stood there, "he came up to me and asked, 'Do you recognize me?' " Summoning her courage, she stammered congratulations on his recovery, then fled to her apartment, where she collapsed.

Catherine was not a simple, romantic young woman. The empress, nevertheless, worried about her reaction to her nephew's appearance.

Fearing that the girl might impulsively reject so appalling-looking a future spouse and ask her parents to withdraw their consent to the match, Elizabeth redoubled her show of affection. On February 10, Peter's seventeenth birthday, with her nephew still in no condition to appear in public, the empress invited Catherine to dine with her alone. During the meal, she complimented Catherine on her letters in Russian, spoke to her in Russian, praised her pronunciation, and told her that she was becoming a handsome young woman.

Elizabeth's efforts were gratifying to Catherine, but unnecessary. Catherine had no intention of breaking her engagement. Not for a moment, whatever her fiancé's appearance, did she think of returning to Germany. There was one promise to which Catherine was faithful throughout her life, one commitment on which she would never renege: this was to her own ambition. She had come not to marry a face, handsome or hideous, but to marry the heir to an empire.

Peter was more affected emotionally and psychologically than Catherine by what smallpox had done to him. But once the disease had done its damage, the fault in behavior lay with Catherine. Her initial reaction was natural enough; most young women would shrink from seeing horrible disfigurement, and probably few would possess the self-control to disguise their feelings. In this case, however, if the relationship was going to surmount this challenge and continue successfully, the moment of meeting demanded something more than Catherine was able to give. And this was something she could not summon: a warm, unrestrained affection, the kind of spontaneous tenderness that came naturally to Empress Elizabeth.

Peter was distressed to feel himself physically repulsive to his fiancée. At the moment they met in the dimly lit hall, Peter was able to read her thoughts in her eyes and voice. Thereafter, he believed himself "hideous" and therefore unlovable. This new sense of inferiority reinforced feelings that had afflicted him all his life. Throughout his bleak and lonely childhood, Peter had never had an intimate friend. Now, just as the cousin he was being forced to marry was becoming a comrade, a shocking ugliness had been added to the list of his disadvantages. When he had asked, "Do you recognize me?" Peter had revealed his anxiety about the effect his changed appearance would have on her. That was precisely the moment that Catherine had unknowingly failed him. Had she managed to give him a compassionate smile and a word of affection, it might have ensured some kind of amicable future. The smile was not given; the word not spoken. The frightened young man saw his trusted playmate shuddering at the sight of him; he knew that he was, in her word, "hideous."

Catherine understood none of this. At first, she was confused; she would have been astonished to learn that her involuntary reaction had alienated him. Once his reaction was clear, her own pride dictated that she respond to his coolness with a corresponding reserve of her own. In turn, her reserved behavior could only reinforce Peter's belief that he had become repulsive to her. It did not take long for his dismay and loneliness to turn to perversity and spite. He decided that when she was friendly to him, it was merely for form's sake. He hated her success. He held it against her that she was blooming into womanhood. The more beautiful, spontaneous, and gay she became in company, the more he felt himself isolated in his own ugliness. Catherine danced and charmed while Peter mocked and withdrew. Both were miserable.

It was Catherine's wish, however, that the deterioration of their private relationship be kept hidden. Peter, lacking both the inner resources and Catherine's consuming ambition, could put on no such show. Smallpox had delivered a shattering blow to his mental as well as his physical health; his gross disfigurement had affected his psychological balance. Under these pressures, the young man retreated into the world of his childhood. In the spring and summer of 1745, Peter made elaborate excuses to remain in his own room, where he was surrounded and protected by his servants. His joy was to dress them in uniforms and drill them. Even as a child, uniforms, military drill, and words of command had helped him to forget his loneliness. Now, unloved and ever more conscious of being alone, he sought relief in the old remedy. His indoor parades with a squad of costumed servants were Peter's way of protesting the prison he considered his life to be and the unwelcome destiny toward which he was being driven.

❧ 12 ❧

Marriage

ELIZABETH'S PATIENCE was exhausted; the nightmare dash to Khotilovo and her long vigil over Peter's bedside continued to haunt her. Her nephew had almost died, but he had survived. He was seventeen, and his sixteen-year-old bride-to-be had been in Russia for more than a year, but they were not yet married, and no infant child was on the way. True, the doctors had told her again that the grand duke was still too young, too immature, and had not recovered yet from the effects of his illnesses. This time the empress dismissed their arguments. She saw only that the succession hung on the health of Peter and his ability to produce an heir. If she waited another year, another fatal illness might carry off the grand duke, but if she went ahead with the marriage, a year might bring Russia a small Romanov heir, stronger and healthier than Peter, as strong and healthy as Catherine. For this reason, there must be a marriage as soon as possible. The physicians bowed and the empress began considering dates. In March 1745, an imperial decree set the wedding for the first of July.

Because the young imperial house of Russia had never celebrated a public royal wedding, Elizabeth decided that it must be so magnificent that her own people and the world would be convinced of the strength and permanence of the Russian monarchy. It must become the talk of Europe; it must be modeled after the great ceremonials of the French court; the Russian ambassador in Paris was instructed to report every detail of recent royal weddings at Versailles. Extensive memoranda and minute descriptions arrived, to be imitated and, if possible, surpassed. Thick folders of sketches and designs were brought back, accompanied by samples of velvet, silks, and gold braid. Enormous fees enticed French artists, musicians, painters, tailors, cooks, and carpenters to come to Russia. As this tide of information and people flowed into St. Petersburg, Elizabeth read, looked, listened, studied, compared, and calculated. She supervised every detail; indeed, through the spring and early summer, the empress was so taken up with wedding preparations that she had no time for anything else. She neglected affairs of state, ignored her ministers, and normal governmental activity almost ceased.

Once the Baltic and the Neva River were free of ice, ships began arriving in St. Petersburg with bales of silk, velvets, brocades, and the heavy cloth of silver from which Catherine's wedding gown was to be made. Senior court officials were given a year's salary in advance in order to equip themselves with finery. A decree ordered members of the nobility to provide themselves with carriages to be drawn by six horses.

While the court churned with excitement, the bride and bridegroom were left curiously alone. Of practical instruction as to what marriage involved, they were given nothing. Peter's lessons on the proper relationship between a husband and wife came haphazardly from one of his servants, a former Swedish dragoon named Romburg whose own wife had been left behind in Sweden. The husband, Romburg declared, must be the master. The wife should not speak in his presence without his permission, and only a donkey would allow a wife to have opinions of her own. If there was trouble, a few well-timed knocks on the head would put things right. Peter liked listening to this kind of talk and—"about as discreet as a cannon ball," as Catherine put it—enjoyed passing along to her what he had heard.

As for sex, Peter had been given a few basic facts, but only partially understood their meaning. His servants passed on information, coarsely expressed, but instead of enlightening him, their words only bewildered and intimidated him. No one bothered to tell him the essential fact that humans often find pleasure in sexual activity. Confused, embarrassed, and lacking in desire, Peter would come to his new wife's bed with no more than a sense of duty and only an elementary, mechanical idea of how this duty was to be performed.

In the spring and summer before their marriage, Catherine saw her future husband frequently, as their apartments were adjoining. But Peter never remained with her for long and, as the days passed, it became increasingly apparent that he was avoiding her company so that he could be with his servants. In May, he moved with the empress to the Summer Palace, leaving Catherine and her mother behind. Catherine wrote later:

> All the attention which the grand duke had previously
> showed me ceased. He sent me word through a servant that he

lived too far away to come and visit me. I was well aware of his lack of eagerness and affection; my pride and vanity suffered, but I would not have dreamed of complaining. I would have felt humiliated if anyone had shown any sign of sympathy which might be interpreted as pity. But when I was alone, I shed many tears, then wiped them away and went to romp with my maids.

That summer, the court moved to the palace and estate of Peterhof on the Gulf of Finland, nineteen miles west of the capital. Catherine described their activity:

> We spent our time walking, riding, or driving. I saw then, clear as day, that the grand duke's retinue, and especially his tutors, had lost all authority over him. His military games, which he had kept secret, now went on practically in their presence. Count Brümmer could now only observe him in public; the rest of the time he spent entirely in the company of servants in childish pursuits incredible for someone his age; he even played with dolls. The grand duke found great amusement in instructing me in military exercises, and owing to him, I can handle a rifle with the precision of an experienced grenadier. He made me stand at arms with my musket, on duty at the door of the room between his and mine.

In many ways, Catherine also remained a child. She loved what she called "romping" with the young women of her small court; together they still played games of blindman's buff. Underneath, however, she was approaching her marriage with apprehension.

> As my wedding day came nearer, I became more melancholy, and very often I would weep without quite knowing why. My heart predicted little happiness; ambition alone sustained me. In my inmost soul there was something that never for a single moment allowed me to doubt that, sooner or later, I would become the sovereign Empress of Russia in my own right.

Catherine's premarital nervousness did not come from fear of the nocturnal intimacies that marriage would demand. She knew nothing

about these things. Indeed, on the eve of her marriage, she was so innocent that she did not know how the two sexes physically differed.
Nor had she any idea what mysterious acts were performed when a
woman lay down with a man. Who did what? How? She questioned her
young ladies, but they were as innocent as she. One June night, she
staged an impromptu slumber party in her bedroom, covering the floor
with mattresses, including her own. Before going to sleep, the eight
flustered and excited young women discussed what men were like and
how their bodies were formed. No one had any specific information;
indeed, their talk was so ill-informed, incoherent, and unhelpful that
Catherine said that in the morning she would ask her mother. She did
so, but Johanna—herself married at fifteen—refused to answer. Instead, she "severely scolded" her daughter for indecent curiosity.

Empress Elizabeth was aware that all was not well in the relationship between Catherine and Peter, but she assumed that the trouble
was temporary. The grand duke might be immature for his age, but
marriage would make a man of him. For this, she counted on Catherine.
Once the young woman was in his bed, applying her charm and freshness of youth, she would make him forget about playing games with his
servants. In any case, the feelings of the nuptial couple about each other
mattered only peripherally; the reality was that neither of the two adolescents had a choice; they were to be married, like it or not. The betrothed pair knew this, of course, and faced the prospect differently.
Peter fluctuated between deep depression and petty revolt. Sometimes
he would grumble that Russia was an accursed country. At other times,
he would lash out angrily at everyone around him. Catherine's response
was different. Despite her apprehensions, there was no turning back.
She had come to Russia, she had learned Russian, she had resisted her
father and converted to Orthodoxy, she had worked hard to please the
empress, she was ready to marry Peter despite his flaws. Having made
all these concessions and sacrifices, she was not going to throw it all
away, go home, and settle down with Uncle George.

Meanwhile, the vast extent and complexity of the wedding preparations had forced even an impatient Elizabeth to postpone the marriage
ceremony, not once but twice. Finally, it was set for August 21. On the
night of August 20, the city was rocked by salvos of artillery and the
pealing of bells. Catherine sat with her mother and, for a while, they
put aside their misunderstandings and animosities. "We had a long,

friendly talk, she exhorted me concerning my future duties, we cried a little together and parted very affectionately."

At this moment, mother and daughter shared a common, humiliating disappointment. By now, Johanna, having incurred the anger and contempt of the empress, was barely tolerated at court. Johanna knew this and had no illusions about the advantages she herself might gain from her daughter's marriage. Her last hope was that her husband, the father of the bride, would be invited to the wedding. Behind this desire lay no overwhelming affection for Christian Augustus, but her own pride. She well understood that Elizabeth's continuing refusal to invite him was a slap at her as well as at her husband; it made plain to Johanna—and to the world—where she stood.

Explaining this to her husband had not been easy. For months, Christian Augustus had been writing from Zerbst, begging Johanna to obtain from the empress the invitation to which he was obviously entitled. Johanna had long held out hope for this invitation, telling her husband to be ready, that the invitation was on the point of being dispatched. But no invitation came. In the end, it was explained to Christian Augustus that the empress did not dare invite him out of consideration for Russian opinion, which, he was told, was strongly opposed to "German princes"—despite the fact that a prince of Hesse, the Duke of Holstein, and other German noblemen were then living at the Russian court. Further, among those invited were two of Johanna's brothers, both German princes, Adolphus Frederick, now heir to the throne of Sweden, and Augustus, who had succeeded him as prince-bishop of Lübeck. Thus, two of Catherine's uncles were to be present at her wedding, but her father was not. It was a flagrant insult, but there was nothing Johanna could do.

Catherine, too, had hoped that her father would be invited. She had not seen him for a year and a half. She knew that he cared for her, and she believed that, in his simple, honest way, he might give her useful advice. But Catherine's wishes and feelings on this matter interested no one. Her position, in its way, was as clear as her mother's: beneath her title and her diamonds, she was only a little German girl brought to Russia for the sole purpose of providing the son of the house with an heir.

On August 21, 1745, Catherine rose at six o'clock. She was in her bath when the empress arrived unexpectedly to examine, unclothed, the virginal bearer of her own dynastic hopes. Then, as Catherine was being dressed, the empress and the hairdresser discussed what coiffure would best hold in place the crown the bride was to wear. Elizabeth supervised everything, and Johanna, allowed to be present, subsequently described the scene for her German relatives:

> Her silver brocade.wedding gown was of the most shimmering cloth I have ever seen, encrusted with glittering embroidery of silver roses. It had a wide skirt, a seventeen inch waist, and a tight bodice with short sleeves. [She wore] superb jewels: bracelets, drop earrings, brooches, rings. . . . The precious stones with which she was covered, gave her a charming appearance. . . . Her complexion has never been lovelier. . . . Her hair was a bright, lustrous black, slightly curled, which set off her air of youthfulness even more.

Because she was pale, a little rouge was added to her cheeks. Then, a cloak of silver lace, so heavy that Catherine could scarcely move, was attached to her shoulders. Finally, the empress placed on her head the diamond crown of a Russian grand duchess.

At noon, Peter arrived dressed in a suit made of the same cloth of silver as Catherine's dress and train. He, too, was smothered with jewels; his buttons, his sword hilt, and his shoe buckles were encrusted with diamonds. Then, together, in matching silver and diamonds, holding hands as the empress instructed, the young couple left to be married.

A blare of trumpets and the thunder of drums signaled the start of the wedding procession. Twenty-four elegant carriages rolled down the Nevsky Prospect from the Winter Palace to the Cathedral of Our Lady of Kazan. The bridal pair sat with Elizabeth in the empress's state coach, "truly a little castle," drawn by eight white horses, their harness adorned by silver buckles, the huge wheels of the coach shining with gilt, the side panels and doors covered with paintings of mythological scenes. "The procession infinitely surpasses anything I have ever seen," reported the English ambassador. Inside the cathedral, Catherine was surrounded by a sea of jeweled icons, lighted candles, clouds of incense, and rows of faces. The service, conducted by the bishop of Novgorod, lasted three hours.

For Catherine, her wedding ceremony, with its chanted liturgy and magnificent a cappella hymns, was a physical ordeal. Her beautiful gown was "horribly heavy"; the weight of the crown crushing her forehead produced a terrible headache, and there still remained the banquet and the ball to follow. Once the wedding ceremony in the cathedral was over, she asked permission to remove the crown, but Elizabeth refused. Catherine persevered through the banquet in the Long Gallery of the Winter Palace, but just before the ball, with her headache worsening, she begged to have the crown lifted for a few minutes. Reluctantly, the empress consented.

At the ball, only the highest male dignitaries, burdened with years as well as honors, were privileged to dance with the sixteen-year-old bride. Fortunately for her, after half an hour the ball was cut short by Elizabeth's impatient desire to get the young bride and groom to bed. Preceded by a train of court officials and ladies- and gentlemen-in-waiting, Elizabeth escorted the seventeen-year-old husband and his wife, again holding hands, to their nuptial chamber.

The apartment consisted of four large, elegantly furnished rooms. Three were hung with cloth of silver; the bedroom walls were covered with scarlet velvet, trimmed with silver. An enormous bed, covered with red velvet embroidered with gold and surmounted by a crown embossed with silver, dominated the middle of the room. Here, the bride and groom separated and the men, including the new bridegroom, withdrew. The women remained to help the bride undress. The empress removed Catherine's crown, the Princess of Hesse helped to free her from her heavy dress, a lady-in-waiting presented her with a new, pink nightgown from Paris. The bride was placed in bed, but then, just as the last person was leaving the room, she called out. "I begged the Princess of Hesse to stay with me a little while, but she refused," Catherine said. The room was empty. Wearing her pink nightgown, she waited alone in the enormous bed.

Her eyes were fixed on the door through which her new husband would come. Minutes passed and the door remained closed. She continued to wait. Two hours went by. "I remained alone not knowing what I ought to do. Should I get up again? Should I remain in bed? I had no idea." She did nothing. Toward midnight, her new principal lady-in-waiting, Madame Krause, came in and "cheerfully" announced that the grand duke had just ordered supper for himself and was waiting to be served. Catherine continued to wait. Eventually, Peter arrived, reeking of alcohol and tobacco. Lying down in bed beside her, he laughed nervously and said, "How it would amuse my servants to see us in bed together." Then he fell asleep and slept through the night. Catherine remained awake, wondering what to do.

The next day, Madame Krause questioned Catherine about her wedding night. Catherine did not answer. She knew that something was wrong, but she did not know what. In the nights that followed, she continued to lie untouched at the side of her sleeping husband, and Madame Krause's morning questions continued to go unanswered. "And," she writes in her *Memoirs*, "matters remained in this state without the slightest change during the following nine years."

The union, although unconsummated, was followed by ten days of court rejoicing in the form of balls, quadrilles, masquerades, operas, state dinners, and suppers. Outside, for the public, there were fireworks, banquet tables set in Admiralty Square, and fountains spurting jets of wine. Catherine, who usually loved to dance, hated the way she spent these evenings because young people her own age were excluded. "There was not a single man who could dance," she said. "They were all between sixty and eighty years old, most of them lame, gouty or decrepit."

In the meantime, a change for the worse had taken effect in the circle of women around Catherine. On her wedding night, she had discovered that the empress had assigned Madame Krause as her new principal lady-in-waiting. "The following day," Catherine said, "I noticed that this woman had already struck fear in all my other ladies because when I went to talk to one of them in my usual manner, she said to me, 'For God's sake, do not come near me. We have been forbidden even to whisper to you.' "

Nor had marriage improved Peter's behavior. "My dear husband did not pay the slightest attention to me," she said, "but spent all his time playing soldiers in his room with his servants, drilling them or changing his uniform twenty times a day. I yawned and yawned with boredom, having no one to speak to." Then, two weeks after their wedding, Peter finally had something to say to Catherine: with a broad smile, he announced that he had fallen in love with Catherine Karr, one of the empress's ladies-in-waiting. Not content with passing this news to his young wife, he also went out and confided his new passion to his chamberlain, Count Devier, telling him that the grand duchess was in no way to be compared with the enchanting Mlle Karr. When Devier disagreed, Peter exploded with anger.

Whether Peter's passion for Mlle Karr was genuine or whether he had merely concocted this story to explain to Catherine (and perhaps also to himself) his lack of sexual interest in his wife, he was aware that he was subjecting her to insult and humiliation. Years later, in her *Memoirs,* Catherine described the situation she found herself in, and the course she chose to take in dealing with it:

> I would have been ready to like my new husband had he been capable of affection or willing to show any. But in the very first days of our marriage, I came to a sad conclusion about him. I said to myself: "If you allow yourself to love that man, you will be the unhappiest creature on this earth. With your temperament, you will expect some response whereas this man scarcely looks at you, talks of nothing but dolls, and pays more attention to any other woman than yourself. You are too proud to complain, therefore, attention, please, and keep on a leash any affection you might feel for this gentleman; you have yourself to think about, my dear girl." This first scar made upon my impressionable heart remained with me forever; never did this firm resolution leave my head; but I took good care not to tell anybody that I had resolved never to love without restraint a man who would not return this love in full; such was my disposition that my heart would have belonged entirely and without reserve to a husband who loved only me.

This was the voice of an older, wiser Catherine, looking back on the difficulties of the young woman she had been many years before. But whether or not her description accurately reflects her thoughts at the earlier time, she was, at least, always more honest and realistic than her mother. Johanna was never able to leave her fantasy world or stop describing life as she wished it were. Writing to her husband to describe their daughter's wedding, she told him that it "was the gayest marriage that has perhaps ever been celebrated in Europe."

❧ 13 ❧

Johanna Goes Home

THE END OF THE wedding celebrations meant the end of Johanna's misadventure in Russia. She had hoped, in coming to that country, to employ her connections and charm and become a significant figure in European diplomacy. Instead, her political plotting had infuriated the empress, her treatment of her daughter had alienated the court, her purported love affair with Count Ivan Betskoy had provided her enemies with titillated gossip. Her reputation was in ruins, but Johanna never seemed to learn. Even now, on the brink of departure, she continued to write to Frederick II. Her letters, however, were no longer secretly intercepted, read, copied, resealed, and sent along. Instead, by command of the empress, they were simply opened, read, and placed in a folder.

Soon after their arrival in Russia, Catherine had become aware that her mother was making mistakes. Because she did not want to provoke Johanna's temper, she had never spoken a word of reproach. But the experience of her wedding night and Peter's "confession" of his love for Mlle Karr had warmed Catherine's feelings about Johanna. It was to her mother that she now looked for companionship. "Since my marriage, being with her had become my greatest solace," Catherine wrote later. "I jumped at every opportunity to go to her rooms, particularly as my own offered but little joy."

Two weeks after the marriage, the empress sent Catherine, Peter, and Johanna to the country estate of Tsarskoe Selo, outside St. Petersburg. The September weather was superb—an intense blue autumn sky and the birch leaves turning to gold—but Catherine was miserable. As her mother's departure approached, her own ambition seemed to waver. Sharing memories with Johanna became a pleasure and, for the first time since coming to Russia, Catherine was homesick for Germany. "At that time," Catherine wrote later, "I would have given much if I could have left the country with her."

Before going, Johanna requested and was granted an audience with the empress. Johanna gave her version of the meeting to her husband:

> Our farewell was very loving. For me, it was almost impossible to take leave of Her Imperial Majesty; and this great monarch, on her side, paid me the honor of being so deeply moved that the courtiers present were also deeply affected. Farewell was said innumerable times and finally this most gracious of rulers accompanied me to the stairway with tears and expressions of kindness and tenderness.

A different description of this interview came from an eyewitness, the English ambassador:

> When the princess took leave of the empress, she fell at Her Imperial Majesty's feet and implored her in floods of tears to forgive her if she had in any way offended Her Imperial Majesty. The empress replied that it was late to talk about such considerations, but that if the princess had had such wise thoughts earlier, it would have been better for her.

Elizabeth was determined to send Johanna away, but she also wanted to appear magnanimous and the princess departed with a cartload of gifts. To console the long-neglected Prince of Anhalt-Zerbst, Johanna carried home diamond shoe buckles, diamond coat buttons, and a diamond-studded dagger, all described as presents from the prince's son-in-law, the grand duke. In addition, before leaving, Johanna was given sixty thousand rubles to pay her debts in Russia. After her departure, it turned out that she owed more than twice that sum. To shield her mother from further shame, Catherine agreed to pay the arrears. Having only her personal allowance of thirty thousand rubles a year, this obligation was beyond her means and helped create a debt that dragged on for seventeen years until she became empress.

When the moment of departure arrived, Catherine and Peter accompanied Johanna on the short first stage of her journey, from Tsarskoe Selo to nearby Krasnoe Selo. The next morning, Johanna left before dawn without saying goodbye; Catherine assumed that it was "not to make me any sadder." Waking up and finding her mother's room empty, she was distraught. Her mother had vanished—from Russia and from her life. Since Catherine's birth, Johanna had always been present, to guide, prompt, correct, and scold. She might have failed as a diplomatic agent; she certainly had not become a brilliant figure on the European stage; but she had not been unsuccessful as a mother. Her daughter, born a minor German princess, was now an imperial grand duchess on a path to becoming an empress.

Johanna would live another fifteen years. She died in 1760, at the age of forty-seven, when Catherine was thirty-one. Now, she was leaving behind a sixteen-year-old daughter who would never see any member of her family again. The daughter was under the control of a temperamental, all-powerful monarch, and was lying in bed every night beside a young man whose behavior was increasingly peculiar.

Traveling slowly, Johanna took twelve days to reach Riga. There, Elizabeth's delayed punishment caught up with her ungrateful, duplicitous guest. Johanna was handed a letter from the empress commanding her to tell Frederick of Prussia, as she passed through Berlin, that he must recall his ambassador, Baron Mardefeld. The letter was phrased with cool, diplomatic politeness: "I consider it necessary to enjoin you to impress upon His Majesty the King of Prussia when you arrive in Berlin, that it would please me if he were to recall his plenipotentiary minister, Baron Mardefeld." The choice of Johanna to deliver this message was a slap at both the princess and the king. La Chétardie, the French ambassador, had been given twenty-four hours to leave Moscow after the scene at Troitsa Monastery; Mardefeld, the Prussian ambassador, who had served in Russia for twenty years, had been spared for an additional year and a half, but now he, too, was to be sent home. And Elizabeth's choice of Johanna to carry the news was explicit recognition of the fact that, while in Russia, the princess had conspired on behalf of the Prussian king to overthrow the empress's chief minister, Bestuzhev. There is no proof that this painful assignment was the work of Bestuzhev—but it sounds like him. If so, Elizabeth had concurred.

Certainly, the letter, its content and its means of delivery, made plain to Frederick how greatly he had overrated Johanna. Regretting his own misjudgment, he never forgave her. Ten years later, after her husband had died and Johanna was acting as regent for her young son, Frederick suddenly reached out and peremptorily incorporated the principality of Zerbst into the kingdom of Prussia. Johanna was forced to take refuge in Paris. There, she died on the fringe of society two years before her daughter became empress of Russia.

PART II
A Painful Marriage

The Zhukova Affair

RETURNING TO St. Petersburg after saying goodbye to her mother, Catherine immediately asked for Maria Zhukova. Before her marriage, the empress had added to Catherine's small court a group of young Russian ladies-in-waiting to help the German-speaking bride-to-be improve her Russian. Catherine was delighted to have them. The girls were all young; the oldest was twenty. "From that moment on," Catherine recalled, "I did nothing but sing, dance, and frolic in my room from the moment I awoke until I fell asleep." These were the playmates with whom Catherine played blindman's buff, used the lid of a harpsichord as a toboggan, and spent a night on mattresses on the floor wondering what men's bodies looked like. The liveliest and most intelligent of these young women, a seventeen-year-old named Maria Zhukova, had become Catherine's favorite.

When she asked for Maria, she was told that the girl had gone to visit her mother. The following morning, Catherine asked again and the answer was the same. At noon that day, when she called on the empress in her bedroom, Elizabeth began to talk about Johanna's departure and said she hoped Catherine would not be too much affected by it. Then, almost in passing, she said something that struck Catherine dumb—"I thought I would faint," Catherine wrote later. In a loud voice and in the presence of thirty people, the empress announced that, in response to Johanna's parting request, she had dismissed Maria Zhukova from court. Johanna, Elizabeth told Catherine, "feared that I had grown too attached to the girl and that a close friendship between two young women the same age was undesirable." Then, on her own, Elizabeth added a stream of insults directed at Maria.

Catherine wondered whether Elizabeth was telling the truth; whether, in fact, her mother had actually asked the empress to send the girl away. Had Johanna felt this much hostility for Maria, Catherine was certain that her mother would have spoken to her before departing; Johanna had never been reticent with criticism. It was true that Johanna had always ignored Maria, but Catherine explained this to herself as stemming from Johanna's inability to speak to the girl: "My mother did not know Russian and Maria spoke no other language." If, on the other hand, Johanna was not to blame and the idea was solely Elizabeth's, perhaps Madame Krause had told the empress about the close friendship between the young women. And perhaps Elizabeth had considered this information relevant to the reports that nothing productive was happening at night in the marital bedchamber. This might explain why, behind the cover of its being Johanna's wish, Elizabeth had summarily removed Catherine's closest friend. If any of this conjectured sequence was true, Catherine never learned.

In any case, Catherine knew that Maria Zhukova was innocent of wrongdoing. Upset, she told Peter that she did not intend to abandon her friend; Peter showed no interest. Catherine then attempted to send money to Maria, but was informed that the girl had already left St. Petersburg for Moscow with her mother and sister. Catherine next asked that the money she wanted to send to Maria be sent instead to Maria's brother, a sergeant in the Guards. She was told that the brother and his wife had also disappeared; the brother had suddenly been posted to a distant regiment. Refusing to give up, Catherine tried to arrange a marriage. "Through my servants and others, I looked for a suitable husband for Mlle Zhukova. A man was located who seemed eligible, a junior officer in the Guards, who was a gentleman of property. This man traveled to Moscow to offer to marry Maria if she liked him. She accepted his proposal." But when word of this arrangement reached the empress, she intervened again. The new husband was assigned (essentially, banished) to a regiment in Astrakhan. "It is difficult," Catherine wrote later, "to find an explanation for this further persecution. Later on, I gathered that the only crime ever attributed to this girl was my affection for her and the attachment she was supposed to have for me. Even now, I find it difficult to find any plausible explanation for all this. It seems to me that people were being gratuitously ruined out of mere caprice, with no shadow of reason."

This was a warning of what lay ahead. Indeed, Catherine soon realized that the harsh treatment of Maria Zhukova was a clear signal to everyone in the young court that those who were suspected of closeness to either Catherine or Peter were liable to find themselves, on one pretext or another, transferred, dismissed, disgraced, or even imprisoned. Responsibility for this policy lay with the chancellor, Alexis Bestuzhev, and, above him, the empress. Bestuzhev hated Prussia and had always opposed the bringing of the two German adolescents to Russia. Now that they were married despite his wishes, he was determined that they should not be in a position to undermine his administration of Russian diplomacy. This meant strict surveillance of the married couple, the curbing of all independent friendships and contacts of any kind, and, eventually, an attempt to isolate them completely. Behind Bestuzhev, of course, stood Elizabeth, whose concerns and fears were personal: she feared for the security of her person, her throne, and the future of her branch of the dynasty. In her plans, of course, Catherine, Peter, and their future child were of supreme importance. For this reason, over the years ahead, Elizabeth's attitudes toward both the young husband and the young wife oscillated dramatically between affection, concern, disappointment, impatience, frustration, and rage.

Not only in appearance but in character, Elizabeth was her parents' child. She was the daughter of Russia's greatest tsar and his peasant wife, who became Empress Catherine I. Elizabeth was tall, like her father, and she resembled him in her energy, ardent temper, and sudden, impulsive behavior. Like her mother, she was quickly moved to sympathy and to lavish, spontaneous generosity. But her gratitude, like her other qualities, lacked moderation and permanence. The moment her mistrust was aroused, her dignity or vanity affronted, or her jealousy incurred, she would become a different person. Because it was difficult to guess the empress's moods, no one could predict her public actions. A woman of extreme, sometimes violent, contradictions, Elizabeth could be easy—or impossible—to get along with.

In the fall of 1745, when Johanna returned to Germany and Elizabeth became the dominant influence in Catherine's life, the empress was nearing her thirty-sixth birthday. She remained handsome and statuesque, but she was tending to heaviness. She continued to move and dance with grace, her large blue eyes remained brilliant, and she still possessed a rosebud mouth. Her hair was blond, but for some reason, she dyed it black, along with her eyebrows and sometimes her eyelashes. Her skin remained so pink and clear that she needed few cosmetics. She cared immensely about what she wore and refused to put on a gown more than once; on her death, fifteen thousand robes and dresses were supposedly discovered in her closets and wardrobes. On formal occasions, she layered herself with jewels. Appearing with her hair flecked with diamonds and pearls, and her neck and bosom covered with sapphires, emeralds, and rubies, she created an overwhelming impression. She intended this always to be so.

Nevertheless, she indulged her appetites without restraint. She ate and drank as much as she pleased. She often stayed up all night. The result—although no one dared to say so—was that her celebrated beauty was fading. Although Elizabeth herself knew this, she continued to live by her own rules. Her daily schedule was a constantly changing mixture of time-honored formality and imperial impromptu. She observed and enforced rigid court protocol when it served her purpose; more often, like her father, she ignored routine and behaved according to impulse. Instead of regularly dining at noon and supping at six, she arose and began the day whenever she felt like it. Often, she postponed the midday meal until five or six in the afternoon, had supper at two or three in the morning, and finally went to bed at sunrise. Until she became too heavy, she went riding or hunting in the morning and then drove out in her carriage in the afternoon. Several times a week there was a ball or an opera in the evening, followed by an elaborate supper and a display of fireworks. For these occasions, she kept changing her gowns and having her elaborate coiffure constantly reshaped. Court dinners offered fifty to sixty different dishes, but sometimes—to the despair of her French chef—the empress herself ate Russian peasant fare: cabbage soup, blini (buckwheat cakes), pickled pork, and onions.

To maintain her dazzling preeminence at court, Elizabeth made certain that no other woman present could shine as brightly. Sometimes, this required draconian coercive measures. During the winter of 1747, the empress decreed that all of her ladies-in-waiting must shave their heads and wear black wigs until their hair grew in again. The women wept but obeyed. Catherine assumed that her own turn would come, but to her surprise, she was spared; Elizabeth explained that Catherine's hair was just growing back after an illness. Soon, the reason for the general pruning became known: after a previous festive occasion, Elizabeth and her maids had been unable to brush a heavy powder out of her hair, which became gray, coagulated, and gummy. The only remedy was to have her head shaved. And because she refused to be the only bald woman at court, bushels of hair were cropped.

On St. Alexander's Day in the winter of 1747, Elizabeth's jealous eye fell specifically on Catherine. The grand duchess appeared at court in a white dress trimmed with Spanish lace. When she returned to her room, a lady-in-waiting appeared to tell her that the empress commanded her to take off the dress. Catherine apologized and put on a different gown, also white but decorated with silver braid and a fiery red jacket and cuffs. Catherine commented:

> As for the previous dress, it is possible that the empress found my dress more effective than her own and that this was the real reason she had ordered me to take mine off. My dear aunt was very prone to such petty jealousies, not only in relation to me, but to all the other ladies also. She had an eye particularly on those younger than herself, who were continually exposed to her outbursts. She carried this jealousy so far that once she called up Anna Naryshkina, sister-in-law of Lev Naryshkin, who, because of her beauty, her glorious figure, superb carriage, and exquisite taste in dress, had become the empress's pet aversion. In the presence of the whole court, the empress took a pair of scissors and cut off a trimming of lovely ribbons under Madame Naryshkina's neck. Another time, she cut off half of the front curls of two of her ladies-in-waiting on the pretext that she did not like their style of hair dressing. Afterwards, these young ladies said privately that, perhaps in her haste, or perhaps in her fierce determination to display the depth of her feelings, Her Imperial Majesty had cut off, along with their curls, some of their skin.

Elizabeth went to bed reluctantly and late. When the festivities and official receptions were over and the crowd of courtiers and guests had retired, she would sit in her private apartment with a small group of friends. Even when these people had left her and she was exhausted, she allowed herself only to be undressed; she still refused to sleep. As long as it was dark—and in winter in St. Petersburg, dark could last until eight or nine o'clock in the morning—she continued to talk to a few of her women, who took turns rubbing and tickling the soles of her feet to keep her awake. Meanwhile, not far away behind the brocaded curtains of the royal alcove, a fully clothed man lay on a thin mattress. This was Chulkov, the empress's faithful bodyguard, who had the strange ability to do without sleep and who for twenty years had not slept in a proper bed. At last, as the pale light of dawn came creeping through the windows, the women would leave, and Razumovsky, or whoever happened to be the favorite of the moment, would appear, and in his arms Elizabeth would finally fall asleep. Chulkov, the man behind the curtain, remained at his post as long as the empress slept, sometimes into the afternoon.

The explanation for these unconventional hours was that Elizabeth feared the night; most of all she feared to sleep at night. The regent Anna Leopoldovna had been asleep when she was overthrown, and Elizabeth was afraid that a similar fate might overtake her. Her fears were exaggerated; she was popular with the public and only a palace coup, organized to elevate some new pretender, could mean loss of the throne. Only the dethroned boy tsar Ivan VI, a helpless child locked in a fortress, was a threat to Elizabeth. But it was the specter of this child that haunted Elizabeth and robbed her of her sleep. Potentially, of course, there was a remedy. Another child, a new baby heir, an offspring of Peter and Catherine, was what was needed. When such a child was born, and was surrounded, guarded, and loved by all of Elizabeth's power, then Elizabeth could sleep.

❧ 15 ❧

Peepholes

ELIZABETH'S INTERVENTIONS in the daily life of the young married couple were often trivial. One night, when Catherine and Peter were having supper with friends, Mme Krause appeared at midnight and announced, "on the empress's behalf," that they were to go to bed; the monarch considered it wrong "to stay up so late." The party broke up, but Catherine said, "It seemed strange to us as we knew the irregular hours kept by our dear aunt . . . it seemed to us more ill-humor than reason." On the other hand, Elizabeth was unusually friendly to Catherine when the younger woman was in difficulty and the empress could play the role of supportive mother. One morning, Peter had a high fever and severe headache and could not get out of bed. He remained in bed for a week and was bled repeatedly. Elizabeth came to visit him several times a day and, observing tears in Catherine's eyes, "was satisfied and pleased with me." Soon afterward, when Catherine was saying her evening prayers in a palace chapel, one of Elizabeth's ladies-in-waiting came in to tell her that the empress, knowing that the grand duchess was upset by the grand duke's illness, had sent her to say that Catherine should have faith in God and should not worry, because under no circumstances would the empress abandon her.

Similarly, in the early months of Catherine's marriage, the people leaving the young court were not always forced to do so by Elizabeth. Catherine's chamberlain, Count Zakhar Chernyshev, suddenly disappeared. He had been one of the young courtiers invited by Catherine and Peter to join them in the large, pillowed cart in which they traveled to Kiev before their marriage. But Count Zakhar's departure in the form of a diplomatic assignment had nothing to do with the empress. Instead, the initiative came from the young man's mother, who had begged Elizabeth to send her son away. "I fear he may fall in love with the grand duchess," the mother had said. "He never takes his eyes off her and when I see that, I tremble for fear that he might do something rash." In fact, her intuitions were sound: Zakhar Chernyshev was indeed attracted to Catherine, as he would make clear a few years later.

The next to go, lamented by no one, was Peter's longtime tormentor, Otto Brümmer. In the spring before his marriage, seventeen-year-old Peter had been formally declared to be of age and had become, in title at least, the reigning Duke of Holstein. In matters concerning his duchy, he now was entitled to make certain decisions. The decision he most wanted to make was to get rid of Brümmer. After reading the document confirming his title, Peter turned to his nemesis and said, "At last my wish is fulfilled. You have dominated me long enough. I shall take steps to have you sent back to Holstein as soon as possible." Brümmer struggled to save himself. To Catherine's surprise, he turned to her, asking her to make more frequent visits to Elizabeth's dressing room and speak to the empress. "I told Brümmer that his suggestion could not help him as the empress almost never appeared when I was there. He begged that I should persevere." Catherine, understanding that "this might serve his purposes but could do me no good," told Count Brümmer that she was reluctant. Desperate, he continued to try to persuade her—"without success." In the spring of 1746, the empress sent Brümmer back to Germany with an annual pension of three thousand rubles.

Living under the eye of Empress Elizabeth was difficult for Catherine, but with the early exception of her vigorous, and ultimately failed, attempt to help Maria Zhukova, the young grand duchess tried to accept her situation. Peter was less pliable. He had little desire to please his aunt; Instead, a belligerent rebelliousness often led him to do foolish things.

The episode of the peepholes was an example: Around Easter in 1746, Peter created a puppet theater in his apartment and insisted that everyone in the young court attend performances. On one side of the room in which he had erected his theater, a door had been walled up because it led into the dining room of the empress's private apartment. One day while working with his puppets, Peter heard voices through the blocked door. Curious to see what was happening in the next room, he took a carpenter's bore and drilled peepholes through the door. To his delight, he found himself witnessing a private, mid-day dinner party with the empress surrounded by a dozen of her friends. Next to his aunt sat Count Razumovsky, who, recovering from an illness, was dressed informally in a brocaded dressing gown.

Then, having already trespassed beyond the limits of discretion, Peter went further. Excited by his discovery, he summoned everyone to come and peek through the holes. Servants placed chairs, footstools, and benches before the perforated door to form an impromptu amphitheater so all could enjoy the spectacle. When Peter and his entourage had finished staring, he invited Catherine and her ladies-in-waiting to come and see this remarkable sight.

> He did not tell us what it was, apparently to give us a pleasant surprise. I did not hurry quickly enough, so he carried off Madame Krause and my women. I arrived last and found them all sitting in front of the door. I asked what was going on. When he told me, I was horrified and frightened by his rashness and said that I wished neither to look nor to take part in this scandalous behavior which would surely upset his aunt if she learned about it. Which she could scarcely fail to do since he had shared his secret with at least twenty people.

When the group that had been peeking through the door saw that Catherine refused to do so, they all began, one by one, to walk away. Peter himself became apprehensive and went back to arranging his puppets.

Elizabeth soon learned what had happened, and on a Sunday morning after Mass, she suddenly burst into Catherine's room and ordered that her nephew be summoned. Peter arrived wearing a dressing gown and carrying his nightcap in his hand. He appeared carefree and rushed to kiss his aunt's hand. She accepted the gesture and then asked how he dared to behave as he had. She said that she had found the door riddled with holes, all of them immediately facing the spot where she sat. She could only suppose that he had forgotten what he owed her. She reminded him that her own father, Peter the Great, had had an ungrateful son whom he had punished by disinheriting. She said that the empress Anne had locked up in the fortress anyone who showed her disrespect. Her nephew, Elizabeth told him, was "no better than a disrespectful little boy who needed to be taught how to behave."

Peter stammered a few words of defense, but Elizabeth ordered him to be silent. Her temper rose; she "let fly at him with the most shocking insults and abuse, displaying as much contempt as anger," Catherine reported. "We were dumbfounded, stupefied and speechless, both of us, and, though this scene had nothing to do with me, it brought tears to my eyes." Elizabeth noticed this and said to Catherine, "What I am saying is not directed at you. I know that you took no part in what he did and that you neither looked nor wanted to look through that door." Then the empress calmed down, stopped talking, and left the room. The couple stared at each other. Then Peter, mingling contrition and sarcasm, said, "She was like a Fury. She did not know what she was saying."

Later, when Peter had left, Madame Krause came in and said to Catherine, "One must admit that the empress behaved today like a real mother." Unsure of her meaning, Catherine was silent. Madame Krause explained: "A mother gets angry and scolds her children and then it all blows over. You ought, both of you, to have said to her, '*Vinovaty, Matush-ka*'—'We beg your pardon, Little Mother'—and she would have been disarmed." Catherine replied that she had been so shaken by the empress's anger that she could do nothing but keep silent. But she learned from the episode. Afterward, she wrote, "the phrase, 'We beg your pardon, Mama,' remained fixed in my memory as a way to disarm the empress's wrath. Later, I used it successfully."

When Catherine first arrived, unmarried, in Russia, Peter's intimate circle included three young noblemen—two brothers and a cousin—named Chernyshev. Peter was immensely fond of all three. It was the eldest of the brothers, Zakhar, who had so worried his own mother with his obvious affection for Catherine that she had arranged to have him sent away from court, out of reach. The cousin and the younger brother remained, however, and the cousin, Andrei, also harbored feelings for Catherine. He began by making himself useful. Catherine had discovered that Madame Krause "had a great liking for the bottle. Often my entourage managed to make her drunk, after which she went to bed, leaving the young court to frolic without being scolded." Her "entourage" in this case was Andrei Chernyshev, who could persuade Madame Krause to drink as much as he chose.

Before Catherine's marriage to Peter, Andrei had fallen into a pattern of lighthearted flirtation with the bride-to-be. Far from opposing or feeling uncomfortable with this intimate but still innocent banter, Peter enjoyed and even encouraged it. For months, he talked to his wife of Chernyshev's good looks and devotion. Several times a day, he would send Andrei to Catherine with trivial messages. Eventually, however, Andrei himself became uncomfortable with the situation. One day, he said to Peter, "Your Imperial Highness should bear in mind that the grand duchess is not Madame Chernyshev"—and, more bluntly—"She is not my fiancée, she's yours." Peter laughed and passed these remarks along to Catherine. To put an end to this uncomfortable joke after the couple was married, Andrei proposed to Peter that he redefine his relationship with Catherine by calling her Matushka (Little Mother) and that she call him *synok* (son). But as both Catherine and Peter continued to show great affection for the "son" and talked about him constantly, some of their servants became concerned.

One day, Catherine's valet, Timothy Evreinov, took her aside and warned her that the whole household was gossiping about her relationship with Andrei. Frankly, he said, he was frightened by the danger into which she was heading. Catherine asked what he meant. "You talk and think of nothing but Andrei Chernyshev," he said.

"What harm is there in that?" Catherine asked. "He is my son. My husband is fonder of him than I am and he is a loyal friend to both of us."

"That is true," Evreinov replied, "and the grand duke can do as he wishes, but it is not the same with you. What you call loyalty and affection because this young man is faithful to you, your entourage believes is love."

When he spoke this word, "which I had not even imagined," Catherine says, she was struck "as if by a thunderbolt." Evreinov told her that, in order to avoid further gossip, he had already advised Chernyshev to plead illness and take a leave of absence from court. And, indeed, Andrei Chernyshev had already departed. Peter, who had been told nothing of this, was concerned about his friend's "illness" and spoke of it worriedly to Catherine.

Eventually, when Andrei Chernyshev reappeared at court a month later, he caused a moment of danger for Catherine. During one of Peter's concerts in which he himself played the violin, Catherine, who hated music in general and her husband's efforts in particular, retreated to her room just off the Great Hall of the Summer Palace. The ceiling of this hall was being repaired, and the space was filled with scaffolding and workmen. Opening the door of her apartment into the hall, she was surprised to see Andrei Chernyshev standing not far away. She beckoned to him. Apprehensively, he came to her door. She said something meaningless. He replied, "I cannot speak to you like this. There is too much noise in the hall. Let me come into your room."

"No," Catherine said, "that is something I cannot do." Nevertheless, she continued talking to him for five minutes through the half-opened door. Then, a premonition made her turn her head and she saw, standing and watching from inside her own room, Peter's chamberlain, Count Devier.

"The grand duke is asking for you, Madame," Devier said. Catherine closed the door on Chernyshev and walked with Devier back to the concert. The following day, the two remaining Chernyshevs vanished from court. Catherine and Peter were told that they had been posted to distant regiments; subsequently they learned that, in fact, they had been placed under house arrest.

The Chernyshev affair had two immediate consequences for the young couple. The lesser was that the empress commanded Father Todorsky to question husband and wife separately about their relationship with the young men. Todorsky asked Catherine whether she had ever kissed one of the Chernyshevs.

"No, my father," she replied.

"Then why has the empress been informed to the contrary?" he asked. "The empress has been told that you gave a kiss to Andrei Chernyshev."

"That is slander, my father. It is not true," said Catherine. Her sincerity apparently convinced Todorsky, who muttered to himself, "What wicked people!" He reported this conversation to the empress, and Catherine heard no more about it.

But the Andrei Chernyshev affair, although lacking in substance, had lodged in the empress's mind, and it played a part in what happened next, something more significant and long-lasting. On the afternoon the Chernyshevs disappeared, a new chief governess, senior to Madame Krause, appeared. The arrival of this woman to rule over Catherine and her daily life marked the beginning of seven years of harassment, oppression, and misery.

❧16❧

A Watchdog

ELIZABETH STILL NEEDED an heir, and she was perplexed, resentful, and angry that no child was on the way. By May 1746, eight months had passed since the marriage, and there were no signs of a pregnancy. Elizabeth suspected disrespect, unwillingness, even faithlessness. She blamed Catherine.

For the chancellor, Bestuzhev, the problem was different. At issue was not only the matter of an unsuccessful marriage that had produced no child but also Russia's diplomatic future. This was Bestuzhev's sphere, and to keep and use the power he needed, he encouraged Elizabeth's suspicion and whipped up her resentments. Personally, he, too, was concerned about the young couple: he was alarmed by Peter's opinions and behavior, and he mistrusted Johanna's daughter, whom he suspected of conspiring secretly with Frederick of Prussia. Because Peter openly admired Frederick, Bestuzhev could scarcely help fearing the accession of such a sovereign to the Russian throne. As for Catherine, the chancellor had always opposed the German grand duke's marriage to a German princess. Accordingly, the young couple and the young court must not be permitted to become an alternative power center, an independent political body made up of faithful friends and loyal partisans; this happened often enough in kingdoms with independent-thinking heirs to thrones. To prevent it, Bestuzhev employed two tactics: first, the isolation of the young couple from the outside world, and, second, the placement of a powerful, vigilant watchdog inside the young court to watch every move and overhear every word.

As the empress's first minister, he had, of course, to address her first concern: her need for an heir. Bestuzhev's approach was to recommend that a strong woman loyal to him be appointed as senior governess to Catherine, to act as the young wife's constant companion and chaperone. This woman's duty be would to superintend the marital intimacies and ensure the fidelity of Catherine and Peter. She was to watch the grand duchess and prevent any familiarity with the cavaliers, pages, and servants of the court. Further, she was to see that her charge wrote no letters and had no private conversations with anyone. This prohibition neatly combined Elizabeth's worries about infidelity with Bestuzhev's insistence on political isolation; it was critically important to the chancellor that Catherine's correspondence and her conversations with foreign diplomats be kept under strict surveillance. Thus, Bestuzhev imposed a new entourage on Catherine, charged to enforce a new set of rules dictated by the chancellor, supposedly aimed at consolidating the mutual affection of the married couple, but also intended to render them politically harmless.

Only the first half of this agenda was made explicit to Catherine. In a decree signed by Elizabeth, the young wife was reminded that:

> Her Imperial Highness has been selected for the high honor of being the noble wife of our dear nephew, His Imperial Highness, the Grand Duke, heir to the empire. . . . [She] has been elevated to her present dignity of Imperial Highness with none other but the following aims and objects: that her Imperial Highness might by her sensible behavior, her wit and virtue, inspire a sincere love in His Imperial Highness and win his heart, and that by so doing may bring forth the heir so much desired for the empire and a fresh sprig of our illustrious house.

The woman carefully selected by Bestuzhev to oversee and administer these tasks was twenty-four-year-old Maria Semenovna Choglokova, Elizabeth's first cousin on her mother's side. She was one of Elizabeth's favorites, and both she and her husband, one of the empress's chamberlains, were also devoted servants of the chancellor. Further, Madame Choglokova had a remarkable reputation for virtue and fertility. She idolized her husband and produced a child with almost annual regularity, a domestic accomplishment meant to set an example for Catherine.

Catherine hated her from the beginning. In her *Memoirs*, she directed a barrage of unflattering adjectives at this woman who was to

rule her existence for many years: "simple-minded ... uneducated ...
cruel ... malicious ... capricious ... self-serving." The afternoon following Madame Choglokova's appointment, Peter took Catherine aside
and told her that he had learned that the new governess had been assigned to watch over her because she, his wife, did not love him. Catherine replied that it was impossible that anybody could believe that this
particular woman could make her feel more tenderness for him. To act
as a watchdog was a different matter, she said, but for that purpose they
should have chosen someone more intelligent.

The war between the new governess and her charge began immediately. Madame Choglokova's first act was to inform Catherine that she
was to be kept at a greater distance from the sovereign. In the future,
she said, if the grand duchess had anything to say to the empress, it
must be passed along through her, Madame Choglokova. Hearing this,
Catherine's eyes filled with tears. Madame Choglokova ran to report
the lack of enthusiasm with which she had been received, and Catherine's eyes still were red when Elizabeth appeared. She led Catherine to
a room where they were completely alone. "In the two years I had been
in Russia," Catherine said, "this was the first time she had ever spoken
to me privately, without witnesses." The empress then unleashed a torrent of complaint and accusation. She asked "whether it was my mother
who had given me instructions to betray her to the King of Prussia. She
said that she was well aware of my wiles and deceitfulness and, in a
word, knew everything. She said that she knew it was my fault that the
marriage had not been consummated." When Catherine again began to
weep, Elizabeth declared that young women who did not love their
husbands always wept. Yet no one had forced Catherine to marry the
grand duke; it had been her own wish; she had no right to weep over it
now. She said that if Catherine did not love Peter, she, Elizabeth, was
not to blame; Catherine's mother had assured her that her daughter
was marrying Peter for love; certainly, she had not forced the girl into
marriage against her will. "Now, as I was married," Catherine reported
Elizabeth saying, "I must not cry anymore. Then she added that, of
course, she knew very well that I was in love with another man, but she
never mentioned the name of the man I was supposed to love." Finally,
she added, "I know quite well that you alone are to blame if you have no
children."

Catherine could think of nothing to say. She believed that at any
moment Elizabeth was going to strike her; the empress, she knew, regu-

larly slapped the women of her household and even the men when she was angry.

> I could not save myself by flight because I had my back against a door and she was directly in front of me. Then I remembered Madame Krause's advice and I said to her, "I beg your pardon, Little Mother," and she was appeased. I went to my bedroom, still crying and thinking that death was preferable to such a persecuted life. I took a large knife and lay down on a sofa, intending to plunge it into my heart. Just then, one of my maids came in, threw herself on the knife, and stopped me. Actually, the knife was not very sharp and would not have penetrated my corset.

Unaware of the degree to which Bestuzhev had agitated Elizabeth on the subject of Prussia, Catherine assumed that there was only one reason for Elizabeth's outburst. None of the empress's criticisms was valid. She was obedient and submissive; she was not indiscreet; she was not betraying Russia to Prussia, she never bored holes through doors, and she did not love another man. Her failure was that she had not produced a child.

A few days later, when Peter and Catherine accompanied the empress on a visit to Reval (today Tallinn, capital of Estonia), Mme Choglokova rode in their carriage. Her behavior, Catherine said, was "a torment." To the simplest remark, however innocent or trivial, she responded by saying, "such talk would displease the empress" or "such things would not be approved by the empress." Catherine's reaction was to close her eyes and sleep through the journey.

Madame Choglokova kept her position for the next seven years. She possessed none of the qualities necessary to assist an inexperienced young wife. She was neither wise nor sympathetic; on the contrary, she had a reputation as one of the most ignorant and arrogant women at court. Not even remotely did it occur to her to win Catherine's friendship or, as a wife and the mother of a large family, to discuss the underlying problem she had been called in to solve. In fact, she had no success in the area about which Elizabeth cared most; her oversight of the marriage bed was fruitless. Nevertheless, her power was real. Functioning as Bestuzhev's jailor and spy, Madame Choglokova made Catherine a royal prisoner.

In August 1746, in the first full summer following their marriage, Elizabeth allowed Peter and Catherine to go to Oranienbaum (Orange Tree), an estate on the Gulf of Finland that Elizabeth had given to her nephew. There in the courtyard and terraced gardens, Peter established a simulated military camp. He and his chamberlains, gentlemen-in-waiting, servants, gamekeepers, even gardeners, walked around with muskets on their shoulders, doing daytime parade ground drill and taking turns standing guard at night. Catherine was left with nothing to do except sit and listen to the Choglokovs grumble. She tried to lose herself in reading. "In those days," she said, "I read romances only." Her favorite that summer was an exaggerated French romance titled *Tiran the Fair,* the story of a French knight-errant who travels to England, where he triumphs in tournaments and battles and becomes a favorite of the daughter of the king. Catherine particularly loved the description of the princess, "whose skin was so transparent that when she drank red wine, you could see it pass down her throat." Peter read too, but his taste lay in tales of "highwaymen eventually hanged for their crimes or broken on the wheel." Of that summer, Catherine wrote:

> Never did two minds resemble each other less. We had nothing in common in our tastes or ways of thinking. Our opinions were so different that we would never have agreed on anything had I not often given in to him so as not to affront him too noticeably. I was already restless enough and this restlessness was increased by the horrible life I had to lead. I was constantly left to myself and suspicion surrounded me on all sides. There was no amusement, no conversation, no kindness or attention to help alleviate this boredom for me. My life became unbearable.

Catherine began to suffer from severe headaches and insomnia. When Madame Krause insisted that these symptoms would disappear if the grand duchess would drink a glass of Hungarian wine in bed at night, Catherine refused. Whereupon Madame Krause always raised the glass to Catherine's health—and then emptied it herself.

❧17❧

"He Was Not a King"

IN ZERBST on March 16, 1747, Catherine's father, Prince Christian Augustus, suffered a second stoke and died. He was fifty-six; Catherine was seventeen. He had not been allowed to come to her betrothal or to her wedding, and she had not seen him since leaving home three years before. In the last year of his life, she had had little contact with him. This was the work of Empress Elizabeth, Count Bestuzhev, and their agent, Madame Choglokova. Relations between Prussia and Russia were worsening, and Bestuzhev insisted to the empress that all private correspondence between Russia and anyone in Germany be stopped. Catherine, therefore, was strictly forbidden to write personal letters to her parents. Her monthly letters to her mother and father were drafted by the Foreign Office; she was allowed only to copy her message from this draft and then to sign her name at the bottom. She was forbidden to slip any personal news or even a single word of affection into the text. And now her father, who in his quiet, undemonstrative way had given her the only disinterested affection she had ever known, was gone, without a final word of tenderness from her.

Catherine's grief was profound. Shutting herself up in her apartment, she sobbed for a week. Then Elizabeth sent Madame Choglokova to tell her that a grand duchess of Russia was not permitted to mourn for more than a week "because, after all, your father was not a king." Catherine replied that "it was true that he was not a reigning sovereign, but he was my father." Elizabeth and Choglokova prevailed, and after seven days Catherine was forced to reappear in public. As a concession, she was allowed to wear black silk in mourning, but only for six weeks.

The first time she left her room, she encountered and spoke a few casual words to Count Santi, the Italian-born Court Master of Ceremonies. A few days later, Madame Choglokova came to tell her that the empress had learned from Count Bestuzhev—to whom Count Santi had reported it in writing—that Catherine had said she found it strange that ambassadors had not offered her condolences on her father's death. Madame Choglokova said that the empress considered her re-marks to Santi highly improper; that Catherine was too proud, and, once again, that she ought to remember that her father had not been a king; for that reason no expressions of sympathy from foreign ambas-sadors should be expected.

Catherine could hardly believe what Madame Choglokova was say-ing. Forgetting her fear of the governess, she said that if Count Santi had written or said that she had spoken a single word to him on this subject, he was a monstrous liar; that nothing of the kind had entered her head; that she had never said a word to him or to anyone else on the subject. "Apparently, my words carried conviction," Catherine wrote in her *Memoirs*, "for Madame Choglokova conveyed my words to the em-press who then directed her rage at Count Santi."

Several days later, Count Santi sent a messenger to Catherine to tell her that Count Bestuzhev had forced him to tell this lie and that he was very ashamed of himself. Catherine told this messenger that a liar was a liar, whatever his reasons for lying, and that in order that Count Santi should not further entangle her in his lies, she would never speak to him again.

If Catherine imagined that the petty tyranny of Madame Choglokova and her sorrow at the death of her father had brought her to the nadir of her early years in Russia, she was in error. In that same spring of 1747, even as she was mourning her father, her situation—and Peter's—became decidedly worse when Madame Choglokova's husband was promoted to become Peter's governor. "This was a dreadful blow for us," Catherine said. "He was an arrogant, brutal fool; a stupid, con-ceited, malicious, pompous, secretive and silent man who never smiled; a man to be despised as well as feared." Even Madame Krause, whose sister was the principal ladies' maid to the empress and one of Eliza-beth's favorites, trembled when she heard about this choice.

The decision had been made by Bestuzhev. The chancellor, dis-trusting everyone who might come in contact with the grand ducal couple, wanted another implacable watchdog. "Within a few days of Monsieur Choglokov taking over, three or four young servants of whom the grand duke was very fond were arrested," Catherine said. Then Choglokov forced Peter to dismiss his chamberlain, Count Devier. Soon after, a master chef who was a good friend of Madame Krause's and whose dishes Peter particularly liked was sent away.

In the autumn of 1747, the Choglokovs imposed more restrictions. All of Peter's gentlemen-in waiting were forbidden access to the grand duke's room. Peter was left alone with only a few lesser servants. As soon as it was noticed that he showed a preference for one of these, that person was removed. Next, Choglokov forced Peter to dismiss the head of his domestic staff, "a gentle, reasonable man who had been attached to the grand duke since birth, and who gave him much good advice." Peter's valet, the rough old Swedish retainer Romburg, who had given him brusque advice on how to treat a new wife, was dismissed.

The restrictions tightened again. An order from the Choglokovs prohibited anyone, on pain of dismissal, from entering either Peter's or Catherine's private rooms without the express permission of Monsieur or Madame Choglokov. The ladies and gentleman of the young court were to remain in the antechamber, where they were never to speak to Peter or Catherine except in a loud voice that everyone in the room could hear. "The grand duke and I," Catherine noted, "were now forced to remain inseparable."

Elizabeth had her own reason for isolating the young couple: she believed that if they were reduced to each other's company they would produce an heir. The calculation was not entirely irrational:

> In his distress, the grand duke, deprived of everyone suspected of being attached to him, and being unable to open his heart to anyone else, turned to me. He often came to my room. He felt that I was the only person with whom he could talk without every word being turned into a crime. I realized his position and was sorry for him and tried to offer all the consolation in my power. Actually, I would often be exhausted by these visits which lasted several hours because he never sat down and I had to walk up and down the room with him all the time. He walked fast and took great strides so that it was difficult to keep up with him and at the same time to continue a conversation about very specialized military details about which he spoke interminably. [But] I knew that it was the only amusement he had.

Catherine could not talk about her own interests; Peter was usually indifferent:

There were moments when he would listen to me, but it was always when he was unhappy. He was constantly afraid of some plot or intrigue which might mean that he would end his days in the fortress. He had, it is true, a certain perspicacity but no judgment. He was incapable of disguising his thoughts and feelings and was so extraordinarily indiscreet that, after he had undertaken not to reveal himself in words, he would then turn around and betray himself through gesture, expression, and behavior. I believe it was these indiscretions that caused his servants to be removed as often as they were.

❦18❦

In the Bedroom

PETER NOW SPENT most of the day with his wife. Sometimes he played his violin for her; Catherine listened, hiding her hatred of his "noise." Often, he talked about himself for hours. Sometimes, he was permitted to hold small evening parties at which he ordered his and her servants to wear masks and dance while he played the violin. Bored by this primitive shuffling, so different from the graceful movement at the great court balls she loved, Catherine, pleading a headache, lay on a couch, still wearing her mask, and closed her eyes. And then at night when they went to bed—during the first nine years of their marriage, Peter never slept elsewhere than in Catherine's bed—he would ask Madame Krause to bring his toys.

Because everyone in the young court detested and feared the Choglokovs, everyone united against them. Madame Krause had suffered from her supplanter's arrogance and so despised Madame Choglokova that she had swung her allegiance entirely to Peter and Catherine. She delighted in outwitting the principal duenna and regularly broke the new restrictions, mostly on behalf of Peter, whom she wanted to please because she, like the grand duke, was a native of Holstein. She rebelled most dramatically by procuring for him as many toy soldiers, miniature cannon, and model fortresses as he wanted. He could not play with them during the day, because Monsieur and Madame Choglokov would have demanded to know from where and whom they came. The toys were hidden in and under the bed and Peter played with them only at night. After supper, Peter undressed and went to bed; Catherine followed. As soon as both were in bed, Madame Krause, who slept in the next room, came in, locked their door, and brought out so many toy soldiers dressed in blue Holstein uniforms that the bed was covered with them. Whereupon Madame Krause, then in her fifties, joined Peter in moving them around as he commanded.

The absurdity of what they were doing, often until two in the morning, sometimes made Catherine laugh, but usually she simply endured. She could not move in bed, the whole surface being covered with toys, some of which were heavy. In addition, she worried that Madame Choglokova would hear of these nocturnal games. Sure enough, one evening toward midnight, she knocked at the bedroom door. It had a double lock, and those inside did not open it immediately because Peter, Catherine, and Madame Krause were scrambling to collect the toys from the top of the bed and cram them under the blankets. When Madame Krause eventually opened the door, Madame Choglokova entered, furious at having been kept waiting. Madame Krause explained that it had been necessary for her to go and get her key. Then Madame Choglokova asked why Catherine and Peter were not asleep. Peter replied curtly that he was not ready to sleep. Madame Choglokova lashed back that the empress would be furious to learn that the couple was not asleep at this late hour. Eventually, she left, grumbling. Peter began playing again and continued until he fell asleep.

The situation was farcical: a newly married couple constantly on guard lest they be caught playing with toys. Behind this farce lay the greater absurdity of a young husband playing with toys in the marital bed, leaving his young wife with nothing to do but to watch. (In her *Memoirs*, an older, more sophisticated Catherine commented wryly, "It seems to me that I was good for something else.") Yet the real context in which these games were played was as dangerous as it was bizarre. Elizabeth was a woman accustomed to having her way. These two impudent grand ducal children were thwarting her. She had done everything for them: she had reached out and brought them to Russia; she had loaded them with gifts, titles, and kindness; she had given them a magnificent wedding; all in the hope of a speedy fulfillment of her wish for an heir.

When, as the months passed, Elizabeth found her hope still frustrated, she was determined to know which of the pair was responsible.

Was it conceivable that Catherine, at seventeen, with her freshness, her intelligence and charm, should leave her eighteen-year-old husband entirely cold? Was it not far more likely that Peter's ugliness and disagreeable nature had repelled his wife, and that she was expressing her revulsion in the privacy of their bedroom by repulsing his advances? If this were not so, what other reason could there be?

Peter was not completely indifferent to women. Proof of this was his constant infatuation with one or another of the ladies of the court. His remark on his wedding night, "How it would amuse my servants . . . ," is proof of his awareness of the role of intimacy in sex, although by mocking it, he was turning intimacy into a vulgar joke.

It may be that the doctors were right and that Peter, in spite of his eighteen years, had not yet fully arrived at physical manhood. This was more or less Madame Krause's opinion as she fruitlessly interrogated the young wife every morning. We do not know why he did not or would not or could not reach over and touch his wife. In her *Memoirs*, Catherine gives no answer. Peter left no records. But two possible explanations, one psychological, the other physical, have been suggested.

The psychological inhibitions brought forward from youth may have prevented Peter from exposing his fragile ego to the physical intimacy of lovemaking. Peter's childhood and youth had been horrendous. He had grown up an orphan in the unloving care of martinet tutors. He had been barred from having companions and playmates his own age. He had known people who gave him orders and people who obeyed him, but never anyone with whom he could share common interests and develop friendship and trust. Catherine, during her first year in Russia, had offered him companionship, but she had unintentionally failed him at the moment in the dimly lit hall when he stood before her bearing the hideous scars of smallpox. In that instant, his new friend had struck his self-confidence a blow. To forgive her, to trust her again, to recommit his shaky self-image to her; these were steps he could not bring himself to take. Peter had some idea of what he was supposed to do with Catherine in bed, but her intelligence and charm, even her close female presence, aroused no initiative in him. Instead, they stimulated his sense of inadequacy, failure, and humiliation.

Another possibility has been offered to explain Peter's apparent indifference. The Marquis de Castéra, a French diplomat who wrote a three-volume *Life of Catherine II* published a year after her death, suggested: "The least rabbi of Petersburg or the least surgeon would have been able to correct his little imperfection." He was talking about a physiological condition called phimosis, a medical term for a tightness of the foreskin that prevents it from easily and comfortably sliding down over the tip of the penis. This problem is normal in a newborn or an infant and sometimes cannot be detected in an uncircumcised boy before the age of four or five because some foreskins remain tight until then. Usually, the problem naturally resolves itself before puberty, when the foreskin loosens and becomes flexible. If this does not happen, however, and the condition continues into adolescence, it can become acutely painful. Sometimes, the foreskin is so tight that the boy cannot have an erection without pain. This, of course, would make sexual intercourse unappealing. If this was true in Peter's case, his reluctance to reach arousal—and to attempt to explain this problem to an uninformed young woman—can be understood.*

If Peter suffered from phimosis when he and Catherine were betrothed, this may have been the reason Elizabeth's doctors recommended that the marriage be delayed. In another context in her *Memoirs*, Catherine says that Dr. Lestocq recommended waiting until the grand duke reached twenty-one; this advice may have stemmed from Lestocq's awareness that the condition should certainly have resolved itself by then. But if Lestocq did discuss this matter with the empress, Elizabeth simply overrode his opinion. She was in a hurry for an heir.

Neither explanation for Peter's persistent coldness in the marriage bed can be proved or disproved. In any case, whether the problem was psychological or physical—or perhaps involved elements of both— Peter was guilty of no wrong. Still, it was inevitable that, just as Catherine's rejection of him when she first saw his ravaged face had affected him, so his physical rejection of her produced a reaction in her. Approaching marriage, she had not been in love with Peter, but she had made up her mind to live with him and to fulfill the expectations of her husband and the empress. Catherine, who knew little about sex, about erections and foreskins, and, certainly, nothing about phimosis, knew well what was expected of wives in a royal marriage. It was not Catherine who said no.

---

*Curiously, a similar "little imperfection" afflicted the sixteen-year-old French dauphin, the future King Louis XVI, at the time of his marriage in 1770 to the fifteen-year-old Austrian archduchess Marie Antoinette. This continued to be the case for the next seven years. Finally, in 1777, Louis was circumcised and a son was conceived.

But Peter made it impossible for her. He scorned her physically and acted moonstruck over other women. He encouraged her to flirt with other men. The whole court witnessed her humiliation. Every foreign ambassador observed that she could not attract her husband's interest; every servant knew the name of whatever young woman the grand duke happened to be pursuing at the moment. And since no one understood why Peter was ignoring his young wife, everyone, including the empress, laid the blame on her. Peter and Catherine continued to live together; they had no choice. But they were estranged by a thousand mutual misunderstandings and mortifications, and a desert of unspoken animosity stretched between them.

❧19❧

A House Collapses

NEAR THE END of May 1748, the empress Elizabeth and the court visited Count Razumovsky's country estate outside St. Petersburg. Catherine and Peter were assigned to a small three-story wooden house built on a hill. Their apartment, in the upper story, had three rooms; they slept in one, Peter dressed in another, and Madame Krause slept in the third. The floor below lodged the Choglokovs and Catherine's ladies-in-waiting. The first night, the party lasted until six in the morning, when everyone went to bed. Around eight, while all were asleep, a sergeant of the guards posted outside heard strange creaking noises. Looking around the base of the house, he saw that the large blocks of stone supporting the building were moving on the damp, slippery earth, detaching themselves and sliding downhill from the bottom timbers of the house. He hurried to awaken Choglokov, telling him that the foundation was giving way and that everyone had to get out. Choglokov rushed upstairs and burst open the bedroom door where Catherine and Peter were sleeping. Tearing aside the curtain around their bed, he shouted, "Get up and get out as fast as you can! The foundation of the house is crumbling!" Peter, who had been fast asleep, made one leap from the bed to the door and disappeared. Catherine told Choglokov that she would follow. While dressing, she remembered that Madame Krause was sleeping in the next room and went in to awaken her.

The floorboards began to rock—"like the waves of the sea," said Catherine—and there was a tremendous crash. The house was settling and disintegrating, and Catherine and Madame Krause fell to the floor. At that moment, the sergeant entered, picked up Catherine, and carried her back to the staircase—which was no longer there. Amid the rubble, the sergeant handed Catherine down to the nearest person below, who handed her down to the next, and the next, from one set of hands to another, until she reached the bottom, from where she was carried into a field. There she found Peter and other people who had walked or been carried from the house. Soon, Madame Krause, rescued by another soldier, appeared. Catherine escaped with bruises and a severe shock, but, on a lower floor, three servants sleeping in the kitchen had been killed when the fireplace collapsed. Next to the foundation, sixteen sleeping workers had been crushed and buried in the rubble.

The house collapsed because it had been hurriedly built in early winter on half-frozen earth. Four limestone blocks had served as the foundation, with the bottom timbers resting on them. With the coming of the spring thaw, the four stone blocks began to slide in different directions and the house was pulled apart. Later that day, when the empress sent for her and Peter, Catherine asked Elizabeth to grant a favor to the sergeant who had carried her from her room. Elizabeth stared at her and, at first, did not reply.

Immediately afterward, she asked if I was very much frightened. I said, "Yes, very much." This displeased her still more. She and Madame Choglokova were angry with me the whole day. I suppose I did not notice that they wished to look upon the whole occurrence as a mere trifle. But the shock was so great, that this was impossible. As she wanted to make light of the accident, everyone tried to pretend that the danger had been minimal and some even said there had been no danger at all. My terror displeased her greatly and she hardly spoke to me. Meanwhile, our host, Count Razumovsky, was in despair. One moment, he seized his pistol and talked of blowing out his brains. He sobbed and wept throughout the day; then, at dinner, he emptied his glass, over and over. The empress could not conceal her distress over her favorite's condition and burst into tears. She had him closely watched; this man, at other times so gentle, was unmanageable and raving when intoxicated. He was

prevented from doing himself harm. The following day, everyone returned to St. Petersburg.

After the episode of the collapsing house, Catherine noticed that the
empress seemed constantly displeased with her. One day, Catherine
walked into a room where one of the empress's chamberlains was standing. The Choglokovs had not yet arrived, and the chamberlain whispered to Catherine that she was being vilified to the empress. At dinner
a few days before, he said, Elizabeth had accused her of getting deeper
and deeper into debt; declared that everything she did was marked by
stupidity; and noted that while she might imagine herself very clever,
no one else shared that opinion because her stupidity was obvious to
everyone.

Catherine was unwilling to accept this appraisal, and, putting aside
her usual deference, flared back:

> That, as to my stupidity, I could not be blamed because
> everyone is just as God has made him; that my debts were not
> surprising because, with an allowance of thirty thousand rubles,
> I had to pay off sixty thousand rubles of debt left me by my
> mother; and that he should tell whoever had sent him that I
> was extremely sorry to hear that I was being blackened in the
> eyes of Her Imperial Majesty to whom I had never failed to
> show respect, obedience and deference and that the more
> closely my conduct was observed, the more she would be
> convinced of this.

The prohibition against any unapproved communication between the
married couple and the outside world remained, but it was porous. "To
show how useless this kind of order is," Catherine wrote later, "we
found many people willing and eager to undermine it. Even the Choglokovs' closest relatives sought to reduce the harshness of this policy."
Indeed, Madame Choglokova's own brother, Count Hendrikov, who
was also the empress's first cousin, "often slipped me useful and necessary information. He was a kind and outspoken man who ridiculed the
stupidities and brutalities of his sister and brother-in-law."

Similarly, there were cracks in the wall Bestuzhev had erected to
block Catherine's correspondence. Catherine was forbidden to write

personal letters; the Ministry of Foreign Affairs wrote them for her. This injunction was underscored when Catherine learned that an official at the ministry had almost been charged with a crime because she had sent him a few lines, begging him to insert them into a letter he was writing over her signature to Johanna. But there were people who tried to help. In the summer of 1748, the Chevalier di Sacrosomo, a Knight of Malta, arrived in Russia and was warmly greeted at court. When he was presented to Catherine, he kissed her hand, and, as he did so, he slipped a tiny note into her palm. "This is from your mother," he whispered. Catherine was frightened, dreading that someone, especially the Choglokovs, who were standing nearby, might have seen him. She managed to slip the note inside her glove. In her room, she found a letter from her mother rolled up inside a note from Sacrosomo. Johanna wrote that she was anxious about Catherine's silence, wanted to know the reason for it, and what her daughter's situation was. Catherine wrote back that she was forbidden to write to her or to anyone, but that she was well.

In his own note, Sacrosomo had informed Catherine that she was to send her reply through an Italian musician who would be present at Peter's next concert. Accordingly, the grand duchess rolled up her response in the same way as the one sent to her and waited for the moment when she could pass it along. At the concert, she made a tour of the orchestra and stopped behind the chair of a cellist, the man described to her. When he saw the grand duchess behind his chair, the cellist opened his coat pocket wide and pretended to take out his handkerchief. Catherine quickly slipped her note into the open pocket and walked away. No one saw. During his stay in Petersburg, Sacromoso passed her three other notes and her replies went back the same way. No one knew.

✤20✤

Summer Pleasures

THE CHOGLOKOVS had been appointed to enforce Bestuzhev's desire to isolate Catherine and Peter from the outside world and also to provide the young couple with a shining example of virtue, marital happiness, and productive fertility. In the first of these assignments, they partially succeeded; in the second, they failed spectacularly.

During a stay at the Peterhof estate on the Gulf of Finland in the summer of 1748, Catherine and Peter, looking out their windows across the garden, frequently saw Monsieur and Madame Choglokov walking back and forth from the main palace on the hill to Monplaisir, Peter the Great's small redbrick Dutch-style house at the edge of the water, where the empress had chosen to stay. They quickly discovered that these recurring trips were all related to a secret affair Monsieur Choglokov had been having with one of Catherine's maids of honor, Maria Kosheleva, and that the young woman was pregnant. The Choglokovs now faced ruin, a possiblity for which the watchers from the upper palace windows fervently prayed.

Carrying out the constant surveillance demanded by Bestuzhev required Monsieur Choglokov, as Peter's principal watchdog, to sleep in a room in the grand duke's apartment. Madame Choglokova, who was also pregnant, and lonely without her husband, asked Maria Kosheleva to sleep near her; she took the girl into her own bed or obliged her to sleep in a small bed next to her own. Kosheleva, according to Catherine, was, "a large, stupid, clumsy girl, but with beautiful blond hair and very white skin." In the mornings, Monsieur Choglokov would come to awaken his wife and find Maria lying next to her in deshabille, her blond hair spread out on the pillows, her white skin bare to inspection. The wife, never doubting her husband's love, noticed nothing.

When Catherine contracted measles, the door of opportunity opened for Monsieur Choglokov. He persuaded his wife that it was her duty to remain day and night at Catherine's bedside, nursing her and making sure that no doctor, lady-in-waiting, or anyone else brought the grand duchess a forbidden message. This gave him ample time with Mlle Kosheleva. A few months later, Madame Choglokova gave birth to her sixth child and Maria Kosheleva's pregnancy became apparent. Once Elizabeth was informed, she summoned the still-unknowing wife and confronted her with the fact that she had been deceived. If Madame Choglokova wished to separate from her husband, she, Elizabeth, would be pleased; from the beginning, she had never really approved of her cousin's choice. In any case, the empress decreed that Monsieur Choglokov could not remain in Peter and Catherine's household. He would be dismissed and Madame Choglokova placed in absolute control.

At first, Madame Choglokova, who still loved her husband, heatedly denied his involvement in any affair and declared the story a slander. As she was speaking, Maria Kosheleva was being questioned. The young woman admitted everything. Informed of this, Madame Choglokova returned to her husband, choking with rage. Choglokov fell on his knees, imploring forgiveness. Madame Choglokova went back to the empress, fell on her own knees, and said that she had forgiven her husband and wished to stay with him because of her children. She pleaded with the empress not to dismiss her husband from court, as this would dishonor her as well as him; her sorrow was so pitiable that Elizabeth's anger subsided. Madame Choglokova was permitted to bring in her husband and, kneeling together before the empress, they begged her to pardon the husband for the sake of the wife and children. Thereafter, although they had appeased the empress, the warmth of their feeling for each other never returned; his deception and her public humiliation left her with an unconquerable repugnance for him and they remained united only by a common interest in survival.

These scenes took place over a span of five or six days, with the young court learning almost hour by hour what was occurring. Everyone, of course, hoped to see the watchdogs dismissed, but, in the end, only the pregnant young Maria Kosheleva was sent away. Both Choglokovs remained, their powers undiminished, although, Catherine commented, "there was no more talk of an exemplary marriage."

The rest of that summer was peaceful. After leaving Peterhof, Catherine and Peter moved to the Oranienbaum estate, nearby on the gulf coast. The Choglokovs, still recovering from their marital disgrace, did not attempt to impose the usual rigid restrictions on movement and conversation. Catherine was able to do what she liked:

> I had the greatest freedom imaginable. I rose before dawn at three in the morning and dressed myself alone from head to foot in a man's clothing. An old huntsman was already waiting for me with guns. We crossed the garden on foot, rifles on our shoulders, and walked to a fishing skiff close to the shore. He, I, a pointer dog, and the fisherman who guided us, got in a skiff and I went to shoot ducks in the reeds that grew along both sides of the Oranienbaum canal which stretches over a mile out into the gulf. We often went out beyond the canal and consequently were sometimes caught in rough weather in the open sea. The grand duke would join us an hour or two later because he always had to have his breakfast before coming. At ten o'clock, I came home and dressed for dinner; after dinner we

rested and in the afternoon the grand duke had a concert or we went horseback riding.

That summer, riding became Catherine's "dominant passion." She was forbidden to ride astride, since Elizabeth believed this produced barrenness in women, but Catherine designed her own saddle on which she could sit as she pleased. This was an English sidesaddle with a movable pommel that made it possible for the grand duchess to set off under the eyes of Madame Choglokova seated demurely, and, once she was out of sight, switch the pommel, swing her leg over the horse's back, and, trusting to the discretion of her groom, ride like a man. If the grooms were asked how the grand duchess rode, they could truthfully say, "On a woman's saddle," as the empress had commanded Catherine to ride. Because Catherine slipped her leg over only when she was sure she was not observed, and because she never boasted or even spoke about her invention, Elizabeth never knew. The grooms were happy to keep her secret; indeed, they found less risk in her riding astride than on an English sidesaddle, which they feared might lead to an accident for which they would be blamed. "To tell the truth," Catherine said, "although I continually galloped with the hunt, the sport of hunting did not interest me, but I was passionately fond of riding. The more violent this exercise, the better I liked it, so that if a horse happened to break loose and gallop away, I was the one who chased it and brought it back."

The empress, who as a young woman had been an expert rider, still loved the sport, although she had become too heavy to ride herself. On one occasion, she sent word to Catherine to invite the wife of the Saxon ambassador, Madame d'Arnim, to accompany her when she rode. This woman had boasted about her passion for riding and her excellence as a horsewoman; Elizabeth wanted to see how much of this was true. Catherine invited Madame d'Arnim to join her.

She was tall, between twenty-five and twenty-six, and she appeared to all of us rather awkward and clumsy; she did not seem to know what to do with her hat or her hands. I knew that the empress did not like me to ride astride like a man, so I used an English lady's side-saddle. Just at the moment I was about to mount my horse, the empress arrived to watch us depart. As I was very nimble and accustomed to this exercise, I leaped easily into my saddle and let my skirt, which was split, fall to either side. The empress, seeing me mount with such agility, cried out in astonishment that it was impossible to mount more skillfully. She asked what kind of saddle I was using and, hearing that it was a woman's saddle, she said, "One would swear that it is a man's saddle."

When it was Madame d'Arnim's turn to mount, her skill was not conspicuous. She had brought her own horse, a large, heavy, ugly, black nag, which our servants claimed was one of her carriage horses. She needed a ladder to mount, this process being managed only with considerable fuss and the aid of several people. Once she was on top, her nag broke into a rough trot that bounced her considerably since she was neither firm in her seat nor in her stirrups and was forced to hold on to her saddle with her hand. I was told that the empress laughed heartily.

Once Madame d'Arnim had mounted, Catherine took the lead, overtaking Peter, who had started before, while their guest and her horse were left behind. Finally, Catherine said, "at some distance from the court, Madame Choglokova, following behind in a carriage, collected the lady who kept losing her hat and then her stirrups."

The adventure was not over. It had rained that morning and the steps and porch of the stable house were covered with puddles of water. Dismounting, Catherine walked up the steps and across the exposed porch. Madame d'Arnim followed, but because Catherine was walking fast, she had to run. She lost her footing in a puddle, slipped, and fell flat. People burst out laughing. Madame d'Arnim rose to her feet in great embarrassment, blaming her fall on her new boots, worn that day for the first time, she said. The party returned from this excursion in a carriage and on the way Madame d'Arnim insisted on talking about the exceptional quality of her horse. "We bit our lips to keep from laughing," Catherine said.

✤ 21 ✤

Dismissals at Court

DURING THE TURMOIL over the Kosheleva affair, Madame Krause, who despised both Choglokovs but especially the wife, had celebrated prematurely what she assumed was the impending fall of her rival. When the Choglokovs did not fall, retribution became inevitable. Madame Choglokova announced to Catherine that Madame Krause wished to retire and that the empress had found a replacement. Catherine had come to trust Madame Krause, and Peter was dependent on her for the toys she brought him at night. Nevertheless, Madame Krause departed, and the next day, Madame Praskovia Vladislavova, a tall woman of fifty, arrived to take her place. Catherine consulted Timothy Evreinov, who told her that the newcomer was an intelligent, spirited, well-mannered woman but was also said to be crafty, and that Catherine should not place too much confidence in her until she saw how Vladislavova behaved.

Vladislavova got off to a good start, doing everything possible to please Catherine. She was sociable, loved to talk, told stories with intelligence, and knew innumerable anecdotes of the past, including the histories of all the great Russian families since Peter the Great. "She was a living archive, that woman," Catherine wrote later. "From her, I learned more about what had happened in Russia over the past hundred years than anywhere else. When I was bored, I got her talking which she was always ready to do. I discovered that she often disapproved of the Choglokovs, both their words and deeds. On the other hand, because Madame Vladislavova often went to the empress's apartments and nobody knew why, everyone remained wary."

Along with Madame Krause, Armand Lestocq, a court figure familiar to Catherine, disappeared. He had been Elizabeth's personal physician since her adolescence, one of her trusted friends, a man who had advised her in seizing the throne, and who, some believed, was one of her former lovers. Catherine had first met Count Lestocq on the night she arrived in Moscow as a fourteen-year-old girl, when he had welcomed her and her mother at the the Golovin Palace. In the late summer of 1748, Lestocq was still in the highest favor when he married one of the empress's maids of honor; Elizabeth and the entire court attended the wedding. Two months later, the newly married couple's fortunes plunged.

The background lay in the constant efforts of Frederick of Prussia to undermine Bestuzhev's pro-Austria policy by attempting to bribe people in the Russian court and government. Catherine's first awareness that something was wrong came one evening when the court was assembled to play cards in the empress's apartment. Suspecting nothing, Catherine went up to speak to Lestocq. In a low voice, he said, "Do not come near me! I am under suspicion." Thinking he was joking, she asked what he meant. He replied, "I am not joking. I repeat to you very seriously that you must keep away from me, because I am a man under suspicion." Catherine, seeing that he was abnormally flushed, assumed that he was drunk and walked away. This happened on a Friday. On Sunday morning, Timothy Evreinov said to her, "Last night, Count Lestocq and his wife were arrested and taken to the fortress as state criminals!" Subsequently, she learned that Lestocq had been interrogated by Count Bestuzhev and others; that he had been accused of sending coded letters to the Prussian ambassador, of taking a ten-thousand-ruble bribe from the king of Prussia, and of poisoning a man who might have testified against him. Catherine was also told that he had tried to take his own life in the fortress by starving himself to death. After eleven days, he had been forced to eat. He had confessed nothing and no incriminating evidence was found. Even so, all of his property was confiscated and he was exiled to Siberia. Lestocq's disgrace was a triumph for Bestuzhev and a warning to anyone in Russia who showed any sign of favoring Prussia. Catherine, herself under Bestuzhev's suspicious eye because she was German, never believed that Lestocq was guilty. Later, she wrote, "The empress did not have the courage to render justice to an innocent man; she feared the revenge such a person might take, and that is why, in her reign, no one, innocent or guilty, left the fortress except to go into exile."

Catherine's greatest concern was Peter. Although the couple stood together in resisting the Choglokovs, and he came to her regularly when he needed help, Catherine found him difficult to live with. Sometimes, it was a small thing. When they played cards, Peter liked to win. If Catherine won, Peter raged, and sometimes sulked for days. When she lost, he demanded payment immediately. Often, she said, "I would deliberately lose to avoid his tantrums."

There were times when Peter made such a fool of himself that Catherine was deeply embarrassed. On occasion, the empress permitted the gentlemen of her court to have dinner with Peter and Catherine in their apartment. The young couple enjoyed these gatherings until Peter began to spoil them by his reckless behavior. One day, when General Buturlin was dining, he made Peter laugh so hard that, throwing himself back in his chair, the heir to the throne burst out in Russian, "This son of a bitch will make me die of laughter." Catherine blushed, knowing that this expression would offend Buturlin. The general was silent. Subsequently, Buturlin reported the words to Elizabeth, who ordered her courtiers not to return to the company of such ill-mannered people. Buturlin never forgot Peter's words. In 1767, when Catherine was on the throne, he asked her, "Do you remember the time at Tsarskoe Selo when the grand duke publicly called me a 'son of a bitch'?" "This," Catherine wrote later, "is the effect that can be produced by a stupid, carelessly spoken word—it is never forgotten."

Sometimes, Peter's behavior could not be excused. During the summer of 1748, Peter collected a pack of dogs in the country and began to train them himself. That autumn, he brought six of these dogs into the Winter Palace and installed them behind a wooden partition that separated the bedroom he shared with Catherine from a vestibule in the rear of the apartment. As the partition consisted only of a few boards to fence in the dogs, the stench of the makeshift kennel suffused their bedroom, forcing them to sleep in a fog of putrid air. When Catherine complained, Peter said he had no choice; the kennels had to be kept a secret and this was the only possible place. "So, in order not to spoil his pleasure, I had to put up with it," she said.

Thereafter, she continued, Peter "had only two occupations, both of which tortured my eardrums from morning to night. One was to scrape his violin; the other was his effort to train his hunting dogs." Violently cracking a whip and yelling huntsmen's cries, Peter made the dogs run from one end of his two rooms to the other. Any dog that tired and fell behind was rigorously whipped, making it howl still more. "From seven in the morning until late at night," Catherine complained, "I had to listen to either the ear-shattering sounds he drew from his violin or the horrible barking and howling of the dogs whom he cudgeled and thrashed."

Sometimes, Peter's cruelty seemed purely sadistic:

> One day, hearing a poor dog cry out piteously for a long time, I opened the door. I saw the grand duke holding a dog by its collar, suspended in the air, while a servant held the same

dog up by its tail. It was a poor little English King Charles Spaniel and the grand duke was beating it with all his strength with the heavy handle of a whip. I tried to intercede for the poor animal, but this only made him redouble his blows. I returned to my room in tears. After the dog, I was the most miserable creature in the world.

❧ 22 ❧

Moscow and the Country

IN DECEMBER 1748, Empress Elizabeth and her court traveled to Moscow, where she would remain for a year. There, before Lent in 1749, the empress was stricken by a mysterious stomach illness. It quickly worsened. Madame Vladislavova, who had connections in Elizabeth's immediate entourage, whispered this information to Catherine, begging her not to reveal that she had told her. Without naming her informant, Catherine told Peter about his aunt's illness. He was simultaneously pleased and frightened; he hated his aunt, but if she were to die, his own future seemed terrifying to him. What made it worse was that neither he nor Catherine dared to ask for more information. They decided to say nothing to anyone until the Choglokovs spoke to them about the illness. But the Choglokovs said nothing.

One night, Bestuzhev and his assistant, General Stepan Apraksin, came to the palace and spent many hours talking in the Choglokovs' apartment. This seemed to imply that the empress's illness was grave. Catherine begged Peter to remain calm. She told him that, although they were forbidden to leave their apartment, if Elizabeth were to die, she would arrange for Peter to escape from their rooms; she pointed out that their ground-floor windows were low enough to enable them to jump down into the street. She also told him that Count Zakhar Chernyshev, on whom she knew she could rely, was with his regiment in the city. Peter was reassured, and several days later, the empress's health began to improve.

During this stressful time, Choglokov and his wife remained silent. The young couple did not speak of it either; had they dared to ask whether the empress was better, the Choglokovs would immediately have demanded to know who had told them that she was ill—and those named would immediately have been dismissed.

While Elizabeth was still in bed recovering, one of her maids of honor married. At the wedding banquet, Catherine sat next to Elizabeth's close friend Countess Shuvalova. The countess unhesitatingly told Catherine that the empress was still so weak that she had not been able to appear at the wedding ceremony, but that, sitting up in bed, she had performed her traditional function of crowning the bride. As Countess Shuvalova was the first to speak openly about the illness, Catherine told her of her worry about the empress's condition. Countess Shuvalova said that Her Majesty would be pleased to learn of this sympathy. Two mornings later, Madame Choglokova stormed into Catherine's room and announced that the empress was angry with Peter and Catherine because of the lack of concern they had shown during her illness.

Catherine furiously told Madame Choglokova that the governess knew very well what the situation had been; that neither she nor her husband had spoken a word about the empress's illness, and that, having been left in complete ignorance, she and her husband had been unable to show concern.

"How can you say you knew nothing about it?" Madame Choglokova asked. "Countess Shuvalova told the empress that you spoke to her at dinner about Her Majesty's illness."

Catherine retorted, "It is true that I spoke to her about it, because she told me that Her Majesty was still weak and could not appear in public. It was then that I asked her for details about the illness."

Later, Catherine found the courage to tell Elizabeth that neither Choglokov nor his wife had informed her or her husband of the illness, which was why it had not been in their power to express concern. Elizabeth seemed to appreciate this and said, "I know that. We will not speak of it any further." In retrospect, Catherine commented, "It seemed to me that the prestige and credibility of the Choglokovs had diminished."

In the spring, the empress began visiting the countryside around Moscow with Catherine and Peter. At Perova, an estate belonging to Alexis Razumovsky, Catherine was seized by a violent headache. "It was the worst I have ever had in my life," she said later. "The extreme pain gave me violent nausea. I vomited repeatedly, and every movement, even the sound of footsteps in my room, increased my pain. I remained in this state for twenty-four hours and then fell asleep. The following day, it was gone."

From Perova, the imperial party went to a hunting ground belonging to Elizabeth forty miles from Moscow. Because there was no house, the imperial party camped in tents. The morning after their arrival, Catherine went to the empress's tent and found her shouting at the man who administered the estate. She had come to hunt hares, she was saying, and there were no hares. She accused him of accepting bribes to permit neighboring noblemen to hunt on her estate; if there had been no such hunting, there would certainly be many hares. The man was silent, pale, and trembling. When Peter and Catherine approached to kiss her hand, she embraced them, and then quickly turned back to continue her diatribe. From her youth in the country, she said, she perfectly understood the administering of country estates; this enabled her to see every detail of the administrator's incompetence. Her tirade lasted three-quarters of an hour. Finally, a servant approached, bringing a baby porcupine, which he presented to her in his hat. She went over to look at it, but the instant she saw the little animal, she screamed. She said that it looked like a mouse and fled to her tent. "She was mortally afraid of mice." Catherine observed. "We saw no more of her that day."

That summer, Catherine's principal pleasure was riding:

> I rode constantly all day; no one stopped me and I could break my neck if I wished. But because I had spent the spring and part of the summer constantly outdoors, I had become very tanned. The empress, seeing me, was shocked by my cracked, red face and told me that she would send me a rinse to get rid of my sunburn and make my face soft again. She sent me a bottle with a liquid composed of lemon juice, egg white and French brandy. In a few days my sunburn disappeared and since then I have always used this mixture.

One day, Catherine and Peter dined with Elizabeth in the empress's tent. The empress sat at the end of a long table, Peter was on her right, Catherine was on her left, next to Catherine was Countess Shuvalova, and next to Peter was General Buturlin. Peter, with the help of General

Buturlin—"himself no enemy of wine," Catherine said—drank so much that he became completely drunk:

> He did not know what he was saying or doing, slurred his words, made horrible grimaces, and cut ridiculous capers. He became such a disagreeable sight that my eyes filled with tears for in those days I always tried to conceal or disguise what was reprehensible in my husband. The empress was sensitive and grateful for my reaction and she got up and left the table.

Meanwhile, Catherine unknowingly attracted another admirer. Kyril Razumovsky, the younger brother of Elizabeth's favorite, Alexis Razumovsky, was living on the other side of Moscow, but he came to visit Catherine and Peter every day.

> He was very cheerful and we liked him very much. Since he was the brother of the favorite, the Choglokovs were glad to receive him. All summer long, his visits continued. He would spend the whole day with us, dine and sup with us, and after supper always returned to his estate; consequently, he traveled twenty-five or thirty miles every day. Twenty years later [in 1769, when Catherine was on the throne], I happened to ask him what could have made him come to share the boredom of our stay. He replied unhesitatingly, "Love." "But my God," I said, "who on earth could you have found to love at our place?" "Who?" he asked. "You, of course." I burst out laughing because I had never suspected it. Truly, he was a fine man, very pleasant and far more intelligent than his brother, who nevertheless equaled him in beauty, and surpassed him in generosity and kindness.

In mid-September, as the weather grew colder, Catherine suffered a severe toothache. She developed a high fever, slipped into delirium, and was moved from the country back to Moscow. She remained in bed for ten days; every afternoon at the same time, the pain in her tooth returned. A few weeks later, Catherine was ill again, this time with a sore throat and another fever. Madame Vladislavova did what she could to distract her: "She sat by my bed and told me stories. One concerned a Princess Dolgoruky, a woman who used to get up often at night and go to the bedside of her sleeping daughter whom she idolized. She wanted to make sure that the daughter was asleep and had not died. Sometimes, to be absolutely certain, she shook the young woman hard and woke her up just to convince herself that slumber was not death."

❧23❧
Choglokov Makes an Enemy and Peter Survives a Plot

IN MOSCOW at the beginning of 1749, it appeared to Catherine that Monsieur Choglokov remained intimate with the chancellor, Count Bestuzhev. They were constantly together, and, to hear Choglokov talk, "one would have thought that he was Bestuzhev's closest adviser." For Catherine, this was hard to believe, because "Count Bestuzhev had too much intelligence to allow himself to be guided by an arrogant fool like Choglokov." In August, whatever intimacy existed abruptly ceased.

Catherine was certain that something Peter had said was responsible. After the affair of Maria Kosheleva's pregnancy, Choglokov had become less flagrantly offensive to the young court. He knew that the empress continued to bear him a grudge; his relationship with his wife had deteriorated; and he sank into depression. One day, Peter, drunk, met Count Bestuzhev, himself tipsy. In this encounter, Peter complained to Bestuzhev that Choglokov was always rude to him. Bestuzhev replied, "Choglokov is a conceited fool with a swollen head, but leave it in my hands. I will see to it." When Peter told Catherine about this conversation, she warned him that if Choglokov heard what Bestuzhev had said, he would never forgive the chancellor. Nevertheless, Peter decided that he could win over Choglokov by confiding in him how he had been described by Bestuzhev. The opportunity soon presented itself.

Soon after, Bestuzhev invited Choglokov to dinner. Choglokov grimly accepted, but remained silent during the meal. Bestuzhev, himself half-drunk after dinner, tried to talk to his guest, but found him unapproachable. Bestuzhev lost his temper and the conversation became heated. Choglokov reproached Bestuzhev for having criticized him to Peter. Bestuzhev rebuked Choglokov for his adventure with

Maria Kosheleva and reminded his guest of the support he, Bestuzhev, had given him in surviving this scandal. Choglokov, the last person to listen to anything critical about himself, flew into another rage and decided that he had been unforgivably insulted. General Stepan Apraksin, Bestuzhev's lieutenant, who was present, tried to make peace, but Choglokov became even more belligerent. Feeling that his services were uniquely valuable; that, whatever he did, everyone would run after him, he swore that he would never again set foot in Bestuzhev's house. From that day on, Choglokov and Bestuzhev were bitter enemies.

With his jailors quarreling, Peter should have been cheerful. Instead, during the autumn of 1749, Catherine found him in a state of intense anxiety. He had stopped training his hunting dogs and he came into her room many times a day with a distracted, even frightened, look. "As he could never keep what was bothering him to himself for long, and had no one to confide in but me, I waited patiently for him to tell what the problem was. At last, he told me and I found the matter more serious than I had supposed."

Through the summer in and around Moscow, Peter had spent most of his time hunting. Choglokov had acquired two packs of dogs, one of Russian dogs, the other of foreign dogs. Choglokov managed the Russian pack and Peter assumed responsibility for the foreign pack. He took charge in minute detail, going frequently to his pack's kennel or having his huntsmen come to talk to him about the pack's condition and needs. Peter became intimate with these men, eating and drinking as well as hunting with them.

At this time, the Butirsky Regiment was stationed in Moscow. In this regiment there was a headstrong lieutenant named Yakov Baturin, a gambler, deeply in debt. Peter's huntsmen lived near the regimental camp. One day, one of the huntsmen told Peter that he had met an officer who expressed great devotion for the grand duke and who had said that, with the exception of the senior officers, his entire regiment agreed with him. Peter, flattered, wanted more details. Eventually, Baturin asked the huntsman to arrange a meeting between himself and the grand duke during a hunt. Unwilling at first, Peter eventually agreed. On the day arranged, Baturin waited in an isolated spot in the forest. When Peter appeared on horseback, Baturin fell to his knees, swearing to recognize no other master and to do whatever the grand duke commanded. Peter later told Catherine that on hearing this oath, he was alarmed and, fearing connection to any sort of plot, had spurred his horse, leaving the other man on his knees in the woods. He also said that none of the huntsmen had heard what Baturin had said. Since then, Peter claimed, he and his huntsmen had had no contact with Baturin. Peter had since learned that Baturin had been arrested for interrogation. Peter feared that his huntsman or even he himself might have been compromised. His fear increased when a number of the huntsmen were, in fact, arrested.

Catherine attempted to calm her husband, telling him that if he had not entered into any discussion beyond what he had told her, then guilty as Baturin might be, she did not believe that anyone could find much to criticize in what he, Peter, had done except the imprudence of speaking to an unknown man in the woods. She could not say whether her husband was telling the truth; in fact, she believed that he was playing down the extent of the discussions. Sometime later, Peter came to tell her that some of his huntsmen had been released and that they had told him that no one had mentioned his name. This reassured him, and there was no more discussion of the matter. Baturin was put on the rack and found guilty. Catherine learned later that he had admitted to planning to kill the empress, set fire to the palace, and, amid this confusion, place the grand duke on the throne. He was sentenced to spend the rest of his life in the Schlüsselburg Fortress. In 1770, during Catherine's reign, he tried to escape, was recaptured, and was sent to the Kamchatka Peninsula, on the Pacific. He escaped again and eventually was killed in a petty fracas on the island of Formosa.

That autumn, Catherine developed another severe toothache accompanied by another high fever. Her bedroom adjoined Peter's apartment, and she suffered from the racket made by his violin and his dogs. "He would not have sacrificed these amusements even if he had known they were killing me." she said. "I therefore succeeded in getting Madame Choglokova's consent to having my bed moved out of reach of the dreadful sounds. The [new] room had windows on three sides and there were fierce drafts but they were preferable to my husband's noise."

On December 15, 1749, the court's year in Moscow came to an end and Catherine and Peter left for St. Petersburg, traveling in an open sleigh. During the journey, Catherine's toothache returned. Despite her pain, Peter would not agree to have the sleigh closed. Instead, grudgingly, he allowed her to draw a little curtain of green taffeta to protect herself from the icy wind blowing directly into her face. When they finally reached Tsarskoe Selo, on the outskirts of St. Petersburg, she was in agony. As soon as she arrived, Catherine sent for the empress's chief physician, Dr. Boerhave, and begged him to extract the tooth that had been tormenting her for five months. With extreme reluctance, Boerhave consented. He sent for the French surgeon Monsieur Guyon to do the extraction. Catherine sat on the floor with Boerhave on her right and Choglokov on her left, holding her hands. Then, Guyon came from behind, reached around, and twisted the tooth with his pliers. As he wrenched and pulled, Catherine felt that her jawbone was breaking. "I have never in my life felt anything like the pain of that moment," she said. Instantly, Boerhave shouted at Guyon, "Clumsy fool!" and having been handed the tooth, he said, "It is just as I feared. This is why I did not want this tooth to be pulled." Guyon, in pulling the tooth, "had pulled out a piece of my lower jaw, to which the tooth had been attached. At this moment, the empress came into the room and, seeing me suffer so terribly, she wept. I was put to bed and was in great pain for four weeks, not leaving my room until the middle of January. Even then, on the lower part of my cheek, I still had in the form of blue and yellow bruises, the imprint of Guyon's five fingers."

❧24❧

A Bath Before Easter and a Coachman's Whip

THE TRANSFER OF THE COURT to Moscow for a year left St. Petersburg socially and culturally as well as politically deserted. Because there were so few horses and almost no carriages in the city, grass grew in the streets. The truth was that most residents of Peter the Great's new capital on the Baltic lived there by necessity, not choice. Once back in Moscow during one of Peter's daughter's yearlong visits, the old families of the nobility were reluctant to leave. Moscow was the place their ancestors had lived for generations, and they cherished their palaces and homes in the old capital. When the time came to return to the new city rising from a northern marsh, many courtiers rushed to ask for leaves of absence from court—for a year, six months, or even a few weeks—in order to remain behind. Government officials did the same, and when they feared they were not succeeding, there came a torrent of illnesses, pretended or real, followed by a stream of lawsuits and other business affairs, all supposedly indispensable, which could be settled only in Moscow. The return to St. Petersburg, therefore, was gradual, and it took months for the entire court to drag itself back.

Elizabeth, Peter, and Catherine were among the first to return. They found the city practically empty and those who were there lonely and bored. In this dreary setting, the Choglokovs invited Catherine and Peter every afternoon to play cards. They included the Princess of Courland, the daughter of the Protestant Duke Ernst Johann Biron, the former lover and minister of Empress Anne. On taking the throne, Empress Elizabeth had recalled Biron from Siberia, where he had been exiled during the regency of Anna, the mother of the child tsar Ivan VI. Elizabeth did not want Biron completely reinstated, however; she preferred not to see him. Rather than bring him back to St. Petersburg or Moscow, Elizabeth had ordered him and his family to live in the city of Yaroslavl on the Volga.

The Princess of Courland was twenty-five years old. She was not handsome—indeed, she was short and hunchbacked—but she had, according to Catherine, "very beautiful eyes, fine chestnut brown hair, and great intelligence." Her father and mother were not fond of her, and the princess complained that she was mistreated at home. One day in Yaroslavl, she ran away to the household of Madame Pushkina, wife of the governor of Yaroslavl, explaining that her parents had refused her to permit her to embrace the Orthodox faith. Madame Pushkina brought the princess to Moscow and introduced her to the empress. Elizabeth encouraged the young woman, stood as godmother at her conversion to Orthodoxy, and gave her an apartment among her maids of honor. Monsieur Choglokov cultivated the princess because in his youth, when her father was in power, her older brother had boosted his career by promoting him into the Horse Guards.

Having made her way into the company of the young court and playing cards for hours every day with Peter and Catherine, the Princess of Courland conducted herself with discretion. She spoke to each person in a manner carefully designed to please that person, and, Catherine said, "her wit made one forget the disagreeable nature of her figure." In Peter's eyes, she had the additional merit of being German, not Russian. She preferred speaking German, and she and Peter spoke only that language together, excluding the people around them. This made her even more attractive to him, and he began to pay her special attention. When she dined alone, he sent her wine from his table; when he acquired some new grenadier's hat or military shoulder belt, he sent them for her to admire. None of this was done in secret. "The Princess of Courland cultivated a faultless attitude towards me and never for one moment forgot herself," said Catherine. "Therefore, this relationship continued."

The spring of 1750 was unusually mild. When Peter, Catherine, and their young court—now including the Princess of Courland—went to Tsarskoe Selo on March 17, it was so warm that the snow had melted and the carriages stirred up clouds of dust from the road. In this rural setting, the group amused itself by riding and hunting during the day and playing cards in the evenings. Peter openly displayed his interest in the Princess of Courland; he was never more than a step away from her. Eventually, with this relationship blossoming before her eyes, Catherine's vanity was stung. Despite her previous dismissal of jealousy as undignified and unproductive, she admitted that she did not like "seeing myself slighted for the sake of this deformed little figure who was preferred over me." One evening, she could no longer control her feelings. Pleading a headache, she rose and left the room. In her bedroom, Madame Vladislavova, who had witnessed Peter's behavior, told her that "everyone was shocked and disgusted that this little hunchback was preferred over me. With tears in my eyes, I replied, 'What can I do?' " Madame Vladislavova criticized Peter for his bad taste in women and his treatment of Catherine. Her tirade, although uttered for Catherine's benefit, made Catherine weep. She went to bed and had just fallen asleep when Peter arrived, drunk. He woke her and began to pour out a description of the qualities of his new favorite. Catherine, hoping to escape this slurred monologue, pretended to fall back asleep. Peter began to shout. When she gave no sign of listening, he clenched his fist and hit her hard, twice. Then he lay down beside her, turned his back to her, and fell asleep. In the morning, Peter had either forgotten or was ashamed of what he had done; he did not mention it. To avoid further trouble, Catherine pretended that nothing had happened.

As Lent approached, Peter and Madame Choglokova collided over taking a bath. Russian religious tradition required that in the first week of Lent, religious believers bathe in preparation for communion; for most of the population, public baths were communal and men and women bathed naked together. Catherine was prepared to bathe at the house of the Choglokovs, and the evening before she was to do so, Madame Choglokova came and told Peter that it would please the empress if he, too, would go to the baths. Peter, who disliked all Russian customs, especially bathing, refused. He had never been to a communal bath before, he said; further, the bath was a laughable ceremony to which he attached no importance. Madame Choglokova told him that he would be disobeying a command of Her Imperial Majesty. Peter declared that whether he went to the bath or not had nothing to do with the respect he owed the empress, and that he wondered how she, Madame Choglokova, dared say that kind of thing to him; he ought not be required to do what was repugnant to his nature and would be dangerous to his health. Madame Choglokova retorted that the empress would punish his disobedience. At this, Peter became angrier and said, "I would like to see what she can do to me. I am not a child any more." Madame Choglokova threatened that the empress would send him to the fortress. Peter asked whether the governess was saying this on her own or in the name of the empress. Then, striding up and down the room, he said that he would never have believed that he, a Duke of Holstein, a sovereign prince, would be exposed to such shameful treatment; if the empress were not satisfied with him, she needed only to release him to go back to his own country. Madame Choglokova continued to shout, the two hurled insults back and forth, and, said Catherine, "both took leave of their senses." Finally, Madame Choglokova departed, announcing that she was on her way to report this conversation to the empress, word for word.

The married couple did not know what happened next, but when Madame Choglokova returned, the subject of conversation had entirely changed. The governess now informed them that the empress, reverting to her primary grievance against them as a couple, was furious that they had produced no children and demanded to know who was to blame. To determine this, she was sending a midwife to examine Catherine and a doctor to examine Peter. Later, hearing this, Madame Vladislavova asked, "How can you be at fault for having no children when you are still a virgin? Her Majesty should hold her nephew responsible."

In 1750, during the last week of Lent, Peter was in his room one afternoon, cracking an enormous coachman's whip. He snapped it right and left with sweeping strokes, gleefully making his servants run from one corner of the room to another. Then, somehow, he managed to slash himself severely on the cheek. The cut extended down the left side of his face and was bleeding profusely. Peter was frightened, fearing that his bloody cheek would make it impossible for him to appear in public on Easter and that if the empress learned the cause, he would be punished. He rushed to Catherine for help.

Seeing his cheek, she gasped, "My God, what happened?" He told her. She thought for a moment and then said, "I'll try to help you. First, go back to your room and try not let anyone see your cheek. I will come as soon as I have what I need. I hope no one will notice what has happened." She remembered that a few years before, when she had fallen in the garden at Peterhof and badly scratched her cheek, Monsieur Guyon had covered the scratch with an ointment of white lead used for burns. It had worked effectively and she had continued appearing in public without anyone ever noticing. She sent for this salve and took it to her husband, where she treated his cheek so well that in the mirror he himself could see nothing.

The following day, as they took communion with the empress in the court chapel, a ray of sunlight happened to fall on Peter's cheek. Monsieur Choglokov noticed and came up, saying to the grand duke, "Wipe your cheek. There is some ointment on it." Quickly, as if in jest, Catherine said to Peter, "And I, who am your wife, forbid you to wipe it." Then Peter turned to Choglokov and said, "You see how these women treat us. We dare not even wipe our faces when they do not like it." Choglokov laughed, nodded, and walked away. Peter was grateful to Catherine for supplying the ointment and for her presence of mind in fending off Choglokov, who never learned what had happened.

❧ 25 ❧

Oysters and an Actor

ON EASTER SATURDAY, 1750, Catherine went to bed at five in the afternoon in order to be up for the traditional Orthodox service, which began later that night. Before she could fall asleep, Peter came running in and told her to get up and come to eat some fresh oysters that had just arrived from Holstein. It was a double pleasure for him: he loved oysters, and these had been sent to him from his native land. Catherine knew that if she did not get up, he would be offended and a quarrel would follow; she rose and went with him. She ate a dozen oysters and then was permitted to go back to bed while he remained, eating more oysters. Indeed, Catherine noted, Peter was pleased that she did not eat too many because this left more for him. Before midnight, she rose again, dressed, and went to the Easter Mass, but in the middle of the long choral service, she was seized with violent stomach cramps. She went back to bed and spent the first two days of Easter suffering from diarrhea, which was finally subdued with doses of rhubarb. Peter had not been affected.

The empress had also left the Easter Mass with a stomach ailment. Gossip ascribed her indisposition not to something she ate but to anxiety over having to maneuver among four different men: one was Alexis Razumovsky, another was Ivan Shuvalov, the third was a chorister named Kachenevski, and the fourth a newly promoted cadet named Beketov.

While the empress and court were away, Prince Yusupov, a senator and the chief of the Cadet Corps, had arranged that his cadets perform Russian and French plays. The lines were pronounced as badly as the scenes were acted and the plays were mangled. Nevertheless, on her return to St. Petersburg, the empress ordered these young men to perform at court. Costumes were made for them in her own favorite colors and then decorated with her own jewels. It was noticed that the leading man, a handsome youth of nineteen, was the best dressed and most adorned. Outside the theater, he was seen wearing diamond buckles, rings, watches, and elegant lace. This was Nikita Beketov.

Beketov's career as an actor and in the Cadet Corps ended quickly. Count Razumovksy made him his adjutant, which gave the former cadet the army rank of captain. At this, the court concluded that if Razumovsky had taken Beketov under his protection, it was to counter the imperial interest being shown Ivan Shuvalov. No one at court was more disturbed by Beketov's rise, however, than Catherine's maid of honor, Princess Anna Gagarina, who was no longer young and was eager to marry. Although she was not beautiful, she was intelligent and possessed her own large property. Unfortunately, this was the second time her choice had fallen on a man who would subsequently be drawn into the close orbit of the empress. The first had been Ivan Shuvalov, who reportedly had been ready to marry Princess Gagarina when the empress intervened. Now the same thing appeared to be happening with Beketov.

The court waited to see whether Shuvalov or Beketov would triumph. Beketov was gaining, when, on impulse, he decided to invite the empress's choir boys, whose voices he admired, to come to his house. He developed an affection for the boys, invited them often, and composed songs for them to sing. Some courtiers, knowing the empress's strong dislike for affection between males, gave these proceedings a sexual interpretation. Beketov, walking with the boys in his garden, was unaware that he was incriminating himself. He went down with a severe fever and, in his delirium, raved about his love for Elizabeth. No one knew what to think. When Beketov recovered his health, he found himself in disgrace and withdrew from court.

Despite her personal troubles with Peter, Catherine's position in Russia was based on her marriage; therefore, when he was in difficulty, she usually tried to help him. One constant concern to Peter was Holstein, the hereditary duchy of which he was the reigning duke. Catherine found his feelings about his native land exaggerated, even foolish, but she never doubted their strength. In her *Memoirs*, she wrote:

> The grand duke had an extraordinary passion for the little
> corner of the earth where he was born. It constantly occupied
> his mind though he had left it behind at the age of thirteen; his
> imagination became heated whenever he spoke of it, and, as
> none of the people around him had ever set foot in what was,
> by his account, a marvelous paradise, day after day he told us
> fantastical stories about it which almost put us to sleep.

Peter's attachment to his little duchy became a diplomatic issue involving Catherine in the fall of 1750 when a Danish diplomat, Count Lynar, arrived in St. Petersburg to negotiate the exchange of Holstein for the principality of Oldenburg, a territory under Danish control on the North Sea coast. Count Bestuzhev urgently desired this exchange in order to remove an obstacle to the alliance he was seeking between Russia and Denmark. To Bestuzhev, Peter's feelings about his duchy counted for nothing.

Once Count Lynar announced his mission, Bestuzhev summoned Baron Johan Pechlin, Peter's minister for Holstein. Pechlin, short, fat, shrewd, and possessing Bestuzhev's confidence, was empowered to open negotiations with Lynar. To reassure his nominal master, Grand Duke Peter, Pechlin told him that to listen was not to negotiate, that negotiation was far from acceptance, and that Peter would always retain the power to break off the discussions whenever he wished. Peter allowed Pechlin to begin, but he counted on Catherine for advice.

I listened to talk of these negotiations with great anxiety and I tried to thwart them as best I could. He had been advised to keep it a close secret, especially around women. That remark, of course, was directed at me, but they were deceived because my husband was always eager to tell me everything he knew. The further negotiations advanced, the more they tried to present everything to the grand duke in a favorable light. I often found him delighted by the prospect of what he would acquire, only to find him later bitterly regretting what he was going to have to give up. When he was seen to be hesitating, the conferences were slowed; they were renewed only after some new temptation had been devised to make things appear more appealing to him. But my husband did not know what to do.

The Austrian minister to Russia at this time was Count de Bernis, an intelligent, amiable man of fifty, respected by both Catherine and Peter. "If this man or someone like him had been placed in the grand duke's service, it would have resulted in great good," she wrote. Peter agreed and decided to consult Bernis about the negotiations. Unwilling to speak to the ambassador himself, he asked Catherine to do it for him. She was willing and, at the next masked ball, she approached the count. She spoke frankly, admitting her youth, lack of experience, and poor understanding of affairs of state. Nevertheless, she declared, it appeared to her that the affairs of Holstein were not as desperate as people were saying. Moreover, concerning the exchange itself, this appeared to be far more profitable for Russia than for the grand duke personally. Certainly, she admitted, as heir to the Russian throne, he must concern himself with the interests of the Russian empire. And, at some point, if these interests made it absolutely necessary to abandon Holstein in order to terminate the endless disputes with Denmark, the grand duke would consent. At present, however, the whole affair had such an air of intrigue about it that if it succeeded, it would make the grand duke appear so weak that he might never recover in the public eye. He loved Holstein, yet, despite this, the negotiators persisted in trying to persuade him to exchange it, without him really knowing why.

Count de Bernis listened and replied, "As ambassador, I have no instructions on this matter, but as Count de Bernis, I think you are right." Peter told her later that the ambassador had said to him, "All I can say to you is that I believe your wife is right and that you will do well to listen to her." As a result, Peter cooled toward these negotiations, and eventually the proposal for an exchange of territories was dropped. And in her first venture into international diplomacy, Catherine had succeeded in besting Count Bestuzhev.

❧26❧

Reading, Dancing, and a Betrayal

PETER'S BEHAVIOR was always unpredictable. For an entire winter, he immersed himself in plans to build a country house near Oranienbaum in the style of a Capuchin monastery. There, he, Catherine, and their court would dress in brown robes as Capuchin friars; each person would have a personal donkey and take turns leading the animal to carry water and bring provisions to the "monastery." The more details he produced, the more excited he became over his creation. To please him, Catherine made pencil sketches of the building and changed architectural features every day. These conversations left her exhausted. His talk was "of a dullness," she said, "that I have never seen equaled. When he left me, the most boring book seemed delightful."

Books were her refuge. Having set herself to learn the Russian language, she read every Russian book she could find. But French was the language she preferred, and she read French books indiscriminately, picking up whatever her ladies-in-waiting happened to be reading. She always kept a book in her room and carried another in her pocket. She discovered the letters of Madame de Sévigné describing life at the court of Louis XIV. When a *General History of Germany* by Father Barre, recently published in France in ten volumes, arrived in Russia, Catherine read a volume every week. She acquired the *Dictionnaire Historique et Critique* by the French philosopher Pierre Bayle, a seventeenth-century philosophical freethinker and precursor of Montesquieu and Voltaire; Catherine read it from beginning to end. Gradually, guided by her own curiosity, she was acquiring a superior education.

As she grew intellectually, Catherine was also becoming perceived as more physically attractive. "I had a slender waist; all I lacked was a little flesh for I was very thin. I liked to go without powder, for my hair was of an exceedingly fine brown, very thick and strong." She had admirers. For a while, the most persistent of these was none other than Nicholas Choglokov, who, after his adventure with Mlle Kosheleva, became infatuated with the grand duchess. Catherine noticed him smiling and nodding foolishly at her. His attention was abhorrent to her. "He was blond and foppish, very fat, and as thick in mind as in body. He was universally hated; everyone considered him a disagreeable toad. I managed to evade all of his attentions, without ever failing to be polite to him. This was perfectly clear to his wife who was grateful to me."

Catherine's charms were most on display when she danced. She chose what she wore carefully. If a gown attracted everyone's praise, she never wore it again; her rule was that if it made a striking impression the first time, it could only make a lesser one thereafter. At private court balls, she dressed as simply as possible. This pleased the empress, who did not like women to appear overdressed on these occasions. When women were ordered to come costumed as men, Catherine appeared in magnificent, richly embroidered outfits. This, too, seemed to please Elizabeth.

Dressing for a particular one of these masked balls at which the court women would be competing in splendor and elegance, Catherine decided to wear only a bodice of rough white cloth and a skirt of the same material over a small hoop. Her long, thick hair was curled and tied in a simple ponytail with a white ribbon. She wore a single rose in her hair and put a ruff of white gauze around her neck, with cuffs and a little apron of the same material. When she entered the hall, she walked up to the empress. "Good God, what modesty!" Elizabeth said approvingly. In high spirits when she left the empress, she danced every dance. "In my life," she wrote later, "I never remember being so highly praised by everyone as on that night. To tell the truth, I have never believed myself to be beautiful, but I had charm and I knew how to please and I think this was my strength."

It was during the masquerades and balls of that winter, 1750–51, that the former gentleman-of-the-bedchamber Count Zakhar Chernyshev, now a colonel in the army, returned to St. Petersburg after a five-year absence. When he had departed, Catherine was an adolescent of sixteen; now she was a woman of twenty-one.

> I was very glad to see him. For his part, he did not miss a
> single opportunity to give me signs of his affectionate feelings.
> I had to decide what interpretation to give to his attentions. He
> started by telling me that he found me much more beautiful.
> This was the first time in my life that anyone had said anything
> like this to me and I found it pleasing. I was simple enough to
> believe him.

At every ball, Chernyshev made this kind of remark. One day, Princess Gagarina, a lady-in-waiting, brought Catherine a printed billet-doux, a little slip of paper containing sentimental verses. It was from Chernyshev. The following day, Catherine received another envelope from Chernyshev, but this time she found inside a note with lines written in his own hand. At the next masquerade, while dancing with her, he said that he had a thousand things to say to her that he could not put on paper. He begged her to give him a brief audience in her room. She told him that this was impossible, that her chambers were inaccessible. He told her that he would disguise himself as a servant if necessary. She refused. "And so," Catherine wrote later, "things went no further than these notes stuffed into envelopes." At the end of the monthlong Carnival, Count Chernyshev returned to his regiment.

During these years when she was in her early twenties, Catherine was living the life of a royal Cinderella. On summer days, she galloped over the meadowlands and shot ducks in the marshes along the Gulf of Finland. Winter nights, she danced as the belle of court balls, exchanging whispered confidences and receiving romantic notes from attentive young men. These moments were elements of her dream world. The reality of her daily life was different: it was filled with frustration, rebuff, and denial.

One shock occurred on the day Madame Choglokova told her that the empress had just dismissed Timothy Evreinov, her chamber valet and friend. There had been a quarrel involving Evreinov and a man who served coffee to Catherine and Peter. During this argument, Peter had walked in unexpectedly and overheard the insults the two men were shouting at each other. Evreinov's antagonist then had gone and complained to Monsieur Choglokov that, without consideration for the presence of the heir to the throne, Evreinov had covered him with abuse. Choglokov rushed to report the incident to the empress, who instantly dismissed both men from court. "The truth," Catherine reported, "is that both Evreinov and the other man were deeply devoted to us." In Evreinov's place, the empress placed a man named Vasily Shkurin.

Soon afterward, Catherine and Madame Choglokova clashed over a matter in which Shkurin played a critical role. From Paris, Princess Johanna, Catherine's mother, had sent her daughter two pieces of beautiful cloth. Catherine was admiring these fabrics in her dressing room in the presence of Shkurin when she let slip that they were so beautiful that she was tempted to present them as a gift to the empress. She waited for an opportunity to speak to the monarch; she wanted the fabric to be a personal present and she wanted to hand it to Elizabeth herself. She specifically forbade Shkurin to repeat to anyone what she had said in his hearing. He immediately ran to Madame Choglokova to report what he had heard. A few days later, the governess came to Catherine and said that the empress thanked her for the fabrics; that Elizabeth was keeping one and sending the other back to the grand duchess to keep. Catherine was dumbfounded. "How is this, Madame Choglokova?" she asked. Madame Choglokova replied that she had been told that Catherine meant the fabrics to go to the empress and so she had brought them to her. Catherine, stammering so badly that she could hardly speak, managed to tell Madame Choglokova that she had looked forward to presenting the empress with these fabrics herself. She reminded Madame Choglokova that the governess could not possibly have known her intentions because she had not spoken of them to her, and said that if Madame Choglokova was aware of what she planned, it was only from the mouth of a treacherous servant. Madame Choglokova replied that Catherine knew that she was not permitted to speak directly to the empress and that she also knew that her servants had orders to report to her, Madame Choglokova, everything Catherine said in their presence. Consequently, her servant had only done his duty, and she hers by bringing the fabrics to the empress. In short, Madame Choglokova declared, everything had been done according to the rules. Catherine was unable to reply; her fury left her speechless.

When Madame Choglokova departed, Catherine rushed to the little antechamber where Shkurin spent his mornings. Finding him there, she slapped him with all her strength and told him that he was an ungrateful traitor for having dared to report to Madame Choglokova what she had forbidden him to speak about. She reminded him that she had showered him with gifts; still he had betrayed her. Shkurin fell to his knees, begging forgiveness. Catherine was touched by his remorse and told him that his future conduct would determine her treatment of him. In the days that followed, Catherine complained loudly to everyone about Madame Choglokova's behavior, intending that the matter reach the empress's ears. Apparently it did and, eventually, when Elizabeth saw the grand duchess, the empress thanked her for her present.

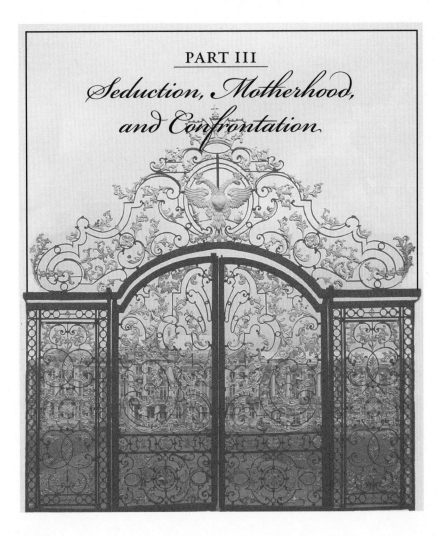

PART III
Seduction, Motherhood, and Confrontation

Saltykov

IN SEPTEMBER 1751, the empress assigned three young noblemen as gentlemen-in-waiting to Grand Duke Peter. One, Lev Naryshkin, came from the family that had produced Natalya Naryshkina, the mother of Peter the Great. Lev himself was an amiable, quick-witted wag whom everybody liked and no one took seriously; Catherine described him as someone who made her laugh more than anyone else in her life.

> He was a born clown and if not of noble birth, he could have made a fortune as a comic actor. He was witty and had heard all the gossip. He had a wide superficial knowledge of almost everything and was able to talk continuously in technical terms on any given art or science for a quarter of an hour. At the end, neither he nor anyone could make any sense of the stream of words flowing from his mouth and everyone simply burst out laughing.

The other two were the Saltykov brothers, sons of one of the oldest and noblest families in Russia. Their father was an aide-de-camp to the empress; their mother was cherished by the empress for her devotion during Elizabeth's seizure of the throne in 1740. Peter, the older of the brothers, was a lout whom Catherine describes as "a fool in every sense of the word. He had the stupidest face I have ever seen: a pair of big, staring eyes, a flat nose, and a gaping mouth, always half open. He was a notorious gossip and, as such, on excellent terms with the Choglokovs."

The second Saltykov brother, Sergei, was entirely different. Sergei was handsome and ruthless; a man who was making the seduction of women his life's purpose. He was dark-complexioned, with black eyes, of medium height, and muscular yet graceful. Constantly on the lookout for a new triumph, he always went straight to work, employing charm, promises, and persistence, in whatever combination worked. Obstacles only increased his determination. When he first noticed

Catherine, he was twenty-six years old and had been married for two years to one of the empress's ladies-in-waiting, Matriona Balk. This marriage had resulted from impulse: he had seen her on a high-flying swing at Tsarskoe Selo and her skirt, flared by the breeze, had exposed her ankles; he had proposed the following day. Now he was tired of Matriona and ready for something new. He observed how blatantly Catherine was ignored by her husband, and how obviously bored she was by the company around her. The fact that the grand duchess was closely guarded added allure; her marriage to the grand duke made the prize more glittering; and the pervasive rumor that Catherine was still a virgin made the challenge irresistible.

Catherine noticed that the young man quickly made himself an intimate of the Choglokovs. She thought this strange: "As these people were neither clever nor amiable, Saltykov must have had some secret purpose in these attentions. Certainly no man with any common sense would have been able to listen to these two arrogant, egotistical fools talking nonsense all day without having some ulterior motive." Maria Choglokova was pregnant again and kept mostly to her room. She asked the grand duchess to visit. Catherine went and usually found Sergei Saltykov, Lev Naryshkin, and others present, along with Nicholas Choglokov. During these afternoons and evenings, Saltykov devised an ingenious way to keep Monsieur Choglokov occupied. He had discovered that this stolid, unimaginative man had a talent for writing simple poetic lyrics. Saltykov praised these lines extravagantly and asked to hear more. Thereafter, whenever the group wanted to rid itself of Choglokov's attention, Saltykov suggested a theme and begged the flattered versifier to compose. Choglokov then would hurry to a corner of the room, sit down by the stove, and begin to write. Once started, he became so absorbed in his work that he would not rise from his seat the entire evening. His lyrics were pronounced wonderful and charming, and he kept writing new ones. Lev Naryshkin set these lyrics to music on the clavichord and sang them with him. Nobody listened and everyone else in the room was free to carry on uninterrupted conversation.

It was in this atmosphere of camaraderie and jolly skullduggery that Sergei Saltykov began his campaign. One evening, he began whispering to Catherine about love. She listened with a mixture of alarm and delight. She did not reply but did not discourage him. He persisted, and the next time she asked him tentatively what he wanted from her. He described the state of bliss he wanted to share with her. She interrupted: "And your wife, whom you married for love only two years ago? What will she say?" With a shrug, Saltykov tossed Matriona overboard. "All that glitters is not gold," he replied, saying that he was paying a high price now for a moment of infatuation. His feelings for Catherine, he assured her, were deeper, more permanent, cast in a more precious metal.

Later, Catherine described the path along which she was being led:

> He was twenty-six years old and, by birth and many other qualities, a distinguished gentleman. He knew how to conceal his faults, the greatest of which were a love of intrigue and lack of principles. These failings were not clear to me at the time. I saw him almost every day, always in the presence of the court and I made no change in my behavior. I treated him as I treated everyone else.

At first, she fended him off. She told herself that the emotion she was feeling was pity. How sad it was that this handsome young man, caught up in a bad marriage, now was offering to risk everything for her, knowing that she was inaccessible, that she was a grand duchess and the wife of the heir to the throne.

> Unfortunately, I could not help listening to him. He was handsome as the dawn and certainly had no equal on this score at the Imperial Court, and still less at ours. Nor was he lacking in that polish of knowledge, manners, and style which are the qualities of society, especially of the court.

She saw him every day. She suggested that he was wasting his time. "How do you know that my heart does not belong to someone else?" she asked. She was a poor actress, and Saltykov, knowing the dialogue of lovemaking, took none of her objections seriously. Later, all Catherine could say was, "I held out all of the spring and part of the summer."

On a summer day in 1752, Choglokov invited Catherine, Peter, and their young court to a hunting party on his island in the Neva River. On arriving, most of the party mounted horses and rode off after the dogs in pursuit of hares. Saltykov waited until the others were out of sight and then rode up alongside Catherine, and, as she put it, "began again on his favorite subject." Here, now without having to lower his voice, he described the pleasures of a secret love affair. Catherine remained silent. He begged her to allow him at least to hope that he had a chance. She managed to retort that he could hope whatever he pleased; she could not control his thoughts. He compared himself to other young men at court and asked whether he was not the one she preferred. Or, if not, who was it? She shook her head wordlessly but said later, "I had to admit that he pleased me." After an hour and a half of this minuet, an old routine for Saltykov, Catherine told him to leave because such a lengthy private conversation would arouse suspicions. Saltykov said he would not go until she consented. "Yes, yes, but go away," she replied. "It is settled, then. I have your word," he said and spurred his horse. She called after him, "No, no!" "Yes, yes!" he shouted and galloped away.

That evening, the hunting party returned to Choglokov's house on the island for supper. During the meal, a strong westerly gale pushed the sea from the Gulf of Finland into the Neva River delta and soon the entire, low-lying island was covered by several feet of water. Choglokov's guests were marooned in his house until three in the morning. Saltykov used this time to repeat to Catherine that heaven itself was favoring his suit because the storm was permitting him to go on seeing her for a longer time. "He already believed himself triumphant," she wrote later. "But it was not at all the same for me. A thousand worries troubled me. I had thought that I would be able to govern both his passion and mine, but now I realized that this was going to be difficult and perhaps impossible." It was impossible. Soon after—sometime in August or September 1752—Sergei Saltykov achieved his goal.

No one knew of their affair, but Peter made an accurate guess. "Sergei Saltykov and my wife are deceiving Choglokov," he told the lady-in-waiting he was pursuing at the moment. "They make him believe anything they want and laugh behind his back." Peter himself did not mind being cuckolded; he saw it as a joke on the foolish Choglokov. More important, neither the empress nor Madame Choglokova was aware of Catherine's new relationship. That summer at Peterhof and Oranienbaum, Catherine went riding every day. Now worrying less about appearances, she had stopped trying to deceive the empress and always rode astride like a man. Watching her one day, Elizabeth had said to Madame Choglokova that it was riding this way that prevented the grand duchess from conceiving children. Boldly, Madame Choglokova replied that riding had nothing to do with the fact that Catherine had no children; that children, after all, could not appear "without something happening first," and that although the grand ducal couple had been married for seven years, "nothing had happened yet." Confronted by this statement—which she still refused entirely to believe—Elizabeth burst out angrily at Madame Choglokova for not persuading the couple to do their duty.

Alarmed, Madame Choglokova began a determined effort to see that the empress's wishes were obeyed. First, the governess conferred with one of the grand duke's valets, a Frenchman named Bressan. Bressan recommended that Peter be placed in the intimate company of an attractive, sexually experienced woman who was also his social inferior. Madame Choglokova agreed, and Bressan located a young widow, Madame Groot, whose late husband, a Stuttgart painter named L. F. Groot, was one of the Western artists brought to Russia by Elizabeth. It took time to explain to Madame Groot what was desired of her and to persuade her to comply. Once the teacher had accepted this assignment, Bressan introduced her to her pupil. And thereafter, in an atmosphere of music, wine, pleasantries—and, on her part, perseverance—Peter's sexual initiation was managed.

Peter's success with Madame Groot meant that the widow had managed to overcome any inhibitions he might have felt regarding his own appearance. If, in fact, he had also been afflicted by phimosis, this problem, too, must have been resolved by the passage of time. Or there is another story, told by the French diplomat Jean-Henri Castéra, who first presented the phimosis theory in his biography of Catherine. According to Castéra, once Saltykov had succeeded in his seduction of Catherine, he became uneasy about the potential danger of being the lover of a woman known to be a virgin and whose husband was the heir to the throne. Suppose the wife became pregnant; where would that put him? He decided to protect himself. During an all-male dinner at which the grand duke was the guest of honor, Saltykov steered the conversation around to the pleasures of sex. Peter, thoroughly drunk, admitted that he had never enjoyed these sensations. Whereupon—the story goes—Saltykov, Lev Naryshkin, and others present begged the grand duke to submit, then and there, to corrective surgery. His head spinning, Peter stammered consent. A doctor and a surgeon, already standing by, were brought in, and the operation was performed immediately. Once the incisions had healed, and after Madame Groot had finished her private lessons, the grand duke was ready to become a complete husband. And thereafter, if Peter's wife became pregnant, who could say that Sergei Saltykov was responsible?

As it happened, Saltykov's worries were unnecessary. Madame

Choglokova, having carried out the empress's command with respect to Peter, was already turning to the problem of Catherine, whom the governess supposed still to be a virgin. There was no certainty that Peter's success in embracing Madame Groot would ensure the same success with Catherine. And even if he managed the physical act, there was no guarantee that this would result in a conception. More certainty was required. Perhaps, even, a more reliable male.

Understanding the wide latitude of the imperial command she had been given, Madame Choglokova took Catherine aside one day and said, "I must speak to you very seriously." The conversation that followed astonished Catherine.

> Madame Choglokova began in her usual way with a long preamble about her attachment to her husband, her own virtue and prudence, and what was necessary and not necessary for ensuring mutual love and facilitating conjugal relations. But then, in midstream, she reversed course and said that there were sometimes situations in which a higher interest demanded an exception to these rules; where one's patriotic duty to one's country took precedence over duty to one's husband. I let her talk without interruption, having no idea what she was driving at, and uncertain whether she was setting a trap for me. While I was deliberating, she said, "I do not doubt that in your heart you have a preference for one man over another. I leave you to choose between Sergei Saltykov and Lev Naryshkin. If I am not mistaken, it is the latter." To this, I cried out, "No, no, not at all." "Well, then," Madame Choglokova said, "if it is not Naryshkin, it can only be Saltykov."

Catherine remained silent, and the governess continued, "You will see that I shall not put difficulties in your way." Madame Choglokova was as good as her word. Thereafter she and her husband stood aside when Sergei Saltykov entered Catherine's bedroom.

The three principals—Catherine, Peter, and Sergei—found themselves in a complicated situation. She loved a man who had sworn he loved her, and who, thrusting aside seven years of virginal marriage, was teaching her about physical love. She had a husband who had not touched her since their marriage, who still did not desire her, who was aware of her lover, and thought it was all a titillating joke. Sergei considered Peter's inclusion a necessary alibi.

Catherine should have been happy, but something in Sergei Saltykov's attitude was changing. In the autumn, when the court moved back to the Winter Palace, he seemed restless; his passion seemed to be waning. When she reproached him, he emphasized the need for caution, explaining that, if she gave it more thought, she would understand the wisdom and prudence of his behavior.

Catherine and Peter departed from St. Petersburg in December 1752 and followed the empress and the court to Moscow. Catherine was already feeling signs of pregnancy. The sleigh traveled night and day, and at the last relay station before Moscow, Catherine suffered violent contractions and heavy bleeding. It was a miscarriage. Soon after, Sergei Saltykov arrived in Moscow, but his attitude remained distant. Nevertheless, he repeated the reasons for his behavior: the need to be discreet and avoid arousing suspicion. She still believed him. "As soon as I had seen and spoken to him," she said, "my worries vanished."

Reassured and hoping to please, Catherine agreed to a political proposal from Saltykov. He asked that she reach out on his behalf and request Chancellor Bestuzhev to help him advance his career. It was not easy for Catherine to agree. For seven years, she had considered the chancellor her most powerful enemy in Russia. He had subjected her to provocation and humiliation; he was behind the campaign against her mother; it was he who had assigned the watchdog Choglokovs; he was the author of the ban on her writing or receiving personal letters. Catherine had never publicly protested; she had carefully avoided alignment with any faction at court; she believed that her own uncertain position dictated that her best course was to cultivate friendships in all directions; she had not seemed interested in political maneuvering. Her priority had been to erase her Prussian identity by enthusiastically adopting every characteristically Russian trait. Now, influenced by her love for the man who had made her pregnant, and frightened by her fear of losing him, she put these considerations aside and did what he asked.

Her first step was to send Count Bestuzhev "a few words that would allow him to believe that I was less hostile to him than before."

She was surprised by the chancellor's reaction. He was delighted by her overture and declared that he was at the grand duchess's disposal. He asked that she indicate a safe channel by which they might communicate. On hearing this news, Saltykov, impatient, decided to visit the chancellor immediately under the pretext of a social call. The old man received him warmly, took him aside, and spoke to him of the inner world of the court, stressing particularly the stupidity of the Choglokovs. "I know that you can see through them as well as I do because you are a sensible young man," Bestuzhev said. Then he spoke of Catherine: "In gratitude for the good will that the grand duchess has shown me, I am going to do her a little service for which I think she will thank me. I will make Madame Vladislavova as gentle as a lamb for her and the grand duchess will be able to do as she pleases. She will see that I am not the ogre she thinks I am." At a stroke, Catherine had transformed the enemy she had feared for many years. This powerful man was now offering to support her and, in the bargain, Saltykov. "He gave him [Saltykov] a good deal of advice which was as useful as it was wise," she said. "All this made him very intimate with us, without any living soul being the wiser."

The new alliance offered advantages to both sides. Despite the humiliations Bestuzhev had heaped on her and her family, Catherine recognized the chancellor's intelligence and administrative skill. This could be useful to her as well as to Saltykov. From Bestuzhev's perspective, Catherine's offer of reconciliation came at an unusually opportune time. The rise of Elizabeth's new favorite, Ivan Shuvalov, was undermining the chancellor's position. The new favorite was not simply amiable and indolent, as Razumovsky had been. Shuvalov was intelligent, ambitious, and strongly pro-French, and he was actively securing influential positions in government for his uncles and cousins. In addition, Bestuzhev worried about Elizabeth's health. Her illnesses had become more frequent and required ever-lengthening periods of recovery. If—or rather, when—the empress died, Peter would inherit the throne. This was Peter who worshipped Frederick of Prussia; Peter who hated the Austrian alliance, the bedrock of the chancellor's diplomacy; and Peter who was quite prepared to sacrifice the interests of the Russian empire to those of tiny, insignificant Holstein. Bestuzhev had long realized that Catherine was far more intelligent than her husband and that she was as sympathetic to Russian interests as Peter was indifferent or hostile. To have Catherine as an ally would mean buttressing his position at the moment and perhaps adding greater strength for the future. When Catherine suggested that they work together, he was quick to agree.

In May 1753, five months after her miscarriage, Catherine was pregnant again. She spent several weeks at a country estate near Moscow, where she restricted herself to walks and gentle carriage rides. By the time she returned to Moscow, she was so overcome by drowsiness that she slept until noon and it was difficult to wake her for midday dinner. On June 28, she felt pain in her lower back. The midwife was summoned, shook her head, and predicted another miscarriage. The following night, the prediction came true. "I must have been pregnant two or three months," she conjectured. "For thirteen days, my life was in danger and it was suspected that part of the after-birth had not been expelled. Finally, on the thirteenth day, it came out without pain or effort."

Peter spent most of this time in his own room, where his servants kept him supplied not only with military toys but with alcohol. During these days, the grand duke often found himself ignored and even flagrantly disobeyed by his servants, they being as drunk as he. Angry, Peter would strike about him with his stick or the flat of his sword, but his entourage dodged and laughed. After Catherine's recovery, Peter asked her to make them behave. "When this happened," she said, "I would go to his rooms and scold them, reminding them of their place and their duties. They always resumed their proper places. This made the grand duke say to me that he did not understand how I managed his servants; he flogged them, but could not make himself obeyed, while I obtained what I wanted with a single word."

Moscow, the largest city of eighteenth-century Russia, was built primarily of wood. Palaces, mansions, houses, and hovels were constructed of logs and planks, sometimes carved and painted to give the appearance of stone, with windows, porches, and gables of many shapes and bright colors. Nevertheless, because they were built in haste, they were often uncomfortable; doors and windows did not shut, stairs wobbled, sometimes whole buildings swayed.

Worst of all was the scourge of fire. Through the icy Russian winters, palaces and houses alike were heated by tall tile stoves standing in the corners of the rooms, rising from floor to ceiling. Often the stoves were old, the tiles had cracked, rooms filled with smoke, the air became unbreathable, and headaches and swollen red eyes afflicted everyone. Sometimes sparks popped through the cracks and alighted on the wooden walls behind. In winter, which lasted for many months, with primitive stoves blazing in every house, a spark could create an inferno. Caught by the wind, flames from one burning house leaped from the roof to the next, reducing entire streets to ashes. To Muscovites the sight of a burning house with firemen struggling to localize the fire by hastily tearing down other buildings in its path was part of daily life. "No one had ever seen more fires in Moscow than in 1753 and 1754," Catherine wrote. "More than once from the windows of my apartment, I saw two, three, four and five fires at a time burning in different parts of the city."

On a November afternoon in 1753, Catherine and Madame Choglokova were together in the Golovin Palace when they heard shouting. The building, constructed entirely of wood, was on fire. It was already too late to save the huge structure. Catherine, hurrying to her room, saw that the stairway in the corner of the grand reception hall was already in flames. In her own apartment, she found a crowd of soldiers and servants carrying and dragging away furniture. She and Madame Choglokova could not help. Retreating to the street, deep in mud from heavy rain, they found the carriage of the choirmaster, who was coming to attend one of Peter's concerts. Both women scrambled into his carriage. They sat and watched the fire until the heat became too great and the carriage was forced to move. Before leaving, however, Catherine saw an extraordinary sight: "An astonishing number of rats and mice were coming down the staircase in a single, orderly line without even appearing to hurry." Eventually, Choglokov arrived and told them that the empress had ordered the young couple to move into his house. It was "a terrible place." Catherine said, "There was no furniture, the wind blew through it on all sides, the windows and doors were half rotten, the floor was split open with cracks, and there were vermin everywhere. Even so, we were better off than the Choglokov children and servants who were living there when we arrived and were expelled to make room for us."

The following day, their clothes and other belongings, collected from the mud where they had been sitting in front of the smoldering ruin of the palace, were brought to them. Catherine was overjoyed to find most of her small library delivered to her undamaged. What had affected Catherine most in the disaster was the thought of losing her books; she had just finished the fourth volume of Bayle's *Dictionnaire historique et critique,* and these volumes were returned to her. It was the empress who suffered the heaviest personal loss in the fire. All of that part of Elizabeth's enormous wardrobe that she had brought with her to Moscow went up in flames. She told Catherine that four thousand dresses had been destroyed and that, of them all, she most regretted losing the one made from the Parisian fabric that Catherine had received from her mother and had given to her.

Peter also suffered a heavy—and embarrassing—loss in the fire. The grand duke's apartment had been furnished with an abnormal number of large chests of drawers. As these were being carried out of the building, some of the drawers, unlocked or badly closed, had slid open and dumped their contents onto the floor. The chests contained nothing but bottles of wine and liquor. The cupboards had served as Peter's private wine cellar.

When Catherine and Peter were moved to another of the empress's palaces, Madame Choglokova, offering various excuses, remained with her children in her own house. The truth was that this mother of seven, famously virtuous and supposedly devoted to her husband, had fallen in love with Prince Peter Repnin. Her meetings with the prince were secret, but, feeling that she needed a discreet confidante, and that Catherine was the only person she could trust, she showed the grand duchess the letters she had received from her lover. When Nicholas Choglokov became suspicious and questioned Catherine, she pretended ignorance.

By February 1754, Catherine was pregnant for the third time. Not long after, on Easter Day, Nicholas Choglokov began suffering severe stomach pains. Nothing seemed to help. That week, Peter went riding, but Catherine remained at home, unwilling to risk the pregnancy. She was alone in her room when Choglokov sent for her and asked her to come see him. Stretched on his bed, he greeted her by unleashing a torrent of complaints against his wife. He said that she was involved in adultery with Prince Repnin, who, during Carnival, had tried to sneak into their house dressed as a clown. As he was about to provide more details, Maria Choglokova entered the room. Then, in Catherine's presence, the husband heaped more blame on his wife, accusing her of adultery and of deserting him in his sickness. Maria Choglokova was anything but repentant. She told her husband that for years she had loved him too much; that she had suffered when he was unfaithful to her; that now neither he nor anyone else could reproach her. She concluded that he was not the spouse who should be complaining; it was she. In this argument, both husband and wife continually appealed to Catherine as a witness and judge. Catherine remained silent.

Choglokov's illness grew worse. On April 21, the doctors declared him beyond hope of recovery. The empress had the sick man carried to his own house for fear he would die in the palace, which she considered bad luck. Catherine found herself surprisingly upset by Nicholas Choglokov's condition. "He was dying just at a time when, after many years of trouble and pain, we had succeeded in making him not only less unkind and malicious, but even tractable. As for his wife, she was now sincerely attached to me, and she had changed from a harsh and spiteful guardian into a loyal friend."

Choglokov died on the afternoon of April 25. During the last days of her husband's illness, Maria Choglokova was also ill and confined to bed in another part of the house. Sergei Saltykov and Lev Naryshkin happened to be in her room at the moment of Choglokov's death. The windows were open and a bird flew in and perched on a cornice opposite Madame Choglokova's bed. She saw it and said, "I am certain that my husband has just died. Please send someone to find out." Told that he was indeed dead, she declared that the bird had been her husband's soul. People told her that it was an ordinary bird and that it had flown away. She remained convinced that her husband's soul had come to find her.

❧28❧

The Birth of the Heir

ONCE HER HUSBAND was buried, Maria Choglokova wanted to resume her duties with Catherine. But the empress relieved her cousin of this assignment, telling her that it was improper for a new widow to appear so soon in public. Elizabeth then appointed Count Alexander Shuvalov, the uncle of her favorite, Ivan Shuvalov, to perform Nicholas Choglokov's former role at the young court. At that time, Alexander Shuvalov was widely feared because of his position as chief of the tribunal for crimes against the state. It was this grim work, according to rumor, that had given him the convulsive movement that seized the entire right side of his face from the eye to the jaw whenever he was anxious or angry.

This was only the first planned change. Catherine heard that the empress planned to appoint Countess Rumyantseva to replace Maria Choglokova. Knowing that this woman disliked Sergei Saltykov, Catherine went to Alexander Shuvalov, the new watchdog, and told him that she did not want Countess Rumyantseva near her. In the past, she said, the countess had harmed her mother by criticizing Johanna to the empress; now she feared she would do the same to her. Shuvalov, not wishing to be responsible for any potential harm to the child Catherine was carrying, said that he would do what he could. He went to the empress and returned to say that Countess Rumyantseva would not become the new governess. Instead, the post was to be given to his own wife, Countess Shuvalova.

Neither Shuvalov was popular with the young court. Catherine described them as "ignorant, ignoble people." Although the Shuvalovs were wealthy, their taste ran to the miserly; the countess was thin, short, and stiff; Catherine called her "a pillar of salt." Catherine also stood back from the countess because of a discovery she had made after the palace fire of November 1753 in Moscow. Some of Countess Shuvalova's belongings, saved from the fire, had been mistakenly delivered to the grand duchess. Examining them, Catherine discovered that "Countess Shuvalova's petticoats were lined with leather because she was incontinent. As a result, the odor of urine permeated all her under-clothing. I sent them back to her as quickly as possible."

In May, when the court left Moscow to return to St. Petersburg, to protect her pregnancy, Catherine traveled slowly. Her carriage was drawn at a walk, moving each day only from one relay station to the next and taking a total of twenty-nine days on the road. In the carriage were Countess Shuvalova, Madame Vladislavova, and a midwife, assigned to be always nearby. Catherine arrived in St. Petersburg suffering from "a depression I could no longer control. At every minute, and on every occasion, I was ready to cry. A thousand preoccupations filled my mind.

The worst was that I could not get it out of my head that everything pointed to the removal of Sergei Saltykov." She went to Peterhof and took long walks, "but my troubles followed me relentlessly." In August, she returned to St. Petersburg, where she was dismayed to learn that the two rooms in the Summer Palace being prepared for her labor and delivery were actually inside the empress's own suite. When Count Shuvalova took her to see the rooms, she realized that because they were so close to Elizabeth's, Saltykov would be unable to visit her. She would be "isolated, with no company."

Her installation in this apartment was planned for a Wednesday. At two o'clock that morning she was awakened by labor pains. The midwife confirmed that Catherine was going into labor. She was placed on a traditional labor bed: a hard mattress on the floor. The grand duke was awakened; Count Alexander Shuvalov was notified, and he informed the empress. Elizabeth swept in and settled down to wait. A difficult labor lasted until noon the following day. On September 20, 1754, Catherine gave birth to a son.

Elizabeth, who had waited so long, was exultant. As soon as the infant had been bathed and swaddled, she called in her confessor, who gave the baby a name, Paul, which had been the name of the first child born to her mother, Catherine I, and her father, Peter the Great. Then the empress departed, commanding the midwife to pick up the new baby and follow. Peter also walked out of the room, and Catherine was left on the floor, with only Madame Vladislavova as company. She was bathed in sweat, and she begged Madame Vladislavova to change her linen and put her back in her own bed, which was two steps away but "to which I had not the strength to crawl." Madame Vladislavova declared that, without the midwife's permission, she did not dare. Catherine asked for water to drink and received the same response. Madame Vladislavova sent several times for the midwife to come and authorize these requests, but the woman did not come. Three hours later, Countess Shuvalova arrived. When she saw Catherine still lying in the labor bed, she said that this neglect could kill a new mother. She left immediately to find the midwife; the woman arrived half an hour later, explaining that the empress had been so preoccupied with the child that she would not allow her leave to attend to Catherine. Finally, Catherine was placed in her own bed.

She did not see the baby for almost a week. She could get news of him only furtively because to ask about him would have been interpreted as doubting the empress's ability to care for him. The infant had been installed in Elizabeth's bedroom, and whenever he cried, the monarch rushed to him herself. What Catherine heard—and later saw for herself—was that

> through excess of care, they were literally stifling and smothering him. He was kept in an extremely warm room, wrapped up in flannel and laid in a cradle lined with black fox fur. Over him was a coverlet of quilted satin, lined with cotton wadding. Above this was another counterpane of rose-colored velvet lined with black fox fur. Afterward, I often saw him lying like this, perspiration pouring from his face and whole body, the result being that when he was older, the least breath of air chilled him and made him ill.

On the sixth day of his life, Paul was baptized. That morning, the empress came into Catherine's bedroom, bringing with her a gold plate on which lay an order directing the imperial treasury to send the new mother one hundred thousand rubles. To this Elizabeth added a little jewel case, which Catherine did not open until the empress had left. The money was very welcome: "I did not have a kopeck and was heavily in debt. But when I opened the box, it did not much improve my mood. It contained only a poor little necklace with earrings and two miserable rings which I would have been ashamed to give my maids. In the whole box there was not one jewel worth a hundred rubles." Catherine said nothing, but the meanness of the gift may have troubled Count Alexander Shuvalov, because eventually he asked whether she liked the jewelry. Catherine replied that "whatever came from the empress was always priceless." Later, when Shuvalov saw that she never wore this necklace and the earrings, he suggested that she put them on. Catherine replied that "for the empress's parties, I was accustomed to wearing my most beautiful jewelry and that the necklace and earrings did not fall within that category."

Four days after Catherine received the gift of money from the empress, the cabinet secretary came to her and begged her to lend this money back to the treasury; the empress needed money for another purpose and no funds were available. Catherine sent the money back and it was returned to her in January. Eventually, she learned that Peter, having heard about the empress's gift to his wife, had become angry and had complained vehemently because nothing had been given to him. Alexander Shuvalov had reported this to the empress, who immediately sent the grand duke an order for a sum equal to what she had given Catherine—which is why the money had to be borrowed back from the original recipient.

While cannonades, balls, illuminations, and fireworks celebrated her son's birth, Catherine remained in bed. On the seventeenth day after the delivery, she learned that the empress had assigned Sergei Saltykov to a special diplomatic mission: he was to deliver the formal announcement of her son's birth to the royal court of Sweden. "This meant," Catherine wrote, "that I was immediately going to be separated from the one person I cared about most. I buried myself in my bed where I did nothing but grieve. In order to stay there, I pretended to have continual pain in my leg which prevented me from getting up. But the truth was that I could not and would not see anybody in my sorrow."

Forty days after Catherine gave birth, the empress came back to her bedroom for a ceremony to mark the end of her confinement. Catherine had dutifully risen from her bed to receive the sovereign, but when Elizabeth saw her so weak and exhausted, she made her remain sitting in bed while prayers were read. The infant Paul was present, and Catherine was permitted to look at him from a distance. "I thought him beautiful and the sight of him raised my spirits a little," Catherine said, "but the moment the prayers were finished, the empress had him carried away and she also left." On November 1, Catherine received the formal congratulations of the court and the foreign ambassadors. For this purpose, a room was richly furnished overnight, and there, on a couch of rose-colored velvet embroidered with silver, the new mother sat and extended her hand to be kissed. Immediately after the ceremony, the elegant furniture was removed and Catherine was returned to the isolation of her room.

From the moment of Paul's birth, the empress behaved as if the child were her own; Catherine had been simply a vehicle for bringing him into the world. Elizabeth had many reasons for holding this point of view. She had brought the two adolescents to Russia in order to create a child. For ten years, she had been keeping them both at the expense of the state. Thus, the child, required for reasons of state, created by her command, was now, in effect, the property of the state—that is, of the empress.

There were other reasons, beyond political and dynastic, for the love and care Elizabeth lavished on Paul. It was not for reasons of state that she took physical possession of the baby. It was also a matter of love welling up from an emotional, sentimental nature; of bottled-up maternal impulses and a desire for family. Now, forty-four years old and in declining health, Elizabeth meant to be the child's mother, even if the motherhood was make-believe. It was as a part of her effort to make this role real to herself that she excluded Catherine from the baby's life. Elizabeth's extreme possessiveness was more than an expression of thwarted maternal need; it was a form of jealousy. In effect, she simply kidnapped the baby.

What Elizabeth took, Catherine was denied. She was not allowed to care for her infant; indeed, she was scarcely allowed to see him. She missed his first smile and his early growth and development. Even in the middle of the eighteenth century, when aristocratic and upper-class women performed little actual child care, leaving most of this work to wet nurses and servants, most mothers still held and fondled their newborn infants. Catherine never forgot the emotional misery attending the birth of her first child. Her son and her lover, the two humans she was closest to, were absent. She was desperate to see them both, but neither of them missed her; one did not know, the other did not care. In those weeks, she was made to understand that, having physically produced the baby, her role in creating an heir to the throne was concluded. Her son, a future emperor, now belonged to the empress and to Russia. The result of these months of separation and suffering was that Catherine's feelings for Paul were never normal. Through the next forty-two years of their shared existence, she was never able to feel or display toward him the warmth of a mother's affection.

Catherine refused to rise from her bed or leave her room "until I felt strong enough to overcome my depression." She remained the entire winter of 1754–55 in this narrow, little room with its ill-fitting windows through which freezing drafts blew in from the icebound Neva River. To shield herself and to make life bearable, she turned again to books. That winter she read the *Annals* of Tacitus, Montesquieu's *L'Esprit des Lois* (*The Spirit of Laws*), and Voltaire's *Essai sur les Moeurs et l'Esprit des Nations* (*Essay on the Manners and Spirit of Nations*).

The *Annals*, a history of the Roman Empire from the death of the emperor Augustus in A.D. 14, through the reigns of Tiberius, Caligula, and Claudius, to the death of Nero in A.D. 68, offered Catherine one of the most powerful works of history of the ancient world. Tacitus's theme is the suppression of liberty by tyrannical despotism. Convinced that strong personalities, good and evil, rather than deep underlying processes, make history, Tacitus painted brilliant character portraits in a spare but telling style. Catherine was struck by his descriptions of people, power, intrigue, and corruption in the early Roman Empire; she saw parallels in people and events surrounding her own life sixteen centuries later. His work, she said, "caused a singular revolution in my brain, to which, perhaps, the melancholy cast of my thoughts at this time contributed. I began to take a gloomier view of things and to look for deeper and more basic causes that really underlay and shaped the different events around me."

Montesquieu exposed Catherine to an early Enlightenment political philosophy that analyzed the strengths and weaknesses of despotic rule. She studied his thesis that there could be contradictions between a general condemnation of despotism and the conduct of a specific despot. Thereafter, for a number of years, she attributed to herself a "republican soul" of the kind advocated by Montesquieu. Even after she reached the Russian throne—where the autocrat was, by any definition, a despot—she tried to avoid excesses of personal power, and to create a government in which efficiency was guided by intelligence; in short, a benevolent despotism. Later, she declared that *L'Esprit des Lois* "ought to be the Breviary of every sovereign of common sense."

Voltaire added clarity, wit, and succinct advice to her reading. He had worked on his *Essai sur les Moeurs* for twenty years (the full text was published as *Essai sur l'Histoire Generale*) and included not only manners and morals, but customs, ideas, beliefs, and laws; he was attempting a history of civilization. He saw history as the slow advance of man by collective human effort from ignorance to knowledge. He could not see the role of God in this sequence. Reason, not religion, Voltaire declared, should govern the world. But certain human beings must act as reason's representatives on earth. This led him to the role of despotism and to conclude that a despotic government may actually be the best sort of government possible—if it were reasonable. But to be reasonable, it must be enlightened; if enlightened, it may be both efficient and benevolent.

Understanding this philosophy required effort from a vulnerable young woman in St. Petersburg recovering from childbirth, but Voltaire made it easier by making her laugh. Catherine, like many of her contemporaries, was charmed by Voltaire. She admired the humanitarian ideas that made him the apostle of religious tolerance, but she also loved his irreligious, irreverent thrusts at the pomposity and stupidity he saw everywhere. Here was a philosopher who could teach her how to survive and laugh. And how to rule.

Catherine gathered her physical strength and attended Mass on Christmas morning, but, while in church, she began to shiver and ache throughout her body. The next day, she had a high fever, became delirious, and returned to her small, temporary room with its freezing drafts. She remained in this nook, avoiding her own apartment and formal bedchamber, because these rooms were close to Peter's apartment, from which, she said, "all day and part of the night, there issued a racket similar to that of a military guard house." In addition, he and his entourage "constantly smoked and there were always clouds of smoke and the foul smell of tobacco."

Toward the end of Lent, Sergei Saltykov returned from Sweden after an absence of five months. Even before his return, Catherine had learned that, once back, he was to be sent away again, this time to Hamburg as resident Russian minister; this meant that their next separation would be permanent. Clearly, Saltykov himself considered the affair to be over and himself lucky to be out of it. He preferred the temporary dalliances of court society to this now increasingly dangerous liaison with a passionate—and annoyingly possessive—grand duchess.

His own ardor had already taken new directions. There had been an irony in his mission to Stockholm; all foreign courts were aware of his liaison with Catherine, and Saltykov could hardly help feeling ridiculous in his role of herald of Paul's birth. But when he reached the Swedish capital, he was quickly relieved of any embarrassment on this account. He found himself a celebrity. He was recognized by everyone as Catherine's lover and the presumed father of a future heir to the Russian throne. He found that men were curious and women fascinated; soon he had his choice of casual affairs. Rumors that he had been "indiscreet and frivolous with all the women he met" reached Catherine. "At the beginning I did not want to believe this," she said, but Bestuzhev, receiving information from the Russian ambassador to Sweden, Nikita Panin, advised her that the rumors seemed to be true. Even so, when Saltykov returned to Russia, she wanted to see him.

Lev Naryshkin arranged a meeting. Saltykov was to come to her apartment in the evening; Catherine waited until three o'clock in the morning. He did not come. "I underwent agonies wondering what could have prevented him," she said later. The next day, she learned that he had been invited to a meeting of Freemasons from which, he claimed, he could not escape. Catherine pointedly questioned Lev Naryshkin:

> I saw as clear as day that he had failed to come because he was no longer eager to see me. Lev Naryshkin himself, although his friend, found no excuse for him. I wrote him a letter bitterly reproaching him. He came to see me and had little difficulty appeasing me for I was only too disposed to accept his apologies.

Catherine may have been appeased, but she was not deceived. When he departed again, this time for Hamburg, Sergei Saltykov was leaving Catherine's private life forever. Their affair had lasted three years and had caused her much anguish, but the worst she could bring herself to say of him later was, "He knew how to conceal his faults, the greatest of which were a love of intrigue and lack of principles. These failings were not clear to me at the time." When she became empress, she made him ambassador to Paris, where he continued to pursue women. A few years later, when a diplomat proposed that he be transferred to a post in Dresden, Catherine wrote to the proposer, "Has he not committed enough follies as it is? If you will vouch for him, send him to Dresden, but he will never be anything but a fifth wheel to the carriage."

✤29✤

Retaliation

D URING THIS SOLITARY WINTER when Paul was born, Catherine decided to change her behavior. She had met her obligation in coming to Russia; she had given the nation an heir. And now, as a reward, she found herself abandoned in a little room without her child. She resolved to defend herself. Examining her situation, she saw it from a new perspective. She had lost the physical presence of her baby, but, by his birth, her own position in Russia had been secured. This realization prompted her decision "to make those who had caused me so much suffering understand that I could not be offended and mistreated with impunity."

She made her public reappearance on February 10 at a ball in honor of Peter's birthday. "I had a superb dress made for the occasion, of blue velvet embroidered with gold," she said. That evening, she made the Shuvalovs her target. This family, believing itself secure in Ivan Shuvalov's liaison with the empress, was so powerful at court, so conspicuous, and so much feared that her attack on them was certain to cause a sensation. She neglected no opportunity to display her feelings.

> I treated them with profound contempt. I pointed out
> their stupidity and malice. Wherever I went, I ridiculed them
> and always had some sarcastic barb ready to fling at them,
> which afterwards would race through the city. Because many
> people hated them, I found many allies.

Uncertain how Catherine's change in behavior would affect their future, the Shuvalovs looked for support from Peter. A Holstein bureaucrat named Christian Brockdorff had just arrived in Russia to serve as chamberlain to Peter in his capacity as Duke of Holstein. Brockdorff heard the Shuvalovs complaining to the grand duke about Catherine, and he urged the husband to discipline the wife. When Peter tried, Catherine was ready for him:

One day, His Imperial Highness came into my room and told me that I was becoming intolerably proud and that he knew how to bring me back to my senses. When I asked him in what my pride consisted, he answered that I held myself very erect. I asked him whether to please him, I must stoop like a slave. He flew into a rage and repeated that he knew how to bring me to reason. I asked how this would be done. Thereupon, he placed his back against the wall, drew his sword half out of its scabbard and showed it to me. I asked what he meant by this; if he meant to challenge me to a duel, I ought to have a sword, too. He put his half-drawn sword back into its scabbard and told me that I was dreadfully spiteful. "In what way?" I asked him. "Well, towards the Shuvalovs," he stammered. To this, I replied that I only retaliated for what they did to me and that he had better not meddle in matters about which he knew nothing and could not understand even if he did know. He said, "This is what happens when one does not trust one's true friends—everything goes wrong. If you had confided in me, all would have been well." "But what should I have confided in you?" I asked. Then he began talking in a manner so extravagant and devoid of common sense that I let him go on without interruption and did not attempt to reply. Finally, I suggested he go to bed because he was clearly drunk. He took my advice. I was pleased because, not only were his words garbled, but also because, he was beginning to give off a perpetual sour odor of wine mingled with tobacco which was insufferable for those near him.

This encounter left Peter confused and alarmed. Never before had his wife confronted him so forcefully; she had always humored him, listened to his schemes and complaints, and tried to keep his friendship. This new woman—self-possessed, unyielding, scornful, dismissive— was a stranger. Thereafter, his attempts at intimidation became more tentative and less frequent. They led increasingly separate lives. Peter continued his relationships with other women; he even continued, from long habit, to describe them to Catherine. She remained useful to him, helping him with duties he found complicated or burdensome. Peter, as heir to the throne, still offered her the likelihood that, when he became emperor, she would become empress. But, as she had come to realize, her destiny no longer depended solely on her husband. She was the mother of a future emperor.

Later in the evening she had confronted Peter, Catherine was playing cards in a drawing room when Alexander Shuvalov approached. He reminded her that the empress had forbidden women to wear the kind of ornamental ribbon and lace on their gowns that Catherine was wearing. Catherine told him "that he could have saved himself the trouble of notifying me because I never wore anything that displeased Her Majesty. I told him that merit was not a matter of beauty, clothes, or ornament; for when one has faded, the others become ridiculous, and only character endures. He listened, his face twitching, and then he left."

A few days later, Peter reverted from bully to supplicant. He told Catherine that Brockdorff had advised him to ask the empress for money to pay his Holstein expenses. Catherine asked whether there was any other remedy and Peter said that he would show her the papers. She looked at them and told him that it seemed to her that he could manage without begging money from his aunt, which she was likely to refuse since, not six months before, she had given him one hundred thousand rubles. Peter ignored her advice and asked anyway. The result, Catherine noted, was that "he got nothing."

Despite the fact that he had been told that he must cut down the Holstein budget deficit, Peter decided to bring a detachment of Holstein troops to Russia. Brockdorff, eager to please his master, had approved. The size of the contingent was concealed from the empress, who loathed Holstein. She was told that it was a trifle not worth discussing, and that oversight by Alexander Shuvalov would keep the project from becoming an embarrassment. On Brockdorff's advice, Peter also tried to keep the impending arrival of these Holstein soldiers hidden from his wife. When she learned of it, Catherine "shuddered to think of the disastrous effect it would have on Russian public opinion, as well as on the empress." When the battalion arrived from Kiel, Catherine stood next to Alexander Shuvalov at the Oranienbaum Palace and watched the blue-uniformed Holstein infantry march past. Shuvalov's face was twitching.

Soon enough, there was trouble. The Oranienbaum estate was guarded by the Russian Ingerman and Astrakhan Regiments. Catherine was told that when these men saw the Holstein soldiers, they said,

"Those accursed Germans are all puppets of the King of Prussia." In St. Petersburg, some people considered the Holstein presence scandalous, others laughable. Catherine herself considered the enterprise "a freakish prank, but a dangerous one." Peter, who in Choglokov's time had worn his Holstein uniform only in secret in his room, now wore nothing else except when he appeared before Elizabeth. Elated by the presence of his soldiers, he joined them in their camp and devoted his days to drilling them. They had to be fed, however. At first, the Marshal of the Imperial Court refused to accept responsibility. Finally, he yielded and ordered court servants and soldiers from the Ingerman Regiment to carry food from the palace kitchen to the Holsteiners. Their camp was some distance from the household, and the Russian soldiers received no compensation for this extra work. They reacted by saying, "We have become the servants of these accursed Germans." Court servants assigned this duty said, "We are employed to serve a set of clowns." Catherine resolved to keep herself "as far away as I could from this ridiculous game. None of the ladies and gentlemen of our court would have anything to do with the Holstein camp, which the grand duke never left. I used to go for long walks with people from the court and we always walked in the opposite direction from the Holstein camp."

❧30❧

The English Ambassador

ONE NIGHT at the end of June in 1755, when the White Nights were at a peak of milky brightness and the sun still remained on the horizon at 11 p.m., Catherine was hostess at a supper and ball in the gardens of the Oranienbaum estate. Among those stepping down from a long line of arriving carriages was the newly appointed English ambassador, Sir Charles Hanbury-Williams. At supper, the Englishman found himself sitting next to Catherine and, as the evening progressed, each was charmed by the other's company. "It was not difficult to talk to Sir Charles for he was extremely witty and had a great knowledge of the world, having visited most of the European capitals," Catherine said. Later, she was told that he had enjoyed the evening as much as she.

Before the supper, Hanbury-Williams had introduced Catherine to a young Polish nobleman, Count Stanislaus Poniatowski, who had come to Russia to act as his secretary. As she and Sir Charles talked at supper, her eyes strayed to this second visitor, whose elegance and grace made him stand out among the dancers. "The English ambassador spoke very favorably of the count," she remembered in her *Memoirs*, "and told me that his mother's family, the Czartoryskis, were a pillar of the pro-Russian party in Poland." They had sent their son to Russia in the ambassador's care in order to enrich his understanding of Poland's large eastern neighbor. Because the subject of foreigners succeeding in Russia applied to Catherine personally, she volunteered an opinion. She said that, in general, Russia was "a stumbling block for foreigners," a yardstick for measuring ability, and that anyone who succeeded in Russia could count on succeeding anywhere in Europe. She considered this rule infallible, she continued, "for nowhere are people quicker to notice weakness, absurdity, or defects in a foreigner than in Russia. One can be assured that nothing will be overlooked because, fundamentally, no Russian really likes a foreigner."

While Catherine was watching Poniatowski, the young man was taking careful note of her. On the journey back from Oranienbaum later that night, he had no difficulty drawing the ambassador into a long, enthusiastic discussion about the grand duchess, and the two men, one forty-seven, the other twenty-three, passed flattering impressions back and forth.

That summer night was the beginning of a close personal and political relationship among the three. Poniatowski became Catherine's lover, and Hanbury-Williams became her friend. For the next two and a half years, the English diplomat helped to assist her financially and then attempted to enlist her influence in the great diplomatic crisis that marked the beginning of the global Seven Years' War.

Sir Charles Hanbury-Williams was born to a wealthy Monmouthshire family. His youth was set in an eighteenth-century English landscape of splendid mansions, formal gardens, clipped green lawns, and portraits by Gainsborough. After Eton, he married, fathered two daughters, and entered Parliament as a Whig under the leadership of Sir Robert Walpole. He became a fixture in fashionable London drawing rooms as an elegant, witty conversationalist and a minor satirical poet. In his late thirties, Sir Charles left his wife and abandoned politics for diplomacy.

In his first two posts, Berlin and Dresden, wit, charm, and elegant English manners were not enough. At the court of Frederick II, he was not to the taste of that intellectual monarch. In Dresden, wit and satire were even less in demand. Political influence at home then saw him appointed to St. Petersburg, where he was warmly welcomed because he was rumored to be bringing a large amount of gold to be used in opening doors and making friends. At Elizabeth's court, however, the elegant Englishman found himself again in an atmosphere where his talents seemed to have little value. He discovered a single exception: a young woman on whom the arrival of a polished diplomat, coming from a world of culture and brilliant repartee, made a strong impression.

Sir Charles had come to St. Petersburg on an important mission. A treaty, originally made in 1742, which traded English payments in gold for the promise of Russian support in any continental war involving England, was on the point of expiring. Simultaneously, fear of Frederick of Prussia's belligerent reputation had stirred King George II's concern for his own small, almost defenseless, north German electorate of Hanover. Hanbury-Williams's mission was to renew the subsidies treaty, which would guarantee Russian intervention if Prussia invaded Hanover. Specifically, the British government wanted Russia to concentrate fifty-five thousand men at Riga with the threat that they would march west into Frederick's province of East Prussia if the Prussians moved against Hanover.

The previous British ambassador, who had attempted to renew this treaty, had found himself at a loss at Elizabeth's court, where diplomatic matters were often settled in a quick conversation at a ball or a masquerade. At his own request, this flustered diplomat withdrew, and a new man, considered better equipped to cope with the nuances of the post, was sought. Charles Hanbury-Williams, who never willingly missed a ball or a masquerade, was considered a good choice. He had proved himself a man of the world, young enough to be attractive to women, but sufficiently mature to remain faithful to his duties. He was not long in St. Petersburg, however, before finding that he could do little better than his predecessor. "The empress's health is very bad," he reported in his first dispatch. "She suffers from a cough and from breathlessness; she has water on the knee and dropsy—but she danced a minuet with me." Hanbury-Williams continued to try, but he had misjudged his quarry. However much it may have amused Elizabeth to listen to the talk of this sophisticated Englishman, the moment he attempted to speak to her of serious matters, she smiled and walked away. As a woman, she was responsive to any compliment; as empress she was deaf. Since his arrival, Sir Charles had not advanced a step.

He looked elsewhere. When he turned to Peter, the future ruler, he was rebuffed again. In their first conversation, he discovered the heir to the throne's obsessive admiration of the king of Prussia. Nothing could be done; he saw that he would be wasting time with the nephew as he had with the aunt. He had come to supper at Oranienbaum that summer evening believing that his mission had failed. Then he found himself seated next to the grand duchess. He discovered a natural ally, a cultured European able to appreciate intelligent conversation, who took a keen interest in books, and who also nourished a dislike of the king of Prussia.

When Sir Charles first saw Catherine, he was as captivated by her appearance as he was impressed by her erudition. Catherine's affair with Sergei Saltykov was well known and had marked her as a susceptible young woman. A cavalier himself in his earlier years, he might briefly have thought of following a romantic path. He quickly confronted reality, however, and recognized that, as a middle-aged widower in less than perfect health, this was no longer open to him. "A man at my age would make a poor lover," he advised a minister in London who had suggested that approach. "Alas, my scepter governs no more." He cast himself, instead, as an avuncular, even paternal, figure to whom Catherine could turn for personal or political advice. He left the other path open for his young secretary, Stanislaus Poniatowski.

Catherine found Hanbury-Williams stimulating and sophisticated; when she learned he had come to renegotiate the alliance between Russia and England aimed at Prussia, her admiration increased. For his part, the ambassador knew Catherine to be a friend of Bestuzhev and therefore a potentially valuable ally. The friendship ripened. When, at a ball, Sir Charles admired her dress, she had a copy made for his daughter, Lady Essex. Catherine began writing letters to him, telling him about her life. This contact with an older man whose intelligence and sophistication she respected was in a sense a reprise of her adolescent relationship with Count Gyllenborg, for whom she had written her "Portrait of a Fifteen-Year-Old Philosopher." In these lengthy epistolary exchanges, she was ignoring the fact that it was indiscreet for a Russian grand duchess to be involved in private correspondence with a foreign ambassador.

Exchanging letters was not the only means Hanbury-Williams employed in his attempt to influence Catherine. He discovered the financial difficulties in which she was mired. New debts had been added to those left behind by her mother. She spent money freely—on clothes, on entertainment, and on her friends. She had learned the power of money to persuade and buy allegiance. She was never guilty of outright bribery; instead, her largesse was driven by her desire to please and be surrounded by smiling faces. When Hanbury-Williams offered financial assistance, using funds from the British treasury, she accepted. The amount Catherine borrowed or took from him is unknown, but it was considerable. Hanbury-Williams had been given carte blanche by his government and had opened a credit account for her with the English consul in St. Petersburg, the banker Baron Wolff. Two receipts signed by the grand duchess bear the dates July 21 and November 11, 1756; the sums totaled fifty thousand rubles. The loan of July 21 was not the first; in asking for it, Catherine wrote to Wolff, "I have some hesitation in coming to you again."

Catherine knew that accepting money from the English ambassador entailed risks, but she also knew that this game was played by everyone at the Russian court. If she allowed herself to be bribed in order to please others, she was only part of a universal corruptibility that was a feature of politics and government in every state in Europe. Money bought friendships, loyalties, and treaties. Everyone in St. Petersburg was corruptible, including the empress herself. When Hanbury-Williams was beginning his effort to persuade the empress to agree to a new Anglo-Russian treaty, he had informed London that Elizabeth had begun to build two palaces but lacked enough money to finish them. The treaty would guarantee Russia an annual payment of one hundred thousand pounds, but Sir Charles thought that an additional contribution to Elizabeth's private purse would bind her even more securely to

England. "In a word, all that has been given so far has served to buy Russian troops," he said. "Whatever may be further given will serve to buy the empress." London approved the additional sum, and Sir Charles was able to report that the treaty negotiations were progressing smoothly. He believed that the same approach would confirm the good-will and anti-Prussian sentiments of the charming grand duchess.

❦31❦

A Diplomatic Earthquake

THE REASON FOR Sir Charles Hanbury-Williams's mission to Russia in 1755 was the political requirement that England defend the electorate of Hanover. In the middle of the eighteenth century, two constant factors dictated British diplomacy and military strategy: one was the permanent hostility of France, whether the two countries were actually at war or passing through an interlude of peace; the other was the need to defend the small, landlocked, north German electoral state. This obligation arose from the fact that the king of England was also the elector of Hanover. In 1714, the fifty-four-year-old elector, George Lewis, had been persuaded by Parliament to accept the British throne, thereby ensuring the supremacy of the Protestant religion in the British Isles. George had become King George I of Great Britain while keeping his German electorate and title. This personal union of the island kingdom and the continental electorate in the figure of the monarch continued until 1837, when, on the coronation of Queen Victoria, it was quietly laid aside.

It was never an easy fit. George I and later his son, George II, greatly preferred their little electorate with its smiling, obedient population of three-quarters of a million people, and no outspoken, interfering Parliament. George I never learned to speak English, and both he and his son frequently went home to Hanover and remained for long periods.

The electorate was always an easy prey for its continental neighbors. Defending Hanover from aggressive neighbors was almost impossible for England, a maritime power lacking a large army. Most Englishmen were convinced that Hanover was a millstone around

England's neck and that Great Britain's larger interests were regularly sacrificed to those of the electorate. There was no escape, however; Hanover had to be protected. Since only the army of a continental ally could do this, England had entered into long-term alliances with Austria and Russia. For many decades, this arrangement had worked.

In 1755, fear of rising Prussian belligerence stirred King George II to worry that his brother-in-law, Frederick II of Prussia (Frederick's wife, Sophia, was George's sister), might be tempted to invade Hanover as he had already invaded Silesia. It was to deter such a Prussian adventure that England had proposed renewal of the treaty with Russia which Sir Charles Hanbury-Williams had come to St. Petersburg to negotiate. When Count Bestuzhev signed the treaty for Russia in September 1755, Sir Charles was exuberant.

Hanbury-Williams's self-congratulation was premature. News that England and Russia were about to sign a new treaty had alarmed the king of Prussia, who, it was said, feared Russia more than he feared God. Appalled by the prospect of fifty-five thousand Russians poised to march against him from the north, he instructed his diplomats to come to terms immediately with Great Britain. They did so by reviving an agreement presumed defunct. Before negotiating with Russia, England had first attempted to ensure the integrity of Hanover by negotiating directly with Prussia. Frederick had rejected this proposal, but now he hastily resurrected and accepted it. On January 16, 1756, Great Britain and Prussia mutually pledged that neither would invade or threaten the other's territories. Instead, should any aggressor disturb "the tranquillity of Germany"—a phrase vague enough to cover both Hanover and Prussia—they would unite to oppose the invader. The potential "invaders" were France and Russia.

This treaty led to a diplomatic earthquake. Allying herself with Prussia cost England her alliance with Austria, as well as implementation of her new treaty with Russia. And when word of the Anglo-Prussian treaty reached Versailles in February 1756, France repudiated her own alliance with Prussia, clearing the way for a French rapprochement with her historic antagonist, Austria. On May 1, Austrian and French diplomats signed the Convention of Versailles, by which France agreed to come to Austria's aid should Austria be attacked.

Six months earlier, these reversals would have been unthinkable; now they were reality. Frederick had overturned his own alliances, forcing other powers to realign theirs; when they did, a new diplomatic structure rose up in Europe. Once these arrangements were made, Frederick was ready to act. On August 30, 1756, his superbly trained, well-equipped Prussian army marched into Saxony. The Prussians quickly overwhelmed their neighbor, and then incorporated the entire Saxon army into their own ranks. Saxony was an Austrian satellite, and the Franco-Austrian treaty, the ink scarcely dry on its pages, now inexorably brought Louis XV to Maria Theresa's aid. And once Russia's longtime ally Austria was involved, Empress Elizabeth joined Austria and France against Prussia. This maneuvering had not improved Hanover's security, however. Freed from the threat of seizure by Prussia, the electorate now stood exposed to danger from both France and Austria.

When Count Bestuzhev sent a note to the British embassy informing Hanbury-Williams of Russia's adherence to the new anti-Prussian alliance between France and Austria, the ambassador was stunned. The newly signed treaty with England, which he had just negotiated with Bestuzhev, had to be set aside, although it was never formally repudiated.* Hanbury-Williams found himself in the topsy-turvy position of being expected by London to further the interests of Britain's new ally, Frederick of Prussia, whom he had originally been sent to Russia to undermine. In this way, the grand reversal of alliances among the European powers was mirrored in miniature by the reversal Hanbury-Williams was forced to make in his own objectives and efforts in St. Petersburg.

The Englishman did his best. He became a diplomatic acrobat. Frederick had no envoy in St. Petersburg; Hanbury-Williams secretly offered to take on the role himself. By using the diplomatic pouch destined for his colleague the British ambassador in Berlin, he would endeavor to keep the Prussian king informed of what was happening in the Russian capital. He would also attempt, through his St. Petersburg connections, to ensure that no serious Russian military effort would be made in the coming war. The most important of these connections, now that Bestuzhev was lost to him, was Catherine. He and the grand duchess had shared an intimate correspondence and many sparkling

---

*Throughout the Seven Years' War (1756–63) that followed, Russia and England were never at war, despite each being allied with the enemies of the other.

conversations; he had given her thousands of pounds; he boasted to the Prussians that she was his "dear friend"; he suggested that he could use her to delay any Russian advance.

The ambassador was betraying his confidante. Catherine knew that the Anglo-Russian treaty was moribund, but she did not know that her friend was secretly assisting Russia's enemy, and that he had used her name as a potential ally in this intrigue. He was deluding everyone, including himself. In January 1757, Catherine expressed her true feelings in a letter to Bestuzhev: "I have heard with pleasure that our army will soon . . . [march]. I beg you to urge our mutual friend [Stepan Apraksin] when he has beaten the King of Prussia, to force him back to his old frontiers so that we may not have to be perpetually on guard."

The truth was that, before his departure, Apraksin had frequently visited the grand duchess and had explained to her that the poor state of the Russian army made a winter campaign against Prussia inadvisable and that it would be better to delay his campaign. These conversations were not the stuff of treason; Apraksin had had similar conversations with the empress, with Bestuzhev, and even with foreign ambassadors. The difference was that Catherine had been commanded by the empress to avoid involvement in political and diplomatic affairs. Perhaps the grand duchess had ignored this command and discussed the matter with Hanbury-Williams, but, if so, she did it unaware that she was speaking not just to her intimate English friend but to someone who would pass along her words to the king of Prussia.

❧32❧

Poniatowski

S TANISLAUS PONIATOWSKI, the young Polish nobleman to whom Catherine had been introduced on the night she met Sir Charles Hanbury-Williams, was one of the adornments of the European aristocracy. His mother was a daughter of the Czartoryskis, one of Poland's great families. She had married a Poniatowski, and Stanislaus was her youngest son. The young man was adored by his mother and patronized by her brothers, his uncles, two of the most powerful men in Poland. Politically, the family hoped, with Russian support, to end the rule of the elected king, Augustus III, a Saxon, and establish a native Polish dynasty.*

At eighteen, Stanislaus had begun touring the capitals of Europe, accompanied by a retinue of servants. He carryied with him an impressive portfolio of introductions. In Paris, he was presented to Louis XV and Madame de Pompadour; in London to George II. He had already met Charles Hanbury-Williams, and when the diplomat was appointed English ambassador to Russia, he invited Stanislaus to accompany him as his secretary. The young man's mother and uncles were pleased; the offer provided the Czartoryskis a means of strengthening their own diplomatic footing in St. Petersburg, and simultaneously gave Stanislaus a chance to begin his public career. Once in the Russian capital, Hanbury-Williams gave his young secretary complete confidence: "He let me read the most secret despatches and code and decode them," said Stanislaus. Sir Charles rented a mansion on the bank of the Neva River to use as an embassy, and the two men lived together, sharing a view across the water of the Peter and Paul Fortress and its golden four-hundred-foot cathedral spire.

Stanislaus Poniatowski, three years younger than Catherine, could not compete in male beauty with Sergei Saltykov. He was short, his face heart-shaped, his eyes shortsighted and hazel. He had prominent eyebrows and a tapering chin, but he spoke six languages, his charm and conversation made him welcome everywhere, and, at twenty-three, he was a model of the young, sophisticated European aristocrat. He was the first of this type to stand before Catherine, and he represented in person the brilliant world for which the writings of Madame de Sévigné and Voltaire had stimulated her taste. He spoke in the language of the Enlightenment, could talk playfully on abstract questions, be dreamily romantic one day and childishly frivolous the next. Catherine was intrigued. Two qualities, however, Stanislaus lacked. There was little originality and no real gravitas in this young Pole, deficiencies that Catherine came to recognize and accept. In fact, no one recognized

*For centuries, elevation to the Polish throne had been by election, with most of the Polish nobility preferring to submit to the weak rule of a foreign king than to sacrifice any of their own privileges by giving preference to one of their own blood. The result was permanent near anarchy.

these limitations better than Stanislaus himself. In his memoirs he confessed:

An excellent education enables me to conceal my mental defects, so that many people expect more from me than I am able to give. I have sufficient wit to take part in any conversation, but not enough to converse long and in detail on any one subject. I have a natural penchant for the arts. My indolence, however, prevents me from going as far as I should like to go, either in the arts or sciences. I work either overmuch or not at all. I can judge very well of affairs. I can see at once the faults of a plan or the faults of those who propose it, but I am much in need of good counsel in order to carry out any plans of my own.

For a man of his sophistication, he was, in many respects, extraordinarily innocent. He had promised his mother not to drink wine or spirits, not to gamble, and not to marry before the age of thirty. Further, by his own account, Stanislaus had another singularity, odd enough in a young man just come from social triumph in Paris and other European capitals:

A severe education had kept me out of all vulgar debauchery. An ambition of winning and holding a place in high life had stood by me in my travels and a concourse of singular circumstances in the liaisons that I had barely entered upon, had seemed expressly to reserve me for her who has disposed of all my destiny.

In a word, he came to Catherine a virgin.

Poniatowski had other qualities appealing to a proud woman who had been rejected and discarded. His devotion showed her that she could inspire more than simple lust. He expressed admiration not merely for her title and beauty but also for Catherine's mind and temperament, which both he and she recognized as superior to his own. He was affectionate, attentive, discreet, and faithful. He taught Catherine to know contentment and security as well as passion in love. He became a part of her process of healing.

At the beginning of this love affair, Catherine had three allies. One was Hanbury-Williams; the others were Bestuzhev and Lev Naryshkin. The chancellor made clear that he was willing to befriend Poniatowski on Catherine's behalf. Naryshkin quickly stepped into the same role of friend, sponsor, and guide for the new favorite that he had performed during Catherine's affair with Saltykov. When Lev was in bed with fever, he sent Catherine several elegantly written letters. The subjects were trivial—pleas for fruit and preserves—but they were written with a style that quickly told Catherine that Lev himself was not the author. Later, Lev admitted that the letters were written by his new friend Count Poniatowski. Catherine realized that, for all his travels and apparent sophistication, Stanislaus was still a shy, sentimental young man. But he was Polish and romantic, and here was a young woman isolated and trapped in a miserable marriage. It was enough to capture him.

This is how Catherine appeared in his eyes :

> She was twenty-five, that perfect moment when a woman who has any claim to beauty is at her loveliest. She had black hair, a complexion of dazzling whiteness, large, round, blue, expressive eyes, long, dark eyelashes, a Grecian nose, a mouth that seemed to ask for kisses, perfect shoulders, arms, and hands, a tall, slim figure, and a bearing which was graceful, supple, and yet of the most dignified nobility, a soft and agreeable voice, and a laugh as merry as her temperament. One moment she would be reveling in the wildest and most childish of games; a little later she would be seated at her desk, coping with the most complicated affairs of finance and politics.

Several months were to pass before the unpracticed lover gathered sufficient courage to act. Even then, but for the persistence of his new friend Lev, the reluctant suitor might have been content to worship from a distance. Eventually, however, Lev deliberately placed Stanislaus in a situation from which the Pole could not retreat without risking embarrassment to the grand duchess. Unaware of what had been arranged, he was led to the door to her private apartment. The door was ajar. Catherine was waiting inside. Years later, Poniatowski remembered, "I cannot deny myself the pleasure of recalling the clothes I found her in that day: a little gown of white satin with a light trimming of lace, threaded with a pink ribbon for its only ornament." From that moment, Poniatowski later wrote, "my whole life was devoted to her."

Catherine's new lover proved to be free of the smiling self-confidence that had led her to capitulate to Saltykov. In this matter, Catherine was dealing with a boy—charming, well traveled, and well spoken, but still a boy. She knew what needed to be done, and, once his hesitation was overcome, she guided the handsome, virginal Pole into manhood.

❖33❖

A Dead Rat, an Absent Lover, and a Risky Proposal

REMARKABLE DIPLOMATIC CHANGES were occurring in Europe, but within the small, closed world of Catherine and Peter's marriage, the arrangements and antagonisms that had marked their lives for ten years continued. Catherine had found a new, supportive lover in Stanislaus Poniatowski; Peter ricocheted among Catherine's maids of honor, making first one and then another the object of his attention. The married couple had extravagantly different tastes and enthusiasms: Peter's were soldiers, dogs, and drink; Catherine's were reading, conversation, dancing, and riding.

In the winter of 1755, most of Peter's Holstein soldiers had been sent home, and Catherine and Peter returned from Oranienbaum to St. Petersburg to resume their separate lives. With the city deep in snow and the Neva River locked under a sheet of ice, Peter's military obsession moved indoors. His soldiers now were toys, made of wood, lead, papier-mâché, and wax. He lined up these figures on so many narrow tables that he could scarcely squeeze between them. Strips of brass with strings attached were nailed to the tables, and when the strings were pulled, the brass strips vibrated and made a noise that, Peter informed Catherine, resembled the rolling fire of musketry. In this room, Peter presided over a daily changing of the guard ceremony in which a fresh detachment of toy soldiers, assigned to mount guard, replaced those who were relieved of duty and removed from the tables. Peter always appeared at this ceremony in full Holstein dress uniform, with top boots, spurs, high collar, and scarf. The servants participating in this exercise were also required to wear Holstein uniforms.

One day when Catherine entered this room, she saw a large dead rat hanging from a model gallows. Appalled, she asked why it was there. Peter explained that the rat had been convicted of a crime that, according to the laws of war, merited the ultimate punishment; therefore, it had been executed by hanging. The rat's crime was to have climbed over the ramparts of a cardboard fortress standing on a table and eaten two papier-mâché sentries standing watch. One of Peter's dogs had caught the rat; the culprit had been court-martialed and immediately hanged. Now, Peter declared, it would remain exposed to public gaze for three days as an example. Catherine listened and burst out laughing. Then she apologized and pleaded ignorance of military law. Nevertheless, he was stung by her facetious attitude and began to sulk. Her last word on the matter was that it could be argued on behalf of the rat that it had been hanged without having been heard in its own defense.

During this winter of 1755–56, Catherine become attached to Anna Naryshkina, Lev Naryshkin's sister-in-law, the wife of his elder brother. Lev was a part of this friendship. "There was no end to his nonsense," Catherine noted. He acquired the habit of running back and forth between Peter's rooms and Catherine's. In order to enter her room, he would meow like a cat at her door. One evening in December, between six and seven, she heard him meowing. He came in, told her that his sister-in-law was ill, and declared, "You ought to go and see her."

"When?" Catherine asked.

"Tonight," he said.

"You know that I cannot go out without permission and they would never give me permission to go to her house," she said.

"I will take you there," he said.

"Are you mad?" Catherine said. "You would be sent to the fortress and heaven knows what trouble I would be in."

"But no one will know about it," Lev said. "I will come for you in an hour or so. The grand duke will be at supper. He will remain at the table for most of the night, and will not get up until he is drunk and ready for bed. To be on the safe side, dress as a man."

Tired of being alone in her room, Catherine agreed. Lev departed, and, pleading a headache, she went to bed early. Once Madame Vladislavova had retired, Catherine got up, clothed herself as a man, and arranged her hair as best she could. At the appointed time, Lev meowed at her door. They left the palace unnoticed, stepping into his carriage and giggling at their escapade. When they arrived at the house where Lev was living with his brother and sister-in-law, she found—unsurprisingly—that Poniatowski was there. "The evening passed," Catherine wrote, "in the wildest gaiety. After staying for an hour and a half, I left and returned to the palace without meeting a soul. The next day, at the morning court and the evening ball, we could not look each other in the face without laughing at the folly of the night before."

A few days later, Lev arranged a reciprocal visit to Catherine's rooms and escorted his friends into her apartment so skillfully that no suspicion was aroused. The group delighted in these secret gatherings. Through the winter of 1755–56, there were two or three of these every week, first in one house, then in another. "Sometimes at the theater," Catherine said, "even if in different boxes or in the orchestra, each of us knew without speaking, by certain private signs, where to go. And no one ever made a mistake. But twice I had to return home to the palace on foot." The happiness of these evenings, Poniatowski's love, and Bestuzhev's political support bolstered Catherine's self-confidence.

Among her own maids of honor, she found occasional opposition, encouraged by Peter's sometimes flagrant belittling of his wife's status and qualities. Now officially recognized as Paul's father, he delighted in playing the untethered male. Singers and dancers, considered by society to be "loose women," appeared at his private suppers. The woman in whom he showed the most interest was one of Catherine's maids of honor, Elizabeth Vorontsova, a niece of Bestuzhev's rival, the vice-chancellor Michael Vorontsov. Placed in Catherine's entourage at the age of eleven, she was neither particularly intelligent nor pretty. Slightly hunchbacked, with a face scarred by smallpox, she had a fiery temperament and was always ready to laugh, drink, sing, and shout. Although she belonged to one of the oldest families in Russia, it was said that she spat when she spoke, and otherwise behaved "like a servant girl in a house of ill-fame." Peter's attachment to her may have grown out of his own sense of inferiority; the grand duke may have concluded that she loved him for himself. At first, Elizabeth Vorontsova was one among many. She had rivals and occasionally she quarreled with Peter, but it was always to Elizabeth that he returned.

At Oranienbaum in the summer of 1756, Catherine's relationship with some of her maids of honor led to a fierce argument. Feeling that these young women had become openly disrespectful, she went to their apartment and told them that unless they changed their behavior, she would complain to the empress. Some were frightened and wept; others were angry. As soon as Catherine left, they rushed to tell the grand duke. Peter, furious, charged into Catherine's room. He told his wife that she had become impossible to live with; that every day she became more insufferable; that they were all young women of rank whom she treated as servants; and that if she complained about them to the empress, he would complain to his aunt about her pride, her arrogance, and her bad temper.

Catherine listened. Then she said that he could say whatever he liked about her but if the matter were placed before his aunt, the empress would probably decide that the best solution would be to dismiss from Catherine's service whichever young women were causing dissension between her nephew and his wife. She said that she was certain that, in order to reestablish peace between the two of them, and to avoid having their quarrels repeatedly dinned into her ears, the empress would take this course. This argument surprised Peter. Imagining that Catherine knew more than he about Elizabeth's attitude regarding these maids of honor, and that she really might dismiss them over this matter, he softened his tone and said, "Tell me how much you know. Has anyone spoken to her about them?" Catherine replied that if the matter went far enough to reach the empress, she had no doubt that Her Majesty would deal with it in her usual decisive way. Peter paced back and forth, worried. That evening, to warn the women to stop making complaints about her, Catherine told the more sensible of them about the scene with the grand duke and what might happen next.

Catherine cared for Stanislaus Poniatowski—how deeply, she learned, when he was forced, temporarily, to leave her. Poniatowski brought this involuntary departure on himself. He disliked his nominal king, Augustus of Saxony, whose German electorate Frederick of Prussia had invaded, and he constantly belittled Augustus. Some took his attacks as expressions of sympathy for Frederick; they were interpreted this way by Peter. But it was not just Peter who mistakenly saw Poniatowski as an admirer of Prussia. It was also the Saxon-Polish court, which now implored Elizabeth to send the young man home. Poniatowski had no choice, and in July 1756 he was obliged to depart. Catherine let him go, determined to bring him back.

Two days before Poniatowski left, he came to Oranienbaum, accompanied by Count Horn of Sweden, to say goodbye. The two counts were at Oranienbaum for two days; on the first, Peter was gracious, but on the second, because he had planned a day of drinking at the wedding of one of his huntsmen, he simply walked away, leaving Catherine to entertain the visitors. After dinner, she showed Horn through the palace. When they reached her private apartment, her little Italian greyhound began to bark furiously at Horn, but when it saw Poniatowski, it greeted him with a frantically wagging tail. Horn noticed and took Poniatowski aside. "My friend," he said, "there is no worse traitor than a small lapdog. The first thing I always do when I am in love with a woman is to give her one of these little dogs. This way, I can always discover whether there is someone more favored than myself. The test is infallible. As you saw just now, the dog wanted to bite me because I am a stranger, but when it saw you, it went mad with joy." Two days after this visit, Poniatowski left Russia.

When Stanislaus Poniatowski departed in July 1756, he assumed that he would return in a matter of weeks. When he failed to come back at the expected time, Catherine began a campaign to bring him back. For the first time, Bestuzhev felt the strong will of the future empress. Through the autumn of 1756, he struggled to do what she asked and persuade the Polish cabinet to return Poniatowski to St. Peterburg. He wrote to Count Heinrich Brühl, the Polish foreign minister: "In the present critical and delicate state of affairs, I find it all the more necessary that an envoy extraordinary should be sent here without delay from the kingdom of Poland whose presence would draw closer the ties of friendship between the two courts. As I have found no one more pleasing to my court than Count Poniatowski, I suggest him to you." Eventually, Brühl agreed.

The way now seemed clear for Poniatowski to return, but, to Catherine's surprise, he remained in Poland. What was the obstacle? In a letter to Catherine, Poniatowski explained that it was his mother:

> I pressed her strongly to consent to my return. She said to me with tears in her eyes that this affair was going to cause her to lose my affection on which she depended for all the happiness of her life; that it was hard to refuse some things, but this time she was determined not to consent. I was beside myself; I threw myself at her feet and begged her to change her mind.

She said, again in tears, "This is what I expected." She went away, pressing my hand, and left me with the most horrible dilemma I have ever experienced in my life.

Aided by his powerful Czartoryski uncles, Poniatowski finally escaped from his mother in December 1756 and returned to Russia as the official representative and minister of the king of Poland. Once back in St. Petersburg, he resumed his role as Catherine's lover. He was to remain in Russia for another year and a half, during which time he fathered her second child.

Empress Elizabeth was frequently ill. No one understood the exact nature of her trouble, but some attributed it to complications with her menstrual periods. Others whispered that her indispositions were caused by apoplexy or epilepsy. In the summer of 1756, her condition became so alarming that her doctors feared for her life.

This crisis of health continued through the autumn of 1756. The Shuvalovs, frantically worried, showered attention on the grand duke. Bestuzhev took a different path. Like everyone else in St. Petersburg, he worried about the future, and he worried most about himself. He was well aware of the prejudices and limited political capacities of Peter, the heir to the throne, and also of the hostility that had been stirred up in Peter's mind against him as chancellor. He could no longer be openly friendly with Hanbury-Williams, since England was now an ally of Prussia. There were other, more general, reasons for him to worry. He was growing old, the years had exhausted him, and, even when she was well, Elizabeth was a difficult mistress. Now, the empress's failing health and the grand duke's hostility left him with only one figure in the imperial family to whom he might turn for support. His relationship with Catherine had strengthened, and the approach of war speeded their rapprochement. By the autumn of 1756, both Catherine and Bestuzhev were deeply concerned about the transition of power that would follow Elizabeth's death.

Bestuzhev began to plan. He had introduced Catherine to his friend General Stepan Apraksin, whom he had appointed commander in chief of the Russian forces mobilizing against Prussia. Next, he sent Catherine a draft of a secret ukase, an imperial decree, to be issued at the moment of Elizabeth's death. This document set forth a restructuring of the administration of the Russian government. It proposed that

Peter immediately be declared emperor, while, at the same time, Catherine be formally installed as co-ruler. Bestuzhev's intention was that Catherine would actually administer the affairs of Russia as she had managed those of Holstein on her husband's behalf. Naturally, Bestuzhev did not forget himself in this new arrangement; indeed, he intended that Catherine's oversight of the empire should be guided by his advice, and he reserved for himself nearly all the real power in the country. The posts he already held would remain his, and others would be added. He would continue as chancellor; he would also become president of three key ministries—foreign affairs, war, and the navy—and he would be appointed colonel of all four regiments of the Imperial Guard. It was a risky, even potentially suicidal, document. He was reaching out to make decisions related to the succession, a prerogative reserved exclusively for the monarch. If Elizabeth were to read this paper, Bestuzhev could pay with his head.

When Catherine received the draft of the proposed document, she reacted cautiously. She did not directly contradict Bestuzhev or discourage his effort, but she did express reservations. If, later, she professed to find its pretensions excessive and its timing inopportune, she could only have been flattered at the central role awarded her. She thanked Bestuzhev verbally for his good intentions but told him that she regarded his plan as premature. Bestuzhev continued writing and revising, making additions and alterations.

Catherine understood that this enterprise was hazardous. On one hand, Bestuzhev was offering her a path that could lead to rule of the empire. On the other, she understood that discovery of this incriminating document could result in mortal danger for herself as well as for the chancellor. Elizabeth's fury, if she read this document, would be a dreadful thing.

❧34❧

Catherine Challenges Brockdorff; She Gives a Party

I N THE SPRING OF 1757, Catherine watched Brockdorff's influence over her husband increasing. The clearest example of this was evident when Peter told her that he must send an order to Holstein to arrest one of the duchy's leading citizens, a man named Elendsheim, who had risen to the top through education and ability. Catherine asked why Elendsheim must be arrested. "They tell me he is suspected of embezzlement," Peter replied. Catherine asked who was accusing him. "Oh, nobody is accusing him because everyone in the country fears and respects him and that is exactly why I must have him arrested," Peter explained. "As soon as that is done, I am assured that there will be a great many accusers."

Catherine shuddered. "If such things are done," she said, "there will not be an innocent man left in the world. Any jealous person will be able to spread a rumor on the strength of which his victim will be arrested. Who is giving you such bad advice?"

"You always want to know more than other people," Peter complained. Catherine replied that she asked because she did not believe that, on his own, the grand duke would commit such an injustice. Peter paced the room and then abruptly left. He soon returned and said, "Come to my apartment. Brockdorff will explain this Elendsheim affair to you. You will be convinced why I must have him arrested."

Brockdorff was waiting. "Speak to the grand duchess," Peter said. Brockdorff bowed. "As Your Imperial Highness orders me, I will speak to Her Imperial Highness." He turned to Catherine "This is an affair that must be handled with great secrecy and prudence," he said. "Holstein is filled with rumors about Elendsheim's embezzlement and misappropriations. He has no accusers because he is feared, but when he is arrested, then there will be as many as one could wish." Catherine asked for details. It turned out that Elendsheim, as head of the Justice Department, had been accused of extortion because after every trial, the loser complained that the other party had won only because the judges were bribed. Catherine told Brockdorff that he was trying to push her husband to commit a flagrant injustice. Using his logic, she said, the grand duke could have him, Brockdorff, locked up, and declare that the accusations would come later. As for litigation, she said, it was easy to understand why those who lost always claimed that they had lost because the judges were bribed.

Both men remained silent and Catherine left the room. Brockdorff then told the grand duke that everything she had said had sprung from her need to dominate; that she disapproved of everything that she, herself, had not proposed; that she knew nothing of the world or of political affairs; that women always liked to meddle in everything, and always spoiled whatever they meddled in; and that any serious measure was beyond their ability. In the end, Brockdorff managed to overrule Catherine's advice, and Peter sent an order to Holstein to arrest Elendsheim.

Catherine, disgusted, struck back, recruiting Lev Naryshkin and others to assist her. When Brockdorff walked past, they shouted, *"Baba Ptitsa!"*—pelican—because they considered the bird's appearance to be hideous and Brockdorff's equally hideous. In her *Memoirs*, Catherine wrote, "He took money from everyone, and he persuaded the grand duke, who always needed money, to do the same thing by selling Holstein orders and titles to anyone who would pay for them."

Despite her efforts, Catherine was unable to weaken Brockdorff's hold on Peter. She approached Alexander Shuvalov and told him that she considered Brockdorff dangerous company for a young prince, the heir to an empire. She advised the count to warn the empress. He asked whether he could mention Catherine's name. She said yes, and added that if the empress wanted to hear it from her personally, she would speak with candor. Shuvalov agreed. Catherine waited, and eventually the count told her that the empress would find a moment to speak to her.

While she waited, Catherine became involved in Peter's affairs in a positive way. One morning, Peter walked into Catherine's room, closely followed by his secretary, Zeitz, who carried a document in his hand. "Look at this devil of a fellow!" Peter said. "I drank too much yesterday and today I am still in a haze, but here he is bringing me papers he wants me to deal with. He even follows me into your room!" To Catherine, Zeitz explained, "Everything I have here only requires a simple 'Yes' or 'No.' It will not take a quarter of an hour."

"Let's see," Catherine said. "Perhaps we can get through them more quickly than you think."

Zeitz began to read aloud and as he spoke, Catherine said yes or no. Peter was pleased by this procedure, and Zeitz said to him, "You see, my lord, if you consented to do this twice a week, your affairs would not fall into arrears. These things are only trifles, but they must be attended to, and the grand duchess has just disposed of all of them with six Yes's and six No's." From that day on, Peter sent Zeitz to Catherine whenever a simple yes or no was required of him. Eventually, she asked Peter to give her a signed order listing the matters she could decide without his permission. Peter obliged.

After this, Catherine mentioned to Peter that if he found decisions regarding Holstein burdensome, he should realize that they were only a small fraction of the work he would have when he was responsible for the Russian empire. Peter reiterated that he had not been born for Russia, that he did not suit the Russians any more than they suited him. She suggested that he ask the empress to acquaint him with the administration of government affairs. Specifically, she urged him to ask to attend meetings of the empress's council. Peter spoke to Alexander Shuvalov, who advised the empress to admit him to these meetings whenever she went herself. Elizabeth agreed, but in the end this turned out to be meaningless, because the empress went with him only once. Neither of them went again.

Looking back on these years, Catherine wrote, "The great problem lay in the fact that I tried to stick as close as possible to the truth, while he left it farther and farther behind." Peter's most outlandish fabrications were personal and petty; often, she says, they originated in a desire to impress a young woman. Relying on this person's innocence, he would tell her that when he was a boy, living with his father in Holstein, he was often placed in command of a detachment of soldiers and sent to round up a band of marauding Gypsies in the countryside near Kiel. Always emphasizing his own skill and valor, Peter described the brilliant tactics he had used to pursue, surround, engage, and capture these opponents, At first, he was careful to tell these stories only to people who knew nothing about him. Then, growing bolder, he told the tales in front of people who knew better, but on whose discretion he relied not to contradict him. When he began to create these fictions in Catherine's company, she asked him how long before his father's death these events had occurred. As she remembered the conversation, Peter replied that it had been three or four years. "Well," she said, "you began very young, because three or four years before your father's death, you were only six or seven years old. You were eleven when your father died and you were left in the guardianship of my uncle, the crown prince of Sweden. What also astonishes me," Catherine continued, "is that your father, whose only son you were—you were a very delicate child at that age—should have sent you, his heir, at the age of six or seven, to fight brigands." It was not she, Catherine concluded, but the calendar that discredited his story.

Still, Peter continued to come to Catherine for help. Because her future was tied to his, she did what she could. She treated him more like a younger brother than a husband: she advised and scolded, listened to his confidences about his love affairs, and continued to assist in the affairs of Holstein. "Whenever he found himself at a loss," Catherine said, "he would come running to me to get my advice, and then, having gotten it, be off again as fast as his legs could carry him."

Eventually, Catherine realized that the empress did not approve of her efforts to help her husband. On the evening Elizabeth finally summoned Catherine for the interview that Catherine had asked for eight months earlier, the empress was alone. The first subject was Brockdorff. Catherine explained the details of the Elendsheim affair and gave the empress her opinion of Brockdorff's harmful influence on her husband. Elizabeth listened without commenting. She asked for details of the grand duke's private life. Catherine told her everything she knew. She started to speak again about Holstein, and Elizabeth interrupted her. "You seem to be well-informed about that country," she said coldly. Catherine understood that her narrative was producing a bad impression. She explained that she was well informed because her husband had ordered her to help him with the administration of his small country. Elizabeth frowned, remained silent, and then abruptly dismissed Catherine. The grand duchess was uncertain what would happen next.

In midsummer 1757, Catherine tried a different approach to appeasing her husband: she gave a party in his honor. For her garden at Oranienbaum, the Italian architect Antonio Rinaldi designed and built a huge wooden cart capable of holding an orchestra of sixty musicians and singers. Catherine had poetic verses written and set to music. She had lamps placed along the grand avenue of the garden, and then she screened off the avenue with an immense curtain behind which tables were set for supper.

At dusk, Peter and dozens of guests entered the garden and sat down. After the first course, the curtain concealing the illuminated grand avenue was raised. Approaching in the distance came the rolling orchestra on its giant cart, pulled by twenty oxen decorated with garlands. Dancers, male and female, performed beside the moving cart. "The weather was superb," Catherine wrote, "and when the cart stopped, it happened by chance that the moon hung directly over it, a circumstance which produced a wonderful effect and astonished the whole company." The diners jumped up from the table to see. Then the curtain dropped, and the guests returned to their seats for another course. A flourish of trumpets and cymbals announced an elaborate free lottery. On either side of the large curtain, a small curtain was raised, revealing brightly lit booths, with porcelain objects, flowers, ribbons, fans, combs, purses, gloves, sword knots, and other finery available. Once all of these items had been taken, dessert was served, and the company danced until six in the morning.

The party was a triumph. Peter and his entourage, including the Holsteiners, praised Catherine. In her *Memoirs,* she basked in her achievement. "The Grand Duchess is kindness itself," she records people as saying. "She gave presents to everyone; she is charming; she smiled and took pleasure in making us all dance, eat, and make merry."

"In short," Catherine purred, "I was found to possess qualities which had not been recognized before, and I thereby disarmed my enemies. This had been my goal."

In June 1757, a new French ambassador, the Marquis de l'Hôpital, had arrived in St. Petersburg. Versailles was well informed about Elizabeth's illnesses and Catherine's growing influence, and the marquis was advised to "please the empress, but at the same time to ingratiate himself at the young court." When l'Hôpital paid his first ceremonial visit to the Summer Palace, it was Catherine who received him. She and her guest waited as long as possible for the empress to appear, but finally sat down together to supper and began the ball without her. It was during the White Nights, and the room had to be artificially darkened for guests to enjoy the full effect of the hundreds of candles. Finally, in the gentler light, Elizabeth appeared. Her face was still handsome, but her swollen legs did not permit her to dance. After a few words of greeting, she retired to the gallery and from there sadly watched the brilliant scene.

L'Hôpital then set about his mission of strengthening France's ties with Russia. He began by pressing for Hanbury-Williams's recall to England and Poniatowski's return to Poland. He was warmly received by the Shuvalovs, but he was rebuffed at the young court. Peter had no sympathy for an enemy of Prussia, and Catherine remained linked to Bestuzhev, Hanbury-Williams, and Poniatowski. Unable to counteract the influence of these three, l'Hôpital reported to his government that attempts to influence the young court were useless. "The grand duke is as completely a Prussian as the grand duchess is an incorrigible Englishwoman," he said.

Nevertheless, the French ambassador did manage to achieve a major goal: he succeeded in getting rid of his English diplomatic rival, Hanbury-Williams. He and his government pressed Elizabeth to force the recall of an envoy whose king, they pointed out, was now an ally of their mutual enemy, Frederick of Prussia. Elizabeth accepted this logic, and, in the summer of 1757, King George II was informed that his ambassador's presence was no longer desired in St. Petersburg. Sir Charles was willing to leave; his liver was failing. But when the moment arrived, he was reluctant. In October 1757 he called on Catherine for the last time. "I love you as my father," she told him. "I count myself happy to have been enabled to acquire your affection." His health worsened. After a stormy passage down the Baltic, he arrived, debilitated, in Hamburg and was hurried by doctors to England. There the elegant, witty ambassador degenerated into an embittered invalid, and, a year later, he ended his life by suicide. King George II, perhaps feeling responsibility for scuttling the alliance that Sir Charles had worked to negotiate, ordered that he be buried in Westminster Abbey.

❧35❧

Apraksin's Retreat

RUSSIA, bound by her alliance with Austria, had been nominally at war with Prussia since September 1756, when Frederick invaded Saxony. By late spring of 1757, however, not a single Russian soldier had marched. It was the first war of Elizabeth's reign, and the victories of her father, Peter the Great, almost four decades earlier, had faded from Russian memory. No money had been spent on the army, and the troops were badly trained and poorly equipped. Morale was low, not only because Elizabeth had promised to send this army against Frederick, the foremost general of the age, but also because the empress's declining health meant that the Russian crown might soon be placed on the head of a young man who was King Frederick of Prussia's fervent admirer.

In the months before the war, Bestuzhev had promoted a friendship between Catherine and his own friend General Stepan Apraksin.

A descendant of Peter the Great's most succesful admiral, Apraksin was described by Hanbury-Williams as "a very corpulent man, lazy, and good-natured." His friendship with the chancellor, rather than his military skill, had earned him command of the army being assembled to invade East Prussia. Once appointed, Apraksin had refused to embark on a winter campaign. He had political as well as military reasons for his caution. The empress's uncertain health and the grand duke's pro-Prussian sentiments made it obvious that the war would end as soon as Peter came to the throne. In these circumstances, even an aggressive general might be forgiven for not risking his own future by plunging ahead. Apraksin might also be excused for uneasiness about Catherine. She was born a German; Frederick had helped arrange her marriage; and her mother had been widely suspected of being a Prussian agent. In this reasoning, he was wrong. Catherine, now caught up in the politics of the Russian court, hoped for a Russian victory that would restore Bestuzhev's prestige and prevent the final triumph of his and her mutual enemies, the Shuvalovs. Before Apraksin left to invade East Prussia, Catherine tried to make certain that he knew her views. When the general's wife came to see her, Catherine spoke of her own worries about the empress's health and said that she greatly regretted the departure of Apraksin at a time when she thought little reliance could be placed on the Shuvalovs. Apraksin's wife repeated this to her husband, who was pleased and passed the grand duchess's words along to Bestuzhev.

In mid-May 1757, the portly, red-faced field soldier, physically unable to mount a horse, climbed into his carriage and set out for East Prussia at the head of eighty thousand men. At the end of June, the army seized the fortress town of Memel, on the Baltic coast. On August 17, Apraksin defeated a part of the Prussian army in a battle at Gross-jägersdorf, in East Prussia. It was not a brilliant victory; Frederick was not present and the Russians outnumbered their enemies by three to one. Even so, Russian national pride and expectations soared. Then, a strange thing happened. Instead of following up his victory by advancing into East Prussia and capturing Königsberg, the provincial capital, Apraksin remained motionless for two weeks, after which he turned around and retreated by forced marches so precipitous that his withdrawal appeared to be a rout. He burned his wagons and ammunition, destroyed his stores and powder, spiked and abandoned his cannon, and burned villages behind him so they could provide no shelter for a pursuing enemy. He halted only when he reached the safety of the fortress of Memel.

In St. Petersburg, elation turned to shock. The public could not understand what had happened, and Apraksin's friends could find no way to justify his behavior. Catherine could not explain the marshal's chaotic retreat, but she speculated that he may have been receiving alarming news about the empress's health. If this were true and Elizabeth were to die, her death would signal an immediate end to the war. He would be needed in Russia, and, rather than advancing farther into Prussia, his duty would be to fall back to the Russian frontier.

Apraksin's retreat provoked angry complaints from the Austrian and French ambassadors. Bestuzhev was alarmed. Because Apraksin was his friend and had received command of the army from him, the chancellor knew that he would bear a share of blame. Faced with the political necessity of a renewed offensive, which would restore Russia's prestige among her allies and his own with the empress, he asked Catherine to write to the general. Catherine did so, warning Apraksin of the harmful rumors circulating in Petersburg and of the difficulty his friends were having in explaining his retreat. She begged him to retrace his steps, resume his advance, and carry out his orders from the government. Ultimately, she wrote three letters, all harmless, although later they were to be produced as evidence that the grand duchess was interfering in matters beyond her concern. Bestuzhev forwarded these letters to Apraksin. The letters were never answered.

Meanwhile, St. Petersburg was a cauldron of recrimination. Elizabeth, pressed by the Shuvalovs and the French ambassador, relieved Apraksin of his command, and sent him to one of his estates to await investigation. General Wilhelm Fermor took over the army, and, despite bad weather, moved forward and seized Königsberg on January 18, 1758. Fermor also tried to clear his predecessor by pointing out that, through no fault of Apraksin's, the Russian soldiers had not been paid, that they were short of ammunition, weapons, and clothing, and that the men were desperately hungry. With endurance and courage, they had defeated the Prussians at Grossjägersdorf, but the effort had proved too much, and Apraksin, unable to supply his troops in enemy territory, had been compelled to retreat.

Fermor's account was only partially accurate. The decision to re-

treat had not been made by Apraksin. After the victory at Grossjägersdorf, the general had informed the war council in St. Petersburg of the
problems he and the army faced. The council had met three times—on
August 27, September 13, and September 28, 1757—and had ordered
Apraksin to withdraw. These facts had been withheld from Vienna,
Paris, and the people of St. Petersburg. Elizabeth had concurred in this
withdrawal but never admitted it. Catherine had not known.

On September 8, at Tsarskoe Selo, Elizabeth went on foot from the
palace to attend Mass at the parish church near the palace gate. Scarcely
had the service begun when, feeling unwell, she left the church, descended a short flight of steps, staggered, and collapsed unconscious on
the grass. The empress's attendants, following behind, found her surrounded by a crowd of people who had come from nearby villages to
hear Mass. At first, no one knew what was wrong. The attendants covered her with a white cloth, and members of the court went to look for
a doctor and a surgeon. The first to arrive was a surgeon, a French refu-
gee, who bled her while she lay unconscious on the ground in the middle of the crowd. The treatment failed to revive her. The doctor, a
Greek, took longer to arrive; being himself unable to walk, he had to be
carried to her in an armchair. Screens and a couch were brought from
the palace. Placed on the couch behind the screens, Elizabeth stirred
and opened her eyes but did not recognize anyone and spoke unintel-
ligibly. After two hours, she was carried on the couch into the palace.
The consternation of the court, already immense, was increased by the
fact that the collapse had occurred in public. Until then, the state of the
empress's health had been a tightly kept secret. Suddenly, it was public
knowledge.

Catherine learned of the incident the following morning at Oranienbaum from a note sent by Poniatowski. She hurried to tell Peter. A
messenger, sent to ask for more news, returned with the information
that Elizabeth was able to speak only with difficulty. Everyone realized
that something more serious than a fainting spell had happened; today
we might realize that Elizabeth had suffered a stroke.

After Elizabeth's collapse, everyone in St. Petersburg linked Elizabeth's
health and Apraksin's retreat with concerns about the succession to the

throne. "If the empress should die," the Marquis de l'Hôpital wrote to Versailles on November 1, "we shall see a sudden palace revolution, for the grand duke will never be allowed to reign." Some believed that the empress would disinherit her nephew in favor of three-year-old Paul. A rumor suggested that with Paul on the throne under the control of the Shuvalovs, his parents, Peter and Catherine, would both be sent back to Holstein.

In mid-January 1758, Alexander Shuvalov interrogated Apraksin. The general's testimony included his sworn denial that he had received any political or military directions from Catherine. Apraksin did admit to receiving correspondence from the grand duchess, and he handed over to Shuvalov all of his personal papers, including the three letters Catherine had written to him. Catherine was to see these letters again.

A year after his dismissal, Apraksin was brought before a judge to receive his sentence: "And there now remains no course but—" Apraksin, overweight and apoplectic, never heard the end of the judge's sentence. Expecting the words "torture" and "death," he fell dead on the floor. The judge's last words were to have been "to set him free."

❧36❧

Catherine's Daughter

IN THE SPRING OF 1757, Catherine realized that she was pregnant with Poniatowski's child. By the end of September, she stopped appearing in public. Her absence annoyed Peter, because when his wife was willing to appear at ceremonial functions, he was able to remain in his apartment. Empress Elizabeth, still unwell, made no public appearances, and with Catherine unavailable, the whole burden of representing the imperial family now fell on him. Irritated, the grand duke said to Lev Naryshkin, in the hearing of others, "God knows where my wife gets her pregnancies. I have no idea whether this child is mine and whether I ought to take responsibility for it."

Lev, true to character, ran to carry this remark to Catherine. Alarmed, she turned to Naryshkin and said, "You fool! Go back and ask the grand duke to swear that he has not slept with his wife. Tell him that if he is ready to swear such an oath, you will go immediately and inform Alexander Shuvalov so that appropriate action may be taken."

Lev raced back to Peter and asked him to swear the oath. Peter, too frightened of his aunt to make such a statement, refused. "Go to the devil!" he shouted. "And don't ever speak to me about this matter again!"

At midnight on December 9, 1757, Catherine began having contractions. Madame Vladislavova summoned Peter, and Alexander Shuvalov went to inform the empress. Peter arrived in Catherine's room wearing his formal Holstein uniform, with top boots, spurs, a sash around his waist, and an enormous sword hanging at his side. Surprised, Catherine asked the reason for this costume. Peter replied that in this uniform he was ready to fulfill his duty as an officer of Holstein (not a grand duke of Russia) to defend the ducal house (not the Russian empire). Catherine's first thought was that he was joking; then she realized that he was drunk. She told him to leave quickly so that his aunt would not have the double annoyance of seeing him reeling and also dressed head to foot in his Germanic Holstein uniform, which Elizabeth loathed. With the help of the midwife, who assured him that his wife would not give birth for some time, she convinced him and he departed.

Elizabeth arrived. When she asked where her nephew was, she was told that he had just left and would soon be back. Catherine's labor pains began to subside, and the midwife said that this respite could last some hours. The empress returned to her apartment, and Catherine lay back and slept until morning. She awoke feeling occasional contractions but was free of them for most of the day. In the evening, she was hungry and ordered supper. She ate and, rising from the table, was seized by sharp pains. The grand duke and the empress returned; both were just entering the room when Catherine gave birth to a daughter. The new mother immediately asked the empress to allow the child to be named Elizabeth. The empress declared that the infant should be named Anna, after her own older sister, Peter's mother, Anna Petrovna. The baby was immediately taken away to the nursery in the empress's apartment, where her three-year-old brother, Paul, awaited her. Six days later, the empress, as godmother, held little Anna over the baptismal font and brought Catherine a gift of sixty thousand rubles. This time, simultaneously, she gave an equal amount to her nephew.

"It is said that the public celebrations were magnificent," Catherine said, "but I did not see any. I remained in my bed alone without company except Madame Vladislavova. No one set foot in my apartment or sent to ask how I was." This was untrue: Catherine's loneliness lasted only a single day. It was true that her newborn was snatched away as Paul had been, but Catherine had expected that this would happen, and she suffered less. Otherwise, she was prepared. Having suffered isolation and neglect after Paul's birth, she had made different arrangements this time. Her bedroom was not subject to drafts from poorly fitted windows. Knowing that only in secrecy would her friends dare to visit her, she had a large screen placed beside her bed, concealing an alcove containing tables, chairs, and a comfortable settee. When the curtain on that side of her bed was drawn, nothing could be observed. When the curtain was opened and the screen drawn aside, Catherine could see the smiling faces of her friends in the alcove. If anyone else who entered the room asked what was behind the closed barrier, they were told that it was the commode. This little fortress, constructed with forethought and guile, remained secure.

On New Year's Day 1758, the court celebrations were to end with another display of fireworks, and Count Peter Shuvalov, Grand Master of the Artillery, came to explain to Catherine what was planned. In the anteroom, Madame Vladislavova told Shuvalov that she thought that the grand duchess was sleeping, but that she would go and see whether he could be received. In fact, Catherine was far from asleep. She was in her bed, and in the alcove was a little group including Poniatowski, still resisting his recall and visiting Catherine every day.

When Madame Vladislavova knocked on her door. Catherine closed the curtain on the screen side of her bed, received Vladislavova, and told her to bring in the visitor. Catherine's friends behind the screen and curtain smothered their laughter. When Peter Shuvalov entered, Catherine apologized for keeping him waiting, having "only just awakened," reinforcing this fib by rubbing her eyes. Their conversation was lengthy and continued until the count said that he had to leave in order not to keep the empress waiting for the fireworks to begin.

Once Shuvalov had gone, Catherine pulled aside the curtain. The screen was pushed back and she found her friends exhausted, hungry, and thirsty. "You should not die of hunger or thirst while keeping me company," she told them. She closed her curtain again and rang her bell. When Madame Vladislavova appeared, Catherine asked for supper—at least six good dishes, she specified. When the supper arrived and the servants were gone, her friends came out and threw themselves on the food. "This evening was one of the merriest in my life," Catherine said. "When the bewildered servants came back to clear away the dishes, I think they were surprised at my appetite." Her guests departed in high spirits. Poniatowski put on the blond wig and cloak he used on all of his nocturnal visits to the palace. In this disguise, when the sentries asked, "Who goes there?" he replied, "One of the grand duke's musicians." The ruse always worked.

Six weeks after the birth, the churching ceremony for Catherine's new daughter was held in the small palace chapel. But little Anna's ceremony was sadly different from the one celebrated for her long-awaited brother, Paul. Indeed, Catherine said that for Anna, the chapel's size was sufficient because "except for Alexander Shuvalov, no one attended." Peter and Poniatowski were absent. Indeed, no one appeared to care much about this daughter, who, frail from birth, survived only fifteen months. When she died, she was buried in the Alexander Nevsky Monastery with Catherine and Elizabeth, but neither Peter nor Poniatowski, present. At the ceremony, both women bent over the open casket and, following the rites of the Orthodox Church, kissed the small figure on her pale, white forehead. Soon, Anna was forgotten. In her *Memoirs*, Catherine never mentions her daughter's death.

❧37❧

The Fall of Bestuzhev

CHANCELLOR BESTUZHEV'S INFLUENCE was waning. The animosity of the Shuvalovs and Vice-Chancellor Michael Vorontsov was stoked by the French ambassador, who blamed him for the retreat of Bestuzhev's friend General Apraksin. The crisis reached a decisive moment when Vorontsov received a visit from the Marquis de l'Hôpital. Waving a paper, the French ambassador said, "Count, I have just received a message from my government. I am told that if, within fifteen days, Chancellor Bestuzhev has not been removed and replaced by you, it is with him that I must deal henceforth." Alarmed, Vorontsov hurried to Ivan Shuvalov. They went together to the empress and warned that Count Bestuzhev's shadow was dimming her own prestige in Europe.

Elizabeth had never particularly liked her chancellor, but he was a legacy from the father she had idolized, and over the years she had grown to rely on him to manage most of the everyday business of government. The Shuvalovs had never been able to persuade the empress to make a change, but now she wavered. She was told that it was common knowledge in Vienna and Versailles that Bestuzhev had been paid a substantial English pension for many years. She was told that letters from Catherine to Apraksin had been passed through the chancellor's hands. She learned that Russia's allies felt they had been betrayed by the corruptibility of her generals and ministers and by the machinations of the young court. If a few unimportant letters had been found, why should not others of a more dangerous nature have been written and then destroyed or hidden? Why was Catherine interfering in matters concerning the crown? It was pointed out that the young court had been going its own way for a long time, flouting her wishes. Was not Poniatowski staying on in St. Petersburg simply because Catherine wanted him and because Bestuzhev preferred to obey the grand duchess rather than the monarch? Was not everybody running to the young court to flatter the rulers of tomorrow? Elizabeth was assured that she had only to arrest Bestuzhev and have his papers examined to find documents that would prove the chancellor's complicity with the grand duchess on matters verging on treason.

Elizabeth ordered a meeting of the war council for the evening of February 14, 1758. The chancellor was summoned. Bestuzhev sent word that he was ill. His excuse was rejected, and he was ordered to come immediately. He obeyed, and, upon arrival, he was arrested. His offices, titles, and orders were stripped from him, and he was sent back to his house a prisoner—without anyone troubling to tell him of what crimes he was accused. To make certain that the overthrow of the leading statesman of the empire would not be challenged, a company of the Imperial Guard was ordered out. As the guardsmen were marching along the Moika Canal, where Counts Alexander and Peter Shuvalov lived, the soldiers were cheerful, telling one another, "Thank God, we are going to arrest those cursed Shuvalovs!" When the men realized that it was not the Shuvalovs but Bestuzhev who was to be arrested, they grumbled, "It is not this man. It is the others who trample on the people."

Catherine learned about the arrest the following morning in a note from Poniatowski. The note added that three other men—the Venetian jeweler Bernardi; her former Russian language teacher Adadurov;

and Elagin, a former adjutant of Count Razumovsky's who had become a friend of Poniatowski's—had also been arrested. Reading this note, Catherine understood that she might be implicated. She was a friend and ally of Bestuzhev's. Bernardi, the jeweler, was a man whose profession gave him entrée to all of the leading houses in St. Petersburg. Everyone trusted him, and Catherine had used him to send and receive messages from Bestuzhev and Poniatowski. Adadurov, her teacher, had remained devoted to her, and she had recommended him to Count Bestuzhev. Elagin, she said, was, "a loyal, honest man; once one gained his affection, one did not lose it. He had always shown marked zeal and devotion for me."

Upon reading Poniatowski's note, she was alarmed, but steeled herself not to display weakness. "With a dagger in my heart, so to speak," she said, "I dressed and went to Mass where it seemed to me that most of the faces were as long as my own. No one said anything to me." In the evening, she went to a ball. There, she marched up to Prince Nikita Trubetskoy, one of the commissioners appointed to assist Alexander Shuvalov in examining the arrested men.

"What do all these wonderful things mean?" she whispered to him. "Have you found more crimes than criminals or more criminals than crimes?"

"We have done what we were ordered to do," Trubetskoy replied stolidly. "But as for crimes, we are still searching for them. Up to now, we have not found any." His response encouraged Catherine, who also noted that the empress, having just ordered the arrest of her senior minister, failed to appear that night.

The next day, Gottlieb von Stambke, the Holstein administrator who was close to Bestuzhev, brought Catherine good news. He said that he had just received a clandestine note from Count Bestuzhev asking him to tell the grand duchess that she should not worry because he had had time to burn all his papers. These included, most significantly, the drafts of his proposal that the grand duchess share power with Peter after Elizabeth's death. Further, the former chancellor had said that he would keep Stambke informed of what happened to him during his interrogation and would pass along the questions put to him. Catherine asked Stambke through what channel he had received Bestuzhev's note. Stambke said that Bestuzhev's horn player had passed it to him, and that, in future, all communications were to be placed in a pile of bricks near Bestuzhev's house.

A few days later, Stambke came back to Catherine's room, frightened and pale, to tell her that his correspondence and that of Count Bestuzhev with Count Poniatowski had been intercepted. The horn player had been arrested. Stambke himself expected to be dismissed, if not arrested, at any moment, and he had come to say goodbye. Catherine was certain that she had done nothing wrong, and she knew that, aside from Michael Vorontsov, Ivan Shuvalov, and the French ambassador, everyone in St. Petersburg was convinced that Count Bestuzhev was innocent of any crime.

Already, the commission charged with prosecuting the former chancellor was struggling. It became known that the day after Count Bestuzhev's arrest, a manifesto had been drafted secretly in Ivan Shuvalov's house, intended to inform the public why the empress had been obliged to arrest her old servant. Unable to find and state any specific offense, the accusers had decided that the crime was to be lèse-majesté: offending the empress by "attempting to sow discord between Her Imperial Majesty and Their Imperial Highnesses." On February 27, 1758, the manifesto was published, announcing the arrest, the charges, the fact that Bestuzhev had been stripped of his offices and decorations and that he would be examined by a special commission. The flimsy document convinced no one in St. Petersburg, and the public found it ludicrous to threaten the former statesman with exile, confiscation of property, and other punishments, with no evidence of a crime, no trial, and no judgment.

The first step taken by the commissioners was equally absurd. They ordered all Russian ambassadors, envoys, and officials at foreign courts to send copies of all dispatches Count Bestuzhev had written to them during the twenty years he had administered Russia's foreign affairs. It was alleged that the chancellor had written whatever he pleased, often in opposition to the wishes of the empress. But because Elizabeth never wrote or signed anything, it was impossible to prove that the chancellor had acted contrary to her orders. As for verbal orders, the empress could hardly have given any significant number of these to the chancellor, who sometimes waited for months without being admitted to see her. Nothing came of this. None of the personnel in embassies bothered to examine archives ranging back over many years in order to search for crimes committed by the man whose instructions these same subordinates had loyally obeyed. Who knew but that this might lead to finding themselves implicated? Besides, once these documents arrived in St. Petersburg, it would take years of research to locate and interpret whatever nuggets, favorable or unfavorable, they might contain. The order was ignored. The inquiry lumbered along for a year. No evidence was produced, but the former chancellor was exiled to one of his own estates where he remained until, three years later, Catherine became empress.

With Stambke's departure for Holstein, Catherine's handling of the affairs of Peter's duchy ended. The empress told her nephew that she disapproved of his wife's involvement in the ruling of his hereditary duchy. Peter, who had enthusiastically encouraged Catherine's participation in that work, now declared that he agreed with his aunt. The empress then formally asked the king of Poland to recall Count Poniatowski.

When she heard of Stambke's dismissal and that Poniatowski was to be sent home, Catherine reacted quickly. She ordered Vasily Shkurin, her valet, to gather all of her papers and account books and bring them to her. Once everything was in her room, she sent him away, and then threw everything—every document, and every paper and letter she had ever received—into the fire; this was how the manuscript of her "Portrait of a Fifteen-Year-Old Philosopher," written in 1744 for Count Gyllenborg, disappeared. When these materials had been reduced to ashes, she called Shkurin back: "You are a witness to the fact that all my papers and accounts are burned. If you are ever asked where they are, you will be able to swear that you saw me burn them." Shkurin was grateful that she had spared him involvement.

✵38✵

A Gamble

ON THE DAY before Lent, the last day of Carnival, 1758, Catherine decided that she had had enough of discretion and timidity. In the weeks that had followed her confinement, she had not appeared in public. Now, she decided to attend a Russian play scheduled for performance at the court theater. Catherine knew that Peter did not like the

Russian theater and that even talk of it upset him. This time, Peter would have another, more personal reason for not wishing her to go: he would not want to be deprived of the company of Elizabeth Vorontsova. If Catherine went to the theater, her maids of honor, including Elizabeth Vorontsova, would be obliged to accompany her. Aware of this, Catherine sent word to Count Alexander Shuvalov to order a carriage. Shuvalov promptly appeared to tell her that the grand duke opposed her plan to go to the theater. Catherine replied that, as she was excluded from her husband's society, it could not matter to him whether she was alone in her room or sitting in her box at the theater. Shuvalov bowed and departed.

Moments later, Peter burst into Catherine's room "in a fearful passion, screaming, accusing me of taking pleasure in enraging him, and saying that I had chosen to go to the theater because I knew he did not like this kind of play." He shouted that he would forbid her having a carriage. She told him that if he did this, she would walk. Peter stamped out. As the hour of the performance approached, she sent to ask Count Shuvalov whether her carriage was ready. He came and repeated that the grand duke had forbidden any carriage being provided. Catherine replied that she would go on foot and that if her ladies and gentlemen were forbidden to accompany her, she would go alone. Furthermore, she said, she would write and complain to the empress.

"What will you say to her?" Shuvalov asked.

"I will tell her," Catherine said, "that in order to arrange for my husband a rendezvous with my maids of honor, you have encouraged him to prevent me from going to the theater where I might have the pleasure of seeing Her Imperial Majesty. Moreover, I will beg her to send me home because I am weary of and disgusted by the role I am made to play here, alone and neglected in my room, hated by the grand duke and disliked by the empress. I do not want to be a burden to anyone any longer or to bring misfortune to whomever approaches me, especially my poor servants, many of whom have already been exiled because I have been good to them. I am going to write to Her Majesty this moment. And I will see whether you can avoid taking this letter to her." It was a masterpiece of manipulative rhetoric.

Shuvalov left the room and Catherine began writing her letter. She began by thanking Elizabeth for all the kindnesses shown her since her arrival in Russia. She said that, unfortunately, events had proved that she had not deserved these favors because she had called down on herself not only the grand duke's hatred but the displeasure of Her Imperial Majesty. Considering these failures, she begged the empress to put a quick end to her misery by sending her home to her family in whatever manner she judged appropriate. As for her children, she said that she never saw them, although they lived in the same building only a few yards away; therefore, it made little difference to her whether she was in the same place or hundreds of miles distant. She knew that the empress gave them better care than anything she could provide. She begged Elizabeth to continue this care, and, confident that the empress would do so, she said she would spend the rest of her life praying for the empress, the grand duke, her children, and all those who had done her both good and evil. Now, however, sorrow had so damaged her that she must concentrate on preserving her own life. For this reason, she begged Elizabeth for permission to go, first to take the waters somewhere so that she could recover her health, and then to go home to her family in Germany.

The letter written, Catherine summoned Count Shuvalov. He arrived and announced that her carriage was ready. She handed him her letter, and told him that he could tell the maids of honor who did not wish to accompany her to the theater that they were excused. Leaving her, Shuvalov told Peter that the grand duchess had said that he should decide which women should go with his wife and which should stay with him. As Catherine passed through the antechamber, she found Peter seated with Elizabeth Vorontsova, playing cards. Seeing his wife, Peter rose—something he had never done before—and Countess Vorontsova rose with him. Catherine responded with a curtsy and went to her carriage. That evening, the empress did not appear at the theater, but when Catherine returned home, Count Shuvalov told her that Elizabeth had agreed to grant her another interview.

Catherine's behavior and her letter to the empress were a gamble. She did not want to leave Russia. She had invested sixteen years, more than half her life, all of her young womanhood, in her ambition to become "a queen." She knew that her tactics were risky, but she believed they would succeed. She was convinced that if the Shuvalovs had any idea of actually sending her home, or of intimidating her by threatening banishment, her plea that she be allowed to leave was the best method of undermining their plan. Catherine knew that, for Elizabeth, the succession was all-important, and that with the young, deposed tsar Ivan VI still alive, the empress would not wish to see this issue reignited. Catherine also realized that the primary complaint against her was that her marriage had not been a success. She also knew that the empress fully shared her views of Peter. When talking or writing about her nephew privately, Elizabeth either burst into tears at the misfortune of having such an heir or showered him with contempt. After Elizabeth's death, Catherine discovered among her papers two such comments in the empress's hand; one addressed to Ivan Shuvalov, the other to Alexis Razumovsky. To the first, she had written, "Today, my damned nephew has greatly irritated me," and to the other, "My nephew is a fool; the devil take him."

In constructing her account of this tense, intricate situation, Catherine, as a much older woman, suspended her narrative of events to look at herself, her life, and her character. Whatever happened, she wrote, "I felt myself possessed of sufficient courage either to rise or fall without being carried away by undue pride on the one hand, or being humbled and dispirited on the other." Her intentions, she told herself, had always been honest. Although she had understood from the beginning that to love a husband who was not lovable and who made no effort to become so was a difficult and probably impossible task, she believed that she had made a sincere effort to devote herself to him and his interests. Her advice had always been the best she could give. If, when she first came to Russia, Peter had been affectionate, she would have opened her heart to him. Now she saw that, among his whole entourage, she was the woman to whom he paid the least attention. She rejected this state of affairs:

> My natural pride made the idea of being miserable intolerable to me. I used to say to myself that happiness and misery depend on ourselves. If you feel unhappy, rise above it and act so that your happiness may be independent of all outside events. I had been born with this disposition, and a face that was, at the very least, interesting, and which pleased at first sight without art or pretense. My disposition was naturally so conciliatory that no one ever spent a quarter of an hour with me without feeling perfectly at ease and talking to me as though

they had known me for a long time. I easily won the confidence
of those who had anything to do with me because everyone felt
that I displayed honesty and goodwill. If I may be allowed to be
frank, I would say about myself that I was a true gentleman
with a mind more male than female, but, together with this, I
was anything but masculine and, combined with the mind and
character of a man, I possessed the attractions of a loveable
woman. May I be pardoned for offering this candid expression
of my feelings instead of trying to cover them a veil of false
modesty.

This evaluation of her qualities—self-laudatory and self-justifying—
led to a general commentary on the conflict between emotion and morality in the lives of human beings. It is a passionate statement—a
personal confession, almost—and it brings to Catherine a sympathy
and understanding that she is sometimes not given:

I have just said that I was attractive; consequently, half the
road of temptation was already traveled, and it is only human in
such situations that one should not stop half way. For to tempt
and to be tempted are closely allied and, in spite of all the finest
maxims of morality, whenever emotion has anything to do with
the matter, one is already much further involved than one realizes. And I have still not learned how to prevent emotion being
excited. Flight, perhaps, is the only remedy. But there are cases
and circumstances, in which flight is impossible. For how can
one escape, fly, or turn one's back, in the middle of a court?
Such an act itself would give rise to gossip. And if you do not
run away, nothing is more difficult, in my opinion, than to escape from something that essentially attracts you. All statements made to the contrary will appear only a prudishness
quite out of harmony with the natural instincts of the human
heart. Besides, one cannot hold one's heart in one's hand, tight-
ening or relaxing one's grasp at will.

The day after going to the theater, Catherine began a long wait for the
empress's reply to her letter. She was still waiting several weeks later
when Count Shuvalov announced one morning that the empress had

just dismissed Madame Vladislavova. After a burst of tears, Catherine gathered herself and replied that, of course, Her Majesty had the right to appoint or dismiss whomever she pleased, but that she was grieved to find, more and more, that all who came near her were doomed to become victims of Her Majesty's disfavor. In order that there be fewer victims, she asked Shuvalov to appeal to the empress to put a quick end to this situation in which she only made other people miserable. She begged to be sent back to her family immediately.

That evening, after a day of refusing to eat, Catherine was alone in her room when one of her younger maids of honor came in. In tears, the young woman said, "We all are afraid that you will sink under these afflictions. Let me to go to my uncle—he is your confessor as well as the empress's. I will speak to him and tell him everything you wish, and I promise that he will speak to the empress in a way that will please you." Trusting her, Catherine described what she had written to the empress. The young woman saw her uncle, Father Theodore Dubyansky, and returned to tell Catherine that the priest advised the grand duchess to announce during the middle of the night that she was seriously ill and wanted to confess, and to ask that he, her father confessor, be sent to her. This way, he would be able to tell the empress what he had heard from Catherine's own lips. Catherine approved this plan, and between two and three in the morning, she rang her bell. A maid entered and Catherine said that she was dangerously ill and wished to make her confession. Instead of her confessor, Count Alexander Shuvalov hurried into the room. Catherine repeated her request for the priest. Shuvalov sent for doctors. When they arrived, she told them that she needed spiritual, not medical, assistance. One of the doctors felt her pulse and reported that it was weak. Catherine whispered that it was her soul that was in danger; that her body no longer needed doctors.

Eventually, Father Dubyansky arrived, and he and Catherine were left alone. The black-robed priest with a long white beard sat by her bed and they talked for an hour and a half. She described to him the past and present state of her affairs, the grand duke's behavior toward her, the Shuvalovs' hostility, how they were poisoning the empress's view of her, and the constant dismissal of her servants, particularly those who were most devoted to her. For these reasons, she said, she had written to the empress and begged to be sent home. She asked the priest to help her. He said he would do his best. He advised her that she should continue asking to be sent home, and he said that she would certainly not be sent away because they could not justify this dismissal in the eyes of the public. He agreed that the empress, having chosen her at a tender age, had largely abandoned her to her enemies; and said that Elizabeth would do far better to dismiss Elizabeth Vorontsova and the Shuvalovs. Moreover, he said, everyone was crying out at the Shuvalovs' injustice in the affair of Count Bestuzhev, of whose innocence everyone was convinced. He concluded by telling Catherine that he would go immediately to the empress's apartment, where he would sit and wait until Her Majesty awakened in order to speak to her and urge her to speed up the interview with Catherine she had promised. Meanwhile, he added, Catherine should remain in bed, which would reinforce his argument that the affliction and grief to which she was being subjected might cause her grave harm unless some remedy was found.

The confessor kept his promise and described Catherine's condition so vividly to Elizabeth that she summoned Alexander Shuvalov and ordered him to inquire whether the grand duchess's health would allow her to come and talk to her the following night. Catherine told Count Shuvalov that for such a purpose she would summon all her remaining strength.

❧39❧

Confrontation

ON THE EVENING of the following day—it was April 13, 1758, a week before Catherine's twenty-ninth birthday—Alexander Shuvalov told Catherine that after midnight he would come to escort her to the empress's apartment. At half past one, he arrived and said that the empress was ready. Catherine followed him through the halls, which seemed empty. Suddenly, she caught a glimpse of Peter ahead of her, also on his way, it seemed, toward his aunt's apartment. Catherine had not seen him since the night she had gone to the theater by herself.

In the empress's apartment, Catherine found her husband already present. Approaching Elizabeth, she fell on her knees and begged to be sent home to Germany. The empress tried to make her get up, but Catherine remained on her knees. Elizabeth, appearing to Catherine to be more sad than angry, said, "Why do you wish me to send you home?

Remember that you have children." Catherine's answer was prepared: "My children are in your hands and could not be better placed. I hope you will not abandon them." Elizabeth asked, "How shall I explain such a step to the people?" Again, Catherine was ready: "Your Imperial Majesty will tell them, if you see fit, all the reasons that have brought upon me your displeasure, and the hatred of the grand duke." "But how will you manage to live at your family's home?" the empress continued. "I will do as well as I did before you did me the honor of choosing me and taking me away," Catherine replied.

The empress again insisted that Catherine rise; this time, Catherine obeyed. Elizabeth paced back and forth. The long room where they were meeting had three windows, between which stood two dressing tables holding the empress's gold toilet service. Large screens had been placed in front of the windows. From the moment she entered, Catherine suspected that Ivan Shuvalov and perhaps others were hidden behind these screens; later, she learned that Ivan Shuvalov had, indeed, been there. Catherine also noticed that one of the basins on the dressing tables contained folded letters. The empress approached her and said, "God is my witness to how I wept when you were so dangerously ill on your arrival in Russia. If I had not loved you, I would not have kept you here." Catherine thanked the empress for her kindness. She said that she would never forget these things and would always consider it the greatest of personal misfortunes that she had incurred Her Majesty's displeasure.

Elizabeth's mood suddenly changed; she seemed to revert to a mental list of grievances drawn up in preparing for the interview. "You are dreadfully haughty," she said. "You imagine that there is no one so clever as you." Again, Catherine was ready: "If I ever had such a conceit, Madame, nothing would be more likely to destroy it than my present situation and this very conversation."

As the two women were talking, Catherine noticed that Peter was whispering to Alexander Shuvalov. Elizabeth saw this too and walked over to them. Catherine could not hear what the three of them were saying until her husband raised his voice and cried out, "She is dreadfully spiteful and very obstinate." Catherine, realizing that she was the subject, said to Peter, "If you are speaking of me, I am glad to tell you in the presence of Her Imperial Majesty that I am indeed spiteful to people who advise you to inflict injustice, and that I have become obstinate because I have seen that, by yielding, I have gained nothing but your hostility." Peter appealed to his aunt: "Your Majesty can see how malicious she is by what she is saying." But Catherine's words were making a different impression on the empress. Catherine saw as the conversation progressed that, although Elizabeth had been advised—or had resolved—to be severe with her, the empress's attitude was wavering.

For a while, Elizabeth continued to criticize. "You meddle in many things that do not concern you. How could you, for instance, presume to send orders to General Apraksin?" Catherine replied, "I, Madame? Send orders? Never has such an idea entered my head."

"How can you deny it?" Elizabeth said. "Your letters are there in the basin." She pointed to them. "You know that you were forbidden to write."

Catherine knew that she must admit to something. "It is true that I transgressed in this respect and I beg Your Majesty's forgiveness. But as my letters are there, these three letters will prove to Your Majesty that I never sent him any orders. In one of them, I told him what was being said of his behavior."

Elizabeth interrupted, "And why did you write this to him?"

Catherine replied, "Because I took an interest in the general, whom I liked very much. I begged him to follow your orders. The two other letters contain only congratulations on the birth of his son and New Year's greetings."

"Bestuzhev says there were many others," Elizabeth said.

"If Bestuzhev says this, he lies," Catherine responded.

"Well, then," the empress said, "since he is lying about you, I will have him put to torture." Catherine replied that, as sovereign, she could do what she liked, but that she, Catherine, had never written more than those three letters to Apraksin.

Elizabeth walked up and down the room, sometimes silent, sometimes addressing herself to Catherine, sometimes to her nephew or Count Shuvalov. "The grand duke showed much bitterness towards me, seeking to anger the empress against me," Catherine wrote in her *Memoirs*. "But because he went about this stupidly and displayed more passion than justice, he failed. She listened with a kind of involuntary approval to my responses to my husband's remarks. His behavior became so objectionable that the empress came up to me and said in a low voice, 'I have many more things to say to you, but I do not want to make things worse between the two of you than they are already.'" Seeing this sign of goodwill, Catherine whispered back, "And I, too, find it difficult to speak, in spite of my great desire to tell you all that is in my mind and heart." Elizabeth nodded and dismissed everyone, saying that it was very late. It was three o'clock in the morning.

Peter left first, then Catherine, followed by Shuvalov. Just as the count reached the door, the empress called him back. Catherine returned to her rooms and had started to undress when there was a knock on her door. It was Alexander Shuvalov. "He told me that the empress had spoken to him for some time, and had instructed him to tell me not to worry too much, and that she would have another conversation with me, alone and soon." She curtsied to Count Shuvalov and asked him to thank Her Imperial Majesty, and to hurry the moment of the second conversation. He told her not to speak of this to anyone, especially the grand duke.

Catherine was certain now that she would not be sent away. While waiting for the promised second interview, she kept mostly to her room. From time to time, she reminded Count Shuvalov that she was anxious to have her fate decided. On April 21, 1758, her twenty-ninth birthday, she was having dinner alone in her room when the empress sent word that she was drinking to Catherine's health. Catherine sent back her gratitude. When Peter learned of the empress's message, he sent a similar greeting. Poniatowski reported that the French ambassador, the Marquis de l'Hôpital, had spoken admiringly of her determination, and said that her resolution not to leave her apartment could only turn to her advantage. Catherine, taking l'Hôpital's remark as the treacherous praise of an enemy, decided to do the opposite. One Sunday, when no one was expecting it, she dressed and left her apartment. When she entered the anterooms where the ladies- and gentlemen-in-waiting of the young court were assembled, she saw their astonishment at seeing her. When Peter arrived, he was equally surprised. He came up and spoke to her briefly.

On May 23, 1758, almost six weeks after the meeting with Elizabeth, Alexander Shuvalov told Catherine that she should ask the empress, through him, for permission to see her children that afternoon. Afterward, Shuvalov said, she would have her second, long-promised private audience with the monarch. Catherine did as she was told and formally asked permission to see her two children. Shuvalov said that she could visit them at three o'clock. Catherine was punctual and remained with her children until Shuvalov arrived to tell her that the empress was ready. Catherine found Elizabeth alone; this time there were no screens. Catherine expressed her gratitude, and Elizabeth said, "I expect you to answer truthfully all the questions I shall ask you." Catherine promised that Elizabeth would hear nothing but the exact truth and that there was nothing she wanted more than to open her heart without reservation. Elizabeth asked if there really had been no more than three letters written to Apraksin. Catherine swore that there were only three. "Then," Catherine wrote, "she asked for details about the grand duke's mode of life."

At this climactic moment, Catherine's memoirs suddenly and inexplicably conclude. Her life continued for another thirty-eight years, and the rest of her story is told by her letters, political writings, official documents, and by other people—friends, enemies, and a multitude of observers, But no part of this story is more remarkable than Stanislaus Poniatowski's description of the episodes involving Catherine and himself that followed in the summer of 1758.

❧40❧

A Ménage à Quatre

STANISLAUS PONIATOWSKI did not leave Russia and Catherine. He resisted departure by feigning illness, sometimes spending the entire day in bed. In the summer of 1758, when the young court moved to Oranienbaum, Poniatowski was with Elizabeth's court at Peterhof, a few miles away. At night, disguised in his blond wig, he visited Catherine at Oranienbaum, where she received him in her separate, private pavilion.

Peter, absorbed with Elizabeth Vorontsova, never interfered in Poniatowski's affair with his wife. An intervention was always a possibility, but when this happened, it was by chance. In July 1758, as Poniatowski told the story in his memoirs, the Shuvalovs and the French ambassador were pressing the empress to send him home, and the Polish government was insisting that he return. He knew that soon he would have to comply.

The knowledge that I would have to leave made my frequent nocturnal visits to Oranienbaum even more frequent.

The good luck that always accompanied me during these visits made me lose all sense of danger. On July 6, I took a small closed carriage whose driver did not know me. That night— although there is no real night in northern Russia during the period of the White Nights—we unfortunately met the grand duke and his entourage, all of them half-drunk, on a road in the woods near Oranienbaum. My driver was halted and asked who was in the carriage. He replied, "a tailor" and we were allowed to proceed. But Elizabeth Vorontsova, who was with him, began making sarcastic remarks about "the tailor" which put the grand duke in a bad humor. The result was that as I was leaving, after spending a few hours with the grand duchess, I was assaulted by three men holding drawn sabers. They seized me by the collar like a thief and dragged me to the grand duke who, recognizing me, simply ordered my escorts to follow him and bring me along. They led me down a path to the sea and I thought my last hour had come. But we turned into a pavilion where the grand duke asked me bluntly whether I had slept with his wife. I said, "No."

"Tell me the truth," Peter said to Poniatowski, "because, if you do, then everything will be arranged. If not, you will go through some bad moments."

"I cannot say that I have done something I have not done," Ponia-towski lied.

Peter went into another room to consult with Brockdorff. Return-ing, he said, "Since you refuse to talk, you will stay here until further orders." He left and stationed a guard at the door. After two hours, Alexander Shuvalov appeared. Shuvalov, his face twitching, asked for an explanation. Instead of responding directly, Poniatowski took another approach: "I am sure you will understand, Count, that it is important to the honor of your court, as well as of myself, that all this should end as quickly as possible, and that you should get me out of here promptly."

Realizing that a scandal of unknown dimensions was looming, Shuvalov agreed and said he would arrange it. He came back an hour later and told Poniatowski that a carriage was ready to take him back to Peterhof. The carriage was so shabby that, at six in the morning, and at a short distance from Peterhof, Poniatowski got out and walked to the palace, wrapped in his cloak, with the brim of his hat pulled down over his eyes and ears; he thought this would arouse less suspicion than if he arrived in the disreputable vehicle in which he had just traveled. Reaching the building where his room was on the ground floor, he decided not to enter by the door; there was a chance of meeting someone. The windows were open to the summer night and Poniatowski climbed through the one he thought was his. He found myself in the room of his neighbor, General Roniker, who was shaving. The two stared at each other, then both burst out laughing. "Do not ask where I come from or why I arrive by the window," Poniatowski said, "but, as a good compatriot, swear you will never mention it." Roniker swore.

The next two days were uncomfortable for Catherine's lover. Within twenty-four hours, his adventure was known to the whole court. Everyone expected that Poniatowski would be required to leave the country immediately. Catherine's only hope of postponing her lover's departure was to placate her husband. Setting aside her pride, she approached Elizabeth Vorontsova, who was delighted to have the proud grand duchess before her as a supplicant. Soon, Catherine managed to send Poniatowski a note saying that she had succeeded in conciliating her husband's mistress, who would, in turn, appease the grand duke. This suggested to Poniatowski an approach that might make it possible for him to stay in Russia a little longer. At a court ball at Peterhof, he danced with Elizabeth Vorontsova, and while they performed a minuet, he whispered to her, "You know that you have it in your power to make several people very happy." Vorontsova, seeing a further opportunity to place the grand duchess under obligation, smiled and said, "Come to the Mon Plaisir villa tonight an hour after midnight."

At the appointed hour and place, Poniatowski met his new benefactress, who invited him in. "And there was the grand duke, very gay, welcoming me in a friendly and familiar way," Poniatowski wrote later. "Are you not a great fool not to have been frank with me from the beginning?" Peter said. "If you had, none of this mess would have happened."

Poniatowski accepted Peter's reproof, and, changing the subject, expressed his admiration for the perfect discipline of the grand duke's Holstein soldiers, guarding the palace. Peter was so pleased by this compliment that, after a quarter of an hour, he said, "Well, now that we are such good friends, I find there is someone missing here." He went to his wife's room, pulled her out of bed, leaving her only time to put a loose robe over her nightgown and a pair of slippers on her bare feet.

Then he brought her in, pointed at Poniatowski, and said, "Well, here he is! Now I hope everyone will be pleased with me." Catherine, imperturbable, responded by saying to her husband, "The only thing missing is that you should write to the vice chancellor, Count Vorontsov, to arrange the prompt return of our friend to Russia." Peter, enormously pleased with himself and his role in this scene, sat down and wrote the note. Then, he handed it to Elizabeth Vorontsova to countersign.

"Afterwards," Poniatowski wrote, "we all sat down, laughing and chattering and frolicking around a small fountain in the room as though we had not a care in the world. We did not separate until four in the morning. Mad as it may seem, I swear that this is the exact truth. Next day, everyone's attitude towards me was much nicer. Ivan Shuvalov spoke to me pleasantly. So did Vice Chancellor Vorontsov."

Not only did this amiability continue; it was enhanced by Peter himself. "The grand duke made me repeat my visit to Oranienbaum four times," Poniatowski said. "I arrived in the evening, walked up an unused staircase to the grand duchess's room, where I found the grand duchess, the grand duke and his mistress. We had supper together, after which he took his mistress away, saying to us, 'Well, my children, you do not need me any more, I think.' And I was able to stay as long as I liked."

No one seemed happier with this situation than Peter. It was his moment of triumph over Catherine. For many years, he had felt himself inferior to his wife. He had tried to humiliate her privately and in public. He had ignored her, shouted at her, ridiculed her, and betrayed her with other women. He had made condescending, usually inaccurate, remarks about her intrigues with other men. Now the moment had come when, with his mistress on his arm, he could smile across a table at Catherine and her lover on an equal basis. He was not embarrassed by being made a cuckold. Rather, for the first time in his life, he felt himself master of a situation. His complaisance was genuine; with nothing to hide, he exposed, and even gleefully helped spread, the scandal. Poniatowski no longer needed to wear a blond wig; there was nothing now to fear from Peter's sentries. Why bother? Why worry? Everyone knew.

For Catherine, however, the situation was different. She had been ready to engage in escapades like slipping out of the palace at night in male clothing. But she did not enjoy sitting down to supper with her gossip-loving husband and his saucy, malicious mistress, listening to their flighty conversation. It was not pleasant to see how much Elizabeth Vorontsova was enjoying the situation. Catherine was not cynical; she believed in love. The degrading of love, which pleased Peter, offended her. And she could not bear that Peter should consider Poniatowski as merely the male equivalent of Elizabeth Vorontsova. She regarded Poniatowski as a gentleman; Vorontsova she considered a trollop. Soon, a warning signal flashed in her mind. This nocturnal camaraderie was based on agreed, mutual adultery, and she realized that these episodes could spell a greater danger to her future than the hostility of the Shuvalovs. Even at the permissive court of Elizabeth, this arrangement between herself and Peter might be a barrier to her ambition. As Catherine feared, awareness of the ménage à quatre began to create a political scandal. L'Hôpital mentioned it when renewing his demands that Poniatowski be dismissed. Elizabeth understood that the reputation of her nephew and heir was being undermined. Poniatowski knew that he must go.

Saying goodbye, Catherine wept. With Poniatowski she had experienced the courtship of a gentle, cultured European. Afterward, her letters and his were filled with hope for a speedy reunion. Many years later, as empress of Russia, Catherine wrote to Gregory Potemkin, in whom she confided almost every detail about her previous life: "Poniatowski was loving and beloved from 1755 to 1758 and the liaison would have lasted forever if he himself had not got bored by it. On the day of his departure, I was more distressed than I can tell you. I don't think I ever cried so much in my life." In fact, Catherine's blaming of boredom on his part was unfair. They both had recognized that the situation had become impossible.

Many years later, as king of Poland, placed on this throne by his former lover Empress Catherine II of Russia, Poniatowski included in his memoirs a brief sketch of Peter. It is a damning portrait, but it also has elements of understanding, even sympathy:

> Nature made him a mere poltroon, a guzzler, an individual comic in all things. In one of the outpourings of his heart to me, he observed, "See how unhappy I am. If I had only entered into the service of the King of Prussia I would have served him to the best of my ability. By this present time, I should, I am

confident, have had a regiment and the rank of major general and perhaps even of lieutenant general. But far from it. Instead, they brought me here and made me a grand duke of this damned country." And then he railed against the Russian nation in his familiar, low, burlesque style, yet at times really very agreeably, for he did not lack a certain kind of spirit. He was not stupid, but mad, and as he loved to drink, this helped scramble his poor brains even further.

PART IV
"The Time Has Come!"

Panin, Orlov, and Elizabeth's Death

A S THE EMPRESS'S HEALTH deteriorated, Catherine considered her own political future. It seemed certain that Elizabeth would make no change in the succession and that Peter would follow his aunt on the throne. Catherine would be alone; her friends and political allies had been stripped away. The chancellor, Bestuzhev, had been disgraced and exiled. General Apraksin, also disgraced, was dead. Hanbury-Williams, the British ambassador, had returned home; now, he too was dead. Her lover, Stanislaus Poniatowski, had departed for Poland and bringing him back would be impossible. With Peter's incompetence now clear, Catherine could not help pondering what political role she might play in a new reign. It could be as Peter's wife and adviser, doing what she had done in helping him to manage the affairs of Holstein. But if Peter acted on his determination to marry Elizabeth Vorontsova, Catherine would have no role. If, somehow, Peter were to be replaced in the line of succession and Paul were to come to the throne, she might act as regent until the boy grew up. A more distant possibility of which Catherine sometimes dreamed was that she would play the supreme role herself. Which path would be open to her was unclear, but one thing was certain: whatever happened, she would need allies.

People were coming to her. One, surprisingly, was Ivan Shuvalov, the favorite of the failing Elizabeth, who began courting the grand duchess in a manner that led to suspicion that he would like to play the same role with the future empress that he had with Elizabeth. She was attracting other, less calculating and less obvious, new adherents and, eventually, a significant trio of dissimilar people gathered around her. One was a fastidious, sophisticated diplomat; another a young war hero; and the third, a passionate and impetuous young woman. Coming from different backgrounds, exhibiting different qualities, there was a single constant: all were Russians, a useful thing for an ambitious German woman with no Russian blood.

The eldest of these three was the diplomat, forty-two-year-old Count Nikita Panin. He was Bestuzhev's protégé and had survived his master's fall by having been absent from Russia when it occurred. The son of one of Peter the Great's generals, Panin was born in Danzig in 1718, educated abroad, and had come home to serve in the Guards. At twenty-nine, he had been appointed Russian envoy to Denmark by Bestuzhev. A few years later, he was transferred to Sweden, where, for twelve years, he had served as ambassador. In Stockholm, Panin was recognized as a cultivated, sophisticated, liberal-minded Russian, and, as such, a rarity. Panin had believed in Bestuzhev's policy of favoring Austria and England and opposing Prussia. When Bestuzhev fell and the Shuvalovs and Vorontsov forged their alliance with France, Panin, still in Stockholm, resisted their demand that he support this new alignment. Out of step, he resigned and, in the summer of 1760, came back to St. Petersburg. Elizabeth, recognizing his ability, shielded him from the Shuvalov-Vorontsov faction and appointed him chamberlain and chief tutor to her beloved Paul, placing him in a politically sheltered post that gave him prestige at court and an avid interest in the succession. Peter, unsurprisingly, was displeased by the choice of Panin. "Let the boy remain for the time being under Panin's supervision," he grumbled. "Soon, I shall take steps to provide for a more suitable military training." Panin, aware of Peter's hostility, was also, by character and education, a natural ally for Catherine, but the two—grand duchess and tutor—had different ideas about the future. Panin, believing that Peter was unfit to rule and should somehow be removed, wished Paul to be placed on the throne as a boy emperor with Catherine as regent. Catherine pretended to agree with Panin; "I had rather be the mother than the wife of the emperor," she told him. In reality, she had no desire to be subordinated to her own child; her ambition was to occupy the throne herself. Panin aligned himself with Catherine because she had been close to his patron, Bestuzhev; because she had faithfully maintained this allegiance throughout the former chancellor's disgrace; and because, in his mind, any arrangement involving her was preferable to seeing Peter on the throne. In addition, he shared her interest in Enlightenment political theory and in the appeal of a government by enlightened monarchy as advocated by Montesquieu. Panin knew that Catherine was discreet and that it was safe to discuss his ideas with her. They had worked out no plan of action—there were too many unknowns—but there was a bond of understanding.

The second of Catherine's new allies was a hero of the war against Prussia, Gregory Orlov. By 1758, Frederick of Prussia was struggling to defend his kingdom against three large allied powers, Austria, France, and Russia. In August that year, a Russian army of forty-four thousand men under General Fermor crossed the Prussian frontier and, on the twenty-fifth, fought a battle with Frederick and thirty-seven thousand Prussians near the town of Zorndorf. The nine-hour battle was among the bloodiest of the eighteenth century: more than ten thousand men were killed on each side; Frederick admitted losing more than a third of his army. In the ferocity of the combat, he and his men also acquired a new respect for the Russians; one Prussian officer wrote afterward that "the terror which the enemy has inspired in our troops is indescribable." After the carnage, both sides claimed victory, and in both camps a Te Deum thanksgiving was sung, but for two days neither of the blood-stained, crippled armies could move. Cannon still fired across the battlefield and cavalry skirmished, but Frederick and Fermor had fought each other to a standstill.

Among the Prussian officers captured at Zorndorf was Frederick's personal adjutant, Count Kurt von Schwerin, a nephew of a Prussian field marshal. When this prisoner was moved to St. Petersburg in March 1760, protocol required that he travel under escort by a Russian officer who would become as much an aide-de-camp as a security guard. The officer assigned this task was Lieutenant Gregory Orlov, who had been at Zorndorf, where he was wounded three times but continued to inspire his men and hold his position. This leadership and courage had made him a hero in the army, and escorting Count Schwerin was a reward for his bravery. When Count Schwerin reached St. Petersburg, Grand Duke Peter, distressed to see an officer close to his own hero, King Frederick, suffer any embarrassment, arranged that Schwerin be treated with the honors and hospitality ordinarily extended to a prominent visiting ally. "If I were emperor you would not be a prisoner of war," he assured Count Schwerin. A mansion was set aside for the prisoner-guest, and Peter dined there often. In addition, he gave Count Schwerin the freedom of the city; he could come and go as he pleased, always accompanied by his escort officer, Lieutenant Orlov.

At twenty-four, Gregory Orlov, was five years younger than Catherine. He came from a line of professional soldiers for whom bravery was a family tradition. His grandfather had been a common soldier in the Streltsy, the corps of bearded pikemen and musketeers founded by Ivan the Terrible that had revolted against the military reforms imposed by the young tsar Peter the Great. In punishment, Peter had sentenced many of the Streltsy—this Orlov among them—to death. When it came his turn to lay his head on the block in Red Square, the condemned Orlov strode unhesitatingly across a platform covered with gore, and, using his foot to push aside the freshly severed head of a comrade, declared, "I must make room here for myself." Peter, impressed by this contempt for death, immediately pardoned him, and placed him in one of his new regiments being formed for Russia's coming war with Sweden. Orlov became an officer. In time, his son rose to be a lieutenant colonel, and then, in turn, begat five warrior sons, Ivan, Gregory, Alexis, Theodore, and Vladimir. All five were officers in the Imperial Guard; all were popular with brother officers and idolized by their soldiers. It was a tightly knit family clan, each brother bound in loyalty to the others. All of the brothers possessed exceptional physical strength, courage, devotion to the army and to Russia. They were drinkers, gamblers, and lovers, equally reckless in war and in tavern brawls; like their grandfather, they were contemptuous of death. Alexis, the third of the five brothers, was the most intelligent. A huge man who had been disfigured by a deep saber cut across the left side of his face, he had earned the nickname Scarface. It was Alexis who one day would accomplish the deed that would secure the throne for Catherine, a deed for which he always accepted full responsibility and for which she gave him her silent, lifelong gratitude.

But it was Gregory, the second of the five brothers, who was the hero. He was considered the handsomest of the Orlovs, with "the head of an angel and the body of an athlete." He feared nothing. One of his conquests followed the Battle of Zorndorf, when, still recovering from wounds, he managed to seduce Princess Helen Kurakina, the mistress of Count Peter Shuvalov, the Grand Master of the Artillery. This trespass on the turf of the mighty Shuvalovs might have imperiled Orlov, but he escaped when Peter Shuvalov suddenly died a natural death. News of this romantic conquest added to his military fame and made Gregory Orlov a conspicuous figure in St. Petersburg. He was introduced to Empress Elizabeth—and eventually he caught the eye of the wife of the heir to the throne.

There are no records describing the circumstances of Catherine and Gregory's first meeting. An oft-told story is that one day the lonely grand duchess was staring out a palace window when she saw a tall, handsome officer in the uniform of the Guards standing in the court-yard. He happened to look up, their eyes met, and the attraction was immediate. No amorous minuet followed, as had been the case with Catherine and Saltykov and again with Poniatowski. Orlov, despite his military reputation, was far below Catherine in rank and had no position at court. But Gregory was neither timid nor hesitant; his success with Princess Kurakina had given him courage to aspire to even a grand duchess, especially one known to be ardent and lonely. There were precedents for the mingling of social ranks: Peter the Great had married a Livonian peasant and raised her to become Empress Catherine I; the great Peter's daughter, Empress Elizabeth, had spent many years with, and perhaps had married, a peasant, the amiable Ukrainian chorister Alexis Razumovsky.

In the summer of 1761, Catherine and Gregory Orlov became lovers. The affair was conducted in secrecy; the empress, Peter, and Catherine's friends were not aware of it, and the couple's assignations took place in a little house on Vassilevsky Island in the Neva River. In August 1761, Catherine was pregnant.

Orlov was a new kind of man for Catherine, neither a sentimental European sophisticate like Poniatowski nor a drawing room predator like Sergei Saltykov. Catherine loved him as he loved her, with an uncomplicated physical passion. Although Catherine's first nine years of marriage had been virginal, she was now a mature woman. She had loved two men outside her marriage, and by each of these men she had borne a child. Now a third man had appeared and he, too, would give her a child.

Orlov's motives were straightforward. Catherine was a powerful, desirable woman, openly and disgracefully neglected and persecuted by her husband, the Prussia-loving grand duke, who was hated by the officers and men of the Russian army. Catherine was exceedingly discreet about their affair, but Gregory kept no secrets from his four brothers, and they all considered that an honor had come to their family. Rumors of this relationship circulated among the men of the Guards regiments; most were impressed and proud.

Catherine had won the support of Nikita Panin, and, with the help of the Orlov brothers, she was winning the sympathy of the Guards. And then she attracted a third, very different, recruit to her cause. This was

Princess Catherine Dashkova, who, oddly enough, was the younger, married sister of Elizabeth Vorontsova, Peter's mistress. Catherine Vorontsova—as Princess Dashkova had been before marrying—was born in 1744, the youngest of three daughters of Count Roman Vorontsov, himself the younger brother of the former chancellor, Michael Vorontsov. Her birth followed soon after the coronation of Empress Elizabeth, and because the Vorontsov family was one of the oldest of the Russian nobility, the infant girl was held over the baptismal font by the new empress herself, while the empress's nephew, Peter, recently summoned from Holstein to be heir to the Russian throne, became the infant's godfather. When she was two, Catherine Vorontsova's mother died. Her father, Count Roman, still a young man, quickly became, in his daughters's words, "a man of pleasure, not much occupied with the care of his children." The child was sent to live with her uncle Michael, who arranged a superior education. "We spoke French fluently, learned some Italian, and had a few lessons in Russian," she wrote in her memoirs. She displayed a precocious intelligence, sometimes staying up all night reading Bayle, Montaigne, Montesquieu, and Voltaire. Catherine met this unusual young person in 1758, when Dashkova was fifteen. The grand duchess, delighted to find a Russian girl who spoke only French and who cherished Enlightenment philosophers, went out of her way to be gracious; the younger woman made Catherine her idol.

In February 1760, sixteen-year-old Catherine Vorontsova married Prince Michael Dashkov, a tall, popular, and wealthy young officer of the Preobrazhensky Guards. She followed her husband when he was assigned to Moscow, and there she had two children within eleven months. She never forgot the grand duchess in St. Petersburg. In the summer of 1761, she and her family moved back to the capital and her relationship with Catherine resumed.

In the capital, Dashkova's sister, Elizabeth, and Elizabeth's lover, Grand Duke Peter, tried to draw her into their circle, but the two sisters differed in almost every way. Elizabeth, whom Peter now had installed in his private apartments and was treating more as a future wife than a mistress, was dowdy, coarse, and ribald. Even so, having decided that she wanted to marry Peter, she pursued her goal with patient, steely determination. She outlasted all of his other diversions, and managed the *ménage à quatre* with Catherine and Stanislaus. Over the years, Peter found that she suited him so well that he could not give her up.

At court, Dashkova also was different. She cared little for elaborate clothes, refused to wear rouge, talked incessantly, and was regarded as intelligent, outspoken, and arrogant. Along with her political idealism, she was prudish and found her sister's behavior a painful embarrassment. Whether or not Elizabeth ever became a crowned empress, Catherine Dashkova considered her to be living in vulgar public concubinage. Worse, her sister's goal was to replace the woman who had become Dashkova's idol, Grand Duchess Catherine.

Princess Dashkova spent the summer of 1761 living in her father's dacha on the Gulf of Finland, midway between Peterhof, where the empress was staying, and Oranienbaum, where Peter and Catherine held their summer court. Paul remained in Elizabeth's household at Peterhof, but the empress now permitted Catherine to drive every Sunday from Oranienbaum to Peterhof to spend the day watching her son play in the palace garden. On the way home, Catherine often stopped her carriage at the Vorontsov dacha and invited the princess to spend the rest of the day with her at Oranienbaum. There, in Catherine's gardens or in her apartment, the two women talked about books and political theory. Dashkova felt that she had reached a rare intellectual summit. "I may venture to assert there were not two women in the empire except the grand duchess and myself who occupied themselves at all in serious reading," she wrote in her memoirs. During these long conversations, the princess convinced herself that Catherine was the only possible "savior of the nation," and that it was essential that she, not Peter, succeed to the throne. Catherine did not encourage the expression of these opinions. She looked on Dashkova as a brilliant, enchanting child, whose adoration was flattering and companionship stimulating, but she realistically saw herself coming to power as Peter's wife—providing she could maintain her position against Elizabeth Vorontsova. Dashkova, for her part, felt something close to worship for the grand duchess: "She captured my heart and mind and inspired me with enthusiastic devotion. I felt a devoted attachment which knew no competition except the love I bore my husband and children."

Grand Duke Peter and Elizabeth Vorontsova persisted in trying to lure Princess Dashkova into their circle. Peter, observing her admiration for his wife, warned her, saying, "My child, you would do well to remember that it is much safer to deal with honest blockheads like your sister and me than with those great wits who squeeze the juice out of the orange and then throw away the rind." Dashkova was not afraid of standing up to Peter. Once at a dinner for eighty at which both Peter and Catherine were present, the grand duke, having drunk too much Burgundy, slurred out that a young officer suspected of being the lover of one of the empress's relatives should be beheaded for his impertinence. Challenging the grand duke, Dashkova said that this punishment appeared tyrannical, "for even if the crime in question were proved, so frightful a punishment was highly disproportionate to the offence."

"You are a mere child," Peter replied, "otherwise you would know that to be sparing of the punishment of death is to encourage insubordination and every kind of disorder."

"But, sir," Dashkova fired back, "almost all who have the honor of sitting in your presence have lived only during a reign in which such a punishment has never yet been heard of."

"As to that," declared the grand duke, "it is the very cause of the present want of discipline and order. But, take my word for it, you are a mere child and know nothing about the matter."

The Holsteiners at the table were silent, but Dashkova persisted. "I am very ready to acknowledge, sir, that I am unable to comprehend your reasoning, but one thing of which I am very sensible is that your august aunt still lives and sits on the throne." All eyes immediately turned, first to the young woman, then to the heir to the throne. But Peter did not answer, and ultimately ended the confrontation by sticking his tongue out at his adversary.

The episode won Dashkova much praise. Grand Duchess Catherine was delighted and congratulated her; the story spread and "gained me a high degree of notoriety," wrote Dashkova. Every episode of this kind increased the contempt the princess felt for the heir to the throne: "I saw how little my country had to hope from the grand duke, sunk as he was in the most degrading ignorance and swayed by no better principle than a vulgar pride in being the creature of the King of Prussia, whom he called, 'the king my master.'"

Princess Dashkova was happy to grant Peter's definition of himself as a blockhead, because she believed that only a blockhead would prefer the company of her sister to that of the dazzling grand duchess. Scandalized that Peter was promising to displace Catherine and marry her sister, the young princess resolved to protect her heroine. One service she could perform was to report every shard of news and gossip that could affect the grand duchess. Catherine did not encourage Dashkova to play this role, although it was useful to have an adherent so close to the talk of the grand duke and Vorontsova. On the other hand, Catherine was careful what she said to her young admirer. Just as Dashkova was a possible source of information, she was also, potentially, a source of leaks. For this reason, Catherine was also careful to compartmentalize her relationships with those who supported her. At the beginning, each of the three primary figures knew little about the others, and each of them knew a different Catherine. Panin knew the levelheaded, sophisticated politician; Orlov, the warm-blooded woman; Dashkova, the philosopher and admirer of the Enlightenment. Eventually, Princess Dashkova came to regard Panin as the kind of Europeanized Russian whom she admired. But Dashkova was completely unaware of Orlov's importance in Catherine's life. She would have been horrified to learn that her idol was submitting to the caresses of a rough, uneducated soldier.

As Elizabeth's physical decline continued, the general anxiety about Peter becoming emperor grew stronger. The longer the war continued, the more flagrantly Peter manifested his hatred and scorn for Russia and his sympathy for Prussia. Certain that his failing aunt would be unable to summon the strength to strip him of his inheritance, he began speaking openly about the changes he would make once he was emperor. He would terminate the war against Prussia. After making peace, he would switch sides and join Frederick against Russia's present allies, Austria and France. Eventually, he meant to use Russia's strength on behalf of Holstein. This meant war with Denmark to reconquer the territory that Denmark had taken from his duchy in 1721. He began to say openly that he intended to divorce Catherine and marry Elizabeth Vorontsova.

Peter was already doing everything possible to assist Frederick. To keep the king informed of the empress's secret war councils, he passed along whatever he could learn of the plans of the Russian high command. This information went to the new English ambassador in St. Petersburg, Sir Robert Keith, who, in forwarding his own diplomatic reports to London, included Peter's information. Keith then sent his couriers by way of Berlin, where his colleague the British ambassador to Prussia made a copy for Frederick before sending the packet along to Whitehall. By this means, the king of Prussia often learned of operations planned by the Russian high command before Russian field commanders were told.

Peter made little effort to keep his betrayal of the empress, the army, the nation, and the nation's allies a secret. The French and Austrian ambassadors complained to the chancellor, but they made no impression because Michael Vorontsov, along with everyone else in the capital, believed that the empress's precarious health soon must fail, and that Grand Duke Peter's first act on taking the throne would be to end the war, recall his armies, and sign a peace with Frederick. In the interim, Vorontsov had no intention of jeopardizing his own future by informing Elizabeth of her nephew's treachery. In the army, however, the contempt and loathing for the heir to the throne rose to the point that even Sir Robert Keith declared, "He must be mad to behave this way."

If the Guards and the army in general had these feelings, the Orlovs particularly hated the man who was passing information to the enemy. In Gregory Orlov, this intense feeling burned even brighter. If Peter were compelled to abdicate, what would become of the grand duchess? Like Peter, she had been born a German, but she had lived in Russia for eighteen years, she was an Orthodox believer, she was the mother of the younger heir, and her absolute allegiance was to Russia. Orlov delivered this message wherever he went and his brothers did the same. Their hatred of Peter, their popularity in the army, and their willingness to act on Catherine's behalf were to bring her to the throne.

Elizabeth was determined to defeat Prussia and Frederick. She had entered the war to honor her treaty with Austria, and she meant to see it through. The end of the war was coming; Frederick no longer led the most effective army in Europe, and both the Austrians and the Russians had become veterans. As Frederick's manpower dwindled, the odds against him lengthened. Proof of this came at the Battle of Kunersdorf, on August 25, 1759, where, fifty miles east of Berlin, fifty thousand Prussians supported by three hundred cannon attacked seventy-nine thousand Russians dug into a strong defensive position.

Frederick's infantry hurled itself against the firmly anchored, well-defended Russian positions. By nightfall, when the fighting ended, Kunersdorf had become Frederick's worst defeat in the Seven Years' War; in the aftermath, Prussian soldiers simply flung away their muskets and ran. Although the Russian army suffered sixteen thousand dead and wounded, it inflicted eighteen thousand casualties on the Prussians. The king himself had two horses killed under him, and a bullet was deflected by a gold snuffbox he carried in his coat. That night, he wrote to a close friend in Berlin, "Of an army of forty-eight thousand, I do not have three thousand left. All flee and I am no longer master of my men. Berlin must look to its own safety. This is a terrible mishap and I shall not survive it. I have no more reserves and, to tell the truth, I believe all is lost." In the morning, eighteen thousand men straggled back to join the king, but the forty-seven-year-old monarch remained in despair. And in pain. "What is wrong with me," he wrote to his brother, Prince Henry, "is rheumatism in my feet, one of my knees and my left hand. I have also been in the grip of an almost continual fever for eight days."

In St. Petersburg, Elizabeth rejoiced in the good news and endured the bad. On January 1, 1760, four months after Kunersdorf, she told the Austrian ambassador, "I intend to continue the war and to remain faithful to my allies even if I have to sell half my diamonds and dresses." The commander of her army in Germany, General Peter Saltykov, repaid her dedication. In the summer of 1760, the Russian army crossed the Oder. Cossack cavalry rode into Berlin and occupied Frederick's capital for three days.

As her pregnancy advanced, Catherine secluded herself. Her excuse— that it mortified her to see her husband publicly according almost royal honors to his mistress—was a convenience to help her protect her real situation. Now, while the grand duke was talking of repudiating her, there was no chance that he would pretend that this new child was his. Determined not to give him any justification for setting her aside, Catherine concealed her pregnancy, wearing wide hooped skirts, spending her days in an armchair in her room, receiving no one.

Catherine's secret was better kept than Elizabeth's. The empress had commanded that news of her condition be hidden from the grand duke and grand duchess. She attempted to conceal the physical ravages of illness: the deathly pale face, the overweight body, the swollen legs. These were hidden beneath rouge and silver gowns. Elizabeth sensed that Peter was waiting impatiently for her death, but she was too exhausted to break her word and carry out her real wish: to transfer the succession to Paul. She had energy and focus enough only to drag herselfy from her bed to a sofa or an armchair. Ivan Shuvalov, her recent favorite, was no longer able to comfort her; she seemed at peace only when Alexis Razumovsky, her former lover and perhaps her husband, was sitting by her bed, soothing her with soft Ukrainian lullabies. As the days passed, Elizabeth lost interest in Russia's future and took less and less interest in her surroundings. She knew what was coming.

Her agony paralyzed Europe. All eyes were on the sickroom, where the outcome of the war hung on the struggle of a woman fighting for life. The allies' dearest hope near the end of 1761 was that the empress's doctors might manage to prolong her life for another six—and, if possible, twelve—months, by which time they hoped that Frederick would be beyond recovery. In private, Frederick himself admitted that he was near the end. The prize for which Russia had struggled for five years was within reach. If only Grand Duke Peter could be held back from his inheritance for a few more months, his enthusiasm for the Prussian king and all of his plans would be meaningless. It was not to be.

By the middle of December 1761, everyone knew that the empress would die soon. When Peter bluntly declared to Princess Dashkova that her sister, Elizabeth Vorontsova, would soon be his wife, Dashkova decided that something must be done to prevent this. On the night of December 20, although she was shivering with fever, she got out of bed, wrapped herself in furs, and had herself driven to the palace. Entering by a little back door, she had one of the grand duchess's servants take her to her mistress. Catherine was in bed. Before the princess could say a word, the grand duchess said, "Before you tell me a thing, come into my bed and warm yourself." In her memoirs, Dashkova described their conversation. She told Catherine that when the empress had only a few days, perhaps a few hours, to live, she could not endure the uncertainty involving Catherine's future. "Have you formed any plan, or taken any precautions to ensure your safety?" the princess asked. Catherine was touched—and alarmed. She pressed her hand to Dashkova's heart, and said, "I am grateful to you, but I declare to you that I have formed no sort of plan and can attempt nothing. I can only meet with courage whatever happens."

To Dashkova, this passivity was unacceptable. "If you can do nothing, Madame, your friends must act for you!" she declared. "I have enough courage and enthusiasm to arouse them all. Give me orders! Direct me!"

For Catherine, this loyalty went too far. It was premature, precipitous. At this stage, Orlov could muster a few men of the Guards, but, without preparation, not enough. And this overwrought, irresponsible young woman might expose and endanger them all before they were ready. "In the name of heaven, princess," Catherine said calmly, "do not think of placing yourself in danger. Were you on my account to suffer misfortunes, that would subject me to everlasting regret." Catherine was still soothing her impetuous visitor when Dashkova interrupted her, kissed her hand, and assured her that she would no longer increase the risk by prolonging the interview. The two women embraced, and Dashkova rose and left as suddenly as she had come. In her excitement, she had not noticed that Catherine was six months pregnant.

Two days later, on December 23, Empress Elizabeth had a massive stroke. The doctors gathered around her bed agreed that this time there would be no recovery. Peter and Catherine were summoned and found Ivan Shuvalov and the two Razumovsky brothers standing beside the bed, staring down at the pale face on the pillow. To the end the empress remained lucid. She showed no sign of wishing to alter the succession. She asked Peter to promise to look after little Paul. Peter, keenly aware that the aunt who had made him her heir could also unmake him with a single word, promised. She also charged him to protect Alexis Razumovsky and Ivan Shuvalov. She had no message for Catherine, who remained at her bedside. Outside the bedroom, the antechamber and corridors were crowded. Father Theodore Dubyansky, the empress's confessor, arrived, and the heavy scent of incense mingled with the smell of medicine as the priest prepared to administer the last rites. As the hours passed, the empress sent for the chancellor, Michael Vorontsov. He replied that he was too ill to come; it was not illness but fear of offending the heir that kept him away.

On Christmas morning, Elizabeth asked Father Dubyansky to read the Orthodox Prayer for the Dying. When he finished, she asked him to read it again. She blessed everyone in the room and, according to Orthodox custom, asked each person in the room for forgiveness. On Christmas Day, December 25, 1761, near four o'clock in the afternoon, Empress Elizabeth died. A few minutes later, Prince Nikita Trubetskoy, the president of the Senate, opened the double doors of the bedroom and announced to the waiting crowd, "Her Imperial Majesty, Elizabeth Petrovna, has fallen asleep in the Lord. God preserve our gracious sovereign, the Emperor Peter III."

❧42❧
The Brief Reign of Peter III

T HE ARCHBISHOP OF NOVGOROD blessed Peter as the new *gosudar* (autocrat), the Senate and the heads of the Colleges of State (government ministries) took the oath of allegiance, and the cannon of the fortress of St. Peter and St. Paul thundered the proclamation of the accession of the new monarch. Peter rode out into the Palace Square to receive the oaths of the regiments of Foot Guards, the Preobrazhensky, Semyonovsky, and Izmailovsky; the Horse Guards; the line regiments; and the Cadet Corps. When the figure of the new emperor, wearing the bottle-green uniform of the Preobrazhensky Guards, appeared, illuminated by torches, the regimental standards dipped in salute. Delighted, Peter returned to the palace and told the Austrian ambassador, Count Mercy, "I did not think they loved me so much." That evening, he presided over a supper for 150 people who had been instructed to dress in light colors to celebrate Peter's accession rather than the usual black customary for mourning. At the table, Catherine sat on one side of the emperor. Ivan Shuvalov, Elizabeth's favorite, in tears at the empress's bedside, stood behind Peter's chair, laughing and joking. The following night, Peter gave another banquet for which ladies were commanded to come "richly dressed." Princess Dashkova refused to attend these festivities, pleading illness. As the evening progressed, she received a message from her sister saying that the new emperor was annoyed by her absence and did not believe her excuse, and that it might go hard with the princess's husband, Prince Dashkov, if she did not appear. Dashkova obeyed. When she appeared, Peter approached and said in a low voice, "If, my little friend, you will take my advice, pay a little more attention to us. The time may come when you will have good reason to repent of any negligence shown your sister. Believe me, it is for your interest alone I speak. You have no other way of making yourself of consequence in the world than by seeking her protection."

Ten days before the funeral, the body of Empress Elizabeth was moved to the Kazan Cathedral, where, in a silver embroidered robe, it was placed in an open coffin, surrounded by candles. A stream of mourners, flowing past the coffin in semidarkness, could not help seeing a veiled figure, draped in black, wearing neither crown nor jewelry, kneeling on the stone floor beside the bier, apparently lost in grief. All knew that this was the new empress, Catherine. Catherine was there in part out of respect but also because she understood that there was no better way to appeal directly to the people than with this demonstration of humility and apparent devotion. Indeed, she played the part so well that the French ambassador reported to Paris that "more and more, she captures the hearts of Russians."

Peter's behavior in the presence of Elizabeth's body was in stark contrast. Through the weeks of public mourning, the new emperor acted out his joy at being released from eighteen years of political and cultural imprisonment. Intoxicated by his new freedom, he resisted conforming to the customs of the Orthodox Church regarding death. He refused to stand in respectful vigil or to kneel beside the coffin. On the few occasions he appeared in the cathedral, he paced restlessly, talking loudly, making jokes, laughing, pointing, and even sticking out his tongue at the priests. Most of the time, he remained in his own apartment, drinking and shouting with an excitement he seemed unable to control.

The climax to this display of mockery came on the day Elizabeth's body was moved from the Kazan Cathedral, across the Neva River bridge, to the mausoleum on the island fortress of St. Peter and St. Paul. Peter, conspicuously alone, walked immediately behind the coffin. He wore a black mourning robe with a long train, carried by elderly noblemen. The new emperor's prank was to lag behind, then stop completely until the coffin had advanced thirty feet ahead of him. Then, with long strides, he would hurry forward to catch up. The older men, unable to manage the emperor's pace, were forced to let go of his train and let it flap wildly in the wind. Delighted by their embarrassment, Peter repeated this sequence over and over. This grotesque buffoonery by a man almost thirty-four years old, walking at the funeral of the woman who had made him an emperor, shocked everyone: the noblemen walking in the procession, the officers and soldiers lining the route, and the crowds of people watching.

Despite this flamboyantly inappropriate behavior, Peter followed a moderate political path in the early weeks of his reign. Michael Vorontsov, restored to the chancellorship after Bestuzhev's fall, retained that post, although in Elizabeth's last years he had sided with the anti-Prussian, pro-French Shuvalovs. Peter immediately recalled long-banished officials. Ernst Johann Biron, Empress Anna's German chancellor and lover and the father of the Princess of Courland, was permitted to exchange his retirement in Yaroslavl for a comfortable residence in Petersburg. Lestocq, Elizabeth's French physician and counselor, and old Field Marshal Münnich, another German, were pardoned and brought back from exile. Nothing was done, however, to ameliorate the disgrace of Alexis Bestuzhev, the former chancellor, who had always supported Austria and opposed Prussia. His exclusion from the general amnesty made a painful impression on many Russians. It seemed that political offenders with foreign names were being allowed to return, but this Russian statesman, who had worked so long for his country's secure position in Europe, remained in disgrace.

A stream of popular administrative changes followed these amnesties. Whether these efforts stemmed from a planned effort to win public favor or were simply an extension of Peter's unpredictable behavior, no one knew. On January 17, he pleased the entire population by reducing the government tax on salt. On February 18, he delighted the nobility by issuing a manifesto ending compulsory service to the state. This obligation was a legacy from the reign of Peter the Great, who, after declaring that he, as tsar, was "the first servant of the state," had then decreed that all landowners and other noblemen owed a similar duty. The result had created a permanent officer corps for the army and navy and a permanent administration staff for the Russian bureaucracy. Now, the descendants of these noblemen were freed from all military and civil obligations; they would no longer be compelled to perform years of state service. They were also granted freedom to travel abroad and, except in wartime, to remain as long as they liked. On February 21, Peter abolished the Secret Chancellery, the dreaded investigative chamber that dealt with those accused of treason or sedition. At the same time, Russian religious dissenters, the Raskolniki, were permitted to return, with full liberty of worship, from the countries to which they had fled to avoid persecution by the the Orthodox Church.

In March, Peter visited the grim Schlüsselburg Fortress, where the former emperor, Ivan VI, deposed by Empress Elizabeth, had been confined for eighteen years. Peter, certain that his own place on the throne was secure, thought of giving Ivan an easier life, perhaps even of releasing him and appointing him to a military post. The condition of the man he found made these plans impossible. Ivan, now twenty-two, was tall and thin, with hair to his waist. He was illiterate, stammered out disconnected sentences, and was uncertain about his own identity. His clothes were torn and dirty, his bed was a narrow pallet, the air in his prison room was heavy, and the only light came from small, barred windows high up in the wall. When Peter offered to help, Ivan asked whether he could have more fresh air. Peter gave him a silk dressing gown, which the former emperor hid under his pillow. Before leaving the fortress, Peter ordered a house to be built in the courtyard where the prisoner might have more air and more room to walk.

Peter rose at seven o'clock and dressed with his adjutants standing by, reading reports and receiving orders. From eight to eleven he consulted his ministers and made a round of public offices, often finding only junior clerks on duty. At eleven, he appeared on the parade ground, where he conducted a rigorous inspection of uniforms and weapons and drilled the troops, assisted by his Holstein officers. At one o'clock, he dined, inviting to his table anyone to whom he wished to speak, regardless of rank. His afternoons often included a nap, followed by a concert in which he played his violin. Then came supper and a party, which sometimes lasted late into the night. Most of these evenings involved heavy smoking, drinking, and carousing. Peter always carried a pipe and was followed by a servant carrying a large basket filled with Dutch clay pipes and a variety of tobaccos. The room quickly filled with smoke, and through this haze, the emperor strutted up and down, loudly talking and laughing. The company, sitting at long tables covered with bottles, and understanding that Peter hated ceremony and liked to be treated as a comrade, let themselves go. Presently, they would all get up and stagger into the courtyard, where they played hopscotch like children, hopping on one leg, butting their comrades, and kicking them from behind. "Imagine our feelings to see the first men of the empire, covered with ribbons and stars, behaving this way," said a onetime guest. When one of the Holsteiners fell to the ground, the others would laugh and clap until the servants came and carried him away. But Peter was always up again at seven o'clock.

This frantic energy displayed little organization or purpose. "The moderation and clemency of the emperor's acts," Count Mercy wrote to Vienna, "do not indicate anything fixed or definite. He has a mind but little exercised in affairs, little given to solid considerations, and continually occupied by prejudices. His natural disposition is heady, violent, and irrational." A few days later, Mercy added, "I can find nobody here of sufficient zeal and courage energetically to resist the vehement and obstinate temper of the monarch. They all flatter his stubbornness for their own private ends."

Severe conflict arose when Peter attempted to impose change on some of the deep-rooted institutions of the Russian empire. His goodwill did not extend to the Orthodox Church. Since coming to Russia eighteen years before, he had hated his adopted form of Christianity. He believed its doctrines and dogmas to be sheer superstition, its services ludicrous, its priests contemptible, and its wealth obscene. The religion he had brought with him from Holstein was Lutheran. Now, as emperor and the official head of the Orthodox Church, he decided that this age-old pillar of Russian life and culture must be remade on the Protestant model practiced in Prussia. Frederick II was a freethinker who sneered at priests and religious belief; why should he, Peter, not do the same? On February 16, a decree secularized all church property, placing it in the hands of a new governmental department. Dignitaries of the Orthodox Church were to become salaried officials paid by the state. When the higher clergy expressed indignation and dismay, Peter bluntly announced that the veneration of icons was a primitive practice that must be eliminated. All icons except those of Jesus Christ—all of the painted and carved renditions of the saints who were a part of Russian history—were to be removed from churches. Then, striking directly at the Russian clergy themselves, he demanded that priests shave off their beards and abandon the long brocaded robes that reached to the floor; in the future, he said, they must wear black cassocks like Protestant pastors. The archbishops replied that if the clergy obeyed these commands, they would be murdered by their flocks. That Easter, the usual open-air religious processions were banned, spurring talk among the people that the emperor was a pagan—or, worse, a Protestant. Indeed, Peter told the archbishop of Novgorod that he meant to establish a Protestant chapel in the new Winter Palace. When the archbishop protested, Peter shouted that the prelate was an old fool and that a religion good enough for the king of Prussia should be good enough for Russia.

To change the beliefs and practices of the Orthodox Church would require a sustained effort, but the clergy and the millions of faithful would have difficulty forming an effective opposition. The army, the other pillar of the Russian state and autocracy, posed a different problem. He considered himself a soldier and was keenly aware of the importance of possessing a loyal, efficient army. Nevertheless, from his first days on the throne, Peter managed to offend the institution that he most needed for support. He was determined to reorganize the Russian army on the Prussian model. Everything was to be reformed or replaced: uniforms, discipline, drill, battlefield tactics, even its commander—all were to be Prussianized. Peter liked neatness and smartness and wanted his soldiers to wear close-fitting German uniforms. He took away the long, loose coats of Russian soldiers, useful in the cold of a northern winter, and put them into lighter, thinner, tight-fitting German uniforms. Before long, some could scarcely recognize the newly costumed, powdered men of the Russian Imperial Guard. Russian officers were expected to appear in new uniforms garnished with shoulder straps and gold knots. Peter himself began wearing the blue uniform of a Prussian colonel. At the beginning of his reign, he was content to wear the broad blue ribbon of the Russian Order of St. Andrew; then he switched to the Prussian Order of the Black Eagle. He often showed off a ring containing a miniature portrait of Frederick, which he announced was his most precious possession.

Peter had never been near a battlefield, but he was an excellent drillmaster, and on the parade ground he made Russian soldiers practice Prussian exercises for hours, enforcing his commands with a little cane. No officer was excused from these drills, and fat, middle-aged generals were obliged to turn out at the head of their regiments and do parade ground drill on their stiff, gouty limbs.

The antics of old generals trying to carry out Prussian exercises gave Peter amusement, but dressing his soldiers as Germans and teaching them Prussian drill was only the beginning. He replaced the traditional Russian sovereign's personal bodyguard, drawn from the Preobrazhensky regiment—a unit founded by Peter the Great and of which Peter III was honorary colonel—with a Holstein Cuirassier Regiment to which he gave the name of Body Guard of the Imperial Household. This created intense indignation in the Guards and in the army generally. He announced that he intended to disband and abolish the regiments of the Russian Imperial Guard altogether and distribute the men among the regular line regiments. As a culminating insult, he placed his uncle, Prince George Lewis of Holstein, who had no military experience, in command of the Russian army.

At the moment Peter was proclaimed emperor in December 1761, Frederick of Prussia was in a precarious position. Nearly a third of his dominions were in enemy hands. The Russians had occupied East Prussia and part of Pomerania; the Austrians had regained most of Silesia: Berlin, his capital, had been pillaged and lay half in ruins. His army now was composed mostly of young recruits, and the king himself resembled "a demented scarecrow." To rid himself of Russia as an enemy, he was prepared to sign a treaty, permanently sacrificing East Prussia. Then came Empress Elizabeth's death and Peter's accession to the throne. When Frederick learned that the new emperor had ordered a cessation of hostilities, he responded by ordering the immediate release of all Russian prisoners and sent a twenty-six-year-old officer, Baron Bernhard von Goltz, to St. Petersburg to negotiate peace. Meanwhile, Prussia's interests were in the care of the English ambassador, Sir Robert Keith, who had followed Sir Charles Hanbury-Williams's practice of sending military information to Frederick in Berlin. Now that Peter was on the throne, Keith's influence was at a peak. The Austrian ambassador, Count Mercy, called him "the chief instrument of the Prussian party. Not a day passes that the emperor does not see Mr. Keith, or send him fruit, or pay him other attentions." Keith's own dispatches also reveal this closeness. Only three days after Peter's accession, Keith informed London that "at a dinner, His Imperial Majesty, with whose good graces I have always been honored, came up to me and smilingly told me in my ear that he hoped I would be pleased with him as the night before he had sent couriers to the different corps of his army with orders not to advance further into Prussian territory and to cease all hostilities." Three weeks later, when Keith was supping with the emperor in Elizabeth Vorontsova's apartment, Peter told him that he wanted to settle matters with the king of Prussia as soon as possible and was "resolved to get free of all commitments to the Court of Vienna."

On February 25, Count Mercy was present at a banquet given by Chancellor Vorontsov for the emperor and for all foreign ambassadors; three hundred people were in the hall. Mercy found Peter uneasy. At nine o'clock the company sat down. During the meal, which lasted four hours, Peter drank Burgundy, became excited, and, at the top of his voice, proposed a toast to the king of Prussia. At two in the morning, the diners rose from the table, baskets of clay pipes and tobacco were brought, and the men began to smoke. Peter, pacing up and down the room, pipe in hand, confronted the new French ambassador, Baron de Breteuil: "We must make peace," he said. "For my part, I have declared it."

"And we, too, sire, would have it," the ambassador replied, then added, "honorably, and in agreement with our allies."

Peter's face darkened. "Just as you please," he said. "For my part, I have declared it. You can do as you please. I am a soldier and I don't joke."

"Sire," said Breteuil, "I will report to my king the declaration Your Majesty has been pleased to make to me."

Peter turned and walked away. The following day, the ambassadors of Russia's allies, Austria and France, were handed an official document which declared that the war had been going on for six years to the detriment of all. Now, the new Russian emperor, anxious to terminate so great an evil, had decided to announce to all the courts in alliance with Russia that in order to restore the blessings of peace to his own empire and to Europe, he was ready to sacrifice all the conquests made by Russian arms. He believed that the allied courts would also prefer restoration of general tranquillity and would agree with him. After reading the declaration, Count Mercy declared to Chancellor Vorontsov that he found the declaration obscure and impertinent. Writing to his own court in Vienna, he described it as venomous; as an effort to avoid the most solemn treaty obligations; and as an excuse to save the king of Prussia from impending destruction.

For Mercy and Austria, worse was to come. Peter's declaration of peace turned out to be a preliminary to the signing of a formal alliance between Russia and Prussia. On March 3, the new Prussian envoy, young Baron von Goltz, arrived in St. Petersburg, where Peter received him enthusiastically. Goltz scarcely had time to congratulate the new monarch on his accession when Peter overwhelmed him with ardent assurances of his own admiration for the king of Prussia. He had a great deal to talk to him about in private, he whispered. Immediately after the audience, Peter thrust his arm through that of this new friend and carried him off to dinner, talking incessantly about the Prussian army and amazing Goltz with his intimate knowledge of the subject, including the names of almost every senior officer of every Prussian regiment. Goltz was provided with a mansion in which Peter visited him twice a day. Within a week, Goltz had completely eclipsed Keith, his English colleague, and, henceforth, until the end of Peter's reign, Prussian influence dominated at the Russian court.

Goltz's mission was to speed the end of the war and the detachment of Russia from her allies. To achieve this, he told Peter that Frederick was willing to consent to the permanent cession of East Prussia. Peter did not require this. On the contrary, he was willing to sacrifice everything to please Frederick. He let Frederick set the terms. When the king sent to St. Petersburg a draft treaty for an eternal peace between Prussia and Russia, it did not go through the normal channel; it was not submitted, or even shown, to Chancellor Vorontsov. Instead, Goltz simply read the text to Peter in private without witnesses, and on April 24, Peter signed it without comment, sending it to Vorontsov for confirmation. By this stroke of a pen on a secret treaty, the new emperor not only restored to Prussia all the territory won from her by Russia during five years of war but contracted an "eternal" alliance with Prussia.

Six days after the signing, the emperor celebrated the peace treaty with a banquet at which every guest was seated according to rank, the first time this precedence had been observed during his reign. Peter and his chancellor, Vorontsov, both wore the Prussian Order of the Black Eagle. The banquet lasted for four hours and four toasts were drunk: an expression of joy at the restoration of peace with Prussia; personal congratulations to Frederick II; a toast to perpetual peace between the two powers; and a toast to the "honor of all the valiant officers and soldiers of the Prussian army." Each toast was accompanied by a triple salvo from the guns of the fortress of Peter and Paul, as well as from fifty cannon planted in the square outside the palace. There was no mention of the achievements, bravery, or losses of the Russian army, and, said Count Mercy, "nothing was omitted in the way of indecency and offensiveness in regard to his ancient ally, Austria."

This sensational diplomatic and military *volte-face* startled the chancelleries of Europe. When Maria Theresa's government in Vienna learned that the Russian emperor meant to sacrifice all his conquests "in the interests of peace," the Austrian reply was guarded, asking for details as to how this was to be achieved. The Russian explanation, arriving in April, was pretentious and pompous: to make peace, it declared, one belligerent must step forward as a general proponent and agent of peace; Russia had chosen this role "out of compassion for suffering humanity and from personal friendship for the king of Prussia. The Austrian court is therefore invited to follow our example." To Vienna, the message was menacing; the threat became real when Peter signed the treaty of alliance with Frederick. Peter explained this by saying that inasmuch as his good offices had proved useless, he found himself regretfully compelled to resort to the extreme measure of assisting the king of Prussia with his army as being the quickest way to restore to humanity the blessings of peace. He ordered General Zakhar Chernyshev, the commander of a Russian corps attached to the Austrian army in Silesia (and Catherine's ardent admirer fourteen years earlier) to join the Prussian army with his force of sixteen thousand infantry and a thousand Cossacks to fight against Austria. At this betrayal and the collapse of all his years of diplomatic effort in Russia, Count Mercy asked to be recalled to Vienna. He recommended sending a third-rank diplomat as his replacement.

With Russia defecting from the alliance and switching sides, France and Austria had no alternative except to negotiate with Prussia. The French were outraged. The Duc de Choiseul, Louis XV's foreign minister, said to the Russian ambassador, "Sir, the maintenance of solemn engagements ought to override every other consideration." Louis himself declared that while he was willing to listen to overtures for a durable and honorable peace, he must act in full accord with his allies; he would consider himself a traitor if he took part in secret negotiations; he would stain the honor of France if he deserted his allies. The result was a rupture of Russian diplomatic relations with France and the recall of ambassadors from both St. Petersburg and Paris.

Peter had provoked and insulted the Orthodox Church, infuriated and alienated the army, and betrayed his allies. Nevertheless, effective opposition still needed a specific cause around which to rally. Peter himself supplied this by endeavoring to impose on his exhausted country a frivolous new war—against Denmark.

As Duke of Holstein, Peter had inherited the grievances of his duchy against the Danish monarchy. In 1721, the small province of Schleswig, then a hereditary possession of the dukes of Holstein, had been seized and handed over to Denmark by England, France, Austria, and Sweden. No sooner was Peter on the Russian throne than he proceeded to insist upon "his rights." As early as March 1, even before peace with Prussia was settled, he demanded to know whether Denmark was prepared to satisfy his claims to Schleswig; if not, he said he would be compelled to take extreme measures. The Danes proposed a conference and the English ambassador recommended negotiations; why should the mighty emperor of Russia make war with Denmark over a few villages? But everyone soon discovered that on the Holstein question, Peter meant to have his way and that even the advice of his new ally, Frederick of Prussia, was powerless to restrain him. Hitherto, Peter had proved pliable in Prussian hands; now even these hardheaded Germans learned about his obstinacy. Ultimately, on June 3, Peter agreed to a conference in Berlin to be mediated by Frederick, but he stipulated that the Russian propositions were to be regarded as an ultimatum to Denmark and that rejection meant war.

Redressing a perceived wrong against his duchy was one motive for provoking a war, but Peter had a second. Having idealized the warrior king of Prussia, having bragged that he had defeated "gypsies" when he was a boy in Kiel, having marched paste soldiers across a tabletop in a palace room and ordered real soldiers around a parade ground, he wanted now to be a hero on a real battlefield. Peter had just proclaimed to his allies and to Europe his passion for peace; now he was preparing to attack Denmark. The Russian army, deprived of its hard-won victory over Prussia, now learned that it was to spill its blood in a new campaign that had nothing to do with the interests of Russia.

Unable to dissuade Peter from undertaking this new war so soon after his accession, Frederick II urged his admirer to take precautions before his departure from Russia. "Frankly, I distrust these Russians of yours," he said to Peter. "What if, during your absence, a cabal were formed to dethrone Your Majesty?" He advised Peter to have himself crowned and consecrated in Moscow before leaving, to lock up all unreliable persons, and to leave St. Petersburg garrisoned by his faithful Holsteiners. Peter refused to be persuaded; he saw no need. "If the Russians had wanted to do me harm," he wrote to Frederick, "they could have done it long ago, seeing that I take no particular precautions, going freely about the streets on foot. I assure Your Majesty that when one knows how to deal with the Russians, one can be quite sure of them."

A Russian army of forty thousand veterans was already assembled in occupied Prussian Pomerania, and Peter, without waiting to arrive himself, ordered these troops to advance. The Danes reacted by moving first and met the Russians in Mecklenburg. Then, to the astonishment of Danish commanders, the Russians in front of them began to retreat.

The riddle was solved a few days later. There had been a coup d'état in St. Petersburg. Peter III had been overthrown, had abdicated, and was a prisoner. Peter's wife, now styled Catherine II, had been proclaimed empress of Russia.

✤43✤

"Dura!"

NO ONE KNOWS EXACTLY when the plot to remove Peter III from the throne first took shape in Catherine's mind. As Peter's consort, she had become empress of Russia. Politically, however, this meant little; from the beginning of her husband's reign, her position was one of isolation and humiliation. "It does not appear that the empress is much consulted," Ambassador Keith reported to London, adding that he and his fellow diplomats "think it not the likeliest way of succeeding to make any direct or particular address to her Imperial Majesty."

Breteuil, the French ambassador, wrote, "The empress is abandoned to grief and dark forebodings. Those who know her say she is scarcely recognizable."

Her position was particularly delicate since she was pregnant. With her physical activity severely restricted, there was little she could do to lead, or even encourage, the overthrow of her husband. The more she examined her situation, the greater appeared the risks, and she concluded that her best course was to withdraw completely from court life, do nothing, and wait to see how Peter managed his role as emperor. Catherine never gave up her ambition; instead, she simply allowed it to be guided by patience.

As she had imagined might happen, Peter's errors and the insults he heaped upon her made her more popular. On February 21, Peter's birthday, Catherine was forced to pin the ribbon of the Order of St. Catherine on Elizabeth Vorontsova's gown, an honor previously conferred only on empresses and grand duchesses. Everyone understood that this was intended as a public insult to Catherine, and it won her increased sympathy. Breteuil, the French ambassador, wrote, "The empress bears the emperor's conduct and the arrogance of Vorontsova nobly." A month later he reported that she was "putting a manly face on her troubles; she is as much loved and respected as the emperor is hated and despised." One factor in Catherine's favor was that the court and the foreign ambassadors all regarded the emperor's choice of a mistress—now the presumed empress-to-be—as farcical. Breteuil described Elizabeth Vorontsova as "having the appearance and manners of a pot-house wench." Another observer described her "broad, puffy, pock-marked face and fat, squat, shapeless figure." A third reported that "she was ugly, common and stupid." Everyone who tried to understand her appeal to the emperor failed.

In her secluded apartment, Catherine's third child, Gregory Orlov's son, was born in secrecy on April 11. Named Alexis Gregorovich (son of Gregory) and later titled Count Bobrinsky, the infant was swaddled in soft beaver skin and spirited out of the palace to be cared for by the wife of Vasily Shkurin, Catherine's faithful valet. Shkurin himself was responsible for the ruse that ensured that the birth would not be noticed. Knowing that the emperor loved fires, Shkurin waited until Catherine's contractions became severe and then set fire to his own house in the city, trusting that Peter and many in the court would rush to watch the blaze. His guess was correct, the fire spread to other houses, and Catherine was left alone with a midwife to bear her child. She recovered quickly. Ten days later, in blooming health, she received dignitaries who came to pay their respects on her thirty-third birthday. Free of the pregnancy that had curtailed her ability to speak publicly and act, she told Count Mercy, the Austrian ambassador, that she heartily detested the new treaty her husband had made with their hated mutual enemy, Prussia.

Through May, tension mounted in St. Petersburg. Preparations for Peter's Danish campaign went forward and some line regiments had moved to Narva, the first stage on the road to the battlefield. With every step in the direction of this unwanted war, resistance grew more intense. The Guards regiments, officers and men, tormented by increasing Prussian influence on their lives, were infuriated by the prospect of a distant, meaningless campaign against Denmark. Peter ignored their opposition.

The poisonous relationship between Peter and Catherine was made unmistakably clear at the end of April when Peter presided over a state banquet to celebrate the alliance with Prussia. Four hundred guests were in the hall. The emperor, wearing a blue Prussian uniform with the Prussian Order of the Black Eagle hanging from an orange ribbon around his neck, sat at the head of the table. The Prussian ambassador was on his right; Catherine was far away. Peter began by proposing three toasts. The first was to the health of the imperial family. The guests pushed back their chairs, rose, and drank. Catherine remained seated. As she put down her glass, Peter flushed with anger, sent his adjutant to ask why she had not risen to her feet. Catherine sent back word that, as the imperial family consisted only of her husband, her son, and herself, she did not think her husband would feel it necessary or appropriate for her to rise. The adjutant returned from Peter to say that the emperor said that she was a fool and ought to have known that the emperor's two uncles, both princes of Holstein and both present, were also members of the imperial family. Then, fearing that his messenger might be softening his message, Peter stood and bawled a single word, *"Dura!"* ("fool"). As this insult reverberated around the room, Catherine burst into tears. To recover, she turned to Count Stroganov, sitting next to her, and asked him to tell a funny story.

Peter had made clear to everyone not only the contempt he felt for his wife but that he scarcely regarded Catherine as his wife any longer. That same night, reeling with drink, he ordered Catherine arrested and taken to the Schlüsselburg Fortress. This command was rescinded on the urgent plea of Catherine's uncle, Prince George of Holstein, the new commander in chief of the Russian army.* After becoming emperor, Peter had brought this Holstein cousin to Russia to command the army in the Danish campaign. In this capacity, George pointed out to Peter that the arrest of the empress would arouse violent indignation in the army. Peter backed away and canceled the order, but the episode was a warning to Catherine. "It was then," she wrote later to Poniatowski, "that I began to listen to the proposals [to depose Peter] which people had been making to me to me since the death of the empress." Of course, she had been listening long before.

The "Dura!" episode turned all eyes on Catherine. Outwardly, she bore this public humiliation with dignity and resignation. But this was a façade; Catherine had never willingly resigned herself to such treatment. It was obvious to her that Peter's hostility had evolved into a determination to end their marriage and remove her from public life. She held positions of strength, however. She was the mother of the heir; her intelligence, competence, courage, and patriotism were widely known; and while Peter was piling blunder on top of blunder, her popularity was soaring. The moment to act was approaching.

On June 12, Peter left St. Petersburg for Oranienbaum to drill his fourteen hundred Holstein soldiers before sending them off to war. Rumors of restlessness in the capital reached him, but his only precautionary response was to order Catherine to leave the city. He instructed her to take herself not to Oranienbaum, where she had spent sixteen summers; (Oranienbaum was now the domain of Vorontsova, the empress-to-be) but to Peterhof, six miles away. Catherine traveled to Peterhof on June 17. As a precaution, she left Paul behind in the cap-

---

*George Lewis was Catherine's mother's younger brother, and Peter's second cousin. This was the young man who had believed himself in love with Catherine— then Sophia, a girl of fourteen.

ital with Panin. Meanwhile, the Orlov brothers, circulating among the Guards, speeded the flow of money and wine to the men in the barracks—all of these good things passed out in the name of the Empress Catherine.

Panin, the Orlovs, and Dashkova understood that the crisis was near. Panin's support was firm. What rapport could there be between a feather-brained, garrulous monarch, pretending to be a soldier and affecting the language of the barracks, and a highly educated statesman, elegant, naturally reserved, of fastidious taste, who had spent half his life at courts, wearing a powdered wig and an elaborate, brocaded costume? There was more than a difference in style. Peter had spoken openly of sending Panin back to Sweden, where his task as Russian ambassador would be to work in the interests of Frederick and Prussia—in direct contradiction to Panin's own political views. This cautious diplomat never intended to be a principal leader in a revolution, but Panin had now become not only the guardian of Catherine's son and heir but also her chief ministerial counselor during this critical moment in her life. He was well qualified.

Another powerful figure had joined the empress. This was Count Kyril Razumovsky, who, twelve years before, had ridden forty miles every day to visit Catherine. Well educated and genial, a court figure whom everyone admired, he was chafing under the regime of Peter III. Razumovsky, grown plump, knew how absurd he looked in a tight-fitting Prussian uniform and that his clumsiness on the parade ground offended as well as amused the emperor. When Peter had boasted to him that King Frederick had made him a colonel in the Prussian army, Razumovsky caustically replied, "Your Majesty can have your revenge by making him a field marshal in the Russian army." Razumovsky had already cast his lot with Catherine and could help in many ways. Besides being hetman of the Cossacks, he was colonel of the Izmailovsky Guards Regiment and president of the Russian Academy of Sciences. At a critical moment, Razumovsky told the director of the academy printing press to begin secretly printing copies of a manifesto, written by Panin and approved by Catherine, declaring that Peter III had abdicated and that Catherine had assumed the throne. Frightened, the director protested that this was premature and dangerous. Razumovsky fixed him with a stare. "You already know too much," he said. "Now your head, as well as mine, is at stake. Do as I say."

Nothing, however, could be done without the Guards. By chance,

Gregory Orlov had been appointed paymaster of the Guards Artillery, giving him access to substantial funds, which he used to pay for the wine he distributed to the soldiers. By the end of June, he and his brothers had won the support of fifty officers, and, they believed, thousands of the rank and file. One of the most enthusiastic officers was a Captain Passek of the Preobrazhensky Guards.

Thus, while Peter at Oranienbaum was preparing his military campaign against Denmark, the conspirators were planning their coup against him. Their first idea had been to seize Peter in his room in the palace and declare him incompetent to rule, just as Empress Elizabeth had seized Ivan VI and his mother while they were asleep, twenty-one years earlier. The departure of Peter for Oranienbaum, where he would be surrounded by hundreds of loyal Holstein soldiers, had thwarted this plan. To replace it, they had agreed to Panin's proposal that Peter be arrested when he returned to the capital to witness the departure of the Guards regiments for the Danish campaign. The Guards, still in the capital and primed by the Orlovs, would depose Peter and swear allegiance to Catherine.

On June 7, members of the emperor's retinue were told to be ready to start within ten days. The Preobrazhensky Guards were ordered to prepare to leave for Germany on July 7. Foreign embassies were informed that when the emperor left to command his armies, he wished all foreign ambassadors to accompany him. But Mercy of Austria had already left for Vienna; Breteuil of France departed quickly for Paris; of the prominent diplomatic envoys in the capital, only Keith of England packed his trunks. The Russian naval squadron at Kronstadt was ordered to be ready to sail. Unfortunately, the admiral reported that many sailors were sick; Peter responded by issuing a decree commanding the sailors "to get well immediately."

The atmosphere at Oranienbaum remained remarkably peaceful. Peter seemed almost reluctant to leave. On June 19, an opera was performed during which Peter played his violin in the court orchestra. Catherine was invited and came from Peterhof. This was the last time husband and wife were to see each other.

On the evening of June 27, one of the conspirators, Captain Passek of the Guards, was accosted by a soldier who asked him whether the rumor was true that the empress had been arrested and a conspiracy discovered. Passek dismissed the story, whereupon the soldier went to another officer, this one ignorant of the conspiracy, and repeated his question and Passek's reaction. This officer promptly arrested the soldier and reported the matter to his superior. The senior officer then arrested Captain Passek and sent a report to the emperor at Oranienbaum. Peter disregarded the warning. He considered the presence of the principal ministers of state with their wives at Oranienbaum to be a guarantee of the good behavior of the capital. He dismissed the idea that Russians would prefer Catherine to himself as ruler. When he was given a second report describing the increasing restlessness in St. Petersburg, Peter, who was playing his violin and resented interruptions, impatiently ordered the note left on a small table nearby so he could read it later. He forgot it.

In the capital, news of Passek's arrest alarmed the leading conspirators. When Gregory Orlov hurried to Panin to ask what should be done, he found the older man with Princess Dashkova. Panin recognized the possibility that Passek might be tortured and that the conspirators could be sure of their freedom for only a few hours. They must act quickly. Catherine must be brought back to the capital and proclaimed empress without waiting for the arrest and deposition of the emperor. Panin, Dashkova, and Orlov agreed that Gregory's brother, Alexis, should hurry to Peterhof and bring Catherine back to the city. The other brothers were to circulate through the barracks of the Guards, sounding the alarm that the empress's life was in danger and preparing the regiments to support her. Gregory himself was to go to the barracks of Kyril Razumovsky's Izmailovsky Guards, which lay at the city's limits on the western road to Peterhof and Oranienbaum. This unit would be the first Guards regiment Catherine would reach when she was escorted back from Peterhof. Alexis Orlov arrived at the meeting, was told what had happened, and immediately went down to the street and hired an ordinary Petersburg street carriage. In this shabby rig, he set off through the luminous, silvery night on the road to Peterhof, twenty miles away.

The next morning, Friday, June 28, Catherine was asleep in Peter the Great's small waterside pavilion of Mon Plaisir in the gardens of Peterhof. Built in the Dutch style, this little building sat on a narrow terrace only a few feet above the gently lapping waves of the Gulf of Finland.

At five o'clock, the empress was awakened by a maidservant. The next moment Alexis Orlov, arriving from St. Petersburg, quietly entered the room and whispered, "Matushka, Little Mother, wake up! The time has come! You must get up and come with me! Everything is ready for your proclamation!"

Startled, Catherine sat up in bed. "What do you mean?" she asked.

"Passek is arrested," Orlov explained. Wordlessly, the empress arose and put on a simple black dress. Without arranging her hair or powdering her face, she accompanied Orlov out the door and through the gardens to the road where his hired carriage was waiting. Catherine got in, accompanied by her maid and her servant Shkurin, while Orlov sat up on the box next to the driver. They set off to return to the capital, twenty miles away, but the two horses, which had already traveled twenty miles that night, were exhausted. Fortunately, a peasant cart drawn by two farm horses appeared on the road. Persuaded by arguments and coins, the peasant driver agreed to exchange his two fresh farm horses for the tired city horses and, in this rustic style, the empress-to-be proceeded toward her destiny. Halfway to the city, they met Catherine's hairdresser on his way to Peterhof to prepare her hair for the day. The empress turned him around, saying that she would not need him. Then, nearing the capital, they encountered another carriage, bringing Gregory Orlov and Prince Bariatinsky to meet them. Gregory took Catherine and Alexis into his carriage and drove directly to the barracks of the Izmailovsky Guards.

It was nine in the morning when they reached the barracks courtyard. Gregory Orlov leaped from the carriage and ran to announce Catherine's arrival. A drummer boy came tumbling out a door, followed by a dozen soldiers, some half-dressed, others fastening on their sword belts. They pressed around Catherine, kissed her hands, feet, and the hem of her black dress. To a gathering, larger crowd of soldiers, the empress said that her life and that of her son had been threatened by the emperor, but that it was not for her own sake, but for that of her beloved country and their holy Orthodox religion that she was compelled to throw herself on their protection. The response was enthusiastic. Kyril Razumovsky, the regiment's popular colonel and Catherine's supporter, arrived, bent his knee before the empress, and kissed her hand. On the spot, the regimental chaplain, holding a cross before him, administered an oath of allegiance to "Catherine II of Russia." It was the beginning.

The Izmailovskys, with Razumovsky riding at their head with a drawn sword, escorted Catherine to the nearby barracks of the Semyonovsky Guards. The Semyonovskys rushed to meet Catherine and swear allegiance. She decided to enter the city immediately. Preceded by chaplains and other priests and followed by a mass of cheering Guardsmen, she rode to the Cathedral of Our Lady of Kazan on the Nevsky Prospekt. There, flanked by the Orlov brothers and Razumovsky, she stood before the iconostasis (icon screen) while the archbishop of Novgorod solemnly proclaimed her *Gosudarina* (sovereign autocrat) Catherine II and her son, Paul Petrovich, heir to the throne.

Surrounded by a cheering crowd, with church bells ringing across the city, the empress walked down the Nevsky Prospect to the Winter Palace. There, an obstacle arose. The senior regiment of the Guards, the Preobrazhensky, had wavered. The majority of the soldiers favored Catherine, but some of the officers, having sworn an oath to defend the emperor, were uncertain. After a debate among themselves, the soldiers buckled on their swords, snatched up their muskets, tore off their tight-fitting Prussian uniforms, and dressed in as many of their old bottle-green jackets as they could find. Then, more like a mob than a military body, they hurried to the Winter Palace, which they found surrounded and guarded by the Izmailovsky and Semyonovsky regiments. The Preobrazhenskys shouted to Catherine, "Matushka, forgive us for coming last. Our officers held us back and, to prove our zeal, we have arrested four of them. We wish the same thing as our brothers." The empress responded by nodding, smiling, and sending the archbishop of Novgorod to administer the oath of allegiance to the latecomers.

Soon after the empress entered the Winter Palace, an older man and a young boy, still in his nightdress, arrived. It was Panin, holding Paul in his arms. On the palace balcony, Catherine presented her eight-year-old son to the crowd as heir to the throne. At this moment, Panin abandoned his thought that Catherine should act as regent for a boy emperor; Catherine now was God's anointed, the sovereign autocrat. Soon, another late arrival came on the scene. Princess Dashkova had been at home that morning when she learned that Catherine had returned to the city in triumph. She had started immediately to join her idol, but was forced to abandon her carriage when it was immobilized by the dense crowd on the Nevsky Prospect. Squirming and elbowing, she made her way through the mass of bodies in Palace Square. In the palace itself, she was recognized by members of her husband's regiment, who lifted her small figure above their heads, and passed her, hand over hand, up Rastelli's magnificent white marble staircase. She landed at Catherine's feet, crying, "Heaven be praised."

In the palace, members of the Senate and the Holy Synod waited to greet the new empress and listen to her first imperial manifesto. It declared that Catherine, moved by the perils threatening Russia and the Orthodox religion, eager to rescue Russia from a shameful dependence on foreign powers, and sustained by divine providence, had yielded to the clear wishes of her faithful subjects that she should ascend the throne.

By early evening Catherine was in a commanding position in the capital. She was sure of the Guards, the Senate, the Holy Synod, and the crowds in the street. Calm prevailed in the city and no blood had been shed. But, as she knew, if she was mistress of St. Petersburg, acclaimed by the regiments there and by the political leaders and the leaders of the church, Peter was unaware of this. He still believed he was emperor. Possibly he still possessed the allegiance of the army in Germany and the fleet at Kronstadt. The Holstein soldiers at Oranienbaum would certainly support their master. To confirm her victory, Catherine must locate Peter and persuade him to abdicate, the Holsteiners must be disarmed, and the fleet and all Russian soldiers near the capital must be persuaded to join her. The key to success was Peter himself; he remained free and had neither abdicated nor been deposed. If he made his way to the Russian army in Germany, calling on the king of Prussia to support him, a civil war was inevitable. Accordingly, he must be found, seized, and forced to accept what had happened.

After this tumultuous, triumphant day, Catherine was exhausted, but, sustained by excitement and ambition, she decided to finish what she had begun. A strong force of the Guards pledged to her must march to Oranienbaum to arrest Peter III. Here, Catherine made another dramatic decision: she would lead this march herself. First, she had herself proclaimed colonel of the Preobrazhensky Guards; this was the traditional privilege and rank of a Russian sovereign. Borrowing different parts of the bottle-green Preobrazhensky uniform from various obliging young officers, she dressed and put on one of their black, three-cornered hats crowned with oak leaves. Still, one piece of equipment was missing. A twenty-two-year-old subaltern of the Horse Guards rode out of the ranks to hand to the empress the sword knot her uniform was lacking. His officers frowned on the impertinence, but his proud, confident bearing pleased the empress, who accepted the gift with a smile. She asked his name; it was Gregory Potemkin. His face, his name, and his action would not be forgotten.

By then, it was ten o'clock at night. Catherine mounted a white stallion, placed herself at the head of the three Guards regiments, the Horse Guards, and two infantry regiments of the line, and led fourteen thousand men out of St. Petersburg to Oranienbaum. It was a dramatic sight, the slim figure of Catherine, a superb horsewoman, at the head of a long column of marching men. At her side rode Kyril Razumovsky, colonel of the Semyonovsky Guards, and Princess Dashkova, also dressed in a Preobrazhensky uniform, which she had borrowed from a young lieutenant. This was her moment of glory, riding beside her beloved empress, and looking—as she described herself—"like a fifteen-year-old boy." She saw herself that night as the central figure in the great adventure. Eventually, this presumption was to lose her the friendship she valued so highly, but on this night nothing clouded her relationship with Catherine. Despite the enthusiasm of their departure, everyone on the march—the empress, the princess, the officers, and the men—all were exhausted. When the column reached a wooden hut on the road to Peterhof, Catherine called a halt. The soldiers watered their horses and bivouacked in the open fields. Catherine and Dashkova, both fully clothed, lay down in the hut, side by side on a narrow bed, but both women were too excited to sleep.

Before leaving St. Petersburg, Catherine had sent off messages. One was to the Kronstadt island fortress and the ships waiting there, informing them of her accession. A special courier was dispatched to the army in Pomerania authorizing Nikita Panin's brother, General Peter Panin, to take over as commander. Another courier went to General Zakhar Chernyshev in Silesia ordering him to bring his army corps back to Russia immediately. If the king of Prussia tried to prevent this, Chernyshev was to "join the nearest army corps of her Imperial Roman Majesty, the empress of Austria." Before leaving, she also wrote to the Senate, "I go now with the army to secure and safeguard the throne and leave in your care as my highest representatives with fullest confidence, the fatherland, the people, and my son."

· · ·

That morning of June 28, even as Catherine was being proclaimed Autocrat of All the Russias in the Kazan Cathedral in St. Petersburg, Peter III, wearing his blue Prussian uniform, was drilling his Holstein soldiers on the parade ground at Oranienbaum. This concluded, he ordered six large carriages to carry him and his entourage to Peterhof, where, he had informed Catherine, he would celebrate his name day, the Feast of St. Peter and St. Paul. In the emperor's party were Elizabeth Vorontsova; her uncle, Chancellor Michael Vorontsov; the Prussian ambassador, Baron von Goltz; Count Alexander Shuvalov; the elderly Field Marshal Count Münnich; and the senior senator, Prince Trubetskoy. Many of these dignitaries were accompanied by their wives, and there were also sixteen young maids of honor who served the presumed empress-to-be. This cavalcade started without the usual escort of hussars; Peter had forgotten to order it.

In high spirits, the company arrived at Peterhof at two in the afternoon. The carriages pulled up in front of the Mon Plaisir pavilion, where Catherine was supposed to be waiting to congratulate her consort on his name day. When they arrived, the doors and windows were tightly closed and no one came out to greet them. No one, in fact, was there at all except a frightened servant, who could tell them only that the empress had left early that morning and that he did not know where she had gone. Refusing to believe what he had seen and been told, Peter rushed inside the empty house, running from room to room, peeping under beds, lifting mattresses, and finding nothing except the gala dress laid out the night before for Catharine to wear at Peter's name day celebration. Infuriated that Catherine had spoiled his moment and his day, he screamed at Vorontsova, "Didn't I always tell you she was capable of anything?" After an hour of tumult and dismay, the chancellor, Michael Vorontsov, volunteered to go to back to St. Petersburg, where Catherine was presumed to have gone, to seek information and "speak seriously to the empress." Alexander Shuvalov and Prince Trubetskoy offered to accompany him. At six o'clock, when they reached the city, Catherine was still there and Vorontsov made an effort to tell her that she should not be taking up arms against her husband and sovereign. Catherine's response was to lead him onto a palace balcony and point to the cheering crowd below. "Deliver your message to them, sir," she said. "It is they who command here. I only obey." Vorontsov was taken to his house where, that evening, he wrote to Catherine as his "most gracious sovereign, whom the inscrutable decree of Providence has raised to the Imperial throne." He asked to be relieved of all his offices and duties and allowed to pass the rest of his days in seclusion. Before nightfall, Alexander Shuvalov swore allegiance to Catherine.

At three in the afternoon, after these three emissaries had departed from Peterhof, Peter received the first sketchy information about the coup. A barge, traveling across the bay from the city, carried the fireworks intended for use that night in the name day celebration. The lieutenant in charge, a specialist in fireworks, told Peter that at nine that morning, when he had left the capital, there was great excitement in the barracks and the streets because of a rumor that Catherine had arrived in the city and that some of the troops had proclaimed her empress. He knew no more because, given orders to deliver fireworks to Peterhof, he had departed.

That afternoon at Peterhof was warm and sunny, and the lesser members of Peter's entourage remained on the terraces near the cool spray of the fountains or wandered through the gardens under the cloudless summer sky. Peter and his primary counselors gathered near the main canal, where Peter paced back and forth, listening to advice. An officer was sent to Oranienbaum to order the Holstein regiments stationed there to march to Peterhof, where, Peter declared, he would defend himself to the death. When the Holstein soldiers arrived, they were posted on the road to the capital, but, not understanding that they might be ordered to fight, they had brought only their wooden parade ground rifles. Another officer was sent to Kronstadt, five miles across the bay, to order three thousand men of the island garrison to come by boat to Peterhof. A uniform of the Preobrazhensky Guards was found so that Peter might replace the Prussian uniform he was wearing. The old soldier Münnich, in an effort to put some steel into Peter, urged him to put on this uniform, ride straight to the capital, show himself to the people and the Guards, and remind them of their oath of loyalty. Goltz offered different advice: he counseled going to Narva, seventy miles to the west, where part of the army destined for the Danish war was assembling; at the head of this force, Peter could march on St. Petersburg and retake his throne. The Holsteiners, knowing their master's character best, advised him bluntly to flee to Holstein, where he would be safe. Peter did nothing.

Meanwhile, the officer sent to Kronstadt arrived at the island fortress and found the commandant of the garrison unaware of any of the turmoil either in the capital or at Peterhof. Soon after, another messenger dispatched by Peter arrived and countermanded the order to send three thousand men to Peterhof, telling the island commander simply to secure the Kronstadt fortress in the emperor's name. Subsequently, he returned to Peterhof to report to the emperor that the fortress was being held for him. Shortly thereafter, Admiral Ivan Talyzin, commander of the Russian navy, who that morning had sworn allegiance to Catherine, arrived at Kronstadt from St. Petersburg and took command of the fortress himself in the name of the new empress. The soldiers of the garrison and the crews of the naval vessels in the harbor swore allegiance to Catherine.

At ten that night, Peter's last envoy returned from Kronstadt to Peterhof with what he thought was good news, although by now it was inaccurate: that the fortress was secure for the emperor. During this messenger's six-hour absence, the situation at Peterhof had deteriorated. Members of Peter's suite were aimlessly walking about or had stretched out to sleep on benches in the park. The Holstein troops, fresh from Oranienbaum but possessing no weapons, now were deployed "to repel attack." Peter, told that Kronstadt was secure, decided to go to the island. A large galley, anchored offshore, was brought alongside the quay and he boarded, taking many of his officers with him. He refused to leave Elizabeth Vorontsova behind and insisted on taking along her sixteen frightened maids of honor.

Out on the bay in the silvery brightness of the White Nights, visibility was almost as clear as daylight. The wind was favorable, and at about one o'clock in the morning, the crowded galley approached Kronstadt Harbor. The entrance was closed by a boom. The vessel dropped anchor outside the walls. Peter climbed down into a small boat and was rowed toward the fortress to command that the boom be raised. The young officer on duty on the ramparts shouted down that the boat should keep away or he would open fire. Peter stood up, throwing aside his cloak in order to display his uniform and the broad blue ribbon of the Order of St. Andrew. "Don't you know me?" he shouted. "I am your emperor!"

"We no longer have an emperor! " came the reply. "Long live the Empress Catherine II! She is now our empress and we have orders to admit nobody within these walls. Another move forward and we fire!" Frightened, Peter hurried back to the galley, clambered aboard, and rushed into the stern cabin, where he collapsed into the arms of Elizabeth Vorontsova. Münnich took charge and and gave the order to steer for the mainland. At four in the morning the galley reached Oranienbaum, which he considered safer than Peterhof.

On disembarking, Peter learned that the empress, at the head of a large military force, was marching toward him. Hearing this, he gave up. He dismissed everyone. In tears, he told Goltz to go back to St. Petersburg because he could no longer protect him. He sent away as many of the women as the carriages could hold, but Elizabeth Vorontsova refused to abandon him. He lay down on a couch, refusing to speak. A little later, he sat up, sent for pen and paper, and wrote a letter to Catherine in French, apologizing for his behavior toward her, promising to do better, and offering to share his throne with her. He gave this letter to the vice-chancellor, Prince Alexander Golitsyn, to deliver to his wife.

At five o'clock in the morning, twenty-four hours after Alexis Orlov had awakened her at Mon Plasir, Catherine and her army had resumed their march. On the road to Peterhof, Prince Golitsyn met Catherine and handed her Peter's letter. Reading it, and understanding that it offered only half of what she already possessed, she remarked that the welfare of the state now demanded other measures and that there would be no reply. Golitsyn's immediate response was to take the oath of allegiance to Catherine as empress.

After waiting in vain for a reply to his first letter, Peter wrote a second, this time offering to abdicate if he could take Elizabeth Vorontsova with him to Holstein. Catherine told his new messenger, General Izmailov, "I accept the offer but I must have the abdication in writing." Izmailov returned to Peter and, finding the despairing emperor sitting with his head in his hands, said to him, "You see, the empress wants to be friendly with you, and if you will voluntarily resign the Imperial crown, you may retire to Holstein unmolested." Peter signed an abdication written in the most abject terms. He declared himself entirely responsible for the decay of the realm during his reign and utterly incapable of ruling. "I, Peter, of my own free will hereby solemnly declare, not only to the whole Russian empire, but also to the whole world, that I forever renounce the throne of Russia to the end of my days. Nor will I ever seek to recover the same at any time or by anybody's assistance, and I swear this before God."

The six-month reign of Peter III was over. Years later, Frederick the Great said, "He allowed himself to be dethroned like a child being sent to bed."

❧44❧

"We Ourselves Know Not What We Did"

RIDING AHEAD of Catherine's advancing army, a group of horse-men led by Alexis Orlov galloped into the Peterhof park and set about disarming the helpless Holstein soldiers. Then, learning that Peter himself had left Peterhof, first for Kronstadt and then for Oran-ienbaum, Alexis hurried on to the second estate, six miles away, to seize the former emperor. At Oranienbaum, he found Peter with Elizabeth Vorontsova. A small carriage, unused for years and covered with dust, was brought out. Surrounded by an escort of mounted guards com-manded by Alexis Orlov, the little carriage with Peter and Elizabeth inside started back for Peterhof.

Simultaneously, Catherine's regiments were arriving at Peterhof. At eleven, the empress, in her uniform of the Preobrazhensky Guards and riding her white horse, reached Peterhof and dismounted into a sea of cheering men. Between noon and one o'clock, the carriage bringing Peter drove into the palace grounds. There was a profound silence. Peter had been warned not to show himself or speak a word to the men through whose ranks his carriage passed. When he stepped out of the carriage, his first request was that he be allowed to see Catherine. It was refused. Not knowing when he would see Vorontsova again, believing that their parting would be temporary, he turned to say goodbye. They were never to see each other again. The former emperor was led up a stairway to a little room in the palace, where he surrendered his sword and the blue ribbon of the Order of St. Andrew. He was stripped of his high black boots and his green Preobrazhensky Guards uniform and left standing in his shirt and stockings, a pathetic, trembling figure. Eventually, an old dressing gown and a pair of slippers were provided.

Later that afternoon, Nikita Panin arrived from St. Petersburg and was sent by Catherine to see her husband. Panin found himself profoundly moved by the former emperor's appearance. Years later, Panin said, "I count it the greatest misfortune of my life that I was forced to see Peter III that day under these conditions." Panin's message was that the former emperor was now a state prisoner and that his future would include "decent and convenient rooms" in the fortress of Schlüsselburg—where Peter had visited Ivan VI three months earlier. It was implied that from Schlüsselburg he would eventually be allowed to return to his duchy of Holstein. While the rooms in the fortress were being prepared, Peter was permitted to choose a place of temporary confinement. He selected Ropsha, a lonely but pleasant summerhouse and estate, fourteen miles away.

Catherine had no wish to add to her husband's humiliation. She did not even trust herself to see him, uncertain whether she would see the boy who had been her friend eighteen years before when she first arrived in Russia or the drunken bully who had just shouted "Fool!" at her across a crowded room and threatened her with prison. Her concern was not to lose her grip on what, after years of waiting, she had finally achieved. Peter would have to be rendered harmless. It was impossible to send him back to his native Kiel, although he remained Duke of Holstein. In Holstein, he would always be an attraction to anyone wishing to use him as a rallying point against her. The king of Prussia would be nearby; why should Frederick not employ Peter as a pawn who might be converted back into a king? Her conclusion was that Peter, like Ivan VI, would have to be imprisoned in Russia.

Even in the countryside at Ropsha, Peter would remain a potential threat. To be certain that he would be guarded adequately, she appointed as chief jailer the stern, rough soldier Alexis Orlov, who already had done much to ensure the success of the coup. Along with Orlov, three other officers and a detachment of a hundred soldiers were given orders to make Peter's life "as agreeable as possible and to provide what he wished for." At six o'clock that evening, Peter left Peterhof for Ropsha in a large six-horse carriage with the blinds down, surrounded by an escort of Horse Guards. Inside the carriage with the former emperor were Alexis Orlov, Lieutenant Prince Bariatinsky, Captain Passek, and another officer.

Nikita Panin, Alexis and Gregory Orlov, and Kyril Razumovsky had all played significant roles in the coup that brought Catherine to power. Princess Dashkova, on the other hand, had been superfluous. She had ridden to Peterhof beside the empress and shared a narrow bed with her during a few hours of rest, but she had played no part in any of the critical decisions or actions. She was aware of the Orlovs but had no knowledge of Gregory's particular role and status. This changed suddenly. After Peter had been driven off to Ropsha, Dashkova happened to enter the empress's private apartment in the Peterhof Palace. She was surprised to find Lieutenant Orlov stretched out full-length on a couch, resting a leg that had been injured in a struggle with some of Peter's Holsteiners. Orlov had before him a heap of sealed official papers which he was opening and reading. Catherine Dashkova, wholly unaware of the empress's relationship with Gregory—whom the princess considered to be far beneath both the empress and herself in social class and intelligence—was infuriated at seeing the soldier so obviously at ease, reading state documents. "By what right are you reading papers which are no concern of yours?" she asked. "No one has a right to read them except the empress and those whom she especially appoints."

"Exactly," Orlov replied, smiling. "The empress asked me to open them."

"I doubt that," Dashkova replied. "They could have waited until Her Majesty had appointed someone who was qualified to read them. Neither you nor I are sufficiently experienced in these matters," she said, and left the room.

Returning later, she found Orlov still reclining on the couch, and, this time, the empress, relaxed and happy, was sitting beside him. A table set for supper for three was drawn up beside the couch. Catherine welcomed Dashkova and invited her to join them. During the meal, the princess noted the deference with which the empress treated the young officer, nodding and laughing at whatever he said, making no effort to hide her affection for him. It was at that moment, Dashkova wrote later, that "I realized with unspeakable pain and humiliation that a liaison existed between the two."

The long day was not over. Catherine was exhausted, but the officers and men of the Guards wanted to return to St. Petersburg to celebrate, and she wished to please them. Accordingly, the victorious empress left Peterhof that same night to return to St. Petersburg. She halted briefly for a few hours of sleep, and on Sunday morning, June 30, still in uniform and still riding her white horse, she made a triumphant entry into the capital. The streets were crowded with excited people; church bells pealed, drums rolled. She attended a mass and a solemn Te Deum—and went to bed. She slept until midnight, when a rumor that the Prussians were coming spread among the Izmailovsky Guards, many of them tipsy from the generous amounts of alcohol they had been drinking. Fearing that she had been kidnapped or assassinated, they left their barracks, marched to the palace, and demanded to see the empress. She rose, put on her uniform, and went out to reassure them that all was well: she was safe, they were safe, the empire was safe. Then she went back to bed and slept another eight hours.

At eight o'clock that night, Peter arrived at Ropsha. The stone house, built during the reign of Peter the Great, was surrounded by a park with a lake in which Empress Elizabeth had liked to fish. She had given it to Peter, her nephew. Alexis Orlov, responsible for the prisoner, lodged him in a small ground-floor room containing little more than a bed. The window blinds were kept closely drawn so that the soldiers posted around the building could not see in. Even at midday, the room remained in twilight. An armed sentry stood guard at the door. Peter, shut up inside, was not permitted to walk in the park or to take the air on the terrace outside. He was permitted, however, to write to Catherine, and over the next days, he wrote three letters to her. The first:

> I beg Your Majesty to have confidence in me and to have the goodness to order the guards removed from the second room as the one I occupy is so small that I can hardly move in it. As Your Majesty knows, I always walk about in the room and my legs swell if I cannot do so. Also I beg you to order that no officers should remain in the same room with me since I must relieve myself and I cannot possibly do that in front of them. Finally, I beg Your Majesty not to treat me as a criminal as I have never offended Your Majesty. I commend myself to Your Majesty's magnanimity and beg to be reunited in Germany with the person named [Elizabeth Vorontsova]. God will repay Your Majesty.
>
> Your very humble, devoted servant,
> Peter

> Your Majesty can rest assured that I will not think or do anything against Your Majesty's person or reign.

The second letter:

> Your Majesty:
> If you do not wish to destroy a man already sufficiently miserable, have pity on me and send me my only consolation, Elizabeth Romanovna [Vorontsova]. It would be the greatest act of charity of your reign. Also, if Your Majesty would grant me the right to see you for a moment, my highest wishes would be fulfilled.
>
> Your humble servant,
Peter

The third letter:

> Your Majesty:
> Once again, I beg you, since I have followed your wishes in everything, to allow me to leave for Germany with the persons for whom I have already asked Your Majesty to grant permission. I hope your magnanimity will not permit my request to be in vain.
>
> Your humble servant,
Peter

Catherine left the letters unanswered.

The first full day of Peter's imprisonment was Sunday, June 30. The next morning, he complained that he had suffered a bad night and would never be able to sleep properly until he could sleep in his own bed from Oranienbaum. Catherine immediately had the bed, a large four-poster with a white satin coverlet, sent to him by wagon. Next, he asked that his violin, his poodle, his German doctor, and his black servant be sent to him. The empress ordered that all of these requests be granted; in fact, only the doctor arrived. Whenever the prisoner asked permission to take the air outside, Alexis opened the door, pointed to the armed sentry barring the way, and shrugged his shoulders.

Catherine and her advisers were still uncertain what to do with the former emperor. The original plan of imprisoning Peter in Schlüsselburg now seemed inadequate. Schlüsselburg was only forty miles from the capital and he would become the second deposed emperor imprisoned in this bastion. Sending him back to Holstein had been ruled out. But if not to Schlüsselburg or Holstein, where was he to go?

There is no evidence that Catherine ever concluded that Peter's death was necessary to her own political—and perhaps physical—survival. She did agree with her advisers that he must be rendered "harmless." Catherine was determined to take no risks, and her friends were aware of this determination. She was, on the other hand, too prudent to hint at the desirability of an unnatural death. It is possible, however, that the Orlovs had already guessed her inner thoughts and persuaded themselves that, as long as their mistress was not admitted into their confidence or given foreknowledge of their plans, they might safely rid her of this danger. Certainly, the Orlovs themselves had a strong motive for ending Peter's life. Gregory Orlov was hoping to marry his imperial mistress, and Peter stood in his way. Even dethroned and imprisoned, Peter still would be, in the eyes of God, Catherine's lawful husband; nothing but death could sever a marriage bond that had received the blessing of the Orthlodox Church. If, on the other hand, the former emperor were to die, there would be no religious bar to a marriage between Catherine and Gregory. Empress Elizabeth had married Alexis Razumovsky, a Ukranian peasant; he, Gregory, an officer of the Guards, was of a higher class and rank.

At Ropsha, mental confusion and fear of the unknown plagued Peter's health. Alternately, he lay prostrate on his bed and rose to pace the small room. On Tuesday, the third day of his captivity, he was stricken by acute diarrhea. On Wednesday evening, he suffered a headache so violent that his Holstein physician, Dr. Luders, was brought from St. Petersburg. On Thursday morning, the former emperor seemed no better, and a second doctor was summoned. Later that day, the two doctors pronounced their patient recovering and, having no desire to share his incarceration, returned to the capital. On Friday, all was quiet. Then, early Saturday morning, Peter's seventh day at Ropsha, while the prisoner still slept, his French valet, Bresson, who had been allowed to stroll in the park, was abruptly seized, gagged, thrust into a closed carriage, and driven away. Peter was not told and did not know. At two o'clock, Peter was invited to dinner with Alexis Orlov, Lieutenant Bariatinsky, and the other officers of his guard.

The only eyewitness to describe the subsequent event confessed to

the empress herself. At six o'clock on Saturday evening, a rider galloping from Ropsha reached St. Petersburg and Catherine was handed a
note from Alexis Orlov. It was written in Russian on a sheet of dirty
gray paper. The handwriting was scrawled and almost illegible; its message verged on incoherence. The letter seemed to have been written by
a man shaking from drink or frantic with worry. Or both.

> Matushka, Little Mother, most merciful Gosudarina, sover-
> eign lady, how can I explain or describe what happened? You
> will not believe your faithful servant, but before God I speak
> the truth, Matushka. I am ready for death, but I myself know
> not how it came about. We are lost if you do not have mercy on
> us. Matushka, he is no more. But no one intended it so. How
> could any of us have ventured to raise our hands against our
> Gosudar, sovereign lord. But, Gosudarina, it has happened. At
> dinner, he started quarreling and struggling with Prince Bariat-
> insky at the table. Before we could separate them, he was dead.
> We ourselves know not what we did. But we are all equally
> guilty and deserve to die. Have mercy on me, if only for my
> brother's [Gregory's] sake. I have confessed my guilt and there
> is nothing further for me to tell. Forgive us or quickly make an
> end of me. The sun will no longer shine for me and life is not
> worth living. We have angered you and lost our souls forever.

What had happened? The circumstances and cause of death, and
the intentions and degree of responsibility of those involved, can never
be known, but perhaps one can merge what is known and what can be
imagined:

On Saturday, July 6, Alexis Orlov, Prince Theodore Bariatinsky,
and others invited the prisoner to join them for midday dinner. It may
be that they had spent the week wondering how long they were to be
separated from their fortunate comrades celebrating in St. Petersburg
while they were assigned to remain watching over this wretched, contemptible man. During the meal, everyone drank heavily. Then, because they had planned it, or because there was quarreling that soared
out of control, they fell on Peter and attempted to suffocate him by
placing him under a mattress. He struggled and escaped. They pinioned
him, wrapped a scarf around his neck, and strangled him.

Whether Peter's death was accidental, the result of a drunken scuffle after dinner that got out of control, or a deliberate, premeditated murder will never be known. The frantic, semicoherent tone of Orlov's scribbled letter, seeming to betray fear of repercussion as well as horror and remorse, suggests that he had not planned to go that far. When he arrived in the capital that night, he was disheveled, bathed in sweat, and covered with dust. "His face," said someone who happened to see him "wore an expression that was frightful to see." Orlov's pleas to Catherine for mercy—"We ourselves know not what we did" and "Forgive us or quickly make an end of me"—suggest that, while admitting that he was present when Peter died, this was not what he had planned.

In either case, whether the death was unintended or was planned in advance by the officers, Catherine herself would seem to have been innocent. However, she was not blameless. She had placed her husband in the hands of Alexis Orlov, knowing that Alexis was a soldier untroubled by violent death and that he hated Peter. But Orlov's letter shocked Catherine. Its frantic language and desperate pleas make it almost impossible to believe that Catherine had previous knowledge of any intent to murder and had given her consent. Nor was Alexis Orlov the kind of sophisticated, duplicitous writer who could manage to concoct so frenzied and abject a story. In the mind of Princess Dashkova, Orlov's letter exonerated Catherine of all suspicion of complicity. When Dashkova visited her friend on the following day, she was greeted by Catherine's words, "My horror at this death is inexpressible. This blow strikes me to the earth!" The princess, still equating her role in events with that of the empress, could not refrain from saying, "It is a death too sudden, Madame, for your glory and for mine."

Whatever happened, Catherine had to deal with the aftermath. Her husband, the former emperor, was dead in the custody of her friends and supporters. Would she arrest Alexis Orlov and the other officers at Ropsha? If she did so, how would Gregory, the father of her three-month-old child, react? How would the Guards react? How would the Senate, St. Petersburg, and the Russian people react? Her decision, made, perhaps, on Panin's recommendation, was to treat the death as a medical tragedy. To deal with the widespread knowledge that the officers guarding her husband were known to have hated him, she ordered a postmortem examination. She had the body dissected by doctors who could be trusted to clear Orlov. The doctors opened the body, and, as they were told to do, looked only for evidence of poisoning. Reporting that there was no such evidence, they declared that Peter

had died of natural causes, probably an acute hemorrhoidal attack—
a "colic"—which had affected his brain and brought on an apoplectic
stroke. Catherine then issued a proclamation, composed with Panin's
assistance:

> On the seventh day of our reign we received the news to
> our great sorrow and affliction that it was God's will to end the
> life of the former emperor Peter III by a severe attack of hem-
> orrhoidal colic. We have ordered his mortal remains to be
> taken to the Alexander Nevsky Monastery. We ask all our faith-
> ful subjects to bid farewell to his earthly remains without ran-
> cor and to offer up prayers for the salvation of his soul.

Panin also advised that the body be exhibited in as nearly normal a
fashion as could be managed; he believed it wiser to display a dead Peter
than to risk fostering the belief that he was still alive, hidden away
somewhere, and might reappear. The former emperor's body, lying in
state in St. Petersburg's Alexander Nevsky Monastery, had been forced
into the blue uniform of a Holstein cavalry officer, apparel that Peter
had delighted in wearing when he was alive but which, on this occasion,
was intended to draw attention to his foreign origins and preferences.
On his chest, he wore no medal or ribbon. A three-cornered hat, a size
too large, covered his forehead, but the part of his face remaining uncovered and visible was black and swollen. A long, wide cravat was
wound around his neck up to his chin around what—had the dead man
been throttled—must have been a bruised and discolored throat. His
hands, which it was the custom of the Orthodox Church to leave bare
and holding a cross, were encased in heavy leather riding gloves.

The body was placed on a bier with candles at the head and feet.
The line of viewers, kept moving quickly by soldiers, saw no Catherine
kneeling and praying over her husband as she had done for Empress
Elizabeth. Her absence, it was explained, was a result of an appeal from
the Senate that she not attend, "so that Her Imperial Majesty might
spare her health out of love for the Russian Fatherland." The site of
Peter's interment was also unusual. Although he was the grandson of
Peter the Great, the dead Peter III had not been crowned, and therefore could not lie in the fortress cathedral with the remains of consecrated tsars and empresses. On July 23, Peter's remains were placed in
the Nevsky Monastery alongside the body of Regent Anna Leopol-

dovna, mother of the deposed and imprisoned Ivan VI. Here Peter was to lie throughout his wife's thirty-four-year reign.

Catherine's explanation of this sequence of events was conveyed in a letter to Stanislaus Poniatowski, written two weeks after her husband's death:

> Peter III had lost the few wits he had. He wanted to change his religion, break up the Guards, marry Elizabeth Vorontsova, and shut me up. On the day of celebrating the peace with Prussia, after publicly insulting me at dinner, he ordered my arrest the same evening. The order was retracted, but from that time I listened to proposals [that she replace Peter on the throne] that had been made to me since the death of Empress Elizabeth. We could count on many captains of the Guards. The secret was in the hands of the Orlov brothers. They are an extremely determined family and much loved by the common soldiers. I am under great obligation to them.
>
> I sent the deposed emperor to a remote and very agreeable spot called Ropsha, under the command of Alexis Orlov with four officers and a detachment of picked, good-natured men, while decent and convenient rooms were being prepared for him at Schlüsselburg. But God disposed otherwise. Fear had caused a diarrhea which lasted three days and ended on the fourth when he drank excessively. . . . A hemorrhoidal colic seized him and affected his brain. For two days he was delirious and then delirium was followed by extreme exhaustion. Despite all the help the doctors could give him, he died while demanding a Lutheran priest. I feared that the officers might have poisoned him so I had him opened up, but not the slightest trace of poison was found. The stomach was quite healthy, but the lower bowels were greatly inflamed and a stroke of apoplexy carried him off. His heart was extraordinarily small and quite decayed.
>
> So at last God has brought everything to pass according to His designs. The whole thing is rather a miracle than a pre-arranged plan, for so many lucky circumstances could not have coincided unless God's hand had been over it all. Hatred

of foreigners was the chief factor in the whole affair and Peter III passed for a foreigner.

Most of Europe held Catherine responsible. Journals and newspapers across the continent wrote of a return to the days of Ivan the Terrible. Many were cynical about the officially proclaimed explanation that the emperor had died of "colic." "Everyone knows the nature of colic," quipped Frederick of Prussia. "When a heavy drinker dies from colic, it teaches us to be sober," deadpanned Voltaire. Frederick nevertheless believed that Catherine herself was innocent. In his memoirs, he wrote:

> The empress was quite ignorant of this crime and learned of it with an indignation and despair which was not feigned. She correctly foresaw the judgment which all the world now passes on her. An inexperienced young woman, on the point of being divorced and shut up in a convent, she had committed her cause to the Orlov brothers. And, even so, she had known nothing of the intention to murder the emperor. Left to herself, she would have kept Peter alive, partly because she thought that once she was crowned, all would be well, and that so cowardly an enemy as her husband would not be dangerous. The Orlovs, more audacious and clear-sighted, foreseeing that the ex-emperor might be turned into a rallying point against them, had been made of sterner stuff and had put out him of the way. She has reaped the fruits of their crime and has been obliged, in order to secure their support, not only to spare, but even to re-tain about her person, the authors of that crime.

Catherine, however much she might pretend to ignore foreign comment and gossip, was never at ease about Europe's reaction to her husband's death. Years later, in conversation with the French Enlight-enment figure and Encyclopedist Denis Diderot, her guest in St. Pe-tersburg, she asked, "What do they say in Paris of the death of my husband?" Diderot was too embarrassed to answer. To relieve his dis-comfort, she turned the conversation in another direction.

There was another interested party in the matter of Catherine's possi-ble involvement, who, years later, after reading Alexis Orlov's letter, exonerated the empress of guilt in the death of Peter III. Having received and read Orlov's letter, Catherine locked it away in a drawer. For the rest of her life, she kept the letter hidden. After her death, her son, Emperor Paul, was told that the letter had been discovered and that the handwriting had been identified as that of Alexis Orlov. Paul read the letter. It convinced him that his mother was innocent.

None of the participants was ever punished. Although, by proceeding against them, she could have established or at least powerfully reinforced her own innocence, Catherine could hardly have punished them. It was to Alexis Orlov and his brothers that she owed her throne. It was Alexis who had come to awaken her at dawn at Mon Plaisir and bring her to St. Petersburg. He and his brothers had risked their lives for her; in return, she was obligated to protect them. She therefore declared that Peter had died of natural causes. Some in Russia believed her; some did not; many did not care.

It was a death she had not planned, but it suited her purpose. She was free of her husband, but had acquired another burden: the shadow over her character and over Russia remained for the rest of her life. This was not the first time in history—nor would it be the last—that this kind of mixed blessing has befallen the ruler of a nation. Henry II of England appointed his former friend and protégé Thomas à Becket, to be archbishop of Canterbury. When, later, Becket confronted and opposed the king on many issues regarding the church, Henry believed himself betrayed. "Will no one rid me of this meddlesome priest?" he burst out in a moment of frustration. Whereupon four of his household knights spurred their horses to Canterbury and murdered the archbishop in front of his cathedral altar. In penance for this act that he did not specifically intend, Henry walked barefoot down miles of dusty roads to the cathedral, where he kneeled before the altar and asked forgiveness. Catherine, less secure on her throne, could not risk a similar gesture.

The dream of the child in Stettin who wanted to be a queen, and the ambition of the grand duchess who knew that she was better suited than her husband to rule, were achieved. Catherine was thirty-three. Half of her life lay ahead of her.

PART V

Empress of Russia

Coronation

S HE SAT ON THE THRONE of Peter the Great and ruled an empire, the largest on earth. Her signature, inscribed on a decree, was law and, if she chose, could mean life or death for any one of her twenty million subjects. She was intelligent, well read, and a shrewd judge of character. During the coup, she had shown determination and courage; once on the throne, she displayed an open mind, willingness to forgive, and a political morality founded on rationality and practical efficiency. She softened imperial presence with a sense of humor and a quick tongue; indeed, with Catherine more than any other monarch of her day, there was always a wide latitude for humor. There was also a line not be crossed, even by close friends.

She had come to the throne with the support of the army, the church, most of the nobility, and the people of St. Petersburg, all of whom assisted her because her personality and character offered stark contrasts to the domineering ineptitude of her husband. The coup itself created few enemies, and in the first weeks of her reign, she faced no opposition. Nevertheless, a multitude of problems awaited her. She had not reached the throne in a traditional Russian way. Most earlier tsars had succeeded by hereditary right and had been accepted and treated as representatives of the divinity. But the last tsar who ruled in this godlike manner was Tsar Alexis Mikhailovich, the father of Peter the Great, and Alexis died in 1676. Peter, as part of his effort to Westernize Russia, had transformed this image, creating for the autocrat a new, secular role as "first servant of the state." Peter had also altered the right of succession, decreeing that the throne would no longer pass down a fixed hereditary male line but that each sovereign would be free to name his successor. Even by these new rules, however, Catherine failed to qualify. Neither Empress Elizabeth, who had brought her to Russia, nor Peter III, who succeeded Elizabeth, had named her heir to the Russian throne. If the old laws of hereditary succession had been observed, Peter III's heir would have been Catherine's seven-year-old son, Paul. Or, as some Russians continued to whisper, the real tsar was the imprisoned Ivan VI, removed from the throne as an infant and locked in a cell for most of his life. Catherine had come to power supported by no right or precedent; she was, in the baldest definition, a usurper. For the first decade of her reign, this cloud hung over her, leaving her vulnerable to challenge, conspiracy, and, finally, to rebellion. In the first summer of her reign, this turmoil lay in the future, but Catherine was aware that it might come. She began her reign, therefore, with the traditional rules reversed. Earlier sovereigns, choosing to favor a subject, could do this by delivering a flow of privileges. Catherine was in the opposite position; it was she who was the supplicant for favor. Writing to Stanislaus Poniatowski, she said wryly, "The least soldier of the guards, when he sees me, thinks that 'this is the work of his own hands.' I am compelled to do a thousand strange things. If I yield, they will adore me; if not, then I do not know what will happen."

She began by seeking support and goodwill. Even before she learned of Peter's death at Ropsha, she showered those who had put her on the throne with promotions, decorations, money, and property. Gregory Orlov was given fifty thousand rubles; Alexis Orlov was given twenty-four thousand rubles; each of the other three Orlov brothers received half that much. Catherine Dashkova was awarded a pension of twelve thousand rubles a year plus a gift of twenty-four thousand rubles to pay her husband's debts. Nikita Panin and Kyril Razumovsky each received life pensions of five thousand rubles a year. Catherine's faithful valet, Vasily Shkurin, who had burned down his house to distract Peter during the birth of Catherine's child Alexis Bobrinsky and then had taken the infant into his family to care for him, was raised to the nobility. The young officer of the Horse Guards, Gregory Potemkin, who had ridden out of the ranks to give his sword knot to Catherine before she led the march to Peterhof, was promoted. All the soldiers of the Petersburg garrison were given half a year's pay, a sum adding up to 226,000 rubles.

Nor did Catherine forget those earlier friends and allies whom Elizabeth in her final years had removed from power and exiled, partly because she thought them too close to Catherine. On the day after her accession, the new empress sent a messenger to Alexis Bestuzhev, the former chancellor who had been the first to imagine her on the throne and who, during interrogation and four years of banishment, had remained silent for her sake. He was summoned back to St. Petersburg, met by Gregory Orlov twenty miles outside the capital, and rode in an imperial coach to the Summer Palace, where Catherine embraced him and announced the restoration of all his titles. She gave him a suite of rooms in the Summer Palace, with all meals furnished from her own kitchens, and, later, an ornate carriage and a large house with a magnificent wine cellar. On August 1, she issued a special manifesto proclaiming his innocence of all the charges levied against him in 1758 and named him the first member of the new imperial council she intended to form. His annual pension was to be twenty thousand rubles.

She was magnanimous to former opponents, never retaliating against supporters of her former husband or other adversaries, personal or official. Elizabeth Vorontsova, Peter III's mistress, who had urged that Catherine be sent to a convent so that she, Vorontsova, might become Peter's wife and future empress, was quietly sent to Moscow, where the empress bought her a house. When Elizabeth married a Muscovite nobleman and quickly produced a child, Catherine became the godmother. Peter's Holstein relatives, including Catherine's uncle and former suitor, Prince George of Holstein, were quickly repatriated to Germany. Peter's Holstein soldiers followed.

Knowing that she needed the assistance of every available person of administrative ability and experience, she drew around her a number of men who had sided with her husband. Many of Peter's high-ranking officials had already come over to her during the climax of the coup. Michael Vorontsov was retained in his position as chancellor; Prince Alexander Golitsyn remained vice-chancellor, and Prince Nikita Trubetskoy kept his post as president of the College of War. To eighty-year-old Field Marshal Münnich, who, as the coup was unfolding, had urged Peter III to put himself at the head of his troops and march on Petersburg to seize Catherine and retake his throne, the new empress remarked, "You only did your duty."

As Catherine was winning allegiance and service from former opponents, she was having difficulty pleasing some of her friends. Her triumph was scarcely achieved when jealousies sprang up among those claiming credit. Each believed that the recognition and reward he or she received was insufficient compared to what others had been given. The most dissatisfied was Princess Catherine Dashkova, who had assumed that she was about to become the new empress's principal adviser, riding in the imperial coach, enjoying a permanent seat at the imperial table. Her complaints were ill-placed; Catherine had treated Dashkova with unusual generosity. Upon her accession, the empress had given Dashkova thousands of rubles and, in addition, a large annual pension. She immediately promoted Dashkova's husband to colonel and gave him command of the Horse Guards, the army's elite cavalry regiment. The young couple moved into an apartment in the Winter Palace and dined almost every day with the empress. However, these imperial favors were not enough for a young woman who regarded herself as the pivotal figure in this chapter of Russian history.

Catherine attempted to make Dashkova understand that their relationship had changed; that there must now be a limit to the claims of friendship. The nineteen-year-old princess continued to make demands and put herself forward. In drawing rooms she spoke loudly of the new policies and reforms she had in mind. To foreign ambassadors, she boasted of her influence over the empress and Count Panin, claiming that she was their closest friend, their confidante, their inspiration.

Catherine Dashkova's ambition extended beyond possible realization; her rudeness beyond deference, courtesy, and common sense. When the empress presented her with the Order of St. Catherine, Dashkova, instead of receiving the honor on her knees, handed the ribbon back, saying loftily, "I implore Your Majesty not to give me this decoration. It is an ornament I do not prize and, as a reward, [it] has no value for me. My services, however they may appear in the eyes of some individuals, never have and never can be bought." Catherine listened to this impertinence; then, forbearing, she embraced Dashkova and placed the order around her shoulders. "At least let friendship have some rights," she said, "and may I not have the pleasure of giving a dear young friend a memento of my gratitude." Dashkova fell to her knees.

Before long, the friendship became a burden. The Dashkova legend was carried to Paris by Ivan Shuvalov, who praised the princess in a letter to Voltaire. Writing to Poniatowski, Catherine begged him to correct the error and inform Voltaire that "the Princess Dashkova played only a minor part in events. She was not trusted because of her family, and she was neither liked nor trusted by the leaders of the coup who told her as little as they could. Admittedly, she has brains, but her character is spoiled by her willfulness and conceit." A few months later, in another letter to Poniatowski, she said she could not understand why Ivan Shuvalov had told Voltaire "that a girl of nineteen had changed the government of Russia." The Orlovs, she said, "had something else to do than put themselves at the command of a little scatterbrain. On the contrary, to the last moment she was kept from knowing the most essential part of this affair."

Catherine had an easier task dealing with another supporter eager to be given exaggerated credit. Count Betskoy, an elderly chamberlain and friend of Catherine's mother, whose role in the coup had been limited to distributing money to some of the Guards already won over by the Orlovs, was to be presented with three thousand rubles and the Order of St. Andrew. At the ceremony, he dropped to his knees and asked the empress to declare before witnesses to whom she owed her crown.

Surprised, Catherine replied, "I owe my accession to God and to the will of my people."

"Then I have no right to wear this mark of distinction," said Betskoy, and he started to remove the Order of St. Alexander that she had draped on his shoulder.

Catherine asked why he was doing this.

"I am the unhappiest of men," he explained. "I am unworthy to wear this order because Your Majesty does not acknowledge me as the sole author of her success. Did I not raise the guards and throw money to them?"

Catherine thought he was joking. Seeing that he was serious, she brought her sense of humor to bear. "I admit that I owe my crown to you, Betskoy," she said, and smiled soothingly. "And that is why I wish to receive it from your hands alone. It is to you whom I confide the task of making it as beautiful as possible. Now I instruct you to see that a crown is made for me. I put at your disposal all the jewelers in the country." Conquered and beaming, Betskoy stood, bowed, and went to work.

During this first summer of her reign, the subject looming largest in Catherine's mind was her coronation. Among the many blunders of Peter's brief reign, none had been more foolishly shortsighted than his refusal to have himself crowned in the Moscow Kremlin, or even to set a date for the ceremony. Catherine did not make this mistake. She understood the religious and political importance of this solemn act of consecration in Moscow, the repository of Russia's national heritage, the holy city where every tsar and empress had been crowned. Moscow was the city most Russians still regarded as their capital; nothing so meaningful could be left to the artificial, Westernized capital forcibly built by Peter the Great. She understood that she would never feel secure on the throne until the crown had been placed on her head in the Kremlin and the people of Moscow had accepted her as empress. In addition, the ceremony would enable her to distribute more titles, decorations, and gifts, thereby purchasing additional favor from her new subjects.

On July 7, the same day that Peter III's death was announced, Catherine proclaimed that she would be crowned in Moscow in September. Prince Nikita Trubetskoy was placed in charge of preparations and sent ahead with fifty thousand rubles for preliminary expenses. As the time came closer, six hundred thousand rubles' worth of silver coins were charged to the empress's privy purse, packed into 120 oaken barrels, and sent to Moscow, where they would be used as largesse and thrown to the crowds.

On August 27, Catherine put seven-year-old Paul on the road to Moscow in the care of his tutor, Nikita Panin. Five days later, she followed. At a relay post halfway to Moscow, the empress caught up with her son, whom she found in bed, shaking with fever. The following day, the fever dropped, but Panin urged the empress to delay her travel until the boy was fully recovered. Catherine was torn; she wanted to stay with Paul, but she hesitated to disrupt the timing of the elaborate coronation program in Moscow. Ultimately, feeling the importance of the ceremony as confirmation of her accession, she decided to go ahead and enter Moscow by herself, if necessary, on the appointed day. Panin was told to follow as soon as the boy's health permitted. As soon as Catherine announced this decision, Panin declared that the boy was better and well enough to travel.

Muscovites lined their streets with green fir branches, hung strings of evergreens across their doorways, and draped silken sheets and Persian carpets from balconies and windows. Along the four-mile passage from the city gate to the Kremlin, four triumphal arches were erected. Viewing stands were built at intersections and in the principal squares to permit Muscovites and the thousands of people from the countryside crowding into the city to see the empress as she passed by. The mood of the city was buoyant; besides pageantry and feasting, the coronation meant a three-day holiday, the distribution of largesse, the lifting of fines and taxes, and pardons for lesser offenses.

On September 13, the day Catherine made her ceremonial entrance into the city, bright sunlight sparkled on the city's gilded onion domes. At the head of the procession rode squadrons of the Horse Guards, the sun flashing off their helmets; next came a cavalcade of the high nobility wearing gold braid and crimson sashes. Catherine's gilded carriage, drawn by eight white horses, followed. The uncrowned empress, smiling and bowing, acknowledged the cheering crowds; when Paul was seen sitting beside her, the cheers were even louder.

On September 22, the day of the coronation, saluting cannon began to thunder at five in the morning when a crimson carpet was laid down the steps of the Kremlin's historic ceremonial outdoor Red Staircase. At nine, Catherine, wearing a dress of silver brocade, trimmed with ermine, appeared at the top of the staircase and slowly descended the steps. At the bottom, she bowed to the crowd in the Kremlin's Cathedral Square and a priest touched her forehead with holy water. She said a prayer, rows of priests kissed her hands, and, walking between lines of soldiers of the Imperial Guard, she came to the door of the Assumption Cathedral.

Beneath the domes of its five golden cupolas, the interior of the fifteenth-century cathedral glowed with light. Its four massive internal columns, its walls and its ceiling were covered with luminous frescoes; before the altar stood the great iconostasis, a golden screen of painted icons studded with jewels. From the central dome hung a gigantic chandelier weighing more than a ton. Before Catherine, in front of the iconostasis, stood ranks of the high clergy: the Metropolitan Timofey, archbishops, bishops, archimandrites, and other priests. From their miters glittered more diamonds, rubies, sapphires, and pearls. Light, filtering down from the cupolas and flickering from thousands of candles, reflected off the surfaces of the jewels and the golden icons.

Catherine walked to the dais draped in red velvet at the center of the cathedral, mounted its six steps, and seated herself on the Diamond Throne of Tsar Alexis. Observing Catherine at that moment, the new English ambassador, the Earl of Buckinghamshire, saw "a woman of middle height, her glossy, chestnut-colored hair massed under the jeweled crown. . . . She was beautiful, and the blue eyes beneath were remarkable for their brightness. The head was poised on a long neck, giving an impression of pride, and power, and will."

The ceremony lasted four hours. Catherine listened as the archbishop of Novgorod described the revolution of June 28 as the work of God and said to her that "the Lord has placed the crown on your head." Next, Catherine personally arrayed herself with the symbols of imperial power. She removed her ermine cloak and draped another cloak of imperial purple over her shoulders. Traditionally, a Russian sovereign crowned himself or herself. Catherine lifted the huge nine-pound imperial crown produced for her under the supervision of Ivan Betskoy and settled this ultimate symbol of sovereignty on her brow. Shaped like a bishop's miter, it was crusted with a cross of diamonds surmounting an enormous 389-carat ruby. Below, set in an arch supporting the cross and in the band surrounding the wearer's head, were forty-four diamonds, each an inch across, surrounded by a solid mass of smaller diamonds. Thirty-eight rose pearls circled over the crown on either side of the central arch. When this glittering masterpiece was in place, she picked up the orb with her left hand, the scepter with her right, and calmly looked out at the cathedral audience.

The final sequence in the ceremony was the acknowledgment that the coronation represented a pact between God and herself. He was the master; she was the servant, now solely responsible for Russia and its people. She was anointed with holy oil on the forehead, the breast, and the hand, and then passed through the doors of the iconostasis into the inner sanctum. She kneeled and, with her own hand, took the communion bread from the plate and administered the sacrament to herself.

The ceremony concluded, the newly crowned and consecrated empress walked from the Assumption Cathedral across the Kremlin square to two ancient, smaller cathedrals, the Archangel Michael and the Annunciation, to kneel before the tombs of previous tsars and a collection of holy relics. She mounted the Red Staircase and turned and bowed three times to the crowd while, from the cannon, more thunder rolled across the city. This sound, amplified by the ringing of thousands of bells in the towers and churches of Moscow, made it impossible for a man to speak to his neighbor.

In the Palace of Facets, Catherine accepted the congratulations of the nobility and the foreign ambassadors. She distributed gifts and honors; Gregory Orlov and his four brothers were created counts; Dashkova became a lady-in-waiting. That night, Moscow glowed with fireworks and special illuminations. At midnight, Catherine—thinking no one would see her—walked alone to the head of the Red Staircase to gaze out over the Kremlin and the city. The crowd, still standing below in Cathedral Square, recognized her and began to cheer. This reaction continued. Three days later, she wrote to the Russian ambassador in Warsaw, "I cannot go out, nor even put my face to the window, without the acclamations beginning all over again."

The eight and a half months Catherine spent in Moscow after her coronation appeared on the surface to be a prolonged carnival, with the court and the nobility competing in the splendor of their balls and masquerades. It was not an easy time for Catherine, however. Some of her problems were familiar: Princess Dashkova complained that Gregory Orlov, who had been placed in charge of banquet arrangements, had decreed that precedence in all ceremonies be based on military rank. As the wife of a mere colonel, Dashkova was relegated to a subordinate seat among people she considered inferiors. Catherine attempted to remedy this situation by promoting Prince Dashkov to the rank of general, but Dashkova continued to grumble.

Paul was stricken again by fever. It was his third serious illness of the year, and the doctors knew neither the cause nor how to treat it. In early October, her son's illness became acute, and, as the news spread, Catherine remained beside his bed. She was concerned not only for Paul but for the effect his illness might have on her own future. She never forgot his superior right to the throne; she knew that Panin and others had preferred that she become regent rather than empress; she had seen the warm reception Paul had received from the Moscow crowds as he rode through the streets at her side. If now, only three months after the sudden death of her husband, her son were also to die, she knew that she would be blamed. Her fears were relieved on October 13, when Paul rose from his bed, and she was able to leave Moscow to make the pilgrimage to the Troitsa (Troitskaya-Sergeeva) Monastery expected of every newly crowned Russian sovereign. In the great white-walled fortress, famous throughout Russia as a place of unique holiness, she received a monarch's blessing.

While Catherine was still in Moscow, another cloud passed over the coronation celebrations. Early in October, the empress learned that there had been loose talk among officers of the the Izmailovsky Guards about restoring the imprisoned Ivan VI to the throne. Alarmed, she ordered Kyril Razumovsky, colonel of the regiment, to investigate, specifying that torture not be used. Fifteen officers were arrested and questioned. The investigtion soon focused on three, who, it turned out, had participated in the coup against Peter III: Ivan and Semyon Gureyev and Peter Khrushchev. Drinking during the coronation celebrations, they had been heard complaining that they had not been rewarded as generously as the Orlovs; for this reason, they said, a real tsar, Ivan VI, should be restored to the throne. The officers also questioned why Grand Duke Paul had been set aside in favor of his foreign mother. Razumovsky, familiar with the behavior of drunken officers, recommended that the guilty men simply be demoted and transferred to other regiments in distant garrisons. Catherine, however, was indignant that this talk had come in the middle of her coronation triumph. She wondered how many others might be grumbling about the Orlovs and talking about the imprisoned "lawful emperor." She believed the recommended penalties were too light; the investigators attempted to please her by condemning Ivan Gureyev and Khrushchev to death. This judgment went to the Senate for confirmation, but before the matter could go further, Catherine intervened. This time she moderated the sentences, sparing the lives of the condemned men, who were dismissed from the army and exiled. By taking this course, Catherine hoped to make clear that she would not forgive but would measure punishments in proportion to crimes. In this case, she decided, drunken men, venting mostly personal grievances, did not deserve decapitation. Soon enough, jealousy of the Orlovs, and an attempted restoration of Ivan VI, would threaten her with something more challenging than inebriated talk.

❧46❧

The Government and the Church

HAVING RECOGNIZED and rewarded those who had helped put her on the throne, Catherine turned next to the two powerful institutions, both pillars of the state, that had given her essential support. Both the army and the church wanted immediate reversal of spe-

cific actions by Peter III. With the army, this was easily done. To cement
the favor of the officers and men, exhausted by seven years of war and
smarting from the humiliation of the dishonorable peace with Prussia,
she canceled the new alliance with Frederick II. She also assured the
Prussians that she had no intention of fighting them or anyone else. She
abruptly halted and withdrew from the barely begun war with Denmark. Russian army commanders in Prussia and central Europe were
given a simple order: Come home! Rewarding the church was more
complicated. Her first step was a temporary suspension of Peter's hastily decreed confiscation of church lands and wealth. The church hailed
her as a deliverer.

These early steps left unresolved other critical problems pressing
on the empire. The Seven Years' War had bankrupted the treasury;
Russian soldiers in Prussia had not been paid for eight months. No
credit was available from abroad. There was a calamitous rise in the
price of grain. Corruption and extortion had spread through all levels
of government. In Catherine's words: "In the treasury there were seventeen millions of rubles' worth in unpaid bonds; almost all branches of
commerce were monopolized by private individuals; a loan of two millions attempted in Holland by the Empress Elizabeth had met without
success; we enjoyed no confidence or credit abroad."

Those who hoped that the overthrow of Catherine's husband and
his pro-Prussian policies would bring about a reinstatement of the
Austrian alliance were disappointed. In the first days of her reign, she
had encouraged these partisans by issuing a manifesto referring to "an
ignominious peace" with the "age old enemy," meaning Prussia. When
the foreign ambassadors were invited to her first official reception, the
Prussian ambassador—Baron Bernhard von Goltz, Peter III's former
confidant—begged to be excused, saying that he "had no suitable costume." But continued hostility with Prussia was not Catherine's intention. During her first week on the throne, couriers were riding to
European capitals with assurances that the new empress wished to live
in peace with all foreign powers. Her letter to the Russian ambassador
in Berlin said, "Concerning the peace lately concluded with His Majesty, the King of Prussia, we command you to convey to His Majesty
our solemn intention of upholding the same so long as His Majesty
gives us no cause to break it." Her one condition was the immediate,
unobstructed return of all Russian soldiers in the war zone. They were
to fight neither for nor against Prussia, and neither for nor against Aus-

tria; they were simply to return home. Only four days after the reception that Goltz had failed to attend, he was back at court, playing cards with Catherine.

Confronted by this array of problems, Catherine sometimes seemed to shrink before the immensity of the task. The French ambassador heard her say, not with pride, but wistfully, "Mine is such a vast and limitless empire." She began her reign with no experience in administering an empire or a large bureaucracy, but she was eager to learn and prepared to teach herself. When it was proposed that, following custom during the reigns of Elizabeth and Peter III, the burdensome task of reading all diplomatic dispatches and ministerial reports be spared the sovereign and only extracts provided, Catherine refused. She wished to know every detail of the problems Russia faced and every ingredient in the decisions she needed to make. "Full reports will be brought to me every morning," she declared.

She was equally forceful in dealing with the Senate. Since the time of Peter the Great, the Senate had administered the laws of the empire, making certain that the decrees handed down by the autocrat were carried out. Having no power to make law, the Senate's role was to administer the state on the basis of existing laws, no matter how useless or out-of-date. During the coup, Catherine had associated herself closely with this body; it was through the Senate that her first orders were issued to Russian troops abroad, and it was to the care of the Senate that she confided her son, Paul, when she rode off at the head of the Guards to Peterhof. Once she was on the throne, the meetings of the Senate were moved to the Summer Palace to make it easier for her to attend. On her fourth day as empress, she was present at a session of the Senate which began with reports that the treasury was empty and that the price of grain had doubled. Catherine replied that her imperial allowance, amounting to one-thirteenth of the national income, should be used by the government. "Belonging herself to the nation," she said, she considered that everything she possessed belonged to the nation. In the future, she continued, there would be no distinction between the national and her personal interests. To deal with the grain shortage, she ordered a prohibition on the export of grain; within two months, the price came down. She abolished many of the private monopolies held by great noble families such as the Shuvalovs, who controlled and made a profit on all the salt and tobacco sold in Russia.

At these meetings, she quickly discovered that in the Senate there were heavy layers of ignorance. One morning, when the senators were discussing a distant part of the empire, it became apparent that none of them had any idea where this territory lay. Catherine suggested looking at a map. There was no map. Without hesitation, she summoned a messenger, took five rubles from her purse, and sent him to the Academy of Sciences, which had published an atlas of Russia. When the messenger returned, the territory was identified and the empress made a gift of the atlas to the Senate. Hoping to improve their performance, she wrote, on June 6, 1763, to the senators as a body: "I cannot say that you are lacking in patriotic concern for my welfare and the general welfare, but I am sorry to say that things are not moving towards their appointed end as successfully as one would wish." The cause of this delay, she said, was the existence of "internal disagreements and enmity, leading to the formation of parties seeking to hurt each other, and to behavior unworthy of sensible, respectable people desirous of doing good."

Her agent in the Senate was the procurator general, an office established by Peter the Great to be the link between the autocrat and the Senate—"the eye of the sovereign," he called it—and to provide supervision over the Senate. Specifically, this official's task was to set and keep track of the Senate's agenda, report to the monarch, and receive and pass along his or her commands. Catherine's newly appointed procurator general, A. A. Vyazemsky, received her analysis:

> In the Senate, you will find two parties. . . . Each of these parties will now try to get you on their side. On the one, you will find honest people, if of limited intelligence. On the other, I think more long-range plans are harbored. . . . The Senate has been established for the carrying out of laws prescribed to it. But it has often issued laws itself, granted ranks, honors, money and lands, in one word . . . almost everything. Having once exceeded its limits, the Senate now finds it difficult to adapt itself to the new order within which it should confine itself.

More important than this admonitory advice to Vyazemsky regarding the behavior of the Senate was Catherine's message to the new procurator general, setting out the relationship she expected to have with him personally:

> You must know with whom you have to deal. . . . You will find that I have no other view than the greatest welfare and glory of the fatherland, and I wish for nothing but the happiness of my subjects. . . . I am very fond of the truth, and you may tell me the truth fearlessly, and argue with me without any danger if it leads to good results in affairs. I hear that you are regarded as an honest man by all. . . . I hope to show you by experience that people with such qualities do well at court. And I may add that I require no flattery from you, but only honest behavior and firmness in affairs.

Vyazemsky justified Catherine's expectations and remained the "eye of the sovereign" for twenty-eight years, until his retirement in 1792.

Within a few days of her accession, Catherine summoned Russia's two most experienced statesmen, Nikita Panin and Alexis Bestuzhev. Each had supported her at a critical time in her life, but the two had never worked together. When Bestuzhev was recalled from exile and restored to his honors and property, he anticipated recovering his place as the empire's leading minister. He was in his seventies and wearied by humiliation and isolation, and Catherine had no intention of elevating him to the chancellorship.

Nikita Panin became the leading political figure in the new government. Combining a keen intelligence with extensive European experience, Panin, her son's tutor, and the counselor who had helped steer her through the planning and execution of the coup, immediately became her chief ministerial adviser. In 1762, Panin was forty-four years old, a short, plump, perfectly mannered bachelor. He got up late, worked during the morning, and, after a heavy midday dinner, took naps or played cards. Catherine valued him for his intelligence and truthfulness, but she began her reign with certain reservations about him. She knew that his twelve years as ambassador in Sweden had instilled in him a respect for constitutional monarchy that she believed would be unworkable in Russia. She also knew that Panin had hoped that she would be satisfied to serve as regent for her son, Paul. The idea of a regency, of course, had no appeal for Catherine; she had never said or even hinted that she might be willing to rule only as caretaker for Paul.

Catherine was also aware that Panin disapproved of the increased prominence she had given the Orlov brothers. He feared that the relationship between Catherine and Gregory Orlov would prove as damaging to orderly, efficient government as the influence on Elizabeth of some of her handsome favorites had been. Panin was a realist, however. He recognized that Catherine had been swept to power primarily by the Orlovs' influence in the Guards, and he understood that her gratitude, along with her continuing personal bond with Gregory, would permit no diminution of the brothers' role. Adjusting to the situation, Panin altered his approach. Before helping Catherine overthrow Peter, he had spoken to her privately about his hope for a more liberal structure of government in Russia—something on the order of the system he had come to admire during his years in Sweden. With Catherine on the throne and seeking to make the imperial government more efficient and responsive to Russia's needs, he began an effort to persuade the empress to agree to a restriction of her authority. He needed to tread carefully. He could not openly propose limitations on the autocrat's absolute power; therefore he suggested the establishment of a permanent executive institution, an imperial council, with precisely defined functions and powers to "assist" the autocrat. In this newly created structure, his council would place organizational limits on the monarch's authority.

Catherine, having attained supreme power, intended neither to share it nor to allow it to be restricted. Catherine's tactic, once in power, was to ask Panin to put his ideas in writing. Panin did so quickly, and before the end of July 1762, he had laid before her his plan to establish a permanent imperial council. In his new structure, the autocrat still retained the principal rule of the state, but, for efficiency's sake, the sovereign would share power with a council of eight imperial councillors. Panin did not explain how or by whom these councillors were to be chosen, although at least four were to be the state secretaries representing the colleges of War, the Navy, Foreign Affairs, and Internal Affairs. (To make his suggestion more palatable to Catherine, Panin included Gregory Orlov on his list of candidates for one of the other places on the council.) All matters outside the legislative responsibility of the Senate were to be taken up by the council "as if by the empress in person." No decree or regulation coming from the imperial council would be valid without the endorsing signature of the autocrat.

Panin knew that in proposing this council, he was on shaky ground:

his plan trespassed on sovereign prerogative. Councillors' appointments were to be for life; they could not be dismissed by the sovereign, but were to be removable only in cases of misconduct, and then only by a full assembly of the Senate. When Catherine read Panin's proposal, she understood immediately that it was designed to limit her authority by infringing on her right to choose and dismiss her leading public officials. From the moment of her first reading, Panin's plan was doomed; she had not waited all these years for the throne to accept limitations.

During her life, Catherine never wavered in her conviction that an absolute monarchy was better suited to the needs of the Russian empire than rule by a small group of permanent officials. She was not alone in opposing the idea of an imperial council. The majority of the nobility opposed it, feeling that a council of this kind would place the imperial government in the hands of a small, permanently entrenched group of bureaucrats rather than leaving it in the hands of the autocrat, the arrangement familiar to them. The opposition of the nobility reinforced Catherine's position, and, by the beginning of February 1763, it was clear that there would be no council. Catherine was careful not to offend Panin by outright rejection. She made a show of pretended interest in his plan, then put it aside and never mentioned it again.

Catherine's decision to bury his plan for an imperial council was a setback for Panin, but in August 1763 the empress made it up to him. She appointed Panin senior member of the College of Foreign Affairs. Bestuzhev, defeated and weary, chose to retire. For the next eighteen years—until 1781—Nikita Panin remained Russia's chief minister for foreign affairs.

While managing the financial crisis, satisfying the army, reorienting Russian foreign policy, and attempting to make government administration more efficient, Catherine also had to deal with the Orthodox Church. She had converted to Orthodoxy, accepted its dogma, and observed its practices, all in striking contrast to her husband, Peter. In the second month of his brief reign, Peter had decreed the secularization of all church property and announced that Russian Orthodoxy must transform itself into a faith akin to the Protestantism of north Germany. Because high church leaders believed that Catherine opposed and would reverse her husband's decisions, they enthusiastically supported her seizure of power. Once it succeeded, the church hierarchy hastened to claim its reward by demanding permanent return of all church properties. On her accession, Catherine had repaid her political debt to the church by revoking Peter's decrees. Inwardly, however, she hesitated. Despite her public displays of conventional faith, she regarded the church's vast wealth as a scandal and refused to accept what she considered the squandering of so large a part of the nation's wealth. Like Peter the Great, she believed that this wealth should be used for the needs of the state. Also like the great tsar, Catherine wanted the church to assume, under state guidance, an active role in social welfare and education. The problem of the disparity between the poverty and needs of the state, and the vast wealth represented in the land and serfs owned by the church, remained to be resolved.

At the time of Catherine's accession, the Russian population included ten million serfs, most of them peasants who furnished the overwhelming majority of the agricultural laborers in an overwhelmingly agricultural state. From the beginning of her reign, Catherine wanted to deal with the fundamental problem of serfdom, but the institution was too deeply interwoven into the economic and social fabric of Russian life for her to approach in her first months. Nevertheless, if a permanent, overall solution must be postponed, she could not put off the question of the church's extensive lands and the one million male serfs who, with their families, worked these lands. She revoked Peter III's decree secularizing church properties, but this act, temporarily restoring all lands and serfs to the church, was not the solution she favored. Catherine's goal lay in the opposite direction.

Confronting the problems of the church's wealth and power, and of the relationship between church and state, Catherine was following in large footsteps. Peter the Great, half a century before, was less concerned with the spiritual salvation of his people than with their material welfare. Disregarding the church's concern with the next world, he wished it to serve his purpose in this one: namely, the education of a population of honest, reliable citizens of the state. To this end, Peter diminished the power of the Russian Orthodox Church hierarchy by eliminating the supreme religious office of Patriarch, who had wielded near-equal power with the tsar. In the place of this single powerful figure, Peter established the Holy Synod of eleven or twelve members, not necessarily churchmen, to administer the temporal affairs and the finances of the church. In 1722, he appointed a civilian Procurator of the Holy Synod, charged with supervising church administration and exercising jurisdiction over the clergy. In this way, Tsar Peter made the church subordinate to the state, and it was his example Catherine meant to follow. After Peter, however, his daughter Elizabeth had partially reversed this relationship. The empress, flamboyantly hedonistic and also deeply religious, had sought absolution for the excesses of her private life by raining wealth and privileges on the church. During her reign, the church hierarchy regained authority to administer its lands and serfs. When Elizabeth was followed by her nephew, Peter III, the pendulum swung back. On taking the throne, Catherine had reversed it again, immediately revoking her dead husband's decree, and granting the church renewed possession and administration of its land and serfs. A few months later, she changed course again.

The unfolding of this political and religious drama was marked by indecision, opposition, and, finally, a major confrontation. In July 1762, Catherine ordered the Senate to investigate and tabulate the immense wealth of the Orthodox Church and to recommend a new policy for the government to follow. The Senate's first response was a compromise proposal: the estates should be returned to the church but the tax on church peasants should be increased. This created a split within the church hierarchy. The majority, led by Archbishop Dimitry of Novgorod, accepted the overall idea of surrendering the burden of administering their agricultural estates and becoming paid servants of the state on the same footing as the army and the bureaucracy. To examine the problem and work out the details, Dimitry proposed setting up a joint religious and secular commission. Catherine agreed, and on August 12, 1762, signed a manifesto confirming her temporary annulment of Peter III's decree and returning church lands to ecclesiastical administration. At the same time, she established Dimitry's recommended commission of ecclesiastical and civil representatives (three clerics and five laymen) to examine the matter.

Catherine had to treat the church hierarchy carefully. She had always exercised a rational flexibility in matters of religious dogma and policy. Brought up in an atmosphere of strict Lutheranism, she had as a child expressed enough skepticism about religion to worry her deeply conventional father. As a fourteen-year-old in Russia, she had been required to change her religion to Orthodoxy. In public, she scrupulously observed all forms of this faith, attending church services, observing religious holidays, and making pilgrimages. Throughout her reign, she never underestimated the importance of religion. She knew that the name of the autocrat and the power of the throne were embodied in the daily prayers of the faithful, and that the views of the clergy and the piety of the masses were a power to be reckoned with. She understood that the sovereign, whatever his or her private views of religion, must find a way to make this work. When Voltaire was asked how he, who denied God, could take Holy Communion, he replied that he "breakfasted according to the custom of the country." Having observed the disastrous effect of her husband's contemptuous public rejection of the Orthodox Church, Catherine chose to emulate Voltaire.

Her principal advisers disagreed as to how to handle the church. Bestuzhev had favored leaving the church hierarchy in control of church affairs; Panin, closer to the beliefs of the Enlightenment, favored state administration of the church and its property. As it was, the manifesto of August 1762, hinting at the desirability of freeing religion from the burden of worldly cares, carried ominous forebodings for the church's future. When the commission began its work, concerns about secularization stirred clerical anxiety, but the majority of priests were uncertain what could or should be done. Few were ready to fight.

One towering exception to this submissive attitude was Arseniy Matseyevich, metropolitan of Rostov, who was a fierce opponent of any state interference in church affairs, and especially of the secularization of church properties. Sixty-five years old, a Ukrainian nobleman by birth, a member of the Holy Synod, he presided over the richest of all the church sees (the see owned 16,340 serfs), and he believed firmly that the church had been granted its property not for secular but spiritual purposes. Fearless, passionate, and equipped with a thorough knowledge of theology, he prepared to use his pen and his voice to challenge the empress. He hoped that a scheduled face-to-face meeting with the new autocrat would provide him an opportunity to convince her that he was right and she was wrong.

Early in 1763, Catherine was to make a pilgrimage from Moscow to Rostov to consecrate the bones of Saint Dimitry Rostovsky, known as Saint Dimitry the Miracle Worker, a newly canonized saint who had been Arseniy's predecessor. The bones were to be placed in a silver shrine in the presence of the empress, after which Arseniy meant to speak to her. But as the time approached, Catherine postponed her visit.

When this delay was announced, Arseniy seized the initiative. On March 6, 1763, he forwarded to the Holy Synod a violent denunciation of the policy of secularization, which, he declared, would destroy both church and state. He reminded the Synod that on her accession, Catherine had promised to protect the Orthodox religion. He railed against the suggestion that the church should be responsible for education in philosophy, theology, mathematics, and astronomy; its only Christian duty, he thundered, was to preach the Word of God. Bishops should not be responsible for establishing schools; this was the duty of the state. If the church were secularized, he said, bishops and priests would no longer be shepherds of their people but "hired servants, accountable for every crust of bread." He aimed harsh words at his clerical colleagues in the Holy Synod, who, in this crisis, "sat like dumb dogs without barking."

He rose before the assembled clergy of Rostov and condemned those who challenged the church's right to its property in land and serfs: these were "enemies of the church ... [who] stretch out their hands to snatch what has been consecrated to God. They want to appropriate the wealth formerly given to the church by the children of God and by pious monarchs."

Arseniy had miscalculated. He had underestimated Catherine's strength and that of other powerful elements in the Russian state arrayed against him. The high nobility were deeply secular; local landowners wanted more access to church-owned land and labor; government officials, struggling with the state's financial condition, agreed with Catherine that the wealth and revenues of the church should be used for secular purposes.

When Catherine read Arseniy's petition to the Synod, she realized that it was aimed directly at her. Describing the metropolitan's arguments as "perverse and inflammatory distortions," she insisted that "the liar and humbug" be punished as an example. Commanding the Synod to act, she signed a decree committing Arseniy for trial. On March 17, the offending cleric was arrested and brought under guard from Rostov to a monastery in Moscow for examination. In a series of nocturnal sessions, the members of the Synod interrogated their former colleague. Catherine, who was present, listened as Arseniy brought up questions of her right to the throne and the death of Peter III. "Our present sovereign is not native and not firm in the faith," the archbishop cried. "She should not have taken the throne which should have gone to Ivan Antonovich [Ivan VI]." The empress, covering her ears, shouted, "Stop his mouth!"

The Synod's verdict was not in doubt. On April 7, Arseniy was found guilty, sentenced to loss of ecclesiastical rank, dismissed from his see, and banished to a remote monastery on the White Sea. He was denied the use of pen and ink and condemned to do hard labor three days a week, carrying water, chopping wood, and cleaning cells. His ecclesiastical degradation was staged at a public ceremony in the Kremlin. Arseniy, appearing in flowing robes, was ritually disgraced: one by one, his ecclesiastical garments were removed. Even during this procedure, he refused to remain silent, shouting insults at his fellow churchmen and predicting that all would die violently. Four years later, incarcerated in the far north, he was still denouncing Catherine as a heretic and despoiler of the church, and still challenging her right to the throne. The empress then deprived him of all religious status and had him transferred to solitary confinement in a cell in the fortress of Reval on the Baltic. Here, the fiery voice was finally silenced: until his death in 1772, his guards, who spoke no Russian, knew him only by the name Andrew the Liar.

Catherine had established the supremacy of the state over the church. A month after sentence was passed on Arseniy, she appeared before the Synod to give her reasons:

> You are the successors to the apostles who were commanded by God to teach mankind to despise riches, and who were themselves poor men. Their kingdom was not of this world. I have frequently heard these words from your lips. How can you presume to own such riches, such vast estates? If you wish to obey the laws of your own order, if you wish to be my most faithful subjects, you will not hesitate to return to the state that which you unjustly possess.

No second Arseniy rose to challenge her.

By imperial manifesto issued on February 26, 1764, all ecclesiastical lands and property became state property, and the church itself became a state institution. All church serfs were upgraded to the status of state peasants; as a result, one million male peasants—more than two million

persons, counting wives and children—came under state control, paying taxes to the state. Power and administrative autonomy were stripped
from the clergy, high and low, and all priests became salaried employees
of the state. Along with loss of administrative autonomy, the church
lost its economic base. Hundreds of churches were forced to close. Of
572 previously existing monasteries, only 161 survived. To this sweeping
change in Russian religious, social, cultural, and economic life, there
was no vocal opposition.

❧47❧

Serfdom

CATHERINE HAD ASSERTED and confirmed the administrative
structure of the imperial government and dealt with the demands
of the Orthodox Church. In the early months of her reign, she also had
to confront a crisis in a basic and chronically unstable institution in the
social and economic life of the empire: serfdom. It was an upheaval involving industrial serf workers in the mines and foundries in the Urals
that first taught the student of Montesquieu and Voltaire that it was
impossible to cure long-established injustice in a society simply by in-
voking philosophy, no matter how beautifully expressed and persuasive
on the page.

In 1762, the Russian population of roughly twenty million consisted of
hierarchal layers: the sovereign, the nobility, the church, merchants and
townspeople, and, at the base, up to ten million peasants. Some of the
peasants were partially free; a few completely; most not at all. Serfs
were peasants in permanent bondage to land owned by the crown, the
state, the church, private owners—almost all in the nobility—or to a
variety of industrial and mining enterprises. According to a census
taken between 1762 and 1764, the crown owned five hundred thousand
serfs who worked on land owned by the ruler and his or her family. Two
million eight hundred thousand serfs were classified as state peasants,
owned by the state and living on land or in villages belonging to the
state but allowed to meet their obligations by paying money or labor

dues to the state. One million had been the property of the Orthodox Church; these were the serfs Catherine had taken from the church and transferred to the state. The largest number of Russian serfs—five and a half million, or 56 percent of the total—belonged to members of the nobility. All Russian noblemen were entitled by law to own serfs. A handful of these nobles were extraordinarily rich (a few owned thousands of serfs), but the vast majority were small squires owning land that required fewer than a hundred—sometimes fewer than twenty—workers to farm. Finally, there was a fourth category of unfree labor, the industrial serfs, working in the mines and foundries of the Urals. They did not belong to the owners or the managers of these enterprises; they were the property of the mines or foundries.

Serfdom had appeared in Russia at the end of the sixteenth century in order to keep laborers clearing and working the enormous expanse of the nation's arable land. The fifty-one-year reign of Ivan the Terrible (1533–84) had been followed by the Time of Troubles and rule by Ivan's lieutenant Boris Godunov. When three years of famine descended on Russia, peasants left the barren land and flocked to towns in search of food. To bind them, Boris decreed a permanent bondage to the land, to be vested in the landowners. In the years that followed, the legal binding of workers to the land was needed to curb the nomadic instincts of Russian peasants; many simply walked away from work they did not like.

Over the years, the status of serfs deteriorated. When workers were first tied to the land, they had possessed some rights, and the system had been based on service duties and payments. Over time, however, the powers of landowners increased and the rights of the serfs were whittled away. By the mid-eighteenth century, most Russian serfs had become possessions, chattel; in fact, slaves. Originally—and supposedly still—attached to the land, serfs were now regarded by their owners as personal property that could be sold apart from the land. Families could be ripped apart, with wives, husbands, sons, and daughters taken separately to market and sold. Sales of talented serfs often took place in cities where their skills were extolled by advertisements in the *Moscow News* or the *St. Petersburg Gazette*:

> For sale, a barber and also four bedposts and other pieces of furniture. For sale, two banqueting cloths and likewise two

young girls trained in service and one peasant woman. For sale: a girl of sixteen, of good behavior, and a ceremonial carriage, hardly used. For sale: a girl of sixteen trained in lace-making, able to sew linen, iron, and starch and dress her mistress, in addition to having a pretty face and being well formed.

Anyone wishing to buy an entire family or a young man and a girl separately, may inquire at the silver-washer's opposite the church of Kazan. The young man, named Ivan, is twenty one years old, he is healthy, robust, and can curl a lady's hair. The girl, well-made and healthy, named Marfa, aged fifteen, can do sewing and embroidery. They can be examined and had for a reasonable price.

For sale: domestics and skilled craftsmen of good behavior. Two tailors, a shoemaker, a watchmaker, a cook, a coach-maker, a wheelwright, an engraver, a gilder, and two coachmen, who may be inspected and their price ascertained . . . at the proprietors's own house. Also for sale are three young racehorses, one colt and two geldings, and a pack of hounds, fifty in number. A maid of sixteen for sale, able to weave lace, sew linen, do ironing and starching and to dress her mistress; furthermore, has a pleasing face and figure.

The price of a serf, even one highly skilled, was often less than that of a prize hunting dog. In general, a male serf could be bought for between two hundred and five hundred rubles; a girl or woman would cost between fifty and two hundred rubles, depending on her age, talents, and comeliness. Serfs sometimes changed owners for no price at all. He or she could be bartered against a horse or a dog, and a whole family could be gambled away in a night of cards.

Most serfs worked the soil. But it was the condition and grievances of industrial serfs working in the mines, foundries, and factories of the Urals that posed Catherine's first challenge. Originally, many Urals workers had been state peasants. To encourage the industrialization of Russia, Peter the Great in 1721 had offered these peasants to non-noble entrepreneurs to buy from the state, remove from the land, convert into industrial serfs, and attach permanently to an industrial enterprise. These serfs did not become the private property of the owners; they belonged instead to the enterprise and were sold along with it, like pieces of machinery. Their living conditions were horrendous, their working hours unrestricted, and the cost of their maintenance negligible. Managers were empowered to inflict corporal punishment. The rate of mortality was high; few industrial serfs reached middle age. Many had been simply worked to death. Not surprisingly, unrest among industrial serfs was acute. Under Empress Elizabeth there had been riots, suppressed by the army. Flight had always been the Russian peasants' principal defense against oppression; industrial serfs attempted escape to the little-populated regions and deserts beyond the lower Volga. Not all of these runaways escaped alive, but the number of those attempting to flee was rising.

This situation confronted Catherine in her first summer as empress. Her reaction was to issue a decree, on August 8, 1762, declaring that, in future, owners of factories and mines were forbidden to purchase serfs for industrial labor apart from purchasing the land to which the serfs were bound. The decree also declared that new serf workers thus acquired were to be enlisted at agreed-upon wages.

News of this imperial decree reverberated through the mining and industrial regions. Hearing mention of agreed-upon wages, serfs in the Urals and along the Volga promptly laid down their tools and went on strike. Production at the nation's mines and foundries came to a standstill. Catherine recognized that her decree had been premature. To force the industrial workers back to work, she was compelled to follow Eizabeth's path and send troops. General A. A. Vyazemsky, the future procurator general, was dispatched to pacify the Urals; in places where former revolts had been suppressed by the lash and the knout, Vyazemsky resorted to cannon.

Before he left on his mission, however, Catherine gave Vyazemsky additional instructions. Having suppressed the strikes, he was to investigate the situation in the mines, study the reasons for the workers' discontent, and ascertain the measures necessary to satisfy them. He was authorized to remove and, where necessary, punish serf managers:

> In a word, do everything you think proper for the satisfaction of the peasants; but take suitable precautions so that the peasants should not imagine that their managers will be afraid of them in the future. If you find managers guilty of great inhu-

manity, you may punish them publicly, but if someone has ex-
acted more work than is right, you may punish him secretly;
thus you will not give the common people grounds to lose their
proper dutifulness.

Vyazemsky toured the Urals and the lower Volga, punishing serf
ringleaders with beatings and sentences to hard labor. But he also took
seriously the second part of his assignment, namely the investigation of
grievances, and administered retribution to managers guilty of cruelty
or extreme mismanagement.

Catherine is said to have read Vyazemsky's report with compassion, but, having used force to put down the strikes, she was caught
between extremes. The industrial serfs, feeling their new power, were
suspicious of any proposals she might make to satisfy their complaints.
Simultaneously, mine owners and local government officials argued
that it was too early to offer reform or even leniency to a savage, primitive people who could only be kept in order by the knout. Thus, except
for the change in the terms of acquiring serf labor made by her initial
decree, the condition of the industrial serf remained unaltered. Troubles continued, violence was frequent, and a few years later, the
Pugachev rebellion swept the entire region of the Urals and the lower
Volga. For Catherine, the lesson was that more than intelligence and
goodwill were needed to break down the traditions, prejudices, and ignorance of both the owners and the serfs.

She continued to try. In July 1765, she established a special commission to "seek means for the improvement of the foundries, bearing in
mind the easing of the people's burdens and their peace of mind as well
as the national welfare." In 1767, she spoke of action necessary to fore-
stall a general uprising by the serfs to throw off "an unbearable yoke."
"If we do not agree to reduce cruelty and moderate a situation intolerable for human beings," she said, "then they themselves will take things
in hand."

Catherine, familiar with the Enlightenment belief in the Rights of
Man, was intellectually opposed to serfdom. While still a grand duchess, she had suggested a way to reform and eventually abolish the institution, although it might take a hundred years to accomplish. The crux
of this plan was that every time an estate was sold, all serfs on the es-

tate should be freed. And since, over a century, a large number of estates were likely to change hands, she said, "There! You have the people
free!"

If she accepted the iniquity of serfdom, why did Catherine, on
reaching the throne, award thousands of serfs to her supporters? In the
first month of her reign, Catherine made gifts of no fewer than eighteen thousand crown and state peasants who had been enjoying a certain measure of freedom. Put in its best light, she may have believed
that this reversal of her belief was temporary. She had to deal with an
immediate situation. The landowning nobility, along with the army and
the church, had put her on the throne. She wished to reward them. In
Russia in 1762, wealth was measured in serfs, not land. If she was going
to reward her supporters beyond granting titles and distributing jewelry, she gave them wealth. Wealth meant serfs.

Because of the compromises imposed by the demands of her new role
as empress, Catherine had to reconcile Russian serfdom and the Enlightenment concept of the Rights of Man. She had no contemporary
European example to guide her. The Encyclopedists condemned serfdom in principle without having to confront it; a remnant of feudalism,
it still existed only in scattered enclaves in Europe. In George III's
England, king, Parliament, and people looked the other way as English
participation in the African slave trade resulted in the shipping of
twenty thousand men and women every year as slaves to the West Indies. The American colonies—and soon the new American republic,
whose leaders often used the language of the Enlightenment—offered
flagrant examples of hypocrisy. The Virginia gentlemen and landowners who advocated American independence were mostly slaveholders.
George Washington still owned slaves at Mount Vernon when he died
in 1799. Thomas Jefferson, who wrote in the Declaration of Independence that "all men are created equal" and have the right to "life, liberty,
and the pursuit of happiness," was a lifelong slave owner. For thirty-eight
years, Jefferson lived with his slave Sally Hemings, who bore him seven
children. Washington and Jefferson were far from alone in this presi-
dential hypocrisy. Twelve American presidents owned slaves, eight of
them while in office.

• • •

In many ways, the condition of Russian serfs resembled that of black slaves in America. They were considered a human subspecies by their owners, and this chasm between serfs and masters was believed to be sanctioned by God. They were bought and sold like animals. They were subject to arbitrary treatment, hardship, and, all too often, cruelty. In Russia, however, there was no color barrier between master and slave. Russian serfs were not aliens in a foreign land; they had not been violently abducted from their homelands, languages, and religions, and carried thousands of miles across an ocean. Serfs in Russia were the descendants of impoverished, uneducated people of the same race, the same blood, and the same language as their owners. Nevertheless, as with slave owners in America, Russian serf owners had complete control over the lives of their human property. A serf could not marry without his master's permission. The law set no limit on the right of owners to administer corporal punishment to their serfs; disobedience, laziness, drunkenness, stealing, fighting, and resisting authority were cause for being beaten with whips, cudgels, and the knout. The only limit on a nobleman's power was that he was not permitted to execute a serf; he was, however, allowed to inflict punishment likely to cause death. A French traveler in Russia wrote, "What has disgusted me is to see men with grey hair and patriarchal beards, lying on their faces with their trousers down and flogged like children. Still more horrible—I blush to write it—there are masters who sometimes force the son to inflict this punishment on his father."

The majority of Russian serfs were agricultural peasants, plowing, sowing, and reaping on land cleared from the forests. Depending on the time of year and the master's whim, they could also be employed as woodcutters, gardeners, carpenters, candle makers, painters, and tanners of leather. Serfs tended cattle or worked at stud farms to breed carriage and riding horses. Serf women lived with constant physical drudgery. Frequently pregnant, they worked without rest in the fields beside their husbands, cooked food, washed clothes, and bore children, thereby creating little serfs to add to the master's wealth. When these women were free of other duties, they were sent to gather mushrooms and berries in the forests, although they were not permitted to keep— or even to eat—any themselves.

It was a grim, patriarchal world. The domestic life of most serf families followed the age-old universal rule that applies in every culture and society: men, brutalized by their superiors, turned and brutalized those under their own power, usually their own wives and children. The male head of the serf household held near-absolute authority over his family. This sometimes included the practice that permitted serf fathers to use their sons' wives for their own sexual pleasure.

The lives of serfs differed, depending on the number of serfs a landowner owned. A wealthy noble landowner might possess tens of thousands of serfs; these Russian grandees employed six times as many personal and domestic servants as people of the same rank in Europe. The household staff of a great nobleman could number several hundred; that of a less wealthy lord might be twenty or fewer. Household serfs were usually taken as children from serf families on the estate. Having been selected for their intelligence, good looks, and prospective adaptability, they were trained in whatever craft or work their master chose for them. The great nobleman had his own shoemakers, goldsmiths, tailors, and seamstresses. In the mansion, males and females, each wearing velvet embroidered with gold thread, would line the hallways and stand at entrances to rooms, waiting ready to obey the commands of the master or his guests. One serf's duty might be simply to open and close a single door; another might stand ready to bring his master's pipe or glass of wine; still another, a book or a clean handkerchief.

Because Russians loved elaborate spectacle, the wealthiest of the nobility created their own theaters, opera companies, one-hundred-piece orchestras, and ballets requiring scores of dancers. To support these performers, the great noblemen might also own composers, conductors, singers, actors, painters, and stagehands—everyone necessary to stage performance arts. Nobles sent their serf musicians, painters, and sculptors abroad in order to perfect their technique with French and Italian masters. Serfs also became engineers, mathematicians, astronomers, and architects. The lives of these talented men and women were easier than those of the field serfs who might be their parents or grandparents; sometimes their masters grew fond of them. Nevertheless, no serf, no matter how intelligent or talented, was ever allowed to forget that he or she remained a form of property; a favorite for a while, perhaps, but always vulnerable to being separated from his family; forbidden to marry or forced to marry someone not of his or her choice; expected to cook, sweep, or wait on tables as well as to dance or play an instrument; always subject to abuse and humiliation; always prey to predatory lust. Against this treatment, there was no protest. The serf could always be sent back to the fields. Or sold.

The history of Russian serf theater is filled with episodes of cruelty. One nobleman suddenly seized a singer who was playing the part of Dido. Slapping her face, he promised that when her performance was over she would be properly beaten in the stable. The singer, her face scarlet from the blow, had to go on singing. A visitor backstage at a princely theater found a man wearing a heavy metal collar lined with sharp spikes; when he moved even slightly, he suffered great pain. "I punished him," the prince explained, "so that he plays the role of King Oedipus a little better next time. I'm having him stand like this for a few hours. His performance is sure to improve." In the same theater, a backstage visitor found a man chained by the neck so that he couldn't move. "This is one of my fiddlers," the host explained. "He played out of tune so I've had to punish him." The same owner would jot down his actors' slightest errors and then go backstage during intermission and whip them.

Ownership of young men, women, boys, and girls gave free rein to serf owners wishing to act out their erotic fantasies. Some female serf performers were forced to act as servants at dinner, then move to the stage to perform, then move on to the bedrooms of the master's male guests. One host assigned each visitor a serf girl for the length of his stay. Prince Nicholas Yusupov treated his guests to orgies that began on stage. When the prince tapped his cane, all of his dancers would strip off their costumes and dance, naked.

Against this backdrop of exploitation and cruelty, one romantic fairy tale stands out. Inevitably, it ended in shame, tragedy, and death.

For generations, the Sheremetevs had been one of Russia's pre-eminent noble families. They had served the grand princes of Moscow, predecessors of the tsars. A Sheremetev was married to Ivan the Terrible's son, Ivan, who was murdered by his father. Field Marshal Boris Sheremetev commanded the Russian army in Peter the Great's historic victory over Charles XII of Sweden at Poltava in 1709. By the mid-eighteenth century, the Sheremetev family was the wealthiest noble family in Russia, with estates totaling two million acres spread across the empire. Some of these estates consisted of dozens of villages, each village including more than a hundred households. Sheremetevs possessed saddles, billiard tables, and hunting dogs imported from England, ham brought from Westphalia, and clothing, pomade, tobacco, and razors, from Paris. Count Nicholas Sheremetev, the head of the family during most of Catherine's reign, owned 210,000 serfs, more people than made up the population of St. Petersburg.

Kuskovo, one of the richest of the Sheremetev estates, lay only five miles east of the Moscow Kremlin. Here, in an Italianate palace, the walls of hallways and ceremonial rooms were hung with Rembrandts and Van Dykes. In the library, busts of Voltaire and Benjamin Franklin faced shelves with twenty thousand volumes, including works by Voltaire, Montesquieu, Diderot, Rousseau, Corneille, Molière, and Cervantes, and French translations of Milton, Pope, and Fielding. Outside the palace, in an artificial lake dug by serfs, floated a fully rigged warship and a Chinese junk.

Nicholas Sheremetev, grandson of the field marshal and heir to this wealth, grew up in a world of luxury and privilege. He was taught Russian, French, and German, the violin and the clavichord, and given lessons in painting, sculpture, architecture, fencing, and riding. As a boy, he was selected by Empress Catherine to became a playmate of her son and heir, Grand Duke Paul.

Nineteen years after Nicholas's birth, a young serf girl named Praskovia was born on a Sheremetev estate. Her father was an illiterate blacksmith with a weakness for the bottle. He was often violent and regularly beat his wife in front of their children. At the age of eight, Praskovia was taken into the palace. Neither she nor her parents had a choice; serfs routinely were forced to give up their children whenever and for whatever purpose the master decided. She was taught to read and write. She met Nicholas when she was nine and he was twenty-six. Nicholas, still unmarried, liked women, and the women he found most appealing—or perhaps simply more available and undemanding—were his own serfs. He and Praskovia became lovers in the mid-1780s, when she was seventeen and he was approaching thirty-five. They grew closer, bound to each other not only because he was the master but by a shared passion for music. She had displayed a rare talent as a singer and he was driven by a vision of creating the finest opera company in Russia. She made her debut on the stage of the new Sheremetev opera theater while still an adolescent and immediately established herself as the star. With dark, expressive eyes, a pale complexion, auburn hair, and a slight, almost fragile build, she performed under the name of "the Pearl." Her soprano voice has been described by her biographer as "a miracle of color and beauty, with amazing range, emotion, power, precision and clarity."

Between 1784 and 1788, Nicholas staged over forty different productions: grand operas, operas comiques, comedies, and ballets. The Russian nobility flocked to see and listen to Praskovia sing. Empress Catherine, on her return from her Crimean trip in 1787, came to Kuskovo and, despite her tin ear, was deeply moved by Praskovia. It was, the empress said, the "most magnificent performance" she had ever attended. After the opera, Catherine asked to meet Praskovia, who was brought forth. The empress spoke to the singer briefly and later sent Praskovia a diamond ring worth 350 rubles—this at a time when giving gifts to serfs was unprecedented.

By 1796, however, Praskovia was suffering from an illness manifesting itself in severe headaches, dizziness, coughing, and pains in her chest. Forced to retire, she last sang on April 25 of that year when she was twenty-eight. Nicholas closed his theater and, in 1798, gave Praskovia her freedom. Later he explained:

> I had the most tender, the most passionate feelings for her. Yet I examined my heart—was it overwhelmed merely by passionate desire, or did it see past her beauty to her other qualities? Seeing that my heart longed for more than love and friendship, more than mere physical pleasure, for a long time I observed the character and qualities of my heart's desire and found in her a mind adorned with virtue, sincerity, a true love for humanity, constancy, fidelity, and an unshakable faith in God. These qualities captured me more than her beauty for they are more powerful than all the external charms and much rarer.

He proposed that they marry. The idea was revolutionary; no nobleman of Nicholas's rank had ever married a woman born a serf. What would it mean—marriage between Russia's wealthiest aristocrat and a serf, even one now liberated? Nicholas ignored the consequences and went ahead. On November 4, 1801, he married Praskovia. On February 3, 1803, at the age of thirty-four, she gave birth to her only child, Dmitry. Three weeks later, on the morning of February 23, Praskovia died. The city's nobility, still enraged that Nicholas had married a former serf, refused to attend the funeral. Nor was Nicholas present; crushed by grief, he was unable to leave his bed. Six years later, at fifty-seven, he died and was laid beside her in St. Petersburg's Alexander Nevsky Monastery. Their son, Dmitry, his only legitimate child, inherited the Sheremetev estates.

The story became a legend. It is said that in 1855, Catherine's great-grandson, Tsar Alexander II, was walking at Kuskovo with Dmitry, listening to stories about Dmitry's mother, Praskovia. Immediately afterward, according to family history, the tsar signed the initial decree that led in 1861 to the emancipation of Russia's serfs. In 1863, Abraham Lincoln's Emancipation Proclamation freed America's black slaves.

❧48❧

"Madame Orlov Could Never Be Empress of Russia"

IN THE FIRST YEARS of Catherine's reign, Gregory Orlov was always at her side in his scarlet uniform, wearing on his chest the emblem of the empress's favor: her portrait set in diamonds. The empress loved him as a man and as the hero who, with his brothers, had put her on the throne. He was also, of the four men with whom she had slept, the one who had given her the most physical satisfaction. He rode in the imperial carriage, sitting next to the sovereign, while men of great aristocratic families rode escort outside on horseback. People wishing to make their way at court sought his ear.

Not everyone was fond of him. Some, like Princess Dashkova, complained of his common origins, his sudden rise, his unpolished manners. Catherine was aware that eminent members of the nobility avoided him and his brothers. Knowing this, she did what she could to smooth Gregory's rough edges and transform him into a grand seigneur. She gave him a French tutor to teach him the language used by cultivated Russians; the effort had little success. Writing to Poniatowski, she tried to explain her situation. "The men who surround me are devoid of education," she said, "but I am indebted to them for the situation I now hold. They are courageous and honest and I know they will never betray me."

Her position on the throne complicated her relationship with Orlov. She showered titles, decorations, and wealth on him and his brothers, but Gregory wanted something else. She was a widow now and he sought the prize he considered his service had earned: he wanted her to become his wife. This was more than political ambition. Orlov was a fearless soldier, the same man who, with three bullets in his body, had stood by his cannon at Kunersdorf, and who later had dared to elope with his general's mistress. Vanity had played a part when he pursued Catherine as a grand duchess, but there was passion, too. Courage was not required; being her lover had not placed him in jeopardy. These relationships, when discreet—and sometimes when indiscreet—were accepted at the Russian court. Empress Anne had had Johann Biron; Empress Elizabeth had had Alexis Razumovsky; Catherine's husband, Peter III, had had Elizabeth Vorontsova; and Catherine herself had already been the lover of Sergei Saltykov and Stanislaus Poniatowski. In western Europe, royal liaisons were common. Charles II, George I, and George II of England, as well as Louis XIV and Louis XV of France, had officially recognized mistresses. Orlov, therefore, was in no danger because of his relationship with Catherine until he became involved with her in a conspiracy to overthrow the sovereign. For him and his brothers, this was a capital offense. On the other hand, during the months their plot was taking shape, he and Catherine had shared the danger as equals. The fact that he was risking his life for her leveled the difference in their stations; in truth, he had been in a position to do more for her than she for him.

This situation had appealed to Orlov. Men can be attracted to women whom they believe need help. Orlov may have mistaken Catherine for a needy women; she was not. She was brave, proud, and confident. While still a grand duchess, she may have seemed and even felt politically and emotionally vulnerable, but she concealed it well. She was Orlov's mistress and had borne his child; he had faced death for her sake. She was on the throne because he had helped put her there. He knew all this, believed it balanced out, and was not disposed to play the role of a subordinate. He wanted Catherine to belong to him during the day, in public, not merely for a few nocturnal hours behind silk curtains.

For Catherine, this was impossible. She was no longer a grand duchess and could not remain simply a loving mistress. She was empress of Russia. The role, as she played it, was demanding. She rose every morning at five or six and worked fifteen hours a day. This left perhaps a single hour between the time her official duties ended— usually late in the evening—and the time she fell asleep, exhausted. This was all the time she could spare to be a man's plaything. She had no time for elaborate lovers' games, for teasing, for weaving and sharing dreams of the future. She knew she was depriving him of what he wanted, but in her mind, she had no choice. Because of this, she carried a burden of guilt, and it was to lessen this burden that she loaded him with titles, jewels, and estates. They were meant as compensation for not being ready to marry him.

They were not the rewards Gregory wanted. He wanted to marry her, not because he desired the role of prince consort but because he wanted to play the dominant marital role of an eighteenth-century Russian husband. He resented that her work stole hours during which he burned to display and satisfy his passion. He was angry that she spent these hours with men like Nikita Panin and Kyril Razumovsky, whose superior education now seemed to trump his passion and military courage. They advised her on matters about which he was completely ignorant. His sense that she was withdrawing from him drove him to clumsy efforts to force her to remember the debt she owed him and his brothers. He sometimes burst out in public and asserted himself with deliberate rudeness to Catherine. One evening before she left to be crowned in Moscow, at a supper of her intimate circle in the Winter Palace, the conversation turned to the coup a few months earlier. Gregory began boasting about his influence with the Guards. Turning to Catherine, he said how easily he had put her on the throne and how, if he wished, he could remove her with equal ease within a month. Everyone at the table was shocked; no one but Orlov would have dared to speak to the empress this way. Then Kyril Razumovsky spoke up. "Perhaps you are right, my friend," he said, smiling coolly. "But long before the month was past, we would have you hanging by the neck." Gregory was stung; it was a reminder that, essentially, he was no more than Catherine's lover, a handsome, muscular pawn.

Catherine looked for a way to restructure and continue the relationship. When she came to the throne, she believed that she could happily spend the rest of her life with Gregory Orlov. He had been her lover for three years; he was the father of her infant child, Alexis Bobrinsky; he and his brothers had risked their lives for her. Further, atop the pinnacle to which ambition had brought her, she felt the loneliness of power. She needed company and affection as much as passion. For this reason, Catherine considered marrying him.

Orlov became insistent, demanding. He declared that he would prefer going back to being a subaltern in the army rather than acting the role of a "male Pompadour." Catherine sorted through her own feelings. She dared not refuse him outright. She was not blind to Orlov's faults. She exaggerated his qualities in front of others, but she knew exactly what he was worth. She knew that there was nothing of the intellectual or man of culture about him and that he was not qualified to participate in the serious business of government.

Orlov could not understand, or would not accept, Catherine's hesitation. He did not comprehend the years of ambition beginning in childhood; the years of waiting, of hungering for power, of always knowing that she was superior in intellect, education, knowledge, and willpower to everyone around her. Through all of this, she had been forced to wait. Now the waiting was over. If she had to choose between having Orlov as a husband or wielding imperial power—if she could have only one—it would not be Orlov.

Yet the marriage question still tantalized her. There were moments when she thought she might have both Orlov and the throne. For a while, she considered saying yes. Later, she did not know how to say no. She could not afford to alienate the Orlovs; at the same time, she could guess the anger and dismay such a match would unleash in other quarters, particularly in Nikita Panin, who was essential to her in administering the government. To all Russians, but to Panin especially, an Orlov marriage would be seen as jeopardizing Paul's right of succession in favor of her younger son by Orlov. Indeed, Panin, who was permitted to speak honestly to Catherine, reacted to marriage talk by coldly declaring, "A Madame Orlov could never be empress of Russia."

At one point, hoping that she might find a precedent for a marriage to Orlov, Catherine decided to explore the rumors that Empress Elizabeth had married her peasant lover, Alexis Razumovsky. She sent Chancellor Michael Vorontsov to call on Razumovsky and tell him that if he would provide proof of his marriage to Elizabeth, he would have the right, as a widower prince consort, to all the honors due a member of the imperial family, a position that would entitle him to a substantial pension. The chancellor found Razumovsky sitting by his fire reading his Bible. The older man listened silently to what the visitor said and then shook his head; already one of the richest men in Russia, he was not interested in honors and did not need money. He rose, went to a locked ivory cabinet, opened it, and took out a scrolled parchment document tied with a pink ribbon. Making the sign of the cross, he touched the scroll to his lips, removed the ribbon, and threw the document into the fire. "Tell Her Imperial Majesty that I was never anything more than the humble slave of the late Empress Elizabeth Petrovna," he said.

Orlov refused to consider this a significant setback. Razumovsky had been only a handsome peasant with a superb voice, whereas he, Gregory Orlov, and his brothers had raised his mistress to an imperial throne. His attempt to arrange a marriage continued. In the winter of 1763, Alexis Bestuzhev, now aligning himself with the Orlovs against Panin, began circulating a petition to gather support from the high nobility, the members of the Senate, and the clergy, requesting that the empress marry again. The petition's argument was that, given the frailty and frequent illnesses of Grand Duke Paul, Russia must be provided with another heir. Whether Bestuzhev alone or the Orlovs or Catherine herself were behind this effort, no one knew. But the petition elicited strong opposition, and when Panin got hold of the document, he took it to Catherine, who refused to authorize Bestuzhev to circulate it.

Once Catherine was on the throne, it did not take long for Gregory Orlov's relationship with the new empress to arouse jealousy in the institution from which the soldier had come. Gregory had always believed that his popularity in the army would be permanent. Now, even as he and his brothers were mounting in imperial favor, they were losing their standing in the army, and even with old comrades in the Guards. The Orlovs' rise had been too rapid; success had led to pride; pride nourished arrogance; arrogance bred jealousy. It was in October, only a month after her coronation in Moscow, that Catherine's relationship with Orlov had aroused the discontent of a group of young officers who had taken part in the coup, and had led them to talk of dethroning her in favor of the deposed emperor Ivan VI. Although this mini-conspiracy was quickly snuffed out, this kind of antagonism remained. What if Catherine should decide to marry the tall, handsome soldier? Six months later, the answer came.

In May 1763, Catherine traveled from Moscow to the Monastery of the Resurrection, in Rostov on the upper Volga, making the pilgrimage she had postponed when the struggle with Archbishop Arseniy Matsey- evich was nearing a climax. Unfortunately for Orlov, this visit coin- cided with Bestuzhev's circulation of a petition asking Catherine to marry again. The result was a rumor that the empress had gone to the monastery in order to marry Orlov in secret. The rumor, spreading through Moscow and greeted first by disbelief, then consternation, triggered a fervent reaction in a young Guards officer, Captain Fedor Khitrovo.

The empress was still in Rostov when she first was told that Khi- trovo was plotting to murder all of the Orlovs in order to eliminate them from Catherine's life. Khitrovo was arrested. Because there also were rumors that people like Nikita Panin and Princess Dashkova were involved, the empress demanded to know who had conceived the con- spiracy and who else was implicated. General Vasily Suvorov was di- rected to investigate.

Khitrovo, Catherine was surprised to learn, had been one of the forty Guards officers rewarded for their services in the coup that put her on the throne. Under interrogation, the young officer declared that he had joined in the coup believing that Catherine was to be proclaimed regent for her son, not reigning empress. In any case, he and his com- rades had done for Catherine exactly what the Orlov brothers had done: all had risked their lives to overthrow Peter III. In gratitude, each of the forty had received a decoration and a few thousand rubles. But Gregory Orlov had been ennobled, granted an annual income of 150,000 rubles, become the empress's favorite, and was strutting about as if he were already prince consort. Khitrovo believed that Catherine's pilgrimage to Rostov was to permit her to marry her lover. He felt that this would be a national calamity and that it must be prevented.

Under interrogation, Khitrovo told the examiners that his plan was inspired solely by love of country. He insisted that he had acted of his own free will and swore that he had no accomplices. At the same time, he declared that he was not at all opposed to the empress marrying again; in fact, that he was wholeheartedly in favor of Catherine remarrying, provided she chose someone worthy of her throne. As the investigation proceeded, it proved beyond doubt that Khitrovo was not an eccentric madman but was voicing the opinion of many in the Guards and the army. His bearing and his replies under questioning made a strong impression, and he earned the support of his examiners, who decided that they were dealing with an honest, determined patriot whose concern was to save Russia from disaster.

Once it was clear that the investigators sided with the prisoner, no charge could be laid against Khitrovo. Far from being a potential assassin, Khitrovo was now regarded as a hero who wished to save his sovereign. Although the investigation had been conducted before a supposedly secret tribunal, everyone in Moscow knew what was happening. All blamed the Orlovs and exonerated Khitrovo. With public sympathy so obviously on Khitrovo's side, even the Orlovs did not dare insist that the case be brought; the interrogation lapsed, and there was no trial. Catherine herself recognized that Khitrovo was not her enemy but an honorable officer who was voicing the opinion of the court, the Guards, the army, and the entire city. Privately, she was grateful to the young captain. By demonstrating the almost universal opposition to a marriage, even Gregory would be forced to acknowledge that it was out of the question. She would be able to evade the painful business of having to reject him personally.

The proceedings, far from secret, had aroused intense public discussion—far more than Catherine liked. To end this chatter, she issued, on June 4, 1763, a so-called Manifesto of Silence. To beating drums, people across the empire were summoned into the public squares to listen to heralds reading her proclamation, which declared that "everyone should go about his own business and refrain from all useless and unseemly gossip and criticism of the government." This had the desired effect, and the Khitrovo affair faded away. Because Khitrovo came from a wealthy family, he suffered no punishment beyond being deprived of his military rank, dismissed from the army, and banished to his country estate near Orel. He died there eleven years later.

Before disappearing completely, however, the Khitrovo affair had repercussions. In the investigation's first phase, Princess Dashkova's name had appeared as being among Khitrovo's alleged accomplices. It was untrue, as Khitrovo himself subsequently made clear, but the Orlovs, knowing how much Dashkova despised them, demanded that she be interrogated. Catherine quashed the idea, but nothing involving Catherine Dashkova could ever remain a secret. The princess publicly declared that she knew nothing about the plot, but she added that if she had known, she would have refused to tell anyone. Then, characteristically, she went on to announce, "If the empress wants me to lay my head upon a block in reward for having placed a crown upon her own, I am quite prepared to die." It was the kind of flamboyant, exhibitionist remark that Catherine found impossible to tolerate. When Dashkova made certain that her statement was repeated everywhere in Moscow, an exasperated empress wrote to Prince Dashkov and asked him to exercise some authority over his wife. "It is my earnest desire," she said, "not to be obliged to forget the services of Princess Dashkova, by her forgetfulness of what she owes herself. Remind her of this, my prince, as she gives herself, I understand, the indiscreet liberty of menacing me in her conversation."

The end of the Khitrovo affair settled a larger problem: there would be no more talk of an Orlov marriage. The public demonstration of how much the Orlovs were hated had shaken Catherine, and she had no desire to further inflame public opinion. There was no further talk of marriage, but Catherine still kept Gregory by her side for another nine years, putting up with his moodiness, his jealousy, and his petty infidelities. "There would never have been anybody else," Catherine would later tell Potemkin, "had he not grown tired." The relationship took on an odd psychological balance: she controlled him because she was his sovereign and far superior in intelligence and culture; he, in turn, had power over her because he knew that she was fond of him, was indebted to him, and that she felt a permanent guilt because she would not marry him. For almost a decade, he was the only man in Russia who could make her suffer. The fact was that Catherine had no time for suffering and little enough for passion; she was simply too busy. To compensate, she made Orlov a prince of the empire; she gave him a palace in St. Petersburg and another at Gatchina, set in the middle of an enormous park. He became lord of vast stretches of land in Russia and Livonia. As always, he alone was privileged to wear the empress's portrait set in diamonds. Officially, he remained one of the empress's advisers. To please her, he attempted to enter the world of scholarship and intellect the empress admired. He supported the scientist Mikhail Lomonosov. He was interested in astronomy and had an observatory constructed on the roof of the Summer Palace. He offered to become the patron of the Enlightenment philosopher Jean-Jacques Rousseau and wrote to persuade Rousseau to come to Russia:

> You will not be surprised at my writing to you, as you know everyone has his peculiarities. You have yours; I have mine. This is natural and the motive of my letter is equally so. I see that for a long time you have been living abroad, moving about from one place to another. . . . I believe that at the moment you are in England with the Duke of Richmond, who no doubt makes you very comfortable. But I have an estate [at Gatchina] which is . . . [forty miles] . . . from St. Petersburg where the air is healthy and the water good, where the hills and lakes lend themselves to meditation, and where the inhabitants speak neither English nor French, still less Greek or Latin. The priest is incapable of arguing or preaching and his flock thinks they have done their duty when they have made the sign of the cross. Should you think this place would suit you, you are welcome to live in it. You will be provided with the necessities of life and find plenty of fishing and shooting.

Catherine was probably pleased when Rousseau declined. Her taste in Enlightenment philosophers ran to Montesquieu, Voltaire, and Diderot, who believed in benevolent despotism, rather than to Rousseau, who advocated government administered by the *volonté générale*—the "general will"—of the entire population.

❧49❧

The Death of Ivan VI

A SHADOWY FIGURE, potentially more threatening than any other who might challenge her right to the throne, loomed over Catherine during the first two years of her reign. This was the silent, imprisoned former tsar, Ivan VI, deposed as an infant. His existence haunted

Catherine as it had haunted Empress Elizabeth. After Catherine's accession, when some were reproaching her for not accepting the superior dynastic claim of her son, Paul, and contenting herself with the role
of regent, others spoke discreetly of releasing Ivan from the cell where
he had spent most of his life. After the Khitrovo affair, Catherine had
issued her Manifesto of Silence, but talk and rumors about the imprisoned former tsar were impossible to stamp out.

During Elizabeth's twenty years on the throne, Ivan had never left
her thoughts. It was because of him that the empress was afraid to sleep
at night. When Elizabeth died, Peter III had assumed the throne without challenge. Peter had been a Romanov; he was the grandson of Peter
the Great and had been named heir to the throne in the manner prescribed by his towering grandfather; that is, he was named by the reigning sovereign, his aunt Elizabeth. Catherine lacked these credentials.
She was a foreigner; she had seized the throne in a coup d'etat, and,
some believed, may have been implicated in her husband's death. For
these reasons, Catherine was concerned about any reports of opposition, conspiracy, or rebellion. In the Khitrovo affair, she had remained
calm and had dealt with it efficiently. But nothing that came before was
quite like the affair involving Vasily Mirovich and the imprisoned Tsar
Ivan VI.

In June 1764, Catherine left St. Petersburg for a tour of the Baltic
provinces. She was in Riga on July 9 when word arrived that there had
been an attempt to free the former emperor that had ended in the
young man's death.

Ivan had been eighteen months old in 1740 when Elizabeth removed
him from the throne. When he was four, he was separated from his
parents. He had received no formal education but in childhood had
been taught the Russian alphabet by a priest. Now twenty-four, he had
spent eighteen years in solitary confinement in an isolated cell in the
Schlüsselburg Fortress, fifty miles up the Neva River from St. Petersburg. Here, designated Prisoner No. 1, he was allowed to see no one
except his immediate jailers. There were reports that he was aware of
his identity; that once, goaded to anger by his guards, he had shouted,
"Take care! I am a prince of this empire. I am your sovereign." A report
of this outburst brought a harsh response from Alexander Shuvalov,
head of Elizabeth's Secret Chancellery. "If the prisoner is insubordinate

or makes improper statements," Shuvalov instructed, "you shall put him in irons until he obeys, and if he still resists, he must be beaten with a stick or a whip." Eventually, the guards reported, "The prisoner is somewhat quieter than before. He no longer tells lies about his identity." Elizabeth continued to worry and, on the empress's command, Shuvalov issued a further instruction: if any attempt to free Prisoner No. 1 seemed likely to succeed, Ivan's jailers were to kill him.

In the turmoil following her own accession, Catherine paid a visit to Ivan in order to judge the prisoner for herself. She found a tall, slender young man with fair hair and a red beard, his skin pale from years hidden from sunlight. His expression was innocent, but his intelligence was stunted by years of solitude. Catherine wrote, "Apart from his painful and almost unintelligible stammering, he was bereft of reasoning and human understanding."

Nevertheless, he, like Peter III, was a Romanov, a direct descendant of Peter the Great's elder brother and co-tsar, Ivan V, and his right to the crown was dynastically impeccable. Had Catherine found him an idiot or insane, she might have had nothing to fear. Citing his obvious unfitness to rule, she could have proclaimed his incapacity, shown mercy, released him and provided him with a quiet, comfortable existence. But if this level of disability were not true, it was possible that Ivan might somehow be rehabilitated, physically and intellectually. Even if obviously unfit to rule, he remained dangerous as a symbol. To protect herself, she ordered a continuation of the severe conditions in which he had previously been held. Nikita Panin was assigned to oversee Ivan's imprisonment.

There was a point at which Catherine hoped the young man might be persuaded to choose a cloistered, monastic life that would disqualify him from returning to the throne. If he accepted tonsure as a monk, it would mean a permanent withdrawal from the political world, and the officers who guarded him were instructed to attempt to guide him along this path. Another possible solution was that Ivan die in prison of genuine natural causes. To enhance this possibility, Panin ordered that medical treatment be denied him; if he became gravely ill, a priest was to be admitted, but not a doctor. Meanwhile, Panin also signed a specific order renewing the previous instructions for guarding the prisoner: if anyone, no matter who, sought to take the prisoner away without an express written order personally signed in the empress's handwriting, Ivan was not to be handed over. Instead, if efforts to liberate him seemed likely to succeed, his guards were commanded to put their prisoner to death. The command reiterated Shuvalov's earlier instruction: "The prisoner shall not be allowed to fall alive into the hands of any rescuers."

Two officers, Captain Danilo Vlasev and Lieutenant Luka Chekin, were assigned to guard Ivan. Only they and the fortress governor had access to the prisoner. As the two guardian officers themselves were never permitted to leave Schlüsselburg, they were, in effect, locked in with the nameless prisoner. The situation, therefore, was that Ivan remained in the hands of two men who were authorized to kill him in certain circumstances and whose own goal was to be free of him so that they could resume living normal lives.

The guards reported bimonthly to Panin. With the passage of time, these reports reflected their growing boredom, frustration, and longing for their own freedom. With every letter, their pleas grew stronger. In August 1763, Panin replied, counseling them to be patient, promising that their duties would end soon. In November, growing more desperate, they addressed an urgent petition to Panin: "Release us for we have come to the end of our strength." Panin's response, on December 28, 1763, was to send each of them one thousand rubles—an enormous sum for them—and the promise that they would not have to wait much longer. "Compliance with your request will not be postponed later than the early months of the summer."

In midwinter 1764, a young officer, Lieutenant Vasily Mirovich of the Smolensk Regiment, was assigned to the garrison at Schlüsselburg. A proud, lonely, embittered young man, in debt and given to drinking and gambling, he harbored a deep and gnawing sense of injustice and persecution. Mirovich was twenty-four and of aristocratic Ukrainian origin. His family's estates had been confiscated in 1709 by Peter the Great because the young man's grandfather had sided with the Ukrainian Cossack hetman Ivan Mazeppa against the tsar during the Swedish invasion of Russia in 1708. Deprived of his family heritage, Mirovich had been brought up in poverty. Without money, he tried to win at cards and was unlucky. His creditors pressed him constantly. His three sisters, living in Moscow, were close to starving, but he could not help them.

He prayed to God, but there was no reply. In hopes of recovering his family lands, he came to St. Petersburg. He petitioned the Senate twice for restoration, but the Senate refused. He appealed twice to Catherine; she rejected him. When he approached Kyril Razumovsky, appointed Ukrainian hetman by Catherine, Razumovsky told him that his claims were hopeless. Razumovsky's only advice was, "Make your own career, young man. Seize fortune by the forelock as others have done." Mirovich filed these words away in memory.

Resentful, without money or connections, he joined the army and was posted to Schlüsselburg. His fellow officers found him moody and difficult. His post was in the outer fortress, where no one was allowed to know what went on in the inner casements. He wondered about the nameless Prisoner No. 1, entombed in the labyrinth of cells in the inner citadel, where he was watched over by special guards who were never relieved. When he learned, eventually, that the prisoner was "Ivanushka," the anointed infant tsar, Mirovich remembered Razumovsky's advice: "Seize fortune by the forelock." This counsel reminded Mirovich of the recent history of another young officer, Gregory Orlov, who had helped Catherine overthrow a sovereign and thereby had promoted himself to spectacular power and wealth. Why should he, Vasily Mirovich, not do the same on Ivan's behalf? Why should not he, like the Orlov brothers, reach fame and fortune by arranging the rescue of the true tsar?

From this ambitious beginning, Mirovich's horizon expanded. His original motive for restoring Ivan to the throne was to alleviate his own misery and poverty by becoming another Orlov. Soon he had a grander vision. Besides being a gambler and a drinker, Mirovich was a churchgoer, and he convinced himself that God had assigned him a sacred mission. Surely God himself would welcome and bless the overthrow of a usurping woman and the restoration of an anointed tsar. Excited by this new idea, Mirovich found a comrade at Schlüsselburg, Appolon Ushakov. Together they considered the layout of the fortress and the means of convincing or overpowering the garrison of the inner fortress. Early in May 1764, Mirovich drew up a manifesto—a tangle of misstatements and grievances—for Ivan to sign and proclaim once he had been liberated.

Not long had Peter III possessed the throne when by the intrigues of his wife and by her hands he was given poison to drink, and by these means and by force, the vain and spend-thrift Catherine seized my hereditary throne. To the day of our accession, she has sent out of my country up to twenty-five mil-lion in gold and silver. . . . And, moreover, her inborn weak-nesses have led her to take as a husband her subject Gregory Orlov . . . for which she will not be able to excuse herself at the Last Judgment.

Their plan was for Ushakov to present himself at Schlüsselburg pretending to be a courier from Catherine, bringing with him an order for Ivan's release. Mirovich would read the order to the garrison, arrest the commandant, release the prisoner, and take him by boat down the Neva River to St. Petersburg, where Ivan would proclaim his accession to the troops in the capital. To seal their bond, the two conspirators went to church and swore an oath. Their moment to act would come when the empress departed on her already announced journey to the Baltic provinces. What Mirovich and Ushakov did not know—only Catherine, Panin, and the two guards, Vlasev and Chekin, knew—was that any effort to free the prisoner would result in his death.

Just before Catherine's departure from St. Petersburg for the Baltic provinces, Ushakov disappeared. He had been ordered by the College of War to to carry funds to Smolensk and give them to the commander of his regiment there. Mirovich waited for his collaborator to return—he did not. His hat and dagger were discovered on a riverbank; a neigh-borhood peasant reported that the body of a drowned officer had washed ashore and that they had buried it. The circumstances of his death were unknown.

Mirovich was dismayed, but, driven by compulsion—and, he may have believed, also bound by his oath—he decided to proceed on his own. He assembled a group of soldiers in the fortress, told them his plan, and asked them to join him. Uneasily, each replied, "If the others agree, I will not refuse." At half past one on the night of July 4, Miro-vich mustered his followers. When the fortress commandant, aroused by the noise, rushed out in his nightshirt, Mirovich clubbed him uncon-scious with a musket butt. Over one hundred shots were fired between the men in the outer and inner bastions; no one was killed or wounded. Impatient to overcome the defenders of the inner casement, Mirovich dragged up an old cannon; a white flag quickly went up. Mirovich crossed the moat to the inner casement and made his way by torchlight to Ivan's cell. Outside the door stood the two wardens, Vlasev and Chekin. Mirovich seized Chekin and demanded, "Where is the emperor?" Chekin replied, "We have no emperor. We have an empress." Pushing him aside, Mirovich stepped into the cell. Ivan's body lay on the floor in a pool of blood. The two officers had obeyed Panin's command and done their duty; when they heard shots fired, they had pulled the sleeping prisoner from his bed and run him through eight times with their swords. Ivan died, only half awake, because a man he had never seen had wished to place him on the Russian throne.

Overcome by what he saw, Mirovich dropped to his knees, embraced the body, and picked up and kissed a bloody hand. His attempted coup having failed, he surrendered. When Ivan's body was carried to the outer fortress, Mirovich cried, "See, my brothers, this is our emperor, Ivan Antonovich. You are innocent, because you were ignorant of my intentions. I assume responsibility and will take all the punishment upon myself."

On regaining consciousness, the Schlüsselburg commandant immediately reported the episode to Nikita Panin, who was at Tsarskoe Selo with Grand Duke Paul. Panin relayed the news by the fastest messenger to Catherine in Riga. She was startled, and then her surprise was followed—she made no attempt to disguise it—by overwhelming relief. "The ways of God are wonderful beyond prediction," she wrote to Panin. "Providence has given me a clear sign of its favor by putting an end to this shameful affair." The Prussian ambassador accompanying the empress's party reported to Frederick that "she left here [Riga] with an air of the greatest serenity and the most composed countenance."

It was difficult for her to believe that the brief uprising had been a desperate act of a single man; a game played for these stakes must be the work a conspiracy. She ordered an immediate investigation. Fifty officers and men from the fortress were arrested. Interrogated by a special commission, Mirovich confessed his guilt frankly and refused to incriminate anyone else. Despite his honesty, once Catherine had examined the documents in the dossier and read Mirovich's manifesto accusing her of being a usurper, of poisoning her husband, and of marrying Gregory Orlov, she put aside any thoughts of leniency. On August 17, an imperial manifesto announced that the investigators had found Ivan insane and that Mirovich would be tried by a special court composed of the Senate, the Holy Synod, the presidents of the colleges of War, the Navy, and Foreign Affairs, and members of the high nobility. In handing Mirovich over for trial, Catherine announced, "As regards the insult to my person, I pardon the accused. But regarding the attack on the general peace and welfare of the country, let the loyal assembly pass judgment."

The two men who had taken Ivan's life were never placed on trial. The court's assignment was to judge the act committed by Mirovich, and the question of guilt for Ivan's death was shifted from those who had actually killed the prisoner to the man who had tried to set him free. Mirovich, brought before the court three times and exhorted to implicate others, doggedly reaffirmed that he had acted alone. During the trial, Catherine herself intervened only once: when a member demanded that Mirovich be tortured to extract the names of his accomplices, Catherine ordered that the examination be conducted without torture. Ironically, in some quarters, this decision damaged her reputation, because it bred suspicion that she feared that pain would bring out incriminating disclosures. In fact, Catherine did attempt to suppress any reference to Panin's secret orders authorizing Ivan's keepers to kill him in the event of an attempt to free him. The few who became aware of this instruction were told that it was based on orders given by Empress Elizabeth.

Mirovich's fate was not in doubt. On September 9, he was condemned to death and sentenced to beheading. Throughout the trial, Mirovich maintained an attitude of composure. This too militated against Catherine; it was said that only the knowledge that he would escape punishment could give a guilty man such calm dignity. Catherine was aware of this, and to rebuff this notion, when the court assigned a death sentence, she, for the first time in her reign, signed it. Mirovich thereby was to become the first Russian executed in the twenty-two years since Empress Elizabeth had vowed never to sign a death warrant.

When the day came, Mirovich faced death with serenity, so much so that many eyewitness were certain that he would be pardoned at the last minute. Mirovich's behavior during his final minutes suggested that he thought so, too. He stood next to the block, exuding calm, while the crowd waited, expecting the arrival of a messenger from the empress bringing an order to commute the sentence. When no messenger arrived, Mirovich laid his head on the block. The executioner raised his axe and paused. Still no one came. The axe fell. Mirovich's remains were left on public display until nightfall, when they were burned.

The details of the Mirovich conspiracy were never made public. The two guards, Vlasev and Chekin, were rewarded with promotion and seven thousand rubles each for "loyally performing their duty." The sixteen soldiers who had been under their command guarding Ivan in the inner Schlüsselburg citadel each received one hundred rubles; in return, they pledged not to speak of what they had seen and heard.

In Russia, public doubts regarding the empress's role in Ivan's death could be managed. Within the Russian government, the court, the nobility, and the army, the opinion was that whether or not Catherine bore some responsibility, she had done what had to be done. In Europe, however, where Catherine had been working to present herself as a daughter of the Enlightenment, it was not so easy. Some supported what Catherine had done; others disapproved; some both approved and disapproved. Madame Geoffrin, the leader and hostess of the dominant literary and artistic salon in Paris, wrote to Stanislaus Poniatowski in Poland criticizing Catherine for becoming too involved in the trial and sentence. "The manifesto she [Catherine] has issued on the death of Ivan is ridiculous," she said. "There was no necessity of her saying anything whatever. Mirovich's trial was entirely sufficient." To Catherine herself, with whom she occasionally corresponded, Madame Geoffrin wrote, "It seems to me that if I were on the throne, I should wish to let my actions speak and impose silence on my pen."

Offended by these judgments from afar, Catherine fired back:

> I am tempted to say to you that you discuss this manifesto as a blind man discussed colors. It was never composed for foreign powers, but to inform the Russian public of Ivan's death. It was necessary to say how he died. To have failed to do so would have been to confirm the malicious rumors spread by the ministers of courts which envy me and bear me ill will. . . . In your country, people find fault with this manifesto; in your country they have also found fault with the Good Lord, and here people sometimes find fault with the French. But it is nonetheless true that here this manifesto and the criminal's head have put an end to all fault-finding. Therefore, the pur-

pose was accomplished and my manifesto did not fail of its object. Therefore, it was good.

With Ivan's death there was no longer a legitimate adult claimant to the throne. Therefore, there was no focal point for a succession crisis. Until nine years later, in 1772, when Paul reached his majority at eighteen, Catherine's crown was secure.

✤50✤

Catherine and the Enlightenment

I N THE MIDDLE of the eighteenth century, most Europeans still regarded Russia as a culturally backward, semi-Asiatic state. Catherine was determined to change this. The intellectual and artistic life of the century was dominated by France, and Catherine's governess in Stettin had made French her second language. During her sixteen years as an isolated, embattled grand duchess, she had read many of the works of the great figures of the European Enlightenment. Of these, the writer with the greatest effect on her was François-Marie Arouet, who called himself Voltaire. In October 1763, after fifteen months on the throne, she wrote to him for the first time, declaring herself to be his ardent disciple. "Whatever style I possess, whatever powers of reasoning, have all been acquired through the reading of Voltaire," she told him.

Voltaire was sixty-one when, in 1755, he had decided to settle down. Two imprisonments in the Bastille; voluntary exile in England; an initially euphoric sojourn at the court of Frederick of Prussia, followed by misunderstanding, estrangement, and, eventually, painful rupture; a complicated warm and cool relationship with Louis XV and Madame de Pompadour—all this was behind him. He was ready to bury himself in work and he believed that he would find a haven of tranquillity in the independent republic of Geneva, governed by a council of aristocratic Calvinists. Already a millionaire from his writing, he bought a villa with a splendid view of the lake and called it Les Délicies. Soon he was in trouble again. A number of Genevois disapproved of an article about their city in Diderot's *Encyclopedia* that seemed to represent the Calvinist clergy of Geneva as rejecting the divinity of Christ. In fact, it was the mathematician and physicist Jean d'Alembert who had written these words, but Voltaire was believed to be the writer's inspiration, and he bore the brunt of the council's complaints. In 1758, he moved to Ferney.

It seemed a safer haven. The Château de Ferney was on French territory, but only just; Geneva was three miles away; Paris and Versailles were three hundred. Should the French authorities decide to make trouble for him again, he needed only an hour to move back across the border to Geneva, where he still had many admirers. Geneva was also the home of the publisher who was then printing *Candide*.

Voltaire had not moved to this new dwelling to live in idleness. Instead, he saw Ferney as well placed to be his command post for an intensification of violent intellectual combat. The philosophical wars of the Enlightenment were being fought in earnest. Louis XV had forbidden Voltaire to return to Paris. The man of letters was eager to fire back, and Ferney became the launching point for his philosophical, intellectual, political, and social fusillades. He wrote books, brochures, histories, biographies, plays, stories, treatises, poems, and over fifty thousand letters that now fill ninety-eight volumes. The Seven Years' War had concluded, and France had lost both Canada and India to England. Voltaire rubbed salt into these wounds by denouncing war as the "great illusion." "The victorious nation never profits from the spoils of the conquered; it pays for everything," he said. "It suffers as much when its armies are successful as when they are defeated. Whoever wins, humanity loses." He fired polemical salvos against Christianity, the Bible, and the Catholic Church. At one point, he considered Jesus a deluded eccentric, *un fou*. At the age of eighty, he rose early on a May morning and climbed a hill with a friend to see the sunrise. At the top, overwhelmed by the magnificent panorama of red and gold, he kneeled and said, "Oh, mighty God, I believe." Then, standing up, he said to his friend, "As to Monsieur the son and Madame his mother, that is another matter!"

A further advantage to Ferney was that the most direct roads between northern and southern Europe passed through Switzerland, and these roads were traveled by many of the European intellectual and artistic brotherhood. Voltaire, in his château, was living in the geographical heart of Europe, and was therefore assured of a swarm of visitors—too many. A multitude came to see him from every quarter: German princes, French dukes, English lords, Casanova, a Cossack hetman. Many were English, to whom Voltaire spoke in their own language: the parliamentary statesman Charles James Fox, the historian Edward Gibbon, the biographer James Boswell. When uninvited people arrived, Voltaire told his servants, "Send them away. Tell them I am very sick." Boswell begged to be allowed to stay overnight and see the patriarch in the morning; he said he would sleep in "the highest and coldest garret." He was sent to a pleasant bedroom.

Nor did Voltaire confine himself to intellectual matters. In 1762 and during the years following, Voltaire became "the Man of Calas." The backdrop to this affair was the persecution of Protestants in France. Protestants were excluded from public office; couples not married by a Catholic priest were considered to be living in sin; their children were considered illegitimate. In the southern and southwestern provinces of France, these laws were grimly enforced.

In March 1762, Voltaire learned that a sixty-four-year-old Protestant Huguenot, Jean Calas, a dealer in linens in Toulouse, had been executed under torture. His eldest son, suffering from depression, had committed suicide in the family's house. The father, Jean, knowing that the law demanded that the body of a suicide be dragged naked through the streets, pelted with mud and stones, and then hanged, persuaded his family to join him in reporting a natural death. The police saw the rope marks on the son's neck, however, and charged that Calas had murdered his son to prevent him from converting to Catholicism. A high court prescribed torture to make Calas confess. He was placed on the rack and his arms and legs were pulled from their sockets; in agony, he admitted that his son's death was a suicide. This was not the confession the authorities wanted; they demanded that he confess to murder. Fifteen pints of water were poured down his throat; he still protested his own innocence. Another fifteen pints were forced into him; he was convinced that he was drowning, but still cried that he was innocent. He was stretched on a cross in the public square before the Toulouse cathedral. The public executioner took a heavy iron bar and crushed each of his four limbs in two places; the old man still proclaimed his innocence. He was strangled and died.

Donat Calas, the youngest of six Calas children, came to Ferney and begged Voltaire to defend his dead father's innocence. Voltaire, appalled and infuriated by this cruelty, undertook the legal rehabilitation of the victim. For three years, from 1762 to 1765, he hired lawyers and mobilized European opinion. During the summer of 1763, he wrote *Traité sur la Tolérance,* which argued that Roman persecution of Christians in the early years of Christianity had now been surpassed by Christian persecution of other Christians who were "hanged, drowned, broken on the wheel, or burned for the love of God." Eventually, Voltaire appealed to the high council of the kingdom, presided over by the king. There, eventually, Jean Calas was posthumously exonerated and his reputation rehabilitated.

This triumph was accompanied by another. Elisabeth, the daughter of Pierre Paul Sirven, a Protestant living near Toulouse, wished to convert to Catholicism and had been spirited away to a convent by a Catholic bishop. There, she ripped off her clothes and demanded to be flogged; prudently, the bishop returned her to her family. A few months later, Elisabeth disappeared. She was discovered drowned in a well. Forty-five local witnesses testified that the girl had committed suicide, but the prosecutor ordered her father's arrest and accused him of having murdered his daughter to prevent her conversion. On March 19, 1764, Sirven and his wife were both condemned to be hanged; their two surviving daughters, one of them pregnant, were to be forced to watch. The family fled to Geneva, reached Ferney, and asked Voltaire to help them. The philosopher again took up his pen. He recruited Frederick of Prussia, Catherine of Russia, Stanislaus of Poland, and other monarchs to take up the cause. After nine years of endless argument, Sirven was acquitted. "It took two hours to condemn this man to death," Voltaire said bitterly, "and nine years to prove his innocence."

With Voltaire in eternal combat, his widowed niece, Mme Denis, acted as mistress of the house—and as his bedroom companion. Voltaire saw nothing wrong in sexual irregularity; he defined morality as "doing good to mankind." In any case, it was an age of sexual irregularity, and Voltaire's relationship with Mme Denis was straightforward. He concealed nothing; she was his mistress; he called her "my beloved." In 1748, in the early years of their relationship (it continued until his death), he had written to her, "I shall be coming to Paris only for you. . . . In the meantime, I press a thousand kisses on your round breasts, on your ravishing bottom, on all your person, which has so often given me erections and plunged me into a flood of delight."

At Ferney, the master usually did not appear until midday dinner. During the day, he read and wrote and then continued far into the night, allowing himself only five or six hours of sleep. He drank an ocean of coffee. He suffered from severe headaches. To help the people of his village, he built a watchmaking factory and then persuaded all of his friends in Europe to buy its products; from St. Petersburg Catherine placed an order worth thirty-nine thousand pounds. By 1777, this once small, impoverished village of forty-nine people had become a prosperous town of twelve hundred. Every Sunday, Voltaire opened the chateau for dancing. On October 4, 1777, Ferney celebrated its patron in the courtyard of his chateau with an evening of singing, dancing, and fireworks. This was the last fete held at Ferney. On February 5, 1778, Voltaire left for Paris, promising to return in six weeks. In Paris, the population, which had not seen him for twenty years, gave him an ovation whenever he appeared. Marie Antoinette asked to meet and embrace him; he could not oblige her because he was still banned from court by her husband, Louis XVI. He met and embraced Benjamin Franklin instead. He never returned to his château. On May 30, 1778, he died in Paris.

While Voltaire lived, Frederick of Prussia told him, "After your death, there will be no one to replace you"; when the philosopher was gone, the king said, "For my part, I am consoled by having lived in the age of Voltaire." Later, Goethe added, "He governed the whole civilized world." Catherine's lament was more specific: it was not his wisdom she mourned; it was his gaiety. "Since Voltaire died," she wrote to her friend Friedrich Melchior Grimm, "it seems to me that honor no longer attaches to good humor. He was the divinity of gaiety. Procure for me an edition, or rather, a complete copy of his works, to renew within me and confirm my natural love of laughter."

After Voltaire's death, the empress told Grimm that she intended to build a replica of the Château de Ferney in the park at Tsarskoe Selo. This "New Ferney" would become the repository of Voltaire's library, purchased by Catherine from Mme Denis for 135,000 pounds. The books went to Russia, but the architectural project was abandoned, and the library of over six thousand volumes, annotated by Voltaire page by page in the margins, was placed in a hall of the Hermitage in St. Petersburg. In the center of this space, the place of honor, was an exact copy of Houdon's remarkable statue of Voltaire seated.

It is there today.

The imperial coronation crown designed for Catherine.
The crown was used in all six of the Romanov coronations that followed.

(RIA Novosti)

Empress Elizabeth, daughter of Peter the Great, who brought Sophia to Russia
at fourteen and changed her name to Catherine. The empress then married
the adolescent girl to her nephew, Peter, and charged her with
immediately producing an infant to secure the dynasty.

Catherine at sixteen, at the Russian court.

(*Portrait of Grand Duchess Ekatrina Alekseyevna, later Catherine II*, c. 1745 by Georg Christoph Grooth (1716–49),
Hermitage, St. Petersburg, Russia/The Bridgeman Art Library)

Catherine preparing to march on Peterhof,
where she would force Peter III to abdicate.

(Equestrian Portrait of Catherine II (1729–96) the Great of Russia (oil on canvas)
by Vigilius Erichsen (1722–82), Musée des Beaux-Arts,
Chartres, France/The Bridgeman Art Library)

Catherine's coronation portrait. She is wearing her new imperial crown.

(RIA Novosti)

Paul, Catherine's son, in one of the Prussian uniforms he delighted in wearing.

(*Portrait of Paul I, 1796–97* by Stepan Semenovich)

The older Gregory Potemkin, the most important man in Catherine's life.

(Portrait of Prince Grigory Aleksandrovich Potemkin (1739–91),
c. 1790 by Johann Baptist I Lampi (1751–1830),
Hermitage, St. Petersburg, Russia/The Bridgeman Art Library)

An aging Catherine with one of her greyhounds
in the park at Tsarskoe Selo.

(*Walking in the Park at Tsarskoye Selo (with the Chessmen Column in the Background)*,
1794 (oil on canvas) by Vladimir Lukich Borovikovsky (1757–1825), Tretyakov Gallery,
Moscow, Russia/The Bridgeman Art Library)

• • •

Voltaire was interested in Russia. In 1757, he had persuaded Empress Elizabeth to commission him to write a history of Russia under her father, Peter the Great. The first volume had been published in 1760; he was still working on the second volume when Elizabeth died and Catherine overthrew Peter III. With rumors of what had happened at Ropsha reverberating throughout Europe, Catherine thought of enlisting Voltaire to help her clear her name. One of her secretaries at the time was a native of Geneva, François-Pierre Pictet, a disciple of Voltaire's and a former actor in the patriarch's amateur theatricals at Les Délices. At Catherine's request, Pictet sent a long account to Voltaire, explaining the intolerable situation in which she had found herself after her coup, and her innocence in the murder itself. Voltaire accepted this account, and brushed it aside by saying, "I know that . . . [Catherine] is reproached with some *bagatelle* about her husband, but these are family matters in which I do not mix."

Originally, Voltaire maintained a certain reserve toward the new empress. European opinion held that she was unlikely to remain on the throne for long, and Voltaire was reluctant to plunge into an epistolary relationship with her. His reluctance increased on news of the sudden death of Ivan VI. "I believe we must moderate a little our enthusiasm for the North," he wrote to d'Alembert. Once it was apparent that the German princess had a firm seat on the Russian throne, Voltaire began to see in her an enlightened monarch who might work to apply the principles of justice and tolerance that he proclaimed. Thereafter, their correspondence flourished, garnished with mutual flattery, until his death. Their political ideology was similar: they agreed that monarchy was the only rational form of government, provided the monarch was enlightened. "Why is almost the whole earth governed by monarchs?" Voltaire asked. "The honest answer is because men are rarely worthy of governing themselves. . . . Almost nothing great has ever been done in the world except by the genius and firmness of a single man combating the prejudices of the multitude. . . . I do not like government by the rabble."

The relationship between an ambitious, politically powerful woman and the most celebrated writer of the age became one of mutual benefit. Both were mindful that they were playing before an immense, influential audience. Catherine recognized that a letter to Voltaire, which could be passed along to his friends, was potentially a message to the intelligentsia of Europe. For Voltaire, what could be more flattering than to have another ruling sovereign become his royal disciple? He addressed her as "the Semiramis of the North," "Saint Catherine," and "Our Lady of St. Petersburg." In return, she showered him with sable pelisses and jeweled snuffboxes, and sent diamonds to Madame Denis. But it was a relationship that thrived on distance; despite the intimacy of their correspondence, the empress and the patriarch never met. Near the end of his life, when Voltaire was toying with the idea of paying Saint Catherine his personal respects, this appeared to be the last thing she wanted. Perhaps nervous about exposing her country or herself to Voltaire's analytical eye, she wrote urgently to Grimm, "For God's sake, try to persuade the octogenarian to stay at home. What should he do here? He would either die here or on the road from cold, weariness and bad roads. Tell him that *Catau* is best seen from a distance."

Even before she first wrote to Voltaire in 1763, Catherine had reached out to another towering Enlightenment figure, Denis Diderot. Diderot, born in a small town near Dijon in 1713, was as warmhearted as Voltaire was cynical, as rough-hewn as Voltaire was sophisticated and polished, and retained though life the innocence of a child and the enthusiasms of adolescence. According to Catherine, Diderot was "in certain ways . . . a hundred, in others not yet ten." Intending as a boy to become a priest, he attended a Jesuit school for seven years (his brother became a priest) and the University of Paris, and became a translator of English books into French. Increasingly, he was fascinated by the whole universe of knowledge: mathematics, biology, chemistry, physics, anatomy, Latin, Greek, history, literature, art, politics, and philosophy. As a young man, he had rejected the biblical God as a monster of cruelty and the Catholic Church as a fountainhead of ignorance. He saw nature, which, he noted, made no distinction between good and evil, as the only permanent reality. He was arrested and imprisoned. Released, he became the founder and chief editor of the new *Encyclopedia,* "the bible of the enlightened." Working with d'Alembert, he brought out the first volume in June 1751; ten more volumes were to follow. The philosophy of the *Encyclopedia* was humanistic; man was placed in nature; he was equipped with reason to make his way. The importance of scientific knowledge, the dignity of human labor were stressed. For denouncing "the myths of the Catholic church," his license to publish was revoked.

This negative attention enormously stimulated desire to acquire and read each of the eleven volumes as it was published.

From the first, Voltaire praised and encouraged. To d'Alembert he wrote, "You and M. Diderot are accomplishing a work which will be the glory of France and the shame of those who persecute you. Of eloquent philosophers, I recognize only you and him." Six years later, when the project was again in trouble, Voltaire urged, "Go on, brave Diderot, intrepid d'Alembert. Fall upon the knaves, destroy their empty declamations, their miserable sophistries, their historical lies, their contradictions and absurdities beyond number."

One of those closely watching these developments was the new empress of Russia. Soon after her accession, and aware of the influence of Diderot and d'Alembert, Catherine set about winning their support. In August 1762, two months after she took the throne, the difficulties of publishing the *Encyclopedia* in France provided her with an opportunity. She offered to have all subsequent volumes printed in Riga, the westernmost city in her empire. But her offer came too soon after the death of Peter III at Ropsha, and the editors of the *Encyclopedia* were wary of trusting their work to a ruler whose tenure seemed uncertain. Ultimately, the French government, learning what Catherine had offered, relented and authorized continued publication in France.

In 1765, Catherine made a grand gesture to Diderot that became the talk of Europe. Three children had been born to Diderot and his wife, and all three had died. Then, when Madame Diderot was forty-three, a fourth child was born, a daughter, Marie Angélique. Diderot idolized this little girl and treasured the time he spent with her. He knew that he must provide for her dowry. But he had no money; everything had gone into the *Encyclopedia*. He decided to sell his only valuable possession, his library. Catherine heard about his decision from Diderot's friend, her ambassador to France and Holland, Prince Dmitry Golitsyn. Diderot had asked fifteen thousand pounds for his books. Catherine offered sixteen thousand but attached a condition: the books should remain in Diderot's possession for his lifetime. "It would be cruel to separate a scholar from his books," she explained. Diderot thus became—without either he or his books leaving Paris—Catherine's librarian. For this service, she paid him a salary of a thousand pounds a year. The following year, when the salary was forgotten and went unpaid, an embarrassed Catherine sent Diderot fifty thousand pounds—to cover fifty years in advance, she said.

The empress's purchase of Diderot's library captured the imagination of literary Europe. Diderot, astonished, wrote to his benefactress: "Great princess, I prostrate myself at your feet. I reach out my arms to you, I would speak to you, but my soul faints, my mind grows cloudy. . . . Oh, Catherine, be sure that you do not reign more powerfully in Petersburg than in Paris." Voltaire joined in: "Diderot, d'Alembert and I—we are three who would build you altars. . . . Would one ever have suspected fifty years ago that one day the Scythians [Russians] would so nobly recompense in Paris the virtue, science, and philosophy that are treated so shamefully among us." From Grimm: "Thirty years of labor have not brought Diderot the slightest recompense. It has pleased the Empress of Russia to pay the debt of France." Catherine's response was, "I never thought that buying Diderot's library would bring me so many compliments."

There was, no doubt, a larger purpose behind her generosity. If so, the gift achieved its objective: Europeans now believed that there were things in the east other than snow and wolves. Diderot threw himself into the task of recruiting artistic and architectural talent for Catherine. His house was turned into an employment agency on her behalf. Writers, artists, scientists, architects, and engineers swarmed to solicit appointments in St. Petersburg.

In 1773, Diderot, who hated to travel and had never before left France, summoned the resolution to embark on the journey to Russia that he felt he owed to Catherine. He was sixty years old, subject to stomach cramps and drafts of cold air, and he was afraid of Russian food. The prospect of crossing Europe to reach a country famous for violence and freezing temperatures was daunting; nevertheless, he felt an obligation to thank his benefactress in person. In May 1773, he set out. He got only as far as The Hague, where he halted for three months to rest with his friend Prince Dmitry Golitsyn.

With autumn approaching, the philosopher set out on the second stage of his journey. Huddled and coughing in a post chaise, he hoped to reach his destination before extreme cold arrived. Unfortunately, it was snowing in the Russian capital when he arrived on October 8, and he collapsed into bed. The day after his arrival he was awakened by the pealing of bells and the booming of cannon celebrating the wedding of the nineteen-year-old heir to the throne, Grand Duke Paul, to Princess Wilhelmina of Hesse-Darmstadt. Diderot, indifferent to ceremonials, avoided the festivities; this inclination was reinforced by his having nothing to wear other than plain black clothes and by his having left his wig behind somewhere during his journey.

Catherine warmly welcomed the famous editor of the *Encyclopedia*. The man she saw before her possessed a "high brow receding on a half-bald head; large rustic ears and a big bent nose, firm mouth . . . [and] brown eyes, heavy and sad, as if recalling unrecallable errors, or realizing the indestructibility of superstition, or noting the high birth rate of simpletons." The empress had her guest inducted into the Russian Academy of Sciences and then began a series of conversations in her private study. "M. Diderot," she told him at their first meeting, "you see this door by which you have entered. That door will be opened to you every day between three and five in the afternoon." Diderot was charmed by her simplicity and the complete informality of their long, intimate sessions. Catherine would sit on a sofa, sometimes with a piece of needlework in her hands, and her guest would take his place in a comfortable armchair opposite her. Diderot, completely at ease, talked interminably, contradicted her, shouted, gesticulated, and called her "my good lady." The empress laughed at his exuberance and familiarities. He took her hands, shook her arm, and tapped her legs in making his points. "Your Diderot is an extraordinary man," Catherine wrote to Mme Geoffrin. "I emerge from interviews with him with my thighs bruised and quite black. I have been obliged to put a table between us to protect myself and my limbs."

Their conversations roamed widely. With some idea of the topic likely to be discussed, Diderot prepared notes and memoranda, which he then read to the empress; after this preliminary, they both spoke freely. He put before her his views on tolerance, the legislative process, the value of competition in commerce, divorce (which he favored in cases of intellectual incompatibility), and gambling. He begged her to provide Russia with a permanent law of succession. He urged her to introduce the study of anatomy in girls' schools to make the young women better wives and mothers, and help them thwart the wiles of seducers.

The cordiality of their relationship encouraged Diderot to hope that he had found a ruler willing to apply the principles of the Enlightenment to her government. He believed that it would be easier to reform Russia than France, since Russia seemed a blank new page on which history had written nothing. He gave his views on the education of Grand Duke Paul: after serving as a statesman's apprentice in the different administrative colleges, the young man should travel all over Russia, accompanied by economists, geologists, and jurists, to familiarize himself with different aspects of the country he would someday rule. Then, after getting his wife pregnant to ensure the succession, he should visit Germany, England, Italy, and France.

If Diderot had confined himself to specific suggestions, he might have had more specific impact. But, having edited a massive encyclopedia that attempted to include the totality of knowledge, Diderot conceived himself as an authority and therefore a suitable adviser on every aspect of human life, culture, and government. He considered it his duty to instruct the empress on the way to govern her empire. He cited examples from the Greeks and Romans, and urged her to reform Russian institutions while she still could. He urged the establishment of an English-style parliament. He subjected Catherine to a questionnaire containing eighty-eight items, including the quality of tar supplied by each province, the cultivation of grapes, the organization of veterinary schools, the number of monks and nuns in Russia, the number and condition of Jews living in the empire, and the relations between master and serf.

If Diderot's irrepressibility made Catherine laugh, his probing questions probably discomfited her. Listening to him, she eventually decided that her learned, garrulous guest had no sense of the reality of Russia. "Monsieur Diderot," she finally said to him,

> I have listened with the greatest pleasure to all the inspirations of your brilliant mind. But all your grand principles, which I understand very well, would do splendidly in books and very badly in practice. In your plans for reform, you are forgetting the difference between our two positions: you work only on paper which accepts anything, is smooth and flexible and offers no obstacles either to your imagination or your pen, while I, poor empress, work on human skin, which is far more sensitive and touchy.

Eventually, however, Diderot realized that the empress did not intend to put into practice any of the advice he had been preaching for so many weeks, and the glow of their first conversations began to fade. His own worsening health, his loneliness in an alien court, the open hostility of courtiers jealous of his easy access to the sovereign, all contributed to Diderot's increasing desire to return home. He had seen much of Catherine but almost nothing of Russia. When he spoke of departing, she did not urge him to stay. He had been her guest for five months, and she had sat with him for sixty afternoons. He was the only one of the *philosophes* she was ever to meet.

Diderot left Russia on March 4, 1774. He had been dreading the return journey, and, to ease his passage, Catherine provided him with a specially constructed carriage in which he could lie down. When she said goodbye, she handed him a ring, a fur, and three bags containing a thousand rubles each. The journey was more difficult than he had feared. The ice was breaking on the rivers along the Baltic coast, and, as his carriage was crossing the river Dvina, the ice cracked and the carriage began to sink. The old man was pulled free, but the horses were drowned, and three-quarters of his baggage was lost. He wound up with a high fever. Eventually, he made it back to The Hague and recuperated in Prince Golitsyn's care.

From Catherine's perspective, the visit had been less than a success. Diderot's ideas did not constitute a practical program for Russia; a noble, idealistic *philosophe* was not a practical politician or administrator. Once physically recovered, Diderot, however, decided that his visit had been a triumph. From Paris, he wrote to Catherine, "Now you sit beside Caesar, your friend [Joseph of Austria], and a little above Frederick [of Prussia,] your dangerous neighbor."

Diderot's exuberant stories about his long stay with Catherine so irritated Voltaire that he became sick with jealousy. For months, he had not received a single letter from St. Petersburg; clearly Catherine had rejected him for another. On August 9, 1774, four months after Diderot left Russia, Voltaire was unable to stand it any longer:

Madame:
    I am positively in disgrace at your court. Your Imperial Majesty has jilted me for Diderot, or for Grimm, or for some

other favorite. You have no consideration for my advanced age. All well and good if Your Majesty were a French *coquette*; but how can a victorious, law-giving empress be so inconstant. . . . I am trying to find crimes I have committed that would justify your indifference. I see that indeed there is no passion that does not end. This thought would cause me to die of chagrin, were I not already so near to dying of old age.

> Signed,
> He whom you have forsaken,
> your admirer, your old Russian of Ferney

Catherine answered lightly: "Live, Monsieur, and let us be reconciled, for in any case there is no cause for quarrel between us. . . . You are so good a Russian that you could not be the enemy of Catherine." Appeased, Voltaire declared that he acknowledged defeat and "returned to her in chains."

Voltaire had exercised the greatest intellectual influence on Catherine, and Diderot was the only one of the major *philosophes* she actually met, but it was in Friedrich Melchoir Grimm that the empress found a lifelong friend. Born a Lutheran in Regensburg in 1723 and educated in Leipzig, Grimm traveled to Paris to make his career. He made his way through the literary salons and became an intimate friend of Diderot's. In 1754, he took over the *Correspondance Littéraire,* an exclusive fortnightly cultural newsletter, reporting from Paris on books, poetry, the theater, painting, and sculpture. The fifteen or so subscribers, all crowned heads or princes of the Holy Roman Empire, received their copies through their embassies in Paris, thus avoiding censorship and enabling Grimm to write freely. Once on the throne, Catherine became a subscriber, but her personal acquaintance with Grimm had to wait until September 1773, when he arrived in St. Petersburg—a month before Diderot—for the wedding of Grand Duke Paul to Princess Wilhelmina of Hesse-Darmstadt. Grimm was present as part of the escort for the bride.

Catherine knew Grimm by his reputation and through his newsletter. Six years older than Catherine, he shared many of her characteristics: German origin, French education, ambition, cosmopolitan interests, love of literature, passion for gossip. Beyond these, Grimm may also have appealed to Catherine because of his sound common sense, his discretion combined with wit, and his quiet charm. From September 1773 to April 1774, he was frequently received in private by Catherine in the same kind of setting as Diderot. She invited him to remain in St. Petersburg and go into her service, but he declined, citing his age, ignorance of the Russian language, and unfamiliarity with the Russian court. Nevertheless, when he left for Italy in April, they began a correspondence that continued until Catherine's last letter in 1796, a month before her death. He returned to St. Petersburg in September 1776 and stayed almost a year, during which time she asked him to head a new commission on public schools. Again, he declined, although he later agreed to serve as her official cultural agent in Paris, managing her artistic and intellectual interests and contacts.

Catherine's friendship with Grimm became one of the most important relationships in her life. He functioned as a confidant and a sounding board—even a safety valve—in whom she had complete trust. She wrote to him with freedom; she could speak frankly of her personal life, including her thoughts about her lovers. Except for her son, Paul, and, later, her grandchildren, she had no family, and to Grimm alone she could pour out her thoughts and feelings as she might have done with a fond uncle or an older brother.

❧ 51 ❧

The *Nakaz*

I N 1766, CATHERINE WROTE to Voltaire that she was working on a special project. This was her *Nakaz,* or *Instruction,* intended to be a guideline for a complete rewriting of the Russian legal code. If all went well, Catherine believed, it would raise the levels of government administration, of justice, and of tolerance within her empire. She also hoped that it would announce to Europe that a new era, informed by the principles of the Enlightenment, was beginning in Russia.

When Catherine took the throne, the Russian legal code, promulgated in 1649 by Tsar Alexis, the father of Peter the Great, was chaotically obsolete. Since the code had first been issued, thousands of new laws had appeared, often without reference to previous laws on the same subject. There was no complete set of statute books. Imperial decrees by successive rulers conflicted, and ministers and officials issued new laws that contradicted earlier laws without the latter being annulled. The result was that government departments were disorganized, administration throughout the empire was inefficient and corrupt, and failure to define the authority of local officials had led to landowners taking ever greater powers at the expense of the peasantry.

Peter the Great's long reign (1689–1725) had aggravated this chaos. Peter's emphasis had been on reform by action; half of his decrees had never been recorded. No successor could have had more respect for the great reforming tsar than Catherine. Peter had made Russia into a European power; he had created a Western capital with access to Europe, launched a navy, mobilized a victorious army, brought women into society, demanded religious tolerance, and promoted the nation's industry and commerce. But he had died at fifty-two, and in the forty years since his death, lazy and incompetent rulers had made the confusion in Russian law worse. Catherine saw it as her task to clarify and complete what Peter had begun. Having absorbed liberal eighteenth-century political theory, which stressed the power of good laws to change society, Catherine concluded that the remedy for the flaws in her empire would be a new legal code. Because she had reached the throne steeped in the ideas of an enlightened European, she decided that these new laws should be based on Enlightenment principles.

Her plan was to summon a national assembly elected from all of the free social classes and ethnic groups of the empire. She would listen to their complaints and invite them to propose new laws to correct these flaws. Before this assembly gathered, however, Catherine decided that she must provide its members with a set of guiding principles upon which she wished the new laws to be founded. The result was her *Nakaz,* published under the full title *Instruction of Her Imperial Majesty Catherine the Second for the Commission Charged with Preparing a Project of a New Code of Laws.* It was the work that Catherine considered the most significant intellectual achievement of her life and her greatest contribution to Russia.

She began working on the *Nakaz* in January 1765 and devoted two to three hours a day to it for two years. The document was published on July 30, 1767, and is, in the view of Isabel de Madariaga, the preeminent historian of Catherine's Russia, "one of the most remarkable political treatises ever compiled and published by a reigning sovereign." In 526 articles, grouped into twenty chapters, she presented her view of the nature of the Russian state and how it should be governed. She began with Locke's belief that in an ordered society, law and freedom were necessary to one another, since the latter could not exist without the former. She drew heavily from Montesquieu's *The Spirit of Law,* published in 1748, which analyzed the structure of societies and the political rights of men in their relationship to the state. Of the total of 526 articles, 294 were taken or adapted from Montesquieu. She also drew 108 articles from the Italian jurist and legal scholar Cesare Beccaria, whose *Essay on Crimes and Punishment* had just been published in 1764. This work was a passionate attack on the relationship between crime and punishment in most states of contemporary Europe. Beccaria declared that the reform of the criminal, rather than his punishment, should be the purpose of laws, justice, and penal incarceration. Above all, Beccaria was revolted by the near-universal use of torture. Catherine, impressed by this work, immediately invited the author to come to Russia. Beccaria chose to stay in Milan.

Catherine's *Nakaz* deals with an immense range of political, judicial, social, and economic questions. It discusses what Russia was at that moment, and what it should be; how society ought to be organized, and how government and the administration of justice ought to be conducted. Her tone was that of a teacher rather than an autocrat. Her preamble reminded delegates and readers that the Christian religion teaches people to do good to one another whenever possible. She expressed the belief that every man wished to see his country happy, glorious, tranquil, and safe, and that people wished to live under laws that protected but did not oppress them. From these opinions and principles, she proceeded to what she believed were the basic facts about her own empire. "Russia is a European state," she declared, meaning with this statement to eliminate the Russian's traditional sense of geographical and cultural isolation, as well as the disdain of Europeans who believed that Russia was only a remote, primitive backwater. From there, she moved directly to an explanation of the need for absolutism in Russia. The sovereign was absolute, she said, "for there is no authority but that which centers in his single person that can act with a vigor proportionate to such a vast dominion." Any other form of government risked weakness.

She accepted from Montesquieu a qualification of her advocacy of absolutism; this was embodied in her acceptance of the limitation of the supreme power of the Russian autocrat by certain "fundamental laws." These "laws" were defined as traditions, habits, and institutions so deeply rooted in the history and life of a society that no monarch, however absolute, could or would act in opposition to them. They included respect for the permanence of the nation's dominant religion, for the law of succession to the throne, and for the existing rights and privileges of dominant social groups, such as the nobility. Montesquieu defined such a state with such a ruler as a "moderate monarchy." In this sense, Catherine was defining and presenting Russia as a moderate autocracy.

Turning to the role of laws in regulating the lives and relationships of people, Catherine wrote: "The laws ought to be so framed as to secure the safety of every citizen as much as possible. . . . Political liberty does not consist in the notion that a man may do whatever he pleases; liberty is the right to do whatsoever the laws allow. . . . The equality of the citizens consists in that they should all be subject to the same laws." In confronting the great issue of crime and punishment, she wholeheartedly accepted the views of Montesquieu and Beccaria, agreeing that "it is much better to prevent than to punish crimes." She insisted that capital punishment be inflicted only in cases involving political murder, sedition, treason, or civil war. "Experience shows," she wrote, "that the frequent use of severe punishment has never rendered a people better. The death of a criminal is a less effective means of restraining crimes than the permanent example of a man deprived of his liberty during the whole of his life to make amends for the injury he has done to the public." Even sedition and treason were given narrow definitions. She distinguished between sacrilege and lèse-majesté. A sovereign may be said to rule by divine right, but he or she is not divine, and therefore it is neither sacrilege nor treason to commit a nonphysical offense against him. Words cannot be called criminal unless accompanied by deeds. Satirical writings in monarchies, even those relating to the monarch— and here she may have had in mind Voltaire's struggles in France— should be regarded as misdemeanors, not crimes. Even here, care should be taken, because censorship can be "productive of nothing but ignorance and must cramp the rising efforts of genius and destroy the very will for writing."

She rejected torture, traditionally used in extracting confessions, obtaining evidence, and determining guilt in Russia. "The use of torture is contrary to sound judgment and common sense," she declared. "Humanity itself cries out against it, and demands it to be utterly abolished." She gave the example of Great Britain, which had prohibited torture "without any sensible inconveniences." She was particularly incensed by the use of torture to force a confession:

> What right can give anyone authority to inflict torture upon a citizen when it is still unknown whether he is innocent or guilty? By law, every person is innocent until his crime is proved. . . . The accused party on the rack, while in the agonies of torture, is not master enough of himself to be able to declare the truth. . . . The sensation of pain may rise to such a height, that it will leave him no longer the liberty of producing any proper act of will, except what at that very instant he believes may release him from that pain. In such an extremity, even an innocent person will cry out, 'Guilty!' provided they cease to torture him. . . . Then the judges will be uncertain whether they have an innocent or a guilty person before them. The rack, therefore, is a sure method of condemning an innocent person whose constitution is weak, and of acquitting the guilty who depends upon his bodily strength.

Catherine also condemned torture on purely humanitarian grounds. "All punishments by which the human body might be maimed are barbarism," she wrote.

Catherine wanted punishments tailored to fit the crimes, and the *Nakaz* provided detailed analysis of different categories of crime and the appropriate punishments. Crimes against property, she said, should be punished by deprivation of property, although she understood that those guilty of stealing property were most often people who had none. She insisted that due process govern legal and courtroom procedures. She demanded that attention be paid to the role of judges, the truth of evidence, and the quality of proof required in reaching verdicts.

> Some judges should be of the same rank of citizenship as the defendant; that is, his equals, so that he will not think him-

self fallen into the hands of people who will automatically decide against him. Judges should not have the right to interpret
the law; only the sovereign, who makes the law, can do that.
Judges must judge according to the letter of the law because
this is the only way of ensuring that the same crime is judged
the same way in all places at all times. If adherence to the law
leads to injustice, the sovereign, as lawgiver, will issue new laws.

Catherine's attempt to address the problems of serfdom was the least
successful part of the *Nakaz*. She began chapter II, her effort to deal
with serfdom, by saying that "a civil society requires a certain established order; there ought to be some to govern and some to obey." In
that context, she believed that even the humblest man had the right to
be treated as a human being, but here her words collided with the general Russian belief that serfs were property. Even a hint of freeing the
serfs met with protest, sometimes from people who prided themselves
on their liberalism. Princess Dashkova was so convinced of the right of
the nobility to own serfs that she attempted to persuade Denis Diderot
of the necessity of serfdom in Russia. Catherine rejected this morally,
even if she was politically powerless to change it. When Diderot was in
St. Petersburg and criticized the squalor of the Russian peasant, the
empress replied bitterly, "Why should they bother to be clean when
their souls are not their own?"

Catherine wrote the *Nakaz* in French; her secretary translated her manuscript into Russian and other languages. She worked in private until
September 1766, when she began to show drafts, first to Orlov, then to
Panin. Orlov's opinion, predictably, was flattering. Panin was cautious;
he saw in the *Nakaz* a threat to the whole political, economic, and social
order. "These are axioms which will bring down walls," he warned. He
worried about the impact that ideas taken from Montesquieu and Beccaria might have on uneducated delegates to the Legislative Commission. He was especially concerned because direct taxation of peasants
and army recruitment were based on the institution of serfdom; he
feared that without these two essential requirements, the state would
wither economically and militarily. Beyond that, he wondered how
freed serfs would live, since they possessed no land. He asked where the

state would find the money to compensate landowners for the serfs taken from them and for the land the serfs must farm to survive.

Catherine did not dismiss Panin's reaction. He was not a large landowner who had many serfs to lose; he had spent twelve years in Sweden and he generally favored reforms. She also found that he was far from alone in his opposition. On completing the original draft of the *Nakaz* early in 1767, she submitted it for review to members of the Senate. "Every part of it evoked division," she said later. "I let them erase what they pleased and they struck out more than half of what I had written." Next, she submitted the draft to certain educated noblemen; they removed half of the remaining articles. With these excisions, the *Nakaz* as finally published amounted to only one-quarter of the text that Catherine had labored two years to produce. This was the limit of absolute monarchy: even an autocrat could not override the views of those whose support she needed to remain in power.

In the version of the *Nakaz* ultimately printed, Catherine's frustration regarding serfdom is apparent in the way she uses language. She writes tentatively, almost apologetically, and then quickly backtracks, contradicts herself, and smothers her message. Thus, her effort to say that serfdom should be a temporary institution, that a ruler should avoid reducing people to slavery, and that the civil laws should guard against the abuse of slaves comes out as a disorganized torrent of jumbled words:

> Since the Law of Nature commands Us to labor to the utmost of Our power for the happiness of all people, We are obliged to render the situation of those who are subjected as easy as sound reason will allow. . . . And therefore, to avoid reducing the people to a state of slavery, unless urgent occasion indispensably obliges us to do it; in that case it ought to be done for no private interest, but for the public benefit. However, such occasions seldom or never occur. Of whatever kind subjugation may be, the civil laws should prevent the abuse of slavery, and guard against the dangers which may arise from it.

Two articles that Catherine had copied from Montesquieu were omitted in the final published document. One declared that serfs should be allowed to accumulate sufficient property to buy their freedom; the other that servitude should be limited to six years. To these

Catherine had added her own belief that once a serf had been freed, he should never be returned to serfdom. This was also omitted, and neither the Legislative Commission nor Russians ever heard, read, discussed, or acted on any these words.

Catherine made no claim to originality of authorship. When sending a copy of the *Nakaz* to Frederick of Prussia, she wrote frankly, "You will see that, like the crow in the fable, I have decked myself out in peacock's feathers; in this work merely the arrangement of the material and here and there a line or a word belong to me." To d'Alembert, she admitted, "For the sake of my empire, I have robbed Montesquieu without mentioning him by name. If he sees my work from the next world, I hope he will pardon me this plagiarism for the good of twenty million people. He loved humanity too well to take offense. His book is my 'prayer book.' "

The *Nakaz* was written in the hope that an updated legal code would lead to a more politically advanced, more culturally sophisticated, and more efficiently productive Russia. This did not happen. However, Catherine addressed the *Nakaz* not only to the Legislative Commission she intended to summon but to the educated public at home and abroad. And when translations appeared outside Russia, even with all the deletions, inconsistencies, and flagrant textual borrowing, it was still a sufficiently impressive document to earn Catherine wide approval. Translations in German, English, and Latin appeared almost immediately. In December 1768 she sent a version to Ferney. Voltaire pretended to believe that the *Nakaz* was a complete, detailed code of laws and declared that neither Lycurgus nor Solon "would have been capable of its creation." His exaggerated praise soared into absurdity when he called the *Nakaz* "the finest monument of the age which will bring you more glory than ten battles because it is conceived by your own genius and written by your own fair little hand."

The government of France thought otherwise. The monarchy viewed the document as so dangerous that by order of the king, publication in France was banned, and two thousand copies on their way from St. Petersburg to Paris were held at the frontier. Voltaire mocked French censors for banning the work, a compliment, he assured Catherine, that would guarantee its popularity. Diderot wrote, "Justice and humanity have guided the pen of Catherine II. She has reformed everything." Frederick of Prussia called the *Nakaz* "a masculine, nervous performance worthy of a great man," and made the empress a member of the Berlin Academy.

The *Nakaz* was not, as Voltaire rhapsodized, a code of laws; rather, it was a collection of principles on which Catherine believed that good government and an orderly society should be based. In a letter to Frederick, she suggested that she was well aware of the discrepancy between the Russia of reality and the nation she hoped it might become: "I must warn Your Majesty that you will find different places in the document which will perhaps seem strange. I beg that you remember that I have often accommodated myself to the present, without closing the path to a more favorable future."

❧52❧

"All Free Estates of the Realm"

CATHERINE HAD WRITTEN the *Nakaz* as a preliminary to summoning an assembly that would assist in creating a new code of laws for the empire. Once the document was published, even in its severely truncated form, in December 1766, she initiated this second stage by issuing an imperial manifesto calling on "all free estates of the realm"—this meant all Russians except serfs—to select delegates to a legislative commission. During the spring of 1767, delegates were chosen, representing the many creeds, ranks, occupations, and social classes of the Russian empire. They included government officials, members of the nobility, townspeople, merchants, free peasants, and the inhabitants of outlying parts of the empire whose people were neither Christian nor racially Russian. Their task would be to inform the empress of the grievances, needs, and hopes of the people they represented, thereby providing her with material to use in drafting a new code of laws.

The basic electoral criteria were geographic territory and class. The central government offices sent 29 delegates. All noblemen living in a particular district were to elect a single delegate for their district; this produced 142 noble delegates (among them three Orlov brothers, including Gregory and Alexis). All property owners in a town were to choose one deputy to represent their town, regardless of the size of the town's population; the result was that the towns, with 209 delegates, had the largest representation in the assembly. The state peasants, working on state lands but legally free, sent one delegate for each province for a total of 56. The Cossacks of the Don, the Volga, the Yaik, and Siberia were to send whatever number of delegates their own chieftains determined; they sent 44. Another 54 delegates came from the non-Russian tribes, Christian, Muslim, and even Buddhist; they sent one delegate for each tribe. Serfs, the overwhelming majority of the Russian population, were considered property and were not represented; they and their interests were presumed to be represented by their owners. When the elections were over, the Legislative Commission was to be composed of 564 delegates.

It was understood that the assembly would limit itself to providing information and advice, and that all final decisions would continue to be made by the empress. Catherine never intended that the Legislative Commission should discuss how Russia was governed. She had no wish to create a body that would limit the absolute power of the Russian autocrat, and she had made clear in the *Nakaz* that she considered absolutism the only form of government workable in Russia; nor was the Legislative Commission to be permitted to aspire to a permanent political role. There was to be no restriction on the expression of general political views, and any grievance, local or national, could be discussed, but the commission was to be purely advisory. As it happened, the delegates in the Legislative Commission showed no inclination to extend their authority. The status and supreme powers of the sovereign were understood and accepted.

Most of the delegates were confused as to exactly what was wanted from them. Any previous demand involving participation in the central government had been regarded with suspicion by the nobility, who considered a summons to the capital for state duty a form of service to be evaded if possible. Catherine endeavored to reverse this perception and make the role of delegate attractive by attaching rewards and privileges to the work. All expenses were to be paid by the state treasury. Delegates were also to receive a salary, ranging from 400 rubles a year for noblemen and 122 rubles a year for town delegates to 37 rubles a year for free peasants. All delegates were to be exempted for life from capital punishment, torture, and corporal punishment, and their property was to be protected from confiscation. Delegates were to wear a special badge of office, which was to be returned to the state when they died. Nobles were entitled to incorporate this badge in their coats of arms so that their descendants would know that they had taken part in this historic work. "By this institution," Catherine's manifesto concluded, "we give to our people an example of our sincerity, of our great belief in them, and of our true maternal love."

Catherine announced that the new Legislative Committee would meet in Moscow and that she would open the proceedings in person. By summoning the assembly to the ancient capital, she hoped to prove to the city's large, conservative population that she, her *Nakaz,* and the new legal code intended to serve Old Russia as well as the new. Before the delegates gathered, she strengthened this message by announcing that she would make a voyage down the Volga, cruising through the heartland of Old Russia. Beside adding to her personal knowledge of her empire, she meant by showing herself among her people to impress observers at home and abroad. In fact, she was excited by this prospective journey. On March 26, 1767, she wrote to Voltaire, "Perhaps at the moment when you least expect it, you will receive a letter from some corner of Asia."

The voyage was on a grand scale. More than a thousand people accompanying her boarded a flotilla of large riverboats at Tver, on the upper Volga, on April 28, 1767. The voyagers stopped at Yarolslavl and then at Kostrama, where, in 1613, a delegation representing "all the classes and all the towns of Russia" had come to petition the first of the Romanov dynasty, sixteen-year-old Michael, to accept the Russian throne. From Kostrama, she and they moved down the river to Nizhny Novgorod, Kazan, and Simbirsk. Catherine delighted in this method of travel. "There can be nothing more pleasant than voyaging as an entire house without fatigue," she wrote to Nikita Panin.

In Kazan, where she stayed for a week, Catherine found herself in a different world. Surrounded by ethnic and cultural diversity, she considered the applicability to Russia of the principles she had inscribed in the *Nakaz*. On May 29, she wrote to Voltaire:

> These laws, about which so much has been said, are . . . not yet enacted, and who can answer for their usefulness? It is posterity, and not we, who will have to decide. Consider, if you will, that they must be applied to Asia as well as Europe, and what difference of climate, people, customs, and even ideas! . . . There are in this city twenty different peoples who do not resemble each other at all. We have, nevertheless, to design a garment to fit them all. They can agree on general principles well enough, but what about the details?

Two days later, in another letter to Ferney, she returned to this theme:

> There are so many objects worthy of a glance, one could collect enough ideas here for ten years. This is an empire to itself and only here can one see what an immense enterprise it is as concerns our laws, and how little these conform to the situation of the empire in general.

Traveling south down the great river, Catherine marveled at the wealth of nature along its banks. To Nikita Panin, she wrote:

> Here, the people along the Volga are rich and extremely well fed. The grain of every kind is so good here and the wood is nothing other than oak and linden. The earth is such dark stuff as is seen nowhere else. In a word, these people are spoiled by God. Since birth I have not eaten such tasty fish as here, and everything is in such abundance that one cannot imagine, and I do not know anything they might need; everything is here.

She and her party disembarked in Simbirsk to return to Moscow. A century and a half later, Alexander Kerensky, the prime minister of the 1917 Russian provisional government, described Simbirsk, which was his birthplace:

The town rose high on a hill overlooking the river and the meadowlands of rich, fragrant grass stretching to the eastern horizon. From the summit right down to the water stretched luxuriant apple and cherry orchards. In the spring the whole mountainside was white with blossoms, fragrant, and at night, breathless with the songs of nightingales.

Back in Moscow, Catherine prepared for the opening of the Legislative Commission. With the delegates arriving in the city, Catherine decided to impress them with the importance of the work they were about to undertake. On the morning of Sunday, July 30, she drove though the streets to the Kremlin, sitting alone in a gilded carriage. After a religious ceremony in the Assumption Cathedral, she walked to the Palace of Facets, where the delegates were presented to her as she sat above them on a raised throne. On her right, a table draped in red velvet displayed copies of the *Nakaz* bound in red leather; on her left stood Grand Duke Paul, the ministers of the government, members of the court, and foreign ambassadors. A welcoming speech compared Catherine to Justinian. She responded by telling the delegates that they had a unique opportunity "to glorify yourselves and your country, and to acquire for yourselves the respect and gratitude of future centuries." She presented each delegate with a copy of the *Nakaz* and a gold medal on a chain. The medal was stamped with an image of the empress. Its inscription read: "For the welfare of one and all." The medals were popular and many were promptly sold.

The following morning, the commission began its work. Over several days, the vice-chancellor, Prince Alexander Golitsyn, read Catherine's *Nakaz* aloud. This was the first of many readings, necessary because many delegates could not read. The impact of this document on moderately educated noblemen, town merchants, peasants whose horizons were limited to their own province, if not their own village, not to mention tribesmen from beyond the Volga, can only be guessed. The difficulty lay in knowing what a Cossack from the Don, or a Kalmuck from the steppes, would make of principles largely borrowed from Montesquieu, and selected and arranged by a German-born princess. Aphorisms such as "Liberty is the right to do all that is not forbidden by law" were ideas so alien to the majority of Russians as to be almost incomprehensible.

In the meeting hall, the delegates sat on benches according to the district from which they had come. The nobility sat in front; behind them were the townspeople, the Cossacks, and the peasant delegates. For the important role of marshal (or president) of the commission, the empress chose General Alexander Bibikov, a soldier; he was charged with organizing and guiding the commission's work. Before the delegates began the work they had been summoned to do, they insisted on debating what title they should present to the empress in gratitude for her calling them together. "The Great" and "All Wise Mother of the Fatherland" were the most popular. Discussion lasted several sessions, provoking Catherine to say impatiently to Bibikov, "I brought them together to study laws, and they are busying discussing my virtues." Eventually, she refused all titles, explaining that she had not earned any of them; that only posterity could impartially judge her achievements, and that God alone could be called "All Wise." Nevertheless, she was far from displeased when the title "Catherine the Great" received the greatest number of votes; she had been on the throne for only five years, whereas Peter the Great had not received this title from the Senate until his fourth decade as tsar. And there was no doubt that the offer of this title by an elected assembly of the free estates strengthened the legitimacy of her position. It eliminated further discussion of her ever reverting to the role of regent, as well as any talk of the accession of Paul when he came of age.

The commission took up rules of procedure and assignment to sub-commissions. The full assembly was to act as a general debating arena, and the main work of analysis, coordination, and drafting of new laws was to be distributed among nineteen subcommissions. The assembly turned to the reports the delegates had brought with them. Catherine believed that discussion of these grievances and proposals, setting forth the needs of each area and class, would be one of the Legislative Commission's most important functions; she expected it to give her a valuable picture of social conditions in Russia. Each delegate was certain that his own list of complaints should be the primary concern of the assembly. Hundreds of these lists and petitions had arrived; the six state peasant delegates from the Archangel region brought with them a mass of seventy-three petitions. Some were simple lists, often unrelated or contradictory; others were relatively sensible proposals for reform. In all, over a thousand peasant petitions were submitted to the Legislative Commission. Naturally, the peasants were less able than the nobles and the townspeople to clearly spell out their grievances, and they tended to limit themselves to descriptions of local problems: fences knocked down, crops trampled by wandering cattle, the scarcity of timber, the cost of salt, the law's delay, the insolence of government officials. Because they were vulnerable to pressure from the local nobility or local government officials, it was difficult for them to be explicit in their complaints. Attempting to hear them all, the sessions went on spawning subcommittees, where much was begun and little finished. Eventually, Catherine realized that the mission assigned to the delegates to find laws suitable for all the citizens of the empire was beyond their reach. Nevertheless, an extraordinary thing was happening: for the first time in Russia, representatives of the people had been brought and were sitting together to speak frankly and publicly without fear of serious retribution about what troubled them and the people they represented.

Catherine was often present, secluded on a platform behind a drawn curtain. She learned something about conditions in her empire, but the commission's stumbling pace irritated her—so much so that at one point she rose from behind her curtain and walked out. Not only did the full assembly sessions disappoint her; some of the subcommittees made her angry. On one occasion, told that the subcommittee on towns had adjourned while waiting for additional copies of the *Nakaz* to be bound, she exploded, "Have they really already lost those copies which they have already been given?" In December, after five months of talk, she decided that she had heard enough and halted the commission session in Moscow. Hopeful that a change of place might revitalize the delegates, she ordered them to reconvene in St. Petersburg two months later. In mid-January, she set off in her sledge over the frozen road. A long string of other sledges, filled with delegates, followed.

When the Legislative Commission met again in St. Petersburg on February 18, 1768, it began by discussing the status of the nobility and the townspeople, the merchants, and the free peasants. Nobles asked that their prerogatives be extended in the form of greater power in provincial and local governments; they also wanted the right to enter commerce and industry in the towns. In addition, the noblemen argued among themselves over definitions of the status and rights of the different layers of nobility. The old hereditary nobility demanded establishment of a strict demarcation between nobility of birth and men recently raised to noble rank for service or merit—men like the Orlovs.

Another bitter debate set noble landowners against town merchants. The nobility claimed the exclusive right to own serf labor and complete freedom in dealing with the serf problem, economically and administratively. The merchants, having heard from the *Nakaz* that all citizens were equal before the law, demanded the same privileges as the nobility, including the right to own serfs. The landowners fought to prevent this, just as the merchants were fighting the attempt by landowners to engage in industry and trade. In the end, both initiatives failed.

In the course of these debates between nobles and merchants on the right to own serfs, the larger, more explosive subject of serfdom arose. The assembly was divided between two fundamentally opposing viewpoints. Those who supported serfdom declared that the institution must be permanent; that it was the only solution to an economic problem that went deeper than the owner's social status and privilege; namely, that serfdom was essential to the supply and control of labor in a huge, primarily agricultural country. Serfdom's opponents spoke of the evils and human misery caused by a form of bondage approaching slavery. With economy and tradition on one side, and philosophy and compassion on the other, there appeared no bridge to span the gulf.

Catherine was no better able to find a solution than anyone else. In her original version, the *Nakaz* had gone as far as to advocate the gradual abolition of serfdom in Russia by allowing serfs, with the permission of their owners, to purchase their own freedom. The Russian nobility overwhelmingly opposed ideas like this, which had been stricken from the document before it went to print. The question of whether serfs should be allowed to own personal property apart from land came before the assembly. It led to heated discussions on the relationship between landowners and serfs, and the administrative and punitive powers landowners should have over their serfs. To the charge that the peasants were lazy and drunk, a liberal delegate replied, "The peasant has his feelings. He knows that all he owns belongs to his landowner. How can he be virtuous when he is deprived of all means of being so? He drinks, not from laziness, but from downheartedness. The hardest worker becomes careless if he is constantly oppressed and owns nothing." Other enlightened landlords spoke in favor of legal limitations on landlords' power over serfs; Bibikov, the marshal, urged that noblemen who tortured their serfs be declared insane, which would allow the law to seize their estates. But when specific improvements in the condition of serfs and the eventual abolition of serfdom were proposed, the speakers were shouted down. Liberals among the noble delegates were vilified and even threatened with death by extremist members of the conservative majority.

Catherine had hoped for support from Count Alexander Stroganov. He had been educated in Geneva and Paris, and it was he who had supported her at the moment when Peter III had shouted *"Dura!"* in a crowded banquet hall. But when Stroganov rose to speak in the Legislative Commission, he defended the institution of serfdom with passion. Prince Michael Scherbatov, who considered the hereditary nobility an institution ordained by God, argued that because Russia was a cold, northern country, peasants would not work without being forced to do so. The state could not force them, he said, because Russia was too large. Only the nobility could do it, but they had to do it in the traditional way, with no interference by the state.

The poet and playwright Alexander Sumarokov objected to the special privileges, such as immunity for life from corporal punishment, granted in advance to peasant delegates to the Legislative Commission. Sumarokov also objected to the principle of majority voting. "The majority of votes does not confirm the truth, but only indicates the wishes of the majority," he said. "Truth is confirmed by profound reason and impartiality." Sumarokov further complained that "if the serfs were freed, the poor nobles would have neither cook nor coachman, nor lackey; their trained cooks and hairdressers would run away to better paid jobs and there would be constant disturbances requiring military force to put them down. Whereas at present landowners live quietly on their estates." ("And have their throats cut from time to time," commented Catherine.) It was known, Sumarakov concluded, that lords loved their serfs and were loved by them. In any case, he said, the common people did not have the feelings of noblemen. ("And cannot have in present circumstances," Catherine noted.) In the end, the empress reacted to Sumarokov's opposition by saying, "M. Sumarokov is a good poet . . . but he does not have sufficient clarity of mind to be a good lawgiver."

Despite Catherine's personal beliefs and misgivings regarding serfdom, the reactions by nobles in the assembly made her back away from further confrontation. Her recognition of the inherent danger in keeping this huge majority of the population in permanent bondage appeared in a letter she wrote to Procurator General Vyazemsky:

> A general emancipation from the unbearable and cruel yoke will not ensue . . . [but] if we do not agree to the diminution of cruelty and the amelioration of the intolerable position of the human species, then, even against our will, they themselves will seize it sooner or later.

As her Enlightenment principles were battered in the assembly, Catherine, aware that she governed primarily through the support of the nobility, decided that she could not go further. Later, she commented:

> What had I not to suffer from the voice of an irrational and cruel public opinion when this question was considered by the Legislative Commission? The mob of nobles . . . began to suspect that these discussions might bring about an improvement in the position of the peasants. . . . I believe that there were not twenty human beings who reflected on the subject with humanity.

The discussions in St. Petersburg were proving even more unproductive and divisive than those in Moscow. The commission continued to stumble along, burdened by procedure, by conflicts of class, and by the generally impossible nature of its task. The twenty-nine Russian peasant delegates played little part in the discussions, except for one indefatigable delegate from the Archangel peasantry who spoke fifteen times. Many peasant delegates simply transferred their limited right to speak to noblemen from their districts. The few free peasants who did speak concentrated on grasping their chance to lay their complaints before the empress herself. Catherine, listening as they jumbled together every abuse, burden, and future fear, realized how far they were—and how far she now was—from Montesquieu. By the autumn of 1768, still without seeing any concrete results, the empress was tired. The commission had dragged on for eighteen months through more than two hundred sessions and not one new law had been written.

In the summer and fall of 1768, the attention of the empress and her ministers was turning in a different direction. Russia's involvement in neighboring Poland and the shadow of a possible war with Turkey loomed over the sessions of the Legislative Commission. Catherine's enthusiasm for a new code of laws faded, and when Turkey declared war in October 1768, her thoughts and energies were directed toward this new challenge. Already, a number of noblemen who were assembly delegates were leaving to serve as officers in the army. On December 18, 1768, Count Bibikov announced that, by order of the empress, the full Legislative Commission would be prorogued indefinitely, although a subcommission would continue to meet. The last session of the full assembly took place on January 12, 1769, after which delegates dispersed to their homes, where they were to await a further summons. The subcommission met intermittently, but by September 1771, even this had ceased. At intervals in 1772 and 1773, the procurator general was informed that the empress intended to summon the full assembly after the conclusion of the Russo-Turkish war. But no summons ever came. The Legislative Commission never met again.

No new code of Russian laws was produced. The distance stretching between an Enlightenment philosopher's definition of an ideal monarchy and the immediate problems of everyday life in rural Russia was simply too great. Catherine looked to Montesquieu, but the nobles wanted confirmation and extension of status and privileges, and the peasants wanted restitution for broken fences, trampled crops, and illegally felled timber. Nevertheless, eighteen months and 203 sessions of effort were not entirely wasted. The documents submitted and discussed by delegates in the full assembly and the subcommissions contained a wealth of valuable information. Studying this mass of detail—these hundreds of grievances and competing claims—reinforced Catherine's conviction that the stability of Russia depended on maintaining the absolute authority of the autocracy.

Along with strengthening Catherine's belief in absolutism, something else had happened. Under the stimulus and protective cover of the *Nakaz,* the discussions in the full assembly and the various subcommissions had furnished delegates with new ideas that had never before been publicly discussed in Russia. In some cases, delegates actually quoted from a specific paragraph of Catherine's *Nakaz,* using the authority of the empress to introduce and support their own ideas. Ultimately, despite the failure of the Legislative Commission to create a new law code, it made a contribution to the nation's history. Taken together, the summons, the elections, and the 203 assembly sessions established a precedent for popular participation in government. It was the first attempt in imperial Russia to give the people a voice in their own political destiny.

Some have believed that the Legislative Commission achieved nothing, and that from the beginning both the *Nakaz* and the Legislative Commission were created simply for show, as no more than propaganda to impress Catherine's Enlightenment friends abroad. This judgment is shallow. Naturally, Catherine welcomed Voltaire's overheated praise for the *Nakaz,* but it does not follow that she wrote it simply to catch Voltaire's eye and win his blessing. Indeed, the Catherine scholar Isabel de Madariaga says:

> The idea that the principal purpose of such an expensive and time-consuming operation . . . was only to throw dust in the eyes of Western intellectuals . . . is difficult to accept. It was possible for Catherine to win their golden opinions by corresponding with them as she did with Voltaire; by buying Diderot's library and leaving it in his possession; by inviting d'Alembert and Beccaria to come to Russia [although both refused]; by appointing Grimm as her personal agent in Paris. . . . This was sufficient evidence of Enlightenment credentials. . . . There was no need for her to embark on an enterprise of such major and time-consuming dimensions as the Legislative Commission.

It is worth noting that Catherine's writing of the *Nakaz* and summons to the Legislative Commission took place nine years before Thomas Jefferson wrote, and the Continental Congress voted to approve, the American Declaration of Independence. It preceded by twenty-two years Louis XVI's summons to the Estates-General. None of Catherine's successors on the Russian throne dared to summon such an assembly again until 1905, when Nicholas II was forced by revolution to sign a document transforming Russia from an absolute autocracy to a semiconstitutional monarchy—and then, in 1906, to summon Russia's first elected parliament, the State Duma.

❧53❧

"The King We Have Made"

A NEW LEGAL CODE adapted to the needs of contemporary Russia was important to Catherine, but conduct of foreign policy ranked first among her concerns. From the beginning of her reign, Catherine pursued an active, forward strategy in the tradition of Peter the Great. As soon as she took the throne, she assumed absolute control of Russia's relations with foreign states. It was to inform her use of autocratic authority that she immediately demanded that she be shown all diplomatic dispatches arriving at the College of Foreign Affairs.

There was much to be done. When Peter the Great took sole possession of the throne in 1694, Russia was a landlocked giant, lacking a year-round, ice-free, saltwater port. Sweden dominated the upper Baltic, and the Black Sea was controlled by the Ottoman Turks. Later, as a result of his triumph in the Great Northern War, Peter broke the Swedish grip, extended Russian possessions down the Baltic coast to include the great port of Riga, and built a new national capital, St. Petersburg, on the Gulf of Finland. In the south, fighting the Turks, he tried to reach the Black Sea, succeeded at first on the mouth of the Don River at Azov, and then lost this prize when the Turks defeated him on the river Pruth. When Peter died in 1725, Russia still had no southern opening to the sea and the outside world. Along Russia's western border lay the huge, chaotically governed kingdom of Poland, which in earlier times had stripped away huge stretches of Russian and Ukrainian territory. For Catherine, therefore, wishing to emulate Peter by expanding her empire and creating new pathways to the world, the places to look were to the south and west. South lay Turkey; west, Poland.

The terminal illness of a king determined that her first objective would be Poland. The Polish Commonwealth, which merged the kingdom of Poland and the grand duchy of Lithuania, was as large as France. It stretched east to west between the Dnieper and the Oder, and north to south from the Baltic to the Carpathians and Turkey's Balkan provinces on the Danube. The frontier between Poland and Russia meandered north and south for nine hundred miles. In earlier centuries, under native kings, Poland had been one of the most powerful states in Europe; in 1611, a Polish army had occupied the Kremlin. More recently, the tsars had won back some of these lost lands—Smolensk, Kiev, and the western Ukraine were Russian again—but large areas of western Russia populated by Orthodox Slavs still remained a part of Poland.

By the middle of the eighteenth century, Poland was in steep decline. The Polish Diet was a weak, quasi-parliamentary body, elected by the Polish and Lithuanian nobility with each of its thousand aristocratic members possessing a single equal vote. The office of king of Poland—not a hereditary position but the result of an election by unanimous vote of the Diet—was weaker still. The king was elected only by unanimous vote and was therefore beholden to every member of the Diet. Furthermore, the Diet had been reduced to choosing a foreigner as king because the powerful figures in the Polish nobility could not agree and unite behind one of their own. Since 1736, the crown had been on the head of the elector Augustus of Saxony, who simultaneously reigned as King Augustus III of Poland. Now Augustus was dying and a successor was needed.

Along with the weakness of being a republic ruled by an elected king, Poland suffered from other uniquely harmful political arrangements. Any single member of the Diet could interrupt and terminate a session by exercising the liberum veto. This procedure empowered one member to veto any decision of the assembly even when the decision had been approved by every other member. This single negative vote also overturned and negated all previous decisions made in that session of the Diet. As one deputy's vote could always be bought, the liberum veto made reform impossible. The Polish government lurched and staggered from crisis to crisis, while powerful, immensely wealthy landowners ruled the country.

There was, however, a political procedure by which the liberum veto could be neutralized. This was the establishment of a temporary "confederation," a gathering of a group of nobles assembled for the purpose of achieving a single specific goal. Once summoned, a confederated Diet could make decisions by majority (rather than unanimous) vote and then, having achieved what it wanted, dissolve itself, allowing Poland to lapse back into routine political anarchy.

Not surprisingly, this repeated convergence of dissension and incompetence opened wide the door to foreign interference; indeed, no system could have been better devised to enable powerful neighbors to intervene in internal Polish affairs. Meddling was never more likely than in 1762, when the king of Poland was on his deathbed. It was generally assumed that his son would succeed him both as Saxon elector and Polish king; he was the candidate favored by Austria and France and by many Poles.

He was not favored by Catherine. Without waiting for Augustus to die, she had made a different choice. The strongest native Polish figure would have been Prince-Chancellor Adam Czartoryski, the leading member of Poland's Russophile party, a strong character and a man of influence and wealth. But strength, experience, and wealth were not the qualities Catherine was seeking in a new king. She wanted someone weaker, more pliable—and in need of money—and she had a candidate who would suit her purpose admirably. This was Adam Czartoryski's nephew—and her former lover—Stanislaus Poniatowski. As early as August 2, 1762, a month after her accession, she had written to Stanislaus, "I am sending Count Keyserling immediately as ambassador to Poland to make you king after the death of August III." Catherine had told Hermann Keyserling that he was authorized to bribe whomever was necessary and could spend up to a hundred thousand rubles. To add steel to gold, she moved thirty thousand soldiers to the Russian-Polish frontier.

Not wishing her candidate's election to be seen as based purely on Russian money and bayonets, she looked for another monarch to support her choice. She knew that Austria and France would prefer the Saxon; she also knew that Frederick of Prussia emphatically did not want another Saxon; that, in fact, he would automatically oppose whomever Maria Theresa of Austria favored. She believed that Frederick would support a native Pole. She understood that if Prussia joined Russia, Poland would feel pressure from both east and west, and that the floundering state would find itself in a diplomatic and military vise.

Frederick carefully considered Catherine's proposal. His own diplomatic situation was weak. Having narrowly escaped defeat in the Seven Years' War, Prussia was exhausted, impoverished, and diplomatically isolated. Frederick needed an ally, and Russia seemed the best—perhaps the only—prospect. But Frederick was too skillful a negotiator to rush into an arrangement in which the Polish crown was the only subject on the bargaining table. He, like Catherine, preferred a native Pole to a Saxon candidate, but he realized that Catherine's interest in the continuation of "fortunate anarchy" in Poland was greater than his own. Cannily, therefore, he declared that he would cooperate with her, but only in return for what he most wanted: a Prussian-Russian alliance. Initially, this bargain suited Catherine not at all; she was aware that a new alliance with Prussia would remind Russians of Peter III's short-lived, highly unpopular alliance with Frederick, whom he had called "the king my master."

She delayed giving a definite answer, attempting to soothe and woo him with exotic gifts. Instead of a treaty, Frederick received watermelons from Astrakhan, grapes from the Ukraine, dromedaries from central Asia, caviar, sturgeon, and furs of fox and marten. Frederick thanked her for the gifts, noting wryly, "There is a vast difference between melons from Astrakhan and the assembly of deputies in Poland, but everything comes within the scope of your activity. The same hand that gives away fruit can distribute crowns and guarantee the peace of Europe, for which I and all those who are interested in the affairs of Poland will eternally bless you."

Mutual interest prevailed. Frederick made a gesture of approval of Catherine's choice for Poland by awarding Stanislaus the Order of the Black Eagle, Prussia's highest military decoration. Catherine allowed herself to forget that not long before, Frederick had bestowed the same award on her husband, Peter III, who was no more a soldier than Stanislaus. But Frederick had the alliance he wanted, a reciprocal defense treaty, binding for eight years. Each of the two powers pledged to assist the other in the event of an attack by a single power, sending an annual financial subsidy of four hundred thousand rubles. Should two hostile powers attack one of the allies, its partner was pledged to send a force of ten thousand infantry and two thousand cavalry. Further, it was understood that Russia and Prussia would cooperate in all matters concerning the Polish political quagmire. In the immediate situation, this meant Prussian support for the candidacy of Stanislaus. There was to be no subtlety and no hesitation. In a secret corollary, the two monarchs declared that both parties were resolved to guarantee "a free and uninfluenced election" and "to resort, if need be, to force of arms, should anyone attempt to prevent the free election of the king in Poland or to meddle with the existing constitution." If certain Poles opposed their new "lawfully elected king" by proclaiming an opposing confederation, the allies agreed to employ "military severity against them and their lands without the slightest mercy."

Negotiation of this treaty was still incomplete when, in September 1763, Augustus III died. By then, the timing of his death was politically irrelevant; Catherine's agreement with Frederick was fixed and the Russian-Prussian candidate had been chosen. The empress received news of the death with mordant wit: "Do not laugh at me for jumping off my chair when I received the news of the death of the Polish king," she wrote to Panin. "The king of Prussia jumped out from behind his desk when he heard it."

For two years after Stanislaus Poniatowski had been summarily sent home from Russia by Empress Elizabeth in 1758, Catherine had remained emotionally tied to the Polish nobleman. She had written to him often as the father of her little Anna, and had tried to secure his recall as ambassador to St. Petersburg. Then she met Gregory Orlov, a man less polished but with greater self-assurance, strength, and drive. Catherine and Stanislaus still corresponded, and their letters were filled with mutual expressions of affection—indeed, the warmth of their language led Poniatowski to consider himself permanently bound to Catherine. The grand duchess, however, was not telling him the whole truth. She managed to omit from her letters details of her affair with Gregory Orlov, including her pregnancy and the birth of her child by Orlov. If Stanislaus learned about Gregory from other sources, he persuaded himself that this raw, uneducated soldier could not be anything more than an infatuation. And once Catherine had taken the throne and her husband was dead, he put Orlov out of his mind and counted the days until she called him back to her side.

Catherine, knowing or sensing his feelings, tried to warn him away. On July 2, 1762, she wrote to him:

> I beg you most urgently not to come here as your arrival in the present circumstances would be dangerous for you and do me much harm. The revolution which has just taken place in my favor is miraculous. Its unanimity is unbelievable. I am deeply engaged in work and would be unable to devote myself to you. All my life I will serve and revere your family, but at the moment it is important not to arouse criticism. I have not slept for three nights and have eaten twice in four days. Good bye. Keep well, Catherine.

The note was affectionate, but it was written in an unmistakable tone of emotional disengagement. Her next letter, written a month later, was an account of the coup and the death of Peter III and included the announcement that she was sending Count Keyserling to make Stanislaus a king. By this point, it had become urgent that she stifle any hope that he would soon rejoin her as her lover and future husband:

> I beg you not to come here now. . . . I received your letter. A regular correspondence would be subject to a thousand inconveniences. I have twenty thousand precautions to take and have no time for harmful little love letters. . . . I have thousands of proprieties to consider and also bear the burden of government. . . . Good bye, the world is full of strange situations.

She still said nothing about her intimate relationship with Gregory Orlov, but she did praise him and his four brothers:

> [The coup was] in the hands of the brothers Orlov . . . [who] shone by their art of leadership, their prudent daring, by the care introduced in small details, by their presence of mind and authority. . . . Enthusiastically patriotic and honest, passionately attached to me and my friends . . . there are five of them in all . . . the eldest of whom [in fact, Gregory was the second] . . . used to follow me everywhere and committed innumerable follies. . . . His passion for me was openly acknowledged and that is why he undertook what he did. . . . I have great obligations to them.

These letters stunned Stanislaus. A desire to wear the Polish crown had never excited him. He did not want to be a king; he did not even wish to live in Poland. Considering himself a European sophisticate, he found that he had little in common with the rough, unruly Polish aristocracy, which rejected all authority except its own and would turn against any elected king at the first sign of a threat to its privileges. If he was to be near a throne, he saw himself more in the role of a prince consort, helping an empress to civilize her empire, than as the ruler of a country in which he had always felt a stranger. Accordingly, Catherine's plan, which would have stranded him on a throne in Poland, had no appeal.

Catherine, however, had three reasons for terminating their personal relationship and making him king: she wanted to make certain that he was permanently disengaged from her personal life; this achieved, she wanted to compensate him for removing herself from his reach; and, more important, she wanted, through him, to dominate Poland. Her letters to her former lover grew cooler. She stopped making a secret of her relationship to Orlov. Stanislaus still believed that his physical presence would reignite her passion for him. He implored that he be allowed to come to Russia, at least for a few months, or even a few weeks. Catherine said no.

Stanislaus refused to accept or even to comprehend his rejection. In his mind, he still carried a picture of a lonely woman coping with the problems of an enormous empire, a woman who desperately needed his help. A more rational man might have seen that Catherine was telling him that she had another lover whose place in her life and contribution to her success had raised him far above himself. Only gradually, Stanislaus grasped this bitter fact, and that the crown of Poland was to be his consolation. He responded with a final, despairing cry:

> I beg of you to listen to me. You, of all women, I never thought would change. Let me be with you in any capacity you will, only do not make me a king. Call me back to you. I will be able to render you far greater service as a private citizen. That any other woman could have changed, I would believe, but you, never! What is left for me? Life without you is nothing but an empty shell, emptiness and frightful weariness of heart. I beg of you to listen to me. Sophie, Sophie, you make me suffer terribly! I would a thousand times rather be an ambassador close to you than a king here.

His appeal was wasted. Catherine had made up her mind. It would be useful to have a man who loved her on the Polish throne, and it was even more convenient that this man was poor and that the Polish crown paid only a pittance. This would ensure that he would always need money and be dependent on her. Stanislaus, although wearing the robes of a king, would become a pawn on the Polish chessboard. The most powerful piece on the board would be a queen—in this case, an empress. Given her former lover's submissive character and disinterest in the bruising business of royal politics, Catherine was certain that it would be only a matter of time before Poland fell completely under Russian influence.

When news of the Russian-Prussian decision in favor of Stanislaus traveled to foreign capitals, it was widely assumed that the empress wanted to make her former lover king of Poland in order to marry him later and then incorporate his kingdom into her empire. Although the announcement raised the danger of antagonizing both Austria and France, neither of these states—both, like Prussia, weakened by war—was prepared to fight over the Polish succession. This did not mean that they approved of Catherine's plan. France lodged its protest through its ally, Turkey, Poland's southern neighbor. French diplomats in Constantinople lost no time in pointing out to the sultan and the grand vizier the danger of having a young, unmarried man on the throne of Poland, one whom the Russian empress had already had as a lover and might well choose as a husband if the marriage settlement brought her territory west of the Dnieper. Skillfully planted, these anxieties quickly took root. In June 1764, the grand vizier sent a note to St. Petersburg declaring that his country was willing to recognize the Russo-Prussian alliance, and also to approve the election of a native king to the Polish throne, but objected to the person of Stanislaus on the grounds that he was too young, too inexperienced, and, above all, unmarried.

In Poland, the Czartoryskis, Stanislaus's family, accepted the logic of Turkey's objections. They proposed a solution: the king-to-be would marry, preferably a Polish Catholic girl—at thirty-two, he was well past the age when most eligible young noblemen were married. They pressed their nephew to do this before election day in the Diet. All parties—Catherine, his family, the Turks, and, behind them, the French—now had a common goal: to force Poniatowski to promise that he would marry only with the approval of the Diet and that he would select a Polish Catholic wife. Stanislaus refused, declaring that no one could force him to become king on these terms and that he would rather forfeit the crown.

Ultimately, it was Catherine who forced a decision on him. Stanislaus received an official message from the Russian foreign ministry in St. Petersburg telling him that it was essential that, before the opening of the election Diet, he marry, or at least select a bride. He realized that the message must have been approved by Catherine. Understanding, finally, that he had lost the woman he loved, he surrendered and signed a declaration that he would never marry anyone other than a Roman Catholic, and then only with the approval of the Polish Diet. He was sufficiently practical, however, to write to Catherine that if she wanted to make him a king, she must provide the money for him to live up to this position. She sent him money. His promise to marry calmed Turkish fears, and the election was allowed to proceed.

Once Stanislaus agreed, Catherine sent the Russian army to help him keep his promise. Fourteen thousand Russian troops surrounded Warsaw to "keep the peace" and "guarantee a free and tranquil election." Some Poles talked of armed resistance and appealing for foreign assistance, but most Diet members were too pleased by the prospect of a native king to oppose Russian intervention.

The "free election" took place by voice vote on a summer day, August 26, 1764, in an open field outside Warsaw where members of the Diet, standing in the meadow grass, had a good view of the large Russian military camp nearby. Stanislaus was elected, and, as he wrote afterward, "The election was unanimous and tranquil." He was now King Stanislaus II Augustus of Poland, and, as it turned out, he had become the last king of Poland. Catherine's former lover, who had dreamed of becoming her husband, became her royal vassal. In St. Petersburg, a relieved empress of Russia saluted the event by sending a note to Panin: "My congratulations on the new king we have made."

❧54❧

The First Partition of Poland and the First Turkish War

CATHERINE WAS PLEASED. Stanislaus's election as king had been a triumph for her, if not for Poland or for Stanislaus. Her victory, however, led to an optimistic view of her ability to influence Polish affairs. Two years later, by attempting to force the Diet to alter policies on the issue of Polish "dissidents," she opened the door to adversity and war.

The "dissident issue" was the official terminology applied to the conflicted status of various religious minorities in predominantly Roman Catholic Poland. These minorities—the Russian Orthodox population in the eastern third of the country, and hundreds of thousands of Protestant Lutherans in the north—had been actively harassed in their religious practices and had been denied most political rights. They were not permitted to elect deputies to the Diet or to occupy high administrative and military posts. For years, their leaders had looked abroad for help: Orthodox believers to Russia; the Protestants to Prussia. Their continuing troubles and recurrent appeals for protection gave Russia and Prussia another common interest in Poland and a further pretext for interference in Polish internal affairs.

From the beginning of her reign, Catherine had heard that Orthodox believers were forbidden to build new churches and frequently barred from attending those that existed. The empress had a reason to respond. She had secularized church lands and serfs in Russia and she wished to do something to earn back the favor of the church at home. A further incentive was that any restriction of the authority of the Catholic Church would be in keeping with Enlightenment principles of religious toleration.

Three months after Stanislaus's election to the Polish throne, the Russian ambassador, Prince Nicholas Repnin, informed the new king that the empress would not permit the reforms in Poland for which the Czartoryskis and other powerful noblemen were asking—abolition of the liberum veto, making the crown hereditary, an increase in the army—until they made concessions to religious minorities: Orthodox and Protestant believers must be allowed to worship in their own churches and to take part in the public life and government of the community. Stanislaus agreed to raise the dissident issue in the next Diet. Antidissident agitation flared immediately, fanned by ardent Catholic churchmen. Both sides were unyielding. By demanding political rights for religious minorities, Catherine was imposing demands on a fervently Catholic people who would rather fight than suffer the slightest alteration of their faith or infringement of their privileges. Religion was the overriding national issue; a threat to the Catholic faith reminded every Pole that he was a patriot. When the 1766 Diet met, it firmly refused to respond to any dissident grievance. Catherine reiterated her position: there were to be no other reforms until Poland permitted dissidents' rights.

Stanislaus was caught in the middle. Familiar with the beliefs of his

Catholic countrymen, he begged the empress not to intrude in religious matters. To his ambassador in St. Petersburg, the king wrote, "[This demand] is a real thunderbolt for the country and for me personally. If it is still humanly possible, try to make the empress see that the crown which she procured for me will become a shirt of Nessus. I shall be burned alive and my end will be frightful."

Catherine ignored his plea. She felt her moral position to be unassailable; she was upholding the rights of a persecuted minority against the Catholic Church. Beyond that, she had given money to Stanislaus; she felt that she had bought and paid for his support. She instructed her ambassador to enforce her policy.

Frederick of Prussia was happy to stand aside in Catherine's struggle with the king and the Diet, and to devote himself to fomenting discontent in the Protestant areas of northern Poland. This served to strengthen the resistance of Polish Catholics to all foreign intervention and make Catherine's effort more difficult. With members of the Diet obdurate and sullen, with Catholic bishops thundering against the wickedness of the dissenters, with some members of the nobility arming their followers, Catherine saw no alternative except to send more Russian troops into Poland. When the next Diet met in October 1767, Warsaw was occupied by a Russian army. Repnin surrounded the Diet building with soldiers and placed some of them inside the Diet chamber to ensure that members voted as he instructed them. At first, the Diet refused to be intimidated. When bishops spoke against dissident rights, members roared approval. Repnin then arrested the two leading bishops, including the elderly bishop of Kraców, and sent them across the border to exile in Russia. Members looked to their king to protest, but Stanislaus accepted Repnin's demands, whereupon they accused the king of betraying his country to the Russians. On November 7, 1767, the Diet, with multiple absentees, with Russian bayonets gleaming everywhere, and finding no one to rally behind, grudgingly submitted and agreed to equal rights for "dissidents." Catherine and Repnin, however, were not finished. In February 1768, they forced the signing of a Polish-Russian treaty of alliance that confirmed the granting of liberty of worship to dissenting minorities and committed the king not to attempt any change in the Polish constitution without Russian consent.

Two days after the Diet in Warsaw dispersed, a group of conservative Catholic noblemen gathered in the southern Polish town of Bar, near the Turkish frontier, and declared themselves to be a Confederated

Diet whose purpose was to defend Polish independence and the Catholic religion. Polish patriotism led to an ill-prepared and uncoordinated uprising. Russian troops marched south and easily dispersed this group of confederates, but other anti-Russian confederations arose elsewhere in Poland, and Catherine was forced to send more troops. The confederates appealed for support from Catholic Austria and from France; both sent money and officers to advise. Catherine responded by flooding the country with even more Russian troops. She realized that she had badly underestimated the strength of Polish Catholicism and national pride, and, to her surprise, she found herself enmeshed in a serious military campaign. The Poles were fighting, she wrote to Voltaire, "in order to prevent a quarter of their nation from enjoying civic rights."

Catherine had succeeded in making Poland a vassal state with a puppet king, but she had also succeeded in arousing the hatred of the Poles, the alarm of Turkey, the anxiety of Austria, and even the nervousness of Prussia. Frederick had not signed a treaty with Russia in order to see the whole of Poland fall under Russian control.

Apprehension caused by events in Poland spread across Europe. Monarchs and statesmen, already astonished by the success of the former Princess of Anhalt-Zerbst in making herself an empress, now watched as she turned her lover into a king and extended Russian influence over his new kingdom. The Turks, neighbors of both Poland and Russia, were greatly alarmed by the growing increase in Russian military power in Poland, which Turkey had assumed would remain a permanently weak buffer state. Russian troops now were in a position to advance down the Dnieper, the Bug, and the Dniester and threaten the Turkish Balkan provinces of Wallachia and Moldavia. If they reached and crossed the Danube, they could threaten the city of Constantinople itself. France, Turkey's traditional ally, was also eager to curtail Russia's growing influence in Poland. It was, therefore, not difficult for French diplomats in Constantinople to convince the sultan and the grand vizier that Russian expansion must be checked and that the wisest course would be to declare war before the Russians were ready. French bribes made this case persuasive in Constantinople. Turkey now needed only a pretext.

An ideal casus belli presented itself in October 1768. Russian troops, fighting Poles in southeastern Poland, pursued them over the border into Turkish territory. The Ottoman Empire responded by issuing an ultimatum to the Russian ambassador, demanding that all Russian troops be removed not only from Turkish territory but from all of Poland. When the Russian ambassador refused even to communicate this demand to St. Petersburg, the Turks escorted him to the Seven Towers and locked him up—the Ottoman protocol for declaring war. Frederick II, following these events from Berlin, clapped his hand to his head and groaned, "Good God, what does one have to endure to make a king of Poland?"

Catherine was undismayed by Turkey's declaration of war. Indeed, she believed that it provided an opportunity to achieve significant Russian goals. Of course, she would be going to war without an ally; as long as Russia was fighting only a single hostile power, Frederick of Prussia was not obliged by treaty to mobilize a single grenadier. He limited himself to the payment of annual subsidies to Russia which the Russian-Prussian treaty required. Privately, he dismissed the war as a contest between "the one-eyed and the blind," but he stopped this talk in 1769 and 1770 when the brilliant successes of Catherine's generals proved him wrong.

In the the spring of 1769, Russian troops occupied and fortified Azov and Taganrog, which Peter the Great had conquered and subsequently, in 1711, had been forced to return to the Turks. Control of these ports and their fortresses meant command of the mouth of the Don, where the river enters the Sea of Azov. The Russians then took Kerch, at the point where the Sea of Azov meets the Black Sea, providing access to the Black Sea itself. Meanwhile, a Russian army of eighty thousand, using Poland as its base, advanced south into the Turkish provinces of Moldavia and Wallachia. General Peter Rumyantsev's forces occupied all of Moldavia and much of Wallachia up to the Danube. In 1770, Rumyantsev led 40,000 men across the Dniester and inflicted two devastating defeats on larger Turkish armies. At the Battle of Larga, on July 7, he defeated 70,000 Turks, and at the Battle of Kagul, on July 21, he routed 150,000. Rumyantsev was promoted to field marshal. Watching from St. Petersburg, an overjoyed Catherine boasted to Voltaire that "at the risk of repeating myself or becoming a bore, I have nothing to report to you but victories." The empress met almost daily with her war council and constantly sent long letters of appreciation and encouragement to her generals. Officers on leave were entertained at the Winter Palace, and at every military parade in the capital, the empress appeared in the uniform of one of the regiments of which she was honorary colonel.

From the first months of the war, Catherine was also looking for ways to use her navy to fight the Turks. Russia had no Black Sea fleet because the Russian empire possessed no foothold on that body of water. Peter the Great had constructed a Baltic fleet, but it had been allowed by his successors to fall into decay. Early in her reign, Catherine had begun to rehabilitate this fleet by repairing old ships, constructing new ones, and asking the British government to permit her to hire some experienced Royal Navy officers. A number of British captains had been recruited, including Captains Samuel Greig and John Elphinstone, both of whom were given the rank of rear admiral and paid twice the salaries they had received in their own navy.

Catherine wished to put this fleet and these officers to use. When, at a meeting of the war council, Gregory Orlov wondered aloud whether this weapon could be employed in the Mediterranean to attack the Turks from the rear, Catherine was interested. It was a daring concept that would involve sending a large part of the Russian navy completely around the ocean periphery of the European continent. The fleet would sail down the Baltic, across the North Sea, through the English Channel, past the coasts of France, Spain, and Portugal, through the Strait of Gibraltar, and into the eastern Mediterranean, carrying the flag of the Russian empress into the Aegean Sea. To make this strategy work, however, Catherine would need the support of a friendly European power. Again, she approached England, and again Whitehall consented. When Russians were fighting Turks—so the British government reasoned— they were also fighting France, which was Turkey's traditional ally. And anything that might damage France, England's permanent enemy, would always be approved in London. Accordingly, Britain offered facilities to the Russian fleet to rest, resupply, and carry out repairs in the English naval harbors of Hull and Portsmouth, and again at Gibraltar and Minorca in the Mediterranean.

On August 6, 1769, Catherine watched the first Russian squadron sail from Kronstadt on the initial leg of its long voyage. The ships resupplied in Hull and then wintered at the British base in Minorca in the western Mediterranean. A second squadron commanded by Admiral John Elphinston followed in October, sailing across the North Sea to winter in Spithead, off the Isle of Wight. In April, these ships put to sea and arrived in Leghorn, where the Grand Duke of Tuscany resupplied them. In May 1770, the combined Russian fleet appeared off Cape Matapan, at the tip of the Peloponnesus, which marked the western entrance to the Aegean Sea. By then, senior command of the fleet had shifted to Gregory Orlov's brother Alexis, who had joined the fleet in Leghorn. The tall, scar-faced Russian, instrumental in Catherine's coup d'etat and the death of Peter III, made up in determination what he lacked in nautical experience, and he had retained Samuel Greig as his technical adviser. Gathering his ships, he began scouring the blue waters of the Aegean for the enemy. Near the end of June, he found them.

The island of Chios lies off Turkish Anatolia, and in the waters of Chios on June 25, a Turkish admiral commanding sixteen ships of the line saw an unexpected sight: fourteen large ships flying the white ensign with the blue cross of St. Andrew—the naval flag of Russia—approaching in line of battle. Orlov engaged immediately near the north end of Chesme Bay, a coastal inlet. A Russian ship rammed the Turkish flagship, and Russian and Turkish sailors grappled on deck in hand-to-hand combat. Fire broke out and both ships exploded. The remaining Turkish vessels scurried into Chesme Bay, where the Turkish admiral believed he was safe in the narrow, shallow waters in which Russian ships would have little room to maneuver. The next morning, Orlov attacked again. Greig entered the bay with three ships and assaulted a 96-gun Turkish ship of the line. Behind them, masked by the smoke and confusion of this engagement, three ancient Greek hulks configured as fireships and crammed with combustibles bore down on the anchored Turkish fleet; the Turkish sailors' first sight was a towering wall of flame moving toward them. Fanned by a stiff breeze in a constricted space, the flames spread quickly, and, one after another, the Turkish ships caught fire and exploded. The result was annihilation; fifteen Turkish ships of the line were destroyed, and only one escaped. Nine thousand Turkish seamen died—and thirty Russians.

Chesme Bay was an astonishing achievement for a fleet and a nation with no naval reputation. The victory allowed Orlov, who now saw himself as the liberator of the Orthodox Greeks, to move his fleet at will around the Aegean, attempting to persuade the Greeks to rise against their Turkish overlords. Lacking the active support of an ally with a land army, he failed. For a while he blockaded the Dardanelles. By autumn, the Russian crews were suffering from dysentery, and the fleet withdrew to winter quarters in Leghorn. In the spring, Orlov was ordered to sail for home. He returned to a hero's welcome. Kneeling before Catherine, he received the Order of St. George.

Russia's surprising 1770 successes—the advance of Russian armies to the Black Sea and the Danube, the presence of a Russian fleet in the Mediterranean, and the total destruction of the Turkish fleet at Chesme—struck Europe with an astonishment heavily freighted with alarm. The rapid expansion of Russian power began to worry her friends as well as her enemies. One of these was Catherine's ally Frederick of Prussia, who took little pleasure in imagining Catherine's permanent domination of all of Poland. Neither Prussia nor Austria liked the prospect of Russia reaching deep into the Balkans or the idea of a Russian seizure of Constantinople. On the other hand, neither Frederick nor Maria Theresa saw how to prevent Russia from achieving these goals. Thus, although Frederick congratulated Catherine ("I cannot keep writing to you for every victory; I shall wait till there are half a dozen"), the last thing he desired was a wider war, which might bring in France and Austria against Russia and, therefore, require the participation of Prussia as Catherine's ally in the fighting. In the 1764 treaty, Prussia had pledged to come to Catherine's aid if Russia were attacked. In the present war, Turkey was clearly the aggressor, and, as a result, Prussia was already sending financial subsidies to Russia. But now Austria, alarmed by Russian penetration of the Balkans, was threatening to ally herself with the Turks. If this led to war, Russia would demand that Prussia fulfill her further treaty obligation, and he, Frederick, would have to fight Austria for the third time in his life. By now, Frederick had had enough of war. At fifty-five, he had already fought two wars against Austria to add Silesia to his kingdom; now the province was his and he had no wish to fight for it again. He preferred diplomacy. Poland's independence was tottering; the Russian ambassador was already the de facto ruler of the kingdom, and it was only a matter of time before Catherine swallowed the country completely. To prevent this and do it peacefully, Frederick scrambled to find a solution that might satisfy all three of Poland's powerful neighbors. Suppose Prussia, Austria, and

Russia could be appeased by each taking an area of the crumbling state? If Catherine would consent to take only the eastern, predominantly Orthodox, part of Poland, and Frederick took only what he wanted in the Protestant northwest, then Austria might be satisfied with the extensive Catholic-populated territory in the south. He was certain that if the three powers could agree on this plan, no one else in Europe could resist such a combination of power—not the Turks or the French, and certainly not the Poles.

At the heart of this cynical appeal to Poland's neighbors to cooperate in joint aggrandizement was the territorial prize Frederick wanted for himself. East Prussia was physically separated from the rest of his Hohenzollern possessions. For years, Frederick had hoped to remedy this flaw by acquiring the Polish Baltic coastal territories that split his country. In the autumn of 1770, Frederick's diplomatic scheming was assisted by the presence of his younger brother, Prince Henry of Prussia, who was making a state visit to St. Petersburg. A short man with an inexpressive demeanor, he had come to the Russian capital reluctantly at the request of his brother to promote Frederick's plan for dividing up Poland. Henry was as little interested in ceremonial pomp as his brother, but his eye was as sharp and his perceptions as keen. Catherine plied him with banquets, concerts, and balls. Henry moved uncomfortably in the luxury of Catherine's court; he was punctual and meticulous, but he did not enjoy himself. Nor did his stolid demeanor and curt Prussian bow please many in the Russian court. But with Catherine, a fellow German, he got on well.

By December, the prince and the empress were seriously discussing Frederick's proposal for the partition of Poland. Would Catherine agree to lower her demands for territorial cessions by a defeated Turkey in exchange for permanent territorial gains in Poland? Catherine pondered the question; savoring her military and naval victories, she was reluctant to compromise. After all, Russia was the only power actually at war with Turkey; it was she who was fighting and had defeated the Turks. Further, having invested so much effort and money in Polish affairs, she would have preferred, through Stanislaus, to make all Poland a permanent Russian satellite. As she considered her situation, however, she became more amenable. She realized that neither her ally Prussia nor an increasingly hostile Austria was likely to allow her to make sweeping Balkan acquisitions at Turkey's expense. In the back of her mind, she feared that Austria and France might enter the war as

Turkey's allies; for months now, both Austria and France had been sending help in the form of money and military advisers to the confederates in Poland. Further, she realized that the deep permanent hatred between Orthodox and Catholic Poles was probably going to make Poland an endless military and financial drain. Finally, she knew that for many Russians, including leaders and believers of the Orthodox Church, bringing the Orthodox population of Poland under Russian protection would be enthusiastically welcomed, and that this would be sufficient to quiet those who had wanted more.

In January 1771, while Prince Henry was edging his way through the Russian Christmas and New Year, Austrian troops suddenly crossed the Carpathians and occupied an area in southern Poland. This news reached the empress and Prince Henry at a concert at the Winter Palace. Henry, hearing the news, shook his head and observed, "It seems that in Poland one only has to stoop and help oneself." Catherine picked up his lead and replied, "Why shouldn't we both take our share?" Henry reported this exchange to Frederick with the comment, "Although this was only a chance pleasantry, it is certain that it was not said for nothing and I do not doubt that it will be very possible for you to profit by this occasion."

In March, soon after his brother returned to Berlin, Frederick wrote to Catherine suggesting that, in view of Austria's aggression, perhaps it would be appropriate if Prussia and Russia simply followed her example and took what they wanted. In mid-May the Prussian minister in St. Petersburg reported to Berlin that the empress had consented to a partition of Poland.

A year of negotiation passed before agreement on partition could be reached with Austria. During this year the diplomatic focus was on Maria Theresa. Already alarmed by Russian victories in the Balkans and objecting particularly to any suggestion that the Turks should be replaced on the Danube by the Russians, the Austrian empress committed herself in July 1771 to a secret treaty with Turkey to come to the assistance of this ancient Muslim enemy of the Hapsburgs. Secrets have short lives, however, and when Frederick and Catherine learned of it, they ignored Austria and, on February 17, 1772, signed an agreement to partition Poland. Meanwhile, Maria Theresa's son and co-ruler, Emperor Joseph II, was struggling to persuade his mother that it was in

Austria's interest to join Frederick and Catherine. This was an excruciating moment for the Austrian empress. She hated and despised these two monarchs; Frederick was a Protestant who had stolen Silesia; Catherine was a usurper who had taken lovers. Maria Theresa was a devout Catholic, and she shuddered at the idea of assisting in despoiling a neighboring Catholic state.

It took time to overcome these scruples, and her son worked hard to set her decision in a larger context than personal feelings. The Austrian empress faced a choice: either she maintained her recently signed treaty with Turkey and had to go to war with Russia with no help from any other European power, or she abandoned the Turks and joined Prussia and Russia in helping herself to another, larger slice of Poland. In the end, Maria Theresa abandoned the Turks. On August 5, 1772, Emperor Joseph II, on his mother's behalf, added his signature to the agreement to partition Poland.

The three partitioning powers sent troops into their newly claimed territories and then demanded that a Polish Diet be called to ratify their aggression. In the summer of 1773, Stanislaus obediently summoned a Diet. Many Polish noblemen and Catholic churchmen refused to attend; some who came were arrested; others accepted bribes and remained silent. The rump Diet then transformed itself into a confederation that did not require a majority decision. In this way, on September 30, 1773, Poland signed the partition treaty formally ceding the land it had already lost.

In what came to be called the First Partition of Poland, the crumbling state lost almost a third of its territory and more than a third of its population. Russia's share was the largest in territory, 36,000 square miles, comprising all of eastern Poland as far as the Dnieper River and the whole course of the river Dvina flowing north toward the Baltic. This area, known as White Russia (now a part of the independent nation of Belorussia) had a population of 1,800,000 people, primarily of Russian stock with Russian identity, traditions, and religion. Prussia's slice of Poland was the smallest, both in area and population: 13,000 square miles, with 600,000 people, predominantly German and Protestant. Frederick was satisfied, at least at that moment. By acquiring the Baltic enclaves of West Prussia and Polish Pomerania, he achieved his goal of uniting his kingdom geographically, stitching the separated province of East Prussia onto Brandenburg, Silesia, and other Prussian territories in Germany. Austria took a substantial piece of southern Poland:

27,000 square miles, including the greater part of Galicia. Maria Theresa acquired the largest number of new subjects: 2,700,000 Poles, overwhelmingly Catholic. A few Poles resisted this aggression, but against the strength of three major powers, they had little success. England, France, Spain, Sweden, and the pope condemned the partition, but no European state was prepared to go to war on behalf of Poland.

Catherine's intervention in Poland was successful. She had returned Russia's frontier to the great trade route of the Dnieper. Two million Orthodox believers could profess their faith unhindered. But she still had important objectives in her war with Turkey. The fact that Russia's western frontier had been brought back to the Dnieper did not mean the opening of that great water route to the Black Sea, because the Turks still controlled the estuary where the river flowed into the sea. Catherine meant to free this river mouth. The war with Turkey continued.

The year 1771 had produced a disappointment on the battlefields. On the Danube, Russian generals had been unable to follow up their victories of 1770. Even though General Vasily Dolgoruky had stormed into the Crimea and overrun the peninsula, this had not inclined the sultan to make peace. Three years of stalemate and frustration followed. Not until the end of 1773 did Russian prospects brighten. In December, Sultan Mustapha III died and was succeeded by his brother, Abdul Hamid. The new sultan, recognizing the unprofitability as well as the danger of continuing the war, decided to end it. Catherine prompted him with a new offensive on the Danube. In June 1774, Rumyantsev crossed the Danube with fifty-five thousand men. On June 9, fifty miles south of the river, a night bayonet attack by eight thousand Russians on forty thousand Turks broke the Turkish lines and led to a crushing Russian victory at Kozludzhi. The grand vizier, fearing that nothing could stop the Russians from reaching Constantinople, sued for peace. Rumyantsev opened direct negotiations in the field, and he and the grand vizier agreed to terms. On July 10, 1774, in an obscure Bulgarian village, the Treaty of Kuchuk Kainardzhi was signed. Rumyantsev immediately sent his son to St. Petersburg with the news, and on July 23, Catherine hurried out of a concert to receive it.

The treaty brought Russia greater gains than she had dared to hope for. Catherine traded her conquests on the Danube for more important acquisitions on the Black Sea coast. The Balkan provinces of Moldavia and Wallachia were restored to Turkey. In exchange, Catherine gained the transfer to Russia of Azov, Taganrog, and Kerch, which provided unfettered access to the Black Sea. Farther west, she acquired the southern delta of the Dnieper River, and the mouth of the river itself, giving her empire another vital outlet to the Black Sea. Although the west bank of the river's broad estuary still retained the massive Turkish fortress at Ochakov, the Russians now had a fort and port at Kinburn on the east bank, and the estuary was large enough to permit Russian commercial navigation and the unhindered construction of Russian warships. The peace terms also included the ending of the sultan's political sovereignty over the Crimean Peninsula, where a Tatar khanate under Turkish protection had existed for centuries. The Crimean Tatars were now declared to be independent of Turkey. Everyone realized that the independence of the Crimea was unlikely to last; indeed, nine years later, Catherine was to annex the peninsula outright.

Russian gains were not purely territorial. The treaty opened the Black Sea to Russian commerce by guaranteeing complete freedom of navigation. The treaty also included the right of Russian merchant ships to unlimited transit through the Bosporus and the Dardanelles into the Mediterranean. Turkey was also to pay to Russia a war indemnity of four and a half million rubles. Persecution of Christians in Moldavia and Wallachia was to cease, and Orthodox believers in Constantinople were to be able to worship at a church of their own. On a grander scale, the war had tipped the balance of power in the region in Russia's favor; Europe was now aware that predominance in the Black Sea had passed to Russia. In Catherine's mind, these were achievements to match those of her predecessor, Peter the Great, who, on the faraway Baltic, had first opened a Russian pathway to the world.

❦ 55 ❦

Doctors, Smallpox, and Plague

THE RUSSIAN PEOPLE considered themselves a national family. The tsar, or emperor, was the Little Father, *Batushka*. His wife, the tsaritsa, or an unmarried soverign empress such as Catherine I, Anna,

Elizabeth, or Catherine II, was the Little Mother, *Matushka*. Catherine liked thinking of herself this way and took seriously the responsibility of maternal care for her people. If she could not give them a new legal code, she could at least address the problem of their health. "If you go to a village and ask a peasant how many children he has," she said," he will say ten, twelve, and sometimes even twenty. If you ask how many of them are alive, he will say, one, two, three, rarely four. This mortality should be fought against."

In 1763, the second year of her reign, Catherine founded Russia's first College of Medicine to train Russian doctors, surgeons, and apothecaries. Until a sufficient number of Russian doctors became available, she attempted to recruit western European physicians by offering generous salaries and pensions. In the same year, to discourage infanticide among unmarried and impoverished mothers, she established with her own funds a foundling hospital with an attached lying-in hospital in Moscow. The anonymity of the mother was assured by a system of baskets, pulleys, and bells. When a bell was rung in the street, a basket was lowered from an upper story, the unwanted baby put in, and the basket raised. All children, legitimate or illegitimate, from any class, were accepted, cared for, and educated, with precautions to ensure that when they left, they were, or remained, free. The hospital was five stories high and had two hundred beds. Dormitories were large and airy. Each child had his or her own bed, with a clean gown, clean sheets, and a small bedside table holding a jug of water, a glass tumbler, and a bell to summon assistance. An English visitor wished "that the same attention to cleanliness was given in English hospitals." The hospital served as a model for similar foundling institutions in St. Petersburg and other places. The empress attacked another problem by creating a hospital for venereal disease, where both women and men were treated. In 1775, Catherine decreed that the capital of every province must have a general hospital, and that every county in the province must have a physician, a surgeon, two surgical assistants, two apprentices, and an apothecary. Since twenty to thirty thousand people lived in some counties, this coverage was thin, but before there had been nothing.

Personally, Catherine did not care for doctors. She was subject to illness; indeed, when she was a grand duchess, her health had frequently worried Empress Elizabeth. Once she reached the throne, Catherine's ailments had political significance. She felt the burden of absolute power: reports had to be studied, advisers consulted, decisions made. She tried to keep herself healthy through adequate rest, dietary restraint, fresh air, and outdoor walks; nevertheless, she often complained privately of headaches and back pains. In 1768 she wrote to Nikita Panin: "I am quite sick, my back hurts worse than I ever felt since birth. Last night I had some fever from the pain, and I do not know what to attribute it to. I swallow and do everything they [the doctors] wish." Again to Panin: "It has been four years since the pain in my head has left me. Yesterday I ate nothing the whole day."

Although she believed that she was healthier because she ignored physicians, she eventually agreed to keep a personal doctor at court. She chose a young Scotsman, Dr. John Rogerson, of Edinburgh University. Still convinced that she had no need of him, she made him the butt of jokes about modern medicine and liked describing him to others as the kind of medical charlatan found in Molière. "You couldn't cure a flea bite," she would say to him. Rogerson would laugh and continue to urge her to take the pill he was offering. When he succeeded, he would pat the empress on the back and say jovially, "Well done, ma'am! Well done!"

There was no joking, however, when Catherine confronted one of the most serious diseases afflicting her contemporary world: smallpox. Here, the imperial family had no greater protection than the poorest peasant. The boy emperor Peter II had died of the disease at fifteen. Empress Elizabeth's Holstein fiancé, Catherine's uncle, had been carried off on the eve of their marriage. Nor could Catherine forget the suffering and disfigurement of her husband, the future Peter III. She considered herself fortunate in having reached adulthood without contracting the pox, but she knew that this reprieve might not last.

The devastating smallpox experience being inflicted on the Hapsburgs frightened Catherine. In May 1767, Empress Maria Theresa and her daughter-in-law, Maria Josepha, the wife of her son and heir, Joseph II, both contracted smallpox. Five days later, Maria Josepha died; Maria Theresa recovered but was scarred. Her widower son, Joseph II, refused to marry again and had no surviving children. The following October, Maria Theresa's daughter, also named Maria Josepha, died of smallpox; two other Hapsburg daughters had the disease but survived, with prominent scars. This succession of tragedies convinced Maria Theresa to have her three youngest children inoculated.

Aware of these personal and dynastic tragedies, Catherine worried about the threat of smallpox to Paul as much as to herself. She knew that the court was never free of talk about the grand duke's uncertain chance of succession, because he had not yet faced and defeated the disease. She and Panin worried constantly about the boy's possible exposure. They sought to isolate Paul from crowds and from anyone who was or might be afflicted. Paul chafed at the restrictions put on him. At twelve, he was asked whether he would attend a masquerade. He replied,

> You know I am a child and cannot be supposed to be a judge whether I ought to go there or not, but I will wager that I do not go. Mr. Panin will tell me that there is a great monster called Smallpox, walking up and down the ballroom. This same monster has very good foreknowledge of my movements for he is generally to be found in precisely those places where I have the most inclination to go.

The disease came close to Catherine and Paul in the spring of 1768 when Nikita Panin's fiancée, Countess Anna Sheremeteva, described by a British diplomat as a woman of "uncommon merit, beautiful, and immensely rich," was struck by smallpox. At Tsarskoe Selo, the empress waited anxiously. When, on May 5, she learned that Panin himself had been placed in quarantine for two weeks, she secretly ordered Paul brought to her. "I am very upset," she said, "not being able to focus on anything better, for everything is awful in this critical situation." Paul arrived at Tsarskoe Selo on May 6, and mother and son waited together. Catherine herself was ill on May 14 and better the next morning; she quickly informed Panin of her overnight recovery and passed along her doctor's assurance that "these difficult days for your fiancée will pass." Two days later she was told that Countess Sheremeteva was dead. "Having this hour learned of the demise of Countess Anna Petrovna, I could not help letting you know my real sorrow," she wrote to Panin on May 17. "I am so touched for you by this grievous misfortune that I cannot sufficiently explain it. Please watch your own health." She spent seven weeks at Tsarskoe Selo, and for the rest of the summer, she and Paul moved between country estates to avoid crowds.

· · ·

Fear for herself, her son, and the nation prompted the empress to investigate a new, controversial method of inoculation that assured permanent immunity: the injection of matter taken from the smallpox pustules of a patient recovering from a mild case. This medical technique was being used in Britain and the British North American colonies (Thomas Jefferson was inoculated in 1766) but was shunned in continental Europe as being too dangerous.

Dr. Thomas Dimsdale was a Scot and a Quaker whose grandfather had accompanied William Penn to America in 1684. Thomas Dimsdale himself, now fifty-six, had a degree from Edinburgh University and had just published *The Present Method of Inoculating for the Small Pox,* describing his success and claiming to have minimized the risks. His book had gone through four editions in Britain, and Catherine, hearing about it, invited the author to St. Petersburg. Dimsdale arrived in Russia at the end of August 1768, bringing with him his son and assistant, Nathaniel. Catherine soon received them privately at dinner.

Dimsdale was charmed by Catherine, finding her, "of all that I ever saw of her sex, the most engaging." He was amazed by "her extreme penetration and the propriety of the questions she asked relative to the practice and success of inoculation." The empress, in turn, liked his common sense, but in her opinion, he was overly cautious. She smiled at his stumbling French and tried to understand his English. She told him that she had feared smallpox all her life, but now she wished to be inoculated as the best way of overcoming the fears of others about the disease and about inoculation. She wanted to be inoculated as soon as possible. Dimsdale asked to first consult her court physicians, but Catherine said that this was unnecessary. Dimsdale then suggested that, as a trial measure, he should first innoculate other women of her age; again, Catherine said no. Bowed by the responsibility, Dimsdale begged her to wait a few weeks while he experimented on several local youngsters. She reluctantly agreed, on condition that he keep his preparations secret. The official court register ignored Dimsdale's presence entirely, although the British ambassador reported on August 29 that the empress's intention "is a secret everybody knows. And which does not seem to occasion much speculation." Finally, the empress and the doctor agreed on a date for inoculation: October 12.

Catherine stopped eating meat and drinking wine ten days before this date and began taking calomel, powder of crab's claws, and a tartar emetic. At nine in the evening on October 12, Dimsdale inoculated

Catherine in both arms with smallpox matter taken from a peasant boy named Alexander Markov, whom she subsequently ennobled. The next morning, Catherine drove to Tsarskoe Selo for rest and isolation. She felt healthy "except for some slight uneasiness" and exercised outdoors for two or three hours a day. She developed a moderate number of pustules that dried up in a week. Dimsdale pronounced the inoculation a success, and three weeks later Catherine resumed her regular schedule. She returned to St. Petersburg on November 1, and Paul was inoculated without difficulty the next day. Congratulated by the Senate and the Legislative Commission, she responded, "My objective was, through my example, to save from death the multitude of my subjects who, not knowing the value of this technique, and frightened of it, were left in danger."

Catherine's example was followed by 140 of the St. Petersburg nobility, including Gregory Orlov, Kyril Razumovsky, and an archbishop. Dimsdale then went to Moscow and inoculated another fifty people. A Russian translation of his treatise explaining his technique was published in St. Petersburg, and inoculation clinics were established in St. Petersburg, Moscow, Kazan, Irkutsk, and other cities. By 1780, twenty thousand Russians had been inoculated; by 1800, two million. As a reward for his service, Catherine made Dimsdale a baron of the Russian empire and awarded him ten thousand pounds plus a life annuity of five hundred pounds. In 1781, Dimsdale returned to Russia to inoculate Catherine's first grandson, Alexander.

Catherine's willingness to be inoculated attracted favorable notice in western Europe. Voltaire compared what she had allowed Dimsdale to do with the ridiculous views and practices of "our argumentative charlatans in our medical schools." At the time, the prevailing attitude toward the disease was fatalistic: people believed that, sooner or later, everyone must have it, and that some would survive and some would die. Most refused inoculation. Frederick of Prussia wrote to Catherine urging her not to take the risk. She replied that she had always been afraid of smallpox and wished more than anything to escape this fear. In May 1774, almost six years after Catherine was inoculated, smallpox killed the king of France. Louis XV took to bed a barely pubescent girl who was carrying smallpox. He died soon after, ending a reign of fifty-nine years. His successor, nineteen-year-old Louis XVI, was inoculated immediately.

· · ·

Catherine's personal confrontation with smallpox occurred three years before Russia was plunged into a desperate struggle with an even more terrible disease: bubonic plague. Plague was a perennial threat along the empire's southern frontiers with European Turkey. It was believed to appear only in warm climates; the link with fleas and rats was unknown. The traditional defense was isolation, ranging from quarantine of suspected individual carriers to cordons of troops sealing off entire regions.

In March 1770, plague appeared among Russian troops occupying the Turkish Balkan province of Wallachia. In September, it reached Kiev, in the Ukraine. Cooler autumn weather slowed the advance of the disease, but by then, refugees were fleeing north. By mid-January 1771, the scare seemed over, but with the first spring thaw, Muscovites began to develop the distinctive dark spots and swollen glands. One hundred and sixty workers died in a single week at one textile factory in the city. On March 17, Catherine decreed emergency quarantine measures in Moscow: theatrical performances, balls, and all large public gatherings were banned. A sudden freeze at the end of March brought an abrupt decline in the death rate. Catherine and the municipal authorities began lifting restrictions. At the end of June, however, plague reappeared. By August, it was ravaging the city. Soldiers removing bodies from the streets fell ill and died. The city's chief doctor requested medical leave for a month to receive treatment for his own illness. On September 5, Catherine was told that the daily death toll was between three and four hundred; that abandoned corpses littered the streets; that the network of checkpoints around the city was collapsing, and that the people were hungry because no supplies were being delivered. Men, women, and children already ill were required to enter quarantine centers.

The imposition of medical precautions led to rioting. Many in Moscow's terror-stricken population came to believe that the physicians and their medicines had brought the plague to the city. They refused to obey orders forbidding them to gather in marketplaces and churches and to kiss supposedly miraculous icons in hope of protection. Instead, they gathered to seek salvation and solace around these icons. A famous icon of the Virgin at Varvarsky Gate became a magnet; day after day, crowds of diseased people swarmed around her feet. She became the deadliest center of contagion in the city.

The doctors knew what was happening but dared not intervene.

The archbishop of Moscow, Father Ambrosius, was an enlightened man who saw that the physicians were helpless. Attempting to reduce infection by preventing the formation of crowds, and relying on his authority as a priest, he had the Varvarsky Virgin removed from the city gate under cover of night and hidden. He believed that once the people knew that he was the one responsible, they would go home and the plague-ridden site would be eliminated. Instead, his well-meaning attempt provoked a riot. The crowd, rather than dispersing, was enraged. Ambrosius fled to a monastery and took refuge in a cellar, but the mob pursued him, dragged him out, and tore him apart. The riot was put down by troops, who killed a hundred people and arrested three hundred.

Catherine realized that Moscow and its population were slipping out of control. The nobles had abandoned the city for their estates in the countryside; the factories and workshops were closed; the workers, serfs, and urban peasants, living in crowded wooden houses that harbored swarms of rats carrying the plague-bearing fleas, had been left to shift for themselves. Late in September, the empress received a message from the governor of Moscow, seventy-two-year-old General Peter Saltykov, saying that, with deaths exceeding eight hundred per day, he was helpless; the situation was out of control. He asked to be allowed to leave the city until winter. The empress was shocked. The rising death toll, Ambrosius's violent murder; Saltykov's desertion of his post. How was she to cope with this? To whom was she to turn?

Gregory Orlov stepped forward and asked permission to go to Moscow to halt the epidemic and restore order. This was the kind of challenge he had sought; after years of idleness, he needed to redeem himself in his own eyes and Catherine's. The empress accepted his "fine and zealous" offer, she told Voltaire, "not without feelings of acute anxiety over the risks he would run." She knew his restlessness and eagerness for action; his frustration at being kept in St. Petersburg while his brother Alexis and other officers won victories and praise on land and sea. She gave him full authority. Orlov assembled doctors, military officers, and administrators and departed for Moscow on the evening of September 21.

Orlov took control of the stricken city. With the death toll between six hundred and seven hundred a day, he asked the physicians what they wanted done and then bullied the people into obedience. He was forceful and effective but also humane. He accompanied doctors to patients' bedsides, he oversaw the distribution of medicines, he supervised the removal of corpses rotting in houses and the streets. He promised freedom to serfs who volunteered to work in hospitals, he opened orphanages, he distributed food and money. Over a period of two and a half months, he spent a hundred thousand rubles on food, clothing, and shelter for survivors. He had victims' clothes burned, and he burned more than three thousand old wooden houses. He reimposed compulsory quarantine, the policy that had caused the riots. He scarcely slept, and his dedication, courage, and effort inspired others. Deaths in the city, which had risen to 21,000 in September, dropped to 17,561 in October, 5,255 in November, and 805 in December. In part, this was a result of Orlov's actions; in part, it was a function of the arrival of cold weather.

Confidence in Gregory, together with hope for the coming of an early winter, sustained the empress during these weeks. She had feared that the epidemic might move northwest toward St. Petersburg; already there had been suspicious outbreaks in Pskov and Novgorod. Precautions were taken to protect the capital on the Neva: checkpoints blocked all roads; extra care was taken in handling mail; a medical examination became mandatory after every suspicious death. She worried about the effect of reports and rumors at home and abroad. At first she tried to suppress stories about mass sickness, terror, and violence. Then, at the peak of the epidemic, to counter further inflammatory rumors—for example, that people were being buried alive—Catherine authorized publication of an official account of the Moscow riots. Foreign newspapers picked up and circulated her version. Privately, however, she was dismayed by what was happening. To Voltaire, she gave her comment on Ambrosius's death: "The famous Eighteenth Century really has something to boast of here. See how far we have progressed!" To Alexander Bibikov, the former president of the Legislative Commission, she wrote, "We have spent a month in circumstances like those that Peter the Great lived under for thirty years. He broke through all difficulties with glory. We hope to come out of them with honor."

By mid-November 1772, the crisis was waning and Catherine allowed public prayers of thanksgiving. When Orlov returned to St. Petersburg on December 4, she covered him with honors. She had a gold medal struck with a likeness of a mythical Roman hero on one side and a likeness of Orlov on the other. The inscription was, "Russia also has such sons." She commissioned a triumphal arch in the park at Tsarskoe

Selo; on it was emblazoned: "To the hero who saved Moscow from the plague."

"Saved" was accurate only in the sense that the losses could have been greater. One contemporary estimate was that the plague had killed 55,000 people in Moscow, one-fifth of the city's population. Another estimate was that 100,000 had died in Moscow and 120,000 throughout the empire. To prevent a recurrence, quarantine was maintained along Russia's southern border for another two years, until the Turkish war ended in 1774.

❧56❧

The Return of "Peter the Third"

D URING THE LAST, climactic year of the war with Turkey (1773–74), another crisis, more threatening than the foreign war, arose inside Russia. This was the rebellion known as the Pugachevshchina, after its leader, the Don Cossack Emelyan Pugachev. In a single year, by uniting Cossacks, runaway serfs, peasants, Bashkirs, Kalmucks, and other discontented tribal groups and malcontents, Pugachev produced a storm of violence that swept across the steppes, at one point menacing Moscow itself. A civil war and a social revolution descended into anarchy, and the upheaval challenged many of Catherine's Enlightenment beliefs, leaving her with memories that haunted her for the rest of her life. Of palace revolutions she had experience. This upheaval, however, occurred in the vast, empty territories of Russia stretching far beyond St. Petersburg and Moscow—out on the Don, the Volga, and in the Urals. It awakened her to the passions seething in the countryside and brought her to the decision that her primary duty as empress was to enforce the authority of the crown. She did this by summoning soldiers, not philosophers.

Most Russians still lived in a world of oppression and discontent. There had been previous uprisings: mine workers had attacked their overseers; villagers had resisted tax collectors and recruiting levies. Pugachev's revolt, however, was the first mass explosion of what might be described as class war. Neither Catherine's *Nakaz* nor the discussions of the Legislative Commission had brought significant change; the serfs and peasants who worked on the land or labored in the mines still worked under a system of forced labor. The empress had tried to change this and had discovered that she could not. The unwieldy machinery of the imperial government, her dependence on the nobility, the vastness of Russia—all these were obstacles to change. In the end, she had been forced to leave things as they were. And then, in the fifth year of the war with Turkey, Russia exploded.

On October 5, 1773, Catherine attended a routine meeting of her war council in St. Petersburg. Presiding was General Count Zakhar Chernyshev, the handsome officer with whom Catherine had enjoyed a flirtation twenty-two years before, and whose military abilities had raised him to leadership of the College of War. Catherine listened closely as Chernyshev read reports from Orenburg, a garrison town three hundred miles southeast of Kazan, describing the appearance of a band of rebellious Cossacks. Restlessness among the Cossacks was not new in Russia, but this disturbance differed from its predecessors. It was led by a man who proclaimed that he was Tsar Peter III, Catherine's husband, miraculously saved from assassination. Now, riding across the southeastern borderlands of Russia, he was issuing incendiary manifestos, promising the people freedom once they had helped him regain his throne.

Cossacks traditionally were adventurers who resented the stream of imperial decrees that restricted their freedom. To escape, they had fled to the borderlands, where, over time, they established their own settlements, chose their own leaders, and lived in their own communities by their their own laws and customs. Some were Old Believers who had fled the reach of the traditional Orthodox Church and now prayed only in their own churches. The men were often splendid horsemen, who, once forcibly recruited into the army, were used as irregular cavalry and, as such, terrified Russia's enemies. The Polish and Turkish wars had brought even more frequent visits by government tax collectors and recruiting parties. By August 1773, the Cossack communities were simmering, needing only a leader to rise in protest. In such an atmosphere, no leader would seem better than a man rumored to be a tsar.

. . .

The appearance of impostors was not rare in Russia; the nation's turbulent history had often featured false tsars whom an uneducated, credulous population was only too ready to accept. In 1605, an adult impostor claiming to be Ivan the Terrible's son Dmitry (who had, in fact, died as a child), seized the throne from Tsar Boris Godunov. Stenka Razin, a Cossack, had defied Peter the Great's father, Tsar Alexis, for two years and, after capture and execution, became a legendary folk hero. Peter the Great himself, in the Great Northern War against Sweden, had been forced to deal with the defection of the Ukrainian Cossacks under hetman, Ivan Mazeppa. Following Peter's death in 1725, the uncertainties surrounding the Romanov succession produced a series of pretenders claiming to be Peter II or Ivan VI. During the first ten years of Catherine's reign, there had already been impostors claiming to be Peter III, all of whom had been arrested before they could make trouble. Catherine had no interest in them beyond a wariness that foreign powers might attempt to sponsor them. But the promises of these earlier impostors had been localized and specific. Their followers, usually few in number, were protesting against local government officials, not against the tsar or even against the nobility. What distinguished Pugachev's rebellion was that it was directed at the empress herself.

The seedbed of the revolt lay between the Don and Ural rivers, intersected by the Volga. It was an unsettled land, with rich grasses, dense forests, and fertile, black soil, watered by the three great rivers. On the west lived the Don Cossacks, who had gradually progressed from an undisciplined, itinerant life to a more organized and settled existence. Although still sending many recruits to the army, they had also developed agriculture and trading and had prospered. The Volga district farther east, with its mixed population of Russians and non-Christian tribes, was less organized and disciplined; in the 1770s, it was a land of trading posts, roaming adventurers, and vagabonds. And still farther east, where the Yaik River flowed west from the Ural Mountains, lay the true frontier, the province of Orenburg, a thinly settled area whose rivers teemed with fish, whose earth was studded with salt mines, and whose forests were a fruitful source of lumber and furs. The principal town, also named Orenburg, was a fortress and trading center standing at the junction of the Orel and Yaik rivers.

Here in Orenburg province, in the village of Yaitsk, Pugachev appeared in September 1773 and proclaimed that he was Tsar Peter III and that he had eluded the assassination plotted by his usurping wife. Now he had returned to regain his throne, punish his enemies, save Russia, and free his people. According to Pugachev, Catherine, aided by the nobility, had driven him from the throne and then tried to kill him because he was planning to liberate the serfs. Some believed his story; for years there had been a rumor that, after Peter III's decree releasing the nobility from compulsory service, his next intention was to liberate the serfs, and that the empress had prevented him. Some even said that his decree was already drawn up but then was suppressed by his wife when she usurped the throne. For those who accepted this story, Peter III, who in his brief reign had been enormously unpopular, now became a hero, while Catherine became his tyrannical wife.

Pugachev bore no resemblance to the tall, narrow-shouldered Peter III, who had spoken mostly German, who had been a parade ground soldier, and who had never seen a battle. This new "Peter" was short, stocky, and muscular; his matted black hair grew in a heavy fringe across his forehead; he had a short, bushy, black beard; he was missing a number of teeth. These physical dissimilarities did not disqualify him, however, because the real Peter III had reigned too short a time for most Russians to know what he looked like. The new Peter who roamed the countryside at the head of his army of Cossacks and tribesmen surrounded by bearded officers and waving banners was a charismatic figure, an experienced soldier who spoke of a bright future in which all Russians would be free. He had little difficulty attracting followers. For people in the southeastern provinces who had never seen a tsar, this short, robust, magnetic fellow with the black beard, crimson caftan, and fur cap satisfied their imagination.

In reality, Emelyan Pugachev was a Cossack born around 1742 in one of the Cossack communities on the lower Don. He owned a small farm, married a local woman, and had three children. He was drafted into the Russian army and served as one of the Cossack cavalrymen in Poland and again in Rumyantsev's army in the 1769 and 1770 campaigns against the Turks. In 1771, he deserted, was captured and flogged, and escaped. He made his way back to the eastern steppes, but not to his homeland and family on the Don. Instead, he moved toward the lower Volga, from one Old Believer community to another. In November 1772, he reached the river Yaik, hoping to find safety among the Yaik Cossacks.

During his wanderings, Pugachev acquired knowledge of the state of mind of the people of the lower Volga: it was a fierce antagonism to authority similar to his own. This shared hatred, added to his military experience, made him a figure around whom the Yaik Cossacks could rally. When he offered to lead discontented Cossacks against their local officials and other oppressors, they accepted. Their plans were postponed when Pugachev was identified, arrested, and taken to Kazan for interrogation. Within six months he escaped again, and in May 1773 he returned to Yaitsk. In September, when the local governor of Yaitsk learned where he was and moved to recapture him, Pugachev and the Cossack dissidents hastily proclaimed their revolt. It was at this point that Pugachev suddenly announced that he was Tsar Peter III.

He promised freedom from a harassing government and a return to the old way of life. He promised an end to the harassment of Cossack Old Believers. He promised "forgiveness of all previous crimes" and "freedom of the rivers from their sources to their mouths and the land and the grass on both sides, and the trees and wild animals that grew thereon." He promised free salt, arms, lead, powder, food, and a gift of twelve rubles a year to every Cossack. In an "imperial manifesto," distributed on September 17, 1773, he declared, "I give eternal freedom to you and your children and your grandchildren. You will no longer work for a lord and you will no longer pay taxes. We make you a gift of the cross and your ancient prayers, of the long hair and beard." He named specific enemies: "If God permits me to reach St. Petersburg," he said, "I shall put my wicked wife Catherine into a convent. Then I will free all the peasants and exterminate the nobles down to the last man."

The message carried beyond the Yaik Cossacks. The Bashkirs declared for him and were followed by the Kalmucks, the Kirghiz, and other seminomadic tribes of the lower Volga. Soon, agricultural serfs and peasants were setting out to join him. A few came on horseback carrying swords and lances, but most brought only farm tools—scythes, axes, and pitchforks. Before winter, the industrial serfs of the mines and foundries of the Urals were rallying to him.

Pugachev first attacked the small fort at Yaitsk, set on a high bank overlooking the Yaik River. He had only three hundred men, and the government commander had a thousand, but many of these soldiers were Cossacks. When they quickly deserted, the government commander retreated into the fort and abandoned the rest of the settlement to the rebels. Pugachev left him there and moved up the river. On October 5, he reached the larger town and government fortress at Orenburg. Pugachev's force now had grown to more than three thousand, outnumbering the garrison except in artillery. Again, the soldiers withdrew into the fortress, which was defended by seventy cannon; again, the rebels were not strong enough to take the fortification by storm. This time, Pugachev settled down to starve the defenders into surrender, and established his headquarters at Berda, three miles away.

By November, the impostor's large following was constantly augmented by the arrival of volunteers. Pugachev's appeals now reached across the area between the Volga, the Yaik, and western Siberia. In December, another thousand Bashkirs joined his army, and in January 1774, two thousand Tatars. Factory serfs and peasants seized the copper foundries and other metalworks in the Urals; soon forty-four foundries and mines were supplying guns and ammunition to the rebel army. There was one interesting exception to this mushrooming support: the Cossacks of the Don, from whom Pugachev came, were glaringly absent.

News of the revolt on the Yaik was slow to reach St. Petersburg. When it arrived, the empress and her advisers were unperturbed; it seemed a local affair, occurring in a perennially unstable region. Catherine and her war council were concentrating on Poland and the Danube, where Russia's armies were deeply committed and where, during the coming summer, they hoped to force an end to the Turkish war, now entering its sixth year. Because the army was straining to mount a fresh offensive, few regular troops could be spared. The best that could be managed was to send General Vasily Kar from Kazan with a small detachment of soldiers. In addition, to counter Pugachev's appeals, Catherine issued a manifesto for distribution only in the areas affected by the revolt; otherwise the troubles were to be kept secret. She denounced Pugachev's imposture as "this madness" and "this godless turmoil among the people" and called for cooperation with General Kar to defeat and capture "the chief brigand, incendiary and impostor." Unfortunately, she and her advisers had grossly underestimated the strength of the enemy Kar had been sent to face. On approaching Orenburg, Kar found the rebel army far more numerous than he had foreseen; moreover, they were being reinforced daily by new recruits. Led by Pugachev, they routed Kar's small force. When Kar escaped and returned to report what had happened, he was dismissed. Another small expedition was immediately dispatched from Simbirsk. Pugachev easily defeated this force and hanged its colonel.

In his Berda headquarters, Pugachev enjoyed playing the role of tsar. Dressed in a scarlet caftan, wearing a velvet cap, and holding a scepter in one hand and a silver axe in the other, he looked down at the supplicants kneeling before him. Unable to read or write, he kept a secretary at his side and dictated his orders, which were signed, "The great sovereign, the Russian Tsar, the Emperor Peter the Third." He would deign to write his name himself, he announced, when he had mounted his throne. Medals were struck with his likeness and inscribed "Peter III."

Every day, he ate heavily, drank continually, and bellowed Cossack songs with his comrades. Many of these men had now become "noblemen." Having sworn to exterminate the real nobility, Pugachev distributed titles among his close companions, naming them after the principal members of Catherine's court. There was a Count Panin, a Count Orlov, a Count Vorontsov, a Field Marshal Count Chernyshev. These newly created grandees were decorated with medals ripped from the tunics of dead officers. They were granted future estates on the Baltic coast; some were even presented with gifts of serfs. In February 1774, Pugachev, who had abandoned his wife and three children on the Don, "married" Yustina Kuznetsova, the daughter of a Yaik Cossack, and surrounded her with a dozen Cossack maids of honor. Prayers were said daily for the emperor and for Yustina, who was addressed and treated as "Her Imperial Majesty."

Pugachev's lieutenants were never in doubt that the man sitting next to them, claiming to be an emperor, was in fact an illiterate Cossack, and that his so-called empress was a Cossack girl from the Urals who was not his legal wife. His real wife was on the Don, and his other, supposed wife, the usurping Empress Catherine, was in St. Petersburg. For most of his brief "reign," both he and his intimate circle lived in overlapping worlds of reality and make-believe. No one complained about this amateur theater, and Pugachev profited from the unspoken agreement to mutual playacting. Believing that the growing momentum of the revolt permitted him everything, the illiterate Cossack could not stop himself.

His costumed make-believe was played against a backdrop of blood and terror. Pugachev's imperial decrees, proclaiming that the nobility must be killed, unleashed a frenzy of hatred. Peasants killed landlords, their families, and their hated overseers. Serfs who had always been considered resigned, submissive to God, the tsar, and the master, now flung themselves into orgies of cruelty. Noblemen were dragged from their hiding places, flayed, burned alive, hacked to pieces, or hanged from trees. Children were mutilated and slaughtered in front of their parents. Wives were spared only long enough to be raped in front of their husbands; then they had their throats cut or were thrown into carts and carried off as prizes. Before long, Pugachev's camp was filled with captured widows and daughters, who were distributed as booty among the rebels. Villagers who persisted in recognizing "the usurper, Catherine," were hanged in rows; nearby ravines were filled with bodies. Desperate townspeople, not knowing what their interrogators wished to hear, gave stock answers when asked whom they considered their lawful sovereign: "Whomever you represent," they replied.

As Pugachev's army, swelling to a torrent, moved down the long roads, flames from landlords' burning mansions glowed in the night, and smoke hung like curtains on the horizon. Towns and villages opened their gates to surrender. Priests hurried to meet and welcome the rebels with bread and salt. Officers of the tiny garrisons were hanged; the men were offered a choice: change sides or die.

At first, before Catherine realized the gravity of the uprising, she attempted to play down its importance in the eyes of western Europe. In January 1774, she wrote to Voltaire that "this impudent Pugachev" was merely "a common highway robber." She personally did not intend that Pugachev's antics should disturb the stimulating conversations she was having in St. Petersburg with her famous visitor Denis Diderot, editor of the *Encyclopedia*. Voltaire agreed that Catherine's dialogue with one of the leaders of the Enlightenment ought not to be interrupted by the "exploits of a brigand." She complained that the European press was making too much fuss over the "Marquis de Pugachev who is giving me a little trouble in the Urals." When she passed along the information that the impertinent fellow was actually claiming to be Peter III, Voltaire picked up her airy, dismissive tone, mentioning to d'Alembert "this new husband who has turned up in the province of Orenburg." But the "new husband" and "Cossack brigand" was giving Catherine more trouble than she admitted. By the spring of 1774, when Pugachev's army had grown to over fifteen thousand men, she understood that a local Cossack revolt was becoming a national revolution. After General Kar failed to capture the "miscreant," and the besieged governor of Orenburg reported severe shortages of food and ammunition, she confessed to Voltaire that "for more than six weeks I have been obliged to devote my uninterrupted attention to this affair."

Determined to crush the rebels, Catherine summoned the experienced General Alexander Bibikov and gave him full power over all military and civilian authorities in southeastern Russia. Bibikov was a veteran of the wars in Prussia and Poland, and had acquired national prestige as president-marshal of the Legislative Commission. Although the Turkish war still prevented the withdrawal of any significant part of the regular army, Bibikov was assigned as many troops as could be found. He arrived in Kazan on December 26, made it his headquarters, and took immediate steps to stabilize the situation. Nobles were persuaded to form a volunteer militia, arming peasants they considered loyal. Catherine had also ordered Bibikov to establish in Kazan a commission of inquiry to investigate the source of the revolt by "this motley crowd which is moved only by seething fanaticism or by political inspiration and darkness." It was to interrogate captured rebels to ascertain whether any foreign influence was at work. Was Turkey implicated? France? What or who had prompted Pugachev to assume the name of Peter III? Were there any traces of conspiracy involving her own subjects? What were his connections with the Old Believers? With disgruntled nobles? Bibikov was instructed not to use torture. "What need is there to flog during investigations?" she wrote to him. "For twelve years the Secret Branch under my own eyes has not flogged a single person during interrogations, and yet every single affair has been properly sorted out, and always more came out than we needed to know." If guilt was established, Bibikov was empowered to execute death sentences, although in cases of nobles or officials found guilty, his judgments were to be referred to the empress for confirmation.

Before sending Bibikov on his mission, Catherine had issued another manifesto, for use only in the region of the rebellion:

> A deserter and fugitive has been collecting . . . a troop of vagabonds like himself . . . and has had the insolence to arrogate to himself the name of the late emperor Peter III. . . . As we watch with indefatigable care over the tranquility of our faithful subjects . . . we have taken such measures to annihilate totally the ambitious designs of Pugachev and to exterminate a band of robbers who have been audacious enough to attack the small military detachments dispersed about these countries, and to massacre the officers who have been taken prisoner.

Two weeks later, after reports confirmed the expansion of the revolt, Catherine decided that the rebellion could no longer be concealed from the public. To explain her decision, she wrote to the governor of the Novgorod region:

> Orenburg has already been besieged two full months by the crowd of a bandit who is committing frightful cruelties and ravages. General Bibikov is departing there with troops who will pass through your *gubernia* in order to curb this distemper which will bring neither glory nor profit to Russia. I hope, however, that with God's aid, we shall prevail. This riffraff is a rabble of miscreants who have at their head a deceiver as brazen as he is ignorant. Probably it will all end on the gallows; but what sort of expectation is that for me who has no love for the gallows? European opinion will relegate us to the time of Tsar Ivan the Terrible. That is the honor we must expect from this contemptible escapade.

On arriving in Kazan at the end of December, Bibikov found the situation more serious than anyone in St. Petersburg realized. His assessment was that, as an individual, Pugachev was not to be feared, but that as a symbol of widespread, popular discontent, he mattered very much. Bibikov's forces struck quickly to relieve Orenburg, which had been under siege for six months and where the shortage of food was acute. Pugachev made a stand with nine thousand men and thirty-six cannon, but the battle was decided by the professionally served artillery of the regular army. Pugachev was routed, four thousand of his men were captured, and "Peter III" galloped away to Berda. The siege of Orenburg was over.

In Pugachev's headquarters in Berda, his lieutenants and camp followers were ready to flee, but all knew that only those with horses would be able to escape. "Leave the peasants to their fate," became the rationale. "The common people are not fighters; they are just sheep." On March 23, Pugachev left his headquarters in Berda, taking with him two thousand men and abandoning the rest of his army. Bibikov's advance guard entered Berda the same day. The scale was balanced, however, when Bibikov, the architect of victory, suddenly developed fever and died. Catherine, saddened, assumed that his subordinate officers would complete his mission. Pugachev disappeared into the Urals.

Before he died Bibikov had assured Catherine that "the suspicion of foreigners is completely unfounded." The empress then wrote to Voltaire attributing "this freakish event" to the fact that the Orenburg region "is inhabited by all the good-for-nothings of whom Russia has thought fit to rid herself over the past forty years, rather in the same spirit that the American colonies have been populated." She defended her policy of leniency in the treatment of rebel prisoners by writing her friend Frau Bielcke of Hamburg, who had complained that the measures taken had not been sufficiently severe: "Since you like hangings so much, I can tell you that four or five unfortunates have already been hanged. And the rarity of such punishments has a thousand times more effect on us here than on those where hangings happen every day."

Catherine believed that the rebellion was over. For the next three months she turned her attention away from Pugachev and back to the Russian offensive on the Danube. She continued to follow the investigation into the causes of the upheaval. A commission report issued on May 21, 1774, restated Bibikov's earlier assessment, discounting the possibility of domestic conspiracy or foreign meddling. The revolt was blamed on Pugachev's exploitation of discontent among the Yaik Cossacks, the tribal peoples, and the serfs assigned to the Urals metalworks. Pugachev was depicted as crude and uneducated, but the investigators cautioned that he was also crafty, resourceful, and persuasive—a dangerous man who should not be ignored or forgotten until he was dead or delivered in chains into the hands of imperial officers.

❧ 57 ❧

The Last Days of the "Marquis de Pugachev"

B Y THE TIME Catherine read the Secret Commission report, at the end of May 1774, she considered it a kind of postmortem on the Pugachev revolt. Then, to her astonishment, on July 11, Pugachev appeared before the town of Kazan on the Volga at the head of an army of twenty thousand men. The following day he stormed, captured, and burned the almost defenseless town. His next objective, he announced, was Moscow. Already he had promised, "If God gives me power over the state, and when I have captured Moscow, I will order everyone to follow the Old Belief and to wear Russian clothes. I will forbid the shaving of the beard, and will have hair cut in Cossack fashion."

Kazan, with its ethnically diverse population of eleven thousand, had fascinated Catherine during her visit in July 1768. Now, Pugachev's attack had quickly overwhelmed the town's outnumbered defenders, and his men reduced the city, built mostly of wood, to ruins by fire. A maelstrom of killing, raping, and looting accompanied the flames. Unbearded men in European dress were instantly killed; women in foreign dress were dragged away to Pugachev's camp. Two-thirds of Kazan's twenty-nine hundred buildings were destroyed. Nobles and their families who could get away fled to Moscow.

The old capital began to prepare its defenses, but Pugachev did not come. A Russian army, already hurrying to Kazan, arrived too late to save the town, but on July 15, it struck and defeated Pugachev. The following day, the false tsar reappeared with fifteen thousand men. In a four-hour battle, the rebel army was routed; two thousand died, and five thousand were taken prisoner. After the battle, ten thousand men and women held captive in Pugachev's camp were freed. The pretender with the remnants of his army fled to the south, down the Volga.

The taking and burning of Kazan was the high-water mark of Pugachev's revolt. Had he not been defeated there, he might have marched on Moscow, carrying the revolt into the heart of serf-owning Russia. Immediately afterward, the impostor learned about the Russian-Turkish peace treaty and realized that regular troops would now be available to the government, By August, a veteran Russian army under General Vasily Suvorov, released from the Danube campaign, was advancing in his direction. Pugachev's men, demoralized by defeat and retreat, began to worry about the consequences of their rebellion. In increasing numbers, they began to desert.

Pugachev was now entering an area populated by small landowners possessing few serfs. Attempting to raise a new army, he called on these serfs to rise against their masters, promising liberty to "be forever Cossacks, free from taxes, levies, recruiting, evil landowners, and corrupt judges." Some serfs slipped away from their owners, but their number was dropping; the revolt was faltering, losing energy and purpose. In turning south, Pugachev was returning to his childhood home, the land of the Don Cossacks. But few impostors can be successful among people with whom they have been raised. "Why does he call himself Tsar Peter?" the Don Cossacks asked. "He is Emelyan Pugachev, the farmer, who deserted his wife Sophia and his children."

After Pugachev's sudden reappearance before Kazan, Catherine knew that the government had relaxed too soon. At a council session on July 14, she had declared that Rumyantsev's victories on the Danube had brought Russia close to peace. And then, on July 21, news of the destruction of Kazan had reached St. Petersburg, two days before Rumyantsev's son arrived with news of peace with the Turks. That morning as Catherine convened her council, she did not know either about Pugachev's defeat after his sacking of Kazan or that a peace had been reached with Turkey. "Extremely shaken" by the news from Kazan, she interrupted the council's discussion and announced that she intended to leave for Moscow immediately to restore confidence. Her councillors were silent until Nikita Panin spoke up, saying that her unexpected arrival might alarm rather than calm the people. It was decided that Panin's younger brother, General Peter Panin, the most experienced general available, then in retirement near Moscow, would be appointed to assume command against Pugachev.

Catherine approved this choice reluctantly. She recognized Peter Panin's military abilities, but she disliked him personally. He had often declared that Russia should be ruled by a man; his preference was Grand Duke Paul. Catherine also worried about his reputation as a military martinet and about his unconventional personal behavior: he sometimes appeared in his headquarters wearing a gray satin night-gown and a large French nightcap with pink ribbons. She had been annoyed by the histrionic nature of his abrupt retirement, taken because he felt inadequately rewarded for his successes in the Turkish war. By the fall of 1773, she had authorized surveillance of "the insolent wind-bag." Now, facing the need to appoint Peter Panin, she confessed to her new admirer Gregory Potemkin: "Before the whole world, frightened of Pugachev, I commend and elevate above all mortals in the empire a prime big-mouth who insults me personally." Nevertheless, Catherine the empress took precedence over Catherine the affronted woman, and on July 22, Peter Panin was appointed general in chief. The following day, July 23, news of the peace treaty with Turkey reached St. Petersburg. Catherine was doubly pleased: the territorial gains of the Treaty of Kuchuk Kainardzhi were substantial, and her army would now be free to confront Pugachev.

Peter Panin demanded authority over all military forces assigned to deal with the revolt and over all officials and people in the affected areas. To Potemkin, Catherine continued, "You see, my friend, that Count [Nikita] Panin wants to make his brother the ruler with unlimited powers in the best part of the empire. If I sign this, not only will Prince Volkonsky [the governor-general of Moscow] be offended and made to look silly, but I myself will be seen publicly to be praising a man who is a first class liar and who has personally offended me."

Catherine did not completely surrender to Peter Panin. Buoyed by her sweeping victory over the Turks and by Pugachev's defeat at Kazan, she restricted his authority to the regions directly affected and declared that the Investigating Commission would remain under her direct personal supervision. Panin was further circumscribed by being given Suvorov as his second in command. Panin, like Bibikov, was encouraged to enlist the nobility in the rebellious provinces. As their reward, all privileges of the aristocracy, including absolute power over their serfs, were guaranteed by the crown. This approach produced results: the noblemen mustered men, money, and supplies of food.

In the field, Panin's methods of retribution were only marginally less cruel than those of Pugachev. Earlier, under Bibikov, the army had dealt leniently with captured rebels. After the relief of Orenburg, the vast majority of Pugachev's followers taken prisoner had been released with a safe conduct pass and told to go home. Most of the prisoners captured in the battles outside Kazan were released with fifteen kopecks travel money. Now, as the revolt entered the final phase with Pugachev's destructive move down the Volga, Panin imposed fierce reprisals. On August 24, he issued a proclamation threatening all who had taken part in the revolt with death by quartering. Panin knew that he was exceeding the authority granted him by Catherine, but she was far away and he ignored her.

Catherine spent August at Tsarskoe Selo anxiously following Pugachev's rampage down the Volga. By the end of the month she told Voltaire that she was expecting "something decisive," because for ten days she had not heard from Panin, and since "bad news travels faster than good, I am hoping for something good." As Suvorov's veterans advanced, Pugachev's army began melting away. Yet even near the end he inspired fear. On July 26, in Saransk, he dined in the house of the governor's widow and then hanged her outside her window. Nobles were hanged upside down in groups with their heads, hands, and feet cut off. On August 1, horsemen announced in the marketplace of Penza that "Peter III" was coming and that if he were not welcomed with the traditional bread and salt, everyone in the town, including babies, would be slaughtered. He came, was welcomed, two hundred men were forcibly recruited, and the governor's house was burned down with the governor and twenty of the gentry locked inside. In another town, a resident astronomer was hanged so that he might be "nearer the stars."

Pugachev's attempts to recruit among his fellow Don Cossacks were mostly ignored. Everyone knew that a reward of twenty thousand rubles had been posted for his capture and that veteran government troops were approaching. Many also knew that Pugachev was not Peter III. When he appeared on August 21 before Tsaritsyn (later Stalingrad, now Volgograd), riding forward to talk to a group of Don Cossack leaders, he was publicly recognized and denounced as an impostor. Two days later, on August 24, he suffered final defeat at Sarepta, south of Tsaritsyn. The defeat became a rout. Pugachev escaped by swimming the Volga with thirty followers. But defeat, fear, and hunger were sapping the loyalty of everyone around him.

On September 15, 1774, almost exactly a year after he had launched his revolt, Pugachev was back where he had begun: at Yaitsk on the Yaik River. There, a group of frightened lieutenants, hoping to save themselves by betrayal, fell on their sleeping chief. "How dare you raise your hands against your emperor?" he shouted. "You will achieve nothing." Unmoved, they delivered him in chains to Peter Panin.

On September 30, Panin wrote to Catherine that he had seen the "infernal monster." Pugachev had made no attempt to sustain his imposture. He fell on his knees, declared that he was Emelyan Pugachev, and admitted that, in parading himself as Peter III, he had sinned before God and Her Imperial Majesty. He was placed inside an iron cage not large enough to allow him to stand, and the cage was bolted onto a two-wheeled cart. In this manner, he was trundled for hundreds of miles to Moscow, through towns and villages where he had been hailed as a liberating hero.

On November 4, 1774, Pugachev and his rolling cage arrived in Moscow. Six weeks of interrogation began. The empress was resolved to satisfy her doubts about the rebellion; she still could not believe that an illiterate Cossack had instigated the revolt on his own. Voltaire lightheartedly proposed that Pugachev be asked, "Sir, are you master or servant? I do not ask who employs you but simply whether you are employed." Catherine wanted more: if there were employers, she wished to know their identities. Catherine carefully monitored the proceedings, but despite the intensity of her curiosity, she refused to allow the use of the rack. Before the investigation began, she had written to Prince Volkonsky, governor-general of Moscow, "For God's sake, refrain from all questioning under torture which always obscures the truth." Behind this command was not only her opposition to barbarism but also political calculation. The rebellion appeared to have spent itself, but that had also seemed the case before the surprise assault on Kazan. Perhaps, even now, there might be another leader waiting to revive the rebellion. Torture of the man whom many peasants had believed was a tsar could provide another spark. Although she was intrigued by the impostor's character and motives, she had no desire to see him. She was already planning a lengthy visit to Moscow to celebrate the peace with Turkey, and she wished the whole Pugachev business to be finished before she arrived. As for foreign influence, even before the interrogators were finished Catherine concluded that there was none. To Voltaire she wrote, "The Marquis de Pugachev has lived like a scoundrel and will die like a coward. He cannot read or write, but he is a bold and determined man. So far there is not a shred of evidence that he was the instrument of any foreign power. It is to be supposed that Monsieur Pugachev is a master brigand and no man's servant. No one since Tamerlane has done more harm than he."

On December 5, the work of the interrogating commission was completed. Pugachev had confessed and expressed hope for mercy, but a death sentence was inevitable. Nevertheless, Catherine wrote to Voltaire, "If it were only me he had harmed, his hopes could be justified and I should pardon him, but this trial involves the empire and its laws." To dissociate herself publicly from the trial and execution, she privately sent Procurator General Vyazemsky to Moscow with instructions to end the affair quickly. She followed by writing to the Moscow governor, Prince Volkonsky: "Please help to inspire everyone with moderation both in the number and in the punishment of the criminals. The opposite will be regrettable to my love for humanity. We do not have to be clever to deal with barbarians."

Vyazemsky did his best to obey. To avoid public pressure in the vengeful atmosphere of Moscow, he established a special court made up of high officials and members of the Holy Synod. The trial was conducted secretly in the Kremlin on December 30 and 31. Pugachev was brought before the court on the second day. He fell on his knees, admitted again that he was Emelyan Pugachev, acknowledged his crimes, and declared that he repented before God and the all-merciful empress. When he was led away, the judges decided that he should be quartered alive and then beheaded. But when the same sentence was awarded to one of his lieutenants, several judges protested that the sentence on Pugachev should be more severe and painful than that on others. "So they wanted to break Pugachev on the wheel," Vyazemsky wrote to Catherine, "in order to distinguish him from the rest." Eventually, the procurator general persuaded the court to leave Pugachev's sentence as it was. Knowing that the empress would never accept the public spectacle of Pugachev being quartered alive, Vyazemsky secretly arranged with Moscow's chief of police to have the executioner "accidentally" behead Pugachev first and afterward chop off his hands and feet. The execution took place before an immense crowd in a Moscow square on January 10, 1775. Pugachev crossed himself and laid his head on the block. Then, to the indignant rage of spectators who included noblemen come to savor their revenge, the executioner seemed to bungle his job by immediately decapitating Pugachev; many were convinced that either the executioner was incompetent or that he had been bribed by someone. Four of Pugachev's lieutenants were quartered first, then beheaded. The lieutenants who had betrayed and handed over their chief were pardoned.

A few days after Pugachev's death, Catherine departed for Moscow to celebrate Russia's victory over Turkey. While there, she also began obliterating all traces of the internal revolt. Pugachev's two wives and three children were incarcerated in the fort of Kexholm in Russian Finland. Pugachev's house on the Don was razed. It was forbidden to speak his name, and his brother, who had not participated in the revolt, was ordered to stop using the family name. The Yaik Cossacks were renamed the Ural Cossacks, and Yaitsk, their capital, and the river flowing past it were renamed Uralsk and Ural, respectively. On March 17, 1775, the empress issued a general amnesty to all involved "in the internal mutiny, uprising, unrest, and disarray of the years 1773 and 1774," consigning "all that has passed to eternal oblivion and profound silence." All sentences of death were commuted to hard labor; lesser sentences were reduced to exile in Siberia; deserters from the army and fugitive state peasants were pardoned. Peter Panin was thanked, and allowed to withdraw and sulk in Moscow for the rest of his life.

In the countryside, few among the nobility shared Catherine's belief in restraint. In reprisal for the massacre of their families and friends, the landowners were determined to exact revenge. Once order was reestablished by the army, the landowners were pitiless. Serfs thought to be guilty were condemned to death without trial. With few exceptions, property owners gave no thought to ameliorating the conditions which had driven the peasantry to its fearful rampage.

The *Pugachevshchina* (time of Pugachev) was the greatest of all violent internal Russian upheavals. One hundred and thirty-four years later, the 1905 Revolution produced nationwide strikes, urban violence, Bloody Sunday in St. Petersburg, the arrival of the mutinous battleship *Potemkin* in Odessa harbor, the storming of barricades in Moscow—and eventually the granting of a parliamentary Duma, which had the right to speak but not to act. The Russian Revolution of 1917, measured in terms of violence, was no more than a peaceful coup d'état, removing from power the Duma ministers who had replaced the abdicated Tsar Nicholas II.

Pugachev's revolt was also the most serious challenge to Catherine's authority during her reign. She took no pride in the defeat of Pugachev and his execution. She was aware that many in Russia and Europe considered her responsible—some for what she had done, others for what she had not done. She noted their criticism, moved on, and never turned back. She never forgot, however, that, after she had reigned for eleven years, her people, whose lives she had hoped to better, had risen against her and rallied to "Peter III." Nor did she forget that, once again, her supporters had been the nobility. There would be no further talk of eliminating serfdom. Landowners were encouraged to treat their serfs and peasants humanely, but the empress now was convinced that enlightenment could not be bestowed on a nation of illiterates until the people had been prepared by education. The *Nakaz,* which embodied the principles of the Enlightenment and the ideals and aspirations of her youth, became no more than a memory. After Pugachev, she concentrated on what she believed to be Russian interests within her power to change: the expansion of her empire and the enrichment of its culture.

PART VI
Potemkin and Favoritism

❧58❧

Vasilchikov

FOR ELEVEN YEARS, from 1761 to 1772, Catherine had been faithful to Gregory Orlov. She was fiercely proud of him, often praising his bravery, generosity, and loyalty to her and the crown. Although his achievements were not balanced by sparkling intelligence and his character defects included selfishness, conceit, and indolence, he still had exhibited the courage and masculine charm that had originally attracted her. Having failed to persuade her to marry him, and finding himself unable to dominate her, he found other women. Catherine suffered but looked away. In 1771, he had rehabilitated himself by his heroic behavior during the Moscow plague. Impressed, she gave him another assignment intended to enhance his prestige. The battlefield stalemate in southern Russia had led to an attempt to negotiate peace with the Turks. Catherine appointed Gregory to be Russia's chief negotiator, and, in March 1772, he left for the Danube. As he departed, she wrote to Frau Bielcke in Hamburg, "He must appear to the Turks as an angel of peace in all his great beauty." In the peace talks, however, his egotistical clumsiness brought him down. He insisted that Russian demands be treated as those of a conqueror and stuck to this position with such arrogance that the offended Turkish emissaries suspended negotiations. Before this denouement, his position in St. Petersburg had already collapsed. On the day he departed for the south, Catherine was told that her "angel" had begun another affair. Orlov's reign had lasted thirteen years and she had forgiven him much—this was too much. Weary of this recurring behavior, Catherine made up her mind to end the relationship. She did not bring herself to this rupture easily, but once decided, she resolved to do it in a way that would make reconciliation impossible. She waited until he was far away.

Nikita Panin, no friend of the Orlovs and seeing the empress oscillating between rage and despair, pushed forward a replacement for Orlov, a twenty-eight-year-old Horse Guards officer, Alexander Vasilchikov. Catherine admitted, "I cannot live one day without love," but it was hardly a question of love with this candidate. Alexander Vasilchikov appeared innocuous. He came from an old noble family; he was modest and sweet-tempered; his manners were polished; he spoke perfect French. Dining at court, Catherine noticed these qualities, along with his handsome face and beautiful black eyes. The Prussian minister noted the empress's good humor in the young man's presence and the corresponding nervousness of Orlov's relatives. When Vasilchikov was presented with a gold snuffbox, his reluctance to accept intensified the donor's desire to give him more. By August, he had become a gentleman-in-waiting; by September, a court chamberlain. Then, suddenly, the young man was installed in Orlov's apartment in the Winter Palace, his rooms linked to Catherine's apartment by the private stairway. He was appointed adjutant general and given a hundred thousand rubles, along with an annual salary of twelve thousand rubles; and jewels, a new wardrobe, servants, and a country estate. This remarkable ascent astonished the court, tempered by the widespread belief that once Orlov returned, Vasilchikov would not last a week.

Gregory was still waiting for negotiations to resume in the Balkans when he received an urgent message from his brother Alexis, in St. Petersburg: the empress had taken a new lover, a young Guards officer, described by Alexis as "good looking, amiable, and a complete nonentity." Russia's chief delegate abandoned the peace talks immediately and rushed back to St. Petersburg. On the city's outskirts, he was abruptly halted; on Catherine's orders he was instructed to retire to his estate at Gatchina. The pretext was that because of plague the previous year, all travelers from the south were required to pass through a period of quarantine before entering the capital. The truth was that Catherine was afraid of Gregory. She had new locks put on her doors and surrounded her apartment with loyal soldiers. Even with this added security, the slightest noise made her imagine that Orlov was coming, and she was always ready to flee. "You don't know him," she said. "He is capable of killing me and the Grand Duke Paul."

From Gatchina, Gregory begged to see her. She refused but sent him messages, telling him that he must be reasonable, must go away and travel for his health. Gregory retorted that he had never felt better. She asked him to send back the jeweled miniature portrait of her which he had worn over his heart. He refused to send the portrait but returned the diamonds from the frame.

After four weeks in "quarantine," Orlov suddenly reappeared in society, behaving as though nothing had happened. He pretended not to notice that Vasilchikov was attending to duties that had been his; he even indulged in his own brand of humor by making friends with the new favorite, praising him loudly and joking about himself. It was Vasilchikov who blushed with embarrassment when, at night in the presence of the entire court, including Orlov, the empress gave him her arm to escort her to her apartment. No one knew how to react. Before long, Orlov realized that the pretty-faced "nonentity" had triumphed. He knew that Catherine was not in love; that she had taken this young man for the same reason he collected mistresses: a need for a companion who would be always available and submissive. Realizing that his own position was becoming ridiculous, he requested permission to travel. Catherine agreed without uttering a word of recrimination. Indeed, before he left, Orlov allowed himself to be awarded a trove of additional rubles and was given the right to use the title of Prince of the Holy Roman Empire.

Gregory Orlov's departure brought peace to court, but for Catherine it was a peace paid for with boredom. Vasilchikov was handsome, but his intellect and personality were so limited as to make conversation impossible. Catherine, wearied by a day of administering her empire, wanted to be intellectually stimulated, amused, and distracted in her hours of relaxation. Vasilchikov had none of these skills, and she soon realized that she had linked herself to a bore incapable of saying anything interesting or funny. He did his best. He was attentive, dutiful, well meaning, and decorative. Nothing helped; she found him increasingly, and then unendurably, boring. Later favorites, picked out by the empress for their physical appearance, had to be acclaimed for their superior mental qualities—or, at least, for the speed with which they were learning. Vasilchikov possessed neither these aptitudes nor prospects. The twenty-two months of his tenure as favorite witnessed some of the most traumatic, challenging, anxiety-producing events of Catherine's reign: the partition of Poland, war with Turkey, the Pugachev rebellion. She needed someone to talk to who could offer support and consolation, if not useful political or military advice. That Vasilchikov was unable to provide anything of this kind was obvious to everyone.

Thus Vasilchikov, not Orlov, had turned out to be the primary victim of this boudoir upheaval, and no one knew better than the wretched favorite himself. He was sufficiently sensitive to realize that he bored his mistress and that he was viewed as only a stopgap. His shy, sweet temper, which had been one of his assets, turned peevish and sour. His description of his life with the empress is the wail of an abandoned child:

> I was nothing more to her than a kind of male *cocotte,* and was treated as such. I was not allowed to receive guests or go out. If I made a request for myself or anyone else, she did not reply. When I wished to have the Order of St. Anne, I spoke to the empress about it. The next day I found a thirty thousand ruble banknote in my pocket. In this way, she always stopped my mouth and sent me to my room. She never condescended to discuss with me any matters that lay close to my heart.

Catherine kept him on because, having made the unfortunate choice of this obscure young guardsman, she thought it would be cruel to dismiss him for faults for which he was not responsible. Finally, however, when she could endure him no longer, she wrote to Potemkin, "Tell Panin that he must send Vasilchikov away somewhere for a cure. I feel suffocated by him and he complains of pains in his chest. Later he could be appointed envoy somewhere as ambassador—somewhere where there is not too much work to do. He is a bore. I burned my fingers and I shall never do it again."

Although Vasilchikov's performance in the role of favorite was probably the weakest of any of Catherine's lovers, she accepted most of the blame. He was a sudden replacement, installed when she was angry at the frequently and flagrantly unfaithful Gregory. "It was a random choice," she admitted later, "made out of desperation. I was more heartbroken at that time than I can say."

The hapless Vasilchikov departed, generously pensioned for his efforts and good intentions. He retired to a large country estate near Moscow—a gift from the empress. Over the years, he aged into a quiet country gentleman, ignored and mostly forgotten by his sovereign.

Once he had gone, she replaced mediocrity with genius and boredom with intellectual fireworks. She sent for Potemkin.

❧59❧

Catherine and Potemkin: Passion

THE OUTSTANDING FIGURE of Catherine's reign, other than Catherine herself, was Gregory Potemkin. For seventeen years, from 1774 to 1791, he was the most powerful man in Russia. No one else during her life was closer to Catherine; he was her lover, her adviser, her military commander in chief, the governor and viceroy of half of her empire, the creator of her new cities, seaports, palaces, armies, and fleets. He was also, perhaps, her husband.

Gregory Potemkin's family had served Russian sovereigns for generations. His seventeenth-century ancestor Peter Potemkin had been sent by Tsar Alexis, the father of Peter the Great, on diplomatic missions to Spain and France. Determined to uphold the rank and dignity of his master, he demanded in Madrid that the king of Spain take off his hat whenever the tsar's name was mentioned. In Paris, he refused to speak to the Sun King, Louis XIV, because an error had been made in the tsar's titles. Later, in Copenhagen, he was received by the king of Denmark, who was ill and confined to bed. The envoy demanded that another bed be brought and placed next to the king so that he could negotiate from a position of absolute equality. This Potemkin, Gregory's grandfather, died in 1700 at the age of eighty-three, demanding and eccentric to the end.

Gregory Potemkin's father, Alexander Potemkin, was not dissimilar. As a young man in 1709, he fought in the Battle of Poltava against Charles XII of Sweden. Retired as a colonel to a small estate near Smolensk, Alexander Potemkin, while traveling, met an attractive, indigent young widow, Daria Skouratova. He was fifty and she was twenty, but he married her on the spot, forgetting to tell her that he already had a wife. Daria was pregnant before she discovered that she was married to a bigamist. She reacted by going to Potemkin's first wife and asking for guidance. The older woman, whose life with her husband was unhappy, resolved the situation by entering a convent, in effect divorcing the colonel. Daria got along with her new husband no better than had her predecessor, but she eventually produced six children, five daughters and a son, Gregory.

The boy was born on September 13, 1739, and began life surrounded and coddled by a loving mother and five sisters. The family was unable to afford a tutor, and Gregory began his education with the village deacon. The pupil loved music, and the deacon had an exceptional voice; he enforced discipline on his precocious, obstreperous student by threatening to sing him no more songs. At five, Gregory was sent to live with his godfather, a senior civil servant in Moscow. With an ear for languages as well as music, he learned Greek, Latin, French, and German. As an adolescent, he was drawn to theology, but also to the army; whichever career he chose, he said, he wished to command. "If I become a general," he declared to his friends, "I will have soldiers under my orders. If I become a bishop, it will be monks." When he entered the recently founded University of Moscow, he won a gold medal for studies in theology. Then, losing interest, he refused to attend lectures and was expelled. He entered the army as a private in the Horse Guards, became a corporal, and, by 1759, a captain. In 1762, he joined the five Orlov brothers and Nikita Panin in the coup that put Catherine on the throne. It was during this tumult that he supplied the missing sword knot that Catherine borrowed for the march on Peterhof. Subsequently, when Catherine was distributing rewards for assistance in the coup, Captain Potemkin was given an army promotion and ten thousand rubles.

At twenty-two, Potemkin was tall and slim, with thick auburn hair. He was intelligent, educated, and spirited. His appearance at court and his introduction to Catherine were sponsored by the Orlovs, who admired the young soldier as an engaging conversationalist and a talented mimic who successfully impersonated the voices of people around him. One evening, Catherine asked him to mimic her. Without hesitation, he spoke to her in her own voice, perfectly imitating her idiom and German accent. Catherine, always seeking wit and humor, could not stop laughing. The impertinence was risky, but Potemkin had guessed that the empress would be amused and would forgive and probably not forget him. He had judged her correctly. Thereafter, he was often invited to her intimate evenings, which included no more than twenty people and from which all ceremony and formality were banned. She decreed that her guests must be good-humored and not speak badly of anyone. Lying and boasting were forbidden, and all unpleasant thoughts were to be deposited with hats and swords at the door. In this uninhibited atmosphere, Gregory—quick-witted, artistic, musical, and able to make the empress laugh—was always welcome.

Others at court noticed that a strong mutual admiration was developing, and there was gossip. It was said that Potemkin, encountering the empress in a palace corridor, had fallen on his knees, kissed her hand, and not been reprimanded. The Orlovs did not like these stories. Gregory was the established favorite and the father of her child, Bobrinsky; he and his brothers had been endowed with enormous power and wealth. It seemed to them that Potemkin had begun to trespass. By some accounts, Potemkin was called to Gregory Orlov's room, where, to teach him a lesson, the two brothers, Gregory and Alexis, fell on him and beat him. Later, it was rumored that it was in this struggle that Potemkin lost the sight in his left eye (a more believable explanation is that he was permanently blinded because of faulty treatment of an infection by an incompetent doctor). Whatever the cause, this disfigurement so upset Potemkin that he withdrew from court. When the empress asked about him and was told that he was suffering from a physical disfigurement, she sent word that this was a poor reason and that he should return. He obeyed.

Catherine began making use of Potemkin's administrative talents in 1763, when, aware of his interest in religion, she appointed him assistant to the Procurator of the Holy Synod, who oversaw church administration and finances. She simultaneously advanced his military career, and, by 1767, he was a senior commander in the Horse Guards Regiment. The following year, he became a court chamberlain. When the Legislative Commission met, he was assigned to be trustee of the Tartars and other ethnic minorities in the Russian empire. Thereafter, Potemkin always had a special interest in Catherine's non-Russian subjects; in later years, holding supreme power in the south, his entourage always included tribal leaders of all faiths. His early love of ecclesiastical controversy continued. He rarely missed an opportunity to discuss points of religious belief with leaders of all faiths. When the First Turkish War began, in 1769, he immediately volunteered for the front. With Catherine's permission, he joined the army of General Rumyantsev, in which he served first as Rumyantsev's aide-de-camp and then as an outstanding leader of cavalry. In recognition of his services, he was promoted to the rank of major general and chosen in November 1769 to carry Rumyantsev's campaign reports to the empress. In St. Petersburg, Potemkin was received as a prominent commander and invited to dine with the empress.

When he returned to the army in the south, it was with Catherine's permission to write to her privately. She was surprised that he was slow to use this privilege. On December 4, 1773, she prompted him:

> Sir Lieutenant General and Chevalier: I suppose you have your eyes so thoroughly trained on Silestra [a Turkish fortress on the Danube under siege by the Russian army] that you haven't time to read letters. . . . Nonetheless I am certain that everything you undertake can be ascribed to nothing but your ardent zeal toward me personally and toward the dear fatherland which you love to serve. But since I very much desire to preserve fervent, brave, clever, and skillful individuals, so I ask you not endanger yourself. . . . Upon reading this letter you may well ask: why was it written? To which I can offer the following
> . reply: so that you had confirmation of my opinion of you, for I am always most benevolent toward you. Catherine.

Potemkin could hardly fail to see an invitation in this language. In January 1774, once the army was in winter quarters, he took leave and hurried to St. Petersburg.

He arrived to find the government and Catherine struggling with multiple crises. The war with Turkey was entering its sixth year, the Pugachev rebellion was spreading, and Catherine's intimate relationship with Alexander Vasilchikov was in its final stage. Potemkin, believing he had been summoned for personal reasons, was dismayed to find Vasilchikov still firmly embedded. He asked for a private audience with Catherine, and on February 4 he went to Tsarskoe Selo. She told him that she wanted him to remain close. He returned to court, where he seemed happy; he continued to make Catherine laugh, and he was generally recognized as the heir presumptive to the office of favorite. One day, supposedly, he was walking up the palace staircase when he met Gregory Orlov descending. "Any news at court?" Potemkin asked. "Nothing in particular," Orlov answered. "Except that you are going up and I am coming down." Vasilchikov managed for a few more weeks to cling to his perch because Catherine worried about the impression a change would make in St. Petersburg and abroad; she was also afraid of alienating Panin by dismissing his nominee. Most important, she wanted to be certain that her new choice was the right one.

Frustrated by Catherine's procrastination, Potemkin decided to force the issue. He came to court only rarely, and when he did, he had nothing to say. Then he disappeared entirely. Catherine was told that Potemkin was suffering from an unhappy love affair because a certain woman did not reciprocate his love; that his despair was so deep that he was thinking of entering a monastery. Catherine complained, "I do not understand what has reduced him to such despair.... I thought my friendliness must have made him realize that his fervor was not displeasing to me." When these words were reported to Potemkin, he knew that Vasilchikov was about to depart.

Employing his flair for the dramatic, Potemkin decided to increase the pressure on Catherine. At the end of January, he entered the Monastery Alexander Nevsky on the outskirts of St. Petersburg. There, affecting melancholy, he began growing a beard and observing the daily routine of a monk. Panin understood Potemkin's game. The counselor requested an audience and told the empress that while the merits of General Potemkin were universally recognized, he had been sufficiently rewarded, and that nothing more need be given this gentleman. In case further advancement were contemplated, Panin observed, he wanted her to understand that "the state and yourself, Madam, will soon be made to feel the ambition, the pride, and the eccentricities of this man. I fear that your choice will cause you much unpleasantness." Catherine replied that the raising of these issues was premature. Given Potemkin's abilities, he could be useful as a soldier and as a diplomat. He was brave, clever, and educated; such men were not so numerous in Russia that she could allow this one to hide in a monastery. Therefore, she would do everything in her power to prevent General Potemkin from taking holy orders.

Catherine did not want to risk Potemkin making his withdrawal permanent. According to one story, she dispatched her friend and lady-in-waiting Countess Prascovia Bruce to the monastery to see Potemkin and tell him that, if he would return to court, he could rely on the empress's favor. Potemkin did not smooth the emissary's path. On her arrival at the monastery, he asked her to wait, saying that he was about to engage in prayer and could not be interrupted. Wearing monastic robes, he walked in procession with the monks, participated in the service, and prostrated himself, murmuring prayers, before an icon of St. Catherine. Eventually, he rose, made the sign of the cross, and came to speak to Catherine's envoy. Countess Bruce's message had a convincing ring; moreover, Potemkin was impressed by the court rank of the messenger. Persuaded, he shed his monastic cassock, shaved off his beard, put on his uniform, and returned to St. Petersburg in a court carriage.

He became Catherine's lover—and immediately became intensely jealous. Apart from lying next to her hapless husband, Peter, Catherine had slept with four men before Potemkin—Saltykov, Poniatowski, Orlov, and Vasilchikov. The existence of these predecessors, and mental images of her as the sexual partner of other men, tormented Potemkin. He accused the empress of having had fifteen previous lovers. In an attempt to calm him, Catherine secluded herself in her apartment on February 21, writing a letter entitled "A Sincere Confession," which gave an account of her previous romantic experiences. It is unique in the annals of written royal confessions; an all-powerful queen attempting to win forgiveness from a demanding new lover for previous actions in her life.

In spelling out the details of her past life, she began with the circumstances of her marriage, and then described the painful disappointments of the love affairs that followed. Her earnest, apologetic, almost pleading tone laid bare how desperately she wanted Potemkin. She began by explaining how Empress Elizabeth's anxiety concerning her failure to produce an heir to the throne had led to her first love affair. She admitted that, under pressure from the empress and Maria Choglokova, she had chosen Sergei Saltykov, "chiefly because of his obvious inclination." Then Saltykov was sent away, "for he had conducted himself indiscreetly:"

> After a year spent in great sorrow, the present Polish king [Stanislaus Poniatowski] arrived. We took no notice of him, but good people . . . forced me to notice that he existed, that his eyes were of unparalleled beauty, and that he directed them (though so nearsighted he doesn't see past his nose) more often in one direction than in another. This one was both loving and loved from 1755 till 1761, [which included] a three year absence. Then the efforts of Prince Gregory Orlov[,] whom again good people forced me to notice, changed my state of mind. This one

would have remained for life had he himself not grown bored. I
learned of . . . [his new infidelity] on the very day of his departure to . . . [the peace talks with the Turks] and as a result I decided that I could no longer trust him. This thought cruelly
tormented me and forced me out of desperation to make some
sort of choice [Vasilchikov], one which grieved me then and
still does now more than I can say. . . .

Then came a certain knight [Potemkin]. Through his merits and kindness, this hero was so charming that people . . . were
already saying that he should take up residence here. But what
they didn't know was that we'd already called him here. . . .

Now, Sir Knight, after this confession, may I hope to receive absolution for my sins? You'll be pleased to see that it
wasn't fifteen, but a third as many: the first [Saltykov] chosen
out of necessity, and the fourth [Vasilchikov] out of desperation, cannot in my mind be attributed to any frivolity. As to the
other three [Poniatowski, Orlov, and Potemkin himself], if you
look closely, God knows they weren't the result of debauchery,
for which I haven't the least inclination, and had fate given me
in my youth a husband whom I could have loved, I would have
remained true to him forever. The trouble is that my heart is
loath to be without love even for a single hour. . . . If you want
to keep me forever, then show as much friendship as love, and
more than anything else, love me and tell me the truth.

Along with Catherine's interpretation of her own romantic history,
this letter displays the impact of Potemkin's personality on her. Potemkin understood this. Assured that he eclipsed everyone who had
gone before, he wrote to Catherine, demanding what he now saw as his
due:

I remain unmotivated by envy toward those who, while
younger than I, have nevertheless received more signs of imperial favor than I, but am solely offended by the possibility that
in Your Imperial Majesty's thoughts, I am considered less worthy than others. Being tormented by this . . . I have been so audacious as to beg that should my service be worthy of your
favor . . . my doubt [would] be resolved by rewarding me with
the title of adjutant general to Your Imperial Majesty. This will
offend no one, and I shall take it as the zenith of my happiness.

The rank of adjutant general was the official status of Catherine's favorites, but that his advancement would offend no one was nonsense. In addition to Vasilchikov, who admittedly no longer counted, it would offend the Orlovs, Panin, most of the court, and Catherine's son, Grand Duke Paul, the heir to the throne. Ignoring all this, Catherine replied the following day in a letter that mingled official wording with private tongue-in-cheek irony:

> Sir Lieutenant General: Your letter was handed to me this morning. I found your request so moderate with regard to your services rendered to me and fatherland, that I ordered an edict prepared rewarding you with the title of Adjutant General. I admit that I am also very pleased that your trust in me is such that you addressed your request in writing directly to me, and did not go through any intermediaries. Rest assured I remain toward you benevolent. Catherine.

Catherine then wrote to General Alexander Bibikov, who was then commander of the troops opposing Pugachev, to tell him that she had appointed Potemkin her personal adjutant, "and, as he thinks that you, being fond of him, will rejoice at this news I am letting you know. It seems to me that considering his devotion and services to me, I have not done much for him, but his joy is hard to describe. And I, looking at him, feel glad that I see near me at least one person who is entirely happy." She also made Potemkin lieutenant colonel of the Preobrazhensky Guards, the most famous regiment of the Imperial Guard, in which she herself, as sovereign, was colonel. A few days later, the British minister, Sir Robert Gunning, informed London of these developments:

> Mr. Vasilchikov, the favorite, whose understanding was too limited to admit of his having any influence in affairs, or sharing his mistress's confidence, is now succeeded by a man who bids fair to possessing them both, in the most supreme form. When I acquaint Your Lordship that the empress's choice is equally disapproved by both the Grand Duke's party [including Panin] and the Orlovs . . . you will not wonder that it has occasioned a very general surprise.

As the news swept through the court, Countess Rumyantseva wrote to her husband, the general, who, a few months before, had been Potemkin's superior in the Turkish war, "The thing to do now, my sweet, is to address yourself to Potemkin."

Panin, despite his warning to Catherine about Potemkin, was pleased by the change because it promised to diminish the influence of the Orlovs. No concern was shown for the hapless Vasilchikov, who, still living in the palace, became simply an inconvenience. Catherine was enraptured by her new favorite; this extended to taking pride in his reputed success with other women. "I'm not surprised that the entire city has ascribed to you a countless number of women as your lovers," she wrote to him. "No one on earth is better at busying himself with them, I suppose, than you." She wanted him now, however, exclusively for herself. Less than a week after writing her "Sincere Confession," she waited at night for Potemkin to come to her. The following day, she wrote to him:

> I don't understand what kept you. And you didn't even come. Please, don't be afraid. We are quite too shrewd. No sooner had I lain down than I rose again, got dressed, and went to the doors of the library to wait for you, where I stood in a drafty wind for two hours. And not till midnight . . . did I return out of grief to lie down in bed where, thanks to you, I spent . . . [a] sleepless night. . . . I want to see you and must see you, no matter what!

Potemkin remained jealous of everyone, flaring up when she paid attention to anyone else. One night at the theater, when she made friendly remarks to Gregory Orlov, he got up and stormed out of the imperial box. Catherine cautioned him to moderate his attitude toward this former lover:

> I only ask you not to do one thing: don't damage, and don't even try to damage, my opinion of Prince Orlov, for I should consider that to be ingratitude on your part. There's no one whom he [Orlov] praised more to me and whom . . . he loved more both in former times and now till your arrival, than you. And if he has his faults, then it is unfit for either you or me to judge them and to make them known to others. He loves you, and they [the Orlov brothers] are my friends, and I shan't part with them. Now there's a lesson for you. If you're wise, you'll

heed it. It wouldn't be wise to contradict it since it's the absolute truth.

In April, Potemkin moved into the apartment immediately beneath the private apartment of the empress; their rooms were now connected by the private, green-carpeted spiral staircase. Because they kept
different hours—Catherine normally rose to begin work at six and retired at night by ten; Potemkin often talked and played cards until dawn
and rose at noon—they did not regularly sleep together in the same
bed. Instead, at night one climbed, or the other descended, the spiral
staircase in order to spend time together.

When they became lovers, Catherine was forty-four, ten years older
than Potemkin. She was inclining toward plumpness, but her mental
acuity and vitality remained exceptional. And Potemkin could see that
his passion for this woman was powerfully reciprocated, which only
added to her attractiveness. He might have settled into the luxurious
life of an imperial favorite and collected the rewards that came with
that position. But Potemkin had no interest in simply becoming the
purveyor of private pleasures to the empress. He wanted a life of action
and responsibility, and he meant to achieve it with the support of the
woman who personified Russia.

Catherine was eager to accept him on this basis. She thought him
the handsomest man she had ever met; she scarcely noticed the damaged eye. At thirty-four, he had gained weight and his body was no longer slim. Biting his nails had become an obsession. None of this
mattered. To Grimm, she wrote: "I have parted from a certain excellent
but very boring citizen [Vasilchikov] who was immediately replaced—
I do not myself quite know how—by one of the greatest, most bizarre,
and most entertaining eccentrics of the iron age."

From the beginning there were quarrels. Hardly a day passed without a
scene, and almost always it was Potemkin who began the quarrel and
Catherine who took the first step toward reconciliation. He questioned
the permanence of her feeling for him and worried her and himself
with questions and reproaches. Because most of his letters and notes
are lost, there is only a slender record of what he wrote to her, but her

letters to him give an idea of what he had said to her. In any case, she had to soothe and flatter him like a spoiled child:

> No, Grishenka, it's quite impossible that my feelings for you will change. Be fair with yourself: how could I love someone after you? I think there's no one like you and I don't give a damn about everyone else. I hate change.

> There is no reason to be angry. But no, it's time to stop giving you assurances. You must be most, most, most certain by now that I love you. . . . I want you to love me. I want to appear desirable to you. . . . If you want, I shall paraphrase this page for you in three words and cross out all the rest. Here it is: I love you.

> Oh, my darling, you should be ashamed. What need do you have of saying that he who takes your place hasn't long to live? Does using fear to compel someone's heart look like the right thing to do? This most loathsome method is utterly contrary to your way of thinking in which no evil dwells.

Not only jealousy, but also Potemkin's sensitivity to the possible impermanence of his new position provided a subject for argument. He refused to be treated as merely the empress's favorite. There is a letter from him, annotated in the margins by Catherine and returned to him, which exhibits one of their arguments and its reconciliation:

IN POTEMKIN'S HAND:	IN CATHERINE'S HAND:
Allow me, my precious dear,	I permit you.
to say these final words that	
I think will end our quarrel.	The sooner the better.
Do not be surprised that I am	Be calm.
uneasy about our love. Beyond	One hand washes the other.
the innumerable gifts you have	
bestowed on me, you have placed	
me in your heart. I want to be there	Firmly and solidly.
alone, preferred to all former ones,	You are and will be.
since no one has so loved you as I.	
And since I am the work of your	I see it and believe it.

hands. So I desire that you should
secure my place, that you should
find joy in doing me good, that you
should devise everything for my
comfort and find therein repose
from the great labors that occupy
your lofty station. Amen.

I am happy with all my soul.

My foremost pleasure.
It will come by itself.
Let your thoughts be calm.
Your feelings are tender and
will find the best way.
End of quarrel. Amen.

Thus began the period in Catherine's life when she had a lover and partner who gave her almost everything she wanted. Their intimacy permitted Potemkin to walk into her bedroom in the morning with only a dressing gown over his naked body, although the room was crowded with visitors and court officials. He scarcely noticed because his thoughts were on the fascinating conversation interrupted a few hours before when Catherine, declaring that she must have some sleep, had left his apartment below and returned to her room.

Because they worked in different parts of the palace during the day, they wrote notes to each other; continuations of their conversations. These were protestations of love mingled with affairs of state, court gossip, reproachful chiding, and discussions of mutual health. Catherine's names for him were "My golden pheasant," "Dearest Pigeon," "Kitten," "Little dog," "Papa," "Twin Soul," "Little parrot," "Grisha," and "Grishenka." Also: "Cossack," "Muscovite," "Lion in the Jungle," "Tiger," "Giaour (Infidel)," "My good sir," "Prince," "Your Excellency," "Your Serene Highness," "General," and "My sweet beauty to whom no king can compare." Potemkin's forms of address to her were more formal, emphasizing the difference in station: *"Matushka,"* "Madame," or "Your Gracious Imperial Majesty." Catherine worried because he carried her little notes in his pocket and often pulled them out to reread. She feared that one would drop out and be picked up by the wrong person.

For a person with an orderly German mind who exercised strict self-control, the emotional intensity Catherine experienced with Potemkin was both liberating and distracting. She had to choose between drawn-out, draining sexual pleasure and her duties as a ruler. She tried to have both, and both ran concurrently in her mind. She was not free to be with him whenever she wanted; she compensated by secretly surrounding herself with thoughts of him; she did this while reading papers or listening to officials delivering reports, hour after hour. Because she was not free to spend these honeymoon days alone with him, Catherine poured her love onto these little scribbled slips of paper.

Potemkin, too, was immersed in passion, but he was uneasy about something else. He realized that he owed his new preeminence exclusively to the empress, and that just as she had summoned and then dismissed Vasilchikov, so, too, she could, at any moment, replace him. There was, of course, a climactic step that would change his status. His plan was extravagant, impracticable—perhaps only a daydream: he wanted to legalize their union by marriage. He spoke to her about it soon after he became the official favorite, and it was a measure of his power over her that she considered it. For Catherine, it would not have been easy; she was wary of surrendering power. This time, because of her love for Potemkin, she may have agreed.

If there was a marriage, this is a widely believed version of how it happened:

No one was to know. But to be a proper Orthodox ceremony, it had to include a chuch, a priest, and witnesses. These arrangements were made. On June 8, 1774, after a dinner in honor of the Izmailovsky Guards, Catherine, wearing the uniform of the regiment, and accompanied only by a favorite maid, set out in a boat from the Fontanka Canal, crossed the Neva River to the Vyborg side, and entered an unmarked carriage, which took her to the St. Sampsonovsky Church. There, Potemkin, wearing his general's uniform, was waiting. Only five people were present: Catherine, Potemkin, her maid, her chamberlain, and Potemkin's nephew Alexander Samoilov. The marriage was performed.

Is this story true? No documents have ever been seen, but there are other forms of evidence. In 1782, Sir Robert Keith, the British ambassador to Austria, walking with Emperor Joseph II, asked about the rumors. "Does it appear, sir, that Prince Potemkin's weight and influence is diminished?" "Not at all," the emperor replied, "but they have never been what the world imagined. The empress of Russia does not wish to part with him, and for a thousand reasons, and as [with] many connections of every sort, she could not easily get rid of him even if she wished to." Why, if Potemkin were merely a favorite, could Catherine not get rid of him? She had gotten rid of Orlov, who, with his brothers, had put her on the throne, and who was also the father of her son, Bobrinsky. A marriage, however, had created a different situation. Perhaps this was what the emperor was saying.

Ambassadors, as well as emperors, like to pose as having inside knowledge. Philippe de Ségur, the French ambassador in St. Petersburg, told Versailles in 1788 that Potemkin had "certain sacred and inalienable rights which secure the continuance of his privilege. . . . A lucky chance enabled me to discover it, and when I have thoroughly researched it, I shall on the first occasion inform the king." No such occasion presented itself. The French Revolution broke out a year later, Ségur returned home, and five years later the king, Louis XVI, was guillotined.

The strongest written evidence appears in the language of Catherine's daily messages to Potemkin beginning in the late spring of 1774. She addresses him as "dear husband" and "my master and tender spouse" and signs herself "your devoted wife." She never called any other lover, before or after Potemkin, "husband," or referred to herself as his "wife." In June and July 1774, immediately after the marriage—if one occurred—she wrote, "I kiss you and embrace you with all my body and soul, dear husband." A few days later: "Dearest darling, dear spouse, pray come and cuddle with me. Your caresses are so sweet and pleasing."

The history of Russia offers the strongest evidence of all. After their physical passion had dimmed, Catherine and Gregory Potemkin continued a special relationship that was often incomprehensible to everyone around them. Marriage would provide an explanation. If they were secretly married and still deeply cared for each other but had agreed on a modus vivendi, it could account for the unique authority wielded by Potemkin in Catherine's Russia for the rest of his life. During this time—over fifteen years—he received and returned Catherine's devoted loyalty and affection. This was true even when both were sleeping with other people.

❧60❧

Potemkin Ascending

POTEMKIN SOARED in rank and power. His appointments as adjutant general to the empress and lieutenant colonel of the Preobrazhensky Guards had been the first visible signs of this ascent, and a stream of titles, honors, and privileges soon followed. On May 6, 1774, Sir Robert Gunning reported to Whitehall, "There has been no instance of so rapid a progress as the present one. Yesterday, General Potemkin was admitted to a seat on the Privy Council." A month later, he was appointed vice president of the College of War and governor-general of New Russia, an immense stretch of territory north of the Crimea and the Black Sea. For his services in the Turkish war, he was awarded a diamond-studded sword and a miniature portrait of the empress set in diamonds to be worn over his heart, a gift previously awarded only to Gregory Orlov. One after another, he received the highest grades of Russian and foreign decorations: first, on Christmas Day 1774, the Order of St. Andrew, the highest order in the Russian empire; then came the Black Eagle from Prussia, the White Eagle from Poland, the White Elephant from Denmark, and the Holy Seraphim from Sweden. Catherine was not universally successful in decorating her hero. Austria declined to make him a Knight of the Golden Fleece because he was not a Roman Catholic, and attempts to obtain the Order of the Garter from Great Britain were flatly refused by King George III. The University of Moscow, which had expelled him for laziness, gave him an honorary degree. When Potemkin spoke to one of the professors who had been active in having him dismissed, he asked, "Do you remember how you got me kicked out?" "At the time, you deserved it," the professor replied. Potemkin laughed and slapped the old man on the back.

Catherine sent him jewels, furs, porcelain, and furniture. His food and wine were charged to her at a cost of one hundred thousand rubles a year. The five daughters of his widowed sister, Maria Engelhardt, were brought to court; all five were created maids of honor. Catherine was attentive to Potemkin's mother. "I have noticed that your mother was most elegant, but that she has no watch," she said at one point. "Here is one I ask you to give her from me."

When Potemkin first asked to be brought onto the Imperial Council, he was rebuffed. Describing what happened next, a French diplomat wrote:

> On Sunday, I happened to be seated at table next to . . . [Potemkin] and the empress, and I saw that not only would he not speak to her, but he did not even answer her questions. She

was quite beside herself and we were utterly upset. Upon getting up from the table, the empress retired alone, and when she returned her eyes were red. On Monday, she was more cheerful. He entered the Council the same day.

Potemkin understood that his rise stirred jealousy and that his future depended not only on his relationship with Catherine but on what he achieved in his work. The court quickly realized that this new favorite would be neither a puppet like Vasilchikov nor an amiable, indolent fixture like Gregory Orlov. Courtiers then divided into those who attempted to ingratiate themselves with the new figure and those who opposed him.

Nikita Panin was between these two groups. He had opposed Potemkin's rapid advancement, but his hatred of the Orlovs was greater than his wariness of the ambitious newcomer. Potemkin at first sought to win Panin's favor for its own value and because it was a path to conciliation with Grand Duke Paul. Panin owed his permanent influence to his years as Paul's childhood tutor and his role in bringing Catherine to the throne. It was this, not his present position at the College of Foreign Affairs, that enabled Panin to continue living at the palace. "As long as my bed remains in the Palace, I shall not lose my influence," he said. Potemkin's efforts to reach out to Paul and the old councillor had mixed results. As long as Potemkin avoided Panin's privileged domain of foreign relations, relations between the two remained correct. Paul, however, was so opposed to everyone personally close to his mother that Potemkin's efforts in this direction were fruitless.

During the spring of 1774, with the Turkish war continuing and the Pugachev rebellion still unresolved, Potemkin was given additional assignments. Catherine ordered that all papers and correspondence regarding the rebellion be addressed to him. Soon, his days were occupied with drafting documents, writing letters, and helping her think through the decisions she had to make. She consulted him about everything from important state affairs to trivial personal matters. He was now correcting her Russian spelling, grammar, and style, not only in official documents but in personal letters: "If there are no mistakes," she wrote to him, "please return the letter and I will seal it. If there are some, kindly correct them. If you want to make any changes, write them out. . . . Either the ukase and the letter are perfectly clear, or else I am stupid today." Meanwhile, outside the palace, Potemkin was dealing with military, financial, and administrative questions at the College of War. He involved himself in decisions on strategy, establishing recruiting quotas, designing soldiers' uniforms, purchasing horses for the army, and drawing up lists of candidates for military honors and decorations. He attended meetings of the Imperial Council, where, increasingly, he began to challenge the arguments and decisions of his older colleagues.

Catherine was impressed and pleased by his efforts, but she complained that they were taking too much of his time. She was not seeing him enough. "This is really too much!" she protested. "Even at nine o'clock I cannot find you alone. I came to your apartment and found a crowd of people who were walking about, coughing, and making a lot of noise. Yet I had come solely to tell you that I love you excessively." Another time, she wrote, "It is a hundred years since I saw you. I do not care what you do, but please arrange that there should be nobody with you when I come. Otherwise, this day will be unbearable; it is sad enough as it is."

Despite love, war, and rebellion, theology and church matters still absorbed Potemkin. He would leave an important political or military meeting to take part in a theological discussion. Any cleric, eminent or obscure, Russian Orthodox, Old Believer, Catholic priest, or Jewish rabbi, was received. He liked to surround himself with new and interesting people and never missed a chance of talking to men and women who had traveled; he stored away what they told him. His relations with foreign diplomats were less close because he felt that it was important to remain on good terms with Panin. At the same time, he was not completely uninvolved. On the anniversary of Catherine's accession to the throne, the diplomatic corps was entertained at a lavish supper at Peterhof. Potemkin, not Panin, was the host.

His first opportunity to reveal his talent for grand-scale showmanship came at the beginning of 1775, when Catherine celebrated the end of the Turkish war. It was Potemkin who persuaded her to stage these celebrations in Moscow, Russia's ancient capital and the heart of the empire, and he became the producer and master of ceremonies of parades, fireworks, illuminations, balls, and banquets. It was in this role that Potemkin had a serious altercation with Nikita Panin. Catherine had given Potemkin instructions regarding honors for the war heroes of the Russian army, and Nikita Panin believed that his brother, General Peter Panin, was to receive insufficient recognition. Potemkin was forced to admit that the empress herself had made the decision and that he was carrying it out. The argument soon moved on to Potemkin's increasingly frequent incursions into Panin's traditional domain, foreign affairs. Panin was annoyed that at meetings of the council, Potemkin had questioned, and sometimes contradicted, his opinions. When a report arrived concerning disturbances in Persia, and Potemkin suggested that it might be in Russia's interest to encourage these disturbances, Panin declared that he would never be a party to such a policy. Potemkin rose and walked out of the room.

There was one foreign policy decision Catherine made at this time in which Potemkin played no part. In the summer of 1775, King George III of England requested the loan—the rental, actually—of Russian troops to fight in America against his rebellious colonial subjects. London's first instruction on this matter came on June 30, 1775, from the Earl of Suffolk at the Foreign Office to Sir Robert Gunning, the British ambassador:

> The rebellion in a great part of his Majesty's American colonies is of such a nature as to make it prudent to look forward to every possible exertion. You will endeavor to learn whether, in case it should hereafter be found expedient to make use of foreign troops in North America, His Majesty might rely on the Empress of Russia to furnish him with a considerable corps of her infantry for that purpose. I need not observe to you that this commission is of the most delicate nature. In whatever method you introduce the conversation, whether with Mr. Panin or the empress, you will be very careful to do it unaffectedly, so as to give it quite the air of an idle speculation of your own and by no means that of a proposition.

Soon, the British government was more specific. What was wanted was a Russian force of twenty thousand infantry and one thousand Cossack cavalry, for which Britain was prepared to meet all expenses—transport to America, maintenance, and pay. Catherine considered the request. She was indebted to the king and England for the assistance rendered five years before when the Russian fleet made its passage from the Baltic to the Mediterranean—the voyage that had led to Russia's naval victory over the Turks at Chesme. She was flattered that her soldiers were respected by England. And she was strongly sympathetic to George III's difficulties—she herself had just dealt with a massive rebellion in Pugachev's uprising. She nevertheless refused the king's request. When she did so, Gunning appealed to Panin and then tried the new man, Potemkin, but Catherine was adamant. Even a personal letter from King George could not persuade her. She wrote back a friendly letter, wishing the king success, but still saying no. An important but unexpressed reason was that she considered that Russia's future lay in the south, along the Black Sea. Despite the peace treaty with Turkey, she sensed that the settlement would not be permanent and that another war would be coming. When this war began, Catherine knew that she would need the twenty thousand soldiers herself.*

❧61❧

Catherine and Potemkin: Separation

DESPITE THE INTENSITY of their early passion, the relationship between Catherine and Potemkin was never smooth. After their first winter and spring together, the notes she wrote to him began spelling out her emotional journey from passion to disappointment, disillusion, frustration, exasperation, and pain. Catherine burned most of his notes to her, but in what she wrote to him, there is evidence of both sides of their arguments:

> My dear friend, I don't know why, but it seems you are angry with me today. If not, and I'm mistaken, so much the better. And as proof, run to me. I'm waiting for you in the bedroom. My soul hungers for you.

> Your long letter and stories are quite excellent, but what's foolish is that there isn't a single affectionate word for me. What need do I have to listen to the huge lies . . . [told you by]

---

*In the eighteenth century, a request of this kind was not extraordinary. Kings and princes, mostly German, happily rented their soldiers to the highest bidder. England eventually hired thousands of Hessians, who made themselves hated throughout the American colonies. The impact that twenty thousand Russians might have had on eighteenth-century America can only be imagined.

other people which you reported to me in such detail? It seems to me that, while repeating all this nonsense, you were obliged to remember that there is a woman in this world who loves you and that I, too, have a right to a word of tenderness.

You were in a mood to quarrel. Please inform me once this inclination passes.

Precious darling, I took a cord with a stone and tied it around the neck of all our quarrels, and then I tossed it into a hole in the ice. . . . And should this please you, pray do the same.

I wrote you a letter this morning devoid of all common sense. You returned this letter to me, I tore it in pieces in front of you and burned it. What more satisfaction could you desire? Even the church aspires to no more once a heretic has been burned. My note has been burned. You should not want to burn me too. . . . Peace, my friend. I stretch out my hand to you. Do you wish to take it?

Do me this one favor for my sake: be calm. I am a bit merrier after my tears, and only your agitation grieves me. My dear friend, my darling, stop tormenting yourself, we both need peace so our thoughts can settle down and become bearable, or else we'll end up like balls in a game of tennis.

It was on January 13, 1776, that Catherine wrote to her ambassador in Vienna, instructing him to ask Emperor Joseph II to grant to her favorite the title of Prince of the Holy Roman Empire. This title, which did not require the holder to profess Catholicism, was awarded to Potemkin in March 1776; thereafter, he was addressed as "Prince" and "Your Serene Highness."

On March 21, 1776, she signed a decree permitting him to use the title. Something between them went wrong, however, and a few days after sending him an angry note, she wrote a plea.

Such rage ought to be expected from Your Highness should you wish to prove to the public as well as to me how great is the extent of your unruliness. This will of course be an indisputable sign of your ingratitude toward me, as well as your slight attachment to me. For this fury is contrary to both my desire and to the difference in our affairs and stations. The Viennese court has no equal and it will now be able to judge how reliable I am in recommending people for their highest honors. And so this is how you show your concern for my reputation.

Then she reversed her approach and made another appeal:

> My Lord and Dear Husband! I shall begin my answer with that line which touches me most of all: who ordered you to cry? Why do you give greater authority to your lively imagination than to the proofs which speak in your wife's favor? Was she not attached to you two years ago by the bonds of Holy Matrimony? My dear, you suspect the impossible of me. Have I changed my tune, could you be unloved? So now consider for yourself: were my words and deeds in your favor stronger two years ago than now?

> Should you not find pleasure in constantly quarreling with me . . . then I beseech you to dampen your hot temper. . . . I am truly someone who loves not only affectionate words and behavior but an affectionate face as well. . . . I remain full of hope, without which, I, like all other people, could not live.

> May God forgive you . . . the injustices you've shown me. . . . Catherine was never insensitive. Even now she is attached to you with all her heart and soul. . . . I don't understand why you call yourself unloved and repugnant, and me gracious to everyone but you. . . . Repugnant and unloved you can never be. I believe that you love me, though quite often your words lack any trace of love. Who desires your peace and tranquility more than I?

In May 1776, Potemkin replied to a letter from her regarding a lack of oversight in the Preobrazhensky Guards. Her letter had spoken of a "blind eye" being turned to the affairs of the regiment. Deeply offended by her probably unintended reference to his physical defect, Potemkin replied:

Your Most Gracious Majesty, when I direct my sight in any direction, then it's not with a blind eye. I renounce any position in which matters will be removed from my oversight. However, should my talents and desire at some time cease, then someone better can be selected to which I shall readily and fully consent.

Catherine responded:

I read your letter. . . . For God's sake, come to your senses. . . . Is it not in your power to do away with this discord? Even the opinion of the foolish public depends on whatever respect you intend to give this matter.

To Catherine, Potemkin now always seemed angry, whereas the theme running through her letters was her desire for peace and harmony. There were moments of reconciliation and assurances of continued affection. Over time, however, she wearied of Potemkin's outbursts. Eventually, she reached the point where she warned that if he did not change his behavior, she would have no choice but to withdraw her love—as a means of self-preservation. She was simply too fatigued by the never-ending quarrels. She had sought in Potemkin a refuge from the pressures and loneliness of exercising power, but now their relationship had become another burden. His bad-tempered anger had started to take on a public face. He had begun talking to his relatives, even describing his fights with Catherine. She wrote to him:

To present this comedy to society is highly regrettable for it's a triumph for your enemies and mine. I did not know till now that they were so thoroughly informed of what goes on between us. I have no confidant in matters that concern you for I honor our secrets and do not disclose them to anyone for discussion. . . . I repeat and have repeated this to you a hundred times: stop your raging so that my natural tenderness might return, otherwise you will be the death of me.

Potemkin replied:

Matushka, here is the result of your agreeable treatment of me over the past several days. I clearly see your inclination to get along with me. But you have let things go so far that it is becoming impossible for you to be kind to me. I came here to see you since without you life is tedious and unbearable. I noticed that you were incommoded by my arrival. I do not know whom or what you are trying to please; I only know that it is not necessary and to no purpose. It seems to me you have never before been so ill at ease. Your Most Gracious Majesty, I shall go through fire for you. But if it has finally been decided that I am to be banished from you, then at least let it not be before the entire public. I do not tarry to withdraw, although this is equal to losing my life.

By the time Potemkin's liaison with the empress had lasted two and a half years, the storms were worsening. He constantly reproached her for condoning intrigues against him and permitting his enemies to remain in her entourage; she complained that he was no longer loving, tender, and cheerful. Moments of truce were followed by continued fighting. Sometimes, his truculent behavior so completely exasperated her that she, normally quick to forgive and take the first step toward reconciliation, would indulge in an outburst of her own. But her anger never lasted, and when Potemkin continued sulking for days and she did not see him, she was miserable. A turning point in their relationship was approaching. Catherine understood this:

> Your foolish acts remain the same; at the very moment when I feel safest, a mountain drops on me. . . . To a madcap like you . . . tranquillity is an unbearable state of mind. . . . The gratitude I owe you has not vanished and I suppose there has never been a time when you haven't received signs of this. But now you take away all my force by tormenting me with new fabrications. . . . Please tell me whether I should be grateful to you for that. Until now I always thought that good health and restful days were esteemed for something in this world, but I would like to know how this is possible with you.

In an embittered effort to analyze their discord, she began with sarcasm:

> Listening to you talk sometimes, some might say that I am a monster who has every possible fault: I am frightfully

two-faced when I am in pain; when I cry, this is not the result of my sensibility, but something entirely different. And therefore you must despise me and treat me with contempt. Such an exceedingly tender way of behaving can only have a positive effect on my mind. Yet this mind, as wicked and horrible as it may be, knows no other way of loving than to make happy the one it loves. . . . Pray tell, how would you behave if I continuously reproached you with the faults of all your acquaintances, all those whom you respect or whose services you employ, if I held you responsible for their silly blunders? Would you be patient or impatient? And if, seeing you impatient, I were to be offended, get up, stomp away, slamming the doors behind me, and if, after that, I were to be cold to you, refuse to look at you, and to add threats to all that? . . . For God's sake, please do all in your power to keep us from quarreling again for our quarrels always arise from nothing but irrelevant rubbish. We quarrel about power, never about love. This is the truth.

This was, indeed, the truth; it was the crux of the problem. The question of power constantly gnawed at Potemkin. He had always craved power, and it had always come to him easily. This had been true when he was a small boy, an only son, and the idol of a mother and five sisters. It had been his goal when he was at the university and declared that he would command either soldiers or monks. It was to seek recognition that he had spurred forward to present the new empress with his sword knot, and when he mimicked Catherine's voice and accent and made her laugh. It was his objective when he left the army and hurried to St. Petersburg, hoping to become the favorite. Now, he had acquired titles, wealth, land, and high office. The empress had raised him to unprecedented heights and even perhaps had sealed their union by marriage. What more did he want? What more power could Catherine bestow? He was the first man in the empire, but he remained unhappy and unfulfilled. He had made clear that all the customary rewards of his position—titles, orders, money—were not enough. He wanted supreme power in an unrestricted sphere.

The problem was that despite everything he had done and everything he had been given, his position rested entirely on Catherine. He knew this. He saw that if their quarreling continued, there was a possibility that, one day, the empress might triumph over the woman and turn on him and dismiss him. He would then be no more than the stumbling Orlov and the pitiable Vasilchikov. He was not willing to risk this. The moment had arrived when he had to choose between love and power. He chose power. It meant withdrawal from love and from Catherine. Not complete withdrawal, however. Mysteriously to all who were watching, even as the nature of their physical relationship was changing, the bonds between the two remained strong, so strong that his political power did not seem to decline. Rather, it seemed to grow.

The court, observing the changing relationship between the lovers, assumed that Potemkin would soon be dismissed. On June 22, 1776, when it was learned that the empress was presenting him with the Anichkov Palace, which Empress Elizabeth had built on the Nevsky Prospect for Alexis Razumovsky, it was believed that this gift was in order to provide Potemkin with a town residence when he moved out of the Winter Palace. This was partially true. In preparing for a physical separation, the question had arisen as to where Potemkin would live. Catherine had encouraged him to remain in the Winter Palace, but she also set about finding another place for him, should he prefer that. Potemkin, having repeatedly threatened to leave, complained when she began to take him at his word. She responded:

> God knows I don't intend to drive you out of the palace. Please live in it and be calm. . . . If you wish to divert yourself by traveling around the provinces for a while, I shan't stand in your way. Upon your return, pray occupy your quarters in the palace as before. As God is my witness, my attachment to you remains firm and unlimited, and I'm not angry. But do me one favor: spare my nerves.

Potemkin thanked her, but with a quibble:

> Your Most Gracious Majesty: Having learned . . . of my being presented with the Anichkov house, I kiss your feet. I express my humblest gratitude. Most merciful mother, God, having given you all resources and power, did not give you, to my misfortune, to know human hearts. God Almighty! Make known to my sovereign and benefactress how grateful I am to her, how devoted I am and that my life is dedicated to her service. Your Most Gracious Majesty, keep in your protection and

care a person devoted to you body and soul, who remains in the most sincere manner till death.

> Your Majesty's most loyal and most devoted servant,
> Prince Potemkin

Potemkin never lived in the Anichkov Palace. Once it had been repaired, he used it for evening entertainments when he was in St. Petersburg. Two years later, he sold it.

The Orlovs, who had introduced Potemkin to Catherine, had grown to hate him. Believing that the favorite's dismissal was imminent, Alexis Orlov, taking advantage of his permanent privilege of speaking frankly to the empress, told her that she should realize the damage her favorite was causing and go ahead and dismiss him. Orlov went further: "You know, Madam, I am your slave. My life is at your service. If Potemkin disturbs your peace of mind, give me your orders. He shall disappear immediately; you shall hear no more of him." Catherine mentioned this conversation to Potemkin, and the generally unexpected result was that, under pretext of illness, Alexis Orlov resigned from his offices and withdrew from court.

❧62❧

New Relationships

I N THE WINTER and spring of 1776, as the passion binding Catherine and Potemkin was ebbing and the rancor between them mounting, she found Gregory's successor. He was Peter Zavadovsky, a protégé of Field Marshal Rumyantsev, the commander of the victorious Russian army in the war with Turkey. When Rumyantstev returned to St. Petersburg, he brought with him two young Ukrainians, Zavadovsky and Alexander Bezborodko. Both were well educated and had served on Rumyantsev's staff during the war and the peace negotiations. When Catherine asked Rumyantsev to recommend talented officials for her personal secretariat, the field marshal gave her these two names. Both were appointed and both were to have brilliant careers.

At first, Zavadovsky appeared to have more of the qualities necessary to succeed. Born of a good family, he had accompanied the field marshal to the battlefield, where his courage had earned him the rank of lieutenant colonel. He was thirty-seven, the same age as Potemkin, had a handsome figure, a classical education, a good mind, and a modest, courteous manner. Bezborodko, on the other hand, was vulgar in appearance and rude in manner, but, in the long run, he was to have the more spectacular career. Zavadovsky lived for a short time in the glow of imperial favor before settling back into life as a highly respected civil servant, while Bezborodko, on the basis of exceptional intelligence and hard work, ended by becoming a prince and chancellor of the empire.

Catherine's notice of Zavadovsky was natural enough. His dark good looks, six-foot form, and quiet dedication appealed to the empress, and, within a month, with Potemkin's agreement, she had attached him to her personal staff as her personal secretary. Bezborodko remained a clerk in the chancellery. At the end of July 1775, Zavadovsky began dining with Catherine and Potemkin.

Zavadovsky's successful appearance in the middle of the stormy relationship between Catherine and Potemkin was achieved with the mutual agreement of the two principals. Both were eager to resolve the situation without further damage, and Zavadovsky assisted by serving as a buffer. At first, the new arrangement worked: the presence of the quiet, discreet Ukrainian provided Catherine with relief from Potemkin's extreme demands and wilder mood swings; she needed this in order to govern the empire. She did not, however, wish to lose the emotional support, the rare energy, and the unique political and administrative qualities supplied by Potemkin. Potemkin also needed a figure like Zavadovsky. He was eager, even desperate, to find a solution that would ensure his position as the most important man in the empress's life while also giving him sufficient autonomy to act freely and not always have to fear that he would wake up one morning to learn that he had been replaced. Both wanted an arrangement that would preserve the valuable core of their relationship; Potemkin wanted to keep his power and banish his insecurities; Catherine wanted a man to love, but she needed stability and predictability. In Zavadovsky, she believed she had found the right man. At the beginning, Potemkin agreed.

By March 1776, Catherine, her relationship with Potemkin still unresolved, was sexually involved with Zavadovsky. The court and diplomatic corps were thoroughly bewildered; except for the fact that it was now Zavadovsky rather than Potemkin who escorted Catherine to her private apartment at the end of the evening, nothing seemed to have changed. Potemkin went on living at the Winter Palace and was always present whenever Catherine appeared. He and Catherine seemed no less affectionate in public, nor was there any sign of strain or jealousy between the incoming and outgoing favorites. In fact, Potemkin's attitude toward Zavadovsky was cheerful, almost like that of an elder brother.

Zavadovsky pleased her as she had hoped he would. He was ardent, and—unique among her lovers—coveted neither honors nor riches. Their language was passionate; Catherine addressed him with loving diminutives and he called her Katya and Katyusha. When he moved into the Winter Palace, all might have been well had he not developed an obsessive love for Catherine and a consequent fierce jealousy of Potemkin. He wanted—then demanded—an exclusive intimacy, and complained that his predecessor's shadow always lay across his path. Catherine tried to explain her situation and feelings; Zavadovsky refused to listen. This was to bring about his downfall.

On June 28, Zavadovsky's position as favorite was made official. Several days earlier, Potemkin had left the capital for Novgorod, not to return for four weeks. During his absence, Zavadovsky remained unhappy; he was not a courtier and court life bored him; his French was too poor to allow him to participate in social conversations. Potemkin was unhappy, too. When he returned at the end of July, he complained that he was lonely and had no place to go. Catherine replied, "My husband has written me, 'Where shall I go? Where shall I find my proper place?' My dear and beloved husband, come to me. You will be received with open arms."

Potemkin, having initially approved of his successor, now realized that Zavadovsky had become a threat, not only to his private but also to his public position. He complained to Catherine. She, who had hoped for domestic peace, found that she had to cope with jealous scenes from both Zavadovsky and Potemkin. In the spring of 1777, Potemkin stayed away from Catherine's birthday celebrations, retreating to a country estate. From there he issued an ultimatum demanding Zavadovsky's dismissal. Catherine refused:

> You ask for Zavadovsky's removal. My reputation will
> greatly suffer should I carry out this request. With this, our dis-

cord will become firmly established, and I'll only be considered the weaker for it. . . . I'll add that this would be to do an injustice to an innocent person. Don't demand injustices, stop your ears against slanderers, heed my words. Our peace will be restored. Should you be moved by my grief, then dispel even the thought of estranging yourself from me. For God's sake, I find just imagining this intolerable, which proves again that my attachment to you is stronger than yours [to me].

Potemkin would not relent; Zavadovsky had to go. In the summer of 1777, after less than eighteen months as the favorite, he left, bitter and disconsolate, taking her parting gift—eighty thousand rubles and an annual pension of five thousand rubles—and closed himself off in his estate in the Ukraine. That autumn, Catherine made a halfhearted effort to bring him back, but 1777 was a year of political crisis; by then Potemkin ruled as viceroy over Catherine's southern empire, and his support was too important to be jeopardized by turmoil in her private life. Zavadovsky remained away from court for three years, returning in 1780 to St. Petersburg, when he was appointed a privy councillor. In 1781, he became the director of the state bank, which was founded on a plan he had submitted. Subsequently, he became a senator and ended his career as minister of education to Catherine's eldest grandson, Alexander I.

The new relationship worked out between the empress and Potemkin had given each of them freedom to choose other sexual partners, while preserving affection and close political collaboration between themselves. Catherine often missed him. "I am burning with impatience to see you again; it seems to me that I have not seen you for a year. I kiss you, my friend. Come back happy and in good health and we shall love each other. . . . I kiss you and I so much want to see you because I love you with all my heart." In her letters, she made a point of informing him that her new favorite—whoever he happened to be at the moment—sent his love or respects. She made her lovers write directly to him, mostly fawning declarations of how much they, too, missed, admired, or even worshipped him. The young men did this because they knew that, in comparison to Potemkin's influence, their own was nonexistent.

• • •

Meanwhile, Potemkin continued to love Catherine in his own way. His physical passion for her had faded, but his affection for and loyalty to her remained. Meanwhile, he was transferring his sexual approaches from one young woman to another. Among these were three of his five nieces, Alexandra, Varvara, and Ekaterinia, the daughters of his sister Maria Engelhardt.

Varvara (Barbara) attracted her uncle first. Golden-haired, flirtatious, and demanding, she knew at the age of twenty how to control the prince, who then was thirty-seven. He made herculean efforts to please her. His letters to her were ardent, far more so than any he had written to Catherine:

> Varinka, I love you, my darling, as I have never loved anybody before. . . . I kiss you all over, my dearest goddess. . . . Good-bye, sweetness of my lips. . . . You were sound asleep and do not remember anything. When I left you I tucked you in, and kissed you. . . . Tell me, my beautiful, my goddess, that you love me. . . . My sweetest, you dare not get out of health; I shall spank you for that. . . . I kiss you twenty-two million times.

Varvara had no difficulty imposing her will on her doting uncle. She teased and misled him. When Potemkin left for the south, she pretended to be lonely and sad. This prompted the empress to write to him, "Listen, my dearest, Varinka is very sick; it is your absence that is causing it. You are wrong. You will kill her while I am getting more and more fond of her." The young woman was actually deceiving them both; she had fallen in love with young Prince Sergei Golitsyn and was trying to find a way to win Potemkin's and Catherine's permission to marry him. She succeeded, married, and, with Sergei, produced ten children.

Her sister Alexandra ("Sashenka") came next. She was two years older than Varvara, and the liaison between her and Potemkin was less passionate but more serious and durable. For the rest of his life, they were devoted to each other, and even after she had married an influential Polish nobleman, Count Xavier Branitsky, Sashenka was often at Potemkin's side. When she was not with him, she was with the empress, having become one of Catherine's favorite ladies-in-waiting. She was slender, with brown hair, blue eyes, high cheekbones, and impeccable dignity. Of his nieces, Sashenka meant the most to Potemkin. It was to her that Potemkin left most of his wealth; as an elderly woman, she estimated her fortune to be twenty-eight million rubles. Nevertheless, until Catherine's death, Sashenka spent most winters in the Winter Palace, and when the empress died, Sashenka quietly retired to a wooden house in the country.

The prettiest and laziest of the Engelhardt sisters was Ekaterina (Catherine), who yielded to Potemkin because she did not want the bother of resisting him. This relationship was less turbulent than the one with Varvara and less affectionate than that with Sashenka. Ekaterina married Count Paul Skavronsky, but when Catherine appointed the count as minister to Naples, his wife refused to accompany him, remaining in St. Petersburg because her uncle wanted her to stay. When she finally departed for Italy, she found her husband chronically ill in bed. She left him there and spent her days and nights reclining on a sofa, wrapped only in a black fur coat, playing cards. She refused to wear the large diamonds Potemkin had given her or the Parisian dresses bought for her by her husband. "What's the use of all this? Who wants it?" she asked. While she was in Italy, Potemkin died, and when her husband also died, she returned to Russia, married an Italian count, and lived with him for the rest of her life.

There was contemporary disapproval of relationships between uncles and nieces, but it was muted, and outright condemnation was almost nonexistent. In Russia and elsewhere in Europe, the glittering, tightly enclosed eighteenth-century worlds of royalty and aristocracy made physical attraction between relatives more likely and criticism more limited. At thirteen, Catherine herself (then Sophia of Anhalt-Zerbst) had dallied with her uncle George before she left for Russia to marry her second cousin, Grand Duke Peter. In Russia, however, there was an exception to the generally lackadaisical attitude toward Potemkin's affairs with his nieces. Gregory's mother, Daria Potemkina, emphatically did not approve of her son's relations with her granddaughters. No one listened to her. Potemkin laughed at her censorious letters, balled them up, and tossed them into the fire.

Catherine was not jealous of these young women because they were sleeping with Potemkin. What she envied them was their youth. Her own youth had been wasted. She had been sixteen when she married a wretched boy. She was a mature woman of twenty-five before she had her first sexual encounter, and this was with a heartless rake. Now approaching fifty, she still saw in Potemkin's nieces the ardent young girl she could have been. She hated growing old. Her birthday, so publicly celebrated, was for her a day of mourning. In a letter to Grimm, she wrote, "Would it not be charming if an empress could be always fifteen?"

❦ 63 ❦

Favorites

WHEN CATHERINE, then Sophia, arrived in Russia at the age of fourteen, she learned that "favorite" was the term used to describe an established and formally recognized lover of the woman on the throne, Empress Elizabeth. While she was still a married grand duchess, Catherine herself had three lovers: Saltykov, Poniatowski, and Gregory Orlov. None of these was her "favorite"; she was not yet the empress. Orlov, of course, remained Catherine's lover after she reached the throne, thereby becoming her first favorite. During her lifetime, Catherine had twelve lovers: the first three, named above, before she reached the throne at thirty-three, the other nine during her thirty-four years as empress. Of the twelve, she loved five: Poniatowsky, Orlov, Potemkin, Zavadovsky, and Alexander Lanskoy. For another three—Saltykov, Ivan Rimsky-Korsakov, and Alexander Mamonov—she felt passion. Three others—Vasilchikov, Simon Zorich and Alexander Yermolov—were quickly chosen and quickly discarded. The twelfth and last, Platon Zubov, was in a category of his own.

Usually there was only a brief interval between the departure of one of Catherine's favorites and the arrival of the next. Most favorites had no influence on government policy, but they were always close to Catherine's ear, and, throughout her reign, reports of their rise and fall filled the dispatches of foreign ambassadors attempting to interpret the significance of each change. Several of Catherine's lovers played a mere decorative role in the life of the woman who drew them from obscurity and eventually sent them back into the shadows. There was always keen competition for the role. The candidate chosen was rewarded with jewels, money, palaces, and country estates. When he was sent away, the parting was almost always managed without tears or recriminations; occasionally a former lover later reappeared at court.

Most of Catherine's favorites were young officers originally selected for their handsome faces, but their selection and presence was not due solely, or even primarily, to sensuality on Catherine's part. She wanted to love and be loved. She had lived with an impossible husband in an emotional vacuum. To read her letters to Potemkin is to realize that, as much as physical satisfaction, she wanted intelligent, loving companionship.

Having accepted that he was no longer the imperial favorite, Gregory Orlov consoled himself by falling in love with, and asking to marry, his fifteen-year-old second cousin, Catherine Zinovieva, with whom he set off on an extended journey to western Europe. The empress, although piqued to find herself replaced so quickly, interceded on his behalf with the Holy Synod, arranging for it to set aside the church ban on marriages of people from the same family. In 1777, Orlov was finally able to marry. But his bride had tuberculosis and her health continued to deteriorate. Despite the fact that Orlov lavished care on her and took her everywhere for treatment, she died four years later in Lausanne. Orlov returned to St. Petersburg, where his own health declined. He suffered from hallucinations and lapsed into dementia. On April 12, 1783, he died at the age of forty-six. His will left his immense fortune to Alexis Bobrinsky, his son with Catherine.

However impetuously Catherine may sometimes have behaved in the first, private stage of a love affair, she was always dignified in public. She never apologized for her favorites or indicated that she considered these arrangements unseemly. All of her favorites were openly acknowledged; indeed, nothing seemed more normal than the matter-of-fact attitude with which these men were regarded by the court and society. Their presence at court was a constant. She was the heavily burdened ruler of a great empire as well as a proud and passionate woman, and she had neither time nor inclination to explain or quibble. She was lonely and she needed a partner, someone with whom to share not power but conversation, laughter, and human warmth. Therein lay one of the problems confronting her: the love of power and the power to attract love were not easy to reconcile.

• • •

Except for Zavadovsky, all of her favorites were Guards officers, and most came from families of the lesser nobility. When a new favorite was named, he was shown to an apartment near hers in the imperial palace. Upon arrival, he found in his dressing table drawer a large bundle of rubles, a welcoming gift from the empress. He began a life of stultifying regularity. At ten every morning, he began his day by calling on the empress in her apartment. In public, he was treated as a high court official. He accompanied Catherine everywhere and was alertly and respectfully attentive to her wishes as she proceeded through her long days. His arm was always ready to escort her at court, dinner, and to her seat at the palace theater. When she drove out in her carriage, he sat beside her. He stood next to her at court receptions, sat with her at card tables, and, at ten every evening, he offered his arm and accompanied her to her apartment. Other than these duties, he lived in near isolation. After Potemkin and Zavadovsky, most of Catherine's favorites were not allowed to make or receive visits. She lavished presents and honors on these young men, but it was unusual for existence in this golden cage to be prolonged for more than two years. On parting, almost all received extravagant gifts; none experienced vindictiveness.

Most of the favorites were young men whose youth and social inexperience offered a striking contrast to the dignified demeanor of their imperial patroness. The differences in age and station confused the court and created a whirlwind of gossip in Europe. But the specific manner and intimate practices by which these favorites pleased Catherine are unknown. Only in the cases of Potemkin and Zavadovsky is private correspondence available, and, in this regard, it is unspecific. Those seeking physical details of Catherine's romantic liaisons will learn nothing; neither in her own words nor in the words of others are there any references to sexual preferences and behavior. Her bedroom door remains closed.

With the exception of her relationships with Potemkin, Zavadovsky, and, at the end, Zubov, Catherine compartmentalized her life, keeping politics, administration, and diplomacy separate from her private life. Fearing that a lover might try to exploit her emotions and reach for political power, she did not permit her favorites to play a role in government. As she grew older, her need for intimacy and support made Catherine more vulnerable, and favorites who showed interest in her intellectual and artistic pursuits were likely to last longer. Lanskoy (1780–84) and Mamonov (1786–89) were examples of this. Then Lanskoy died and Mamonov betrayed her by falling in love with someone else.

Until the procession of young Guards officers began, Catherine's love affairs had not shocked Europe. The example set by other contemporary monarchs left scant grounds for rebuke. Monarchs everywhere had mistresses or lovers. In Russia, Peter the Great had children by his mistress before marrying her and making her an empress. Empress Anne and Empress Elizabeth had both paved the way for the acceptance of favoritism in Russia. Catherine's political achievements also made flaws in her private life easy to overlook or discount; beyond that, she conducted her court "with the greatest dignity and exterior decorum," said Sir James Harris, the British ambassador in the 1780s.

The problem, as the years went by, was not the institution of favoritism but the extreme youth of the favorites and the discrepancy between their ages and Catherine's. As attention focused increasingly on the question of age, Catherine explained that these relationships served an important pedagogical function. Her young men, she said, were being schooled to ornament a sophisticated, cosmopolitan court; they were to be accomplished and useful, not just to the monarch personally but ultimately to the empire. In her correspondence with Grimm, she explained that these young men were so extraordinary that she was obliged to give them opportunity to develop their talents.

When Peter Zavadovsky fell from favor, Potemkin looked around for a candidate whom Catherine might accept and whose loyalty to him he could trust. His choice was thirty-two-year-old Simon Zorich, a Russian officer of Serbian descent. Zorich was tall, handsome, and polite, although he lacked notable intelligence. He had an honorable war record; he had displayed bravery in battle against the Turks and had borne up well during five years as a prisoner of war. Returning to Russia in 1774, he became an aide to Potemkin. In May 1777, with Zavadovsky's departure, he became the new favorite.

Zorich's tenure was briefer than Zavadovsky's. His new position went to his head. Catherine made him a count, but he demanded to be made a prince like Orlov and Potemkin. His complaints offended the empress; Zorich had been in favor for only ten months when she told Potemkin, "Last night I was in love with him; today I cannot stand him any more." Potemkin had ignored the fact that Catherine needed someone she could talk to. As the relationship deteriorated, Zorich could not understand why the woman who had covered him with riches had suddenly retreated. Blaming Potemkin, he determined to fight for his place. He challenged Potemkin; the prince disdainfully turned his back and walked away. In May 1778, only a year after his arrival, Zorich was dismissed with a pension. A compulsive gambler, he was later discovered embezzling army funds and died in disgrace.

Zorich was replaced by a twenty-four-year-old Guards officer, Ivan Rimsky-Korsakov, whose term lasted two years. The new favorite was handsome, played the violin, and had a fine tenor voice. In Catherine's eyes, his male beauty evoked the heroes of ancient Greece, and in her letters to Grimm she refers to her new lover as "Pyrrhus, king of Epirus whom every painter should paint, every sculptor should sculpt and every poet should sing. . . . He makes no gesture, no movement, that is not graceful and noble."

His brilliance did not encompass the intellect, however. When Catherine gave him a mansion in St. Petersburg, he decided that it needed a library to proclaim his new status. He had shelves built and then called on the capital's leading bookseller. What books were wanted, he was asked. "You understand that better than I," said the new bibliophile. "Big books at the bottom, then smaller books, and so on up to the top." The bookseller unloaded many rows of unsold German Bible commentaries bound in fine leather. Soon afterward, the British ambassador probed the favorite's background and discovered that he had "changed his original common name of Ivan Korsak to the better-sounding one of Ivan Rimsky-Korsakov."*

Despite Catherine's praise, most in the Russian court expected Rimsky-Korsakov to last only briefly, because everyone except the em-

---

*The family decided to keep the new name, and the nineteenth-century composer Nicholas Rimsky-Korsakov came from a collateral branch.

press saw that his heart was not in his work. He was expected to be in constant attendance, was forbidden to leave the palace, and became bored and restless. He escaped into the arms of Countess Bruce, Catherine's principal lady-in-waiting and for years one of her closest friends. Foolishly, the couple believed that they could carry on their affair inside the palace. They managed for almost a year, but it ended abruptly one day when the empress opened a door and discovered them making love. Catherine sent a message to Rimsky-Korsakov informing him that she would be generous provided he left St. Petersburg immediately. Countess Bruce was commanded to return to her husband.

There was more to this tangled plot. Catherine, the court, and Countess Bruce soon learned that Rimsky-Korsakov had been using Bruce as a decoy with whom to pass the time and alleviate his boredom. His real object was a beautiful young countess, Catherine Stroganova, married to one of the wealthiest men in Russia. The Stroganovs had just returned from six years of living in Paris, and, on first seeing the handsome "king of Epirus," the young countess fell in love. Only when the disgraced Rimsky-Korsakov left for Moscow and Countess Stroganova immediately followed him, was the extent of this operatic, labyrinthine double betrayal fully revealed. Count Stroganov behaved with patrician dignity. Worried that his young son would be affected by public scandal, he installed his wife in a Moscow palace, where she and her lover lived happily for thirty years. There, they brought up the three children they had together.

For six months following the Rimsky-Korsakov debacle, Catherine remained alone, but at Easter in 1780 a new favorite, Alexander Lanskoy, appeared. Then twenty-two, he came from an impecunious family of the provincial nobility and had served as an officer in the Horse Guards. When he found that he lacked sufficient funds to keep pace with his brother officers, he asked for reassignment to a provincial garrison, where his expenses would be lower. His application was rejected at the College of War by Potemkin himself, who then, surprisingly, appointed the young man his personal aide-de-camp and introduced him to Catherine. Lanskoy had an elegant bearing and a sensitive face; Catherine described him as "kind, gay, honest, and full of gentleness." In November 1779, he was was officially installed in the palace apartment vacated by Rimsky-Korsakov. The usual shower of riches descended: jewels, a hundred thousand rubles, and a country estate. Two cousins became officers in the Preobrazhensky Guards; three sisters came to court as maids of honor, married noblemen, and became ladies-of-the-bedchamber.

Catherine's admiration for this adoring acolyte stimulated her pedagogical belief that more Russians should be trained to serve the empire. Lanskoy responded wholeheartedly to this approach. His education had been modest, and his devotion to Catherine was based on her role as his teacher as much as her position as empress. When she discovered his desire to learn, she helped him write to Grimm in French.

Lanskoy did not arouse in Catherine the passion she had for Orlov or Potemkin, but his gentleness and devotion inspired in her an almost maternal affection. He was intelligent and tactful; he refused to take any part in public affairs; he was artistic, had good taste, and was seriously interested in literature, painting, and architecture. He became an ideal companion, accompanying her to concerts and the theater, sitting quietly and listening as she talked, even helping her to design new gardens at Tsarskoe Selo.

As the months stretched into years, Catherine's young lover became indispensable to her. Even the cynical Bezborodko admitted that "compared to the others, he was an angel. He had friends, did not try to harm his neighbors, and often he tried to help people." From time to time, there were rumors that Potemkin was jealous of this nonthreatening young man and that Lanskoy was on the brink of dismissal. This was far from the truth. Potemin was thoroughly satisfied, and Catherine was free to devote herself to Lanskoy, whose good humor, she said, had made Tsarskoe Selo "into the most charming and pleasant of places where the days passed so quickly one did not know what had become of them."

Four years passed, a longer period than Catherine had spent with any lover since she had separated from Orlov twelve years earlier. On June 19, 1784, Lanskoy complained of a sore throat. It grew worse. A high fever set in. Suddenly, five days from the onset, he died of inflammation of the throat. It was said to have been diphtheria.

The suddenness of this death was overwhelming, and the reaction of the woman left behind was uncontrollable grief. She collapsed into bed and for three weeks refused to leave her room. Her son, his wife, and her beloved grandchildren all were refused admittance; they heard only endless sobbing behind her bedroom door. Potemkin came immediately from the south. He and others tried to comfort her, but, as Catherine later told Grimm, "they helped, but I could not endure the help. No one was able to speak, to think in accord with my feelings. One step at a time had to be taken, and with each step a battle had to be endured; one to be won; one to be lost." Eventually, Potemkin managed to calm and distract her. "He succeeded in awakening us from the sleep of the dead," she said.

Her weeping stopped, but her depression remained. As she described it to Grimm:

> I am plunged into the most profound grief and my happiness no longer exists. I thought that I myself would die from the irreparable loss of my best friend. I had hoped that he would become the support of my old age.... This was a young man whom I was educating, who was grateful, gentle and honest, who shared my pains and who rejoiced in my joys.... I have become a desperate, monosyllabic creature. I drag myself about like a shadow. I cannot set eyes on a human face without the tears choking my mouth. I do not know what will become of me, but I do know that in all my life I have never been so unhappy as now that my best, dearest, and kindest friend has abandoned me like this.

Lanskoy left to Catherine the fortune he had acquired as her favorite; she divided it equally among his mother, brother, and sisters. She could not face spending the rest of the summer at Tsarskoe Selo without him, did not appear in public until September, and refused to return to the Winter Palace until February. Eventually, when she went back to Tsarskoe Selo, it was to place a Grecian urn dedicated to his memory in the garden where they had worked together. The inscription read, "From Catherine to my dearest friend."

In the procession of Catherine's favorites, it seemed that the ending of a significant relationship was often followed by the appearance of a lesser figure. Orlov had been followed by Vasilchikov, and Zavadovsky by Zorich. Now, this sequence recurred: after the death of Lanskoy came Alexander Yermolov, although not immediately. The deep wound caused by Lanskoy's death healed slowly, and the favorite's apartment remained vacant for a year. When she resumed life, she found only tepid consolation in the thirty-year-old Yermolov.

He, like most of the others, was a Guards officer, and he, like Lan-

skoy, had served as an aide to Potemkin. The prince approved of Yermolov, whom he thought to be safe and knew to be ignorant and
uninterested in being taught anything. He was handsome and seemed
honest, which suited Catherine at that moment. She was in no mood
for another ardent young student; in her mind, no one could compete
with the charm, brilliance, and devotion of Lanskoy. By the spring of
1785, she was writing to Grimm, "I am once more inwardly calm and
serene. . . . I have found a friend who is very capable."

During his seventeen months as favorite, Yermolov made little
claim on Catherine's time or interest. In the end, he engineered his
own demise. He had been Potemkin's protégé, but he began behaving
toward Potemkin as if he considered himself the prince's equal. Secure,
he thought, in his position, he began to criticize the prince to Catherine. He reported every scandalous story, true or false, that reached his
ears. He passed along an accusation that Potemkin was pocketing the
pension intended for the deposed khan of the Crimea. The denouement was predictable. In June 1786, an infuriated Potemkin descended
on Yermolov at court and shouted, "You cur, you monkey, who dares to
bespatter me with the mud of the gutters from which I have raised
you." Yermolov, who was proud, put his hand on his sword hilt, but a
sudden blow from Potemkin sent him reeling. Then Potemkin burst
into Catherine's's apartment and roared, "Either he or I must go! If this
nonentity of nonentities is allowed to remain at court, then I quit the
state's services as of today." Yermolov was dismissed immediately and
was given 130,000 rubles in cash and permission to live abroad for five
years. Catherine never saw him again.

After Yermolov's dismissal, Catherine followed her pattern of replac-
ing a nonentity with a seeming paragon, someone she believed was another Lanskoy. Alexander Mamonov, then twenty-six, was another
Guards officer, handsome, educated, fluent in French and Italian, and
the nephew of the generous Count Stroganov, whose young wife had
run off with Rimsky-Korsakov. Only one evening after Yermolov's dismissal, Mamonov escorted Catherine to her apartment. "They slept
until nine o'clock," Catherine's secretary wrote in his notebook the following morning. The new favorite was immediately promoted to high
rank in the Preobrazhensky Guards and in May 1788 was elevated to
the rank of lieutenant general. Later that month, Catherine made him

a count. Her private name for him was "L'habit rouge" (the Red Coat), after the color of his favorite uniform. Because he was more intelligent than most of his predecessors, she occasionally asked his advice on political matters. Although she treated him seriously to his face, she spoke of him to others as a doting mother might speak of her child: "We are as clever as the very devil; we adore music; we hide our fondness for poetry as though it were a crime," she wrote to Grimm. To Potemkin, she reported enthusiastically: "Sasha is beyond price . . . an inexhaustible source of gaiety, original in his outlook and exceptionally well-informed. . . . Our whole tone is that of the best society. We write Russian and French to perfection; our features are very regular; we have two black eyes and eyebrows, and a noble, easy bearing."

Despite Catherine's initial enthusiasm, her relationship with Mamonov began to cool after eighteen months. By January 1788, the favorite was showing signs of weariness, and there were rumors that he was attempting to evade his intimate duties. In fact, Mamonov found the restrictions involved in life with Catherine burdensome. In St. Petersburg, he was rarely permitted out of her sight, and he hated trips outside the capital, when he was shut up for days on a boat or in a coach; he complained that he found traveling in her coach "stifling."

In the spring of 1788, he began a clandestine affair with twenty-five-year-old Princess Darya Scherbatova. Soon he was writing to Potemkin, begging to be released from his relationship with Catherine. Potemkin replied sternly, "It is your duty to remain at your post. Don't be a fool and ruin your career." By December 1788, Mamonov was in a state of decline, warning that he could no longer perform. Nevertheless, at the beginning of 1789, he was still the official favorite, and Catherine remained deaf to any suggestions that he be replaced. Then, on the evening of February 11, 1789, they quarreled, he asked to resign, and she wept all the next day. Potemkin briefly patched things up, but Mamonov confided to a friend that he considered his life "a prison." On February 21, Catherine tearfully complained that Mamonov was "cold and preoccupied." In the weeks that followed, the empress saw him infrequently; on April 21, 1789, her sixtieth birthday, she passed the day in seclusion. By then, Mamonov's affair with Scherbatova was known to many at court, although still not to Catherine. On June 1, Peter Zavadovsky, the former favorite, was told that Mamonov was determined to marry Scherbatova, whom he described as "a girl most ordinary, not possessing either looks or other gifts." On June 18, Mamonov finally came to the empress to confess. Beginning his argument with duplicity, he complained that she was cold to him and asked her advice as to what he should do. She understood that he was asking to be released, but, in order to keep him at court, she suggested that he marry Countess Bruce's thirteen-year-old daughter, one of the richest heiresses in Russia. Catherine was surprised when he declined—and then suddenly the whole truth came out. Trembling, Mamonov admitted that for a year he had been in love with Scherbatova, and that six months earlier, he had given his word to marry her. Catherine was shocked, but she was too proud not to be magnanimous. She summoned Mamonov and Scherbatova and saw immediately that the young woman was pregnant. She pardoned Mamonov and granted the couple permission to marry, even insisting that the ceremony be performed in the palace chapel. She did not attend, but gave them a hundred thousand rubles and a country estate. "God grant them happiness," she said, stipulating only that they leave St. Petersburg.

She had been generous, but behind her generosity was a woman badly hurt. "I cannot express how I have suffered," she wrote to Potemkin. "Can you imagine?" He was guilty of "a thousand contradictions and contradictory ideas and irrational behavior." That anyone should think she had kept him against his will made her indignant. "I have never been anybody's tyrant and I hate constraint," she said.

The greater misfortune was Mamonov's. Somehow, he mistook the empress's parting generosity for lingering embers of passion. In 1792, tiring of his wife, he began writing the empress from Moscow, pleading for a renewal of the imperial liaison, lamenting his youthful "folly" in precipitating the loss of her favor, a memory, he said, that "constantly tortures my soul." Catherine did not reply.

What was Catherine seeking in these ornamental young men? She has suggested that it was love. "I couldn't live for a day without love," she had written in her *Memoirs*. Love has many forms, however, and she did not mean sexual love alone, but also companionship, warmth, support, intelligence, and, if possible, humor. And also respect—not just the respect automatically due an empress, but the admiration a man gives an attractive woman. As she grew older, she wanted assurance that she could still attract a man and keep his love. A realist as well as a romantic, she knew and accepted the fact that because she was their sovereign, young men were drawn to her for reasons and with goals different from hers. Desire for love and sex played little part in attracting her lovers to her; they were motivated by ambition, desire for prestige, wealth, and, in some cases, power. Catherine knew this. She asked them for things other than simple sexual congress. She wanted an indication of pleasure in her company, a desire to understand her point of view, a willingness to be instructed by her intelligence and experience, an appreciation of her sense of humor, and an ability to make her laugh. The physical side of her relationships offered only brief distraction. When Catherine dismissed lovers, it was not because they lacked virility but because they bored her. One need not be an empress to find it impossible to talk in the morning to a person with whom one has spent the night.

The history of her youth and young womanhood helps explain her relationships with favorites. She had been a fourteen-year-old stranger brought to a foreign land. At sixteen, she had married a psychologically crippled and physically blemished adolescent. She spent nine years untouched by this man in their marriage bed. She had no family: her mother and father were dead; her three children were spirited away at the moment of birth. As the years passed, she became caught up in a search for the Fountain of Youth. Today, there are various ways of prolonging the illusion of youth, but in Catherine's day there were not. She attempted to preserve her youth by identifying it with the affection—simulated, if necessary—of young men. When they were unable to prolong that illusion, either they or she ended the charade, and she tried again with someone else.

Catherine had twelve lovers. What shocked her contemporaries was not this number, but the age difference between Catherine and her later favorites. She crafted an explanation: she categorized these young men as students whom she hoped to develop into intellectual companions. If they did not completely measure up—and she did not pretend that one would become another Voltaire or Diderot, or even another Potemkin—then she could at least say that she was helping to train them for future roles in administering the empire.

How severely should her young favorites be judged for allowing themselves to be used; specifically, for submitting to a sexual liaison with someone they did not love? This is not just an eighteenth-century question, nor one to be asked only of young men. Women have always submitted to sexual relationships with men they do not love. Beyond physical force, and arrangements made by family, they usually have reasons similar to those of Catherine's young men: ambition, a desire for wealth, for some form of power, and possible future independence. Catherine's young men did not always independently aspire to become favorites. Rising from the lesser nobility, they were frequently urged on by relatives who hoped that the shower of imperial benevolence would also fall on them. Nor was it widely seen as immoral. Indeed, there was no case involving one of Catherine's favorites in which the young man's family raised a warning finger and said, "Stop! This is wrong!"

Catherine conducted the public side of her romantic life on an open stage. Privately, writing in her memoirs or to Potemkin or other correspondents, she included glowing descriptions of the young men who became her favorites. These descriptions erred on the side of poor judgment and excess sentimentality, nothing else. About herself, she was honest; she admitted to Potemkin that she had taken four lovers before him; she wrote in her memoirs about the difficulty of resisting temptation in a setting like the Russian court. Who she was and where she came from helped determine her relationships with men. Perhaps if she had been the daughter of a great king, as Elizabeth I of England had been; perhaps if she, like Elizabeth, had been able to use virginity and abstinence as prizes to tempt and manipulate powerful men, the lives of these two preeminent woman rulers in the history of European monarchy would have been more similar.

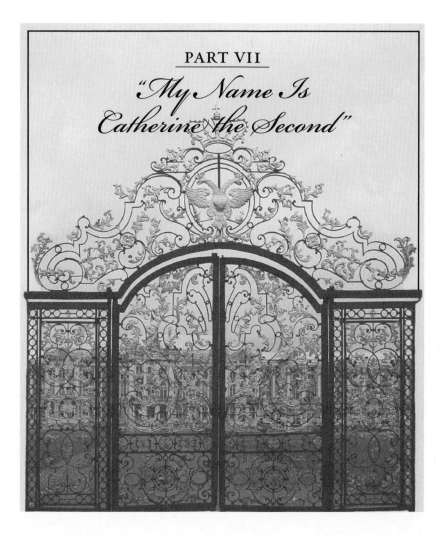

PART VII

"My Name Is Catherine the Second"

Catherine, Paul, and Natalia

CATHERINE HAD BEEN brought to Russia to produce an heir and ensure the succession. Her obligation to conceive a child with her husband, Peter, had stretched over nine wasted years. Failure had prompted Empress Elizabeth to insist that Catherine choose between two potential surrogate fathers, Sergei Saltykov and Lev Naryshkin. And then, the moment success was achieved, Elizabeth had snatched the newborn infant away.

This cruel mischief permanently affected the lives of both Catherine and her son, Paul. Catherine was permitted no complete experience of motherhood, and her memories of the birth and infancy of this child were painful. Saltykov, almost certainly Paul's father, had abandoned her to boast about his conquest. Paul thereafter became a reminder of a man who had ruthlessly deserted her. Peter, her husband, was worse. Peter humiliated her for years and threatened to seal her away in a convent. Both of these men, Paul's dynastically recognized father and his biological father, left her with bitter memories of misery, disillusionment, and loneliness.

In 1762, when Catherine reached the throne and retrieved her son, it was too late to repair their relationship. Paul was eight years old, small for his age, frail, and frequently ill. At first, he missed Elizabeth, the tall, overwhelmingly affectionate woman who had spoiled him by surrounding him with nurses and women who refused to let him do anything for himself. When Catherine was allowed to see him, she came, but she was usually accompanied by the giant figure of Gregory Orlov, who claimed the attention Paul felt should be his.

Catherine's relationship with Paul, involving as it did the question of the succession, was the most psychologically difficult personal and political problem of her reign. From the beginning, Catherine realized that anyone plotting against her could always point to a Romanov heir in the person of her son. The issue was clouded by the question of whether Paul was the son of Peter III or the child of Catherine's lover, Sergei Saltykov. In her memoirs, Catherine strongly implies that Paul was Saltykov's son, and, at the time of Paul's birth, almost no one at court believed the child to be Peter's son. There was general knowledge of Peter's sexual incapacity, of the emotional and physical breach between the married partners, and of Catherine's affair with Saltykov. The mass of the Russian people, however, were not privy to this information, and believed that the heir to the throne was the son of Catherine's husband, the future Tsar Peter III. The Moscow crowds cheering Paul at Catherine's coronation believed that Paul was the legitimate great-grandson of Peter the Great. Catherine, riding in the coronation procession, heard the cheers and understood their meaning: that Paul was her rival. Officially, however, Paul's status as heir did not hinge on the question of his paternity. Once proclaimed empress, Catherine had made certain that Paul's succession rights derived from her. Basing her proclamation on Peter the Great's decree that the sovereign could name his or her successor, she publicly proclaimed Paul her heir. No one ever challenged her right to make this decision.

Then a strange thing happened: Paul's face began to change. A lengthy illness when Paul was nine eroded his childhood prettiness; his face and features, which had been pleasing, became distorted in a manner that was more than temporary adolescent asymmetry. He developed thin brown hair, a receding chin, and a protruding bottom lip. He looked more like Peter than Sergei, and had the same abrupt, clumsy movements as Peter. Some who had known Peter began to believe that Paul really was the dead tsar's son.

By the time Paul reached adolescence he, at least, was convinced that he was Peter's son, and Peter was the paternal figure the boy came to revere. He began to ask people about the death of his father, and why the throne had come to his mother instead of himself. If they hesitated to answer, he said that when he was grown up, he would find out. When he asked about his own chances of ruling, there were long, uncomfortable silences. There were other gaps in his knowledge. He heard rumors that the brother of Gregory Orlov, his mother's favorite, was suspected of being responsible for his father's death. Thereafter, the sight of the

Orlov brothers at court, and the knowledge of his mother's relationship with Gregory Orlov, tormented him. At the same time, he was constructing an idealized image of Peter, modeling himself on Peter and imitating Peter's traits and behavior. Aware that Peter had been passionately fond of everything connected with the army, Paul began playing with soldiers, first toys, then real soldiers, as Peter had done. Again following Peter's lead, he turned to admire the greatest soldier of the age, Frederick of Prussia.

Since 1760, when Paul was six, Nikita Panin had been his governor and senior tutor. Paul's lessons had included languages, history, geography, mathematics, science, astronomy, religion, drawing, and music. He learned to dance, ride, and fence. He was intelligent, impatient, and highly strung. "His Highness has the bad habit of rushing things; he rushes to get up, to eat, to go to bed," said one of his tutors. "At dinner-time, how many ruses will he think of to gain a few minutes and sit down sooner.... He eats too fast, doesn't chew properly, and so charges his stomach with an impossible task."

At ten, Paul began to study the works of Jean d'Alembert, the French mathematician and co-editor of Diderot's *Encyclopedia*. Catherine invited d'Alembert to come to Russia to teach mathematics to her son. When the Frenchman first declined, she tried again, this time offering him a house, a large salary, and the status and privileges of an ambassador.

Unfortunately, this approach to d'Alembert elicited a personally humiliating response. Not only did d'Alembert reiterate his refusal to come to Russia, but he privately uttered a remark that traveled far. Referring to the official reason given by Catherine for Peter III's death, he said, "I am too prone to hemorrhoids which in Russia is a severe complaint. I prefer to have a painful behind in the safety of my home." The empress never forgave him.

In the summer of 1771, Paul, then seventeen, endured a five-week battle with influenza. Catherine and Panin watched anxiously as he struggled with a high fever and debilitating diarrhea. Once he began to recover, the question of the succession reasserted itself. Catherine knew that she could not postpone his official coming of age much beyond his eighteenth birthday in September 1772. It was Panin who, in this context, suggested that marriage to some healthy young woman might help mature the difficult young man. This way, too, the tutor added, Her Majesty would probably soon have a grandson whom she could raise according to her own views. This reasoning appealed to Catherine.

Three years earlier, in 1768, when Paul was fourteen, Catherine had already begun thinking of a suitable bride for him and had made a list of candidates. Characteristically, she sought a bride in her own image: a sensible German princess from a minor court. The one who appealed to her most was Sophia of Württemburg, but Sophia was then only fourteen, too young for marriage. The empress's eye shifted to the younger daughters of the landgrave of Hesse-Darmstadt. Catherine's plan was to invite the landgravine and her three still-unmarried daughters, Amalie, Wilhelmina, and Louise, to Russia. They were eighteen, seventeen, and fifteen, respectively. Paul would be asked to chose among them. As had been true in her own case years before, the invitation did not include the father.

During the summer of 1772, after Gregory Orlov had been replaced, the relationship between Catherine and her son improved. Living together with Paul at Tsarskoe Selo, Catherine made a companion of her son, and the long estrangement seemed to be over. "We have never had a jollier time at Tsarskoe Selo than these nine weeks I have spent there with my son, who is becoming a nice lad. He really appears to enjoy my company," she wrote to her Hamburg friend Frau Bielcke. "I return to town on Tuesday with my son who does not want to leave my side, and whom I have the honor to please so well that he sometimes changes his place at the table to sit next to me." Then, after what Paul assumed was Orlov's final disappearance, Gregory reappeared at court. Paul was dismayed.

In the spring of 1773, the three Hessian princesses and their mother were invited to Russia. They stopped first in Berlin, where, as he had done with Sophia of Anhalt-Zerbst thirty-one years earlier, Frederick reminded them always to remember they had been born Germans. At the end of June, four Russian naval vessels arrived in Lübeck to carry the Hessian party up the Baltic. The commander of the frigate transporting the young women and their mother was Paul's best friend, Andrei Razumovsky, the son of Catherine's friend Kyril Razumovsky. Andrei was captivated by the middle daughter, Wilhelmina, and she by him.

In St. Petersburg, Paul took only two days to make his choice: it was the same as Andrei Razumovsky's—Princess Wilhelmina. Unfortunately, Wilhelmina's reaction to the small, strange young man soon to be her husband was not enthusiastic. Catherine noticed her hesitation; so did the girl's mother. Nevertheless, the machinery of diplomacy and protocol ground ahead. As had been the case with Catherine and her own mother, both the bride-to-be and the landgravine were indifferent to the requirement for a religious conversion. Predictably, as the date of the wedding approached, the landgrave wrote from Germany, objecting to his daughter changing her religion. Also predictably, he surrendered to his wife's decision. On August 15, 1773, Wilhelmina was received into the Orthodox Church as Natalia Alekseyevna. The next day she was betrothed to Paul and became a Russian grand duchess.

There were banquets, balls, and late-summer picnics at which Catherine enjoyed the company of the landgravine, an energetic woman who was a friend of Goethe's. Prince Orlov invited the three princesses, their mother, Catherine, and the court to Gatchina, where he gave a lavish reception: five hundred guests dined from Sèvres porcelain and gold plate. Orlov, hoping to irritate the empress, who had brought along her new favorite, Vasilchikov, immediately began to flirt with Louise, the youngest of the visiting princesses. To Berlin, the Prussian minister described "the extraordinary attentions which Prince Orlov pays the landgravine and the freedom of manner with which he treats the princesses, especially the youngest one."

The wedding of nineteen-year-old Paul and seventeen-year-old Natalia took place on September 29, 1773. It was followed by ten days of court balls, theatrical performances, and masquerades, while people in the streets drank free beer, ate hot meat pies, and watched fireworks soaring above the St. Peter and St. Paul Fortress. Paul was exultant; a new life and a new freedom seemed to be offering itself. Natalia consoled herself because Andrei Razumovsky was always nearby.

As Paul's wedding approached, Nikita Panin had been waging a battle to retain his influence over Paul and his wife-to-be. Catherine realized that, once married, Paul would become more independent of her; she was determined that, simultaneously, he also become more independent of Panin. Paul's marriage would be both the pretext and the moment for severing this tie with Panin. With the loss of his role as tutor, however, Panin would be deprived of the base at court that entitled him to live at the palace and see his charge daily. He would no longer be able to influence Paul's political views, which, Catherine believed, had helped steer her son toward what she regarded as an excessive admiration of Prussia and Frederick II.

Panin, who had held his position for thirteen years, was unprepared for this maneuver. Being governor and tutor to the heir to the throne gave him a commanding position in government and society. As the guardian of the physical well-being and the education of the future sovereign, he had chosen, directed, and dismissed tutors, librarians, doctors, and all servants at the grand ducal court. The establishment over which he presided had its own table, famous as one of the best in the city. There, Panin received guests every day—supposedly on behalf of the grand duke, who was present to listen—including senior state officials, court dignitaries, foreign guests, writers, scientists, and many of his own relatives. His position as tutor, in short, was the foundation of Panin's political influence. To avoid jeopardizing it, he had always refused to accept any other official post. On assuming the real leadership of the College of Foreign Affairs in 1763, he remained only at the second level of rank, leaving the senior title to the largely absentee chancellor, Michael Vorontsov. Being in constant contact with the empress, Panin was also able to offer frequent counsel to her on personal subjects; a year before, in the autumn of 1772, he had helped Catherine break with Orlov by producing Vasilchikov. Given these many duties and services, he had believed himself invaluable and invulnerable.

Unfortunately for Panin, in May 1773 Orlov had returned to the capital and been readmitted to the council. There, he was eager to retaliate against Panin and assist Catherine in breaking the tutor's hold on the grand duke. The result was that as Paul was about to be married, Panin was informed that the education of the grand duke was completed and that his mission as tutor was fulfilled. He responded by threatening to retire altogether to his estate near Smolensk if he were separated from Paul. Catherine, who did not wish to lose Panin completely, found a compromise. Panin would cease to be Paul's tutor and give up administration of the grand ducal household. When he balked at vacating his rooms in the palace, Catherine announced that the rooms needed remodeling. To pacify Panin, she raised him to the equivalency in rank of the chancellor or a field marshal, and gave him the title of minister of Foreign Affairs. He was awarded a special grant of one hundred thousand rubles, an annual pension of thirty thousand rubles, and a salary of ten thousand rubles. Paul regretted the separation, but, caught up in his marriage to Natalia, he did not complain.

After the wedding, the empress told the landgravine that the new grand duchess was "a golden young woman" with whom her son appeared to be deeply in love. Over time and on closer examination, however, Catherine's praise of her new daughter-in-law turned to irritation. She complained to Grimm:

> Everything is done to excess with this lady. If she goes for a walk, it is for . . . [thirteen miles]; if she dances, it's twenty quadrilles and as many minuets . . . in order to avoid the apartments being overheated, she has no fire lit in them at all . . . in short, the middle way is unknown here. . . . There is neither grace, nor prudence, nor wisdom in any of this and God knows what will become of her. . . . Just think that after more than a year and a half, she still doesn't speak a word of the language.

With Potemkin, she shared a different complaint:

> The grand duke . . . came to tell me himself that he and the grand duchess are in debt again. . . . He told me that her debt was from this, that, and the other thing to which I answered that she has an allowance, just as he does, like no one else in Europe; that this allowance is simply for clothing and passing fancies, but that the rest—servants, table, and carriage—is provided them. . . . I fear there will be no end to this. . . . If you count everything, then more than five hundred thousand has been expended on them during the year, and still they are in dire straits. But not a single thank you or a word of gratitude.

Catherine also heard rumors that Natalia's relationship with Andrei Razumovsky had grown excessively warm. To her lectures to Paul on his wife's extravagance, she added suggestions that he should keep an eye on her private behavior. Paul was aware that something was wrong. His marriage was a disappointment; his frivolous wife never encouraged his affection. But when his mother talked of sending Razumovsky away, Paul declared that he would never part with Andrei, his best friend, the person second only to his wife in his affections.

Catherine's real complaint against Natalia was not financial, but that after two and a half years of marriage, her daughter-in-law showed no signs of producing an heir. These complaints were forgotten, however, when, in the fall of 1775, the grand duchess believed herself to be pregnant. "Her friends are, with reason, very anxious that she should prove so," reported the British ambassador. A month later, it was officially announced that Natalia was pregnant; a baby was expected in the spring. By March 1776, Natalia's pregnancy was proceeding so smoothly that the empress ordered wet nurses for the coming infant. Frederick II's brother, Prince Henry of Prussia, was on his way from Berlin to be present at the important dynastic event.

At four on Sunday morning, April 10, Paul awakened his mother to tell her that his wife had been in labor since midnight. Catherine rose, put on a robe, and hurried to the bedside, and, although serious contractions had not yet begun, she stayed with the couple until ten in the morning. She left to be dressed and returned at noon, when the contractions became powerful and Natalia was in such pain that birth seemed imminent. But the afternoon and evening passed without result, and pain alternated with exhausted sleep. Monday was the same. On Tuesday, the midwife and doctors announced that there was no possibility of saving the child; all agreed that the baby was probably dead. On Wednesday, the thirteenth, they also despaired of saving the mother, and Natalia was given last rites. Toward six in the evening on Friday, April 15, after five days of agony, Natalia died.

Catherine and Paul had both remained with her through the five days. "Never in my life have I found myself in a more difficult, more hideous, more painful position," the empress told Grimm. "For three days, I neither ate nor drank. There were moments when her suffering made me feel that my own body was being torn apart. Then I went stony. I, who am tearful by nature, saw her die, and never shed a tear. I said to myself, 'If you cry, others will sob. If you sob, others will faint.' " Catherine's anguish was magnified by the knowledge that her dead grandchild had been a "perfectly formed boy." The autopsy revealed that the baby had been too large to pass through the birth canal; the cause was an inoperable malformation of the bone, which the empress was told would have prevented Natalia from ever giving birth to a living child. After the young woman's body was opened after her death, Catherine reported that "it was found that there was only a space of four fingers' breadth; the child's shoulders were eight fingers wide."

Despite fatigue, Catherine maintained her presence of mind. She had to; Paul, in a frenzy of grief, was refusing to allow his wife to be removed, and insisting on remaining beside her body. He did not attend the burial at Alexander Nevsky Monastery. His mother was accompanied by Potemkin and Gregory Orlov.

Beyond Natalia's death and Paul's uncontrolled grief, Catherine now faced the fact that three years of marriage and a pregnancy had produced no heir. Further, the grand duke's emotional state was such that no one could predict when he would be willing and able to fulfill his dynastic duty. At one moment rigid with grief, the next sobbing and screaming, throwing himself around the room, smashing furniture, threatening to kill himself by jumping out a window, he refused ever to think of marrying again.

To subdue this emotional storm, Catherine chose a cruel remedy. She broke into Natalia's desk. There, as she expected, she found the love letters exchanged by the dead woman and Andrei Razumovsky. Furious at seeing her son weep over a wife who had betrayed him with his best friend, Catherine decided to use the letters to wrench him back to reality. She thrust the pages under Paul's eyes. He read the proof that the two people he had loved most had deceived him; he did not even know whether the dead child had been his. He groaned, wept—and then erupted with rage. He demanded that Razumovsky be sent to Siberia, but the empress, loyal to Andrei's father, refused and simply ordered Andrei to leave the capital immediately. Exhausted, almost unable to function, Paul then agreed to all of his mother's decisions. He was ready to marry again immediately, long before the year of official mourning had passed. To Grimm, Catherine wrote, "I have wasted no time. At once, I put the irons in the fire to make good the loss, and by so doing I have succeeded in dissipating the deep sorrow that overwhelmed us. The dead being dead, we must think of the living."

Catherine was distressed by Natalia's death, not because she had lost a daughter-in-law but because she had lost a grandson. In a letter to Frau Bielcke, she addressed the situation with an icy absence of sympathy: "Well, since it has been proven that she could not give birth to a living child, we must not think about her any more." The essential thing now was to replace the dead wife quickly. The future of the dynasty and the empire were at stake; ensuring them was a sovereign's duty. On the day Natalia died, Catherine was already considering possible replacements.

❧65❧

Paul, Maria, and the Succession

THREE YEARS BEFORE, Princess Sophia of Württemburg had been Catherine's first choice as a bride for Paul, but Sophia had been ruled out because she was only fourteen. Now, Sophia, almost seventeen, was in every respect exactly what Catherine sought: a German princess whose family was aristocratic but of modest circumstances, prolific with nine children, the three sons tall and strong, the six daughters handsome and wide-hipped. The presence of Prince Henry of Prussia in St. Petersburg made Catherine's new project easier to achieve. Sophia of Württemburg was a great-niece of Frederick II and Prince Henry, and, as Paul idealized Prussia and the Prussian monarch, Catherine hoped that Prince Henry could help persuade her distraught son to marry a relative of his hero. Henry, knowing that his brother was always eager to strengthen ties with Russia, sent a message to Frederick by the fastest courier.

Frederick did everything he could to satisfy and please Catherine. He urged Sophia and her parents to accept the marriage, stressing its political advantages for Prussia and potential financial benefits for the house of Württemburg. He pointed out that Catherine had pledged a dowry for all three Württemburg daughters. An obstacle had to be overcome: Sophia was already engaged to Lewis (Ludwig), prince of Hesse-Darmstadt, who happened to be the brother of the recently deceased Natalia and therefore Paul's former brother-in-law. On the king's orders, the Hesse engagement was broken off, and, with the promise of a pension from Catherine and the hand of another Württemburg daughter, Prince Lewis was appeased.

The next step was to arrange a meeting of the prospective bride and groom. Frederick summoned Sophia to Berlin, where Paul would travel to meet her. This plan suited everyone. Foreign travel was what Paul needed as a distraction from thoughts of Natalia's death and the stinging humiliation of her betrayal. Further, the prospect of a trip to Berlin appeared certain to delight the young widower, who had never been abroad. The opportunity to meet Frederick II provided another powerful incentive.

The journey to Berlin began on June 13, 1776, with Paul sitting in a large, comfortable carriage and Prince Henry at his side. During Paul's absence, Catherine wrote frequently, praising his letters and worrying about his health. With her encouragement, Paul inspected local Russian government offices, military garrisons, and commercial enterprises along the road to the frontier. She responded to Paul's praise of the orderliness and manners of Livonia by saying, "I hope that in time the main part of Russia will not yield to . . . [Livonia] in anything, neither in order nor in the correction of manners, and that your lifetime will be sufficient to see such a change." While Paul was traveling, Frederick was briefing Sophia of Württemburg about the Russian court, just as he had briefed Sophia of Anhalt-Zerbst thirty-two years before. As he had done with the earlier Sophia, he emphasized that conversion from Lutheranism to Orthodoxy was of little consequence, especially when high matters of state were involved.

When Paul reached Berlin, Frederick made every effort to impress and honor the twenty-three-year-old grand duke. Paul was saluted by cannon, rode beneath triumphal arches, and passed between double lines of soldiers. He attended receptions, dinners, and balls. Few were more practiced and effective in the art of political flattery than the king. Paul, accustomed to playing an insignificant role at his mother's court, now found himself honored and celebrated by the great Frederick. For the first time in his life, he received the consideration due to the heir to a great throne. "Nothing can exceed the attention His Prussian Majesty pays to the grand duke, nor the pains he takes to captivate and please him," reported the British ambassador from Berlin. Paul reveled in this attention, which cemented his view that the king of Prussia was the greatest man and greatest monarch in Europe. He wrote to his mother that the level of civilization in Prussia was two centuries ahead of that in Russia.

Not only did Paul's reception in Berlin thoroughly reconcile him to the idea of a second marriage, but he also developed an immediate liking for Sophia. She was tall, blond, wholesome, amiable, and sentimental. And, because she had been recommended by Frederick, she seemed to Paul twice as desirable. As for Sophia, she made no protest when her engagement to the handsome Lewis of Hesse was suddenly broken off and her great uncles Frederick and Henry introduced the small, less attractive Paul. Whatever her innermost feelings when she first saw Paul, she dutifully accepted him. "The grand duke is exceedingly amiable," she wrote to her mother. "He has every charm."

Catherine was pleased by what Paul wrote in his letters about Sophia's appearance and good sense, her determination to be a good wife, and her resolve to learn Russian. The empress sent her blessing, but, in order to make certain that she would keep absolute control, she insisted that Sophia leave her mother behind in Berlin and come to Russia alone. She wrote to the princess, praising her willingness to make herself "my daughter. . . . Be assured that I shall not neglect a single occasion where I may prove to Your Highness the sentiments of a tender mother." She also stressed that she wanted the marriage to take place as soon as possible. She wrote to Grimm:

> We shall have her here within ten days. As soon as we have her, we shall proceed with her conversion. To convince her, it ought to take about fifteen days, I think. I do not know how long will be necessary to teach her to read intelligibly and correctly the confession of faith in Russian. But the faster this can be hurried through, the better. . . . To accelerate that . . . [a cabinet secretary] has gone to Memel to teach her the alphabet and the confession en route; conviction will follow afterwards. Eight days from this, I fix the wedding. If you wish to dance at it, you will have to hurry.

Meanwhile, the empress sent a diamond necklace and earrings to the bride-to-be, and a jewel-encrusted snuffbox and a sword to her parents. On August 24, Sophia crossed the Russian frontier at Riga, and on August 31, she and Paul were received by Catherine at Tsarskoe Selo. The empress greeted Sophia warmly, and, a few days later, she wrote to Madame Bielcke:

> My son has returned very much taken with his princess. I confess to you that I am enchanted with her. She is precisely that which is desired; shapely as a nymph, a complexion the

color of the lily and the rose, the most beautiful skin in the world, tall, but still graceful; modesty, sweetness, kindness, and innocence are reflected in her face.... The whole world is enchanted with her ... she does everything to please.... In a word, my princess is everything that I desired. So there, I am content.

On September 6, Catherine, Paul, and Sophia traveled from Tsarskoe Selo to St. Petersburg. A Lutheran pastor and an obliging Orthodox priest confirmed Frederick of Prussia's opinion that the differences between Lutheranism and Orthodoxy were minimal. On September 14, Sophia Dorothea's official conversion took place; she accepted Orthodoxy and became Maria Fyodorovna. Her formal betrothal followed the next day, on which occasion she wrote to Paul, "I swear to love and adore you all my life and to be always attached to you, and nothing in the world will make me change with respect to you. Those are the sentiments of your ever affectionate and faithful betrothed."

On September 26, 1776, only five months after Natalia died, Paul and Maria were married and the new grand duchess set about her duty. Fourteen and a half months later, on December 12, 1777, after only a few hours of labor and without complications, Maria gave birth to a healthy boy, Catherine's first grandchild, a future emperor. Catherine, ecstatic, named him Alexander. A second child arrived eighteen months later, another healthy boy, insurance for the dynasty. Again, Catherine rejoiced. She named him Constantine.

Paul's second marriage probably gave him the greatest happiness of his life. "This dear husband is an angel, the pearl of husbands. I am madly in love with him and I am perfectly happy," Maria wrote to a friend in Germany. She was an excellent wife for Paul. She did her best to make him happy and to calm his anxieties, becoming not only his wife but his friend. She encouraged Paul's best qualities at home and treated him with respect and deference in public. Paul was grateful and wrote to Henry of Prussia, "Wherever she goes, she has the gift of spreading gaiety and ease. And she has the art of not only driving out all my melancholy thoughts, but even of giving me back the good humor that I had completely lost during these last three unhappy years." Together, Paul and Maria produced nine healthy children.

• • •

In 1781, Catherine, hoping to convince her Prussophile son of the advantages of her new friendship with Joseph II of Austria, arranged for Paul and Maria to make a European tour. It would take them a year and carry them to Vienna, Italy, her home in Württemburg, and Paris, but would pointedly exclude Berlin. Maria Fyodorovna was eager to see her family, but her pleasure faded when she was told that her children would remain behind. Paul's disappointment was political; his mother's refusal to let him revisit Berlin meant that he could not renew his acquaintance with Frederick. Tension between mother and son was heightened by the almost simultaneous dismissal of Nikita Panin from leadership of the College of Foreign Affairs. In fact, Panin's removal and Catherine's refusal to let Paul visit Berlin were linked. The close relationship between Russia and Prussia, which had been the centerpiece of Panin's foreign policy, was crumbling even as Catherine's friendship with Joseph II of Austria was growing stronger. Joseph had visited Catherine and St. Petersburg the year before, and the empress was hoping to embrace Austria as a partner and ally against the Turks.

On October 1, 1781, the journey began with the couple traveling incognito as the Comte et Countess du Nord—the Count and Countess of the North. Maria, upset to be leaving her children, fainted three times before the carriage could get under way. Once on the road, however, she recovered and the tour was a triumph. Catherine had been generous, supplying three hundred thousand rubles for travel expenses. She wrote affectionate letters to "my dearest children," telling them to come straight home if they became homesick and that three-year-old Alexander "had been given a map of Europe so that he could follow his parents' itinerary."

Their first stop was in Poland, where Stanislaus charmed Maria Fyodorovna. Catherine, curious about her former lover, asked Paul "whether his Polish majesty was still such a delightful conversationalist or whether the cares of royalty had destroyed these qualities." She added, "My old friend must have had difficulty in tracing any resemblance between my contemporary portraits and the face he remembers from the past."

The warm reception in Poland was a taste of what was to come. Joseph II traveled to the Austrian frontier to welcome the heir to the

Russian throne. Vienna celebrated the couple's presence, and Maria reveled in the elegance of the Austrian court and aristocracy. A visit scheduled to last a fortnight was extended to a month, during which Paul moderated his pro-Prussian sentiments and gravitated toward Joseph II. When his guests were leaving for the south, Joseph instructed his relatives in Tuscany and Naples that the grand duchess "prefers stewed fruit to rich deserts and neither she nor her husband touches wine. She has a fondness for mineral water."

The Hapsburg princes in Italy continued the warm welcome, but the culmination of their long journey was Paris. Crowds cheered the young couple wherever they appeared: at the theater, the racetrack, or walking in the Tuileries Gardens. At Versailles, Marie Antoinette, Joseph II's sister, concentrated on pleasing Paul and reported, "The grand duke has the air of an ardent and impetuous man who holds himself in." The queen treated the grand duchess as an old and dear friend. Presented with a rare porcelain dinner set produced at Sèvres, Maria thought it was intended for the empress, her mother-in-law, until, with astonishment, she saw the arms of Russia and Württemburg intertwined on the plates.

Their return to Russia was painfully anticlimactic. The Count and Countess of the North had been absent for fourteen months; on first meeting their sons, the boys looked at them as strangers and clung to their grandmother's skirts. The empress appeared determined to deflate the couple's sense of accomplishment. The welcome Paul had received everywhere had enhanced his sense of self-worth; now Catherine told him that his travels had spoiled him. The young grand duchess was met with a more specific rebuff. She had gone to Marie Antoinette's milliner, the famous Mlle Bertin, and made a number of purchases. The trunks from Paris were still being unpacked in St. Petersburg when Catherine forbade the wearing at court of tall headdresses with feathers, exactly the fashion which Maria had brought home to emulate the queen of France. Paul's wife was commanded to return the purchases, having been told that a tall woman looked better in simple Russian costume than in these gaudy Parisian trappings. Paul, meanwhile, found that Nikita Panin's health had collapsed. In 1783, the grand duke and his wife were at the deathbed of the man who had been Paul's teacher, adviser, protector, and friend for twenty-three years.

• • •

Paul was fortunate in his second marriage, but in most other areas of life, he suffered constant frustration. At different times he exhibited two distinctly different personalities, and people meeting him often took away entirely opposite views of the heir to the throne. In 1780, Emperor Joseph II of Austria paid his first visit to Russia, and he reported his impressions to his mother, Maria Theresa. Like everyone, he admired Maria Fyodorovna. More surprisingly, his verdict on Paul was largely favorable:

> The grand duke is greatly undervalued abroad. His wife is very beautiful and seems created for her position. They understand each other perfectly. They are clever and vivacious and very well educated, as well as high-principled, open, and just. The happiness of others is more to them than wealth. With the empress, they are ill at ease, especially the grand duke. There is a lack of intimacy [between Paul and his mother] without . . . which I could not live. The grand duchess is more natural. She has great influence over her husband, loves him, and rules him. She will certainly play an important part some day. . . . The grand duke has many qualities deserving respect, but it is extremely difficult to play second fiddle here when Catherine II plays the first. The more I learn of the grand duchess, the greater is my admiration. She is exceptional in mind and heart, attractive in appearance and blameless in conduct. If I could have met a princess like her ten years ago, I should have been most happy to marry her.

The French ambassador, the Comte de Ségur, who arrived in St. Petersburg in 1784, also had a generally positive opinion of Paul, although it was tinged with qualifications:

> When they admitted me into their society, I learned to know all the rare qualities which at this period won general affection. . . . Their circle, though fairly large, seemed, especially in the country, more like a friendly gathering than a stiff court. No private family did the honors of the house with more ease and grace . . . everything bore the imprint of the best tone and the most delicate taste. The grand duchess, majestic, affable and natural, pretty without coquetry, amiable without affecta-

tion, created an impression of virtue without pose. Paul sought to please and was well-informed. One was struck by his great vivacity and nobility of character. These, however, were only first impressions. Soon, one noticed, above all when he spoke of his personal position and future, a disquiet, a mistrust, an extreme susceptibility; in fact, oddities which were to cause his faults, his injustices and his misfortunes. In any other rank of life he might have made himself and others happy; but for such a man the throne, above all the Russian throne, could not fail to be dangerous.

Years later, after his return to France and after Paul's reign had ended in assassination, Ségur had more to say about the emperor. It was less favorable:

He combined plenty of intelligence and information with the most unquiet and mistrustful humor and the most unsteady character. Though often affable to the point of familiarity, he was more frequently haughty, despotic, and harsh. Never had one seen a man more frightened, more capricious, less capable of rendering himself or others happy. It was not malignity . . . it was a sickness of mind. He tormented all who approached him because he unceasingly tormented himself. . . . Fear upset his judgement. Imagined perils gave rise to real ones.

After the death of Gregory Orlov in 1783, Catherine purchased the palace at Gatchina, thirty miles south of the capital, which she had given her favorite; now she presented it to Paul. Living there with his family, he complained bitterly about his exclusion from power and responsibility. "You tax me with my hypochondria and black moods," he wrote to Prince Henry. "It may be so. But the inaction to which I am condemned makes the part excusable." On another occasion, he wrote to Prince Henry, "Permit me to write you often; my heart has need to unburden itself, especially in the sad life that I lead." The letter stopped abruptly: "My tears prevent me from continuing."

At Gatchina, Paul was free to indulge his version of Peter III's mania for soldiering. To console himself for the humiliation of being barred from a regular army command, he engaged a Prussian drillmas-

ter and proceeded to create his own small, private army. By 1788, he had
five companies of men dressed in tightly buttoned Prussian uniforms
and powdered wigs. Every day, Paul appeared, wearing high boots and
elbow-length gloves, and drilled his men to exhaustion—just as Peter
III had done. He was short-tempered and, when displeased, would lash
out with his cane. Count Fyodor Rostopchin wrote to a friend:

> One cannot see everything the grand duke does without
> being moved to pity and horror. One would think he was trying
> to invent ways to make himself hated and detested. He has got-
> ten it into his head that people despise him and want to show
> their disrespect; starting from that conception, he seizes on
> anything and punishes indiscriminately. The least delay, the
> least contradiction . . . and he flies into a rage.

A humiliation Paul could never overcome and which kept him away
from court was the presence of his mother's favorites; they automatically became his enemies. As a child, he had hated Orlov. Then Orlov
was replaced by Vasilchikov and other nobodies like Zorich, Yermolov,
Rimsky-Korsakov, and Zubov. The vast sums continually bestowed on
these young men emphasized to Paul, himself always in debt, the difference between the way she treated them and him. Potemkin, upon becoming all-powerful, stopped bothering even to be polite to the grand
duke and openly dismissed him as a fool.

When she seized the throne, Catherine had proclaimed Paul to be her
heir. Conceivably, when he reached his majority, she might also have
enthroned him as co-ruler with significant responsibilities, as Maria
Theresa had done with her son Joseph. In Vienna, Paul had seen the
results of this other mother giving her son opportunities to learn by
assisting her in ruling. There was never a chance that Catherine would
do this. She saw her son as a rival, not a helpmate, and she gave Paul no
role in the government of Russia. He and his wife were required to appear at official ceremonies; otherwise, mother and son saw little of each
other.

To keep Paul in his place as a political cipher, Catherine found
constant fault with him; at times he was too childish; at others too independent. One minute, she would accuse him of paying insufficient

attention to serious matters; the next, she complained that he was in-terfering in matters beyond his competence. Unable to decide how or where to use him, she gave up and decided not to use him at all. When he asked to become a member of the Imperial Council, he was re-jected. "I told you that your request needs mature consideration," his mother said. "I do not think your entrance into the Council would be desirable. You must be patient until I change my mind." On the out-break of her second war with Turkey in 1787, Paul, who was thirty-three, asked to join the army as a volunteer. At first, she refused permission; then she gave in, but she reversed course again when Maria became pregnant. Her reasoning, she told Paul, was that if he deserted his wife at the moment of childbirth, his absence might jeopardize a precious Romanov life. He bitterly resented this veto on military ser-vice. When war suddenly broke out with Sweden a year later, Cathe-rine relented sufficiently to allow Paul to visit the army in Finland. His passion for this duty was reflected in the degree to which his wife wor-ried about his safety; she believed that he was actually going to fight. "I shall be separated from my beloved husband," Maria wrote. "My heart is almost broken by anxiety for the life of him for whom I would will-ingly sacrifice my own." Paul put on his uniform and left St. Petersburg on July 1, 1788, but his service was brief. He criticized the hastily as-sembled Russian soldiers in Finland because they did not live up to the parade ground standards of Gatchina; he quarreled with the Russian commander in chief; he was not allowed to see maps or discuss mili-tary operations. By mid-September he was back in the capital; he never went to war again.

During the childhood of Paul and Maria's first son, Alexander, Catherine began to think seriously about disinheriting Paul and passing the succession directly to her grandson. There was no constitutional barrier to this: the law of succession decreed by Peter the Great em-powered every reigning Russian sovereign to overrule the tradition of primogeniture and name his or her successor, male or female. Cathe-rine could make that decision right up to the moment of death. That the empress was thinking of naming her gifted and handsome grandson to succeed her was widely suspected, especially by Paul. He had another reason to hate his mother: not only had she stood between him and any training for the throne; now she was confronting him with his own son—precocious, attractive, and beloved by the empress—as a rival for the prize for which he had been waiting most of his life.

As years of frustration warped Paul's character, his eccentricities became more pronounced. Already, he was melancholy and pessimistic; now he began to appear unbalanced. His behavior sometimes worried even his loyal wife. "There is no one who does not every day remark the disorder of his faculties," Maria said. Ironically, Paul's shaky reputation and strange behavior reinforced Catherine's hold on the throne; everyone desired the reins of government to remain in her strong hands as long as possible. When she felt her own strength declining, and she worried about the future of Russia, she never spoke of the reign of her son. It was Alexander of whom she spoke as her heir. Otherwise, she said gloomily, "I see into what hands the empire will fall when I am gone." In a letter to Grimm in 1791, referring to the bloody turmoil of the French Revolution, she predicted the coming of a Genghis Khan or a Tamerlane to Europe. "This will not come in my time," she said, "and I hope not in the time of M. Alexander." In the last months of her life, she may have thought of changing the succession. Thirty years later, Maria, as Paul's widow, confided to her daughter Anna that a few weeks before Catherine's death, the empress had invited her to sign a paper demanding that Paul renounce his right to the throne. Maria had indignantly refused. A subsequent appeal by Catherine to Alexander to save his country from rule by his father was equally fruitless.

Paul, enduring this long nightmare, had no idea how it would end. For years, he had been aware that disinheritance was in his mother's mind. In 1788, as he was leaving for the army in Finland, he dictated a will instructing his wife to find and secure the empress's papers at once in the event of her death; he wanted to make sure that no last testament would affect his claim to the throne. Until her final hours, many people at court believed that Catherine intended to disinherit Paul. A manifesto announcing this decision and proclaiming her grandson as her successor was expected on January 1, 1797. Whether she left such a will that was then destroyed by Paul, no one knows. More likely, she was still undecided when she died.

The schism between mother and son stretched beyond the grave. When finally, in 1796, he reached the throne, Paul immediately restored primogeniture as the basis of succession to the crown. Thereafter, until the fall of the monarchy and the Romanov dynasty in 1917, the eldest son of the deceased sovereign—or, lacking a son, the eldest male closest in the direct family line—would succeed. Never again would an heir have to go through what Paul had been through. And never again would Russia be ruled by a woman.

❧ 66 ❧

Potemkin: Builder and Diplomat

GREGORY POTEMKIN had fought in Catherine's first war against Turkey, from 1769 to 1774, which had pushed Russia's border to the Black Sea. He understood that the acquisition of new territory was not enough; the new possessions also had to be protected and developed. The most lasting part of his life work took place in these southern regions, where he took the dreams and plans he had shared with Catherine and turned them into reality.

Catherine had given him power—power subject only to her own—in many areas. Potemkin then proved what he could do as an organizer, administrator, and builder. Whether it was a matter of government, diplomacy, a military campaign, the planning of a trip, or simply a theatrical performance, concert, or parade, it was Gregory who ruled, managed, negotiated, produced, and directed. The primary focus of his work was in the south, where the sum of his accomplishments during the thirteen years that separated the first and second Turkish wars was extraordinary.

Potemkin ruled southern Russia like an emperor, although he always did so in the name of the empress in St. Petersburg. His most visible and permanent achievements were the cities and towns he built. Kherson, on the lower Dnieper River, was the first. Conceived as a port and a place to build warships, he began in 1778 with docks and a shipyard. Twenty miles upriver from the Black Sea, Kherson's access to it lay through the Dnieper estuary called the Liman. The Russians controlled the eastern bank, where a narrow sand spit named Kinburn extended into the water; the Turks controlled the western bank with their massive fortress at Ochakov. Despite this formidable obstacle, Potemkin decided to build. Thousands of workers were brought to Kherson, and the first warship keels were laid down in 1779. In 1780, he launched a sixty-four-gun ship of the line and five frigates. When Kyril Razumovsky visited Kherson in 1782, he found stone buildings, a fortress, barracks housing ten thousand soldiers, and many Greek merchant ships anchored in the harbor. In 1783, after Catherine had annexed the

Crimea, Potemkin began constructing a second naval base on the peninsula's south shore. Called Sebastopol, it lay on a deep, protected bay that offered anchorage for scores of ships.

In 1786, Potemkin designed and began to build a new capital for this southern empire. The site he chose was on a bend in the Dnieper at a point where the river was almost a mile wide. He named it Ekaterinoslav (Catherine's Glory). He planned a cathedral, a university, law courts, a musical conservatory, public parks and gardens, and twelve factories for making silks and wool. In 1789, he founded Nikolaev, another seaport and shipyard twenty miles upriver from Kherson. And once the Turkish war was over, Potemkin chose the site and made plans to build the city that is now Odessa; he died before this work began.

As he was transforming the southern provinces, Potemkin was also reforming the army and taking control of Russia's foreign affairs. In February 1784, Catherine promoted him to the presidency of the College of War, with the rank of field marshal. He immediately introduced practical reforms: Russian soldiers were to wear the simplest, most comfortable uniforms, with loose tunics, wide breeches, boots that did not pinch, and easy-fitting helmets. He ordered soldiers to stop cutting, curling, and powdering their hair. "Is that a solider's business?" he asked. "They have no personal valets." A year later, he took control of the staff of the Black Sea Fleet. In his hands, thereafter, he had complete authority over everything relating to Russia's relationship with Turkey, except the ultimate decision of war or peace.

As Russian influence extended over eastern and central Europe, the efforts of other states to win Russia's friendship and support intensified. Britain had tried to rent Russian soldiers to assist in defeating her American colonies, and Catherine had rejected this request. In the spring of 1778, Britain suffered a heavier blow when France, eager to avenge the loss of colonial possessions to England in the Seven Years' War, recognized the independence of the rebellious American colonies. By June, England and France were at war again. London sent a new ambassador to St. Petersburg. He was James Harris, later Sir James Harris, later still Earl of Malmesbury. Born in 1746, the son of a distinguished Greek scholar, Harris was only thirty-two, but his thatch of thick, prematurely white hair gave him a reassuring air of maturity. Already, he had served as British head of mission in Madrid and as minister in Berlin, where he had negotiated successfully with Frederick II. Now he was assigned to bring Russia into an offensive-defensive alliance with Great Britain. In St. Petersburg, Harris met Panin and Catherine; both were friendly but diplomatically noncommittal. Panin, in fact, was strongly opposed to an English alliance, and Catherine had no desire to involve Russia in a British war with France and her ally Spain. Harris was instructed to push ahead with a new request for Russian assistance in the struggle against "His Majesty's misguided subjects in America." To smooth this path, Harris was authorized to give formal assurance that England had no objection to Russian expansion along the Black Sea.

Harris had been negotiating with Panin, but, in August 1779, eighteen months after his arrival in St Petersburg, the ambassador concluded that Panin's stature at court had become so diminished that little could be hoped for from him. On arriving, Harris had been wary of Potemkin, but he transferred his approach to the prince, whom he described as "such a mixture of wit, levity, learning, and humor, as I never met in the same man." In July 1789, Potemkin arranged an informal meeting between Harris and the empress after an evening card game. As Harris reported their conversation:

> She had the strongest desire to help us; she had withheld it from reluctance to plunging her empire into fresh troubles and probably ending her reign in a state of war. . . . She had the highest opinion of our national strength and spirit, and did not doubt that we should overmatch the French and Spaniards. Her Imperial Majesty then discoursed on the American war, lamented at our not having been able to stop it at the beginning, and hinted at the possibility of restoring peace by our renouncing our struggle with our colonies. I asked her, if they belonged to her, and a foreign power was to propose peace on such terms, whether she would accept it. "I would rather lose my head," she said with great vehemence.

Harris realized that Catherine was conflicted: she admired England, but she was not sorry to see the British government distracted by its new war with France. An over-powerful England was not in the interests of the Russian empire; the empress feared that England might alter its policy and oppose Russia's continued expansion along the Black Sea. Harris did not report this to London, but he also realized that if Catherine ever led Russia into war again, it would not be against France. It would be against the Turks.

Emperor Joseph II of Austria was nurturing his own ambitions regarding the Turks. Eager to repair the damage and humiliation inflicted on his country and his mother by Frederick II's seizure of Silesia, his goal was the acquisition of Turkish territories in the Balkans and eastern Mediterranean. In an alliance of Austria and Russia, he saw the means of achieving this. In pursuit of this goal, the emperor asked to pay a personal visit to Catherine at Mogilev, a Russian town near the Austrian frontier. Catherine, understanding that in any future war with Turkey, Austria would be a far more useful ally than Prussia, instructed Potemkin to make the arrangements.

In May 1789, the two monarchs met in Mogilev. Catherine was pleased to be receiving this particular guest. Although he was traveling incognito as Count Falkenstein, Joseph was the co-ruler, with his mother, of the possessions of the ancient house of Hapsburg, and he was also the Holy Roman Emperor. His effort to come to Russia was unprecedented among foreign sovereigns; none had ever visited in Russia's history. At Catherine's request, the emperor accompanied her from Mogilev back to St. Petersburg, where he remained for three weeks, spending five days at Tsarskoe Selo. Because he was traveling incognito with no retinue of courtiers and attendants, and because he preferred to sleep at ordinary inns, a palace annex was transformed into an inn and servants were costumed accordingly. Catherine's English-Hanoverian gardener, John Busch, whose first language was German, assumed the role of innkeeper. By the time Joseph left, a regular correspondence and the foundations of a military alliance had been agreed to between the emperor and the empress. The subject of their discussions was the dismemberment and partition of the European territories of the Ottoman Empire. Catherine's vision was of the restoration of a Greek empire under her grandson Constantine, with Constantinople as its capital. Joseph coveted the Ottoman provinces in the Balkans, along with as much as possible in the Aegean and eastern Mediterranean.

Joseph's visit to Mogilev and St. Petersburg occurred in May and

June 1780. In November of that year, his mother, Empress Maria Theresa, died at sixty-three, and thirty-nine-year-old Joseph became the
sole ruler of Austria and the Hapsburg empire. In May 1781, Joseph
signed a treaty with Catherine pledging Austria's aid to Russia in the
event of war with Turkey. The signing of this treaty marked the end of
Nikita Panin's influence on Russian foreign policy. Always an advocate
of alliance with Prussia against Austria, he declared that "he could not
soil his hand" by putting his name on such a treaty, and he asked permission to retire to the country. In September 1781, the aging counselor
who, nineteen years before, had helped put Catherine on the throne,
was dismissed.

Potemkin stepped forward in Panin's place. The British ambassador,
James Harris, still struggling to arrange a Russian alliance with England,
persuaded King George III to write a warm personal letter to Catherine, but even this failed to persuade her. When Harris pressed him,
Potemkin explained, "You have chosen an unlucky moment. The favorite [Lanskoy] lies dangerously ill; the cause of his illness and the uncertainty of recovery have so entirely unhinged the empress that she is
incapable of employing her thoughts on any subject, and all ideas of
ambition, of glory, of dignity, are absorbed in this one passion. Exhausted, she avoids everything involving activity or exertion."

Lanskoy worsened. Harris himself developed influenza and jaun-
dice; then Potemkin fell ill for three weeks. When this tide of illness
began to ebb, Potemkin told Harris that the empress still remained par-
tial to England. Catherine herself told Harris, "The interest I take in
everything that concerns your country has made me resolve in my mind
every kind of means by which I could assist you. I would do everything
to serve you except involve myself in a war. I would be answerable to
my subjects, my successor and perhaps to all Europe for the consequences of such a conduct." Her position regarding an English alliance
remained unchanged.

England did not give up. In October 1780, Lord Stormont at the
Foreign Office instructed Harris to go back to Catherine and offer
"some object worthy of her notice, a cession of territory of a nature to
increase her commerce and naval strength that would persuade the empress to conclude an alliance with the king, assisting us against France
and Spain, and our revolted colonies." Harris replied, "Prince Potem-

kin, though he did not directly say so, clearly gave me to understand that the only cession which would induce the empress to become our ally was that of Minorca." This island in the western Mediterranean with a fortified harbor and naval base, Port Mahon, was a treasured British possession. Harris asked for an interview with Catherine. Potemkin, arranging it, advised him, "Flatter her as much as you can. You cannot use too much unction, but flatter her for what she ought to be, not for what she is."

When he saw the empress, Harris said: "You can demand of us whatever you like. We could not refuse anything to Your Imperial Majesty if we only knew what could please you." Catherine remained determined not to become involved in England's war with France, Spain, and America. The dialogue then returned to Harris and Potemkin, both still hopeful that something could be salvaged

"What can you cede to us?" Potemkin asked Harris.

"We have extensive possessions in America, in the East Indies, and on the Sugar Islands [in the Carribean]," Harris replied.

Potemkin shook his head. "You would ruin us if you gave us distant colonies. Our ships can scarce get out of the Baltic. How would you have them cross the Atlantic? If you give us anything, give us something nearer home. . . . If you would cede Minorca, I promise you, I believe I could lead the empress any lengths."

Harris reported to London: "I told him . . . that I believed the cession he required to be impossible."

Potemkin had replied: "So much the worse. It would insure us to you forever."

Despite the magnitude of the gift requested and the pain that would be involved in giving it, the British government went ahead and prepared a draft of the terms of alliance that Britain wanted: "The empress of Russia shall effectuate the restoration of peace between Great Britain, France, and Spain. . . . It shall be an express condition that the French immediately evacuate Rhode Island and every other part of His Majesty's colonies in North America. No agreement whatever shall be made with respect to His Majesty's rebellious subjects."

Catherine still would not agree. She remained convinced that the alliance treaty was an attempt to draw her and her subjects into a European war. When Potemkin went back to her, she told him: *"La mariée est trop belle; on veut me tromper"* ("The bride is too beautiful; they wish to deceive me"). She emphasized her friendly feelings toward England but otherwise rejected the entire proposition. By the end of 1781, the issue was moot. In December of that year, the British army in North America surrendered when Lord Cornwallis handed his sword to George Washington at Yorktown. In March 1782, the Lord North government fell and was replaced by a Whig ministry. The idea of a Russian alliance was dropped.

Catherine had another reason for rejecting a treaty with England: her rapprochement with Austria had led to a formal alliance. On the strength of this alliance, she and Potemkin were preparing for the annexation of the Crimea, which both considered far more important than the acquisition of Minorca. It was Potemkin who had proposed and managed this peaceful annexation. The Treaty of Kuchuk Kainardzhi, which ended the first Turkish war in 1774, had established the independence of the Crimea, but the khanate still remained a nominal vassal state of the Ottoman sultan. Potemkin worried that geographically the peninsula split Russia's Black Sea possessions, and he explained to Catherine the difficulty of guarding her southern frontier while the Crimea remained outside her empire. "The acquisition of the Crimea can make us neither stronger nor richer, but it will ensure our peace," he said. In July 1783, Catherine announced the annexation of the Crimean peninsula into the Russian empire. Potemkin managed this acquisition without a war or a battle, although it came at a long-term personal cost: in the Crimea, he acquired a severe case of malaria that never entirely left him during the rest of his life.

❧67❧

Crimean Journey and "Potemkin Villages"

OVER TIME, the story of Catherine the Great's journey down the Dnieper River to the Crimea in the spring of 1787 has passed from history into legend. It has been described as the most remarkable journey ever made by a reigning monarch and as Gregory Potemkin's greatest public triumph. It has also been disparaged as a gigantic hoax: the prosperous villages shown to the empress were said to have been made of painted cardboard; the happy villagers were declared to be cos-tumed serfs, marched from place to place, appearing and reappearing, waving and cheering as Catherine passed by. These accusations became the basis of the myth of "Potemkin villages," the settlements Potemkin supposedly fabricated along the Dnieper in order to deceive Catherine and her guests about the actual state of her southern territories. In time, the expression "Potemkin village" came to mean a sham, or some-thing fraudulent, erected or spoken to conceal an unpleasant truth. As such, it became a cliché; now, it is part of the language. In evaluating the allegation, two facts should be considered. The first is that those who mocked and condemned were not present on the journey. The other is that the results of Potemkin's work were personally observed by many eyewitnesses, including three sharp-eyed and sophisticated foreigners: the Austrian emperor, Joseph II; the French ambassador, the Comte de Ségur; and the Austrian field marshal Prince Charles de Ligne. Over two centuries, no one has produced any evidence that what these three said and wrote about their journey was untrue.

For nine years Potemkin had worked to transform the newly acquired areas of southern Russia into a prosperous part of Catherine's empire. Proud of what he had achieved, he had been urging the empress to come and see what he had done. Finally, she agreed to come in the spring and summer of 1787, the year of her silver jubilee, the twenty-fifth anniversary of her accession to the throne. The planning and prepara-tion of Catherine's Crimean journey began. It was to be the longest journey of her life and the most spectacular public spectacle of her reign. For more than six months and over four thousand miles, she traveled by land and water, by sledge, river galley, and carriage. In doing this, she confirmed the future of this vast region. From the year of her journey until the German invasion in 1941, and then the independence of Ukraine in 1991, these lands never passed from Russian hands.

The Crimean Peninsula, which Potemkin most wanted the em-press to see, had a history embracing many peoples and cultures. In the fifth and fourth centuries B.C., the Greeks had established colonies along the Crimean coast. Then called the Taurus, it was the site where Iphigenia, daughter of Agamemnon and Clytemnestra, is said to have served as a priestess in the Temple of Diana. Three hundred years later, these Greek colonies became part of the Roman Empire; later, the

Crimea was conquered and occupied by the Mongols. When Catherine annexed the peninsula in 1783, she instructed Potemkin to build roads, cities, and ports, enrich and broaden agriculture, and integrate the Muslim population into her empire without destroying their religion or culture. Potemkin then built cities, created parks, and planted vineyards and botanical gardens. He brought in cattle, silkworms, mulberries, and melon seeds. He began building warships, and at Kherson, Nikolaev, and on the Bay of Sebastopol he constructed naval bases for the new Russian Black Sea Fleet.

Catherine was eager to see and know these lands about which she had heard so much, and in which she had invested so many rubles. She also had diplomatic reasons for going: she wished to impress Europe and intimidate the Turks. On her journey, she would be meeting a king and an emperor: Stanislaus of Poland and Joseph II of Austria. Stanislaus, her former lover, was to join her at a point where the Dnieper River constituted the border between Russia and Poland. Joseph, her ally, had been persuaded to come so that together they could advertise the strength of the Russo-Austrian alliance. Her journey, therefore, was to be simultaneously a pleasure trip, a royal inspection, and a strong diplomatic statement.

Catherine was fifty-eight when she began this journey, and it was an unusual effort for a woman of her age to undertake. It displayed not only her vitality and enthusiasm but also her trust in the mastermind who for three years had been planning this enterprise. Once on her way, she said to Ségur:

> Everything was done to deter me from this journey. I was assured that my progress would be bristling with obstacles and unpleasantness. They wished to frighten me with stories of the fatigue of the journey. These people had a very poor knowledge of me. They do not know that to oppose me is to encourage me, and that every difficulty they put in my way is an additional spur.

Primarily, she wanted to endorse and set her imperial seal on Potemkin's achievements in the south. For years, his enemies at court had belittled his efforts, asserting that he had wasted or stolen the vast sums, now millions of rubles, allotted for the development of these new territories. Potemkin himself knew that the success of Catherine's journey would make him unassailable—and that failure would ruin him. He knew also that the courts of Europe would be watching. He urged, therefore, that Catherine bring with her the foreign ambassadors stationed in St. Petersburg so that they could report to their governments what they had seen.

Potemkin hurled himself and all of his talents for organization and showmanship into this enormous effort. He decided where the immense imperial caravan would stop every night. He erected or borrowed houses, mansions, and palaces to accommodate the travelers. He chose sites for balls, fireworks, and celebrations. He ordered the construction of a fleet of large, luxurious galleys to carry the empress and her guests down the Dnieper River. He had guidebooks printed giving detailed descriptions of the towns and villages the galleys would pass and naming the distances the fleet would travel each day.

Catherine made up the guest list. There were omissions. The Prussian ambassador was not included because the death of Frederick the Great a year before had brought his nephew, Frederick William, to the throne in Berlin, and the nephew's dislike of Catherine was warmly reciprocated. The Saxon ambassador, Georg von Helbig, was left behind because he had made a practice of denigrating Potemkin and his achievements.

More conspicuous were the absentees from among the members of Catherine's own family. Until the last minute, she planned to take her two oldest grandchildren, ten-year-old Alexander and eight-year-old Constantine. She wanted them to see the territories, the towns, and the fleet she was adding to their inheritance. But as the time to depart drew closer, the protests of the boys' parents grew louder. The usually serene Maria Fyodorovna became almost hysterical at the thought of her sons traveling to a region where plague and malaria were perennial hazards. Dr. Rogerson supported her. Catherine persisted, arguing that it was cruel to let a grandmother go off on a long journey without a single member of her own family to accompany her. To Paul and Maria, she wrote: "Your children belong to you, they belong to me, they belong to the state. From their earliest childhood, I have made it my duty and my pleasure to give them the tenderest care. I reasoned as follows: it will be a consolation for me, when I am far from you, to have them near me. Am I to be the only one who is deprived, in my old age, for six months, of the pleasure of having some member of my family with me?" Receipt of this letter only made Maria more desperate. Paul then suggested that both he and Maria as well as their sons should accompany his mother. Or, if this was not acceptable, he offered to be the only family member to go with her. He was, after all, heir to the throne; presumably the lands to be visited would one day be his to rule. Why should he not see them? This suggestion, like the other, was coldly rejected. "Your latest proposal would cause the greatest of upsets," she wrote. The truth was that she did not want the "heavy baggage" of Paul's presence to detract from her enjoyment of Potemkin's triumph.

In the end, the question became moot. On the eve of departure, both grandsons developed chicken pox. Six doctors had to be summoned to testify to this fact before Catherine surrendered and agreed that her grandsons should stay home. Paul, too, remained behind, embittered because he had not been delegated any authority over anything during her absence.

On New Years Day 1787, Catherine received the diplomatic corps at the Winter Palace, and then drove to Tsarskoe Selo. At eleven in the morning on January 7, in brilliant sunshine and bitter cold, she left Tsarskoe Selo in the first of fourteen large, comfortable carriages mounted on broad runners to convert them into sledges. Catherine's carriage had seats for six, and she began the journey riding with her current favorite, Alexander Mamonov, Lev Naryshkin, Ivan Shuvalov, and a lady-in-waiting. All were wrapped in soft furs, with bearskins draped over their laps. Behind her, other carriage-sledges carried the foreign ambassadors, members of the court, government officials, and her personal staff. Aware that, despite the traditional hostility between their two countries, they liked each other privately, she had placed the French and English ambassadors, Philippe de Ségur and Alleyne Fitzherbert (later Lord St. Helens), in the same carriage. One hundred twenty-four smaller sleighs and sledges followed, carrying doctors, apothecaries, musicians, cooks, engineers, hairdressers, silver polishers, washerwomen, and scores of other male and female servants.

In January in northern Russia, everything vanishes beneath a deep blanket of whiteness. Rivers, fields, trees, roads, and houses disappear, and the landscape becomes a white sea of mounds and hollows. On days when the sky is gray, it is hard to see where earth merges with air. On brilliant days when the sky is a rich blue, the sunlight is blinding, as if millions of diamonds were scattered on the snow, refracting light. In

Catherine's time, the log roads of summer were covered with a smooth coating of snow and ice that enabled the sledges to glide smoothly at startling speeds; on some days, her procession covered a hundred miles. "It was a time," wrote Ségur, "when every animal stayed in its stable, every peasant by his stove, and the only sign of human life were the convoys of sleighs passing like small ships over a frozen sea." In those northern latitudes at this time of year, daylight lasts no more than six hours, but this did not hinder Catherine's progress. When darkness fell in the afternoon—as early as three o'clock on the first days of the journey—the road was illuminated by bonfires and blazing torches.

Travel did not alter Catherine's daily schedule. She rose at six as she did in St. Petersburg, drank coffee, and then worked alone or with her secretary or ministers for two hours. At eight, she summoned her close friends to breakfast, and at nine, she entered her carriage to resume the journey. At two, she halted for midday dinner, then resumed an hour later. At seven, long after the fall of darkness, she stopped for the night. Usually, Catherine was not tired and would go back to work or join her companions for conversation, cards, or games until ten.

Speeding over the snow, Catherine shuffled the passengers in her sledge in order to shift topics and diversify her amusement. Frequently, Ségur and Fitzherbert were exchanged for Naryshkin and Shuvalov. Ségur, sophisticated and intelligent, a born storyteller, was her favorite. She laughed at most of what he said, but, at one point, he discovered the limits of her tolerance:

> One day when I was sitting opposite her in her carriage, she indicated to me the desire to hear some snippets of light verse which I had composed. The gentle familiarity which she permitted to the people who were traveling with her, the presence of her young favorite, her gaiety, her correspondence with . . . Voltaire and Diderot, had made me think that she could not be shocked by the liberty of a love story and so I recited one to her which was admittedly a little risqué, but nevertheless decent enough to have been well received by ladies in Paris.
>
> To my great surprise, I suddenly saw my laughing traveling companion reassume the face of a majestic sovereign, interrupt me with a completely unrelated question, and so change the subject of conversation. Several minutes later, to make her

aware that I had learned my lesson, I begged her to listen to another piece of verse of a very different nature, to which she paid the kindest attention.

In Smolensk, the journey was delayed for four days by massive snowdrifts and by a feverish sore throat that had stricken Mamonov. But a letter from Potemkin, still in the Crimea, urged Catherine on: "Here, the greenery in the meadows is starting to break through," he said. "I think the flowers are coming soon."

On January 29 the cavalcade reached Kiev, standing on the high, west bank of the Dnieper River. The empress, whose only previous visit had been forty-three years earlier when she was a fifteen-year-old grand duchess accompanying Empress Elizabeth, was welcomed with saluting cannon and pealing bells. Each ambassador was assigned his own palace or mansion, handsomely furnished, staffed with servants and stocked with excellent wines. At night, there were games, music, and dancing. Catherine often played whist with Ségur and Mamonov.

Potemkin arrived from the Crimea. At first, he remained in seclusion, away from all the excitement he had created, declaring that he intended to observe Lent in the company of monks rather than courtiers and diplomats. He chose the Pecherskaya Lavra, the famous Monastery of the Caves, hollowed out of the cliff rising from the river. Here, in a labyrinth of caves and low, narrow tunnels, seventy-three mummified saints lay in open niches, close enough for passersby to reach out and touch. Catherine, knowing Potemkin's moods, warned, "Avoid the prince when you see him looking like an angry wolf." The cause of the prince's behavior was worry; in overseeing this journey he had accepted an enormous responsibility, and the most difficult parts lay ahead.

Along with Potemkin, another new traveler joined the party at Kiev. This was Prince Charles de Ligne, a fifty-year-old Belgian-born aristocrat, now an Austrian field marshal in the service of Emperor Joseph II. Arriving from Vienna, Ligne was a welcome addition. A European cosmopolitan, at ease corresponding with Voltaire or Marie Antoinette, he was witty, wise, sophisticated, cynical, and sentimental, and, at the same time, diplomatic and discreet. A friend of sovereigns and princes, affectionate with equals, popular with inferiors, he put everyone at ease. He was delighted to be invited by Catherine, whom he later described as "the greatest genius of her age." Of all Catherine's guests on the journey, Ligne remained most consistently in favor, not only with Catherine but with everyone else. Catherine herself described him as "the pleasantest company and the easiest person to live with that I have ever met." When his master, friend, and confidant Joseph II joined the party, Ligne was asked to share the imperial carriage and overhear the conversation between the two monarchs. Ligne joined in when asked to do so; the other occupant, Alexander Mamonov, too bored to listen, slept.

Catherine and her guests remained in Kiev for six weeks. Thereafter, the journey was to be resumed in large galleys built for the voyage down the river. On April 22, cannon signaled that the ice on the river had cracked. At noon, the empress and her guests boarded seven opulently decorated and furnished Roman-style galleys, all painted in red and gold, with the Russian imperial double eagle emblazoned on their sides. Catherine's galley, named *Dnieper,* had a bedroom hung with gold and scarlet silk brocade, a drawing room, a library, a music room, and a dining room. A private canopied deck offered her the opportunity to take the air while avoiding the sun. The six galleys following hers were almost as luxurious: also painted red and gold with interiors lined with expensive brocades. Potemkin's galley housed the prince, no longer an "angry wolf," two of his nieces and their husbands, and his new friend, the raffish soldier of fortune Prince Charles de Nassau-Siegen. This forty-two-year-old Franco-German, the impoverished heir to a tiny principality, had sailed around the world, fought on land and sea, married a Polish woman, and then come to Russia, where he had met Potemkin. Catherine was dubious. "It is odd that you like Prince Nassau considering his universal reputation as a hothead," she told Potemkin. "Still, it's well known that he is brave."

On the day of embarkation, with the galleys still tethered to the shore, Catherine invited fifty guests to dine on board the special dining galley. At three in the afternoon, the fleet cast off and headed downstream with the seven large galleys followed by eighty smaller vessels carrying three thousand people who serviced this unusual flotilla. At six, a smaller number of guests were rowed back to the empress's private galley for supper; this became the habitual pattern during the days to come.

Under a blue sky, with the river sparkling in sunlight, painted oars dipped rhythmically into the river and this "Cleopatra's fleet," as Ligne christened it, moved down the Dnieper. Travel along the great river waterways was normal in Russia, but no one had ever seen anything like this, and crowds of people stood on the banks, watching and waving as the galleys swept by. The fleet passed meadows carpeted with spring wildflowers, herds of cattle and flocks of sheep, and villages with churches and houses gleaming with new paint. As the large galleys passed by, a swarm of little boats darted among the larger vessels, carrying visitors from one to another, transporting wine and food as well as musicians who played at meals and evening concerts. By day, Catherine would lie on the deck of her galley under her silken awning. For her guests and those passengers who were not on the empress's working staff, the mornings were free and passengers visited one another, talked business, gossiped, and played cards. At midday, the empress's galley fired a gun to announce dinner; sometimes it would be for only ten guests who were rowed to her galley; sometimes for fifty, summoned to the special dining galley. Often, the fleet stopped and anchored so that the passengers could picnic or simply walk along the riverbanks.

Six days brought the fleet to Kaniev, a point on the Dnieper where the east bank was Russian and the west bank Polish. Here Catherine was to meet Stanislaus Ponitowski, whom she had created king of Poland. The two had not seen each other since 1759, twenty-eight years earlier. Even now, at fifty-six, Stanislaus remained handsome, sensitive, cultured—and also well-meaning and weak. But Catherine was uneasy. At fifty-nine, she was aware of how the years had affected her own appearance, and she was not looking forward to subjecting herself to the gaze of a former lover.

When the fleet anchored off Kaniev, the king was rowed out to Catherine's galley. The morning had seen gusts of wind and rain, and the king's clothing was sodden when he came aboard. Catherine received him with state honors, and Stanislaus responded with his old sophistication. As king, he was forbidden by the Polish constitution to leave Polish soil; accordingly, he had assumed a temporary incognito. Bowing to those who received him on deck, he said, "Gentlemen, the king of Poland has asked me to commend Count Poniatowski to your care."

Catherine was cool. Stanislaus now seemed insipid, his manners too exquisite, his compliments excessively elegant and long-winded. As Catherine wrote to Grimm, "It was thirty years since I'd seen him and you can imagine that we found each other changed." She presented him to her ministers and foreign guests and then, walking stiffly, retired with him for a private half-hour talk. When they returned, her manner was strained and his eyes were sad. At dinner, Ségur sat opposite the empress and the king and later he recorded, "They spoke little, but each was watching the other. We listened to an excellent orchestra and drank the king's health to a salvo of artillery fire." On departing, the king, rising from the table, could not find his hat. Catherine handed it to him. Stanislaus thanked her and, smiling, said that it was the second article of headgear she had given him; the first had been the crown of Poland.

He tried and failed to persuade her to prolong her visit and remain his guest for several days. He had arranged dinners and a ball in her honor at a palace he had built especially for the occasion. She declined, having already resolved that their reunion should not exceed a single day. Stanislaus was told that she had to meet the Emperor Joseph II in Kherson, downstream; the emperor would be waiting and her schedule could not be changed. Potemkin, who liked Stanislaus, was annoyed, and warned her that her refusal would undermine the king's position in Poland. Catherine was adamant: "I know of our guest's desire that I remain here for another day or two, but you yourself know that this is impossible, given my meeting with the emperor. Kindly let him know, in a polite manner, that there is no possibility of making changes in my journey. And moreover, as you yourself know, I find any change in plan disagreeable." When Potemkin continued to argue, she grew testy: "The dinner proposed for tomorrow was suggested without any regard for what is possible.... When I make a decision there's a reason for it ... and so I'm leaving tomorrow as planned.... I'm truly tired of this!" To appease Potemkin, she permitted her guests to attend the first of Stanislaus's balls, to be given that night, but she remained on her galley and watched the fireworks from the deck, attended by Mamonov. The following morning, the galley fleet sailed at dawn. To Potemkin, Catherine said, "The king bores me." She never saw Stanislaus again.

Meanwhile, downriver in Kherson, Joseph had arrived and was waiting. A man who loved to travel unencumbered, Joseph was once again traveling incognito as Count Falkenstein. With little baggage, and accompanied by a single equerry and two servants, he usually arrived early on his travels. In Kherson, he tired of waiting and decided to go upriver by land to meet Catherine in Kaidek, where her fleet of galleys would halt on reaching the first of the Dnieper cataracts. When the galleys arrived in Kaidek, Catherine was informed that Count Falkenstein was waiting downriver at Kherson. Soon, further news arrived that he was already on his way by road to meet her. Determined not to be outdone, Catherine hastily disembarked and hurried by carriage to intercept her ally. The two met by the road, and, riding together in her carriage, returned the twenty miles to Kaidek. Joining her traveling party, Joseph insisted on maintaining his incognito, attending the empress's levees with other gentlemen of the court, and always being introduced as Count Falkenstein. He was delighted to see his friend and army commander, Ligne, and to strike up a new friendship with Ségur. He spoke admiringly to the French ambassador about the vitality of the extraordinary woman ten years his senior who had become his ally, but he had few compliments for Mamonov. "The new favorite is good-looking," Joseph wrote, "but does not appear to be very brilliant and seems astonished to find himself in this position. He is really no more than a spoiled child."

After twenty-four hours at Kaidek, Catherine and Joseph left to the courtiers and diplomats the pleasure of shooting the rapids by galley, and traveled together by carriage to the site where Potemkin intended to build the new city of Ekaterinoslav. There, with Joseph at her side, Catherine laid the foundation stone of the city's new cathedral. The emperor, dubious about building a large church before there was a town or a population, wrote to a friend in Vienna, "I performed a great deed today. The empress laid the first stone of a new church, and I laid—the last."

Once the galleys had passed safely through the rapids and the two sovereigns reembarked, they made their entry into Kherson by water. Nine years before, when Potemkin had first chosen this site twenty miles up the estuary from the Black Sea, Kherson had been no more than a few huts in a marsh. Now it was a fortified city with two thousand white houses, straight streets, shade trees, flower gardens, churches and public buildings, barracks for twenty thousand men, crowds in the streets, shops filled with goods, and a thriving shipyard with warehouses along the quays and two completed ships of the line and a frigate ready to be launched. More than a hundred ships, many of them Russian, were riding at anchor in the port. On May 15, Catherine and Joseph launched the three warships, including the ship of the line *Vladimir* and a powerful eighty-gun ship of the line diplomatically named *St. Joseph*.

The proximity of the Turks loomed in the minds of both sovereigns. They saw the arch Potemkin had erected over the entrance to the town, provocatively emblazoned with the inscription in Greek "This is the way to Byzantium." They met Yakov Bulgakov, the Russian minister in Constantinople, who had come to report to the empress and remind her of what she and Potemkin already knew: that the Ottoman Empire had never fully accepted the annexation of the Crimea or, indeed, any Russian presence on the Black Sea. The Turks were only biding their time, Bulgakov warned. Catherine and Potemkin understood, and because Russia would not be ready for war for at least two years, they urged Bulgakov to be conciliatory.

Catherine herself was now obliged to be cautious. Originally, she had hoped to travel the full length of the Dnieper, which meant going from Kherson down the estuary all the way to the Black Sea. The Turks forestalled this final stage of her river voyage by sending four men-of-war and ten frigates to cruise in the estuary. It was a reminder that the Dnieper was not yet fully open.

Despite this disappointment, Catherine was determined to impress her imperial ally and the foreign ambassadors by taking them on a tour of the Crimea. Leaving Kherson and the Dnieper on May 21, they traveled overland by carriage. Once out on the steppe, Joseph was astonished when twelve hundred Tartar horsemen suddenly appeared in a cloud of dust; here were tribesmen, only recently conquered, now considered to be sufficiently loyal to serve as an imperial guard of honor. Impressed by what he was seeing, Joseph left the encampment at dusk one evening and walked with Ségur out into the flat wasteland of grass stretching to the horizon. "What a peculiar land," the emperor said. "And who could have expected to see me with Catherine the Second, and the French and English ambassadors wandering through a Tatar desert? What a page of history!"

Passing through the Perekop Isthmus connecting the Crimean Peninsula with Ukraine and Russia to the north, the procession of carriages rolled down the steep, rocky road leading to Bakhchisarai, the former capital of the Crimean khans. Here, the private apartments in the palace of the khans became the temporary residence of the two visiting monarchs. Months before, Catherine had sent Charles Cameron, her Scottish architect, to repair and decorate the palace. Cameron had preserved the atmosphere of Islam. There were inner courts and secret gardens enclosed by high walls and hedges of myrtle. There were cool, uncluttered rooms with tiled walls in glowing colors, thick carpets, elaborate tapestries, and, in the center of every room, a marble fountain. Through her open windows, Catherine could see minarets rising above the walls and breathe the scents of roses, jasmine, orange trees, and pomegranates. Surrounding the palace was the town, dominated by nineteen mosques and their high minarets, from which, five times a day, voices summoned the faithful to prayer; while she was there, Catherine ordered the construction of two new mosques. Outside, too, were other sights, sounds, and smells of Islam: teeming street bazaars; Tatar princes and men in flowing robes; their wives and other women, covered except for their eyes.

Because Potemkin was eager to show Catherine and the emperor what he considered his greatest achievement in the south, they spent only three days and two nights in Bakhchisarai. On May 22, they drove across the mountains through forests of cypress and pine to the rugged headlands of the Crimea's Black Sea south coast. Here they entered a lush, Riviera-like region of mild temperatures the year around, with olive trees, orchards, vineyards, pastures, and gardens of jasmine, laurel, lilacs, wisteria, roses, and violets. Every spring, the sudden, massive flowering of fruit trees, shrubs, vines, and wildflowers, with their swirl of colors and odors, transformed the coast into a vast perfumed garden.

Their destination was Inkerman, on the heights overlooking the Black Sea, where they dined in a new pavilion. After a midday banquet, Potemkin stood and drew back the curtains at one end of the room. Before them, under the cloudless blue Crimean sky, the travelers saw an amphitheater of rugged mountain peaks rising from emerald blue waters. This was the great bay of Sebastopol, glittering in the sunlight. In the bay lay the ships of Potemkin's growing Black Sea Fleet. On a signal from the pavilion, the ships thundered a salute to the two monarchs. To conclude, one of the new ships raised the emperor's flag and fired a salute specifically for him.

Catherine led Joseph to a carriage and together they drove down to the port to tour the harbor and the city. They saw its new dockyards and wharves, its fortifications, admiralty buildings, magazines, barracks, churches, two hospitals, shops, houses, and schools. Joseph, who had been skeptical and critical of Kherson, was astonished by Sebastopol; it was, he declared, "the most beautiful port I have ever seen." Impressed by the quality and readiness of the Russian ships, the emperor added, "The truth is that it is necessary to be here to believe what I see."

From Sebastopol, Catherine had intended to escort her visitors through the Crimea as far as Taganrog on the Sea of Azov. But summer heat and Joseph's desire to return to Vienna convinced her that everyone had seen enough. They returned to the Dnieper, riding together in her carriage, still talking politics and future plans. On June 2, they parted. Catherine continued north to Poltava, where Potemkin staged a re-creation of the 1709 Battle of Poltava, at which Peter the Great had annihilated Charles XII's invading Swedish army. She watched as fifty thousand Russian soldiers, some costumed as Russians, some as Swedes, reenacted the battle.

On June 10 at Kharkov, Catherine and Potemkin parted. Before leaving, he presented her with a magnificent necklace of pearls, purchased and brought to him from Vienna. She bestowed on him the title of prince of Tauris. Afterward, traveling north through Kursk, Orel, and Tula, Catherine's carriage bumped along roads no longer offering the smooth glide of a sledge on snow. When she reached Moscow on June 27, she was overjoyed to see her grandsons, Alexander and Constantine, whose parents had permitted them to travel to welcome their grandmother. This was Catherine's last visit to the old capital, and when she reached Tsarskoe Selo on July 11, she was exhausted.

She was immensely proud of Potemkin's achievements. After leaving him at Kharkov, she had written him grateful, emotional letters during her journey: "I love you and your service which comes from pure zeal. . . . Please be careful. . . . With the intense heat you have at midday, I beg of you most humbly: do me the favor of looking after your health, for God's and our sake, and be as pleased with me as I am with you."

Potemkin replied with gratitude and a devotion that was almost filial:

> Your Majesty! How I appreciate the feelings you expressed is known to God! You are more than a real mother to me. . . . What I owe you, what numerous distinctions you have given me, how far you have extended your favors on those close to me; but chief of all, the fact that malice and envy could not prejudice me in your eyes and all perfidy was devoid of success. That is what is really rare in this world; such firmness is given to you alone. This country will not forget its happiness. . . . Goodbye my benefactress and mother. . . . I am unto death your faithful slave.

Regarding the "malice and envy" of his enemies, she wrote back: "Between you and me, my friend, I will tell you the state of affairs in a few words: you serve me and I am grateful. And that's all there is to it. With your zeal toward me and your fervor for the affairs of the empire, you rapped your enemies across the knuckles."

Potemkin had built new cities and seaports, created new industries and a fleet, imported and planted new agriculture, and given Russia access to a new sea. One interested party did not believe that these cities and towns, or the shipyards and warships that Potemkin had shown to Catherine, were made of cardboard. The Turks were keenly aware of the strength of the new empire spreading along the north shore of the Black Sea. They did not wait to react. Catherine had returned to Tsarskoe Selo to rest, but she was to have little rest. Immediately following her return from the south came the news that Turkey had declared war.

❧ 68 ❧

The Second Turkish War and the Death of Potemkin

THE PEACE BETWEEN Russia and Turkey signed in 1774 was precarious. The Turks had never been reconciled to loss of territory in the south and the opening of the Black Sea to Russian merchant vessels. Once Potemkin began building a Black Sea Fleet, Turkish concern mounted. Then Catherine annexed the Crimea. She had made her triumphant personal tour of the south, accompanied by the Austrian emperor, culminating in her inspection of the new naval base at Sebastopol, filled with warships only a two-day sail from Constantinople. This seemed a deliberate provocation. The sultan declared war.

This sudden move caught Russia by surprise. Catherine and Potemkin were both aware of Turkey's permanent hostility, but both had expected her triumphant journey to the south to intimidate the Turks, not provoke them; certainly, they had not thought it would precipitate an immediate war. For the Turks, however, there was a price to pay for the advantage of striking first: the Turkish declaration of war triggered

Russia's secret treaty with Austria, obliging Joseph II to come to Catherine's aid. Two weeks after the Turkish declaration, the emperor told Catherine that he would honor their treaty, and in February 1788, Austria declared war on the Ottoman Empire.

Turkey's objectives in the new war were simple: to regain the Crimea and eliminate the Russian Black Sea Fleet. Catherine's objectives were more layered. Her ultimate purpose was still to drive the Turks from Europe and seize Constantinople, but her immediate effort was directed at the mighty fortress of Ochakov, which controlled the estuary of the Dnieper River. Once this strategic strong point, garrisoned by twenty thousand men, had fallen, Catherine and Potemkin intended their armies to advance westward along the north shore of the Black Sea and occupy the land between the Bug and the Dniester rivers. At that point, they would weigh the prospects for a march on Constantinople.

It was clear that Potemkin would be in supreme command of the Russian war effort. All the necessary reins of power were in his hands. He had been viceroy and commander in chief of the armed forces in the southern provinces for a decade. He had created the cities and the fleet. Moreover, he was president of the War College and was familiar with the military resources available, the disposition of forces, and the administrative and political details involved. He became commander in chief by merit, and even the most senior Russian general, Peter Rumyantsev, agreed to serve under him. Suvorov, the most successful Russian battlefield commander of the age, already was under Potemkin's command.

Potemkin and Suvorov were both eccentrics. In pure military genius, Suvorov surpassed Potemkin. The prince was a resourceful soldier, but he was cautious and distracted by political affairs. He excelled as a statesman, an administrator, and a military strategist, but he lacked Suvorov's aptitude for quick, intuitive battlefield decisions. They complemented each other. Potemkin provided Suvorov with the strategy, the troops, and the supplies; Suvorov provided Potemkin and Russia with the victories. Potemkin always insisted that the highest rewards be given to Suvorov, demanding, for example, that he be given the Order of St. Andrew before other, more senior generals.

The Turks began the war with an assault on the Russian fort on Kinburn, the spit of land on the eastern bank of the Dnieper estuary across from Ochakov. Two attempted landings at Kinburn were beaten off by Suvorov, whose battlefield preference was the use of cold steel. "The bullet is a fool, the bayonet a brave lad" was his philosophy. Employing these tactics, the Russians charged the Turks as they disembarked from their boats and slaughtered most of them while their feet were still wet. This Russian victory was offset, however, by the wounding of Suvorov in the battle, and by a subsequent gale, which caught the Russian fleet sailing from Sebastopol; one large ship went down and others were damaged. Dismayed by this harm to his beloved ships, Potemkin spoke of evacuating the Crimea and resigning all his commands. Catherine's response was indignation. "You are impatient like a five-year-old child, while the affairs of which you are now in charge require an imperturbable patience," she wrote to him. "You belong to the state and you belong to me. My friend, neither time nor distance, nor anyone in the world will change my thoughts of you and about you." To which she added her guess (correct, as it turned out) that the storm had damaged the Turkish fleet equally. Potemkin apologized, blaming his loss of nerve on his sensitivity, his headaches, and his hemorrhoids.

When winter ice formed on the Dnieper, both sides suspended campaigning, and it was not until the following May that Potemkin had fifty thousand men positioned before Ochakov. Even then, he seemed not to be in a hurry. Assuming that the fortress must eventually fall, and fearing the losses that would accompany an all-out attempt to storm the ramparts, he deliberately held back an assault and waited for a voluntary surrender. Personally, he was not a coward; during the long siege, he continually exposed himself to danger. Convinced that he was protected by God, he would appear in the line of fire wearing his parade uniform, making himself a prime target. His self-confidence was reinforced when a cannonball killed an officer standing just behind him. To his men, he said, "Children, I forbid you to get up for me and wantonly expose yourselves to Turkish bullets." Suvorov disagreed with this strategy of caution; he believed in the sudden, decisive blow, accepting whatever losses he must. When Potemkin restrained him from storming Ochakov, saying, "Relying on God's help, I will try to get it cheaply," Suvorov replied, "You cannot capture a fortress merely by looking at it." They continued to admire each other. When Suvorov was wounded, Potemkin wrote, "My dear friend, you alone mean more to me than ten thousand others." Suvorov replied, "May the Prince Gregory Alexandrovich live long! He is an honest man, he is a good man, he is a great man, and I would be happy to die for him!"

The siege continued; an unpleasant feature was the Turkish practice of beheading Russian prisoners and mounting the heads on stakes along the ramparts. Finally, in December 1788, the second winter of the siege, when the army was suffering from the cold, Potemkin yielded. Promising his men that they could sack the city once the fortress was taken, he organized his assault force into six columns of five thousand men each and sent them forward at four o'clock in the morning on December 6. The assault lasted only four hours and was one of the bloodiest battles in Russian military history; it is said that twenty thousand Russians and thirty thousand Turks died that morning. But with the taking of Ochakov, the path to the Dniester and the Danube lay open.

During the following year, 1789, the whole course of the Dneister fell to the Russian army. The fortress towns of Ackkerman and Bender capitulated without a fight—and Bender alone had a garrison of twenty thousand men. That same year, Belgrade and Bucharest were taken by the Austrians. In February 1790, however, Catherine's friend and ally Emperor Joseph II died of tuberculosis. Joseph was childless, and he was succeeded by his brother, Leopold, Grand Duke of Tuscany, who became Emperor Leopold II. Leopold had little interest in continuing Austria's war with Turkey. In June 1790, he and the sultan agreed on an armistice, and in August, they concluded a peace, leaving Catherine to fight alone. Despite Austria's withdrawal, the Russian army reached the lower Danube, capturing one town after another until they reached Izmail, one of the most formidable fortresses in Europe. This massive bastion of towers and ramparts, defended by thirty-five thousand men and 265 cannon, was surrounded by thirty thousand Russians with six hundred cannon. By late November 1790 no progress had been made, and the three Russian generals commanding the army were preparing to withdraw. Worried, Potemkin sent for Suvorov, giving him the freedom to launch an assault or abandon the siege, as he thought best. "Hurry up, my dear friend," he wrote. "My only hope is in God and your valor. There are too many generals there equal in rank and the result is a kind of indecisive parliament." Suvorov arrived on December 2, resited the Russian artillery, began a punishing bombardment, and informed Potemkin that he would begin the assault within five days. He called on the Turks to surrender, warning, "If Izmail resists, no one will be spared." The Turkish commander spurned the demand. The Russian assault began at dawn. The Turks fought on the ramparts, at the gates, and in every street and house. They were overwhelmed by the fury of the Russian attack. Then, as he had promised the army before the assault, Suvorov unleashed his men for three days of looting.

During the years 1788–90, Russia was fighting two wars, in the north as well as the south. In June 1788, Gustavus III, king of Sweden, seeing an opportunity to recover the lands lost to Peter the Great in the early century, succumbed to the temptation offered by the concentration of the Russian army in the south. His objectives were to retake Finland and strip away Russia's Baltic provinces; if he failed to do this, he melodramatically promised to follow the path of Queen Christina a century before, renounce the throne, convert to Catholicism, and move to Rome. On July 1, 1788, Catherine received his ultimatum, which went beyond demanding the return of all former Swedish territories on the Baltic. He now also insisted that the empress accept Swedish mediation in the Russo-Turkish war and restore to Turkey the Crimea and all other Ottoman territory won since 1768. A final insult in this provocative document referred to the "aid" he had given Russia by not attacking the empress during her first Turkish war and during the Pugachev rebellion. In Stockholm, Gustavus boasted that he would soon be breakfasting in Peterhof, and then go on to St. Peterburg, where he would tear down a statue of Peter the Great and replace it with one of himself. Catherine categorized the ultimatum as "this insane note," which she had received from "Sir John Falstaff." To Potemkin, she described the king as donning "breastplate, thigh pieces, armlets and a helmet with an enormous number of plumes. . . . What have I done that God should choose to chastise me with such a feeble instrument as the king of Sweden?"

In July 1789, Gustavus invaded Finland and sent his fleet up the Gulf of Finland; his army failed on land and his navy was only partially successful at sea. In the end, the war was inconclusive, the more so for Sweden, because Catherine, fully engaged against Turkey, had only to maintain the status quo in the Baltic in order to succeed. In the summer of 1790, Gustavus asked for peace. The Swedish-Russian peace agreement of August 3 left all frontiers exactly where they had been before the king had posted his "insane note." Catherine was relieved. Writing to Potemkin, who was still fighting the Turks, she said, "We have pulled one paw out of the mud [in the Baltic]. As soon as we pull out the other [in the south], we'll sing alleluia."

. . .

The second war with Turkey proved a rich source of colorful stories to add to the legend of Gregory Potemkin. One was the tale of the subterranean headquarters he had constructed for himself while his army was besieging Ochakov. It told of an enormous underground hall of marble, rows of pillars made of lapis lazuli, enormous chandeliers, myriads of candles, huge mirrors, and platoons of lackeys in powdered wigs and gold brocade waiting to serve. It is not much easier to believe the report that Potemkin was keeping an entire theater company and a symphony orchestra of one hundred musicians to provide inspiration or distraction. There are also extravagant accounts of the love affairs Potemkin supposedly conducted while in the Ochakov camp. It was said that he kept a harem of beautiful women, including both Princess Catherine Dolgoruky, whose husband was serving under his command, and the beautiful Prascovia Potemkina, wife of his kinsman Paul Potemkin.

The most remarkable phenomenon at Ochakov, however, was Potemkin himself. The Prince de Ligne, the Austrian field marshal who had joined Catherine and Potemkin on the Crimean journey, was at Russian headquarters to urge Potemkin to storm the fortress in order to draw Turkish troops away from the Austrian campaign in the Balkans. Despite Potemkin's protracted refusal to attack, Ligne was overwhelmingly impressed by the man before him. To his friend Philippe de Ségur in St. Petersburg, he wrote:

> I here behold a Commander in Chief who looks idle and is always busy; who has no other desk than his knees, no other comb than his fingers; constantly reclined on his couch, yet sleeping neither in night nor in daytime. A cannon shot, to which he himself is not exposed, disturbs him with the idea that it costs the life of some of his soldiers. Trembling for others, brave himself, alarmed at the approach of danger, frolicsome when it surrounds him, dull in the midst of pleasure, surfeited with everything, easily disgusted, morose, inconstant, a profound philosopher, an able minister, a sublime politician, not revengeful, asking pardon for a pain he has inflicted, quickly repairing an injustice, thinking he loves God when he fears the Devil; waving one hand to the females that please him, and with the other making the sign of the cross; receiving number-

less presents from his sovereign and distributing them immediately to others; preferring prodigality in giving, to regularity in paying; prodigiously rich and not worth a farthing; easily prejudiced in favor of or against anything; talking divinity to his generals and tactics to his bishops; never reading, but pumping everyone with whom he converses; uncommonly affable or extremely savage, the most attractive or most repulsive of manners; concealing under the appearance of harshness, the greatest benevolence of heart, like a child, wanting to have everything, or, like a great man, knowing how to do without; gnawing his fingers, or apples, or turnips; scolding or laughing; engaged in wantonness or in prayers, summoning twenty aides de camp and saying nothing to any of them, not caring for cold, though he appears unable to exist without furs; always in his shirt without pants, or in rich regimentals; barefoot or in slippers; almost bent double when he is at home, and tall, erect, proud, handsome, noble, majestic when he shows himself to his army like Agamemnon in the midst of the monarchs of Greece. What then is his magic? Genius, natural abilities, an excellent memory, artifice without craft, the art of conquering every heart; much generosity, graciousness, and justice in his rewards; and a consummate knowledge of mankind.

There is another story related to this Russian war with Turkey—this one is true—which centers on a figure few connect with Catherine of Russia or Gregory Potemkin. This figure is John Paul Jones, whom Americans know as the father of the United States Navy.

Jones began as nobody and he died alone, rejected, and, once again, nobody. In the interim, however, he achieved the fame he desperately craved. He was born John Paul—Jones was added later—an obscure, impoverished gardener's son on the bank of Solway Firth in Scotland. At thirteen, he went to sea as an unpaid cabin boy aboard a merchant vessel bound for Barbados and Virginia. In 1766, at nineteen, he joined an African slave ship as third mate and remained in the slave trade for four years. At twenty-three, he became master of a merchant vessel on which his seamanship was unchallenged but men were wary of his prickly temper. He was slight and wiry, five feet five inches tall, with hazel eyes, a sharp nose, high cheekbones, and a strong cleft chin. He dressed neatly, more like a naval officer than a merchant captain, and always wore a sword. This blade was used in the West Indies to run through the ringleader of a group of mutineers in his crew. Uncertain whether the law would applaud him for suppression of mutiny or try him for murder, he changed his name from John Paul to John Jones and sailed on the next ship leaving the harbor.

In the summer of 1775, Jones was in Philadelphia seeking a place in the infant navy of the rebellious American colonies; he became the first naval first lieutenant commissioned by the Continental Congress. A year later, after the signing of the Declaration of Independence, he sailed for Europe, hoping to find a frigate to command. The French government, spurred by news of British general John Burgoyne's surrender at Saratoga, was moving toward full recognition of America's independence, and Benjamin Franklin, the American representative in Paris, became Jones's patron. With Franklin's help, Jones took command of a French East Indiaman, a travel-worn merchant ship of nine hundred tons. Jones armed her with thirty cannon and named her *Bonhomme Richard,* after Franklin's famous work *Poor Richard's Almanack.*

On August 14, 1779, Jones sailed on the voyage that made him famous. Off the North Sea Yorkshire coast, he encountered a forty-four-ship Baltic convoy laden with naval stores for England, under escort by a fast, maneuverable, fifty-gun British frigate, HMS *Serapis,* commanded by a veteran Royal Navy captain. Jones attacked. The battle, beginning at 6:30 p.m., continued for four hours under a harvest moon. The two ships, locked together yardarm to yardarm by American grappling hooks, pounded each other with shot. At one point amid the carnage, the British captain called across his deck to Jones, "Has your ship struck her colors?" He was referring to the signal of surrender. Someone heard—or perhaps a writer sitting at his desk later imagined—Jones call back, "I have not yet begun to fight." The battle continued until, with *Bonhomme Richard* sinking and *Serapis* on fire, the British captain suddenly struck. Jones transferred his wounded and the rest of his crew to his captured prize, put out the fire, and returned to France. In Paris, he was a hero. At Versailles, Louis XVI made him a chevalier of the Military Order of Merit and presented him with a gold-hilted sword. His celebrity and self-confidence attracted women and he had a succession of affairs, one of which apparently resulted in a small, unexpected son.

Jones never gave up wanting to become an American admiral, but no American naval officer was promoted to that rank until the American Civil War. He returned to Paris, and in December 1787, Thomas Jefferson, who had succeeded Franklin as American minister to France, told him that the Russian minister in Paris wished to know whether Jones would be interested in a high command in the Russian navy: command of the Black Sea Fleet with an admiral's rank. Jones grasped the offer: if not an American admiral, perhaps a Russian admiral.

The new admiral arrived in St. Petersburg on May 4, and Catherine wrote to Grimm, "Paul Jones has just arrived here; he has entered my service. I saw him today. I think he will suit our purpose admirably." Jones's view of her was equally optimistic: "I was entirely captivated and put myself into her hands without making any stipulation for my personal advantage. I demanded but one favor: that she would never condemn me without hearing me." He traveled south and met Potemkin at Ekaterinoslav. Assuming that he was to take supreme command of the Black Sea Fleet, he passed through Kherson to the Liman estuary. There, to his dismay, he found himself in the company of three other rear admirals, including the prince of Nassau-Siegen, none of whom was willing to concede superiority in rank to Jones. Potemkin refused to intervene.

The theater of operations was the Liman estuary, thirty miles long, nowhere more than eight miles wide, and nowhere more than eighteen feet deep; large warships, whose movements were subject to the direction of the wind, found it difficult to maneuver without running aground. Jones was given command of the squadron of larger ships that included one ship of the line and eight frigates. If his enemy, the Turks, decided to enter these narrow, congested waters in force, they could bring as many as eighteen ships of the line and forty frigates, along with numerous oar-propelled galleys, rowed by slaves chained to their seats. The Russians also had a flotilla of twenty-five oar-propelled, shallow-draft galleys, but their commander, the prince of Nassau-Siegen, was independent of Jones, and took orders only from Potemkin. A battle with the Turks on June 5 was inconclusive, and afterward Russian commanders argued about tactics and credit for their success in forcing the Turks to withdraw. Potemkin sided with Nassau-Siegen. "It is to you alone that I attribute victory," he wrote. To Catherine, Potemkin wrote, "Nassau was the real hero and to him belongs the victory." The battle resumed ten days later, and Jones found himself in difficulty—not with the Turks, but with the Russians. He did not speak Russian, and there was no agreed-on method of signaling between his ships; the admiral had to have himself rowed in a small boat so that he could shout instructions to his captains; even these had to be given through an interpreter. Nevertheless, he won; the Turkish flagship ran aground and was destroyed. Nassau-Siegen took the credit. "Our victory is complete," he wrote to his wife. "My flotilla did it. Oh what a poor man is Paul Jones! I am master of the Liman. Poor Paul Jones! No place for him on this great day!" Throughout his life, Jones had displayed an intense desire to have his merit recognized. He wrote to Potemkin, "I hope to be subjected to no more humiliation and to find myself soon in the situation that was promised me when I was invited to enter Her Imperial Majesty's Navy." Instead, Potemkin relieved Jones of command, explaining to the empress that "nobody wished to serve under him." By the end of October, Jones was back in St. Petersburg, where he was received by Catherine and told to wait for an assignment with the Baltic Fleet.

He waited through the winter, passing time with his friend the French ambassador, Philippe de Ségur. During the first week of April 1789, the capital was startled by a report that Rear Admiral Jones had attempted to rape a ten-year-old girl, the daughter of a German immigrant woman who had a dairy business. The police had been told that the girl was peddling butter when Jones's manservant told her that his master wanted to purchase some and led her to Jones's apartment. There, the girl said, she found her customer, whom she had never seen before, dressed in a white uniform wearing a gold star and a red ribbon. He bought some butter, locked the door, knocked her down, dragged her into his bedroom, and assaulted her. She ran home and told her mother, who went to the police. Ségur defended his friend, both at the time and later in his memoirs. He said that the young girl had called on Jones to ask whether he had any linen to mend. He said no. "She then indulged in some indecent gestures," Ségur quotes Jones as saying. "I advised her not to enter on so vile a career, gave her some money and dismissed her." As soon as she left his front door, the girl ripped her dress, screamed "Rape!" and threw herself into the arms of her mother, who, conveniently, was standing nearby.

Two weeks later, Jones wrote to Potemkin that he had learned that the mother had admitted that a gentleman with decorations had given her money to tell a damaging story about the American. She confessed that her daughter was twelve, not ten, and had been seduced by Jones's manservant three months before she visited the admiral. Further, Jones said that immediately after the alleged rape, rather than rushing home to her mother, the girl had continued peddling butter. "The charge against me is an unworthy imposture," Jones continued to Potemkin. "Shall it be said that in Russia, a wretched woman who abandoned her husband, stole away her daughter, lives in a house of ill repute and leads a debauched, lecherous life, has found credit enough on a simple complaint unsupported by any proof to affect the honor of a general officer of reputation who has merited and received the decorations of America, France and this empire? I love women, I confess, and the pleasures that one only obtains from that sex, but to get such things by force is horrible to me. I cannot even contemplate gratifying my passions without their consent, and I give you my word as a soldier and an honest man, that if the girl in question has not passed through hands other than mine, she is still a virgin."

There was, however, a third version. Before talking to Ségur or writing Potemkin, Jones had informed the chief of police: "The accusation against me is false. It was invented by the mother of a depraved girl who came to my house several times and with whom I have often *badine*,* always giving her money, but whose virginity I have positively not taken. I thought her to be several years older than Your Excellency says she is and each time she came to my house she lent herself very willingly to do all that a man would want of her. The last time passed off like the rest and she went out appearing content and calm, and having been in no way abused. If one has checked on her being deflowered, I declare that I am not the author of it, and I shall easily prove the falseness of this assertion." This letter was supported by affidavits from three witnesses who swore that they saw the girl leave Jones's apartment quietly without blood, bruises, torn clothing, or tears.

In any case, if not a crime, this encounter between a restless, lonely, middle-aged man and an underage girl was tawdry. Nobody knew exactly what had happened, but Jones was ostracized by St. Petersburg society. Ségur believed that Jones had been duped and that the prince of Nassau-Siegen was responsible. "Paul Jones is no more guilty than I," the ambassador declared, "and a man of his rank has never suffered

---

*Jones wrote this letter in a mixture of French and English, and it was he who chose the French word *badiner*. This can mean "played with," "bantered with," "joked with," "toyed with," or "trifled with." In today's vernacular, it could mean "fooled around with." No one will ever know now how intimate this encounter became. Jones, however, was not denying that something had happened. He was insisting that he did not have sexual intercourse with a ten- or twelve-year-old girl.

such humiliation through the accusation of a woman whose husband certifies that she is a pimp and whose daughter solicits the inns." Criminal charges against Jones were dropped, but the offer of a command in the Baltic Fleet also evaporated. (This command went to Nassau-Siegen, who promptly lost a naval battle to Sweden.) In lieu of outright dismissal, Catherine granted Jones a two-year leave of absence. On June 26, she gave him her hand to kiss in a public farewell and nodded a cool "Bon voyage."

What remained of his life was brief and anticlimactic. Never again did he command a ship, much less a fleet. Still in his early forties, he lived alone in Paris during the first years of the French Revolution; neither Gouverneur Morris, the American minister, nor Lafayette found time to see him. He died on July 18, 1792, two weeks after his forty-fifth birthday, of nephritis and bronchial pneumonia. After his death, Gouverneur Morris refused to allot public funds for a funeral or to save Jones from a pauper's grave. Instead, the French National Assembly, which remembered him as a hero, paid for what little was done.

A century passed. In 1899, the American ambassador to France, Horace Porter, used his own money to search for Jones's body. It was found in a lead coffin, under a pavement, in an obscure cemetery outside Paris. When Theodore Roosevelt was president and creating a great American navy became one of his passions, he sent four American armored cruisers to Cherbourg to carry Jones back across the Atlantic to his adopted country. In 1913, 121 years after his death, the body of John Paul Jones, proclaimed to be the father of the United States Navy, was placed in a marble sarcophagus in the crypt of the U.S. Naval Academy chapel. Since then, every midshipman has been taught Jones's words, whether they were exactly his words or not: "I have not yet begun to fight."

By the summer of 1791, the Russian army had forced the Turks to the peace table. In the treaty concluded at Jassy in Moldavia in December 1791, Catherine's greatest goals were not achieved: the Turks kept Constantinople, and the crescent remained atop the Haigia Sophia; there was no Greek empire for Grand Duke Constantine. Still, Catherine gained much. The Turks formally ceded the Crimea, the mouth of the Dnieper with Ochakov, and the territory between the Bug and the Dniester rivers, making the Dniester Russia's western frontier. Formal acquisition by treaty of the naval base at Sebastopol and Turkish acceptance of the fleet based there provided Russia with a permanent naval presence on the Black Sea. The subsequent development of the commercial port of Odessa provided an outlet for the export of large quantities of Russian wheat.

The second Turkish war had been Potemkin's war; he had borne responsibility for strategy, command, and logistics. Catherine had sustained him. She was the more stable, avoiding his alternating moods of optimism and pessimism, his doubts, fears, and occasional despair. Neither could have achieved victory without the other. When military operations were over, Potemkin turned the negotiations at Jassy over to others and headed back to St. Petersburg, where Catherine was preparing a conqueror's welcome. Even as he traveled north, however, Potemkin was worried. For the first time in seventeen years, Catherine had acquired a new favorite of whom he vehemently disapproved: a handsome young man named Platon Zubov. Poorly educated, he was vain and greedy for wealth, estates, honors, and titles, not only for himself but also for his father and his three brothers; all soon became counts. The most prominent men of the court and the empire began lining up to humble themselves at his morning levee. When the doors to his reception room opened, they were likely to reveal Zubov stretched out in a lounge chair before his mirror, having his hair dressed and powdered. He could be wearing a silk colored frock coat sewn with jewels, white satin trousers, and green ankle-length boots. Conspicuously ignoring the ministers, generals, courtiers, foreigners, and petitioners who stood motionless and silent before him, he paid attention only to his pet monkey. When, with a gesture, the master cued the creature's performance, it leaped across the furniture, hung from the chandeliers, and finally jumped onto a visitor's shoulder to pull off his wig or muss his hair. When Zubov laughed, everyone laughed.

Potemkin knew that he and Zubov would now be competing for the empress's confidence. So far, he had remained foremost; Catherine consulted him on everything; she told him that if war were to break out in Poland, he was to take supreme command of the Russian army. Nevertheless, he was uneasy. "Zub" means "tooth" in Russian. As his carriage rolled north to the capital, Potemkin repeatedly reminded himself, "I must pull out the tooth."

Arriving in St. Petersburg on February 28, 1791, Potemkin quickly demonstrated that his character had not changed. When Kyril Razumovsky called to tell him that he was giving a ball in Potemkin's honor, Potemkin met his visitor wearing a tattered dressing gown and nothing underneath. Razumovsky good-naturedly retaliated a few days later by publicly receiving the prince wearing a nightgown with a nightcap on his head. Potemkin laughed and embraced his host.

He turned to the problem of Zubov, which, he believed, had to be solved as much to shield Catherine as for his own reasons. He saw that he could no longer use his political power as he had done with Yermolov; if this young man were to be displaced, it must be done more subtly. The best approach, he concluded, would be to re-create the aura of their old romance. Surprisingly, he partially succeeded. In a letter to Grimm on May 21, Catherine spoke of Potemkin with the same enthusiasm that she had years before.

> When one looks at the Prince-Marshal Potemkin, one must say that his victories, his successes, beautify him. He has returned to us from the army as handsome as the day, as gay as a lark, as brilliant as a star, more witty than ever, no longer biting his nails, giving feasts every day, and behaving as a host with a polish and courtesy by which everybody is enchanted.

Potemkin's success was incomplete, however. It was obvious that Catherine wanted her relationship with Zubov to continue. The competition between the two men became a standoff: Potemkin openly displayed his contempt for Zubov, who, in return, smiled and bided his time. Meanwhile, when Potemkin's bills came due, Catherine paid them, instructing the treasury that it was to treat Prince Potemkin's expenses as if they were her own.

Potemkin tried to distract himself by giving and attending receptions, dinners, and balls. The evening that surpassed anything ever seen in Russia occurred on April 28, 1791, at Potemkin's Tauride Palace. Three thousand guests had been invited; all were present when the empress arrived. The prince was at the door, wearing a scarlet tailcoat with solid gold buttons, each button encasing a large solitaire diamond. Once the empress was seated, twenty-four couples, including Catherine's two grandsons, Alexander and Constantine, entered to dance a quadrille. Afterward, the host led his guest through the rooms of the palace. In one, poets were reciting verse; in another, a choir was singing; in still another, a French comedy was being performed.

At the end of the evening, following a ball and an extravagant supper, Catherine and Potemkin withdrew alone to the winter garden to walk between the fountains and marble statues. When they spoke, he mentioned Zubov; she did not reply. Catherine stayed until two in the morning, later than she had ever remained at a party. Escorted to the door by Potemkin, she stopped to thank him. They said goodbye. Overwhelmed, he threw himself at her feet; when he looked up, both were in tears. After she left, Potemkin stood quietly for a few minutes, then walked alone to his room.

At five o'clock in the morning on July 24, 1791, Potemkin left Tsarskoe Selo for the last time. He was already tired, and the journey to the south further exhausted him. He was still deeply unhappy about Zubov, and, as if Catherine did not realize how much she was wounding him, she continued to fill her letters with talk of her young lover: "The child sends his greetings. . . . The child thinks that you are more intelligent . . . and far more amusing and pleasant than all those who surround you." Years later, when both Potemkin and Catherine were dead, "the child" revealed his true feelings about his rival: "I could not remove him from my path, and it was essential to remove him because the empress always met his wishes halfway and simply feared him as though he were an exacting husband. She loved only me, but she often pointed to Potemkin as an example for me to follow. It is his fault that I am not twice as rich as I am."

Sunk in melancholy, Potemkin began by traveling slowly—the jolting of the carriage was painful—then, suddenly, he demanded speed. Hurtling down dusty roads and through towns and villages, he reached Jassy only eight days after leaving the Neva. The journey drained his declining strength; on arriving, he wrote to Catherine that he felt the the touch of the hand of death. His illness showed symptoms of the malaria that had infected him in the Crimea in 1783. Traveling south, he refused to take quinine and other medicines prescribed by the three doctors accompanying him; like Catherine, he was convinced that the best way to recover from illness was to let the body itself solve the problem. Instead of dieting, as the doctors recommended, he ate huge meals and drank heavily. To ward off pain, he wrapped his head in wet towels. When he reached Jassy, his staff sent for his niece, Sashenka Branitsky, hoping that she could persuade him to be reasonable and accept treatment. She hurried from Poland. In the middle of September, he had an attack of fever and shivered uncontrollably for twelve hours. He wrote to Catherine, "Please send me a Chinese dressing gown. I badly need one." The Russian ambassador in Vienna, Andrei Razumovsky, wrote suggesting that he send "the first pianist and one of the best composers in Germany" to soothe him. The offer was made and the composer accepted, but Potemkin did not have time to respond and Wolfgang Amadeus Mozart did not make the journey.

Oppressed by the humid air of Jassy, he twice drove out seeking country air, only to give up and come back. In St. Petersburg, Catherine waited for messages and letters and asked Countess Branitsky to write to her every day. On Potemkin's behalf, Catherine reversed her position on doctors and medicines. "Take that which in the doctors' estimation will give you relief; and having taken it, I beg you also to save yourself from food and drink that opposes the medicine." With this support, Sashenka and the doctors finally persuaded the sick man to take medicine. For a few days he seemed better. Then, shivering and sleeplessness returned. Saying that he was "burning up," he demanded more wet towels, drank cold liquids, and had bottles of eau de cologne poured over his head. He asked that all windows be opened and, when that failed to cool him, insisted on being carried into the garden. Every day, he asked repeatedly whether any messages had come from the empress; when a new letter arrived, he wept and read it, then reread it and kissed it repeatedly. When state documents were brought and read to him, he could barely scribble his signature at the bottom. It was clear that he was dying; Potemkin himself realized this. He refused to take quinine. "I'm not going to recover. I have been ill for a long time . . . God's will be done. Pray for my soul and do not forget me when I am gone. I never wished anybody any harm. To make people happy has always been my desire. I am not a bad man and not the evil genius of our mother, the Empress Catherine, as has been said." He asked for the Last Sacrament, and once it had been given, he relaxed. A courier from Moscow brought another letter from Catherine, a fur coat, and the silk dressing gown he had asked for. He cried. He said to Sashenka, "Tell me frankly, do you think I shall recover?" She assured him that he would. He took her hands and caressed them. "Good hands," he said. "They have often soothed me."

Gradually, the passionate, ambitious man, still only fifty-two, became calm; those around him watched him dying in serenity. He begged everyone to forgive him for any pain he might have caused them. They must promise to convey to the empress his humblest gratitude for everything she had done for him. When a new message arrived from her he wept. He agreed to try quinine but could not hold it down. He began to faint; he was conscious only half the time; he felt that he was suffocating. He wrote to Catherine, "Matushka, oh how sick I am!" He asked to be moved from Jassy to Nikolaev; its cooler air might do him good. On the day he started out on the journey, he dictated a note to Catherine: "Your most gracious Majesty. I have no more strength to endure my torments. My only remaining salvation is to leave this town and I have ordered myself be taken to Nikolaev. I do not know what is to become of me."

At eight on the morning of October 4, he was carried to his carriage. He went a few miles and said that he could not breathe. The carriage stopped. Carried into a house, he fell asleep. After three hours' rest, he talked cheerfully until midnight. He tried to sleep again but could not. At daybreak, he asked that the journey resume. The procession had gone only seven miles when he ordered it to stop. "This will be enough," he said. "There is no point in going on. Take me out of the carriage and put me down. I want to die in the field." A Persian carpet was unrolled on the grass. Potemkin was placed on it and covered with the silk gown Catherine had sent him. Everyone searched for a gold coin to close his eye in the Orthodox fashion, but no gold coin was found. An escorting Cossack offered a copper five-kopeck piece and with this his eye was covered. At midday on Sunday, October 5, 1791, he died. A message went to the empress: "His Serene Highness the prince is no longer on this earth."

At five in the evening on October 12, a courier bringing the news reached the Winter Palace in St. Petersburg. Catherine collapsed. "Now I have no one left on whom I can rely," she cried. "How can anybody replace Potemkin? Everything will be different now. He was a true nobleman." The days passed and her secretary could only report: "Tears and despair . . . tears . . . more tears."

❧69❧

Art, Architecture, and the Bronze Horseman

THE FOUNDATION of the superb collection of art in St. Petersburg's Hermitage Museum today was laid by Catherine only a year after she reached the throne. In 1763, she learned that a collection of 225 paintings accumulated by a Polish art dealer in Berlin who regularly supplied pictures to Frederick II had not been paid for. The dealer had been buying and holding the paintings for the king's Potsdam palace, Sans Souci, but Frederick had decided that he could not afford them. His finances, personal and national, had been ravaged by the cost of the Seven Years' War, and the need to pay his army and to begin reconstruction of his devastated country took precedence over the purchase of paintings for his palace walls. The art dealer was, therefore, deeply in debt and urgently needed a customer. Catherine stepped forward and, without serious bargaining, bought the entire collection.

There may have been an element of spite in her purchase of a collection originally destined for Frederick. When Elizabeth was on the throne, Russia had been at war with Prussia; then Peter III had succeeded his aunt, had switched sides, and had become Frederick's ally. Now, pulling Frederick's paintings out from under him would partially balance the ledger. Not all of her new paintings were masterpieces, but they included three Rembrandts, a Franz Hals, and a Rubens.

When the paintings arrived in St. Petersburg, Catherine was so pleased that she sent word to her ambassadors and agents in Europe to be alert for other collections that might come up for sale. Fortunately, the Russian ambassador in Paris was Prince Dmitry Golitsyn, a polished Enlightenment figure, a friend of Voltaire's and Diderot's, and a habitué of the intellectual and artistic salon of Madame Geoffrin. Golitsyn arranged Catherine's purchase of Diderot's library in 1765 and continued to buy paintings for Catherine as long as he remained in Paris. When he left France to become Russian ambassador in The Hague, Diderot agreed to become Catherine's scout, selecting and buying paintings for her. The most prestigious and best-informed art critic in the world now was acting for the richest and most powerful woman in the world.

A few years later, in 1769, Catherine scored a coup when the famous Dresden collection of the late Count Heinrich von Brühl, minister of foreign affairs to Augustus II, king of Poland and elector of Saxony, came on the market. She paid 180,000 rubles to acquire the collection, which included four more Rembrandts, a Caravaggio, and five works by Rubens. The paintings were delivered by sea, up the Baltic and into the Neva River, where the ships tied up at the Winter Palace quay only fifty feet from the palace doors. For the next quarter of a century, this was a frequent sight in St. Petersburg: vessels from France, Holland, and England lying against the quay, unloading packing crates and boxes containing paintings by Rembrandt, Rubens, Caravaggio, Franz Hals, and Van Dycks. Inside the palace, Catherine had the crates opened in her presence alone so as to see and judge them first. As the containers were unpacked and the paintings emerged and were propped against the walls, she stood in front of them and walked back and forth studying them, trying to understand them. In her first years of collecting, Catherine valued the paintings she bought less for their visual beauty or artistic technique than for their intellectual and narrative content and for the notice and prestige their acquisition conferred on her.

On March 25, 1771, the empress surprised Europe again by buying the famous collection of Pierre Crozat, which, since the collector's death, had passed through many hands. It included eight works by Rembrandt, four by Veronese, a dozen by Rubens, seven by Van Dyck, and several by Raphael, Titian, and Tintoretto. The entire collection came to her with a single exception: Van Dyck's portrait of King Charles I of England, who had been beheaded by Oliver Cromwell. Madame du Barry, mistress of Louis XV, bought this painting because she was convinced that she had Stuart blood. Catherine was pleased when Diderot told her that he had succeeded in acquiring the collection for half its value. Four months later in the same year, Catherine bought 150 paintings from the collection of the Duc de Choiseul. Again, Diderot, who arranged the purchase, estimated that she had paid less than half the market value.

In 1773, Diderot and Grimm both came to St. Petersburg. Once back in France, Grimm took over Diderot's role as Catherine's agent in Paris. She felt more at ease with Grimm; Diderot, like Voltaire, seemed to her a great man who had to be handled carefully; Grimm was a clever, congenial man with whom she exchanged an informal correspondence of more than fifteen hundred letters. Grimm spread his net wide on Catherine's behalf: it was Grimm, for example, who acquired for her a copy of the sculptor Houdon's extraordinarily lifelike statue of a seated Voltaire. The original is now in the Comédie Française; Catherine's copy is in the Hermitage Museum.

In 1778, the empress received news from her ambassador in London that George Walpole, the spendthrift grandson and heir of Sir Robert Walpole, intended to sell the family's collection of paintings. Robert Walpole, a Whig who had been prime minister for more than twenty years under George I and George II, had been a lifelong collector of paintings. For thirty-three years, since Robert Walpole's death, they had been hanging in the family home at Houghton Hall in Norfolk. Walpole's grandson, in order to pay his debts and support his passion for raising greyhounds, had decided to sell the entire collection, the finest and most famous private art collection in England, and among the finest in the world. There were almost two hundred paintings, including Rembrandt's *Abraham's Sacrifice of Isaac,* fifteen works by Van Dyck, and thirteen works by Rubens. Catherine wanted them all. After two months of negotiations, she acquired the entire collection for thirty-six thousand pounds.

The consequence was a storm of public indignation in England. That a foreign empress should be allowed to buy and carry away a British national treasure was intolerable. More than a collection of paintings was being removed from the country; a whole chapter of British history and culture was being shipped away. Horace Walpole, the writer and aesthete who was the grandson's uncle, had always coveted the collection and expected that one day it would come to him. He called what had happened a "theft." If he couldn't have the paintings, he said, "I would rather they were sold to the crown of England than to that of Russia, where they will be burned in a wooden palace at the first insurrection." A public subscription campaign to buy back the paintings failed. Catherine was never worried. Writing to Grimm, she said, "The Walpole paintings are longer to be had for the simple reason that your humble servant has already got her claws on them and will no more let them go than a cat would a mouse."

The Walpole purchase confirmed Catherine's reputation as Europe's foremost collector of art and as the leading prospective customer for all owners with major collections to sell. She continued buying, although more selectively. In 1779, when Grimm recommended purchasing the collection of the French Comte de Baudouin, which contained nine Rembrandts, two Rubenses, and four Van Dycks, she held back, complaining about the price. Grimm reported, "The Comte de Baudouin leaves it to your Majesty to decide conditions, timing, and all other considerations." Catherine admitted, "It would indeed be discourteous to refuse such a generous offer," but she did not concede until 1784. "The world is a strange place and the number of happy people very small," she wrote to Grimm. "I can see that the Comte de Baudouin is not going to be happy until he sells his collection and it appears that I am the one destined to make him happy." She sent Grimm fifty thousand rubles. When the paintings arrived and were uncrated, Catherine wrote to Grimm, "We are prodigiously delighted."

Many wealthy Europeans wished to be considered connoisseurs, and competition in the art market was keen. Catherine was the leader; she was an immensely rich collector who trusted her agents and possessed the self-confidence of one who wants only the best and is willing to pay for it. Later, she confessed that ego and prestige played a part; that she loved to possess, to amass. "It is not love of art," she admitted, in part facetiously. "It is voracity. I am a glutton." Her agents continued to buy everything available of beauty and value. During her reign, Catherine's collection expanded to almost four thousand paintings. She became the greatest collector and patron of art in the history of Europe.

Catherine was more than a collector; she was also a builder. It was through architecture as well as her collection of paintings that she was determined to leave on St. Petersburg a cultural mark that time would not obliterate. During her reign, architects of genius were commissioned to create elegant public buildings, palaces, mansions, and other structures, all examples and reminders of the larger world she wished Russia to join. Elizabeth had also been a builder, but now Elizabethan baroque exuberance, as manifested by Rastrelli, was succeeded by a sober, pure, neoclassical style. Catherine's buildings were intended to represent in form and stone her personal character and taste. She preferred to combine simplicity with elegance, employing stately columns and geometrical façades built of granite and marble rather than Rastrelli's brick and painted plaster.

The huge, baroque Winter Palace, Rastrelli's signature masterpiece, had taken eight years to build and was completed in 1761, the year Elizabeth died. Painted apple-green and white, with a façade that rose 450 feet, it was a massive structure of 1,050 rooms and 117 staircases. Six months later, when Catherine reached the throne, she found this palace crushing in size and herself stifled by its lush decor. With her love of rationality and order, she rejected the ornate atmosphere of gold, blue, and glitter and looked for an escape. She disliked pomp and crowds, as well as architectural frills; she preferred informal gatherings in small rooms where she could enjoy the intimate companionship of a few close friends. She also wanted a spacious, well-lighted hall nearby to serve as a gallery in which to hang the paintings now arriving on the quay below. To create such a refuge, she turned to a French architect brought to Russia by Ivan Shuvalov, Elizabeth's favorite during the final years of her reign. Shuvalov had persuaded the empress to permit the founding of a permanent Academy of Art and subsequently had persuaded the French architect Michel Vallin de la Mothe to come to St. Petersburg and build a gallery to house this academy. Catherine, then a grand duchess, had admired Mothe's new building when it was finished in 1759, and, once on the throne, she commissioned the architect to build something for her.

In 1765, Mothe designed for Catherine a private retreat and art gallery in which to hang her new paintings. She called it her Hermitage, and subsequently it became known as the Little Hermitage. Mothe attached the three-story building as an annex to Rastrelli's enormous Winter Palace, and, somehow, perhaps because of its far smaller size, its neoclassical façade was compatible with the huge, ornate Winter Palace next door. Throughout her reign, she used the smaller building as a European town house in which to read, work, and talk. It was here that she met Diderot on his visit to St. Petersburg, Grimm on his two visits, the British ambassador James Harrris, and many others. She could also stroll through its gallery, by herself or surrounded by friends, and reflect on her latest treasures.

"You should know our mania for building is stronger than ever," Catherine wrote to Grimm in 1779. "It is a diabolical thing. It consumes money and the more you build, the more you want to build. It's a sickness like being addicted to alcohol." She built mostly for others, however. In 1766, she had commissioned Antonio Rinaldi to construct a country palace for Gregory Orlov at Gatchina, thirty miles south of St. Petersburg. It was to Gatchina that Orlov invited Jean-Jacque Rousseau; it was to Gatchina, too, that Catherine placed Orlov in a month's "quarantine" when, in a rage, he rode back from the south having learned that he had been replaced as Catherine's favorite by the hapless Vasilchikov. In 1768, she commissioned Rinaldi to build the Marble Palace for Orlov in St. Petersburg, set in a garden facing the Neva River. Rather than constructing a palace of brick and then coating the brick with thick layers of stucco painted in bright colors as Rastrelli might have done, Rinaldi built Orlov's palace of gray and red granite, faced with different shades of marble: pink, white, and blue-gray. On the façade, Catherine inscribed, "In grateful friendship."

Of all the private palaces built for others by Catherine, the largest and most spectacular was constructed for Potemkin. She chose a Russian architect, Ivan Starov, who had spent a decade studying in Paris and Rome. Starov built the unique neoclassical Tauride Palace; when it was finished in 1789, it was considered the finest private residence in Russia. Its domed entry hall led to a gallery of 230 feet lined by Ionic columns and opening onto an enormous winter garden. In 1906, when Tsar Nicholas II established the first Russian State Duma, or parliament, this body, soon to become irrelevant, sat in the Tauride Palace.

For all the responsibility she gave to Starov, he was not the architect who worked most closely with Catherine and who most fully reflected her personal taste. This was a quiet, unpretentious Scotsman, Charles Cameron. Born in 1743, Cameron was a Jacobite who had studied in Rome. Fascinated by the design of classical antiquities, he had written a book on ancient Roman baths. When he arrived in Russia in the summer of 1779, he was already well known as a designer of neoclassical interiors and furniture. Catherine commissioned him to redesign and decorate her private apartments in the palace at Tsarskoe Selo where she spent her summers. Just as she disliked Rastrelli's Winter Palace in St. Petersburg, she found equally unlivable the enormous, bright blue, pistachio green, and white baroque palace Rastrelli had built for Elizabeth at Tsarskoe Selo. Its façade of 326 feet was too large for her; its endless row of elaborately decorated public rooms seemed to her like an ornamented army barracks. Catherine's first commission for Cameron was to remodel and redecorate the private apartment she used in the palace. This assignment was a test of Cameron's taste and skill. He created simple, elegant rooms, gentle in color: milky white, light blues, greens, and violet. "I never cease to be surprised by this work," Catherine wrote Grimm. "I have never seen anything to equal it." Thereafter, she allowed, and then encouraged, Cameron to use only the most expensive materials: agate, jasper, lapis, malachite, and bronze.

In 1780, the empress asked Cameron to build a palace for her son, Grand Duke Paul, and his wife, Maria, at Pavlovsk, three miles from Tsarskoe Selo. In 1777, at the birth of her grandson Alexander, the empress had given the couple a thousand acres and a large English park with ponds, bridges, temples, statues, and colonnades. Cameron went to work on the palace, which became Maria's place of refuge during her many years of widowhood. Today, restored from the terrible damage it suffered during World War II, it is considered a masterpiece.

Cameron's next commission was the transformation of another

part of the great palace at Tsarskoe Selo. He created the Agate Pavilion, three rooms with walls of solid jasper interspersed with red agate. His ultimate triumph followed: the terrace and colonnade that bears his name, the Cameron Galley. This marble gallery is 270 feet long, set on a granite base with an open-air colonnaded balcony featuring slender Ionic columns. It was placed at the far end of Rastrelli's palace near Catherine's new, private apartment and at a sharp left angle, making it perpendicular to the long line of the main building. Between the columns in this covered gallery, Catherine placed more than fifty bronze busts of Greek and Roman philosophers and orators. Surrounded by figures she admired, she sat and read during the summer. When she rose, she could walk to the end of he gallery, which opened onto a sweeping curved staircase divided into two branches, one with steps, the other with a ramp, leading down to the park. In her later years, she could choose to walk slowly up or down, or be pushed in a wheelchair, to or from the park.

After Cameron, Catherine's favorite architect was Giacomo Quarenghi, an Italian also designing and building in neoclassical style. Quarenghi arrived in Russia in 1780, two years after Cameron. He began by designing the neoclassical Palladian Theater at the Litttle Hermitage, decorating it with marble columns and statues of playwrights and composers. Quarenghi also designed the austere Alexander Palace at Tsarskoe Selo for Catherine's beloved grandson Alexander, who became Tsar Alexander I. A century later this palace became the country home of Catherine's great-great-great-grandson, Russia's last tsar, Nicholas II, and his family.

Not all of the artists encouraged and supported by Catherine came from abroad. The best Russian students at the Academy of Art were being sent abroad in groups of twelve at state expense to spend two, four, or more years studying in France, Italy, or Germany. The greatest portraitists of Catherine's time were both Ukrainians, Dmitry Levitsky and Vladimir Borovikovsky; Borovikovsky's best-known portrait depicts an elderly Catherine walking her dog in the park of Tsarskoe Selo. Another Russian-born artist of Catherine's day was the architect Georg Friedrich Velten, whose father had come to Russia as Peter the Great's master cook. The younger Velten studied architecture abroad and, on returning, was commissioned to remove the wooden quays along the Neva River and to face the embankments with Finnish granite. The architectural continuity of this work, stretching for twenty-four miles along the river, gave the waterfront a stately elegance. At the same time, the solid granite quays served as landing stages where both river traffic and seagoing vessels could tie up and discharge cargo.

If Catherine sought straight, pure classical lines in her buildings, she wanted the opposite in her parks and gardens. When she transformed the formal Dutch and French gardens at Tsarskoe Selo, her adviser and chief gardener was John Busch, an Englishman of Hanoverian origin, who spoke to the empress in German. Busch's language ability had been useful when he was cast as the German "innkeeper" during Emperor Joseph II's visit to Tsarskoe Selo as "Count Falkenstein." Busch retained the post of gardener for years, and when he retired, he was succeeded by his son, Joseph. Busch also found himself related to Cameron. On arriving in Tsarskoe Selo, the Scottish architect, speaking no Russian or French, moved into Busch's house; eventually, he married Busch's daughter.

Catherine helped design the new park. She liked flowers, shrubs, monuments, obelisks, triumphal arches, canals, and winding paths, and Busch laid these out for her. She wrote to Voltaire, "Now I love to distraction gardens in the English style, the curving lines, the gentle slopes, the ponds like lakes . . . and I hold in contempt straight lines. . . . I hate fountains that torture water and force it into a course contrary to its nature. . . . In a word, Anglomania rules my plantomania." At the end of her working day, she walked in the park in a plain dress, exercising her dogs and mingling with the public, which, if decently dressed, was freely admitted. It was in the park at Tsarskoe Selo that Alexander Pushkin set the penultimate scene in his story of the Pugachev rebellion, *The Captain's Daughter,* written forty years after Catherine's death. A young woman, the distressed eighteen-year-old betrothed of an imprisoned and wrongly condemned young officer caught up in the rebellion, is walking in the park. She happens to meet a plainly dressed, unaccompanied, middle-aged woman sitting on a bench. The older woman asks why she is upset. The young woman tells her story and says she hopes to find a way to beg for mercy from the empress. The questioner, who "seemed to be about forty," has "a plump and rosy face . . . an expression of calm and dignity . . . blue eyes . . . a slight smile . . . and an indescribable charm." She tells the anxious girl that she often goes to court and will pass her story along to the empress, encouraging her not to lose hope. Soon after, the young woman is summoned to the palace and taken to the empress's dressing room, where she realizes that the woman she met in the park was Catherine herself. The young officer is pardoned and despair is transformed into joy.

It was not simply her unmatched collection of paintings or the elegant neoclassical palaces she built for herself and others that made Catherine's reputation as a patron of the arts. The single most famous artistic work produced in Russia during her reign was Étienne Maurice Falconet's equestrian statue of Peter the Great. Since its unveiling in 1782, this unique masterpiece, commissioned by Catherine in a deliberate effort to assert her claim to the legacy of the greatest of Russian tsars, has stood for two and a quarter centuries on the bank of the Neva River in the middle of the city Peter founded.

Empress Elizabeth, Peter's daughter, idolized her father, but she had never erected what Catherine considered an appropriate monument to him. Now Catherine, not born a Russian but hoping to be accepted as the great tsar's true political heir, decided that there should be a supreme visual tribute to the figure who had made Russia a great European power. She considered herself, a daughter of Europe coming to Russia eighteen years after Peter's death, as resuming his journey to civilization and greatness. She wanted Russians to understand and accept this connection between them.

Because she believed that no one in Russia had sufficient talent to do the work she wanted done, she instructed her ambassador in Paris, then Prince Dmitry Golitsyn, to find a French sculptor to design and cast a heroic equestrian statue in bronze. The price originally offered was 300,000 livres. Golitsyn approached three well-known French sculptors; they asked 450,000, 400,000, and 600,000 livres. Golitsyn then spoke to his friend Diderot, and Diderot spoke to the sculptor Étienne Maurice Falconet, director of the sculpture workshop of the Royal Sèvres porcelain factory. Falconet seemed an unlikely candidate. The son of a poor carpenter, he was considered competent but not brilliantly talented. Although Catherine had told Golitysn and Diderot that her monument was to be on a grand scale, Falconet was known for his small figures in porcelain, greatly admired by Louis XV's mistress Madame de Pompadour. At fifty-one, he had never worked on a large scale. Nevertheless, he succumbed to Diderot's persuasion, accepted the empress's offer, and agreed to work for 25,000 livres per year, saying that he was ready to devote eight years to the work. In fact, he remained in Russia for twelve years.

Falconet arrived in St. Petersburg in 1766, and Catherine greeted him enthusiastically. It pleased her that Falconet had asked less in payment than the sum offered and far less than others had asked. Although in Paris Falconet had a reputation for a prickly ego, once he reached St. Petersburg and began working on the first clay models of the statue he seemed in constant need of his patron's approval. Catherine obliged by showing him not only enthusiasm but deference. In 1767, when Falconet submitted his first design for the statue of Peter, she protested her lack of knowledge and excused herself from expressing an opinion. She recommended that the artist rely on his own judgment and the probable views of posterity. Falconet argued back, "My posterity is Your Majesty. The other may come when it will."

"Not at all," Catherine replied. "How can you submit yourself to my opinion. I do not even know how to draw. The merest schoolboy knows more about sculpture than I do."

Pleased by the value the empress placed on his judgement, Falconet began to offer advice on the paintings that Diderot was buying and sending. His comments were often obsequious. "What a charming picture," he wrote of a painting by a lesser-known artist. "What magnificent brushwork! What beautiful tones! What a sweet little head of Aphrodite! What an admirable consistency!" Concerning another painting, he said, "We should fall on our knees before it. Anyone who dares to think otherwise has neither faith nor morals. After all, I do know something about it; it is practically my profession." To which Catherine replied, "I think you are right. I am well aware of the reason I cannot approve. It is because I don't understand enough to see in it all that you do." Often, after taking a private first look at her new paintings, Catherine wanted to share them with Falconet. "My paintings are beautiful," she wrote about one arriving shipment. "When would you like to come and see them?"

Catherine may have assumed an ignorance of art, but in imagining her statue of Peter, she knew what she wanted. Falconet had never hoped to work on the scale that the empress was demanding, but her high expectations elevated his design and effort. In order to help him understand the appearance and movements of a rearing horse, the empress made available two of her favorite animals, along with their trainers, who could make them rear as the artist wished. Meanwhile, Falconet's apprentice, eighteen-year-old Marie-Anne Collot, who had come with him from Paris, began working on the head and face of the tsar, using Peter's death mask and the portraits available. She remained in Russia as long as Falconet and later married the sculptor's artist son who came to visit.

By the summer of 1769, Falconet's work on the statue was sufficiently advanced to allow the public to see the model. Not every reaction was favorable. One point of contention was the presence of the serpent the sculptor had placed beneath the horse's rear hooves. Falconet was told that the creature was inappropriate and should be removed by people who did not realize that the support given by attachment to the serpent was essential. Without the three points made up by the hooves and tail resting on the serpent's back, the horse would not stand. "They have not made, as I have, the calculation of forces which I need," the sculptor declared of his critics. "They do not know that if their advice were followed, the work would not survive at all." Catherine had no intention of getting involved in the controversy and replied to Falconet, "There is an old song which says 'what will be, will be.' That is my response to the serpent. Your reasons are good."

By the spring of 1770, the model was complete, and there were more complaints. Falconet was said to have represented the Russian hero dressed as a Roman emperor, provoking leaders of the Orthodox Church to complain that this Frenchman had made Peter resemble a pagan monarch. Catherine calmed these critics by declaring that Peter was wearing an idealized representation of Russian costume. Later, Catherine wrote again to reassure her sensitive artist: "I hear only praise of the statue. I have heard from only one person a comment which was that she wished the clothing was more pleated, so that stupid people would not think it was a chemise, but you can't please everybody." Finally when the completed clay version was unveiled, Catherine still had to reassure the nervous Falconet, who now was worrying that there seemed to be no reaction to his work; people weren't speaking to him, he complained. Again, Catherine tried to reassure him. "I know that . . . in general everyone is very happy," she told him. "If people don't say anything to you, it is out of delicacy. Some feel they aren't qualified enough; others are perhaps afraid of displeasing you by telling you their opinion; still more can't see a thing. Don't take everything the wrong way."

While the colossal statue was being molded, the sculptor and his patron were trying to find a base on which to mount the work. Prospectors searching in nearby Finnish Karelia for granite for the new Neva quays had discovered an enormous, monolithic rock, deeply embedded in marsh. When unearthed, it was twenty-two feet high, forty-two feet long, and thirty-four feet wide. Its weight, experts calculated, was fifteen hundred tons. Catherine decided that this Ice Age boulder must serve as the pedestal for her statue. To bring it to St. Petersburg, a system was worked out that in itself was an engineering feat. Once winter came and the ground was frozen, the boulder was dragged four miles to the sea. It was cradled in a metallic sledge, which rolled over copper balls serving the function of modern ball bearings; the balls rolled in tracks hollowed out in logs laid end to end. It took capstans, pulleys, and a thousand men to inch the stone along, a hundred yards a day, from the forest clearing to the coast of the Gulf of Finland. There, a specially constructed barge was waiting; once it was loaded, the barge was supported on each side by a large warship to prevent its capsizing. In this fashion, the boulder moved slowly across the gulf and was towed up the Neva River, to be brought ashore, maneuvered into position, and deposited at its final site on the riverbank.

By this time, five years had gone by. Another four years were spent finding the right casting master and constructing a mold to cast the immense mass of copper and tin into the form of the statue. Horse and rider together would weigh sixteen tons, with the thickness of the bronze varying from one inch to a quarter of an inch. At one point in the casting, the mold broke, pouring out molten bronze. Fires started and were extinguished, and then the melted, hardened metal had to be pried and scraped up, remelted and recast. Failure followed failure and money drained away. Falconet's relations with Catherine frayed. What had been enthusiasm and encouragement on her part turned to indifference and irritation. Falconet, nervous and irascible, was unable to stand up to the empress, who could not understand the constant delays. At first, he had pleased her with his artistic temperament; eventually she wearied of it. Writing to Grimm and commissioning him to hire two Italian architects, she expressed her frustration: "You will choose honest and reasonable people, not dreamers like Falconet; [I want] people who walk on the earth, not in the air."

Falconet remained in Russia for nearly twelve years, but eventually, he could not continue. In 1778, tired of the delays, exasperated by criticism, and broken in spirit and health, Falconet asked permission to leave, Catherine paid him what was due but refused to see him. He returned to Paris, where he became director of the Académie des Beaux-Arts. In 1783, he suffered a stroke, although he lived another eight years. He continued to write about art, but he never sculpted again.

After Falconet's departure, another four years—sixteen years in all since the sculptor had come to Russia—were to pass before his statue was unveiled. Catherine did not invite the sculptor to return for the ceremony. But time has made up for her ingratitude. The result of his twelve years of work became a permanent landmark in St. Petersburg, Russia's best-known monument and, then and now, one unparalleled in the world. During the nine-hundred-day siege in the Second World War, the city suffered constant German air and artillery bombardment. Falconet's statue, exposed on the riverbank, was never touched.

On August 7, 1782, Catherine presided over the formal unveiling of the statue. Looking down from a window of the nearby Senate building at the massed Guards regiments and an immense crowd in the square below, the empress gave a signal. The drapery fell away and cries of admiration and awe burst from the crowd.

There was Peter, immortalized in bronze, his head almost fifty feet in the air. He wore a simple Roman shift and was crowned with a laurel wreath. He faced the Neva flowing before him. His left hand grasped the reins of his horse, rearing on the crest of a wave frozen in stone. His right arm was outstretched, the hand pointing across the river to the fortress and the first buildings of the city he had created. The serpent, symbolizing the difficulties he had overcome, lay trodden and crushed under the horse's rear hooves. The horse's tail rested on the serpent, providing the three points needed to give the statue balance. On either side of the granite base, metallic letters embedded in the stone bore the inscriptions TO PETER THE FIRST, FROM CATHERINE THE SECOND— on one side in Russian, on the other in Latin. Thus the empress paid tribute to her predecessor and identified herself with him.

In his classic poem "The Bronze Horseman," Alexander Pushkin wrote:

> The Image with an arm flung wide,
>   Sat on his brazen horse astride . . .
> Him, Who moveless and aloft and dim
>   Our city by the sea had founded,
> Whose will was Fate. Appalling there,

He sat, begirt with mist and air.
What thoughts engrave his brow!
     What hidden Power and Authority He claims!
Proud charger, whither art thou ridden
     Where leapest thou? And where, on whom
Wilt plant they hoof?

This was the greatest of all Russian poets' description of a French sculptor's representation of the greatest of Russian emperors, created by the inspiration and determination of a German-born empress. The statue was the culmination and embodiment of Catherine's effort to identify herself with her predecessor. Catherine was Peter's equal—his only equal—in vision, strength of purpose, and achievement during the centuries that Russia was ruled by tsars, emperors, and empresses.

❧70❧

"They Are Capable of Hanging Their King from a Lamppost!"

HIS MOST CHRISTIAN MAJESTY, Louis XVI, king of France and Navarre, was a gawky, amiable, well-intentioned man whose joys in life came from eating heartily, hunting stags, and tinkering with the inner workings of locks. Surrounded by ministers offering contradictory advice, he had difficulty making decisions. Demands that he choose one way or another threw him into confusion; once he had chosen, he continued to vacillate and sometimes changed his mind. This unfortunate thirty-five-year-old monarch was in his sixteenth year on the throne when, in May 1789, he summoned the Estates-General to meet at Versailles. Louis did not do this because he wished to, or because it was part of the usual practice of French kings. Rather, Louis acted because he had no choice; his government desperately needed to raise money to avoid national bankruptcy.

Outwardly, France still seemed to be at the summit of European culture and power. Its population of twenty-seven million was the largest in Europe. It possessed the richest, most productive agriculture on the continent. It was the center of intellectual thought, and its language was the lingua franca of literate, educated people everywhere. Since William of Normandy had triumphed at Hastings in 1066, it had been the victor on numberless battlefields. From the beginning of the sixteenth century, the great kings of France—Francis I, Henri IV, Louis XIV—had been preeminent among the monarchs of Europe. But when, in 1715, the Sun King had been succeeded by his great-grandson, Louis XV, and still the endless wars continued, success had become intermittent. In the Seven Years' War, ending in 1763, England had stripped away most of France's important colonial possessions in North America and India. In return, by backing the American colonists in their fight for independence, France had taken revenge. The euphoria following the military triumph in America was as great in Paris as in Philadelphia.

But wars cost money and the bills had to be paid. The nation's finances had been depleted, then ravaged, by war; still, government expenditures continued to mount. The treasury responded by borrowing, and by 1788 interest on the debt absorbed half the government's spending. Taxes, levied most heavily on the lower class, were crushing, and in the fertile land of France, common people were impoverished. Poor harvests in 1787 and 1788 resulted in grain shortages and rising food prices. Facing financial collapse, the king and the government had no choice but to call a meeting of the Estates-General, France's long-dormant representative body. By summoning this assembly, the government was admitting that it could raise taxes no further without the consent of the nation.

The Estates-General met at Versailles on May 5, 1789. Three estates—classifications of people—were represented by twelve hundred delegates. The clergy, considered the First Estate, owned 10 percent of the land in France, were exempt from most taxes, and had three hundred delegates. The nobility, the Second Estate, owned 30 percent of the land, enjoyed many tax exemptions, and made up another three hundred delegates. One hundred of these noblemen were liberal-minded, and fifty, under forty years old, were ready, even eager, for change. The commoners of the Third Estate, represented by six hundred delegates, were there to speak for the people who made up 97 percent of the French population. The great majority of these people were agricultural peasants, although the Third Estate also included urban laborers. Bread constituted three-fourths of an ordinary person's diet and cost one-third to one-half of his or her income. The bourgeoisie, or middle class—bankers, lawyers, doctors, artists, writers, shop-keepers, and others—were also reckoned among the Third Estate. Plagued by heavy taxes, food shortages, unemployment, poverty, and general restlessness, the Third Estate was anxious, even desperate, for change. Its delegates were aware, however, that they had been summoned not for the purpose of improving the condition of the people they represented but because the government was desperate for money.

Within a few weeks of the first meeting, delegates from the two privileged estates, the clergy and the nobility, succeeded in making the commoners feel their inferior status. On June 20, members of the Third Estate arrived at the usual meeting place to find themselves locked out by armed guards and forced to stand and wait in a heavy rain. Someone remembered the existence of a covered tennis court nearby and it was to this place that the six hundred delegates hurried. Once there, they vented their feelings by declaring themselves to be the true National Assembly and swore "to God and the country never to be separated until we have written a solid and equitable constitution as our constituents have asked us to." Forty-seven members of the liberal nobility joined this new National Assembly and swore to what became known as the Tennis Court Oath.

The Third Estate had no permission to declare itself or act as a national assembly, and the king threatened to dissolve the entire Estates-General, by force if necessary. The Count of Mirabeau, a nobleman elected as a commoner who quickly became the leading presence among the delegates of the Third Estate, confronted the king's messengers. "Go tell those who have sent you," he said, "that we are here by the will of the people and that we will not be dispersed except at the point of bayonets." On June 27, a decree from Louis terminated all meetings of the Estates-General, declaring them "null, illegal, and unconstitutional." Riots in cities and uprisings in the countryside were the result. The most famous of these was the storming of the Bastille.

The Bastille, a fourteenth-century fortress with eight round towers and walls five feet thick, had been converted into a state prison to which men who had broken the law or offended the government were spirited away, sometimes never to reappear. By 1789, however, this had changed and the prison had become more a symbol of tyranny than a grim place of incarceration. The Marquis de Sade, a prisoner in the Bastille until a week before the fortress was stormed, hung family portraits on his walls and kept a wardrobe of fashionable clothing and a library of dozens of volumes. On the day of the attack, the fortress contained only seven prisoners: five forgers and two people who were mentally adrift. Still, because it was considered a royal arsenal and possessed a garrison of 114 soldiers, the government decided to use it as a place to deposit 250 barrels of gunpowder.

On July 14, twenty thousand Parisians, incensed by the royal dismissal of the Estates-General, the presence of a growing number of soldiers in Paris, and the stocking of gunpowder, marched on the Bastille. A few hours later, the fortress had surrendered, and the mob had liberated the seven prisoners and taken possession of the gunpowder. The governor of the fortress was stabbed with knives, swords, and bayonets, his neck was sawed through with a pocket knife, and his head, mounted on a pike, was bobbing at the head of a street parade.

The fall of the Bastille was a political and psychological turning point. The National Assembly wrote a new constitution and voted on August 4 to abolish most of the aristocratic rights and fiscal privileges of the nobility and clergy. On August 26, the assembly adopted the Declaration of the Rights of Man, a charter of liberties whose wording reflected the ideas of the Enlightenment and the language of the American Declaration of Independence.

Louis XVI and his family remained at Versailles. On October 5, a procession of five thousand women (and men disguised as women; it was rightly believed that the king would not order soldiers guarding the palace to fire on women) walked ten miles from Paris, invaded the palace built by the Sun King, and, the following day, forced the royal family to return with them to Paris. The family was installed in the Tuileries Palace in a state of semidetention (afternoon carriage rides in city parks were permitted). They remained there for nine months while the leaders of the National Assembly, most of them intellectuals and lawyers, with a few noblemen, all of whom thought in terms of maintaining order while bringing reform, tried to create a new form of constitutional monarchy. While they worked, and until the spring of 1791—twenty-four months after the summoning of the Estates-General, and twenty-two months after the storming of the Bastille—France was governed by a National Assembly with a monarchist majority led by Mirabeau.

On the night of March 25, 1791, Mirabeau took two dancers from the opera home with him, slept with them, became violently ill, and, eight days later died. His departure removed the one figure whose political reputation and oratorical powers might have ensured the establishment of a constitutional monarchy. Even without him, on May 3, the National Assembly proclaimed a new constitution, establishing a limited monarchy. The monarch now would be titled King of the French rather than King of France, but France remained a monarchy and bourgeois politicians remained in control.

On June 20, Louis and Marie Antoinette opened the door to personal and political catastrophe. Managing to escape from the Tuileries disguised as servants, the king and queen fled Paris with their children and headed toward the eastern frontier and the Austrian Netherlands. The royal carriage traveled no faster than seven miles an hour because the queen insisted that the whole family remain together in a single large overweight vehicle. Believing that they were out of danger, they stopped for the night at Varennes, only a few miles from the border. There, the awkward figure wearing a bottle-green coat and a lackey's hat was recognized, apprehended, and, with his family, ignominiously brought back to Paris.

Politically, the failure of the flight to Varennes cut the ground from under the king. It discredited the leaders of the National Assembly, who had been negotiating with Louis to create a new form of monarchy and who now felt themselves betrayed. Many abroad also condemned the king. Until Louis's capture and return from Varennes, Catherine had still regarded him as a free agent—weak, but free. But after he had been trundled back to Paris like an animal in a cage, any illusion of freedom disappeared. "I fear that the greatest obstacle to the escape of the king is the king himself," Catherine said. "Knowing her husband, the queen does not leave him, and she is right, but it complicates the problem."

The disastrous muddle of the escape attempt spurred talk elsewhere of the need to rescue the monarch and his family. Before the end of June, Marie Antoinette's brother, the new emperor Leopold II of Austria, appealed to all European powers to assist in the restoration of the French monarchy. Leopold, succeeding his older brother, Joseph II, on the imperial throne, had been emperor for only a year. His appeal was halfhearted, even duplicitous, since at that moment he had no intention of leading, or even joining, an anti-French military crusade. But Leopold's concern did precipitate a meeting with King Frederick William of Prussia, at the spa of Pillnitz, in Saxony. The two monarchs were joined by Louis XVI's arrogant brother the Count of Artois, who arrived uninvited and demanded immediate armed intervention.

The Declaration of Pillnitz, signed on August 27, 1791, stopped short of the demand made by Artois. It restated Leopold's argument that the fate of the French monarchy was of "common interest" and invited other European monarchs to assist in taking "the most effective means of putting the king of France back on his throne." No concrete steps were proposed. Leopold was cautious because the empire he had inherited from his brother was in a state of revolt in the Netherlands and dissent elsewhere. At the same time, he could not ignore the fate of his sister and brother-in-law in Paris, who, he realized, could now be in physical danger. On the other hand, Leopold worried that the kind of military action Artois was urging might increase his sister's peril. Leopold's final decision was that he could act against France only in concert with other powers, and, in this stipulation, he knew he was safe. Therefore, the Pillnitz Declaration committed Austria to nothing. In fact, its only achievement was to so outrage the French National Assembly that, eight months later, in April 1792, France declared war on Austria. By then, Leopold, who died suddenly in March, had been replaced by his inexperienced twenty-four-year-old son, Francis II.

During the first two years of the French Revolution—from the spring of 1789 to the summer of 1791—information about events in France was freely available in the Russian press. No censorship was imposed on news from France, just as news about the newborn United States, which had just drafted its own republican constitution, was openly presented. The summoning of the Estates-General, the declaration by the Third Estate that it had transformed itself into the National Assembly, the storming of the Bastille, the surrender of noble privileges, the Declaration of the Rights of Man—all this was published in full Russian translation in the *St. Petersburg Gazette* and the *Moscow Gazette*. According to Philippe de Ségur, the fall of the Bastille aroused widespread enthusiasm: "French, Russians, Danes, Germans, Englishmen, and Dutch . . . all congratulated and embraced each other in the street."

When the Third Estate proclaimed itself the National Assembly and Catherine realized that the peasants and the bourgeoisie had been joined by a group of noblemen willing to give up their own political and social privileges, she was astonished. "I cannot believe in the superior talents of cobblers and shoemakers for government and legislation," she wrote to Grimm. As the weeks went by, astonishment turned to alarm. "It's a veritable anarchy," she exclaimed in September 1789. "They are capable of hanging their king from a lamppost!" She was especially concerned about Marie Antoinette. "Above all, I hope that the situation of the queen will match my lively interest in her. Great courage triumphs over great perils. I love her as the dear sister of my best friend, Joseph II, and I admire her courage. . . . She may be sure that if I can ever be of use to her, I shall do my duty." But as long as Russia was fighting wars on two fronts—against Turkey in the south and Sweden in the Baltic—she could not do her "duty," however she might interpret it.

By October 1789, Catherine had realized that if France slid into genuine revolution, it could threaten all European monarchies. This put her in a difficult position with Philippe de Ségur. When the ambassador's four years of service in Russia were concluded, he came to say goodbye to the empress. Catherine gave him a friendly message for his king and also some personal advice,

> I am sad to see you go. You had far better stay here with me than to throw yourself into the eye of the storm which may spread further than you think. Your leanings toward the new philosophy, your passion for liberty will probably lead you to adopt the popular cause. I shall be sorry for I am and shall remain an aristocrat. It is my *métier*. Remember, you will find · France very feverish and very sick.

Ségur, equally distressed, replied, "I am afraid so, Madame, and that is what makes it my duty to return." When she invited him to stay for dinner and displayed the warmth of her feelings toward him, the parting became difficult. "When I went, I thought I was only going on leave," he wrote later. "The departure would have been still more painful had I known I was seeing her for the last time."

Catherine's comments about events in France became increasingly caustic. The National Assembly was "the Hydra with twelve hundred heads." In the new governing figures, she discerned "only people who set in motion a machine which they lack the talent and skill to control. . . . France is the prey of a crowd of lawyers, fools masquerading as philosophers, rascals, young prigs destitute of common sense, puppets of a few bandits who do not even deserve the title of illustrious criminals." Her defense of monarchy followed from her belief in the need for efficiency in administration and the preservation of public order: "Tell a thousand people to draft a letter, let them debate every phrase, and see how long it takes and what you get." She hated to see order crumbling and anarchy looming in France because she knew something about anarchy; she had seen it in the Pugachev rebellion.

She was unable to support her views with military action half a continent away, but even before the flight to Varennes, she was not wholly passive. She told her ambassador in Sweden that she wanted the future of France to become the concern of all European monarchs. It was not merely a question of crushing revolution, she wrote, but also of France resuming its role in the European balance of power. Knowing that Gustavus III of Sweden, always in search of glory, coveted the leadership of a monarchist crusade against the revolution in France, she chose him as the figure to support. In October 1791, only a year after the end of the short, pointless Baltic war between Russia and Sweden, she offered to provide Gustavus a subsidy to maintain a corps of twelve thousand Swedish soldiers to be used in an invasion of France. The date discussed for this operation was the spring of 1792.

A violent event in Sweden prevented this military enterprise. On March 5, 1792, Gustavus III was shot in the back and gravely wounded at a masked ball in Stockholm; he died at the end of the month. Although the assassin was a Swedish aristocrat and the issue was peculiar to Swedish politics, Catherine immediately saw it as part of a rising tide of antimonarchical violence. There were police reports that a French agent was on his way to St. Petersburg to assassinate the empress, and the number of guards at the Winter Palace was doubled. There was no further talk of landing Swedish troops in France.

In the spring of 1792 Catherine issued a ten-page memorandum, suggesting measures to suppress anarchy in France, reestablish the monarchy, and set France back on the road to tranquillity and greatness. She began by writing that "the cause of the king of France is the cause of all kings. . . . All the works of the [French] National Assembly have been devoted to the abolition of the form of monarchy established in France for a thousand years. [Now] it is important to Europe to see France resume her position as a great power." As to how this could be achieved, she said, "A body of ten thousand men would suffice to march across France from one end to the other. . . . Perhaps mercenaries—the best would be the Swiss—could be hired, and perhaps others from the German princes. With this force, one could deliver France from the bandits, reestablish the monarchy, chase away the impostors, punish the rascals and deliver the kingdom from oppression." Once a restoration was achieved, the empress advised against widespread, vindictive repression. "A few genuine revolutionaries should be punished and amnesty should follow for those who have submitted and returned to their allegiance." She believed that many delegates in the National Assembly would accept forgiveness, realizing that "they had gone beyond their powers because the electorate had not demanded the abolition of the monarchy, much less the Christian religion." It was essential in the newly restored kingdom, she continued, that there be a balance of the original three estates: the nobility, the clergy, and the common people. The property of the clergy should be restored, the nobility should regain their privileges, and the popular and valid demand for liberty "could be satisfied by good and wise laws." Before everything else, she wrote, the royal family must be liberated: "As the troops advance, the princes and the troops must focus on the most essential point: the deliverance of the king and the royal family from the hands of the population of Paris."

This document, written only months before the September massacres, the formal abolition of the French monarchy, and the beheading of the king, was hopelessly naïve; it displays Catherine's complete misunderstanding of the evolving political, economic, social, and psychological condition of the people of France. Even as Catherine was writing, the radicalization of France was accelerating. The Jacobin Club, immensely powerful in Paris, was extending its membership and influence across the country. Meeting at a former convent of the Jacobins in the rue St.-Honoré, it had begun its revolutionary role as a place for reading and discussion of needed reforms; then it evolved into an arena of radical thought, fiery speeches, and demands for drastic action. Its leaders, Georges Danton, Jean Paul Marat, and Maximilien Robespierre, were reaching the summit of political power. By the summer of 1792, the Paris Commune, the new municipal government supported by the sansculottes—ordinary citizens "without fine knee breeches"— controlled the city. Danton, the new, thirty-year-old minister of justice, assumed responsibility for the royal family at the Tuileries.

On August 10, a mob, organized by the Commune, stormed the

Tuileries Palace. Six hundred members of the Swiss Guard protecting the royal family resisted until the king, to prevent bloodshed, ordered them to surrender. The Swiss obeyed, were taken prisoner, and slaughtered. The royal apartments were invaded and the king, his wife, and their children were seized and carried off to the prison of the Temple.

That spring of 1792, Prussia had entered the Austrian war against France. By midsummer, a Prussian army stood on the Rhine, ready to march on Paris. As the army began to move, the Duke of Brunswick, commanding the Prussian forces, learned that Louis XVI and his family had been taken from the Tuileries. The duke's response was to issue a manifesto threatening that Paris would be singled out for "an exemplary and unforgettable act of vengeance . . . if the king and his family came to any harm." This threat produced a result opposite to that intended. The Brunswick manifesto seemed to expose Paris to a terrible retribution. Having been told that they had already committed acts for which they would be punished, Parisians were persuaded that they had nothing more to lose. Rumor declared that when the enemy arrived, the population of the city would be massacred.

On July 30, 1792, five hundred men wearing red caps arrived in Paris from Marseilles and the south. Described by one member of the Assembly as "a scum of criminals vomited out of the prisons of Genoa and Sicily," they had been hired by the Commune to come to Paris to help defend the city. To further bolster these ranks, the Commune drew on the local criminal population. Prisoners were released on condition that they would obey orders given by the Commune.

The savagery of the prison massacres of September 2–8, 1792, was planned. During the final two weeks of August, hundreds of Parisians, described as "presumed traitors," were arrested. Destined to be killed, they were gathered in prisons to make this more convenient. Many of the prisoners were priests taken from seminaries and churches and accused of antirevolutionary beliefs. Some were former personal servants of the king and queen. Those arrested also included the playwright Pierre Beaumarchais and Marie Antoinette's close friend the Princesse de Lamballe, who had fled to London and then returned to Paris to be with the queen. Most were ordinary people. Danton was not an instigator, but he was aware of what was about to happen. "I don't give a damn about the prisoners," he said. "Let them fend for themselves." Later, he added that "the executions were necessary to appease the people of

Paris." Robespierre said simply that the will of the people had been expressed.

News that the Prussians had seized Verdun reached Paris on Sunday morning, September 2. The massacres began that afternoon. Twenty-four priests being brought to the prison at the Abbaye de St.-Germain-des-Prés were pulled from the carriages transporting them and, before entering at the prison gate, slaughtered with swords, knives, axes, and a shovel on the cobbles of the narrow street. Prisoners already held in the abbey were pushed, one by one, down steps into a garden, where they were hacked to death with knives, hatchets, and a carpenter's saw. Other bands attacked other prisons: 328 prisoners were slaughtered in the Conciergerie; 226 at the Châtelet; 115, including an archbishop, at a Carmelite convent. At the Bicêtre, 43 adolescent boys were butchered. Thirteen were fifteen-year-olds, three were fourteen, two were thirteen, and one was twelve. Women of all ages including adolescent girls were brutally violated. When the Princesse de Lamballe refused to swear an oath of hatred against the royal couple, she was hacked to death. Her head was taken to the Temple to dance on a pike before the eyes of the king and queen.

On September 9, the French defeated the Prussians at Valmy, ending the allied invasion and forcing the Prussian army to retreat to the Rhine. The French did not stop there; they swept on to capture Mainz and Frankfurt. On September 21, three weeks after the massacres, the French monarchy was abolished and a republic established. In December, the National Assembly proclaimed that wherever France's armies marched, the existing form of government would be replaced by the rule of the people.

On January 21, 1793, Louis XVI was executed. This was too much for some who, until then, had believed in the revolution. General François Dumouriez, the military victor of Valmy, who had been Danton's friend, deserted to the Austrians; Lafayette had defected after the storming of the Tuileries. The provinces rose against the Paris government and then paid dearly. When Lyon, France's second city after Paris, capitulated, those to be killed, most of them peasants or laborers. were roped together in groups of two hundred, herded to fields outside the city, and executed by cannon firing grapeshot into the bunched human mass. One of Robespierre's agents was present and reported to his master: "What delights you would have tasted could you have seen national justice wrought on two hundred and ninety scoundrels! Oh, what majesty! What a lofty tone! It was thrilling to see all those wretches chew the dust!"

A new executive committee of the government, the Committee of Public Safety, was created that included Danton and Robespierre. Eventually, Robespierre decided that the revolution was ideologically impure. A Reign of Terror was instituted "to protect the republic from its internal enemies . . . those who whether by their conduct, their contacts, their words, or their writings, showed themselves to be supporters of tyranny or enemies of liberty" or those "who have not constantly manifested their attachment to the revolution." Over nine months, the official count of those executed was sixteen thousand; there were estimates that the Terror actually claimed two or three times that number.

Informed that Louis of France had been sent to the guillotine, a shaken Catherine became physically ill. She remained in seclusion for a week and ordered six weeks of court mourning. She ordered a total break in relations with France. The French chargé d'affaires, Edmond Genet, was expelled. The Franco-Russian commercial treaty of 1787 was annulled and all trade between the two countries was prohibited. No vessel flying the tricolor flag of the revolution was allowed in Russian waters. All Russian subjects living or traveling in France were recalled, and all French citizens in Russia were given three weeks to publicly pledge allegiance to the king of France or leave Catherine's empire. Of fifteen hundred French citizens in Russia, only forty-three refused to take this oath. In March 1793, two months after his brother's death, she welcomed the Count of Artois to St. Petersburg, agreed to finance him, and exhorted him to work together with other émigrés. But she still held back from military involvement in the war against France. With Austria and Prussia rebuffed, she believed that little could be achieved without Britain and that Britain had no intention of going to war. William Pitt, the prime minister, had said as much: that British policy was concerned with the security of Europe, not with the nature of the French government. The execution of Louis XVI changed Pitt's mind. The king's execution, Pitt said, was "the foulest and most atrocious act the world has ever seen."* The French ambassador was ordered to leave

---

*Pitt had perhaps forgotten that in 1588, England had beheaded Mary Stuart, a former queen of France and, subsequently, of Scotland. And that in 1649, the English, after overthrowing their monarchy, had beheaded King Charles I.

England. Once again, France acted first. On February 1, 1793, France declared war on Great Britain.

Six months after her husband's death, the widowed Marie Antoinette, her hair white at thirty-seven, was taken from her children in the Temple tower and placed in the prison of the Conciergerie. The former queen of France—a Hapsburg archduchess, the daughter of an Austrian empress, the sister of two Austrian emperors, and the aunt of a third—remained alone for two months in a cell eleven feet by six feet. On October 5, 1793, she was placed in a tumbrel and taken through the streets to the guillotine.

The tumbrels continued to roll. The massive blade rose and fell forty, fifty, sixty times a day. Terrified politicians guillotined one another in order to escape the guillotine themselves. Hundreds went to their deaths for no better reason than personal quarrels or neighborhood jealousies; their crime was being "under suspicion." The victims included twenty peasant girls from Poitou, one nursing a baby while sleeping on the cobbles of the Conciergerie courtyard, awaiting execution. The poet André Chénier was guillotined because he was mistaken for his brother; then, informed of its mistake, the Commune guillotined the brother, too. Antoine Lavoisier, the scientist, requested a short stay of his execution in order to complete an experiment. "The revolution has no need of scientists" was the reply. One of the condemned was the eighty-year-old Marshal Duke de Mouchy, whose elderly wife did not understand what was happening. "Madame, we must go now," her husband said gently. "God wishes it, let us therefore honor His will. I shall not leave your side. We shall depart together." As they were taken from the prison, someone shouted, "Courage!" Mouchy replied, "My friend, when I was fifteen, I went into the breach for my king. At eighty, I go to the scaffold for my God. I am not unfortunate." French émigrés and refugees told these stories to Catherine.

The Terror crested and began to ebb. On July 13, 1793, Marat was stabbed in his bathtub by Charlotte Corday. It was on April 5, 1794, that Danton was sent to the guillotine by Robespierre. Three and a half months later, on July 27, 1794, Robespierre's head rolled into a basket.

With the death of Robespierre, the worst of the Terror came to an end. The Directory followed, and, in 1799, the Consulate. A young army general, Napoleon Bonaparte, became first consul until 1804, when he crowned himself emperor. The wars begun by revolutionary France in 1792 continued under Napoleon, until they had spanned twenty-three years. With the downfall of Napoleon, the former Count of Provence, the older of the surviving brothers of Louis XVI, returned to France and ascended the throne as Louis XVIII. He was succeeded by his younger brother, the former Count of Artois, who became King Charles X. Then followed the last king of France, Louis Philippe. None of these three kings was an improvement on the amiable, indecisive Louis XVI, who failed as a monarch but was devoted to his country, endured his imprisonment with dignity, and went to his death bravely and without bitterness.

The lasting symbol of the French Revolution is the guillotine. The executions of Louis XVI and Marie Antoinette, reinforced in literature by Dickens's image of Madame Defarge sitting and knitting at the foot of this implacable machine, have imprinted this method of inflicting death deep on cultural memory.

Originally, the guillotine was designed to give practical effect to the belief that the purpose of capital punishment was the ending of life rather than the inflicting of pain. Until it took its first victim, in April 1792, condemned prisoners in France had sometimes died horribly; they could be broken on the wheel or torn apart by four horses, each tied to one limb of the victim. More generally, noblemen were beheaded by sword or axe and commoners were hanged. But headsman were clumsy and swords and axes dull, while nooses often strangled slowly while the choking victim danced in the air. The guillotine was meant to be humane and deliver an instant, painless death; its inventor, Dr. Jospeh Guillotin, described its operation: "The mechanism falls like thunder; the head flies off; blood spurts; the man is no more." It was also considered more equitable because it was to be used on all condemned people regardless of class. In any case, it had a long life of service. It was used in imperial Germany, the Weimar Republic, and Nazi Germany, where, between 1933 and 1945, sixteen thousand people were guillotined. It remained a form of execution in France until 1977; four years later France abolished the death penalty.

Whether the guillotine was more humane than the axe, the noose, the electric chair, the firing squad, and lethal injection is a medical, as well as a political and moral, question. The most effective resolution would be to let the question fade away by the universal prohibition of state-inflicted death penalties. While societies struggle toward this goal, a second medical or scientific question may be asked: was death by guillotine so instantaneous as to be truly painless? Some believe not. They argue that because the blade, cutting rapidly through the neck and spinal column, had relatively little impact on the head encasing the brain, there may not have been immediate unconsciousness. If this is true, should one believe that some victims were aware of what was happening? Witnesses to guillotining have described blinking eyelids and movement of the eyes, lips, and mouth. As recently as 1956, anatomists experimenting with the severed heads of guillotined prisoners explained this by saying that what appeared to be a head responding to the sound of its name or to the pain of a pinprick on the cheek might only have been a random muscle twitch or an automatic reflex action; that no intelligent awareness was involved. Certainly, the shock of the blow to the spinal column and a sudden, massive drop in cerebral blood pressure must bring a loss of consciousness rapidly, if not instantaneously. But in that flicker of time, was there awareness?

In June 1905, a respected French medical doctor was permitted to experiment with the freshly severed head of a prisoner named Languille. He reported that "immediately after the decapitation . . . the spasmodic movements ceased. . . . It was then that I called out in a strong sharp voice: 'Languille!' I saw the eyelids slowly lift up . . . with an even movement, quite distinct and normal. . . . Next, Languille's eyes very definitely fixed themselves on mine and the pupils focused themselves. . . . I was dealing with undeniably living eyes which were looking at me. . . . After several seconds, the eyelids closed. . . . I called out again, and once more the eyelids lifted and living eyes fixed themselves on mine with perhaps even more penetration than the first time. Then there was a further closing of the eyelids . . . [and] no further movement."

What awareness, if any, a severed head might have is something that Louis XVI, Marie Antoinette, Georges Danton, Maximilien Robespierre, and tens of thousands of others who died by the guillotine may have discovered. We cannot know.

❧71❧

Dissent in Russia, Final Partition of Poland

T HE FRENCH REVOLUTION had a dramatic impact on Catherine, not only because the empress was horrified by the degradation, humiliation, and violent destruction of the French monarchy but because she feared that revolutionary fervor would spread. Her belief that she must act to protect herself and Russia precipitated a significant reversal in her early liberal thinking about freedom of thought and expression. In the political and military sphere, her fear of what she called the "French poison" resulted in—or was used to justify—a rare event in European history: the complete disappearance of a large, proud nation-state.

In the beginning, as a young woman and new empress, Catherine had been the admiring friend of the *philosophes.* Voltaire and Diderot had acclaimed her as the most liberal sovereign in Europe, the Semiramis of the North. By them and from her reading of Montesquieu, she been taught that the best form of government was benevolent autocracy, informed and guided by the principles of the Enlightenment. In her first years on the throne, she had hoped that she could correct or at least ameliorate the workings of some of the more inefficient and unjust institutions in Russia, among them serfdom. She had summoned the Legislative Commission in 1767 and listened to the complaints and recommendations of different classes of people, including peasants. But then had come the Pugachev rebellion. After this, she still had cordial friendships with various *philosophes,* but she was no longer a disciple. She questioned and often challenged their utopias.

By 1789, after twenty-seven years on the throne, Catherine had achieved some of the liberal goals formulated in her youth. She had helped to create a Russian intelligentsia. Among the nobility, more people attended universities, traveled abroad, spoke foreign languages, and wrote plays, novels, and poetry. Promising young men were sent at state expense to study and acquire knowledge in foreign schools and universities. Educated men, not born to the nobility, had become senior government officials, poets, writers, doctors, architects, and painters. But then, seeming to call into question her early efforts and goals, came the grim reality of Pugachev, followed, twenty years later, by the events in France.

Catherine had observed with dismay the destruction of the French monarchy and the Old Regime. Every month, French émigrés and refugees arrived in Russia with frightful stories. More than any other European monarch, she felt that the ideology of radical France was also directed at her, and the more radical France became, the more defensive and reactionary were her responses. She now discovered dangers implicit in Enlightenment philosophy. Some responsibility for the excesses of the revolution seemed traceable to the writings of philosophers she had admired. For years, their writing had attacked and undermined respect for authority and religion. Were they not, therefore, at least partly responsible? How had they and she failed to see where this path was leading?

In 1791, she ordered all bookshops to register with the Academy of Sciences their catalogs of available books that were opposed to "religion, decency, and ourselves." In 1792, she ordered the confiscation of a complete edition of the works of Voltaire. In 1793, she ordered provincial governors to forbid the publication of books that appeared "likely to corrupt morals, concerned with the government, and, above all, those dealing with the French revolution." She began to fear the ease with which revolutionary ideas could cross frontiers, and the importation of French newspapers and books was prohibited. In September 1796, the first formal system of censorship during her reign was established. All private printing presses were closed; all books were to be submitted to a censorship office before publication. One of the first to be affected by these new restraints was a young, intellectual nobleman who had risen to a significant position in the imperial administration.

Alexander Radishchev was born in 1749 in Saratov province, the oldest of eleven children of an educated, noble landowner who possessed three thousand serfs. At thirteen, Alexander entered the Corps des Pages in St. Petersburg and served at court. At seventeen, he was among twelve young men chosen to study philosophy and law at the University of Leipzig at state expense; there, he knew Goethe, a fellow student. In

1771, at twenty-two, he returned to Russia, where he served first as a clerk in the offices of the Senate and then on the legal staff of the College of War. In 1775, Radishchev married and took a post in the College of Commerce, presided over by Alexander Vorontsov, a brother of Catherine's friend Princess Dashkova. Eventually, he became the director of the St. Petersburg Customs House.

During the 1780s, Radishchev began writing a book, *A Journey from St. Petersburg to Moscow.* In 1790, he printed a few copies on his private home printing press. As required, he submitted a copy to the chief police censor in St. Petersburg. This official glanced briefly at the book's title, assumed it to be a travelogue, approved it, and returned it to the nobleman in the Customs House. Radishchev then printed six hundred copies anonymously. His timing was unlucky, coming a year after the fall of the Bastille, and while Russia was still at war with Turkey and Sweden.

Radishchev's *Journey* was not a travelogue. Instead, it was a passionate indictment of the institution of serfdom and a criticism of the government and social structure that permitted serfdom to exist. He began with an emotional appeal:

> Shall we be so devoid of humane feeling, devoid of pity, devoid of the tenderness of noble hearts, devoid of brotherly love, that we endure under our eyes an eternal reproach to us . . . [by keeping] our comrades, our equal fellow citizens, our beloved brothers in nature, in the heavy fetters of servitude and slavery? The bestial custom of enslaving one's fellow men . . . a custom that signifies a heart of stone and a total lack of soul, has spread over the face of the earth. And we Slavs, sons of glory among earth-born generations . . . have adopted this custom, and, to our shame . . . to the shame of this age of reason, we have kept it inviolate even to this day.

Radishchev illustrated the effects of serfdom by creating numerous scenes described by "the traveler" as he passed through villages, towns, and staging posts during his journey. He portrayed the abuse of serf labor, the shocking verdicts of corrupt judges, and the defenseless situation of serf women at the mercy of predatory owners. In one episode, three brutal sons of a landlord attack, bind, and gag a beautiful serf maiden on the morning of her wedding day, intending to use her for their "beastly purpose." The serf bridegroom sees what is happening, charges the three evildoers, routs them, and "breaks the head" of one of them. As punishment, the landlord then orders a merciless flogging of the bridegroom. The young serf accepts this—until he sees the landlord's three sons dragging his future wife back into their house. He breaks free, saves the girl, and faces his three enemies, whirling a fence-post over his head. At this point, other serfs arrive, and in the ensuing melee, the landlord and his three sons are beaten to death. All of the serfs involved are condemned to penal servitude for life. Radishchev told this story not only as an example of the nature of master-serf relationships but also to warn his readers that many serfs, driven to desperation, were only awaiting a chance to rise in revolt:

> Do you know, dear fellow citizens, what destruction threatens us and in what peril we stand? . . . A stream that is barred in its course becomes more powerful. Once it has burst the dam, nothing can stem its flood. Such are our brothers whom we keep enchained. They are waiting for a favorable chance and time. The alarm bell rings. And the destructive force of bestiality breaks loose with terrifying speed. . . . Death and fiery desolation will be the answer to our harshness and inhumanity. The more procrastinating and stubborn we have been about the loosening of their fetters, the more violent they will be in their vengefulness. Bring back to your memory the events of former times [Pugachev]. . . . They spared neither sex nor age. They sought more the joy of vengeance than the benefit of broken shackles. This is what awaits us. This is what we must expect.

As a palliative to this grim prospect, Radishchev offered a plan for the gradual emancipation of serfs. All domestic serfs were to be emancipated at once; agricultural serfs would be granted full ownership of private plots and then be allowed to use their profits to buy their own freedom. They would be allowed to marry without asking their masters' permission. And they would be judged in courts of their peers—that is, by other peasants.

Catherine read the book in June 1790 and filled the margins with notes. She gave Radishchev intellectual credit: "[The author] has learning enough, and has read many books . . . he has imagination enough, and he is audacious in his writing." She guessed that he acquired his education in Leipzig, "hence the suspicion falls on M. Radishchev, the more so because he is said to have a printing press in his house." Had the book been written thirty or even twenty years earlier, Catherine might have recognized some of her own views; now, from her new perspective, she declared that "the purpose of this book is clear on every page. Its author, infected and filled with the French madness, is trying in every possible way to break down respect for authority and the authorities, to stir up in the people's indignation against their superiors and against the government." She rejected Radishchev's portrayal of the behavior of landowners and the condition of serfs and was outraged by his warnings of serf rage and impending revenge. The author, she declared, is "a rabble-rouser, worse than Pugachev . . . inciting the serfs to bloody rebellion." And he was inciting not only the peasants but the general population to disregard the authority of all rulers, from empresses down to local officials. In Radishchev's denunciations of her government and his mingling of the Pugachev horrors with the new "poisons" being concocted in France, she saw an effort to propagate the beliefs of the revolutionaries in Paris and destabilize Russia at a time when the country was fighting two wars. The book, she wrote in a margin, "could not be tolerated."

Radishchev was identified, arrested, and taken to the Peter and Paul Fortress for interrogation. He was not tortured. Even so, aware of the consequences for his family, he began to renege. He declared that his book had stemmed from vanity; he said he had wanted to win literary fame. He did his best to minimize retribution by admitting that his language had been exaggerated and that his accusations against government officials were inaccurate. He denied any intention of attacking Catherine's government; he meant only to point out certain correctable shortcomings. He had not intended to rouse peasant against landowner; he had only wished to force bad landowners to be ashamed of their behavior. He admitted that he hoped for the freedom of the serfs but declared that he wanted to achieve this through legislative action, such as that already taken or proposed by the Empress Catherine. He threw himself on Catherine's mercy. He was tried by the Central Criminal Court in St. Petersburg, charged with sedition and lese-majesté, and sentenced to death by beheading. The Senate routinely confirmed the verdict. In the interim, however, Catherine had forwarded the book to Potemkin for comment. Despite the personal attacks on himself as well as the empress, the prince advocated leniency. "I've read the book you sent me. I am not angry," he wrote to Catherine. "It seems, Matushka, he has been slandering you, too. And you also won't be angry. Your deeds are your shield." Potemkin's moderate response calmed Catherine, who did what she always did: she commuted the death penalty and changed it to a sentence of ten years of Siberian exile.

Thereafter, Radishchev was treated with relative leniency. After sentencing, he was taken from the court in chains, but the following morning the chains were struck off by Catherine's order. He was allowed sixteen months to reach his place of exile four thousand miles east of St. Petersburg. Minister of Commerce Alexander Vorontsov, his patron and friend, sent him clothes, books, and a thousand rubles a year. Eventually, Radishchev, by now a widower, was joined in Siberia by his two youngest children, brought to him by his sister-in-law, who remained with him and bore him three more children. He constructed a large house for his family, his servants, and his books. He worked as an amateur doctor, taught his children, and read the books sent to him by his friends. Soon after Catherine's death in 1796, her son, Paul, terminated Radishchev's exile and allowed him to return to his estate near Moscow. In 1802, deeply depressed, he committed suicide, leaving behind the dying words of Cato: "Now I am my own master." His *Journey* was published in London in 1859. Three years later—sixty years after Radishchev's death—Catherine's great-grandson, Emperor Alexander II, abolished serfdom.

When partitioning Poland in 1772, Russia, Austria, and Prussia had imposed on that nation a constitution that limited the authority of the king and the Diet and left power in the hands of an independent, conservative aristocracy that refused to govern or be governed, leaving the country in a perpetual state of near-anarchy. Stanislaus Augustus, the king installed by Catherine, reigned for the next sixteen years, but in all important matters, Poland's government was overseen by St. Petersburg. Territorially, Poland remained large, and through these years the resentment of many Poles against the partitioning powers, particularly Russia, continued to fester. In September 1788, with both Catherine and her ally Joseph II of Austria involved in war with Turkey, Poles saw their chance to make a change. A Polish Diet, hostile to Polish dependence on Russia, met and was almost immediately confederated. The liberum veto was set aside, enabling the Diet to make decisions by majority vote. Amid an eruption of anti-Russian feeling and much verbal abuse of Catherine, Stanislaus warned of the danger of making unilateral changes in a constitution approved by the empress. He was ignored. During the following months, the confederated Diet proceeded to overturn the governmental structure endorsed by Russia for sixteen years. With her army in the south, Catherine could do nothing—for the moment, at least—but pretend not to notice.

The following year, 1790, Catherine suffered a series of political setbacks. In March, King Frederick William of Prussia, who in 1886 had succeeded his uncle Frederick the Great, surprised Russia and Austria by signing a defensive treaty with Poland, pledging military assistance against foreign interference. On May 3, 1791, the emboldened Polish confederated Diet, knowing that Russia was still enmeshed in war on the Black Sea, and also believing that Poland was now protected by its treaty with Prussia, voted to adopt a new constitution, providing for a hereditary, rather than elective, monarchy. The present ruler, Stanislaus, would be allowed to remain during his lifetime, but on his death, the crown was to become hereditary, passing from father to son in the house of the electors of Saxony. The liberum veto was to be abolished and replaced in the Diet by majority rule. The purpose of the new constitution was to weaken the old nobility and provide Poland with a more effective national government.

Catherine, realizing the extent to which the new constitution diminished the power of the old Polish nobility, on whom she relied to keep Poland weak, was alarmed. The Russian-Polish treaty of 1772 had been unilaterally scrapped. She had no troops available to uphold the old constitution, but, in her anger and frustration, she quickly found allies among the Poles themselves. The conservative Polish nobility, knowing that a weak central government was necessary if they were to keep power in their hands, also rejected the May 3 constitution. These noblemen, meeting in Grodno, formed their own new federation, proclaimed the restoration of the 1772 constitution, and sent a delegation to St. Petersburg to ask Catherine to help them.

Catherine was eager to help. The May 3 constitution was far from radical, but to Catherine there seemed a disturbing similarity between it and the developing attack on the monarchy in France. By July 1791, peace with Turkey was near, and the Russian army would soon be available to support the conservative Poles. She had already told Potemkin, during his last visit to St. Petersburg, that she intended to appoint him commander in chief in this new campaign. There were risks to be considered. Both Leopold of Austria and Frederick William of Prussia, concerned about the deteriorating situation in France, and hoping to calm the increasing turmoil behind their backs in eastern Europe, had agreed to accept Poland's new May 3 constitution. Frederick William did so as Poland's new ally; Leopold because he wished to be free to concentrate on France. Both monarchs urged Catherine to join them.

Catherine, who had already decided to act alone if necessary, refused. She tried instead to persuade the Prussians and Austrians to support her approach. She bluntly told her own College of Foreign Affairs in December 1791 that she would never agree to the new Polish political structure, and that she was determined to act. Prussia and Austria "will oppose us with only a pile of written paper," she predicted. She anticipated protest, but Austria, facing war with France, would do nothing, and if Prussia's agreement to ignore its treaty with Poland had to be bought with additional Polish territory, she would agree to another partition. As for the Poles themselves, she understood that to restore the 1772 constitution, an invasion by the Russian army would be necessary.

Behind Catherine's militant new Polish policy was the fact that, despite her talk of a crusade against France, her real worries lay closer to home. She was angered by the steps the Poles had already taken and alarmed by what might follow. An effective, potentially revolutionary regime in Poland would be dangerous to Russia. Was she to ignore this possible threat in order to fight Jacobinism in France? Her duty was to deal with the enemy in the place most threatening to her. She was determined, she told Grimm, to "exterminate that nest of Jacobins in Warsaw." This was the façade of her argument, but she revealed her real strategy in an outburst to her private secretary on November 14, 1791: "I am breaking my head to push the courts of Vienna and Berlin to involve themselves in the affairs of France. The Austrian court is willing but the court of Berlin refuses to move. . . . There are reasons which I cannot explain [to them]. I wish to engage them in these affairs in order to have elbow room. I have in mind much unfinished business and it is necessary that they be kept busy so that they cannot hinder me." Her "unfinished business" was to restore Russian control of Poland.

On April 9, 1792, France unintentionally assisted Catherine by declaring war on Austria. The empress could now be certain that Austria would not honor its promises to Poland to support the May 3 Polish constitution. At the end of April, she informed Berlin and Vienna of her intention to invade Poland; on May 7, sixty-five thousand Russian troops crossed the Polish border, followed by another thirty-five thousand a few weeks later. Poland immediately appealed to Frederick William of Prussia on the basis of the 1790 defensive treaty. The king of Prussia behaved as Catherine had foreseen. Anticipating war with France, he betrayed his treaty obligation to assist Poland, declaring that he had not been consulted about the May 3 constitution and that this absolved him of treaty commitments. He was not, he declared, "obliged to defend a constitution drawn up without his knowledge." Stanislaus, again playing both sides, first swore to fight for the May 3 constitution and then attempted to negotiate with Catherine by offering to give up the throne to her grandson Constantine. She was not interested. Having nothing further to offer, the Polish king ordered the Polish army to lay down its arms.

The military occupation proceeded smoothly, but Russia soon found itself caught in a thicket of political difficulties. The conservative Polish leaders Catherine was supporting fell to squabbling among themselves and proved unable to govern. By December 1792, Catherine had decided that the only solution to growing chaos was to formalize the occupation in a second partition. Frederick William was offered the areas in the north and west that Prussia had long desired. He accepted. Both Russia and Prussia declared that their actions were aimed at fighting Jacobinism in Poland. Frederick William announced that he was forced to send his army to protect Prussia from the raging Jacobinism across his border. Catherine continued to use this argument. "Apparently you ignore that the Jacobiniere of Warsaw were in correspondence with the Jacobin Club in Paris," she wrote to Grimm. In January 1793, Russia and Prussia secretly signed a treaty that sealed the Second Partition of Poland.

Unaware of this treaty, Poland's conservative leaders asked Catherine for assurance that she would protect the physical integrity of their country. It was too late; early in April 1793, Russian and Prussian manifestos announcing the new partition were published. Attempting to give their actions a cloak of legality, Catherine and Frederick William forced Stanislaus to leave Warsaw for Grodno, the center of the failing conservative confederation, and there to preside over a Diet that was to come to "an amiable understanding with the partitioning powers." To help the Diet make this decision, the Russian ambassador announced that "soldiers of Her Imperial Majesty would occupy the lands of any deputy who opposed the will of the nation." In July, members of the Diet sullenly gave consent to the new partition treaty with Russia, but, hating Prussia more, they refused to ratify the cession of territory to a nation that had betrayed them. The Diet building in Grodno was surrounded by Russian troops, and the deputies were told that no one would be allowed to leave until the partition treaty was approved. The session continued into the night. At first, the deputies shouted and refused to sit; then they lapsed into total silence and sat immobile in their seats. At 4 in the morning, the marshal of the Diet asked three times: "Does the Diet authorize the delegates to sign the treaty?" No deputy replied. Whereupon, the marshal announced: "Silence means consent." In this manner, the partition treaty was approved by the Polish Diet.

In effect, the treaty with Russia turned newly truncated Poland into a protectorate—or, as one Polish deputy said bitterly, "a Russian province." All domestic and foreign policies were to be submitted for Russian approval; the personnel of the government would be approved by St. Petersburg; the Polish army would be reduced to fifteen thousand men. Stanislaus kept his throne. Politically impotent, superfluous, and pathetic, he returned to his palace in Warsaw, despised by his subjects.

Russia's new share of Poland was large: eighty-nine thousand square miles of eastern Poland, including the rest of Belorussia, with the city of Minsk; further extensive slices of Lithuania, including Vilnius; and the remaining Polish Ukraine. In all, three million people were added to Catherine's empire. Prussia took twenty-three thousand square miles, finally acquiring the long-coveted regions of Danzig and Thorn, as well as other territory in western Poland; Prussia's gain was one million inhabitants. Austria had no share in the spoils this time, but Francis II was promised that Prussia would remain an active ally in Austria's war against France. Poland now was reduced to one-third its original size and a population of four million. When the treaties were signed, Catherine told herself that not only had she fended off the revolutionary virus spreading from France, but she was simply reoccupying lands that had once belonged to the great sixteenth-century principality of Kiev, "lands still inhabited by people of the Russian faith and race."

By the spring of 1794, when Robespierre was supreme in France, many Poles had concluded that the further mutilation of their country and the humiliating constitutional settlement imposed were intolerable. In

March, when the disarming of the Polish army was attempted, the nation rose up. Thaddeus Kosciuszko, a Polish officer trained in France who had fought beside Washington and Lafayette in the American War of Independence, suddenly appeared in Krac\'ow and took command of Polish rebel forces. On March 24, with four thousand soldiers and two thousand peasants armed with scythes, he defeated seven thousand Russian soldiers near Kraców. The revolt spread, moving so quickly that when it reached Warsaw, the Russian occupation garrison of seven thousand men was caught by surprise. Three thousand Russian soldiers were killed or taken prisoner; the bodies of the dead were stripped and thrown naked into the streets. Frederick William of Prussia was denounced as a betrayer, and a portrait of Catherine, taken from the Russian embassy, was publicly torn to pieces.

When reports of these events reached St. Petersburg, Catherine told Prussia and Austria that the time had come "to extinguish the last spark of the Jacobin fire in Poland." Frederick William, smarting from the personal insults hurled at him by the Poles, asked for the honor of personally strangling Polish resistance. Catherine suggested that he take charge of putting down the revolt in Poland west of the Vistula River, and then advised Francis II of Austria to move into the south. Both hurried to oblige, and both expected to be paid for their efforts; thus, still another partition of Poland became an expectation of all parties. Frederick William divided the army he had deployed against France and sent twenty-five thousand men to the east against Poland. By mid-July, these twenty-five thousand Prussians and fourteen thousand Russians were advancing on Warsaw from two directions. Late in July, Frederick William himself arrived before Warsaw to direct a siege of the city. The Prussians made little progress, and in September, the king, declaring that he needed his troops to face threats from France, lifted his siege and withdrew.

By then, the Russians needed no help. Indeed, Catherine had realized that if Russia were to crush the revolt without assistance, she would be able to dictate a settlement. She placed Rumyantsev in overall command of her army in Poland and Suvorov in tactical command. On October 10, Suvorov defeated Kosciuszko in a battle in which thirteen thousand Russians overwhelmed seven thousand Poles. Kosciuszko was severely wounded, captured, and sent to St. Petersburg, where he was locked in the Schlüsselburg Fortress. Suvorov next appeared before Praga, the fortified suburb across the Vistula from Warsaw.

Before launching his attack, Suvorov reminded his soldiers of the April slaughter of the Russian garrison in Warsaw. The assault began at dawn; "three hours later," Suvorov reported, "the whole of Praga was strewn with bodies, and blood was flowing in streams." Estimates of the dead ranged between twelve and twenty thousand. The Russians later claimed that Suvorov was unable to restrain his soldiers from taking revenge for the slaughter of their comrades in the spring—an argument that failed to explain the killing of women, children, priests, and nuns. Suvorov then used the carnage as an example to warn Warsaw that if it did not surrender, it would be treated as another Praga. Warsaw capitulated immediately, and armed resistance throughout Poland came to an end.

Catherine regarded Kosciuszko as an agent of revolutionary extremism and believed him to be in correspondence with Robespierre. It was in this context that she and her council decided what was to be done with a prostrate Poland. They agreed that because the dangers of Jacobinism continued to threaten Russia, it was unwise to allow any Polish government to exist. Bezborodko insisted that centuries of experience had shown that it was impossible to make friends with the Poles; they would always support any future enemy of Russia, be this Turkey, Prussia, Sweden, or somebody else. Further, the buffer state concept did not apply to ideas that could cross frontiers. The council's decision, therefore, was to treat Poland as a conquered enemy: all Polish regalia, banners, and state insignia, along with archives and libraries, were collected and sent to Russia. Suvorov was to govern by decree.

The next step was to agree on a new division of territory. Catherine would have preferred outright Russian annexation of all that remained of Poland, but she knew that this would be unacceptable to Prussia and Austria. Accordingly, she proposed a third and final partition. Austria hesitated, suggesting a return to the status quo but with greater supervision from outside. Prussia favored partition, either total or leaving a small, insignificant buffer state between the partitioning powers. Catherine's proposal was the most extreme: she wanted to subdivide the entire remaining territory of Poland and thereby simply erase this dangerous neighbor from the map. Her proposal was accepted.

On January 3, 1795, Russia and Austria agreed to the third and final partition of Poland. Prussia, still at war with France, was told that the territory it desired could be taken whenever it was ready to do so. On May 5, Prussia made peace with revolutionary France and occupied its allotted slice of Poland. Russia's prizes were Courland, what was left of Lithuania, the remaining part of Belorussia, and the western Ukraine. Prussia took Warsaw and Poland west of the Vistula. Austria took Kracòw, Lublin, and western Galicia. Afterward, Catherine repeated that she had annexed "not a single Pole," and that she had simply taken back ancient Russian and Lithuanian lands with Orthodox inhabitants who were "now reunited with the Russian motherland."

On November 25, 1795, Stanislaus, his kingdom dismembered, abdicated. When Catherine died a year later, the new emperor Paul invited the former king to St. Petersburg, where he was housed in the Marble Palace that the empress had built for Gregory Orlov. He died there in 1798. For Poland, the Third Partition meant national extinction. Not until the signing of the Versailles Treaty after the First World War, when the Russian, German, and Austrian empires had collapsed, did Poland physically reemerge. In the interim, for 126 years, the people and culture of Poland did not possess a nation.

✤72✤

Twilight

I N 1796, CATHERINE, in her thirty-fifth year on the Russian throne, was the preeminent royal personage in the world. Age had affected her appearance, but not her devotion to work or her positive attitude toward life. She was heavier, and her gray hair had turned to white, but her blue eyes were youthful, bright, and clear. Even at sixty-seven, her complexion was fresh, and dentures preserved the illusion that her teeth were intact. Dignity and grace were embodied in her bearing, particularly in the way she held her head high and nodded graciously in public. From friends, officials, courtiers, and servants, she drew deep affection as well as respect.

She rose at six and wrapped herself in a silk dressing gown. Her movements awakened the family of small English greyhounds sleeping on a pink satin couch next to her bed. The oldest of them, whom she had named Sir Tom Anderson, and his spouse, Duchess Anderson, were gifts from Dr. Dimsdale, who had inoculated her and her son, Paul, against smallpox. They, with the help of Sir Tom's second wife, Mademoiselle Mimi, had produced numerous litters. Catherine attended them; when the dogs wanted to go out, Catherine herself opened the door into the garden. This done, she drank four or five cups of black coffee and settled down to work on the mass of official and personal correspondence awaiting her. Her sight had weakened, and she read with spectacles and sometimes used a magnifying glass. Once when her secretary saw her reading this way, she smiled and said, "You probably don't need this contrivance yet. How old are you?" He said that he was twenty-eight. Catherine nodded and said, "Our sight has been blunted by long service to the State and now we have to use spectacles." Promptly at nine, she put down her pen and rang a little bell, which told the servant outside her door that she was ready for her daily visitors. This meant a long morning of receiving ministers, generals, and other government officials; of reading or listening to their reports; and of signing the papers they had prepared for her. These were working sessions; visitors were expected to object to her ideas and offer their own when they thought she was wrong. Her attitude almost always remained attentive, pleasant, and imperturbable.

An exception to this demeanor was her reaction to the visits of her brilliant general Alexander Suvorov. Devout as well as eccentric, Suvorov entered her room, bowed three times to the icon of Our Lady of Kazan hanging on a wall, and fell on his knees before the empress, touching the ground with his forehead. Catherine always tried to stop him, saying, "For heaven's sake, are you not ashamed of yourself?" Unabashed, Suvorov sat down and repeated his request to be allowed to fight the French army in northern Italy, commanded by a young general named Napoleon Bonaparte. "Matushka, let me march against the French!" he pleaded. After many visits and many pleas, she agreed, and in November 1796, Suvorov was ready to march at the head of sixty thousand Russians. Catherine died on the eve of his departure, and the campaign was canceled. No battlefield meeting of these two famous soldiers ever took place.

At one in the afternoon, her morning work was finished, and Catherine retired to dress, often in gray or violet silk, for midday dinner. Ten to twenty guests sat down with her: personal friends, noblemen, senior officials, and her favorite foreign diplomats. She was not interested in food, and the fare was Spartan; afterward guests discreetly retreated to the apartments of courtiers living in the palace where they could supplement their meal.

In the afternoon, Catherine read books or was read to while she sewed or embroidered. At six, if there were a court reception, she moved among her guests in the drawing rooms of the Winter Palace. Supper was served, but Catherine never ate, and at ten she withdrew. When there was no official court reception, she entertained privately in the Hermitage. The company listened to a concert, watched a French or Russian play, or simply played games, performed charades, or played whist. During these gatherings, her long-standing rules remained in force: formality was banned; it was forbidden to rise when the empress stood; everyone talked freely; bad tempers were not tolerated; laughter was required. To her friend Frau Bielcke, she wrote: "Madame, you must be gay; only thus can life be endured. I speak from experience for I have had to endure much, and have only been able to endure it because I have always laughed whenever I had the chance."

In the 1790s, Catherine's health was declining. For years, she had suffered from headaches and indigestion; now colds and rheumatism were added. By the summer of 1796 she was afflicted by open leg sores. Sometimes swollen and bleeding, her legs bothered her so much that she tried soaking them daily in fresh, ice-cold seawater; Dr. Rogerson's skepticism regarding this unconventional treatment only made her more certain that it was having "marvelous effects."

Her physical infirmities were an inconvenience, but she was not immobilized. She spent autumn and winter at the Winter Palace and the Hermitage. After Potemkin's death, she had another residence in the capital and lived for a few weeks in spring and again in autumn in the Tauride Palace, which she had bought from the prince's heirs. Living there helped her keep fresh the memory of the man who had been her partner, lover, and perhaps her husband. In preference to the estates at Peterhof and Oranienbaum on the Gulf of Finland, which could summon unhappy memories from the past, Tsarskoe Selo, where she could be surrounded by her friends and grandchildren, was her favorite summer retreat. No serious barriers were placed between the imperial family and the public; all parks in the capital and the nearby countryside were open to all who were "decently dressed." This included the park at Tsarskoe Selo. One day, Catherine was seated on a bench with her favorite personal maid after their early morning walk. A man passed by, glanced briefly at the two elderly women, and, failing to recognize the empress, walked on, whistling. The maid was indignant, but Catherine merely remarked, "What do you expect, Maria Savichna? Twenty years ago this would not have happened. We have grown old. It is our fault."

Catherine was forty-eight when, in 1777, her daughter-in-law, Maria, gave birth to the empress's first grandson. She, not the child's mother or father, named him Alexander. Motherhood had provided Catherine with few joys; now, as a grandmother, she had an opportunity to catch up. Setting aside her long-ago grief when Empress Elizabeth had taken away her firstborn, Paul, Catherine assumed the dominant role in the new infant's life. Her reason was similar to Elizabeth's. Both women had been frustrated by their inability, in one case to conceive, in the other to mother a child. Both used the same excuse for their subsequent behavior: a young, inexperienced mother could not be given the responsibility of raising and educating a future tsar.

Catherine did not take complete possession of Alexander, as Elizabeth had done with Paul. She had him brought to her every afternoon to be placed on the carpet next to her desk. When he arrived, she stopped whatever she was doing to play with him. She lay on the floor next to him, told him stories, invented games, corrected his mistakes, and hugged him repeatedly. "I have said it to you before and I say it again," she wrote to Grimm. "I dote on the little monkey. . . . In the afternoon, my little monkey comes as often as he likes and spends three or four hours a day in my room." She called him "Monsieur Alexander" and announced, "It is astonishing that, although he cannot yet talk, at twenty months he knows things that are beyond the grasp of any other child at the age of three." When he was three, she said, "If you only knew what wonders Alexander achieves as a cook, and an architect; how he paints, mixes colors, chops wood; how he plays being the groom and the coachman; how he is teaching himself to read, draw, calculate and write." These conceits are no different from the effusions of any grandmother eager for the world to know—indeed, insisting that the world must know—of the extraordinary qualities and accomplishments of her grandchild. In any case, Catherine was convinced that Alexander was unique and that this was due exclusively to her. "I am making a delicious child of him," she said. "He loves me instinctively." She designed a loose, one-piece garment that could be put on him easily and would not restrict his arms and legs. "It is sewn together and goes on at once, and fastens behind with four or five little hooks," she told Grimm. "The king of Sweden has demanded and received a pattern of the dress of Monsieur Alexander."

Her second grandson was born eighteen months after Alexander. The empress named him Constantine to indicate the throne she had in mind for him: one day, she hoped, he would reign over a great new Orthodox Greek empire based on Constantinople. When Constantine was old enough, he joined his brother to play on her carpet. As they were intended for different thrones, they were given different educations. Alexander, who would become the future occupant of Catherine's own throne, was brought up on the English model. He was given an English nanny and was taught the history of Europe and the literature of the Enlightenment. Constantine, destined for Constantinople, was given a Greek nurse, Greek servants, and Greek playmates so that he could begin speaking the language early. His lessons included the histories of Greece, Rome, and Byzantium, as well as of Russia.

When Alexander was seven and Constantine almost six, and they had reached the age for tutors, Catherine wrote thirty pages of instructions to guide their education. They were to be truthful and courageous. They were to be courteous to servants as well as to elders. They must go to bed early in rooms with plenty of fresh air circulating at a temperature of sixty degrees Farenheit. They were to sleep on flat beds with leather mattresses. They were to wash every day in cold water, and, in winter, to go to Russian steam baths. In summer, they were to learn to swim. Food was to be plain; fruit of all kinds was to serve as breakfast in summer. They were to plant their own gardens and grow their own vegetables. Any necessary punishment would consist of teaching the child to be ashamed of his misbehavior. Rebukes were to be delivered in private; praise in public. Corporal punishment was forbidden.

In 1784, Catherine appointed a Swiss, Frédéric-César de La Harpe, to be the boys' primary tutor. A republican, skeptical of autocracy, he won Alexander's respect and affection and, with Catherine's permission, continued to preach the blessings of liberty and the duties of a sovereign toward his people. Alexander listened to these teachings; Constantine rebelled against them. Once he shouted at La Harpe that when he came to power, he would enter Switzerland with his army and destroy the country. La Harpe replied calmly, "There is in my country, near the little town of Morat, a building in which we keep the bones of those who pay us such a visit."

From Alexander's earliest years, Catherine nourished a hope that she could put him in place of her son, Paul, as her successor. Just as it had not taken Paul long to suspect that his mother's intention to disinherit him was behind her possessive behavior regarding his son, Alexander, as he grew older, realized that he was the object of a struggle between his parents and his grandmother. He learned to adapt himself to the company he was in. At Gatchina, he listened to his father's diatribes against the empress; back at court, he concurred with whatever his grandmother said. Unable to choose, he retreated into irresolution and equivocation; throughout his life, Alexander had difficulty making straightforward, unambiguous decisions.

Paul and Maria's ten children were produced over a period of nineteen years. There were four boys and six girls. Their third son, Nicholas, arrived in 1796, the last year of Catherine's life, and he escaped her strict supervision. The girls, unlike their older brothers, were left with their parents, who were allowed to educate them however they wished. Alexander remained Catherine's primary concern, and her anxiety about the succession and the future of the dynasty led her to push him to marry early. Although his tutors believed that he was too immature for marriage, Catherine, in October 1792, invited two German princesses from Baden to visit St. Petersburg for scrutiny. The elder sister, Louisa, was fourteen; Fredericka was a year younger. Louisa was shy but quickly fell in love with the Russian prince. Alexander admitted that he liked her. This was sufficient for Catherine. In January 1793, Louisa converted to Orthodoxy and became the Grand Duchess Elizabeth Alekseyevna. The wedding of Alexander when he was still fifteen and the newly named Elizabeth was fourteen took place in September 1793. Unfortunately for Catherine's dynastic hopes, Elizabeth never gave birth to a living child. Constantine, who refused the throne at the end of Alexander's reign in 1825, remained without legitimate children. That left Nicholas, the grandson Catherine had left to his mother to educate, to inherit the throne and, through his descendants, to carry on the dynasty.

Catherine permitted Paul and Maria to keep their daughters at home, but when she believed that the young women were ready to marry she took charge. The eldest of her granddaughters, Alexandra Pavlovna, was thirteen years old when the empress decided the time had come. Catherine wanted a marriage to Gustavus Adolphus, the young un-crowned king of Sweden, the son of Gustavus III, who had been assassinated four years earlier. A marriage to young Gustavus would ameliorate the long-standing hostility between Russia and Sweden and secure the Russian position on the upper Baltic.

There was an obstacle. In November 1795, Gustavus's engagement to Princess Louisa, the Protestant daughter of the Duke of Mecklenburg-Schwerin, had been announced. Catherine was not deterred. Word was passed to the Swedish regent, the Duke of Sudermania, brother of the murdered Gustavus III and uncle of the young uncrowned king, that hundreds of thousands of rubles would be available to subsidize the Swedish treasury once the empress's wish was granted. At the beginning of April 1796, the regent agreed to postpone his nephew's marriage until the young man reached his majority at eighteen in November of that year.

Catherine invited Gustavus and his uncle to visit St. Petersburg. As the king was still uncrowned, it would be a "private" visit, and the royal Swedes would come incognito; Gustavus would arrive as "Count Haga" and the regent as "Count Vasa." On August 15, the two "counts" arrived. The king turned out to be a solemn young man with fair hair down to the shoulders of his black suit. He was introduced to Alexandra, and the pair opened the ball that evening by leading a minuet. Catherine, contrary to custom, stayed until midnight. The next three weeks were crowded with entertainment, but the couple was given time to be alone. The empress was pleased to see that Gustavus was losing some of his stiffness and was often observed speaking in a low voice to Alexandra. Eventually, during a dance, he went so far as to squeeze her hand. "I didn't know what would become of me," she whispered to her governess. "I was so frightened I thought I would fall." Two days later, after a dinner in the Tauride Palace, Gustavus joined Catherine on a bench in the garden and confided that he would like to marry her granddaughter. Catherine reminded him that he was already engaged to someone else; Gustavus promised to break that engagement immediately. Negotiations began regarding the Russian-Swedish alliance that would accompany the marriage. The annual subsidy promised Sweden was to be three hundred thousand rubles.

Pleased with this progress, Catherine set a formal betrothal ceremony for September 11. One significant matter remained to be confirmed: the bride's religion after marriage. Catherine was determined that Alexandra be free to practice Russian Orthodoxy. Gustavus said he did not see how this would be possible; that he thought it had always been clear that, were he to marry Alexandra, she would be expected to embrace Lutheranism. Catherine reacted by insisting that he guarantee that, even as queen of Lutheran Sweden, her granddaughter would remain a member of the Russian Orthodox Church. In fact, Catherine was surprised; it never occurred to her that an uncrowned adolescent monarch would expect a Russian grand duchess, the granddaughter of an empress, to abandon her religion. For Catherine, personal and national prestige were as important as—perhaps more important than—religious observance. Further, she believed that she was entitled to set the terms because her large subsidies to Sweden would, in effect, be paying for the marriage.

There was still another reason. She had been the same age as Alexandra when she had received a marriage proposal that had been accepted for her and which had forced her, over her father's objection, to change her religion. Now, she promised herself, her granddaughter would not have to endure what she had been through half a century before. She inserted into the marriage contract a clause not only guaranteeing Alexandra's right to remain Orthodox as queen of Sweden but permitting her to have a private chapel with an Orthodox priest and confessor in the Swedish royal palace. Gustavus, devoted to his kingdom's established Protestant religion, and believing that his queen should share his faith, refused. To Catherine's protest that his ministers had already pledged the guarantees she desired, the young man replied that his ministers and the Russian officials with whom they were negotiating must have misunderstood each other. Catherine then demanded that the king now put his private pledge in his own handwriting. Gustavus hesitated; then, under pressure from his uncle, he agreed to amend the contract.

The way seemed clear for the betrothal ceremony, which was to be followed by a ball at the Tauride Palace. The families and the plenipotentiaries met at noon to witness the signing of the treaty. The Russians quickly discovered, however, that the clause regarding Alexandra's religion was missing from the treaty text. Gustavus had removed it so that he could discuss the matter again with the empress. That afternoon, he refused to go beyond a promise that "the grand duchess will never be troubled in her conscience with regard to religion." Catherine interpreted this as a new commitment and suggested to the regent that the couple go ahead with the formal betrothal. After consulting Gustavus, the regent agreed. "With the church's blessing?" asked Catherine. "Yes," the regent said. "According to your rite." Confident that the matter was settled, Catherine saw no need to continue her personal discussions with Gustavus and left the final drafting of the document to Platon Zubov.

At seven, Catherine entered the throne room and took her seat on the throne. Beside her stood the Orthodox metropolitan, Gavril; on a table lay two rings. Two armchairs, upholstered in blue velvet, awaited the king and his bride-to-be. Paul, Maria, and the entire imperial family were present. All eyes were on Alexandra, standing by her grandmother's throne, waiting for her intended fiancé. Time passed . . . half an hour . . . then a full hour. Officials glanced at one another. Something was wrong; under Catherine II, the Russian court stressed promptness. At last the double doors opened. But it was not Gustavus, only a secretary who whispered to Zubov and handed him a paper. Zubov hurried out. The king had refused to sign the amended marriage contract in which he read the new clause reinserted by Catherine. He had reverted to his earlier position: that a queen of Sweden must be Lutheran. Zubov, increasingly desperate, tried to convince him to change his mind. Catherine, her family, and her court continued to wait.

Suspense filled the room. At first, Catherine was calm. Then, as time passed, her smile disappeared and her face became red. Nearby, her granddaughter was in tears. The hands of the clock passed nine and moved toward ten. At last the double doors opened. Zubov appeared and handed Catherine a paper. The king had changed his mind again. His last word was that he had given his word of honor that Alexandra would not be hindered in the practice of her religion, but that he would put nothing in writing and would not sign the marriage contract as long as it contained the clause Catherine demanded.

Catherine could scarcely believe what she was reading. Rising from her throne, she tried to speak, but her words were unintelligible. To some, it seemed that she was suffering from dizziness; others thought it was a mild stroke. The attack, whatever it was, was temporary, and, a minute later, she was able to announce, "His Majesty King Gustavus is not well. The ceremony is postponed." She left the room on the arm of Alexander. Although the regent sent an apology for his nephew's behavior, Catherine was shaken. The next morning she reappeared and spoke briefly to the regent and the king. The regent was in despair, but Gustavus, "stiff as a ramrod," kept repeating, "What I have written, I have written. I will never change what I have written."

Catherine refused to admit that a seventeen-year-old could defeat the empress of Russia in her own palace. More time, she decided, would overcome his stubbornness, and she insisted that Gustavus and his uncle remain in St. Petersburg for another two weeks. Gustavus agreed to an additional ten days but would not retreat from his position. In the end, there was no marriage.

Catherine's humiliation and her effort to suppress her anger in public affected her health. Later, she learned that a strict Lutheran pastor had taught Gustavus that his subjects would never forgive him if he took a wife belonging to any but the Lutheran faith. Catherine also discovered that, during their long moments together, when the young king appeared to be wooing the young grand duchess, he was in fact attempting to convert her to Lutheranism. She wrote bitterly to Paul:

> The fact is that the king pretended that Alexandra had promised him to change her religion and take the sacrament the Lutheran way and that she had given him her hand on it. . . . She told me with the candor and naivete natural to her how he had told her that on the coronation day she would have to take the [Luthernan] sacrament with him, and that she had replied, "Certainly, if I can, and if Grandmama consents."

Alexandra, the bride-to-be, never completely recovered. After her grandmother's death, her father, the new emperor, Paul, married her to a Hapsburg archduke. The marriage was unhappy, and at seventeen Alexandra died in childbirth. On November 1, 1796, Gustavus was crowned as King Gustavus IV. He subsequently married Princess Fredericka of Baden, a younger sister of Grand Duchess Elizabeth, the wife of Catherine's grandson Alexander.

❧73❧

The Death of Catherine the Great

ON TUESDAY EVENING, November 4, 1796, Catherine appeared in public for the last time when a small number of close friends gathered at the Hermitage. One was Lev Naryshkin, who, more than forty years before, had been proposed, along with Sergei Saltykov, as a potential father of the child Catherine urgently needed to bear, and, subsequently, had meowed like a cat to spirit her out of the palace at night to visit her lover Poniatowski. Now, still playing the role of court jester, Lev, costumed as a peddler, shuffled up to Catherine with a tray full of toys and trinkets, pretending to hawk them. His performance made her shake with laughter. She retired early, explaining that she had laughed so hard that she needed to rest.

The next morning, November 5, she rose at six, drank black coffee, and sat down to write. At nine, she asked to be left alone for a moment and went into her dressing room. She did not reemerge. Her attendants waited. Her valet knocked, entered the room, and saw no one. He waited a minute, then pushed on the door of the adjacent water closet. It was partially jammed. He and a maid forced the door open and discovered the empress unconscious on the floor against the door. Her face was scarlet and her eyes were closed. When he gently raised her head, she issued a low groan. He called for help and with other servants managed to carry and drag her into her bedroom. There, finding her limp body too heavy to lift onto her high bed, they placed her on a leather mattress on the floor. Dr. Rogerson arrived and opened a vein in her arm.

The empress was alive, but her eyes were closed and she did not speak. The officials who gathered agreed to send urgently for Grand Duke Paul. Platon Zubov immediately sent his brother Nicholas galloping to Gatchina to notify Paul. Soon after, nineteen-year-old Alexander, in tears, asked Count Fyodor Rostopchin to go to Gatchina and officially inform his father of what had happened; Alexander wanted to assure Paul that no one—and certainly not he—thought of seizing the throne. Rostopchin followed Nicholas Zubov on the road to Gatchina.

Nicholas Zubov arrived at Gatchina at 3:45 p.m. with the news that Catherine had probably suffered a stroke. Paul ordered a sleigh and left immediately with Maria for St. Petersburg. At a staging post on the road, halfway to the capital, they met Rostopchin. The count later recalled:

> The grand duke got out of his sleigh to satisfy a need of nature. I got out too and drew his attention to the beauty of the night. It was extremely calm and light . . . the moon was visible through the clouds, every sound was muffled and silence

reigned. . . . I saw the grand duke fix his gaze on the moon; tears filled his eyes and flowed down his face. . . . I seized his hand. "My lord, what a moment this is for you!" He pressed my hand. "Wait, my dear friend, wait. I have lived forty-two years. Perhaps God will give me the strength and good sense to bear my appointed destiny."

Paul and Maria arrived at the Winter Palace at 8:25 p.m. They were greeted by Alexander and Constantine, who had already changed into Prussian-style "Gatchina" uniforms with stiff, buttoned tunics and high boots. The grand duke found his mother lying on the leather mattress, motionless, her eyes closed. Kneeling, Paul kissed her hands. There was no response, and he and Maria sat down near her for the rest of the night.

Everywhere in the palace, the stricken woman became an object of pity and calculations. Would she recover? Would she at least regain consciousness long enough to disinherit Paul and name Alexander? Courtiers wondered whether to declare their allegiance. And to whom. And when. One who said nothing, sitting alone in a corner, shunned by everyone, was Platon Zubov.

The vigil lasted through the night. At dawn, the doctors told Paul that Catherine had suffered a stroke and that there was no hope. Paul sent for Bezborodko and told him to prepare a manifesto announcing his accession. At noon, the grand duke ordered Bezborodko to sort and seal the papers in his mother's study under the supervision of his sons, then to lock the study and bring him the key. At five that afternoon, with Catherine struggling to breathe, Rogerson informed Paul that the end was near. Metropolitan Gavril administered the last rites, anointing Catherine with holy oil on the forehead, cheeks, mouth, breast, and hands.

Hours passed. No one spoke. At 9:45 on the night of November 6, 1796, thirty-six hours after she was stricken and without ever recovering consciousness, Catherine died. To courtiers assembled in an antechamber, an official announced, "Gentlemen, the Empress Catherine is dead and His Majesty Paul Petrovich has deigned to mount the throne of all the Russias."

On November 8, two days after his mother's death, the new emperor went to the Alexander Nevsky Monastery, where the coffin of the man he believed was his father, Peter III, was opened. The body had not been embalmed, and the coffin contained only bones, dust, a hat, gloves, boots, and buttons. On December 2, a procession left the monastery to escort the coffin to the Winter Palace. Paul, his family, the court, and the diplomatic corps walked behind, through streets lined by the Guards regiments. A figure from the past also walked. Eighty-year-old Alexis Orlov, who had commanded the guard at Ropsha and written the note informing Catherine of her husband's death, had been commanded by Paul to walk behind Peter's casket, carrying Paul's crown on a cushion held before him. Orlov endured this humiliation, his head erect, his face carved in stone. At the palace, Peter's coffin was placed beside that of Catherine for a lying-in-state honoring both. On December 5, the two coffins were carried across the ice of the frozen Neva River to the Cathedral of St. Peter and St. Paul, where they were placed near the tomb of Peter the Great. They are there today.

Catherine believed in enlightened autocracy. Supporting her belief and the practice of it was the keen attention she paid to public opinion. It was with this in mind that she said to Diderot, "What I despair of overthrowing, I undermine." Her wielding of absolute power rested on her sensitivity to the nuances of the possible. Years later, Potemkin's aide, V. S. Popov, elaborated on this by telling the young Emperor Alexander I of a conversation he had once had with the empress:

> The subject was the unlimited power with which the great Catherine ruled her empire. . . . I spoke of the surprise I felt at the blind obedience with which her will was fulfilled everywhere, of the eagerness and zeal with which all tried to please her.
> "It is not as easy as you think," she replied. "In the first place, my orders would not be carried out unless they were the kind of orders which could be carried out. You know with what prudence and circumspection I act in the promulgation of my laws. I examine the circumstances, I take advice, I consult the enlightened part of the people, and in this way I find out what sort of effect my laws will have. And when I am already convinced in advance of good approval, then I issue my orders, and have the pleasure of observing what you call blind obedience.

That is the foundation of unlimited power. But, believe me, they will not obey blindly when orders are not adapted to the opinion of the people."

She was aware that aspects of her personal life were criticized; her reply was that her life had been unique. "Before I became what I am today, I was thirty-three years the same as other people. It is only thirty years since I have become what they are not, and that teaches one to live."

After Potemkin's death, Catherine wrote an epitaph for herself:

HERE LIES CATHERINE THE SECOND

Born in Stettin on April 21, 1729.

In the year 1744, she went to Russia to marry Peter III. At the age of fourteen, she made the threefold resolution to please her husband, Elizabeth, and the nation. She neglected nothing in trying to achieve this. Eighteen years of boredom and loneliness gave her the opportunity to read many books.

When she came to the throne of Russia she wished to do what was good for her country and tried to bring happiness, liberty, and prosperity to her subjects.

She forgave easily and hated no one. She was good-natured, easy-going, tolerant, understanding, and of a happy disposition. She had a republican spirit and a kind heart.

She was sociable by nature.

She made many friends.

She took pleasure in her work.

She loved the arts.

This description is, of course, both idealized and excessively modest. She always refused extravagant titles, whether from the Legislative Assembly in 1764, which wished to name her Catherine the Great; from Voltaire, who filled his letters with flowery tributes; or from Grimm, who called her Catherine the Great in a letter in 1788. Replying to Grimm, she wrote, "I beg you no longer to call me Catherine the Great, because . . . my name is Catherine II." It was after her death that Russians began speaking of her as "Catherine the Great."

She was a majestic figure in the age of monarchy; the only woman to equal her on a European throne was Elizabeth I of England. In the history of Russia, she and Peter the Great tower in ability and achievement over the other fourteen tsars and empresses of the three-hundred-year Romanov dynasty. Catherine carried Peter's legacy forward. He had given Russia a "window on the West" on the Baltic coast, building there a city that he made his capital. Catherine opened another window, this one on the Black Sea; Sebastopol and Odessa were its jewels. Peter imported technology and governing institutions to Russia; Catherine brought European moral, political, and judicial philosophy, literature, art, architecture, sculpture, medicine, and education. Peter created a Russian navy and organized an army that defeated one of the finest soldiers in Europe; Catherine assembled the greatest art gallery in Europe, hospitals, schools, and orphanages. Peter shaved off the beards and truncated the long robes of his leading noblemen; Catherine persuaded them to be inoculated against smallpox. Peter made Russia a great power; Catherine magnified this power, and advanced the nation toward a culture that, during the century that followed, produced, among others, Derzhavin, Pushkin, Lermontov, Gogol, Dostoevsky, Tolstoy, Turgenev, Chekov, Borodin, Rimsky-Korsakov, Mussorgsky, Glinka, Tchaikovsky, Stravinsky, Petipa, and Diaghilev. These artists and their work were a part of Catherine's legacy to Russia.

In 1794, when she was sixty-four, she wrote to Grimm:

> Day before yesterday, on February ninth, it was fifty years since I arrived with my mother in Moscow. I doubt if there are ten people living today in St. Petersburg who remember. There is still Betskoy, blind, decrepit, gaga, asking young couples whether they remember Peter the Great. . . . There is one of my old maids, whom I still keep, though she forgets everything. These are proofs of old age and I am one of them. But in spite of this, I love as much as a five-year-old child to play blind-man's buff, and the young people, including my grandchildren, say that their games are never so merry as when I play with them. And I still love to laugh.

It was a long and remarkable journey that no one, not even she, could have imagined when, at fourteen, she set off for Russia across the snow.

ACKNOWLEDGMENTS

In writing this book, I drew heavily from the rich collections of the Sterling Memorial Library at Yale University. Thanks to the library's Privileges Office, I was able to spend days in the stacks, gather the books I wanted to bring home, and withdraw them for a reasonable period. I am grateful to the library for this generous policy and for the members of its staff who were always helpful. I also used the New York Public Library extensively and I thank the staff of this crown jewel of New York's cultural life.

Among those who by word and deed gave me steady encouragement during the years of working on this book were Andre Bernard, Donald Bitsberger, Kenneth Burrows, Janet Byrne, Georgina Capel and Anthony Cheetham, Robert and Ina Caro, Patricia Civale, Robert and Aline Crumb, Donald Holden, Melanie Jackson and Thomas Pynchon, James Marlas and Marie Nugent-Head, Kim, Lorna, and Miranda Massie, Jack and Lynn May, Lawrence and Margaret McQuade, Gilbert Merritt, Eunice Meyer, David Michaelis and Nancy Steiner, Edmund and Sylvia Morris, Mary Mulligan, Sara Nelson, Sydney Offit, George Paine, Heather Previn, David Remnick and Esther B. Fein, Peter and Masha Sarandinaki, Richard Weiss, and Brenda Wineapple. Douglas Smith generously allowed me to use his translations of the Catherine-Potemkin correspondence. Doug Smith also permitted me to draw heavily on his book *The Pearl* and its descriptions of the institution of Russian serfdom, particularly in the areas of serf opera, ballet companies, theatrical companies, symphony orchestras, and other forms of the performing arts.

I have again been fortunate to have Random House, a gathering of extraordinary talents, as my book's publisher. The members of this family who have worked to help me this time are Avideh Bashirrad, Evan Camfield, Gina Centrello, Jonathan Jao, Susan Kamil, London King, Carole Lowenstein, Jynne Martin, Sally Marvin, Tom Perry, Robbin Schiff, Ben Steinberg, and Jessica Waters. I have also been helped by Dolores Karl, Lane Trippe, and Alex Remnick.

For many years, my essential friend, counselor, and supporter at Random House has been Bob Loomis, who, in the summer of 2011, retired after fifty-four years of sustained effort and brilliant achievement at the same publishing house. I am one of hundreds of authors whose work has been guided and improved by his wisdom, enthusiasm, kindness, and firm but gentle admonitions, usually beginning, "Let's see if we can find a way to make this even better." There are no others like him.

Manuscript in hand, Deborah Karl, my wife, literary agent, and the best-read person I know, made many suggestions; every one is now in the book. Three of my children, Bob, Jr., Elizabeth, and Christopher, also read the manuscript and asked good questions. My daughter Susanna keeps track from far away, and at home, my daughters Sophia and Nora have sustained me with their love, unfailing optimism, and soaring artistic talent.

Finally, I must acknowledge the extraordinary pleasure I have had in the company of the remarkable woman who has been my subject. After eight years of having her a constant presence in my life, I shall miss her.

SELECTED BIBLIOGRAPHY

Alexander, John T. *Catherine the Great*. New York: Oxford University Press, 1989

Anderson, Fred. *Crucible of War*. New York: Vintage, 2001

Anderson, M. S. *Britain's Discovery of Russia, 1553–1815*. London: Macmillan, 1958

Anthony, Katharine. *Catherine the Great*. New York: Alfred A. Knopf, 1925

Asprey, Robert. *Frederick the Great*. New York: History Book Club, 1986

Bain, R. Nisbet. *Peter III, Emperor of Russia*. Westminster: Constable, 1902

———. *The Pupils of Peter the Great*. Westminster: Constable, 1897

Billington, James H. *The Icon and the Axe*. New York: Alfred A. Knopf, 1966

Catherine II. *Memoirs*. Translated by Alexander Herzen. New York: D. Appleton, 1859

———. *Memoirs of Catherine the Great*. Translated and with notes by Katharine Anthony. New York and London: Alfred A. Knopf, 1927

———. *The Memoirs of Catherine the Great*. Edited by Dominique Maroger and translated by Moura Budberg. New York: Macmillan, 1955

———. *The Memoirs of Catherine the Great*. Edited and translated by Mark Cruse and Hilde Hoogenboom. New York: Modern Library, 2005

Coughlan, Robert. *Elizabeth and Catherine: Empresses of All the Russias*. New York: G. P. Putnam's Sons, 1974

Crankshaw, Edward. *Maria Theresa*. New York: Viking Press, 1969

Cranston, Maurice. *Philosophers and Pamphleteers*. Oxford: Oxford University Press, 1986

Cronin, Vincent. *Catherine, Empress of All the Russias*. New York: William Morrow, 1978

Dashkova, Princess Catherine. *Memoirs*. Two volumes. London: Henry Colburn, 1840

Descargues, Pierre. *The Hermitage Museum, Leningrad*. New York: Harry Abrams, 1961

Dixon, Simon. *Catherine the Great*. London: Longman-Pearson, 2001

Duffy, Christopher. *Frederick the Great*. London: Routledge, 1988

———. *The Military Experience in the Age of Reason*. New York: Atheneum, 1988

———. *Russia's Military Way to the West*. London: Routledge, 1981

Dukes, Paul. *Catherine the Great and the Russian Nobility*. Cambridge University Press, 1967

Durant, Will, and Ariel Durant. *The Story of Civilization*. Vol. 9, *The Age of Voltaire*. New York: Simon and Schuster, 1965

———. Vol. 10, *Rousseau and Revolution*. New York: Simon and Schuster, 1967

Figes, Orlando. *Natasha's Dance*. New York: Metropolitan-Holt, 2002

Fisher, Helen. *Why We Love*. New York: Henry Holt, 2004

Gooch, G. P. *Catherine the Great and Other Studies*. Hamdon, Conn.: Archon Books, 1966

Gorbatov, Inna. *Catherine the Great and the French Philosphers of the Enlightenment*. Bethesda, Md.: Academica Press, 2006

Grey, Ian. *Catherine the Great*. Philadelphia: Lippincott, 1962

Haslip, Joan. *Catherine the Great*. New York: G. P. Putnam's Sons, 1977

Hubatsch, Walther. *Frederick the Great*. London: Thames and Hudson, 1973

Kaus, Gina. *Catherine: The Portrait of an Empress*. New York: The Literary Guild, 1935

Kerensky, Alexander. *The Crucifixion of Liberty*. New York: Day, 1934

Lariviere, Ch. *Catherine II et la Revolution Francaise*. Paris: Librairie H. Le Soudier, 1895

Lincoln, W. Bruce. *Between Heaven and Hell*. New York: Viking-Penguin, 1998

Longworth, Philip. *The Three Empresses*. New York: Holt, Rinehart and Winston, 1973

Loomis, Stanley. *Paris in the Terror*. London: Jonathan Cape, 1964

Madariaga, Isabel de. *Russia in the Age of Catherine the Great*. New Haven: Yale University Press, 1981

———. *Catherine the Great*. New Haven: Yale University Press, 1990

Marsden, Christopher. *Palmyra of the North: The First Days of St. Petersburg*. London: Faber and Faber, 1942

Masson, Charles. *Secret Memoirs of the Court of Petersburg*. New York: Arno Press and New York Times, 1970

Montefiore, Sebag. *Prince of Princes: The Life of Potemkin*. New York. St. Martin's Press, 2001

Morison, Samuel Eliot. *John Paul Jones*. Boston: Little, Brown, 1959

Oldenbourg, Zoe. *Catherine the Great*. New York: Pantheon, 1965

Oliva, L. Jay, ed. *Catherine the Great*. Englewood Cliffs, N.J.: Prentice Hall, 1971

Pipes, Richard. *Russia Under the Old Regime*. New York: Scribners, 1974

Plumb, J. H. *The First Four Georges*. London: Fontana-Collins, 1966

Pomeau, Rene, ed. *Voltaire Chez Lui*. Yens sur Morges: Editions Cabedita, 1999

Poniatowski, Stanley-August. *Memoires du Roi*. St. Petersburg: L'Academie Imperiale Des Sciences, 1914

Radishchev, Alexander. *A Journey from St Petersburg to Moscow*. Translated by Leo Wiener. Cambridge, Mass.: Harvard University Press, 1958

Raeff, Marc. *Origins of the Russian Intelligentsia*. New York: Harbinger, Harcourt Brace, 1966

———, ed. *Catherine the Great: A Profile*. New York: Hill and Wang, 1972

Ransel, David L. *The Politics of Catherinian Russia: The Panin Party*. New Haven: Yale University Press, 1975

Reddaway, W. F. *Documents of Catherine the Great: Correspondence with Voltaire and the Nakaz of 1767*. Cambridge University Press, 1931

Rice, Tamara Talbot. *Elizabeth, Empress of Russia*. London: Weidenfeld and Nicolson, 1970

Richter, Melvin. *The Political Theory of Montesquieu*. Cambridge, U.K.: Cambridge University Press, 1977

Ritter, Gerhard. *Frederick the Great*. Berkeley: University of California Press, 1984

Rounding, Virginia. *Catherine the Great*. London: Hutchinson, 2006

Schama, Simon. *Citizens: A Chronicle of the French Revolution*. New York: Alfred A. Knopf, 1989

Scott Thomson, Gladys. *Catherine the Great and the Expansion of Russia*. London: Hodder & Stoughton, 1947

Smith, Douglas. *Love and Conquest: Personal Correspondence of Catherine the Great and Gregory Potemkin*. DeKalb, Ill.: Northern Illinois University Press, 2005

———. *The Pearl*. New Haven: Yale University Press, 2008

Soloveytchik, George. *Potemkin: A Picture of Catherine's Russia*. London: Thornton Butterworth, 1938

Thomas, Evan. *John Paul Jones*. New York: Simon & Schuster, 2003

Thompson, J. M. *French Revolution Documents*. Oxford University Press, 1933

Troyat, Henri. *Catherine the Great*. New York: Meridian, 1994

Williams, Basil. *The Whig Supremacy, 1740–1760*. Oxford: The Clarendon Press, 1962

Winik, Jay. *The Great Upheaval*. New York: HarperCollins, 2007

Waliszewski, Kasimierz. *The Romance of an Empress*. Archon Books, 1968

Yarmolinsky, Avrahm, ed. *The Poems, Prose, and Plays of Alexander Pushkin*. New York: Modern Library, 1936

Zweig, Stefan. *Marie Antoinette*. New York: Viking Press, 1933

NOTES

Catherine's life divides into two halves almost equal in length. From 1729 to 1762, she was a German princess and a Russian grand duchess; from 1762 until her death in 1796, she was the empress of Russia. The primary source of information about the first half of her life is her own *Memoirs,* which begin with her earliest recollections and continue to 1758, when she was twenty-nine and under stress at the court of Empress Elizabeth. Naturally, her memoirs display the subjective perspective of any memoir writer; even so, they are invaluable.

Catherine wrote her memoirs in French, and at least four translations have been published in English. The first of these was by Alexander Herzen, a celebrated Russian author and exile in London; this work appeared in 1859. An American, Katharine Anthony, retranslated and edited the memoirs and published them in London and New York in 1927. Catherine's memoirs in the original French were edited and published by Dominique Maroger in Paris, then translated into English by Moura Budberg, appearing in New York in 1955. Modern Library brought out a new translation by Mark Cruse and Hilde Hoogenboom in 2005 that put Catherine's reminiscences in correct chronological sequence, which Catherine herself and previous translators never achieved. I have used the first three of these translations. They are identified in the notes as follows: Maroger and Budberg's version is denoted simply as *Memoirs.* Herzen's translation is identified as Herzen. The Anthony translation is denoted by *Memoirs* (Anthony).

I. SOPHIA'S CHILDHOOD

3   "that idiot": Haslip

6   "It was told me": *Memoirs,* 25–26

6   "He lived to be only twelve": Ibid., 41

7   "Very early it was noticed": Anthony, 27

8   "circumcision": Ibid., 31

8   "every night at dusk": *Memoirs,* 30

8   "I am convinced": Anthony, 27

8   "All my life": *Memoirs,* 30

8   "He always brought with him": Anthony, 27

8   "Music to my ears": *Memoirs,* 31

8   "She had a noble soul": Ibid., 26

8   "the pupil": Oldenbourg, 8

8   "One cannot always know": Kaus, 11

10   "A large number of parrots": *Memoirs,* 36

11   "I don't know whether": Anthony, 13

11   "agreeable and well-bred": *Memoirs,* 33

12   "I knew that one day": Ibid., 34

12   "Madame, you do not know": Ibid., 49

13 "Galloped until": Ibid., 38
13 "I was never caught": Ibid.
13 "I knew nothing about love": Ibid., 46
13 "My parents will not wish it": Memoirs (Anthony), 28
13 "He was very good looking": Memoirs, 46

2. SUMMONED TO RUSSIA

15 "The empress is charmed": Kaus, 19
16 "At the explicit command": Ibid., 25
17 "I will no longer conceal": Ibid., 26
17 "She lacked only wings": Ibid., 27
18 "Next to the empress": Ibid., 28
18 "The prince, my husband": Ibid.
19 "She told me": Memoirs, 50

3. FREDERICK II AND THE JOURNEY TO RUSSIA

21 "ambition, the opportunity for gain": Ritter, 7
23 "opera, comedy, poetry, dancing": Memoirs, 54
23 "the entire company": Oldenbourg, 21
23 "Accept this gift": Memoirs, 54
23 "The little princess of Zerbst": Haslip, 24
25 "My Lord: I beg you": Oldenbourg, 59
26 "The bedchambers were unheated": Waliszewski, 23
26 "I had never seen anything": Memoirs, 54
26 "In these last days": Anthony, 69
26 "I found ready to wrap us": Ibid., 71
27 "Here everything goes on": Ibid.
28 "It is the bride": Kaus, 42

4. EMPRESS ELIZABETH

29 "loved both his girls": Rice, 15
30 "My father often repeated": Bain, Peter III, 13
30 "She is a beauty": Massie, Peter the Great, 806

33 "I was too young then": Rice, 48
36 "knew of no other family": Ibid.
36 "Your Majesty may create me": Ibid., 61
36 "In public": Longworth, 162
38 "exceedingly obliging and affable": Rice, 47
38 "Madame, you must choose": Ibid., 57

5. THE MAKING OF A GRAND DUKE

40 "I don't belive there is a princess": Massie, 806
41 "I am Russian, remember": Bain, Pupils of Peter the Great, 125
42 "the happiest day of my life": Oldenbourg, 48
45 "I see that Your Highness": Bain, Peter III, 11
46 "utterly frivolous": Ibid.,14
46 "extremely weak": Ibid., 15
46 "This will be your last": Oldenbourg, 52
47 "I cannot express": Bain, Peter III, 13
47 "One promised": Oldenbourg, 53
48 "as he spoke": Ibid.

6. MEETING ELIZABETH AND PETER

49 "I could wait no longer": Kaus, 43
50 "All I have done for you": Ibid.
50 "It was quite impossible": Memoirs, 60
50 "one of the most handsome men": Ibid., 61
51 "We are living like queens": Kaus, 53
51 "for the first ten days": Memoirs, 62
51 "because his aunt wished it": Ibid.
52 "I blushed to hear": Ibid.

7. PNEUMONIA

53 "the external forms ": Madariaga, Russia in the Age, 6
53 "Search yourself with care": Anthony, 82

53 "The change of religion": Ibid., 81

53 "There I lay with a high fever": Memoirs, 63

54 "the devil would take her": Oldenbourg, 68

55 "Call Simon Todorsky": Anthony, 83

55 "the ladies would speak": Herzen, 28,

55 "my mother's behavior": Memoirs, 64

56 "I had become as thin as a skeleton": Memoirs, 65

56 "My Lord, I make so bold": Oldenbourg, 68

57 "Our good prince": Kaus, 58

57 "I have had more trouble": Ibid., 59

8. INTERCEPTED LETTERS

59 "If the empress would give": Kaus, 50

60 "frivolous, indolent, running to fat": Haslip, 34

60 "This horseplay will stop": Herzen, 29

61 "If your mother has done something wrong": Memoirs, 66

9. CONVERSION AND BETROTHAL

62 "She slept soundly": Oldenbourg, 74

62 "I thought she was lovely": Ibid., 75

62 "The forehead, eyes, neck, throat": Ibid., 76

63 "I had learned it by heart": Anthony, 84

63 "Her bearing . . . through the entire ceremony": Ibid.

64 "real little monsters, both of them": Oldenbourg, 77

64 "The ceremony lasted four hours": Ibid., 78

64 "Our situation is the same": Ibid.

64 "one was almost suffocated": Memoirs, 71

65 "My daughter conducts herself": Oldenbourg, 79

65 "There was not a day": Memoirs, 72

65 "I know that Your Highness has sent my brother": Kaus, 65

65 "use my influence": Memoirs, 72

10. A PILGRIMAGE TO KIEV AND TRANSVESTITE BALLS

67 "pedagogues": Memoirs, 73

67 "got into ours": Ibid., 74

67 "We allowed only the most amusing": Ibid.

67 "While we were enjoying ourselves": Ibid.

68 "Knowing how easily excited": Ibid., 75

68 "When my mother was in a temper": Ibid.

69 "In truth, at that time": Ibid.

69 "Never in my whole life": Ibid., 76

69 "I was afraid of not being liked": Ibid., 77

70 "My respect for the empress": Ibid.

70 "I must say": Ibid., 78

70 "The very tall Monsieur Sievers": Ibid.

71 "washed her hands": Ibid., 79

11. SMALLPOX

72 "uncontrollable in his whims": Ibid., 82

72 "he confided his childish pranks": Ibid.

74 "and was on such bad terms": Ibid., 84

74 "was very much to my liking": Ibid.

75 "she ordered me to go": Ibid., 91

76 "Your Highness, my very dear niece": Troyat, 39

76 "He was a man of great intelligence": Memoirs, 85

77 "I read his remarks again": Ibid., 86

77 "What a pity": Ibid., 86, footnote

77 "semi-darkness": Ibid.

77 "almost with terror": Ibid.

77 "he came up to me": Kaus, 79

12. MARRIAGE

81 "About as discreet as a cannon ball": *Memoirs,* 88
82 "All the attention": Ibid., 92
82 "We spent our time walking": Ibid. 93
82 "As my wedding day came nearer": Ibid., 97
83 "severely scolded": Ibid.
84 "We had a long, friendly talk": Ibid., 97
85 "Her silver brocade wedding gown": Oldenbourg, 95
85 "The procession infinitely surpasses": Kaus, 85
86 "horribly heavy": *Memoirs,* 98
86 "I begged the Princess of Hesse": Ibid., 99
86 "I remained alone": Ibid.
87 "How it would amuse my servants": Ibid.
87 "And matters remained in this state": Kaus, 86
87 "There was not a single man": *Memoirs,* 100
87 "The following day": Ibid.
87 "My dear husband": Ibid., 100
88 "I would have been ready": Ibid., 101
88 "was the gayest marriage": Kaus, 85

13. JOHANNA GOES HOME

89 "Since my marriage": *Memoirs,* 101
89 "At that time I would have given much": Ibid., 102
90 "Our farewell was very loving": Kaus, 89
90 "When the princess took leave": Ibid.
90 "not to make me any sadder": Anthony, 102
91 "I consider it necessary": Kaus, 90

14. THE ZHUKOVA AFFAIR

95 "From that moment on": Herzen, 46
95 "I thought I would faint": *Memoirs,* 103

95 "feared that I had grown": Ibid.
96 "My mother did not know Russian": Ibid., 104
96 "Through my servants": Ibid., 105
96 "It is difficult to find an explanation": Ibid.
99 "As for the previous dress": Ibid., 149

15. PEEPHOLES

100 "on the empress's behalf": Ibid., 106
100 "It seemed strange to us": Ibid.,
100 "satisfied and pleased with me": Ibid., 107
101 "I fear he may fall in love": Ibid., 104
101 "At last my wish is fulfilled": Kaus, 84
101 "this might serve his purposes": *Memoirs,* 112
102 "He did not tell us what it was": Ibid., 109
103 "a disrespectful little boy": Ibid., 110
103 "let fly at him": Ibid.
103 "We were dumfounded": Ibid.
103 "She was like a Fury": Ibid., 111
103 "One must admit": Ibid
103 "We beg your pardon, Mama": Ibid.
104 "had a great liking for the bottle": Ibid., 112
104 "Your Highness should bear in mind": Ibid., 116
104 "You talk and think of nothing": Ibid.
105 "I cannot speak to you like this": Ibid., 117
105 "The grand duke is asking for you": Ibid.
106 "No, my father": Ibid., 123

16. A WATCHDOG

107 "Her Highness has been selected": Oldenbourg, 110
108 "In the two years I had been in Russia": *Memoirs,* 113
109 "Now, as I was married": Herzen, 66

109   "I know quite well": *Memoirs*, 114
109   "I could not save myself by flight": Ibid.
109   "such talk would displease the empress": Ibid., 119
110   "In those days": Ibid., 123
110   "Never did two minds resemble each other less": Ibid., 129

17. "HE WAS NOT A KING"

111   "your father was not a king": Ibid., 130
112   "Apparently, my words carried conviction": Ibid.
112   "This was a dreadful blow for us": Ibid., 127
113   "Within a few days": Ibid., 128
113   "a gentle, reasonable man": Ibid.
113   "The grand duke and I": Ibid., 133
113   "In his distress, the grand duke": Ibid., 128
114   "There were moments": Ibid., 129

18. IN THE BEDROOM

114   "It seems to me that I was good for something else": Kaus, 101
117   "The least rabbi of Petersburg": Kaus, 94

19. A HOUSE COLLAPSES

118   "Get up and get out": *Memoirs*, 141
119   "like the waves of the sea": Ibid., 142
119   "Immediately afterward": Herzen, 89
120   "That, as to my stupidity": *Memoirs*, 136
120   "To show how useless this kind of order is": Herzen, 84
120   "often slipped me useful . . . information": Ibid.
121   "This is from your mother": *Memoirs*, 144

20. SUMMER PLEASURES

122   "a large, stupid, clumsy girl": *Memoirs* (Anthony), 132
123   "I had the greatest freedom imaginable": Ibid., 147

124   "dominant passion": Herzen, 78
124   "On a woman's saddle": Ibid., 131
124   "To tell the truth": *Memoirs*, 183
124   "She was tall": Ibid., 181
125   "We bit our lips": Ibid., 182

21. DISMISSALS AT COURT

126   "She was a living archive": *Memoirs*, 164
127   "Do not come near me!": Ibid., 150
127   "Last night, Count Lestocq and his wife": Ibid.
127   "The empress did not have the courage": Ibid., 151
128   "This son of a bitch": Ibid., 140
128   "Do you remember the time": Ibid., 141
128   "This is the effect": Ibid.
128   "So, in order not to spoil his pleasure": Ibid., 133
128   "only two occupations": Ibid., 154
128   "From seven in the morning": Ibid.
128   "One day, hear a poor dog cry": Ibid., 159

22. MOSCOW AND THE COUNTRY

130   "Countess Shuvalova told the empress": *Memoirs*, 156
130   "I know that. We will not speak of it": Ibid., 157
130   "It was the worst I have ever had": Ibid., 160
131   "She was mortally afraid of mice": Ibid., 163
131   "I rode constantly all day": Ibid., 161
132   "himself no enemy of wine": Ibid., 163
132   "He did not know what he was saying": Ibid.
132   "He was very cheerful": Ibid., 161
132   "She sat by my bed": Ibid., 164

23. CHOGLOKOV MAKES AN ENEMY

133   "one would have thought": Herzen, 101

133 "Choglokov is a conceited fool with a swollen head": *Memoirs,* 165

134 "As he could never keep": Ibid., 167

136 "I have never in my life felt anything like the pain": Ibid., 170

24. A BATH BEFORE EASTER AND A COACHMAN'S WHIP

137 "beautiful eyes": *Memoirs,* 173

137 "her wit made one forget": Herzen, 118

138 "seeing myself slighted": Ibid., 120

138 "everyone was shocked and disgusted": Ibid.

139 "I would like to see what she can do": *Memoirs,* 174

139 "both took leave of their senses": Ibid.

140 "My God!, what happened?": Ibid., 177

140 "Wipe your cheek": Ibid.

140 "You see how these women treat us": Ibid.

25. OYSTERS AND AN ACTOR

142 "an extraordinary passion": *Memoirs,* 148

143 "I listened to talk": Herzen, 126

143 "If this man or someone like him": Ibid., 124

144 "As ambassador, I have no instructions": *Memoirs,* 192

26. READING, DANCING, AND A BETRAYAL

144 "of a dullness that I have never seen equaled": Herzen, 148

145 "He was blond and foppish": Ibid., 132

145 "Good God, what modesty!": *Memoirs,* 190

146 "I was very glad to see him": Ibid., 189

146 "And so, things went no further": Herzen, 149

147 "The truth": *Memoirs,* 181

147 "How is this, Madame Choglokova?": Herzen, 151

27. SALTYKOV

151 "He was a born clown": *Memoirs,* 194

151 "a fool in every sense": Herzen, 132

152 "As these people": *Memoirs,* 199

153 "And your wife": Ibid., 200

153 "All that glitters": Ibid.

153 "He was twenty-six years old": Ibid.

153 "handsome as the dawn": Ibid.

153 "How do you know": Ibid., 201

153 "his favorite subject": Herzen, 155

154 "I had to admit": *Memoirs,* 201

154 "Yes, yes, but go away": Ibid.

154 "He already believed himself": Ibid., 202

154 "Sergei Saltykov and my wife": Ibid.

154 "without something happening first": Herzen, 158

156 "I must speak to you": *Memoirs,* 208

156 "Madame Choglokova began": Ibid.

156 "You will see": Ibid.

157 "As soon as I had seen": Ibid., 207

157 "a few words that would allow him": Ibid.

158 "I know that you can see through them": Ibid.

158 "He gave him": Ibid., 208

159 "I must have been pregnant": Herzen, 168

159 "When this happened": Ibid., 169

160 "No one had ever seen": Alexander, 45

160 "There was no furniture": Herzen, 173

162 "He was dying just at a time": *Memoirs,* 220

162 "I am certain that my husband": Herzen, 184

28. THE BIRTH OF THE HEIR

163 "a pillar of salt": *Memoirs,* 248

163 "Countess Shuvalova's petticoats": Herzen, 174

163 "a depression": *Memoirs,* 223

164 "my troubles followed me": Ibid.
164 "isolated, with no company": Herzen, 187
164 "I had not the strength to crawl": Ibid., 189
165 "through excess of care": Ibid., 192
165 "I did not have a kopeck": *Memoirs*, 228
165 "whatever came from the empress": Ibid.
166 "This meant that I was": Ibid., 229
166 "I thought him beautiful": Ibid.
167 "until I felt strong enough": Ibid.
168 "a singular revolution in my brain": Herzen, 196
168 "ought to be the Breviary": Durant, 10:435
169 "all day and part of the night": *Memoirs*, 230
169 "constantly smoked": Ibid.
170 "I underwent agonies": Herzen, 197
170 "I saw as clear as day": *Memoirs*, 231
170 "He knew how to conceal his faults": Ibid., 200
170 "Has he not committed": Alexander, 63

29. RETALIATION
171 "I had a superb dress made": *Memoirs*, 232
171 "I treated them with profound contempt": Herzen, 198
172 "One day, His Imperial Highness": *Memoirs*, 233
173 "he could have saved himself": Herzen, 201
173 "he got nothing": *Memoirs*, 234
173 "shuddered to think": Herzen, 203
174 "Those accursed Germans": *Memoirs*, 235
174 "a freakish prank": Ibid., 236
174 "We have become the servants": Ibid.
174 "as far away as I could": Ibid

30. THE ENGLISH AMBASSADOR
174 "It was not difficult to talk": *Memoirs*, 239

175 "a stumbling block": Ibid.
175 "nowhere are people quicker": Ibid., 240
176 "The empress's health": Kaus, 138
177 "A man at my age": Cronin, 105
178 "I have some hesitation": Troyat, 87
179 "Whatever may be further given": Kaus, 143

31. A DIPLOMATIC EARTHQUAKE
182 "I have heard with pleasure": Kaus, 144–45

32. PONIATOWSKI
184 "An excellent education": Haslip, 71
184 "A severe education": Poniatowski, 157
185 "She was twenty-five": Madariaga, *Russia in the Age*, 48
185 "I cannot deny myself the pleasure": Oldenbourg, 178

33. A DEAD RAT
187 "You ought to go and see her": *Memoirs*, 242
188 "The evening passed": Ibid., 243
188 "Sometimes at the theater": Ibid., 244,
188 "like a servant girl": Haslip, 76
189 "Tell me how much you know": *Memoirs*, 252
190 "there is no worse traitor": Ibid., 249
190 "in the present critical and delicate": Haslip, 82
190 "I pressed her strongly": Anthony, 137

34. CATHERINE CHALLENGES BROCKDORFF
193 "They tell me he is suspected": *Memoirs*, 254
193 "If such things are done: Ibid., 249
193 "Come to my apartment": Ibid., 255.
193 "Speak to the grand duchess": Ibid.

194   "*Baba Ptitsa*": Ibid., 256
194   "He took money from everyone":
         Ibid.
194   "Look at this devil of a fellow":
         Ibid., 257
195   "The great problem lay in the
         fact": Ibid., 258
195   "Well, you began very young":
         Ibid., 259
196   "You seem to be well-informed":
         Ibid., 264
196   "The weather was superb": Ibid.,
         276
197   "The Grand Duchess is kindness":
         Ibid., 277
197   "please the empress": Kaus, 147
197   "The grand duke is as completely a
         Prussian": Ibid., 148
198   "I love you as my father": Cronin,
         110

35. APRAKSIN'S RETREAT
199   "a very corpulent man": Cronin,
         109
202   "If the empress should die":
         Haslip, 89
202   "And there now remains": Kaus,
         171

36. CATHERINE'S DAUGHTER
202   "I have no idea": *Memoirs*, 280
202   "You fool! Go back": Ibid.
203   "Go to the devil!": Ibid.
203   "It is said that the public celebra-
         tions": Ibid., 283
204   "only just awakened": Ibid., 284
204   "You should not die of hunger":
         Ibid.
205   "the grand duke's musicians":
         Ibid., 285
205   "except for Alexander Shuvalov":
         Ibid.

37. THE FALL OF BESTUZHEV
205   "Count, I have just received a
         message": *Memoirs*, 286
206   "Thank God, we are going to ar-
         rest": Ibid., 287
207   "a loyal, honest man": Ibid.

207   "With a dagger in my heart": Ibid.,
         288
207   "What do all these wonderful
         things mean?": Ibid.
208   "attempting to sow discord": Ibid.,
         292
209   "You are a witness to the fact":
         Ibid., 294

38. A GAMBLE
210   "in a fearful passion": *Memoirs*,
         297
210   "What will you say to her?": Ibid.
212   "Today, my damned nephew":
         Ibid., 299
212   "I felt myself possessed": Ibid
212   "My natural pride": Ibid., 300
213   "I have just said": Ibid., 301
214   "We are all afraid": Ibid., 302

39. CONFRONTATION
215   "Why do you wish me": *Memoirs*,
         305
216   "My children are in your hands":
         Ibid.
216   "Your Imperial Majesty will tell
         them": Ibid.
216   "God is my witness": Ibid.
216   "You are dreadfully haughty":
         Ibid., 306
216   "She is dreadfully spiteful": Ibid.
217   "You meddle in many things":
         Herzen, 288
217   "And why did you write": Ibid.,
         289
217   "The grand duke showed much
         bitterness": Ibid.
217   "I have many more things to say":
         Ibid., 290
218   "He told me that the empress had
         spoken": Ibid., 291
219   "I expect you to answer truth-
         fully": Ibid., 296

40. A MÉNAGE À QUATRE
219   The quotations appearing in
         this chapter are taken from
         Poniatowski's *Memoires*, translated
         by R. Massie

41. PANIN, ORLOV, AND ELIZABETH'S DEATH

228 "Let the boy remain": Kaus, 176
228 "I had rather be the mother": Ibid., 177
229 "the terror which the enemy": Duffy, *Frederick*, 171
229 "If I were emperor": Alexander, 55
230 "I must make room here": Kaus, 183
230 "the head of an angel": Ibid.
232 "a man of pleasure": Dashkova, 1:3
232 "We spoke French fluently": Ibid., 4
233 "I may venture to assert": Ibid., 13
233 "She captured my heart": Ibid., 29
233 "My child, you would do well": Ibid., 27
234 "You are a mere child": Ibid., 29
234 "gained me a high degree of notoriety": Ibid., 30
234 "I saw how little": Ibid., 31
236 "He must be mad": Oldenbourg, 230
237 "Of an army of forty-eight thousand": Asprey, 520
237 "What is wrong with me": Duffy, *Frederick*, 192
237 "I intend to continue the war": Oldenbourg, 222
238 The account of Dashkova's nocturnal visit and conversation with Catherine is from Dashkova, 1:32–35
240 "Her Imperial Majesty, Elizabeth Petrovna": Haslip, 108

42. THE BRIEF REIGN OF PETER III

240 "I did not think": Bain, *Peter III*, 40
241 "If, my little friend, you will take my advice": Dashkova, 1:38
244 "The moderation and clemency": Bain, *Peter III*, 49
244 "I can find nobody here": Ibid.
246 "the chief instrument of the Prussian party": Ibid., 56

246 "at a dinner": Ibid.
247 "resolved to get free": Ibid., 57
247 "We must make peace": Ibid., 63
249 "honor of all the valiant officers": Ibid., 74
249 "nothing was omitted": Ibid.
249 "out of compassion": Ibid., 77
249 "the maintenance of solemn engagements": Ibid., 79
251 "Frankly, I distrust these Russians": Ibid., 116
251 "If the Russians had wanted": Ibid., 117

43. "DURA!"

251 "It does not appear": Bain, *Peter III*, 123
252 "The empress is abandoned": Ibid., 130
252 "pot-house wench": Ibid., 126
252 "broad, puffy, pock-marked face": Ibid.
253 *"Dura!"*: Madariaga, *Russia in the Age*, 27
254 "It was then that I began to listen": Bain, *Peter III*, 192
255 "Your Majesty can have your revenge": Ibid., 134
255 "You already know too much": Kaus, 214
258 "Matushka, Little Mother, wake up!": Anthony, 165
259 "Matushka, forgive us": Madariaga, *Russia in the Age*, 29
260 "Heaven be praised!": Dashkova, 1:81
261 "like a fifteen-year-old boy": Ibid., 1:98
261 "I go now with the army": Alexander, 9
262 "Didn't I always tell you": Bain, *Peter III*, 154
264 "We no longer have an emperor!": Ibid., 160
265 "I accept the offer": Ibid., 161
265 "I, Peter, of my own free will": Kaus, 233
266 "like a child being sent to bed": Ibid.

44. "WE OURSELVES KNOW NOT WHAT WE DID"

266 "the greatest misfortune of my life": Madariaga, *Russia in the Age*, 31

268 "By what right": Dashkova, 1:89

268 "I realized with unspeakable pain": Ibid., 1:90

269 "I beg Your Majesty": Peter's letters from Ropsha to Catherine, Anthony, 176–77

272 "Matushka, Little Mother": Madariaga, *Russia in the Age*, 32,

273 "His face wore an expression": Oldenbourg, 252

273 "We ourselves know not what we did": Kaus, 244

273 "My horror at this death": Dashkova, 1:107

274 "On the seventh day of our reign": Kaus, 246

274 "might spare her health": Troyat, 139

275 "Peter III had lost the few wits": Bain, *Peter III*, 191

276 "it teaches us to be sober": Cronin, 156

276 "The empress was quite ignorant of this crime": Haslip, 133

276 "What do they say in Paris": Anthony, 180

45. CORONATION

282 "The least soldier of the guards": Alexander, 67

283 "You only did your duty": Cronin, 172

284 "I implore Your Majesty": Dashkova, 1:97

284 "the Princess Dashkova played only a minor part": Haslip, 144,

285 The exchange between Catherine and Betskoy is from Dashkova, 1:101–2, and Kaus, 240

287 "a woman of middle height": Scott Thomson, 85–86

288 "the Lord has placed the crown": Grey, 119

289 "I cannot go out": Ibid.

46. THE GOVERNMENT AND THE CHURCH

291 "In the Treasury": Waliszewski, 313

291 "an ignominious peace": Kaus, 239

291 "no suitable costume": Ibid.

291 "Concerning the peace": Ibid.

292 "such a vast and limitless empire": Haslip, 137

292 "Full reports will be brought to me": Ibid.,

292 "Belonging herself to the nation": Ibid.

293 "I cannot say that you are lacking": Madariaga, *Russia in the Age*, 44

293 "the eye of the sovereign": Ibid., 40

293 "In the Senate": Ibid., 44–45

294 "You must know": Ibid., 58

300 "sat like dumb dogs without barking": Ibid., 116

300 "stretch out their hands": Kaus, 254

300 "Our present sovereign": Madariaga, *Russia in the Age*, 116

301 "Stop his mouth!": Ibid.

301 Andrew the Liar: Ibid., 117

301 "You are the successors": Kaus, 255

47. SERFDOM

303 "For sale, a barber": Oldenbourg, 285

304 "Anyone wishing to buy": Waliszewski, 304

304 "For sale: domestics and skilled craftsmen": Grey, 122

306 "If we do not agree": Ibid., 164

307 "There! You have the people free!": Cronin, 262

308 "What has disgusted me": Grey, 122

310 "I punished him": Smith, *Pearl*, 105

310 "This is one of my fiddlers": Ibid.

312 "a miracle of color": Ibid., 70

312 "I had the most tender": Ibid., 71

48. "MADAME ORLOV COULD NEVER BE EMPRESS OF RUSSIA"

313 "The men who surround me": Haslip, 143

315 "Perhaps you are right": Alexander, 74

317 "Tell Her Imperial Majesty": Kaus, 271

319 "everyone should go about his own business": Ibid., 273

320 "If the empress wants me to lay my head": Haslip, 149

320 "It is my earnest desire": Dashkova, 1:128

320 "There would never": Smith, *Love and Conquest*, 9

321 "You will not be surprised": Haslip, 178

49. THE DEATH OF IVAN VI

322 "Take care!": Kaus, 277

322 "If the prisoner is insubordinate": Ibid.

323 "The prisoner is somewhat quieter": Ibid.

323 "painful and almost unintelligible stammering": Ibid., 278

324 "The prisoner shall not be allowed": Ibid., 280

324 "Release us": Ibid.

324 "Compliance with your request": Ibid.

325 "Make your own career, young man": Ibid., 282

325 "Not long had Peter III possessed": Madariaga, *Russia in the Age*, 35

326 "If the others agree": Kaus, 285

327 "Where is the emperor?": Alexander, 91

327 "See, my brothers": Kaus, 285

327 "The ways of God are wonderful": Madariaga, *Russia in the Age*, 36

327 "she left here with an air": Waliszewski, 264

328 "As regards the insult": Kaus, 287

329 "loyally performing their duty": Ibid., 288

329 "The manifesto she has issued": Troyat, 167

329 "It seems to me that if I were on the throne": Ibid.

329 "I am tempted to say to you": Ibid.

50. CATHERINE AND THE ENLIGHTENMENT

330 "Whatever style I possess": Haslip, 157

331 "The victorious nation never profits": Durant, 10:151

331 "Oh, mighty God, I believe": Ibid., 9:750

332 "Tell them I am very sick": Ibid., 10:133

332 "the highest and coldest garret": Ibid.

333 "hanged, drowned, broken on the wheel": Ibid., 9:731

333 "It took two hours": Ibid., 9:733

333 "I shall be coming to Paris": Ibid., 10:392

334 "For my part, I am consoled": Ibid., 10:139

334 "He governed the whole civilized world": Ibid., 9:784

334 "Since Voltaire died": Anthony, 229

335 "these are family matters": Gorbatov, 70

335 "I believe we must moderate": Ibid.

336 "Semiramis of the North": Durant, 9:448

336 "try to persuade the octogenarian": Madariaga, *Russia in the Age*, 336

336 "in certain ways . . . a hundred": Gorbatov, 177

337 "You and M. Diderot": Durant, 9:719

337 "Go on, brave Diderot": Ibid.

337 "It would be cruel": Gooch, 60

338 "I prostrate myself": Troyat, 177

338 "we are three who would build you altars": Ibid., 178

338 "Thirty years of labor": Ibid.

338 "I never thought": Gorbatov, 156

339 "That door will be opened to you": Oliva, 119

339 "my good lady": Troyat, 207

339 "an extraordinary man": Durant, 9:448

340 "I have listened": Troyat, 207

341 "Now you sit beside Caesar": Ibid., 209

341 "Madame, I am positively in disgrace": Reddaway, 198

342 "Live, Monsieur": Ibid., 199

342 "returned to her in chains": Ibid., 200

51. THE *NAKAZ*

344 "one of the most remarkable political treatises": Madariaga, *Russia in the Age*, 151

345 "Russia is a European state": Ibid., 153

346 "it is much better to prevent than to punish crimes": Reddaway, 225

346 "productive of nothing": Ibid., 288

347 "The use of torture is contrary": Ibid., 231

347 "without any sensible inconveniences": Ibid., 232

347 "What right can give anyone authority": Ibid., 244

347 "All punishments by which the human body": Ibid., 227

347 "Some judges should be of the same rank": Ibid., 232

348 "a civil society requires a certain established order": Ibid., 256

348 "Why should they bother to be clean": Haslip, 162

348 "These are axioms which will bring down walls": Madariaga, *Russia in the Age,* 158

349 "I let them erase what they pleased": Ibid.

349 "Since the Law of Nature": Reddaway, 256

350 "I have decked myself out in peacock's feathers": Grey, 147

350 "I have robbed Montesquieu": Troyat, 179

350 "would have been capable": Troyat, 182

350 "the finest monument of the age": Gooch, 67

351 "A masculine, nervous performance": Troyat, 182

351 "I must warn Your Majesty": Madariaga, *Russia in the Age,* 151

52. "ALL FREE ESTATES OF THE REALM"

353 "By this institution, we give to our people": Alexander, 102

353 "you will receive a letter": Ibid., 103

353 "There can be nothing more pleasant": Ibid., 108

354 "These laws, about which so much has been said": Ibid., 109

354 "There are so many objects": Ibid.

354 "Here, the people along the Volga": Ibid., 110

355 "The town rose high on a hill": Kerensky, 3

355 "to glorify yourselves and your country": Alexander, 112

356 "I brought them together to study laws": Troyat, 181

357 "Have they really already lost": Alexander, 115

358 "The peasant has his feelings": Madariaga, *Russia in the Age,* 176

359 "The majority of votes": Ibid., 159

359 "And have their throats cut from time to time": Ibid., 160

359 "cannot have in present circumstances": Ibid.

360 "A general emancipation": Alexander, 116

360 "What had I not to suffer": Anthony, 215

362 "The idea that the principal purpose": Madariaga, *Catherine,* 34

53. "THE KING WE HAVE MADE"

365 "I am sending Count Keyserling": Kaus, 262

366 "fortunate anarchy": Alexander, 123

366 "There is a vast difference between melons": Kaus, 264

366 "to resort, if need be, to force of arms": Ibid., 265

366 "without the slightest mercy": Alexander, 126

367 "Do not laugh at me": Kaus, 263

367 "I beg you most urgently not to come here": Coughlan, 228

368 "a thousand inconveniences": Ibid.

368 "in the hands of the brothers Orlov": Ibid., 229

369 "I beg of you to listen to me": Kaus, 263

371 "the new king we have made": Ibid., 266

54. THE FIRST PARTITION OF POLAND AND THE FIRST TURKISH WAR

373 "a real thunderbolt for the country and for me": Coughlan, 233

374 "to prevent a quarter of their nation": Gooch, 64

375 "what does one have to endure": Alexander, 129

375 "at the risk of repeating myself": Haslip, 182

378 "I cannot keep writing to you": Ibid.

380 "in Poland one only has to stoop": Anthony, 203

55. DOCTORS, SMALLPOX, AND PLAGUE

384 "If you go to a village": Cronin, 167

384 "the same attention to cleanliness": Madariaga, *Russia in the Age*, 560

385 "I am quite sick": Alexander, 144

385 "It has been four years": Ibid., 143

385 "You couldn't cure a flea bite": Cronin, 169

385 "Well done, ma'am!": Ibid., 169

386 "You know I am a child": Alexander, 145

386 "uncommon merit, beautiful, and immensely rich": Ibid.

386 "I am very upset": Ibid.

386 "Having this hour learned": Ibid.

387 "of all that I ever saw of her sex": Cronin, 168

387 "a secret everybody knows": Alexander, 146

388 "except for some slight uneasiness": Ibid., 147

388 "My objective was": Ibid.

388 "our argumentative charlatans": Ibid., 148

390 "fine and zealous": Reddaway, 135

391 "The famous Eighteenth Century": Ibid.

391 "We have spent a month in circumstances": Alexander, 158

56. THE RETURN OF "PETER THE THIRD"

396 "freedom of the rivers": Madariaga, *Russia in the Age*, 243

396 "I give eternal freedom": Oldenbourg, 299

396 "If God permits me to reach St. Petersburg": Kaus, 296

397 "this godless turmoil": Alexander, 170

398 "The great sovereign": Madariaga, *Russia in the Age*, 270

399 "Whomever you represent": Kaus, 298

399 "a common highway robber": Oldenbourg, 301

399 "exploits of a brigand": Troyat, 213

399 "Marquis de Pugachev": Alexander, 177

400 "this new husband who has turned up": Haslip, 211

400 "for more than six weeks I have been obliged": Grey, 162

400 "this motley crowd": Alexander, 171

400 "What need is there to flog": Madariaga, *Russia in the Age*, 249

401 "Orenburg has already been besieged": Alexander, 171

402 "Leave the peasants": Madariaga, *Russia in the Age*, 248

402 "the suspicion of foreigners": Alexander, 174

402 "inhabited by all the good-fornothings": Ibid.

402 "Since you like hangings so much": Ibid.

57. THE LAST DAYS OF THE "MARQUIS DE PUGACHEV"

403 "If God gives me power over the state": Madariaga, *Russia in the Age,* 271

404 "Why does he call himself Tsar Peter?": Cronin, 180

404 "Extremely shaken": Alexander, 176

405 "the insolent windbag": Ibid.

405 "You see, my friend, that Count Panin": Madariaga, *Russia in the Age,* 264

406 "bad news travels faster than good": Alexander, 177

407 "How dare you raise your hands": Madariaga, *Russia in the Age,* 255

407 "infernal monster": Oldenbourg, 302

407 "Sir, are you master or servant?": Alexander, 178

407 "refrain from all questioning under torture": Madariaga, *Russia in the Age,* 267

407 "Pugachev has lived like a scoundrel:" Oldenbourg, 304

408 "Please help to inspire everyone": Alexander, 179

408 "they wanted to break Pugachev on the wheel": Ibid.

409 "all that has passed to eternal oblivion": Ibid., 180

58. VASILCHIKOV

413 "He must appear": Kaus, 311

414 "good looking, amiable, and a complete nonentity": Haslip, 198

414 "He is capable of killing me": Oldenbourg, 310

416 "a kind of male *cocotte*": Kaus, 313

416 "he must send Vasilchikov away": Smith, *Love and Conquest,* 21

416 "It was a random choice": Kaus, 311

59. CATHERINE AND POTEMKIN: PASSION

418 "If I become a general": Soloveytchik, 43

420 "Sir Lieutenant General and Chevalier": Smith, *Love and Conquest,* 8

420 "Any news at court?": Soloveytchik, 67

421 "I do not understand what has reduced him": Ibid., 68

421 "the state and yourself, Madam": Ibid., 69

422 "he had conducted himself indiscreetly": Smith, *Love and Conquest,* 9

422 "After a year spent in great sorrow": Ibid., 9–10

423 "I remain unmotivated by envy": Ibid., 18

424 "Sir Lieutenant General": Ibid., 20

424 "Mr. Vasilchikov, the favorite": Soloveytchik, 73

425 "The thing to do now, my sweet": Ibid., 75

425 "I'm not surprised": Smith, *Love and Conquest,* 19

425 "I don't understand what kept you": Ibid., 17

425 "I only ask you not to do one thing": Ibid., 19

426 "I have parted from a certain excellent": Soloveytchik, 78

427 "No, Grishenka": Smith, *Love and Conquest,* 24

427 "There is no reason to be angry": Ibid., 27

427 "Oh, my darling, you should be ashamed": Ibid., 35

427 "Allow me, my precious dear": Smith, Ibid., 78

429 "Does it appear, sir": Soloveytchik, 101

430 "certain sacred and inalienable rights": Montefiore, 139

430 "I kiss you and embrace you . . . dear husband": Smith, *Love and Conquest,* 38

430 "pray come and cuddle with me": Ibid., 40

60. POTEMKIN ASCENDING

431 "There has been no instance": Soloveytchik, 107

431 "Do you remember how": Ibid., 110
431 "I have noticed that your mother": Smith, *Love and Conquest*, 61
431 "On Sunday, I happened to be seated": Soloveytchik, 112
432 "As long as my bed remains": Ibid., 119
432 "If there are no mistakes": Smith, *Love and Conquest*, 50
433 "This is really too much!": Soloveytchik, 131
433 "It is a hundred years": Smith, *Love and Conquest*, 55
434 "The rebellion in a great part": Soloveytchik, 143

61. CATHERINE AND POTEMKIN: SEPARATION

435 "My dear friend, I don't know why": Smith, *Love and Conquest*, 51
435 "Your long letter and stories": Ibid., 57
436 "You were in a mood to quarrel": Ibid., 67
436 "Precious darling": Ibid.
436 "I wrote you a letter": Ibid., 75
436 "Do me this one favor": Ibid., 77
436 "Such rage ought to be expected": Ibid., 80
437 "My Lord and Dear Husband!": Ibid., 77
437 "Should you not find pleasure": Ibid., 81
437 "May God forgive you": Ibid., 82
438 "Your Most Gracious Majesty": Ibid., 83
438 "I read your letter": Ibid., 84
438 "To present this comedy to society": Ibid., 85
438 "Matushka, here is the result": Ibid.
439 "Your foolish acts remain the same": Ibid., 68
439 "Listening to you talk sometimes": Ibid., 74
441 "God knows I don't intend": Ibid., 87
441 "Your Most Gracious Majesty": Ibid.

442 "You know, Madam, I am your slave": Soloveytchik, 195

62. NEW RELATIONSHIPS

444 "My husband has written me": Smith, *Love and Conquest*, 76
444 "You ask for Zavadovsky's removal": Ibid., 85
446 "Varinka, I love you": Soloveytchik, 167
446 "Listen, my dearest, Varinka is very sick": Smith, *Love and Conquest*, 96
447 "What's the use of all this?": Soloveytchik, 170
448 "Would it not be charming": Anthony, 315

63. FAVORITES

451 "with the greatest dignity": Coughlan, 294
452 "Last night I was in love with him": Haslip, 257
452 "Pyrrhus, king of Epirus": Kaus, 326,
452 "Big books at the bottom": Cronin, 256
452 "changed his original common name": Haslip, 261
453 "kind, gay, honest": Madariaga, *Russia in the Age*, 354
454 "compared to the others, he was an angel": Haslip, 288
454 "they helped, but I could not endure": Alexander, 217
455 "I am plunged into the most profound grief": Ibid., 216
455 "From Catherine to my dearest friend": Haslip, 290
456 "I am once more inwardly calm": Ibid., 292
456 "You cur, you monkey": Ibid., 299
456 "Either he or I must go!": Ibid.
456 "They slept until nine o'clock": Alexander, 218
457 "We are as clever": Coughlan, 295
457 "Sasha is beyond price": Haslip, 305
457 "stifling": Ibid., 306

457 "It is your duty to remain": Ibid., 330

457 "cold and preoccupied": Alexander, 219

457 "a girl most ordinary": Ibid., 220

458 "God grant them happiness": Gooch, 51

458 "I have never been": Alexander, 222

458 "constantly tortures my soul": Ibid.

64. CATHERINE, PAUL, AND NATALIA

466 "We have never had a jollier time": Gooch, 26

466 "I return to town on Tuesday": Ibid.

469 "Everything is done to excess": Alexander, 227

469 "The grand duke": Smith, *Love and Conquest,* 58

470 "Her friends are, with reason": Alexander, 228

470 "Never in my life": Ibid.

470 "For three days": Haslip, 239

471 "perfectly formed boy": Alexander, 229

471 I have wasted no time": Troyat, 232

472 "since it has been proven": Ibid., 231

65. PAUL, MARIA, AND THE SUCCESSION

473 "I hope that in time": Ibid., 231

473 "Nothing can exceed": Gooch, 29

474 "The grand duke is exceedingly amiable": Ibid.

474 "my daughter. . . . Be assured": Alexander, 232

474 "We shall have her here": Anthony, 277

474 "My son has returned": Alexander, 233.

475 "I swear to love and adore you": Troyat, 234

475 "This dear husband is an angel": Gooch, 30

475 "Wherever she goes": Ibid.

476 "had been given a map of Europe": Haslip, 285

476 "whether his Polish majesty": Ibid., 286

477 "prefers stewed fruit": Ibid.

477 "an ardent and impetuous man": Waliszewski, 403

478 "The grand duke is greatly undervalued": Gooch, 30

478 "When they admitted me": Ibid., 32

479 "He combined plenty of intelligence": Ibid., 33

479 "You tax me with my hypochondria": Anthony, 287

479 "Permit me to write you often": Ibid.

480 "One cannot see everything": Troyat, 323

481 "I told you that your request": Gooch, 27

481 "I shall be separated": Gooch, 34

482 "There is no one": Anthony, 288

482 "I see into what hands": Gooch, 35

482 "I hope not in the time of M. Alexander": Ibid., 36

66. POTEMKIN: BUILDER AND DIPLOMAT

484 "Is that a soldier's business?": Soloveytchik, 177

485 "such a mixture of wit": Ibid., 221

485 "She had the strongest desire to help us": Ibid., 201

487 "You have chosen an unlucky moment": Ibid., 212

487 "The interest I take in everything": Ibid., 216

488 "Flatter her as much as you can": Ibid., 225

488 "You can demand of us": Ibid.

488 The dialogue between Potemkin and Harris regarding an Anglo-Russian alliance is drawn from Soloveytchik, 227–45

488 "*La mariée est trop belle*": Ibid., 234

489 "The acquisition of the Crimea": Soloveytchik, 180

67. CRIMEAN JOURNEY AND "POTEMKIN VILLAGES"

491 "Everything was done to deter me": Haslip, 308

492 "Your children belong to you": Troyat, 271

493 "Your latest proposal": Rounding, 424

493 "heavy baggage": Madariaga, *Russia in the Age,* 569

494 "It was a time": Haslip, 307

494 "One day when I was sitting": Rounding, 429

495 "Here, the greenery in the meadows": Smith, *Love and Conquest,* 176

495 "Avoid the prince": Haslip, 310

495 "the greatest genius of her age": Ibid., 303

496 "the pleasantest company": Ibid., 304

496 "It is odd": Smith, *Love and Conquest,* 175

497 "Gentlemen, the king of Poland": Montefiore, 365

497 "It was thirty years": Ibid., 366

498 "They spoke little": Haslip, 314

498 "our guest's desire that I remain here": Smith, *Love and Conquest,* 178

498 "The king bores me": Haslip, 315

499 "The new favorite is good-looking": Ibid., 317

499 "I performed a great deed": Cronin, 130

500 "What a peculiar land": Montefiore, 371

501 "the most beautiful port I have ever seen": Ibid., 374

502 "I love you and your service": Smith, *Love and Conquest,* 180

502 "How I appreciate the feelings": Ibid., 182

503 "Between you and me, my friend": Ibid.

68. THE SECOND TURKISH WAR AND THE DEATH OF POTEMKIN

505 "You are impatient": Madariaga, *Russia in the Age,* 398

505 "Children, I forbid you": Soloveytchik, 301

505 "I will try to get it cheaply": Ibid., 308

505 "You cannot capture a fortress": Ibid.

505 "My dear friend, you alone mean more to me": Ibid.

505 "May the Prince Gregory Alexandrovich": Ibid., 309

506 "Hurry up, my dear friend": Ibid.

506 "If Izmail resists": Montefiore, 450

507 "this insane note . . . Sir John Falstaff": Alexander, 270

507 "breastplate": Haslip, 346

507 "We have pulled one paw out": Madariaga, *Russia in the Age,* 414

508 "I here behold a Commander in Chief": Ibid., 314

510 "Has your ship struck": Morison, 230

511 "Paul Jones has just arrived: Ibid., 364

511 "I was entirely captivated": Ibid.

511 "It is to you alone": Montefiore, 400

512 "Our victory is complete": Ibid.

512 "I hope to be subjected": Morison, 382

512 "nobody wished to serve:: Ibid., 384

512 "She then indulged": Ibid., 387

513 "The charge against me is an unworthy": Ibid., 388

513 "The accusation against me is false": Ibid.

513 "Paul Jones is no more guilty than I": Montefiore, 421

515 "I must pull out the tooth": Soloveytchik, 326

516 "When one looks at the Prince-Marshal Potemkin": Ibid., 327

517 "The child sends his greetings": Ibid., 335

517 "I could not remove him from my path": Montefiore, 478

517 "Please send me a Chinese dressing gown": Ibid., 338

518 "the first pianist and one of the best composers": Montefiore, 482

518 "Take that which": Smith, *Love and Conquest,* 389

518 "I'm not going to recover": Soloveytchik, 340

518 "Tell me frankly": Ibid.

518 "Good hands": Ibid., 341

519 "Matushka, oh how sick I am!": Smith, *Love and Conquest,* 390

519 "I have no more strength": Ibid., 390

519 "This will be enough": Soloveytchik, 342

519 "the prince is no longer on this earth": Ibid., 343

519 "Now I have no one left": Ibid.

69. ART, ARCHITECTURE, AND THE BRONZE HORSEMAN

522 "The Walpole paintings are no longer to be had": Descargues, 42

522 "The Comte de Baudoin leaves it": Ibid., 44

522 "The world is a strange place": Ibid.

523 "We are prodigiously delighted": Ibid.

523 "I am a glutton": Waliszewski, 344

524 "You should know our mania": Madariaga, *Russia in the Age,* 532

527 "Now I love to distraction": Waliszewski, 390

527 *The Captain's Daughter* appears in Yarmolinsky, ed., 599–727

529 "My posterity is Your Majesty": Waliszewski, 341

529 "What a charming picture": Descargues, 26

529 "My paintings are beautiful": Ibid., 29

530 "They have not made, as I have": Rounding, 221

530 "There is an old song": Ibid., 222

530 "I hear only praise": Ibid.

530 "in general, everyone is very happy": Ibid.

531 "You will choose honest and reasonable people": Waliszewski, 350

532 The lines from Pushkin's "The Bronze Horseman" are cited in Yarmolinsky, ed., 106–107

70. "THEY ARE CAPABLE OF HANGING THEIR KING FROM A LAMPPOST!"

535 "to God and the country never to be separated": Schama, 359

535 "Go tell those who have sent you": Schama, 363

535 "null, illegal, and unconstitutional": Winik, 124

537 "I fear that the greatest obstacle": Gooch, 103

538 "French, Russians, Danes": Madariaga, *Catherine,* 189

539 "I cannot believe in the superior talents": Gooch, 99

539 "They are capable of hanging their king": Madariaga, *Russia in the Age,* 421

539 "Above all, I hope": Gooch, 99

539 "I am sad to see you go": Haslip, 341

539 "I am afraid so, Madame": Ibid.

539 "the Hydra with twelve hundred heads": Waliszewski, 351

539 "only people who set in motion a machine": Gooch, 100

540 "Tell a thousand people to draft a letter": Cronin, 269

540 "the cause of the king of France": This summary of Catherine's memorandum is based on Lariviere, 101 ff.

542 "an exemplary and unforgettable act": Schama, 612

542 "a scum of criminals vomited": Loomis, 75

542 "I don't give a damn about the prisoners": Schama, 633

544 "to protect the republic": Thompson, 258–9

544 "the foulest and most atrocious act": Schama, 687

545 "The revolution has no need": Loomis, 335

545 "Madame, we must go now": Ibid., 333

546 "The mechanism falls like thunder": Schama, 621

547 "immediately after the decapitation": www.guillotine.dk/Pages/30sek/html.

71. DISSENT IN RUSSIA, FINAL PARTITION OF POLAND

549 "Likely to corrupt morals": Madariaga, *Russia in the Age,* 546

551 "beastly purpose": Radishchev, 96

551 "breaks the head": Ibid., 97

551 "Do you know, dear fellow citizens": Ibid., 153

551 "has learning enough": Ibid., 239

552 "hence the suspicion falls on M. Radishchev": Ibid., 241

552 "the purpose of this book is clear": Ibid., 239

552 "a rabble-rouser, worse than Pugachev": Ibid., 11

552 "I've read the book you sent me": Montefiore, 440

553 "Now I am my own master": Radishchev, 19

555 "will oppose us with only": Madariaga, *Russia in the Age,* 430

555 "exterminate that nest of Jacobins": Haslip, 353

555 "I am breaking my head": Madariaga, *Russia in the Age,* 428

556 "Apparently you ignore": Ibid., "435

557 "soldiers of Her Imperial Majesty": Haslip, 356

557 "Does the Diet authorize": Madariaga, *Russia in the Age,* 439

557 "Silence means consent": Ibid.

557 "a Russian province": Ibid., 440

559 "the whole of Praga": Ibid., 446

72. TWILIGHT

561 "You probably don't need this contrivance": Cronin, 289

561 "are you not ashamed of yourself?": Waliszewski, 376

561 "let me march against the French!": Kaus, 376

562 "Madame, you must be gay": Ibid., 367

563 "Twenty years ago": Waliszewski, 391

563 "I have said it to you before": Ibid., 412

563 "It is astonishing": Troyat, 236

563 "If you only knew what wonders": Kaus, 306

564 "I am making a delicious child": Troyat, 236

564 "He loves me instinctively": Oldenbourg, 331

564 "It is sewn together": Waliszewski, 413

565 "There is in my country": Troyat, 323

566 "I didn't know what would become of me": Cronin, 295

567 "the grand duchess will never be troubled": Madariaga, *Russia in the Age,* 576

568 "With the church's blessing?": Cronin, 296

568 "King Gustavus is not well": Ibid., 297

568 "What I have written": Madariaga, *Russia in the Age,* 576

569 "The fact is that the king pretended": *Memoirs* (Anthony), 321

73. THE DEATH OF CATHERINE THE GREAT

570 "The grand duke got out of his sleigh": Cronin, 299

571 "Gentlemen, the Empress Catherine is dead": Ibid., 300

572 "The subject was the unlimited power": Madariaga, *Russia in the Age,* 580

573 "Before I became what I am today": Haslip, 361

573 "HERE LIES CATHERINE": Anthony, 325

573 "my name is Catherine II": Alexander, 265

574 "Day before yesterday": Haslip, 361

INDEX

ABOUT THE TYPE

This book was set in Requiem, a typeface designed by the Hoefler Type Foundry. It is a modern typeface inspired by inscriptional capitals in Ludovico Vicentino degli Arrighi's 1523 writing manual, *Il modo de temperare le penne*. An original lowercase, a set of figures, and an italic in the "chancery" style that Arrighi helped popularize were created to make this adaptation of a classical design into a complete font family.